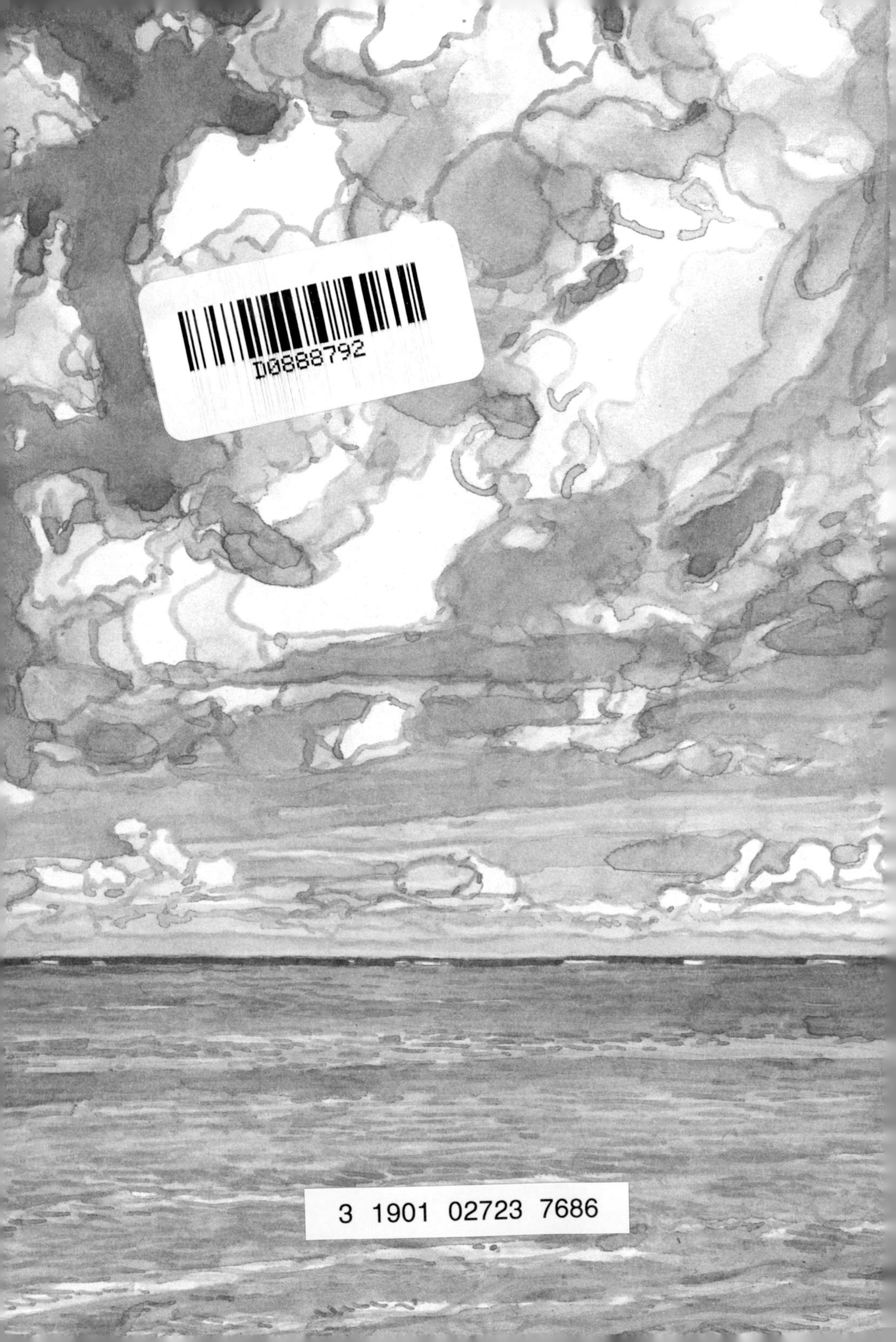

CHILDREN OF THE SEA

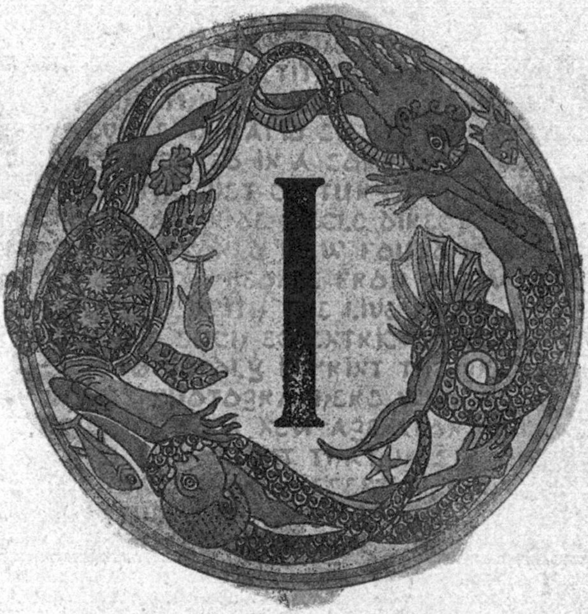
I

DAISUKE IGARASHI

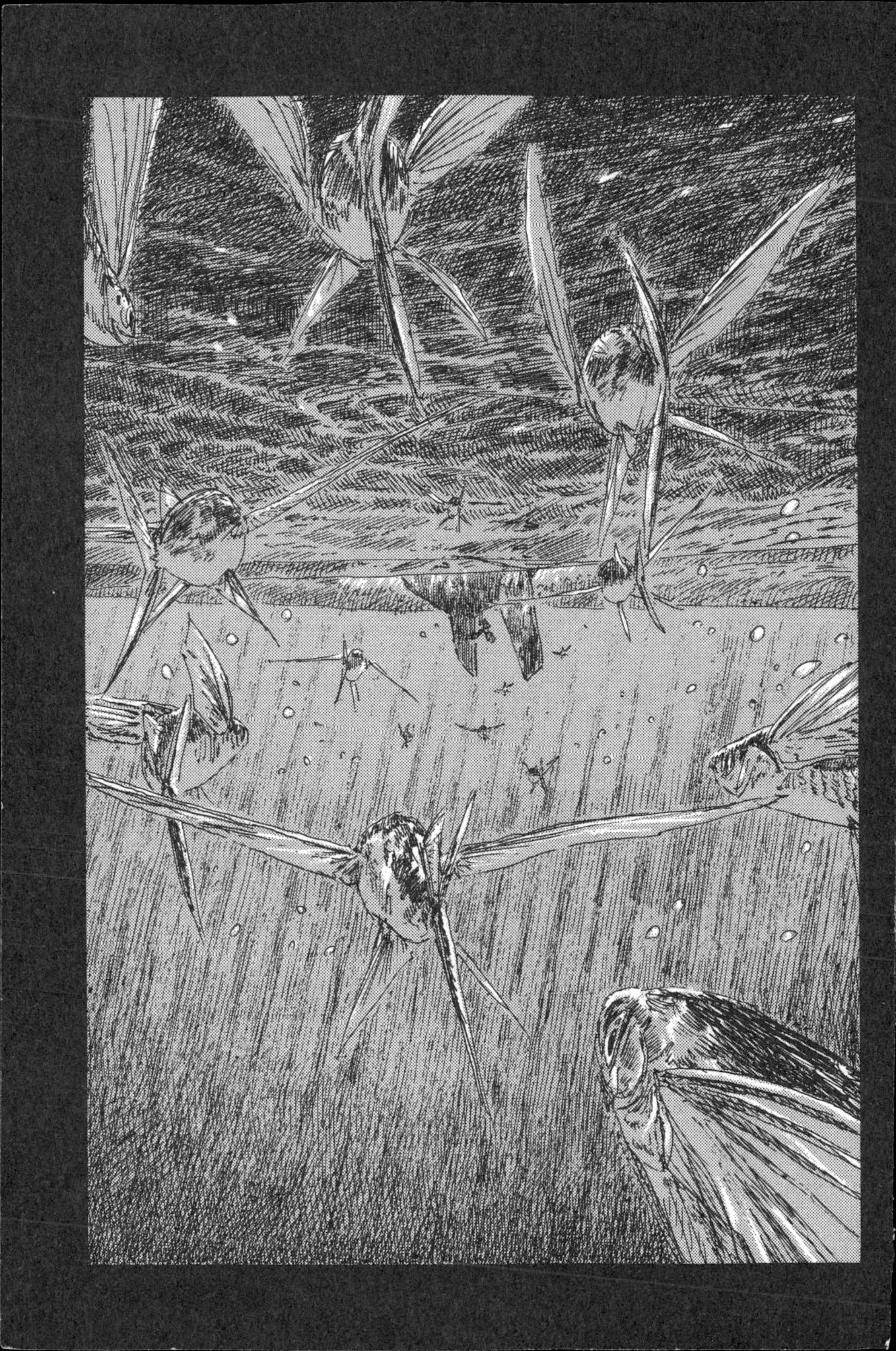

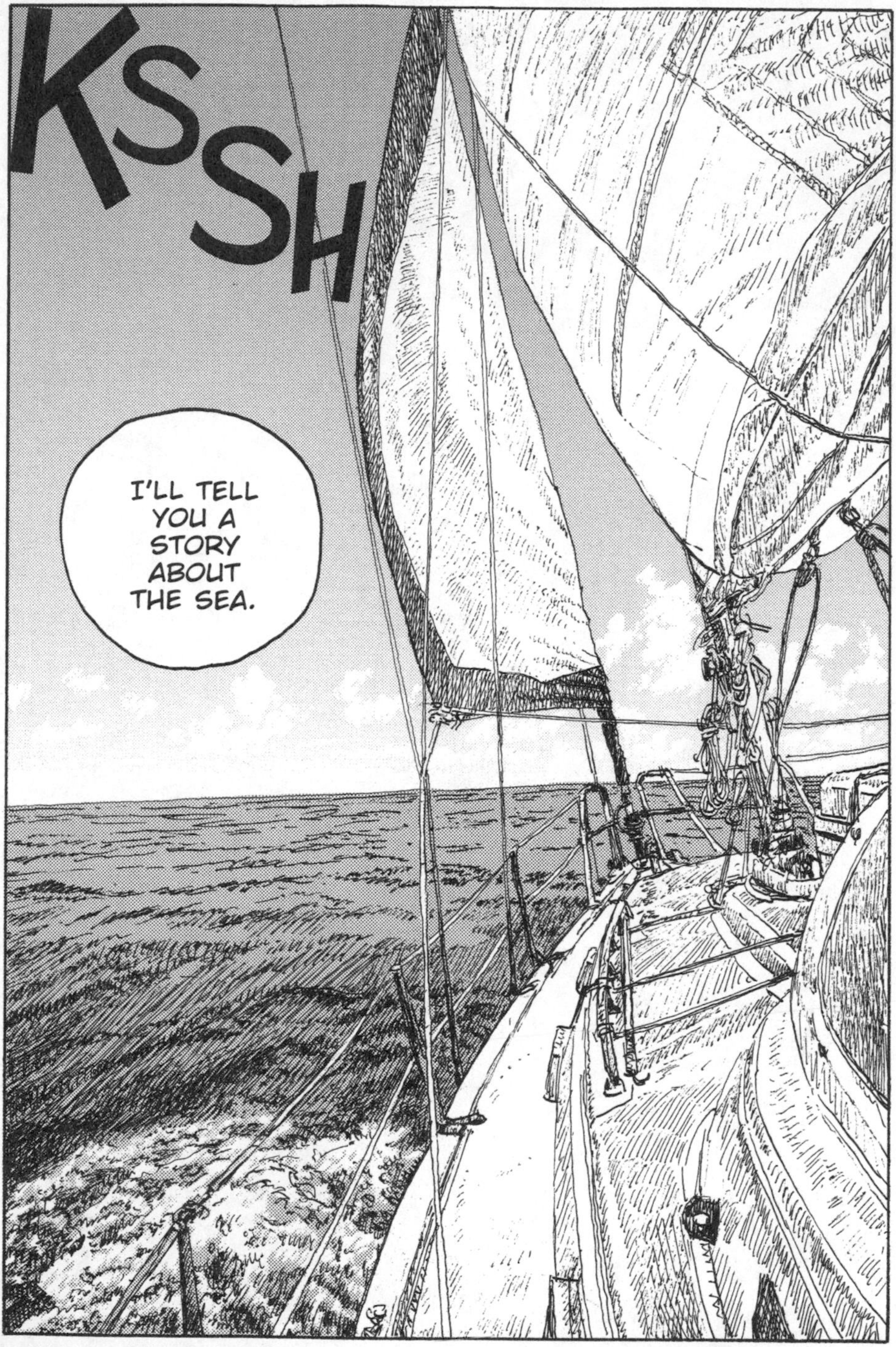
KSSH
I'LL TELL YOU A STORY ABOUT THE SEA.

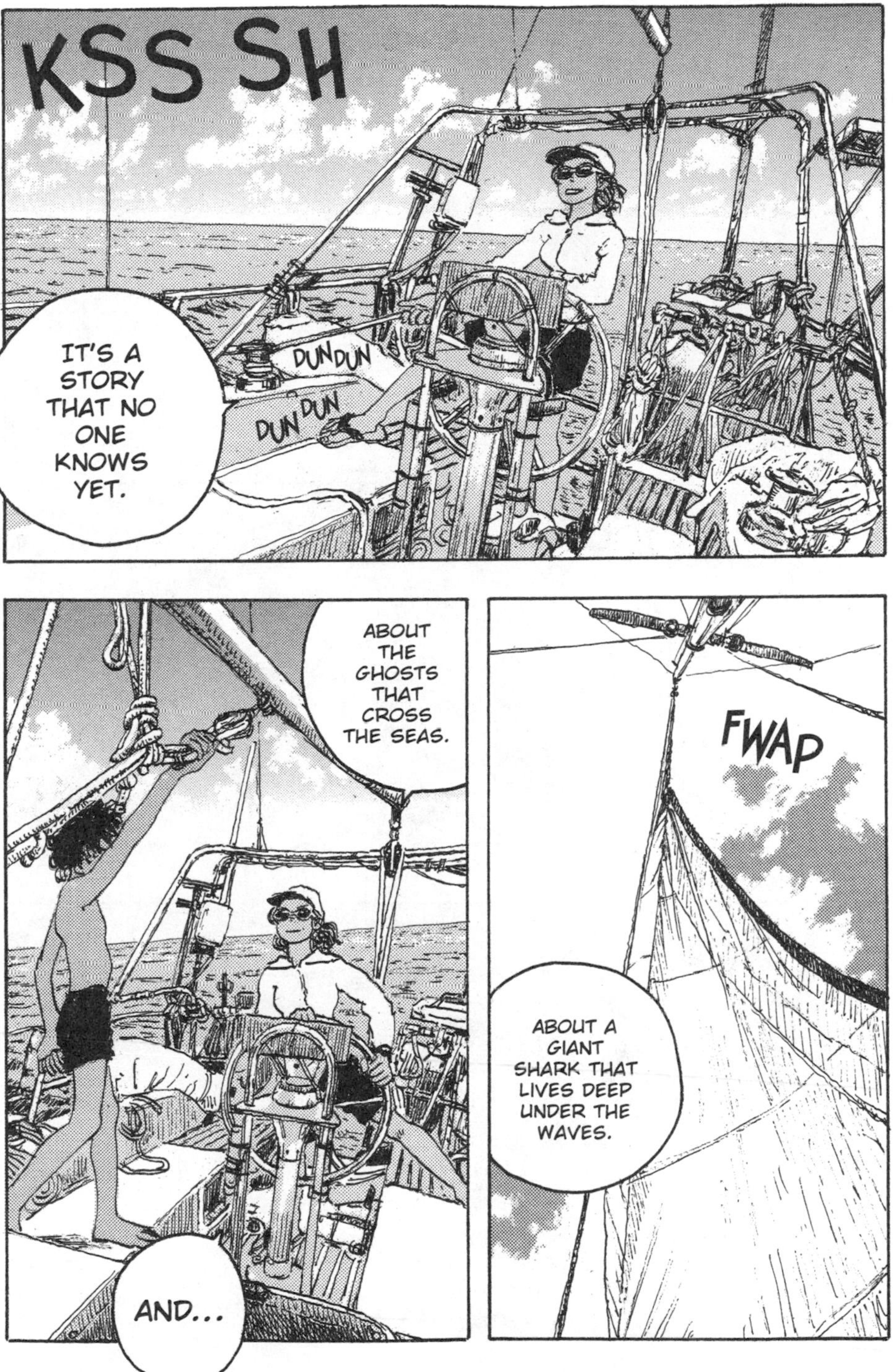
KSS SH
DUN DUN
DUN DUN
IT'S A STORY THAT NO ONE KNOWS YET.
FWAP
ABOUT A GIANT SHARK THAT LIVES DEEP UNDER THE WAVES.
ABOUT THE GHOSTS THAT CROSS THE SEAS.
AND...

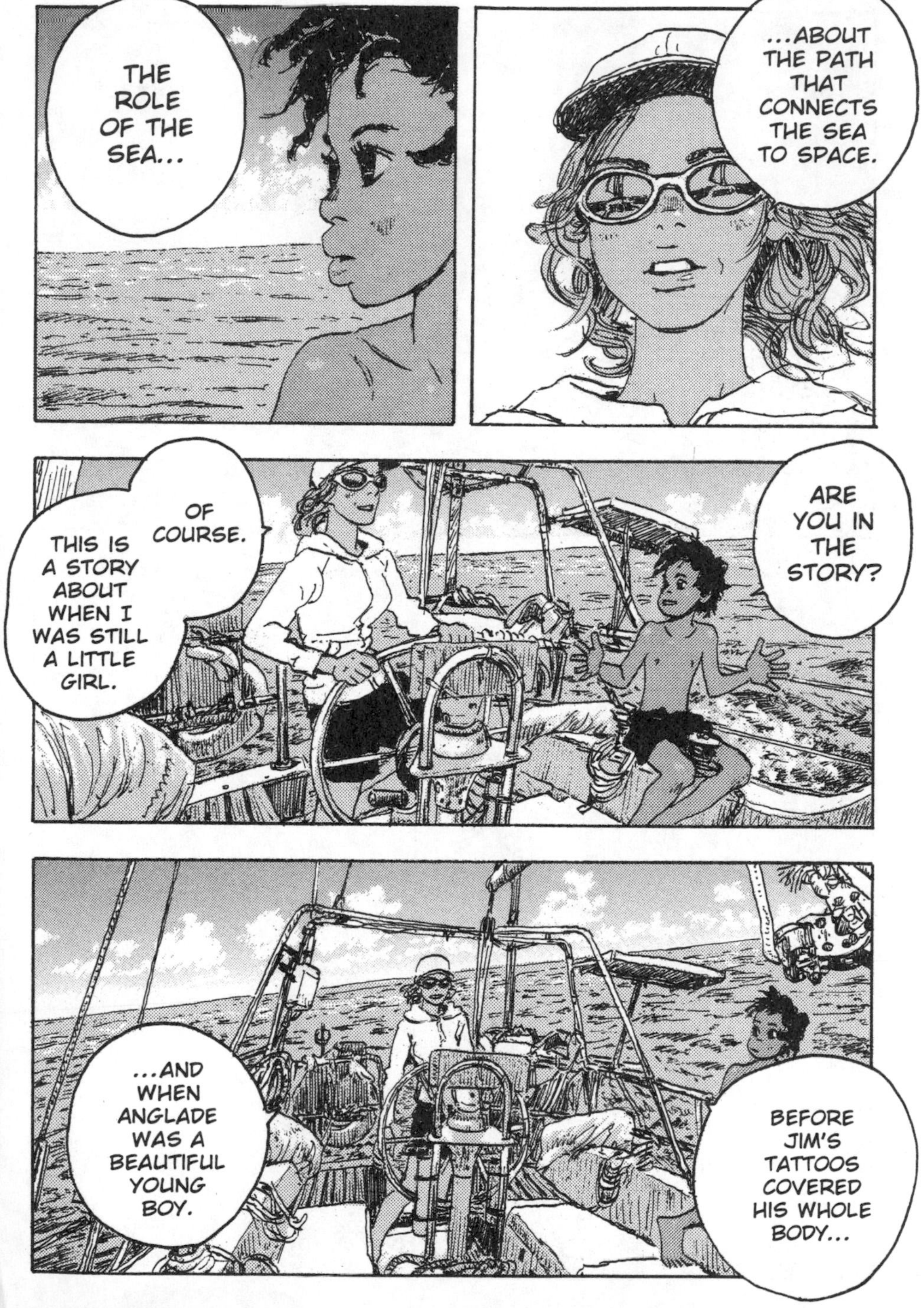
...ABOUT THE PATH THAT CONNECTS THE SEA TO SPACE.
THE ROLE OF THE SEA...
ARE YOU IN THE STORY?
OF COURSE.
THIS IS A STORY ABOUT WHEN I WAS STILL A LITTLE GIRL.
BEFORE JIM'S TATTOOS COVERED HIS WHOLE BODY...
...AND WHEN ANGLADE WAS A BEAUTIFUL YOUNG BOY.

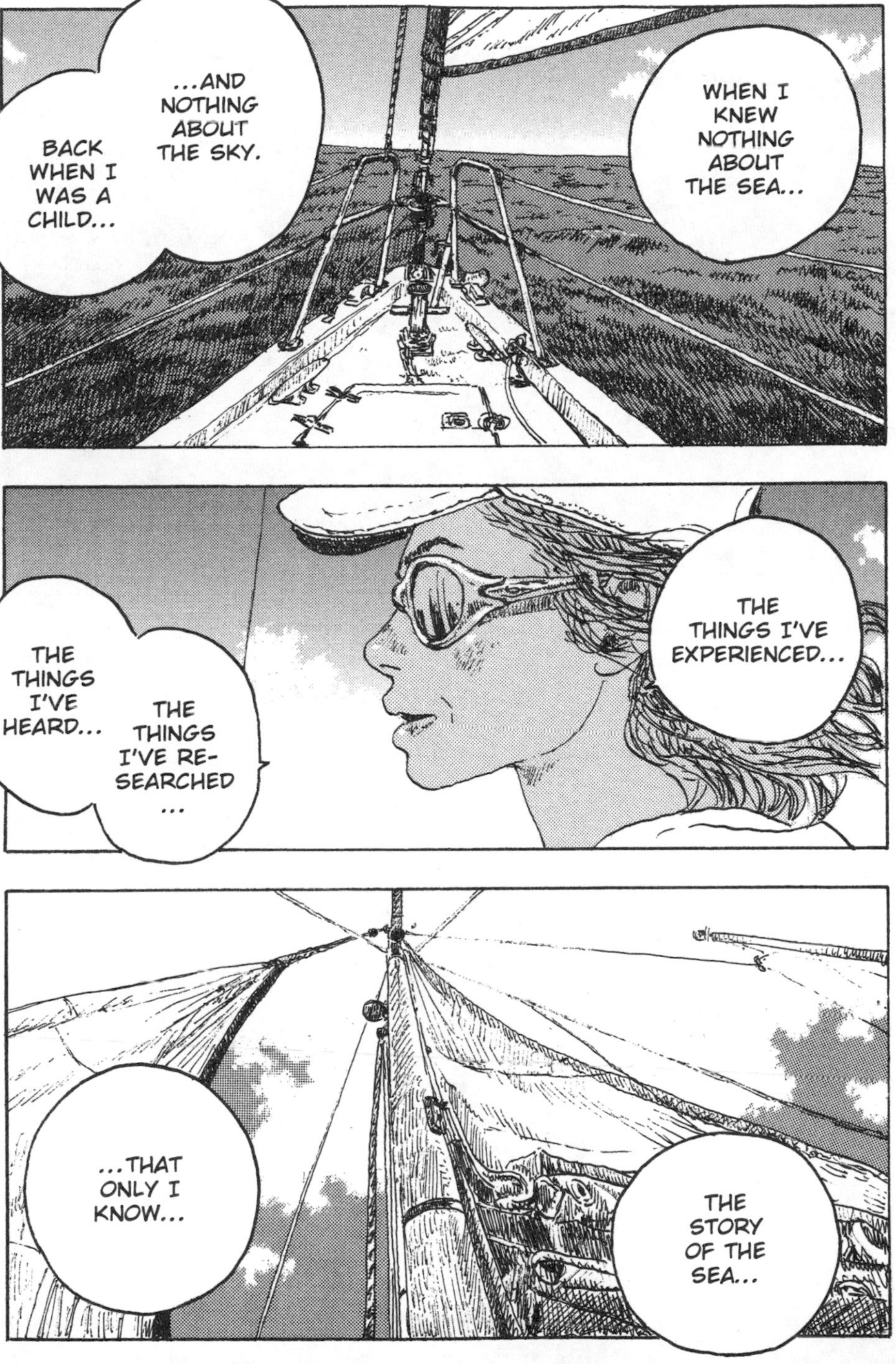
WHEN I KNEW NOTHING ABOUT THE SEA...
...AND NOTHING ABOUT THE SKY.
BACK WHEN I WAS A CHILD...
THE THINGS I'VE EXPERIENCED...
THE THINGS I'VE HEARD...
THE THINGS I'VE RE-SEARCHED ...
THE STORY OF THE SEA...
...THAT ONLY I KNOW...

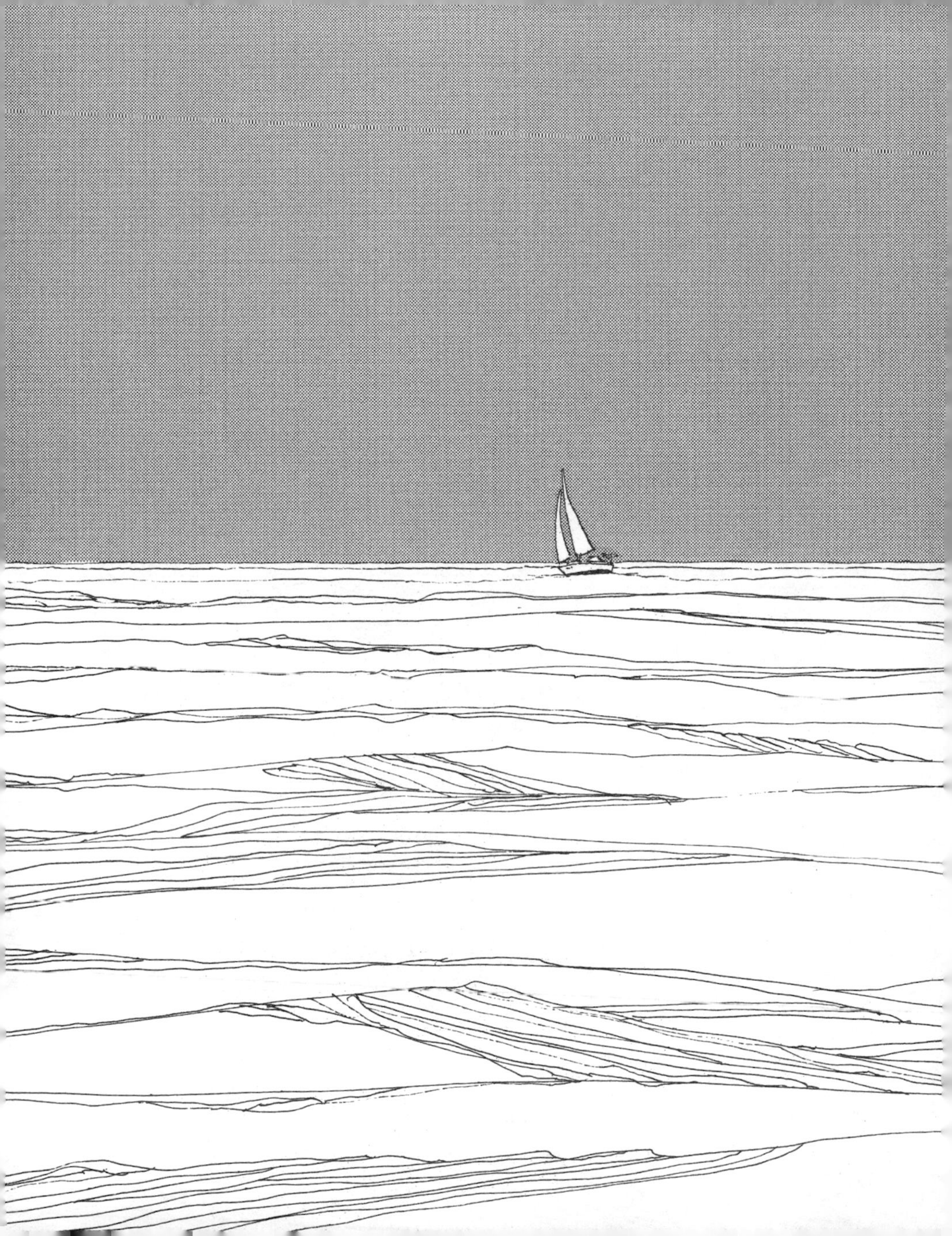

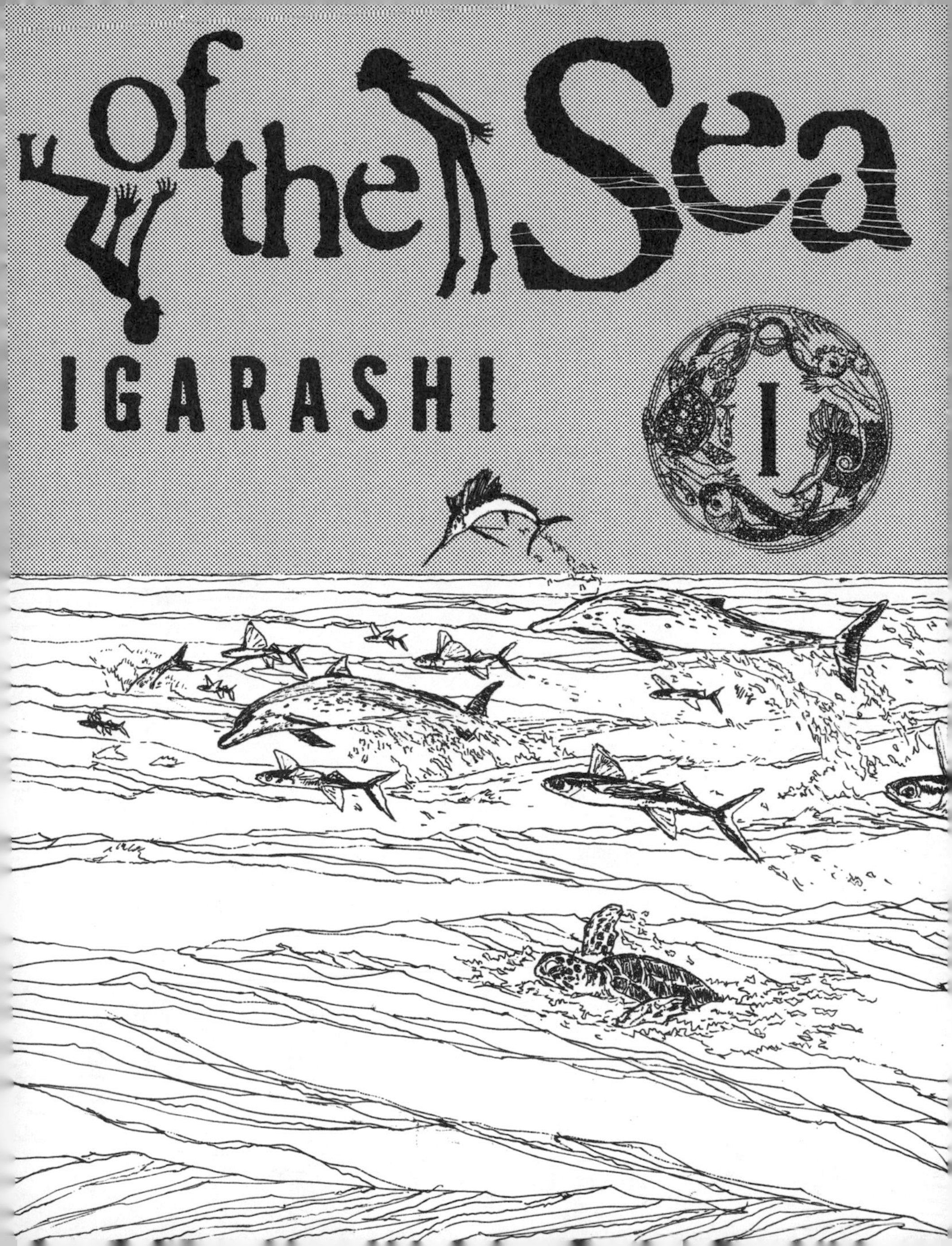
of the Sea
IGARASHI
I

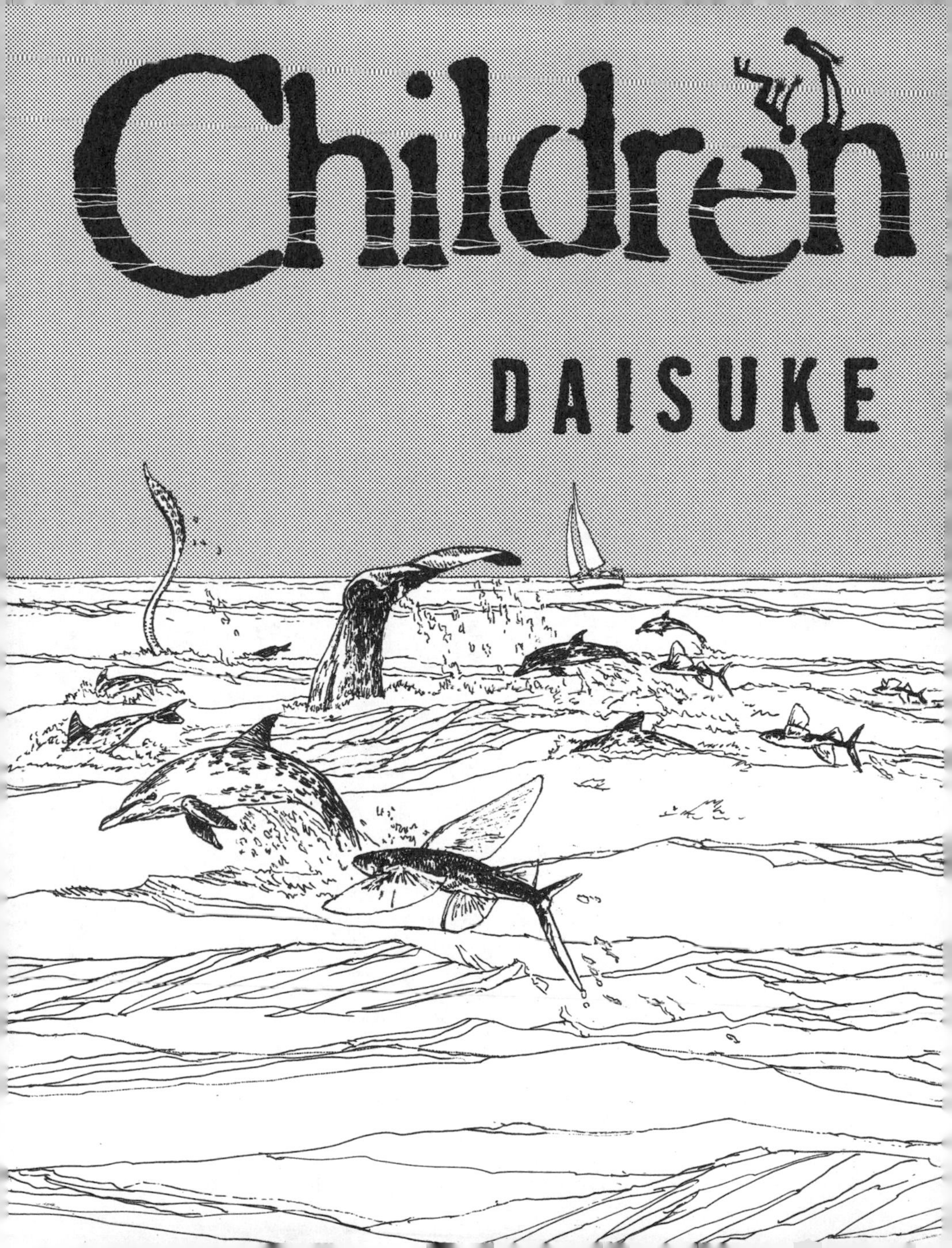
Children
DAISUKE

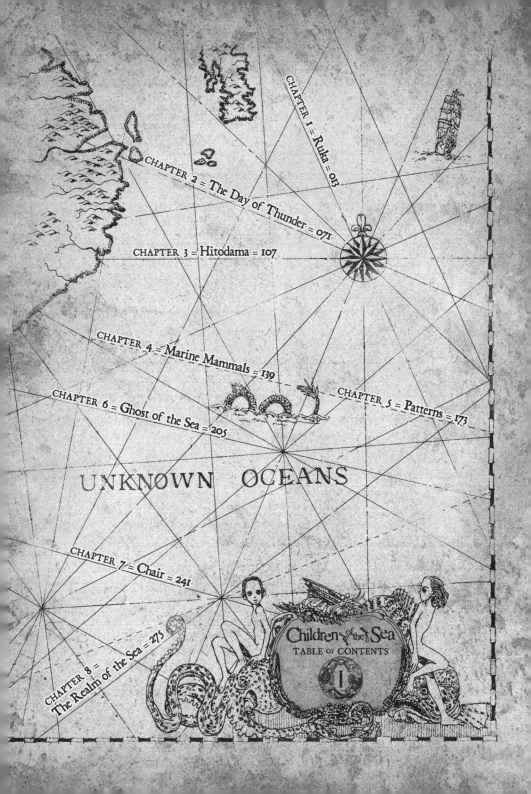

UNKNOWN OCEANS

Children of the Sea

TABLE OF CONTENTS

1

Chapter 1: Ruka

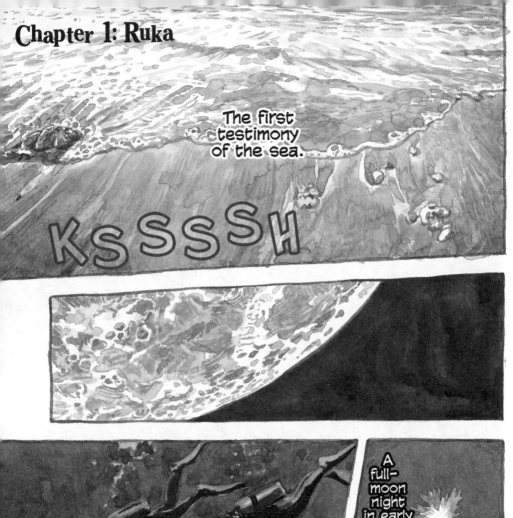

The first testimony of the sea.

KSSSSH

A full-moon night in early summer.

My assistant and I were taking pictures in the local waters.

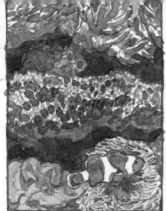

We were there for the coral spawning.

Fish gather to eat the eggs...

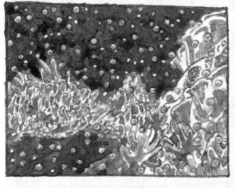

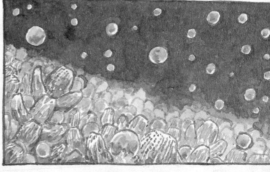

Man, it was just like...

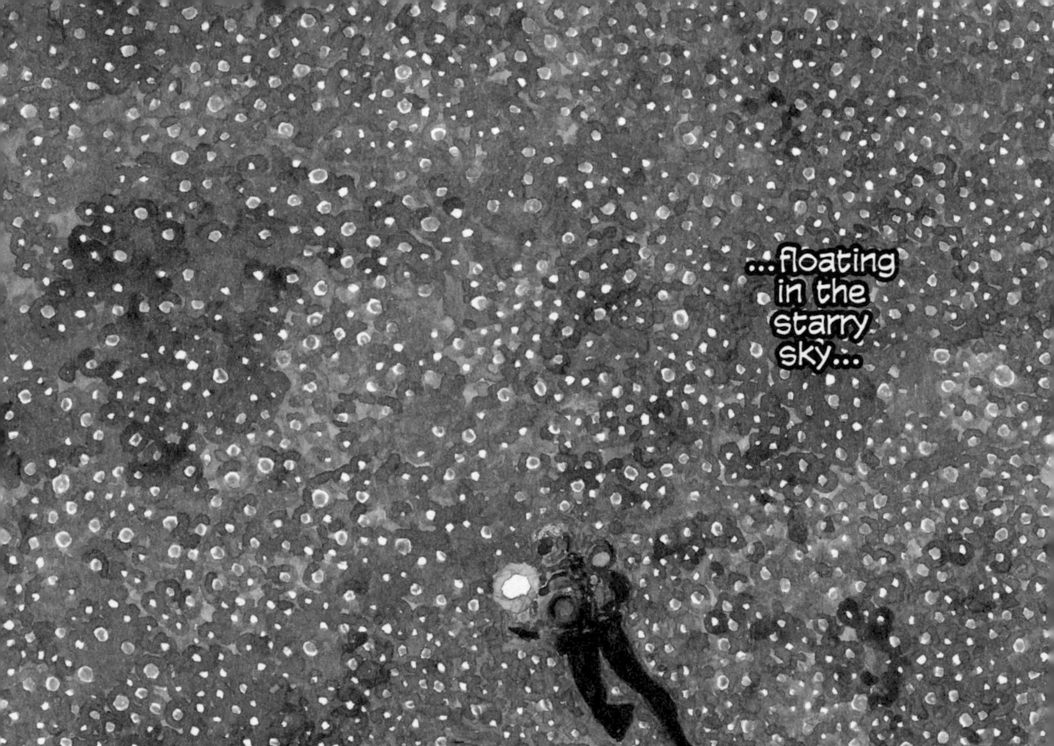
...floating in the starry sky...

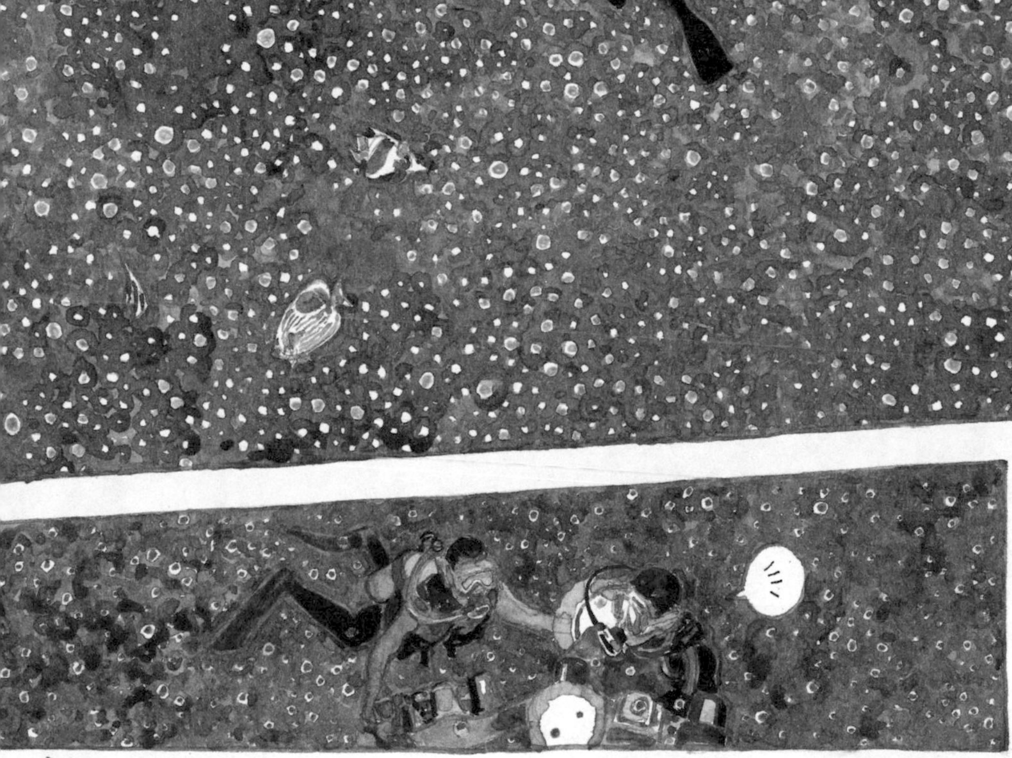

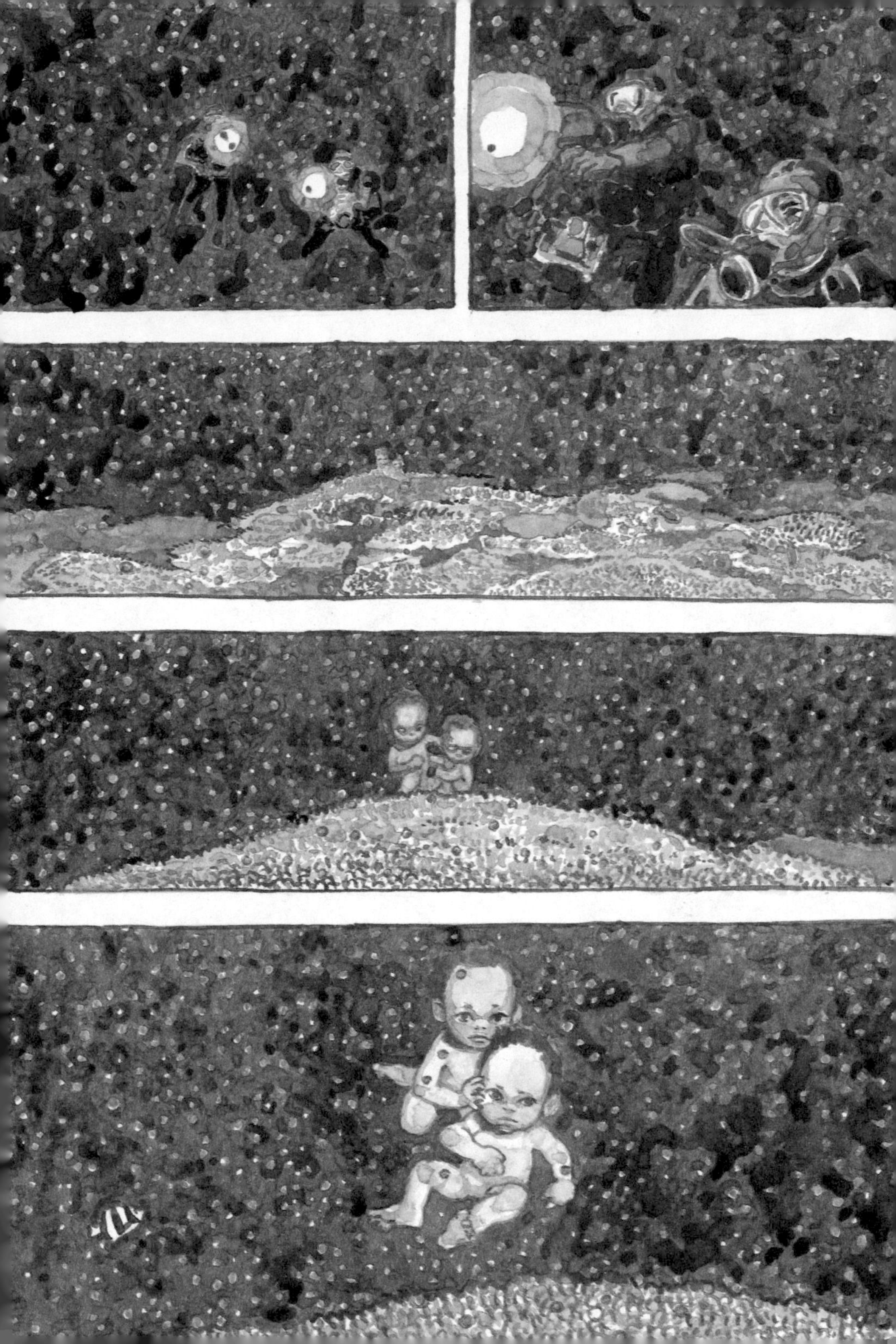

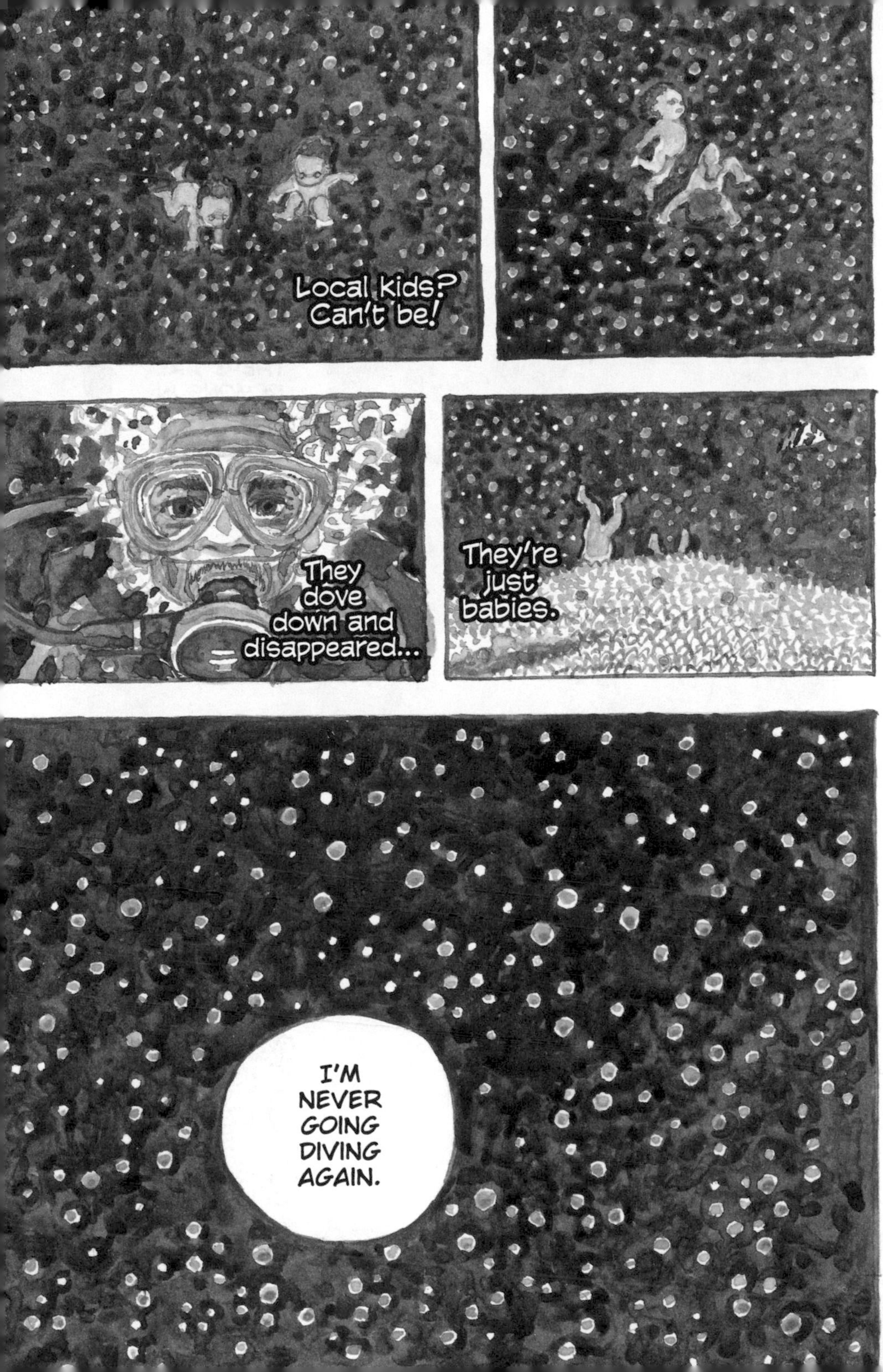
Local kids? Can't be!
They're just babies.
They dove down and disappeared...
I'M NEVER GOING DIVING AGAIN.

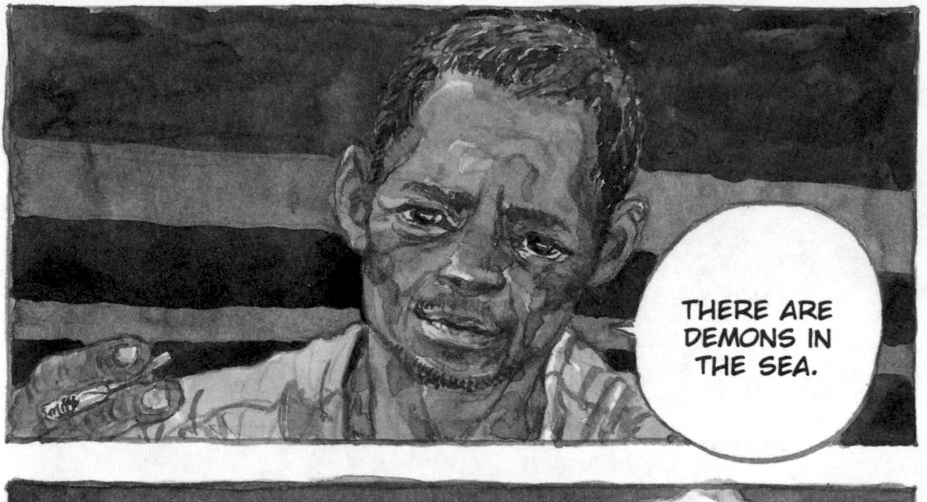
THERE ARE DEMONS IN THE SEA.

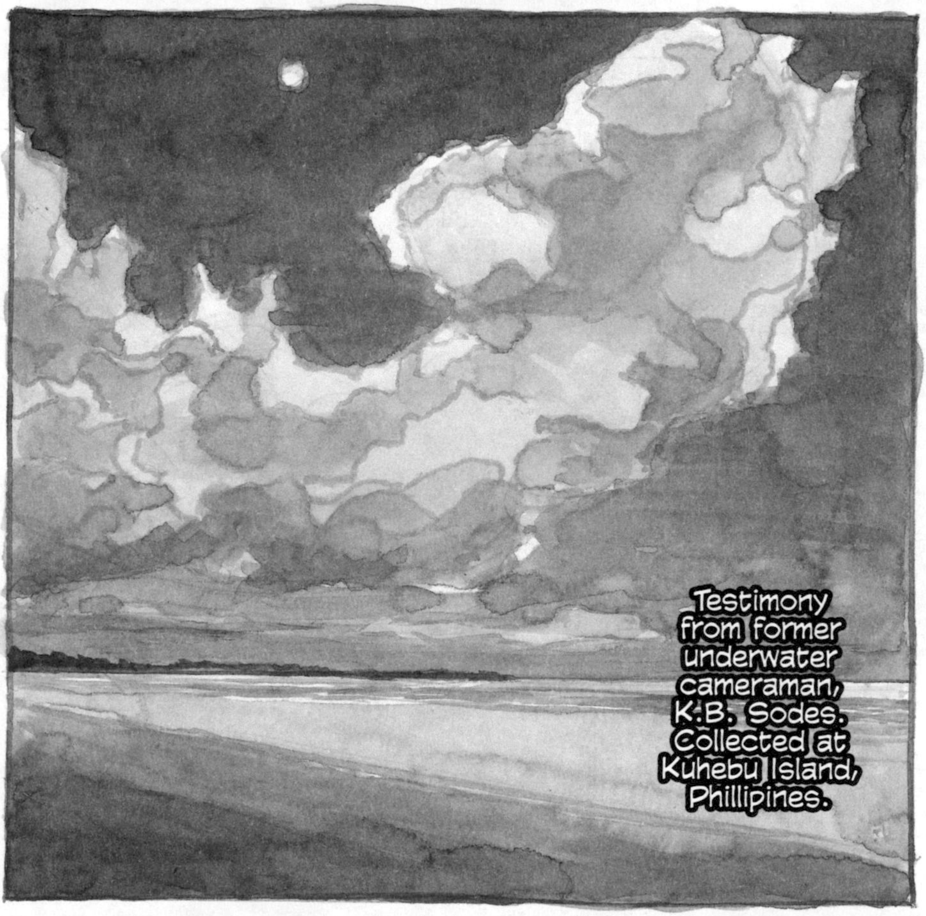
Testimony from former underwater cameraman, K.B. Sodes. Collected at Kuhebu Island, Phillipines.

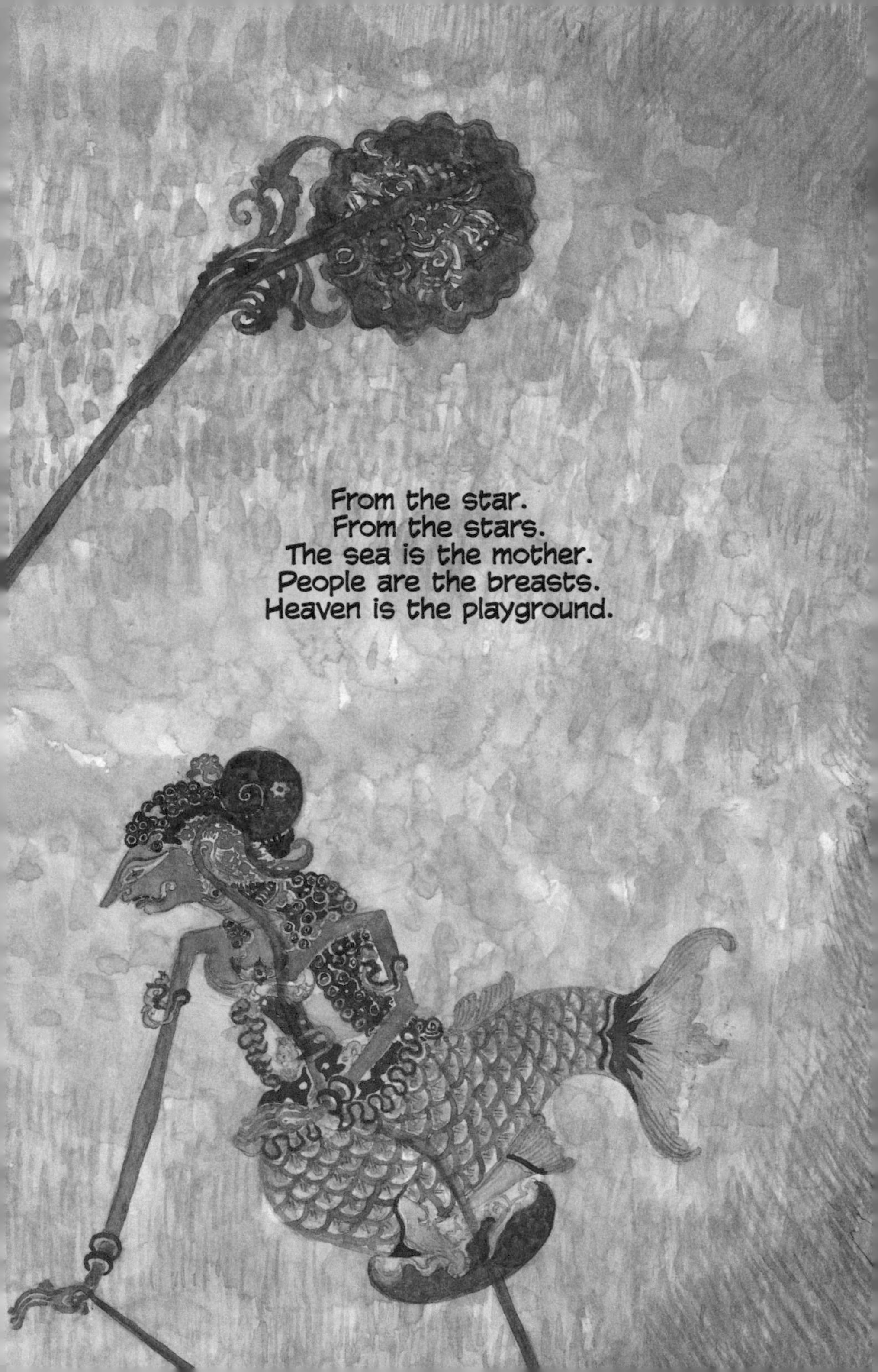
From the star.
From the stars.
The sea is the mother.
People are the breasts.
Heaven is the playground.

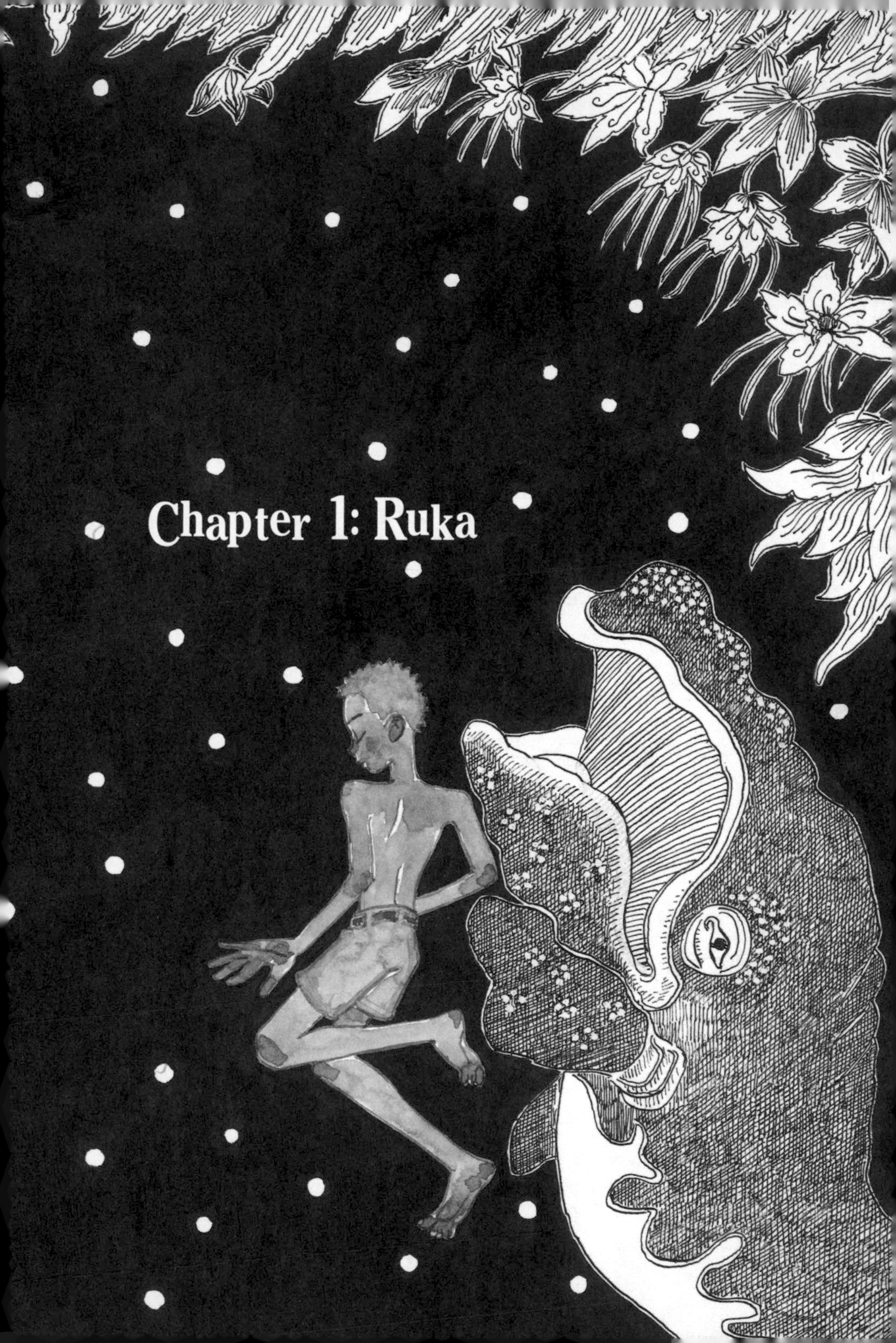
Chapter 1: Ruka

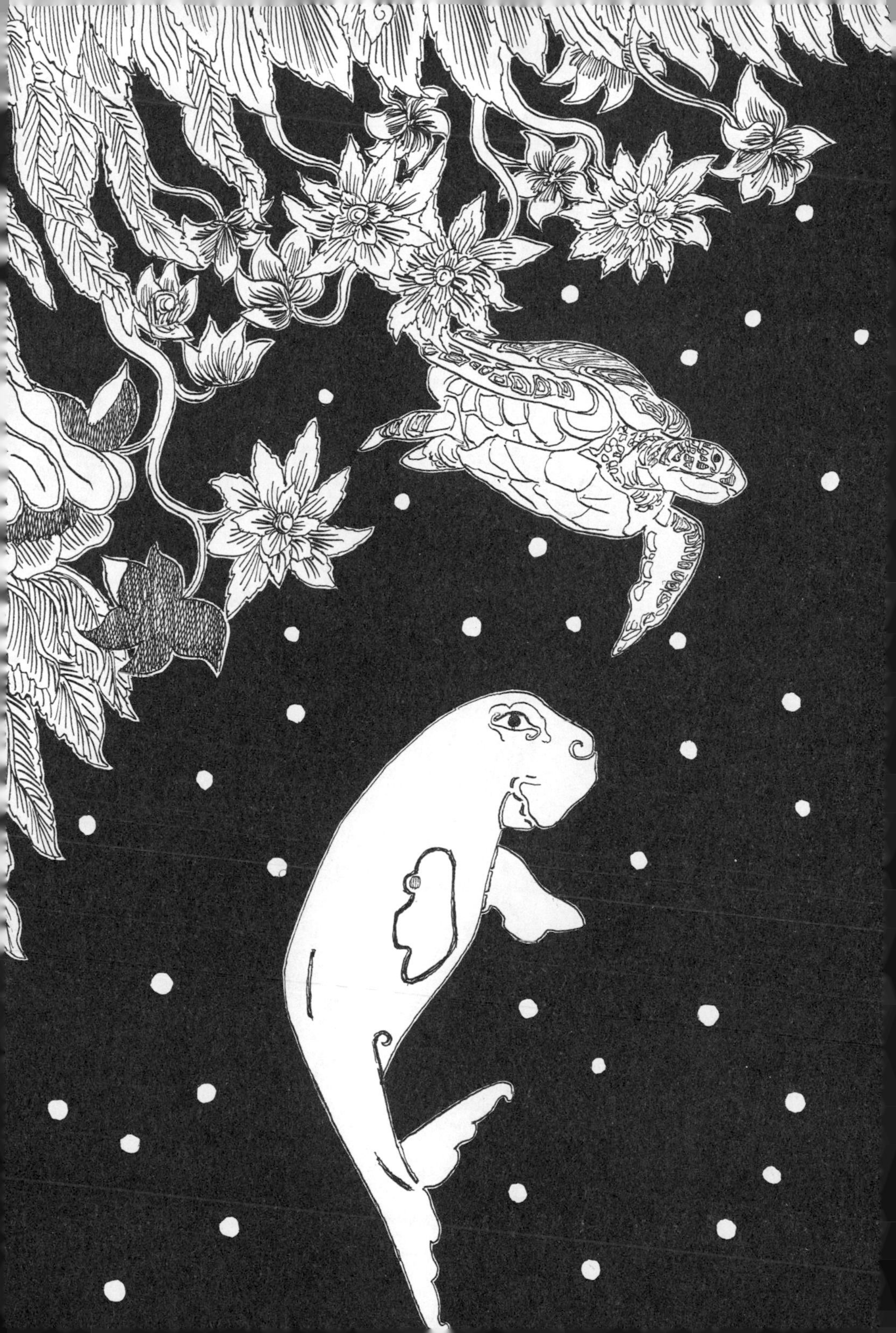

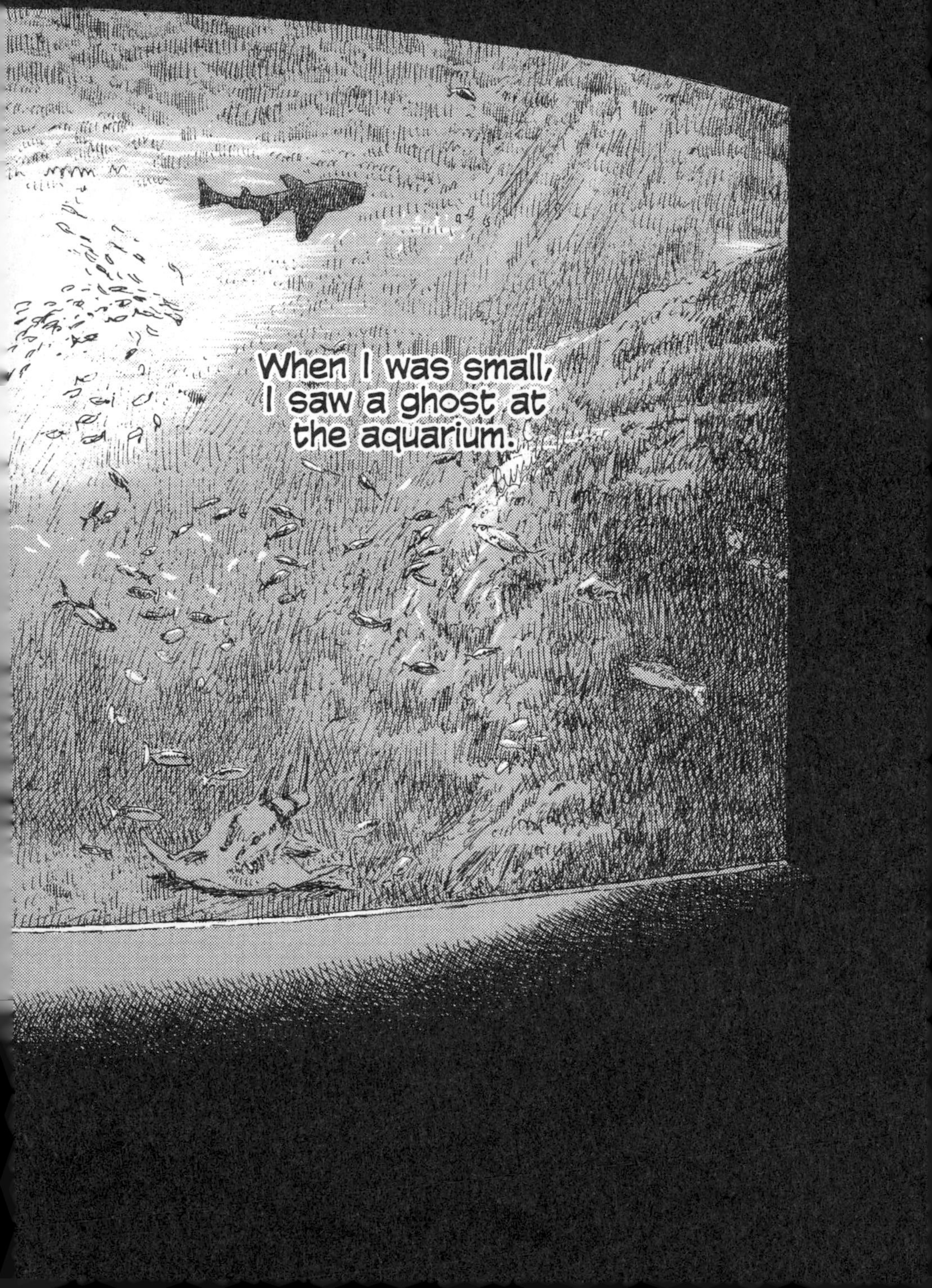
When I was small, I saw a ghost at the aquarium.

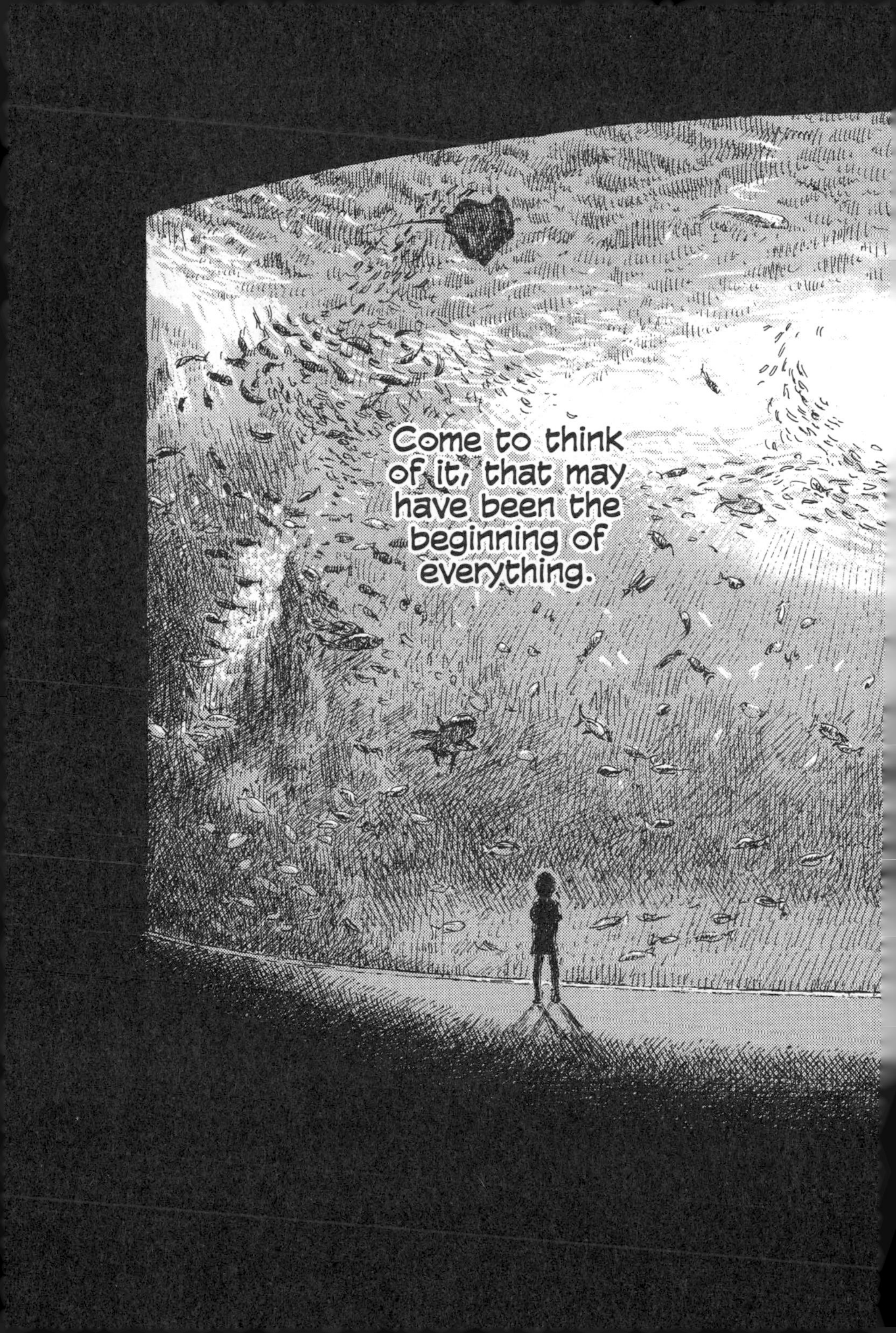
Come to think of it, that may have been the beginning of everything.

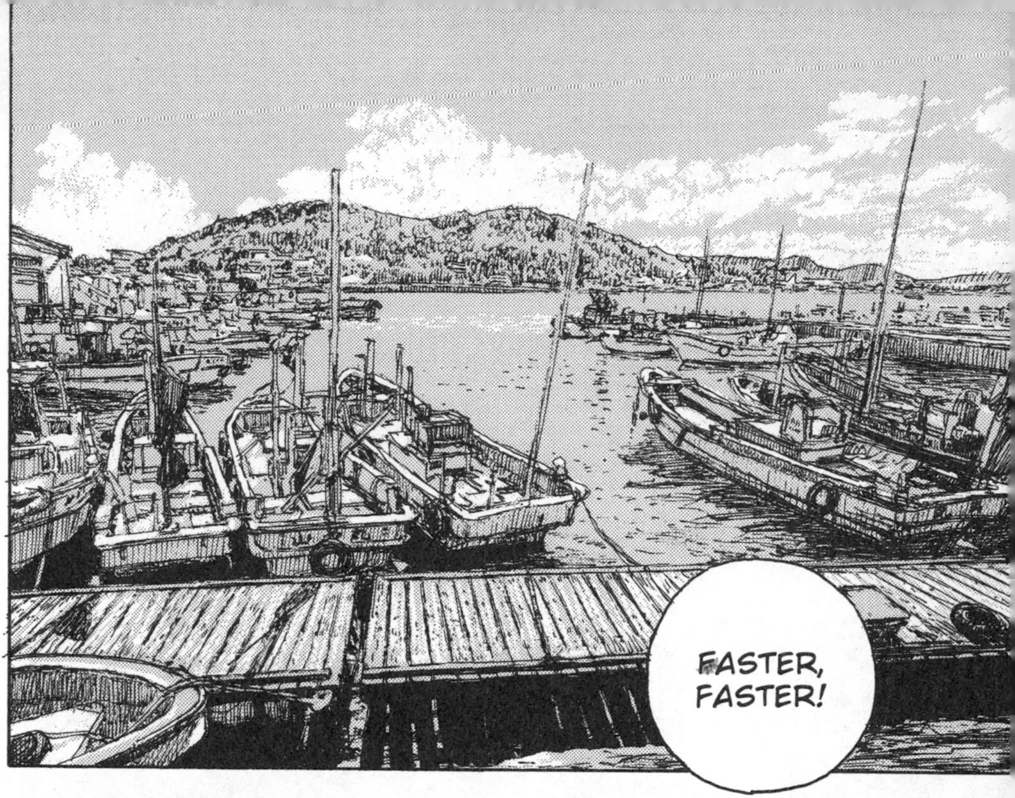
FASTER, FASTER!
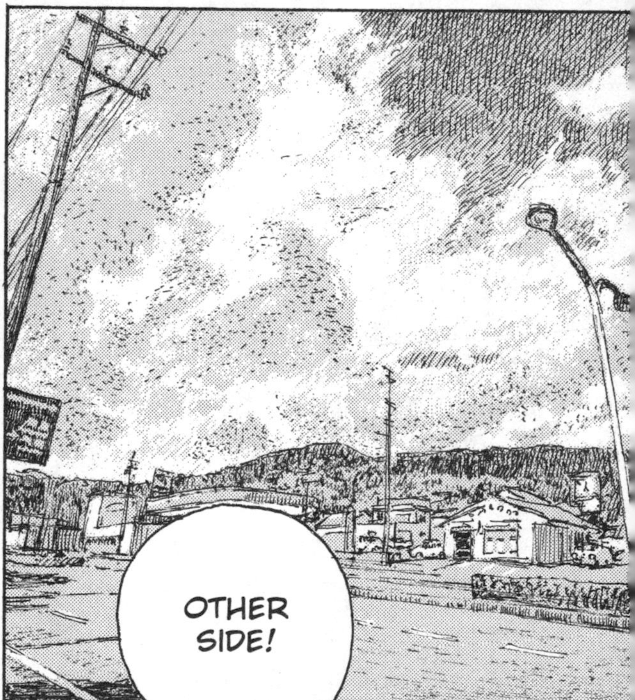
OTHER SIDE!
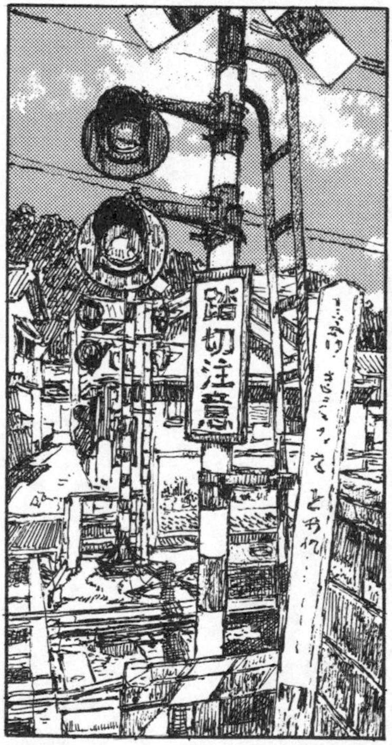
踏切注意

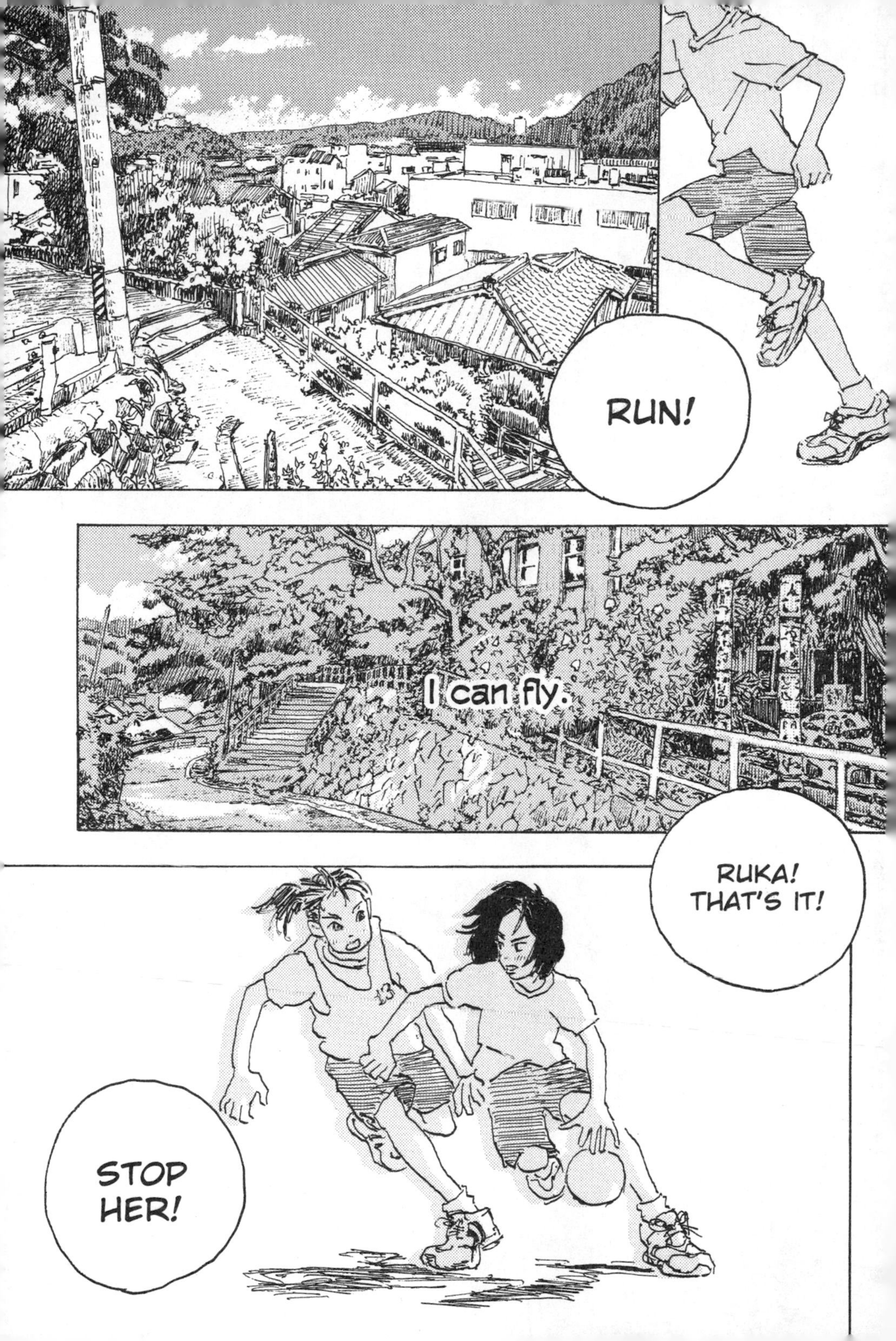
RUN!
I can fly.
RUKA! THAT'S IT!
STOP HER!

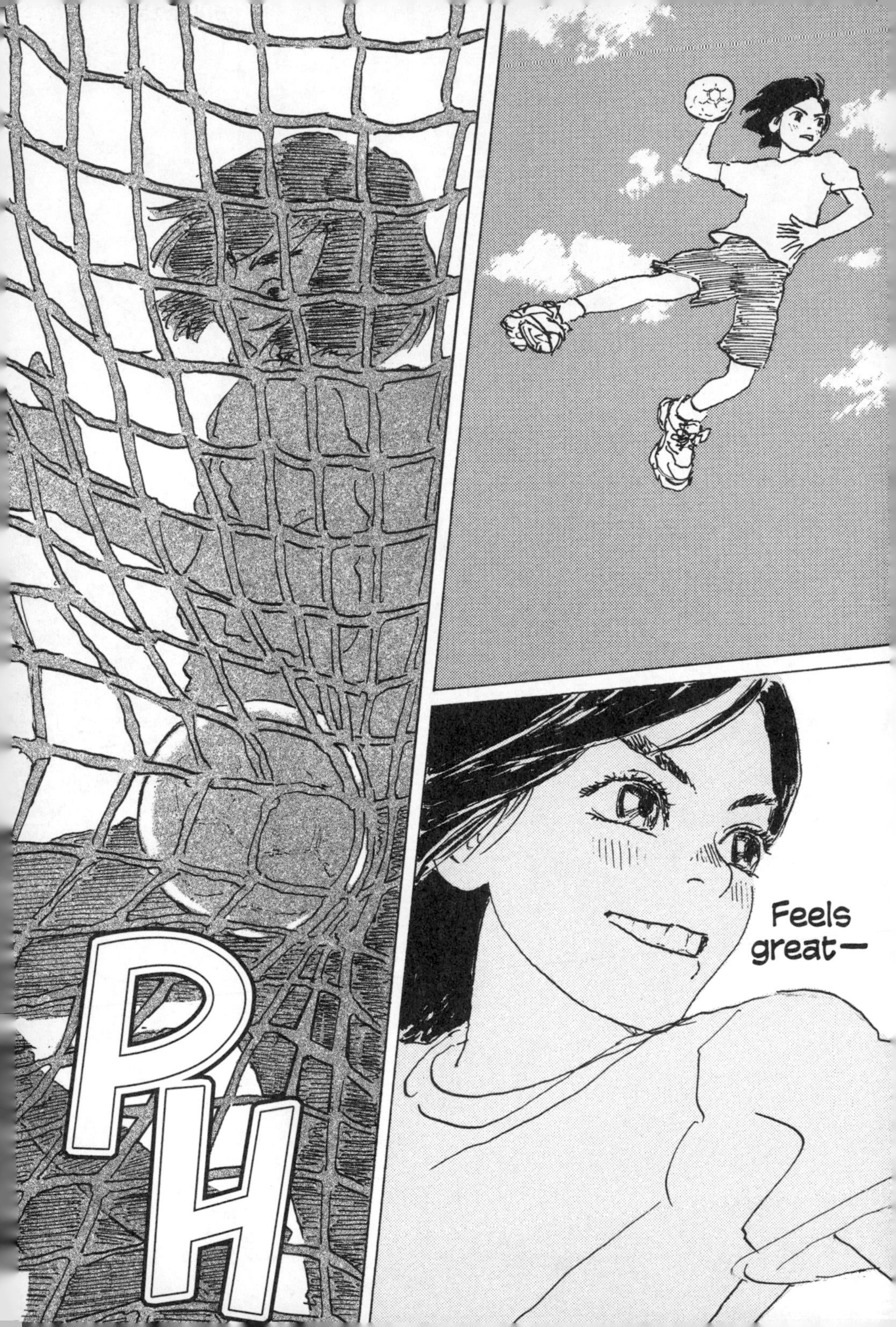
Feels great—
PH

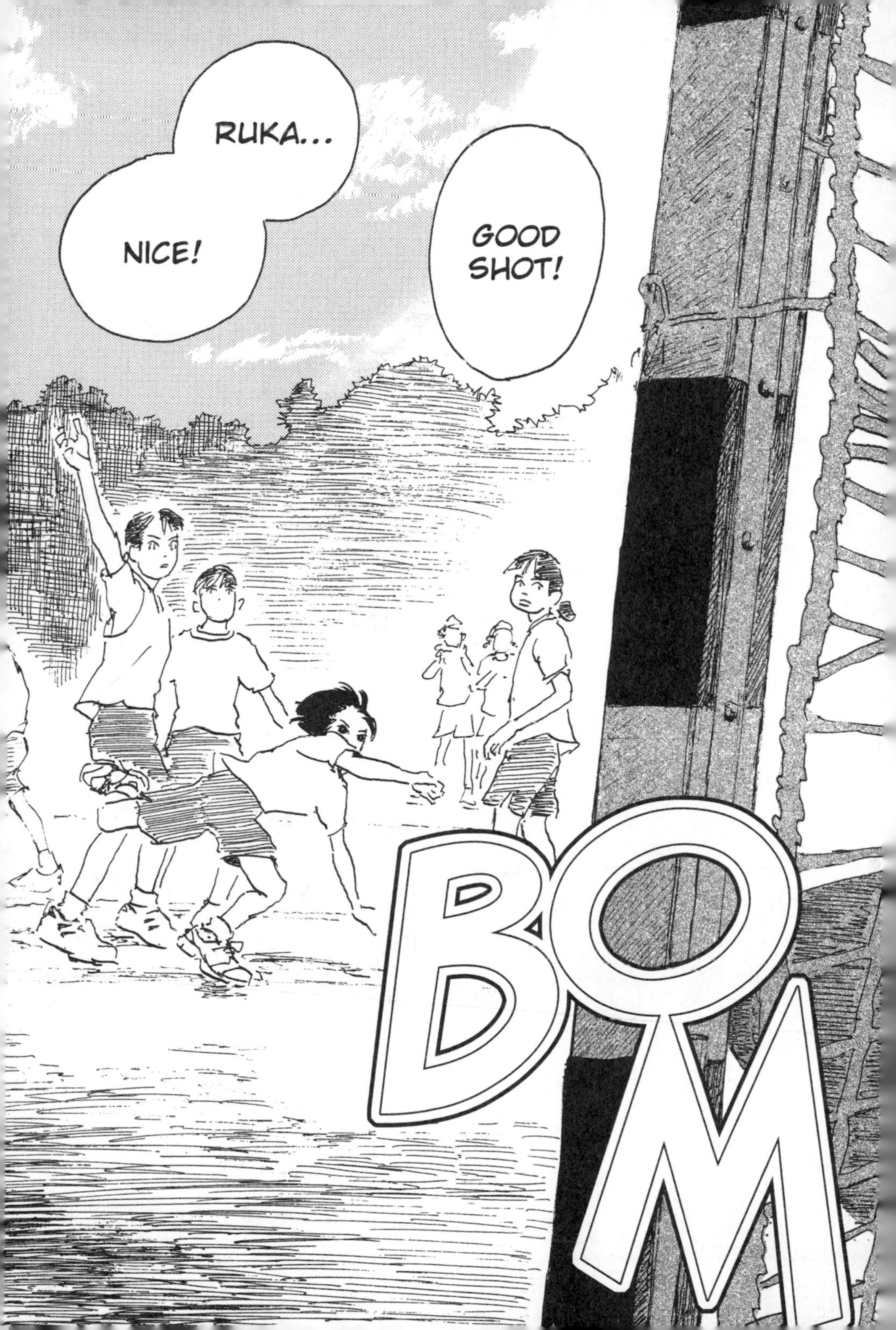
GOOD SHOT!
RUKA...
NICE!
BOM

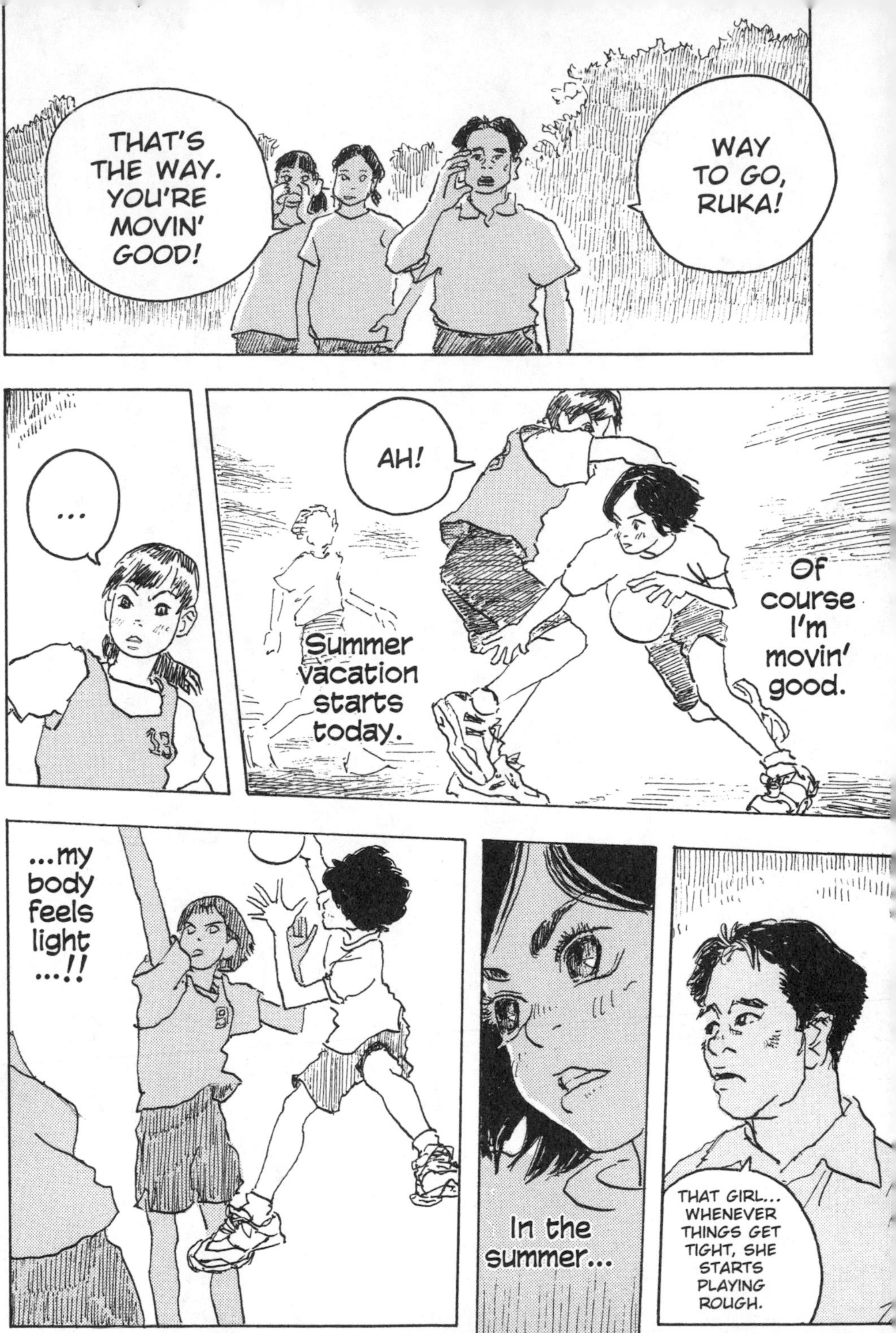
WAY TO GO, RUKA!
THAT'S THE WAY. YOU'RE MOVIN' GOOD!
AH!
Of course I'm movin' good.
Summer vacation starts today.
...
THAT GIRL... WHENEVER THINGS GET TIGHT, SHE STARTS PLAYING ROUGH.
In the summer...
...my body feels light ...!!

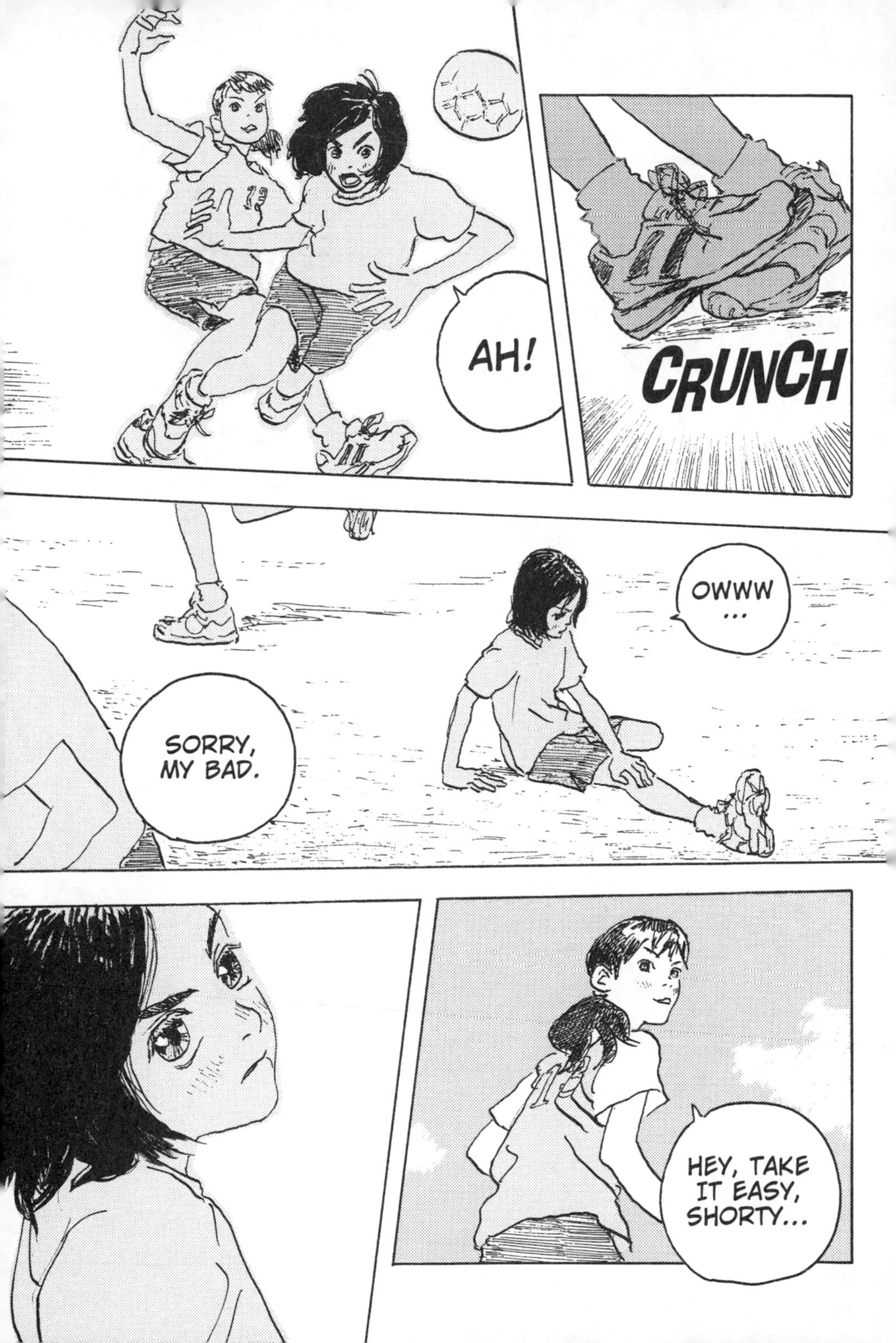
CRUNCH
AH!
OWWW ...
SORRY, MY BAD.
HEY, TAKE IT EASY, SHORTY...

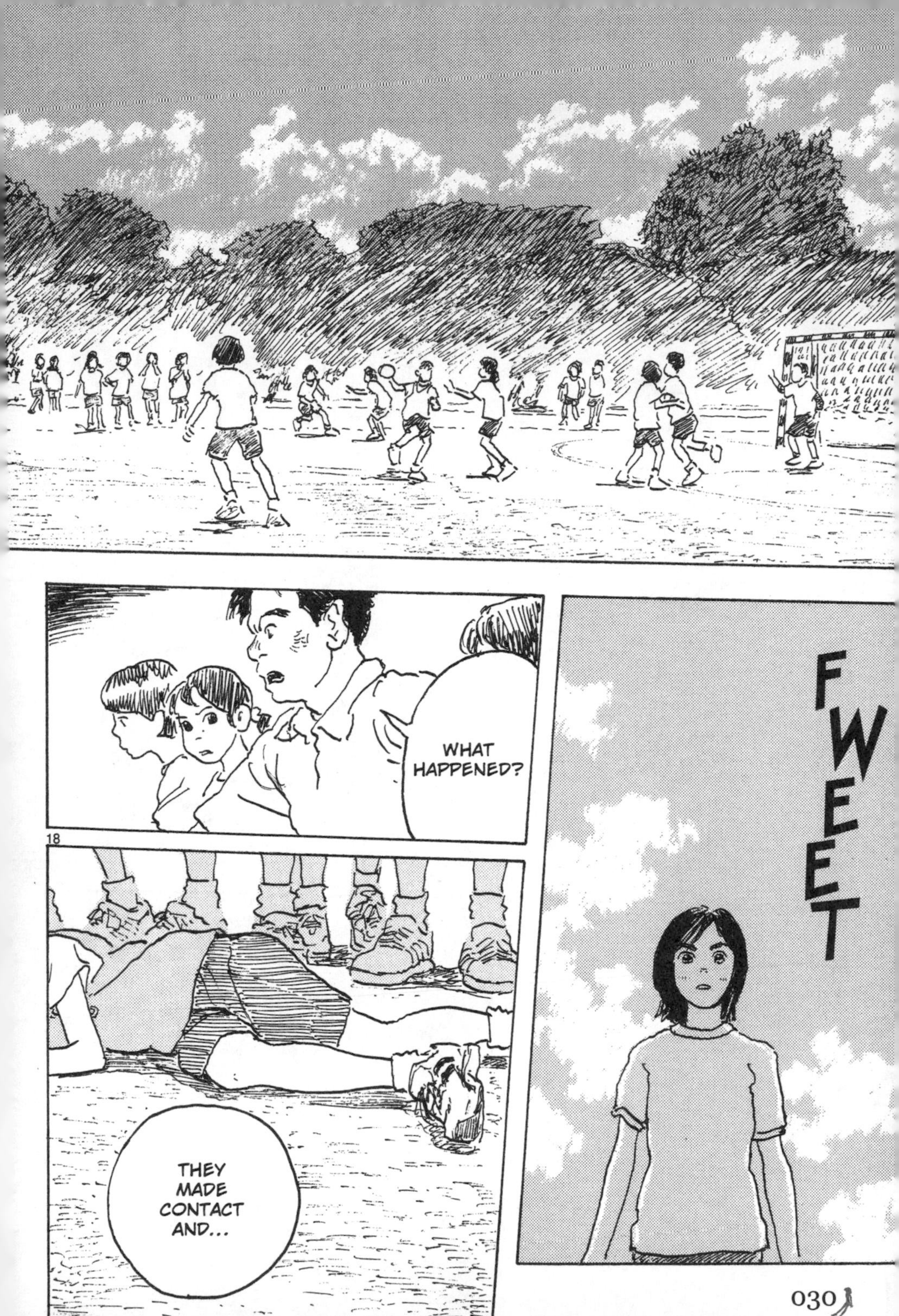
FWEET
WHAT HAPPENED?
THEY MADE CONTACT AND...

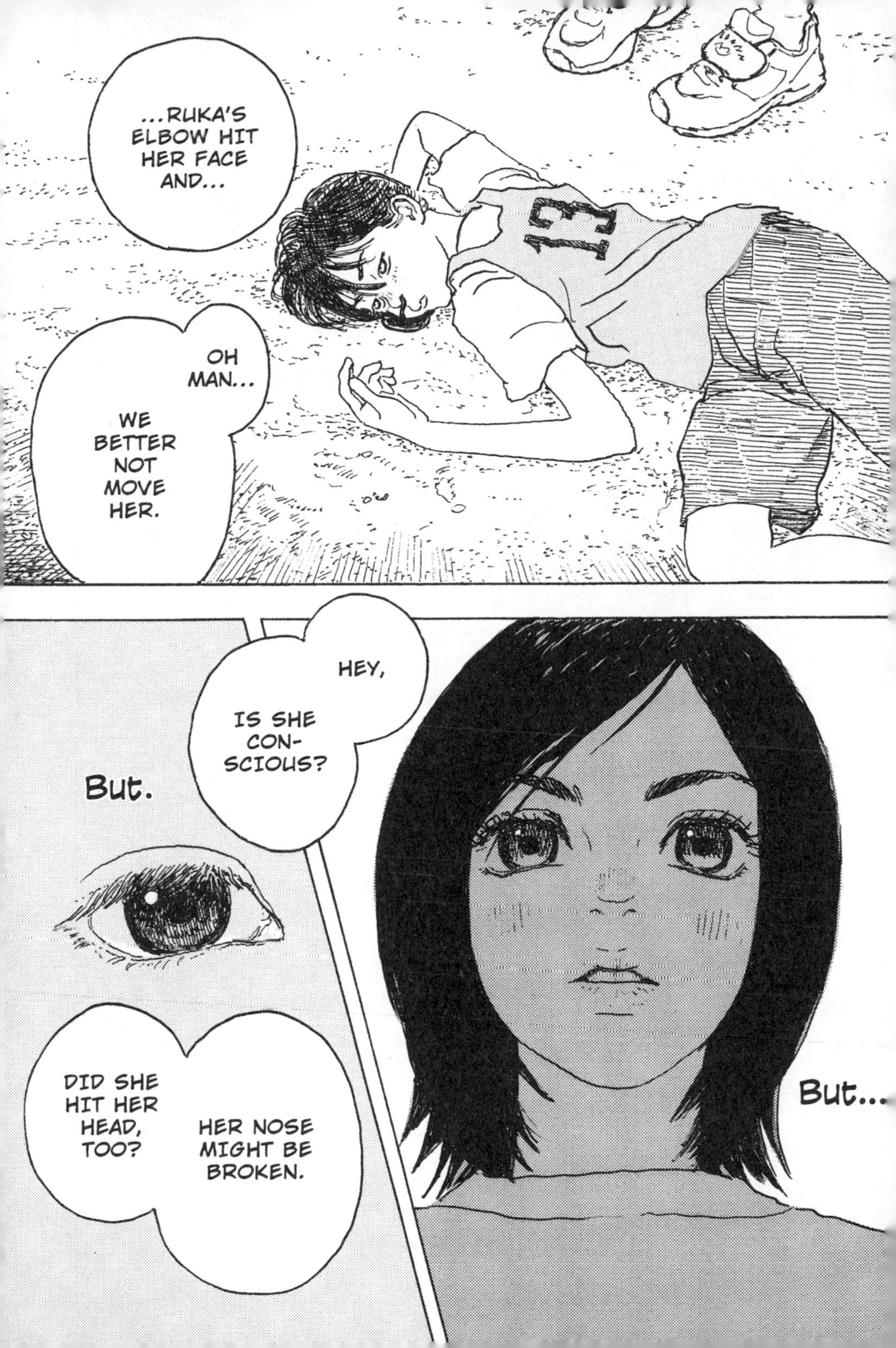
...RUKA'S ELBOW HIT HER FACE AND...
OH MAN...
WE BETTER NOT MOVE HER.
HEY,
IS SHE CON-SCIOUS?
But...
But.
DID SHE HIT HER HEAD, TOO?
HER NOSE MIGHT BE BROKEN.

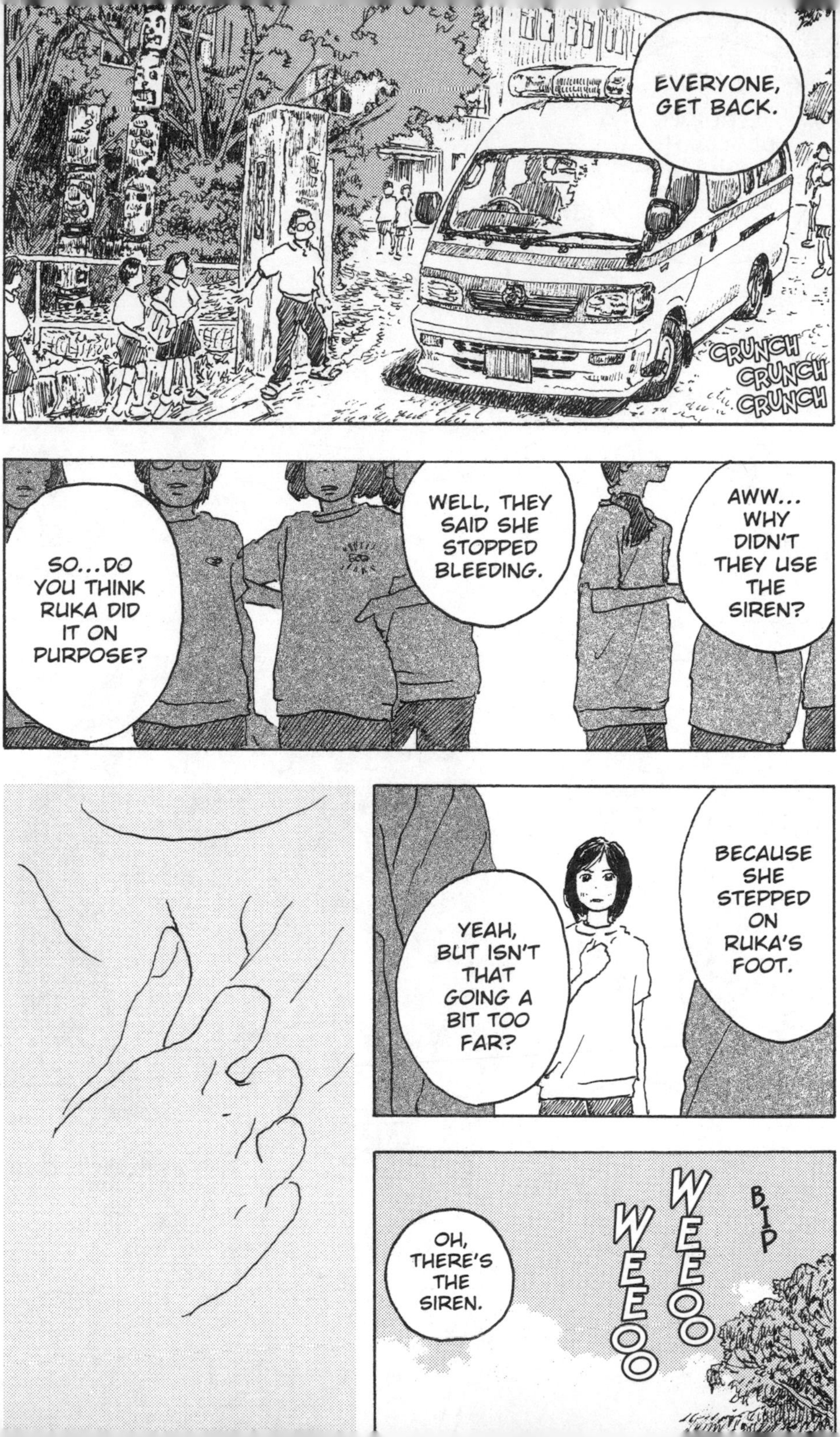
EVERYONE, GET BACK.
CRUNCH CRUNCH CRUNCH
AWW... WHY DIDN'T THEY USE THE SIREN?
WELL, THEY SAID SHE STOPPED BLEEDING.
SO...DO YOU THINK RUKA DID IT ON PURPOSE?
BECAUSE SHE STEPPED ON RUKA'S FOOT.
YEAH, BUT ISN'T THAT GOING A BIT TOO FAR?
BIP
WEEOO
WEEOO
OH, THERE'S THE SIREN.

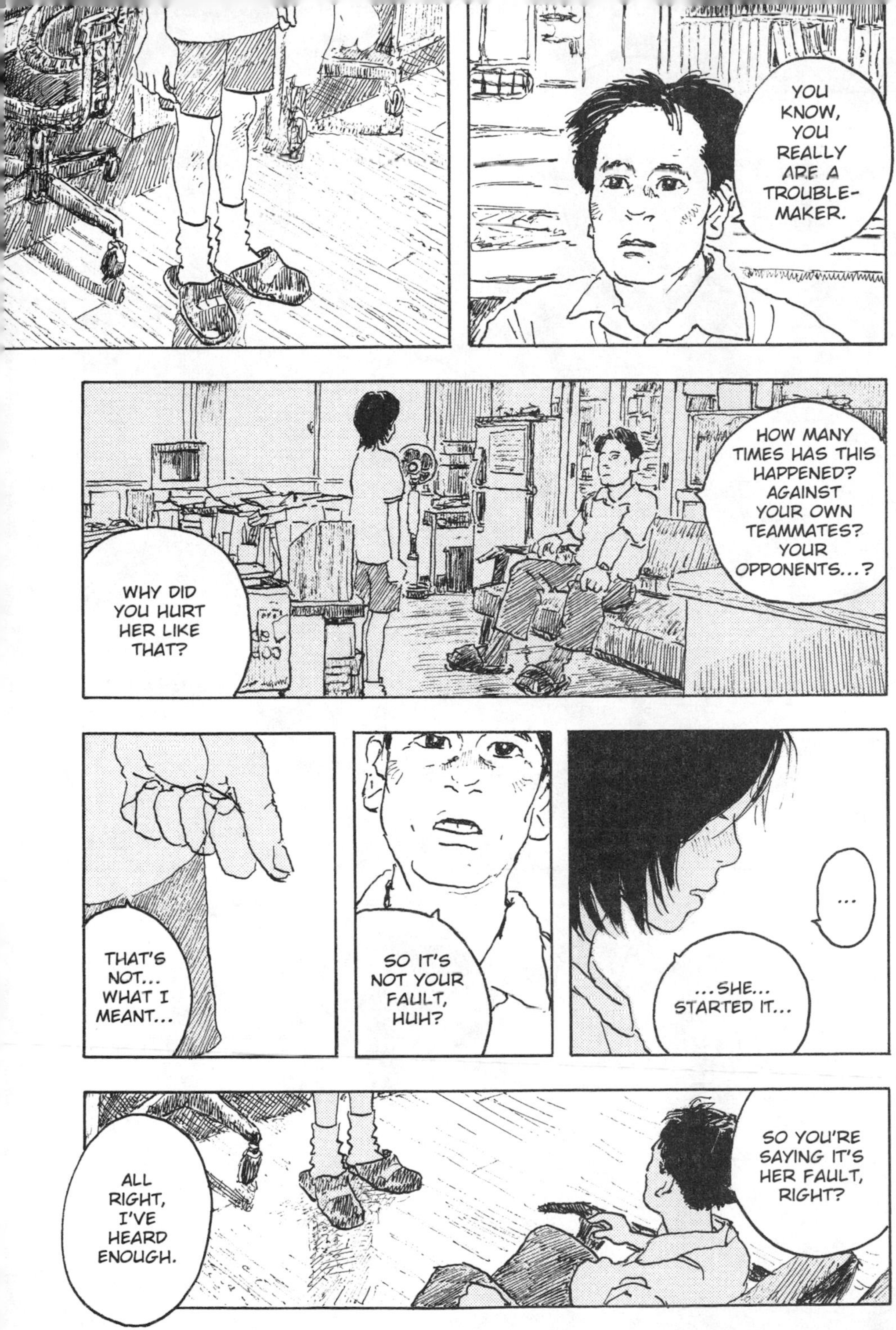
YOU KNOW, YOU REALLY ARE A TROUBLE-MAKER.
HOW MANY TIMES HAS THIS HAPPENED? AGAINST YOUR OWN TEAMMATES? YOUR OPPONENTS...?
WHY DID YOU HURT HER LIKE THAT?
...
...SHE... STARTED IT...
SO IT'S NOT YOUR FAULT, HUH?
THAT'S NOT... WHAT I MEANT...
SO YOU'RE SAYING IT'S HER FAULT, RIGHT?
ALL RIGHT, I'VE HEARD ENOUGH.

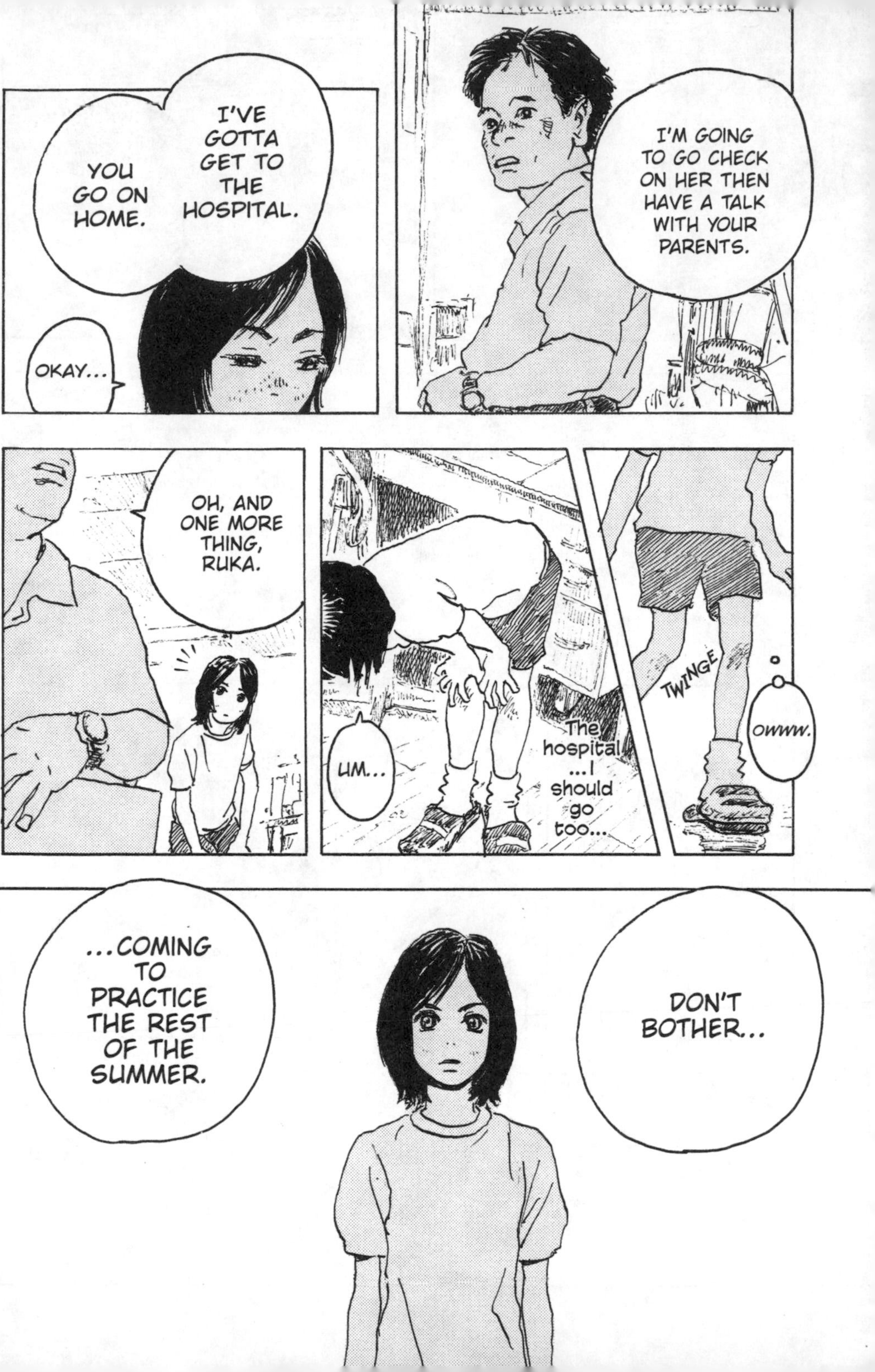
I'M GOING TO GO CHECK ON HER THEN HAVE A TALK WITH YOUR PARENTS.
I'VE GOTTA GET TO THE HOSPITAL.
YOU GO ON HOME.
OKAY...
TWINGE
OWWW.
The hospital ...I should go too...
UM...
OH, AND ONE MORE THING, RUKA.
DON'T BOTHER...
...COMING TO PRACTICE THE REST OF THE SUMMER.

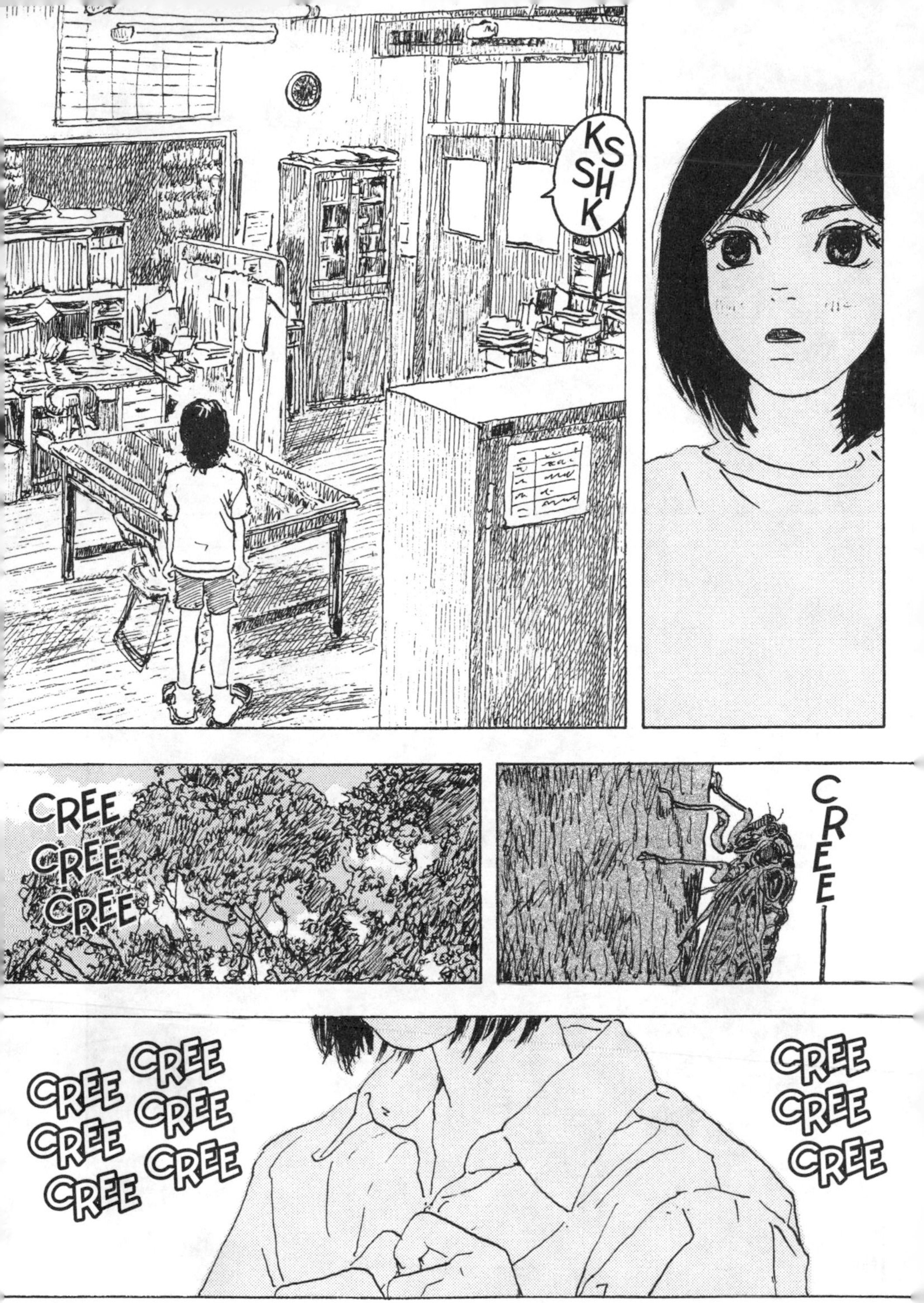
KSSHK
CREE—
CREE CREE CREE
CREE CREE CREE
CREE CREE CREE
CREE CREE CREE

DASH

THROB

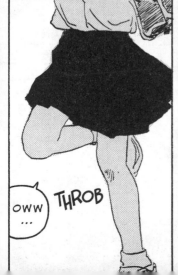

oww
...
THROB

THROB   THROB

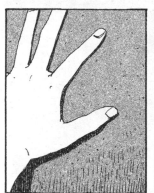

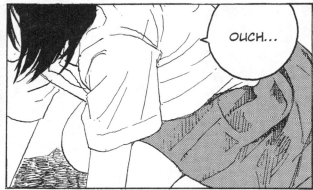

OUCH...

EVEN THOUGH TODAY IS THE FIRST DAY OF SUMMER VACATION...

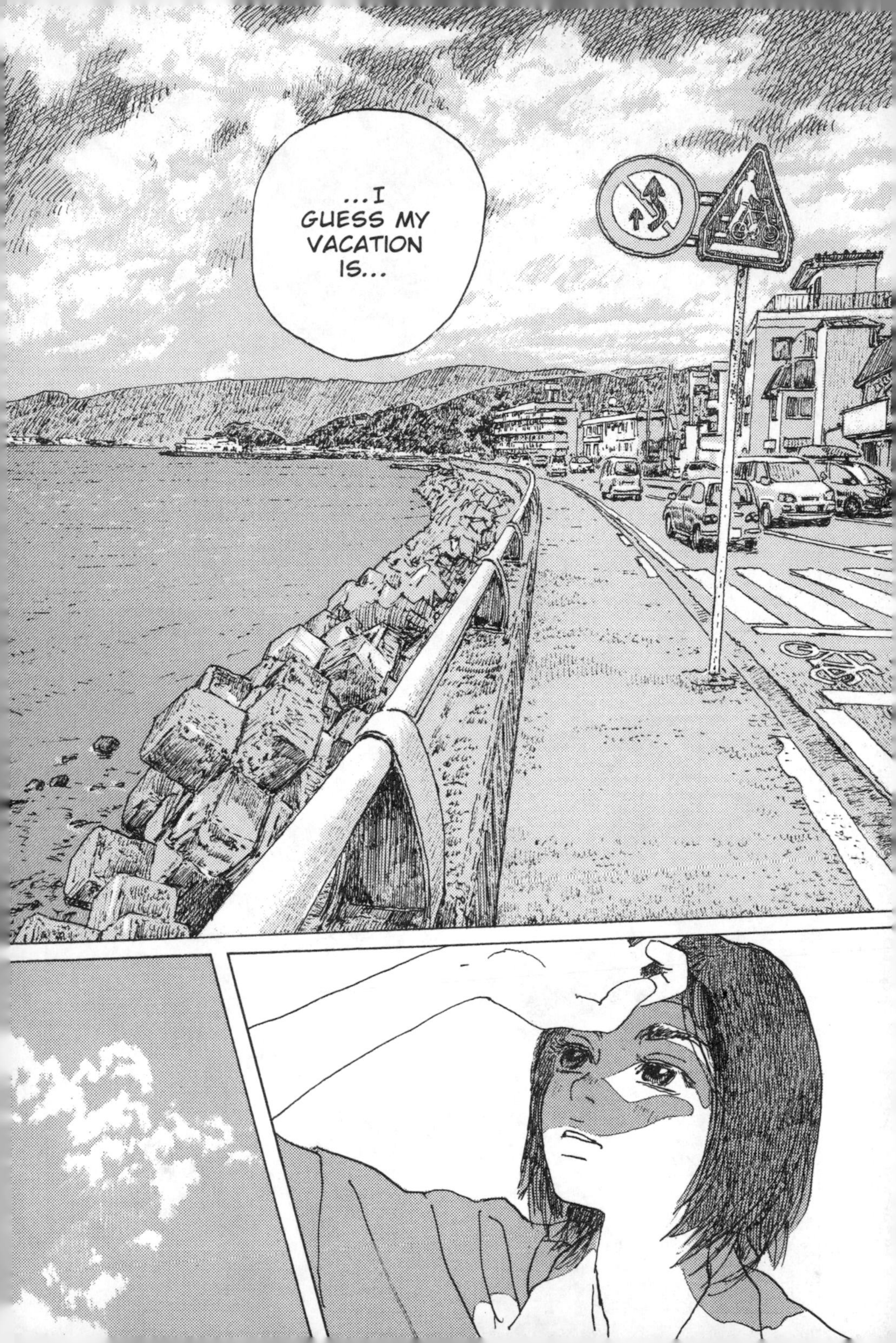
...I GUESS MY VACATION IS...

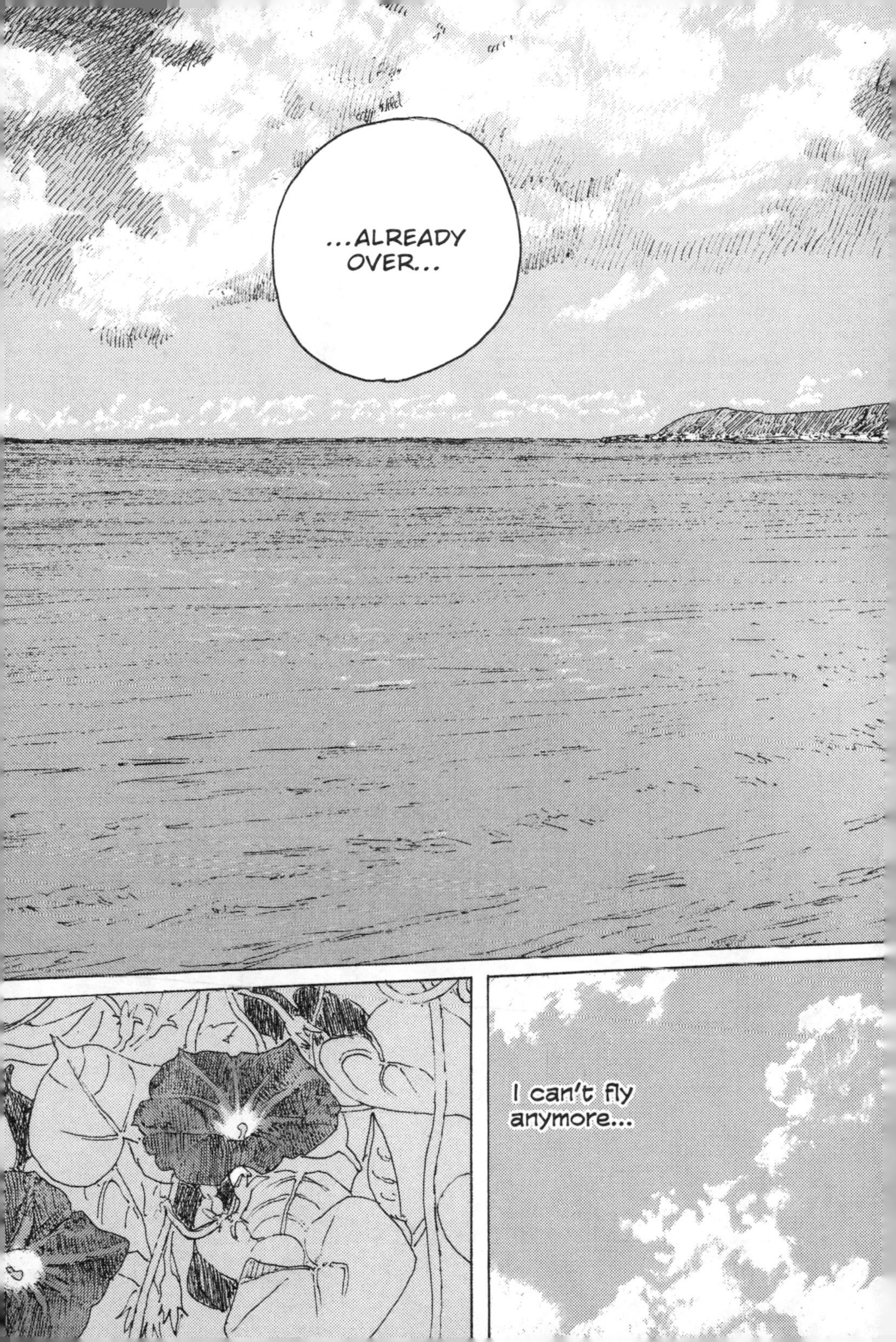
...ALREADY OVER...
I can't fly anymore...

BZZZ

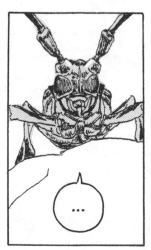

...

CREE—

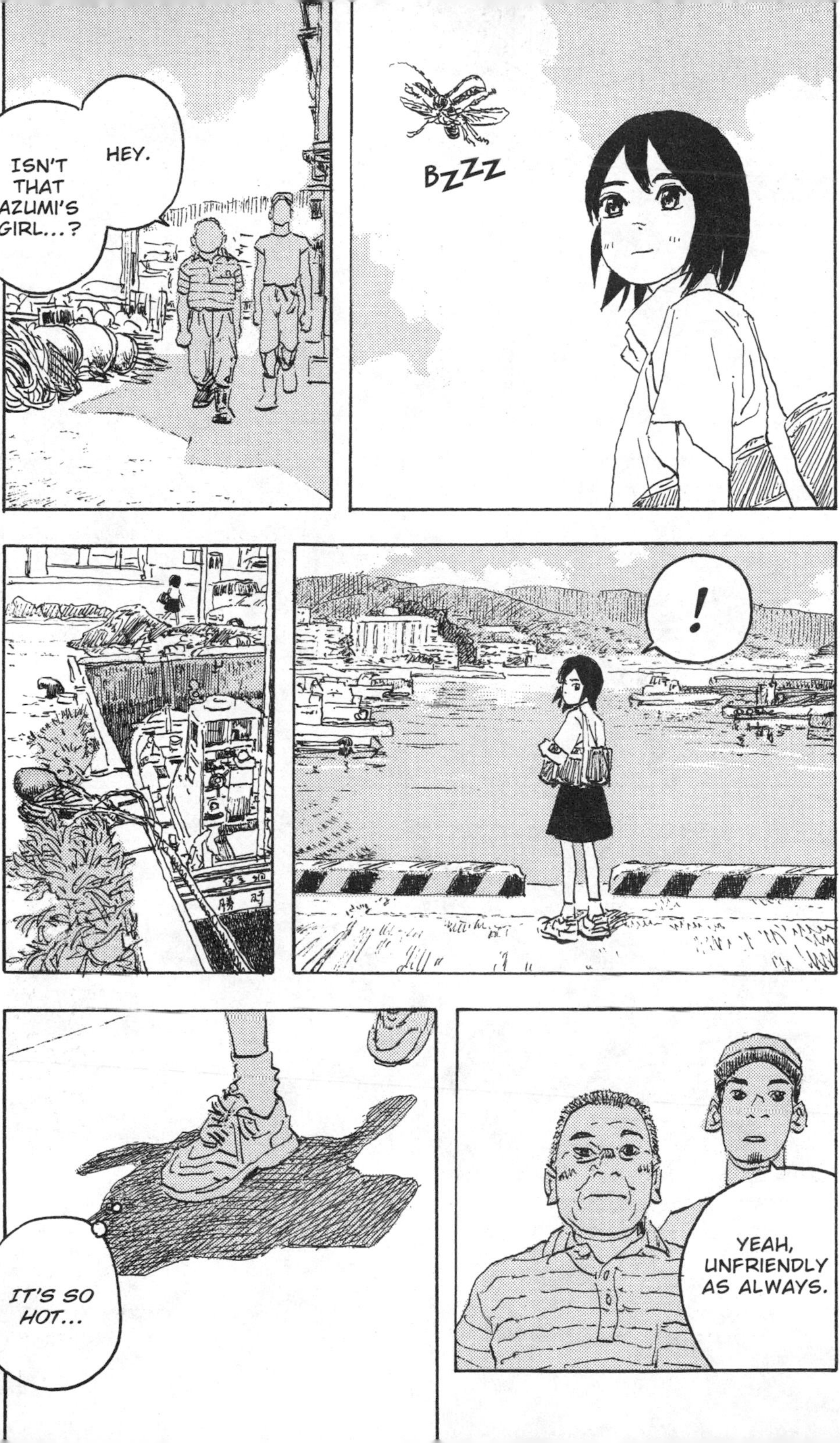
BZZZ
HEY.
ISN'T THAT AZUMI'S GIRL...?
!
YEAH, UNFRIENDLY AS ALWAYS.
IT'S SO HOT...

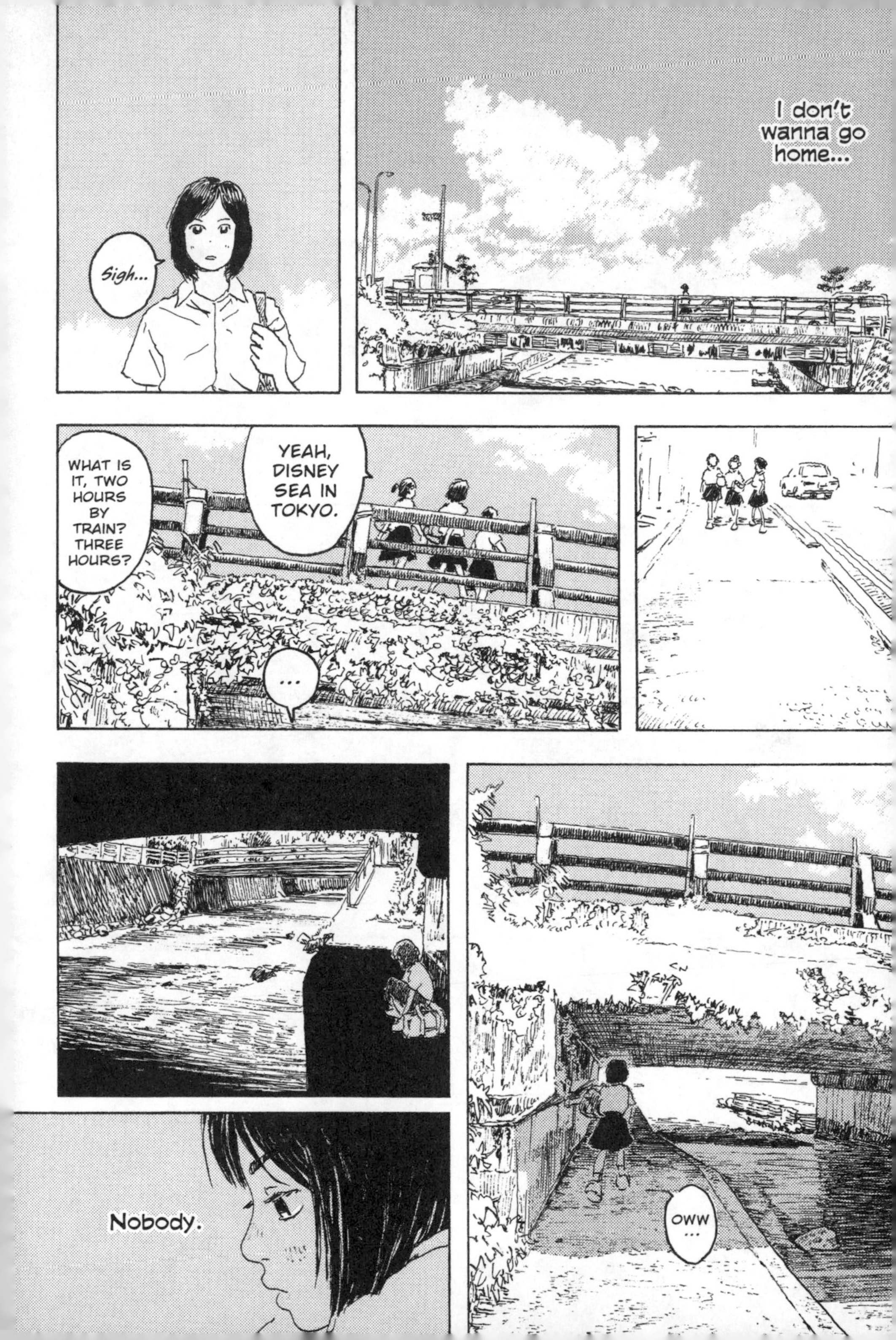
I don't wanna go home...
Sigh...
YEAH, DISNEY SEA IN TOKYO.
WHAT IS IT, TWO HOURS BY TRAIN? THREE HOURS?
...
OWW ...
Nobody.

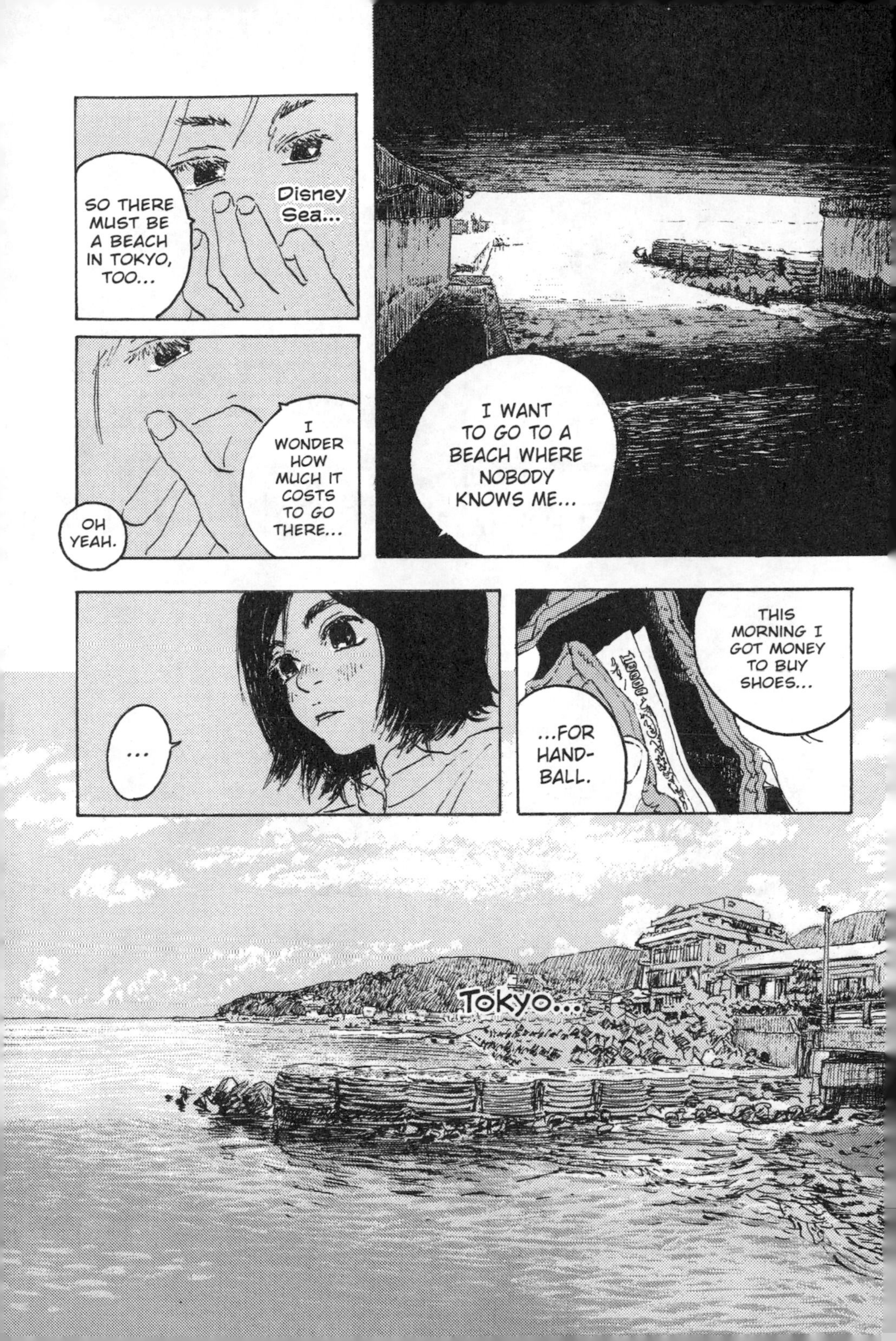
I WANT TO GO TO A BEACH WHERE NOBODY KNOWS ME...
Disney Sea...
SO THERE MUST BE A BEACH IN TOKYO, TOO...
I WONDER HOW MUCH IT COSTS TO GO THERE...
OH YEAH.
THIS MORNING I GOT MONEY TO BUY SHOES...
...FOR HAND-BALL.
...
Tokyo...

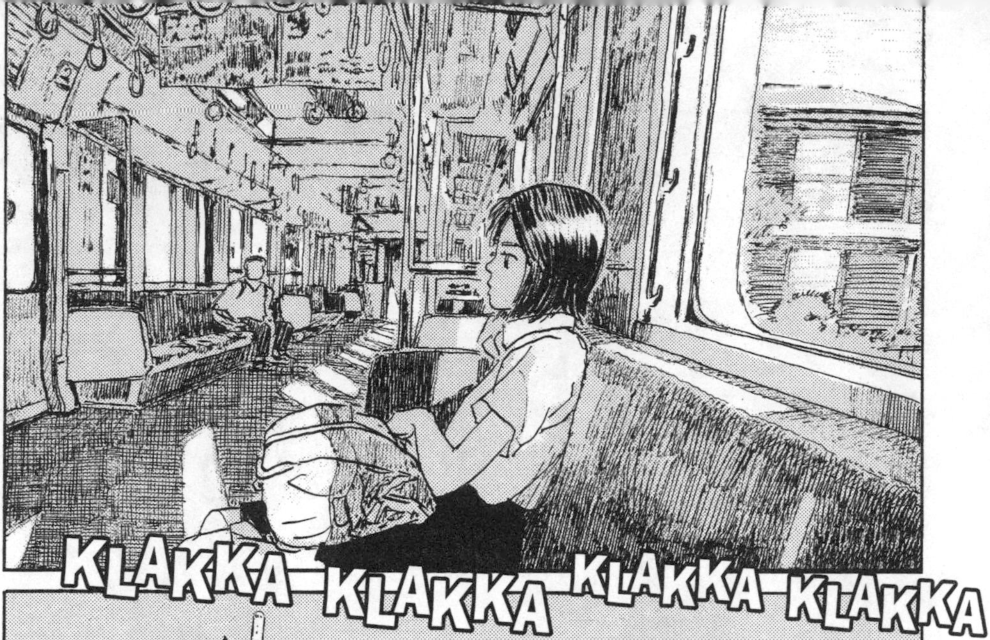
KLAKKA KLAKKA KLAKKA KLAKKA
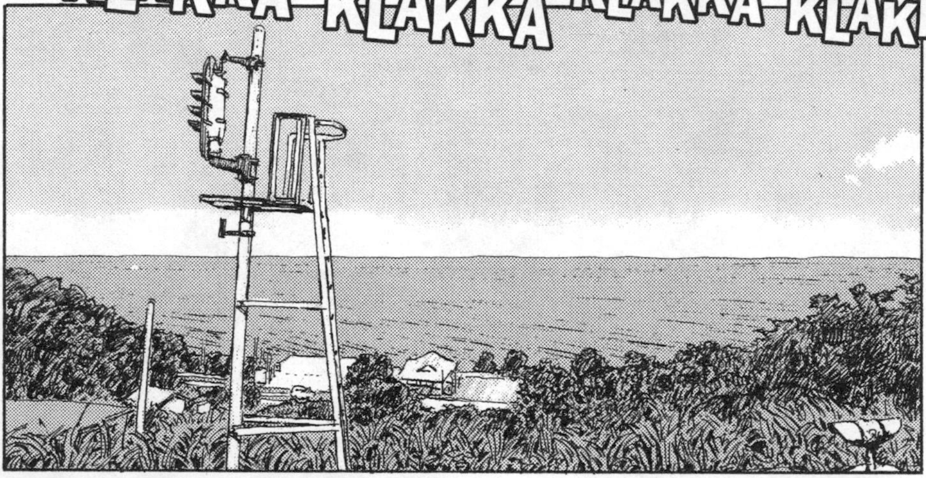
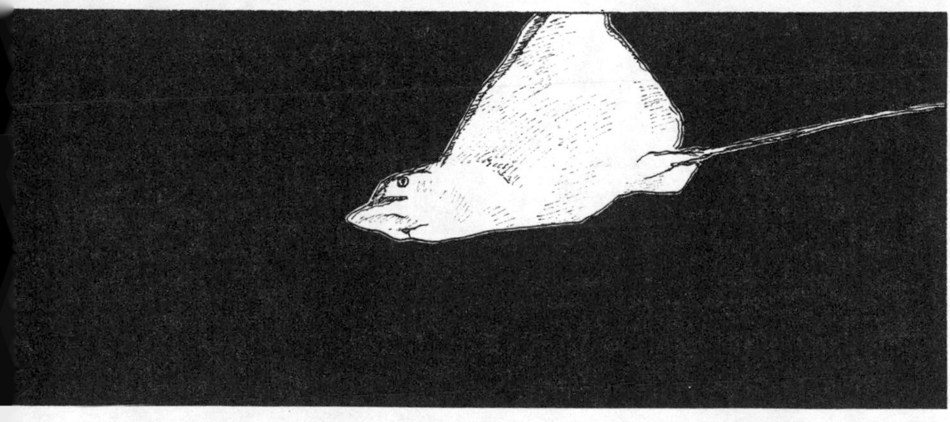

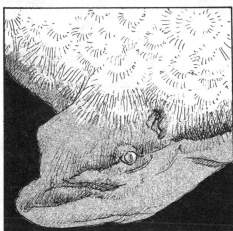
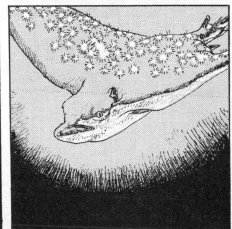

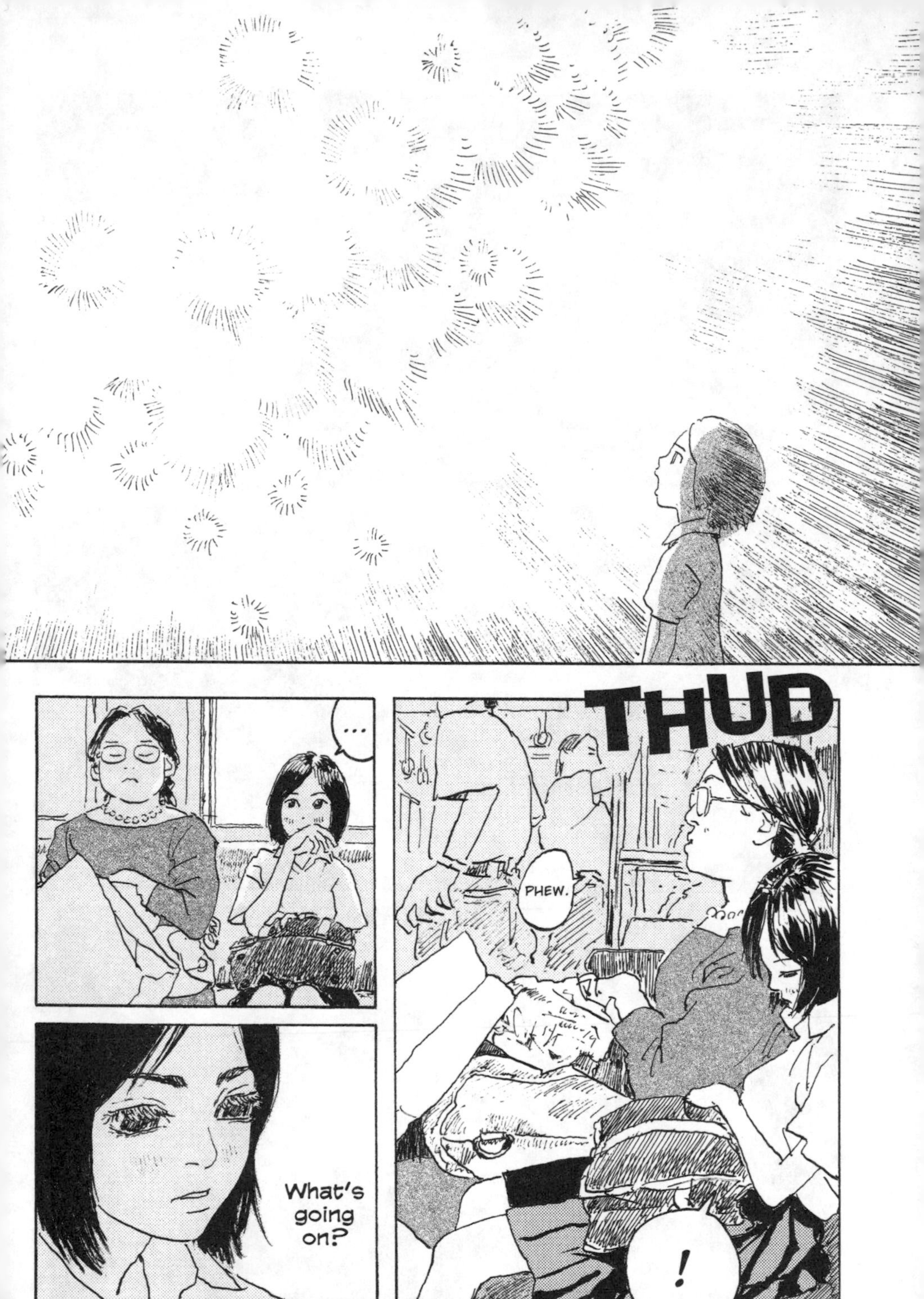
THUD
PHEW.
!
...
What's going on?

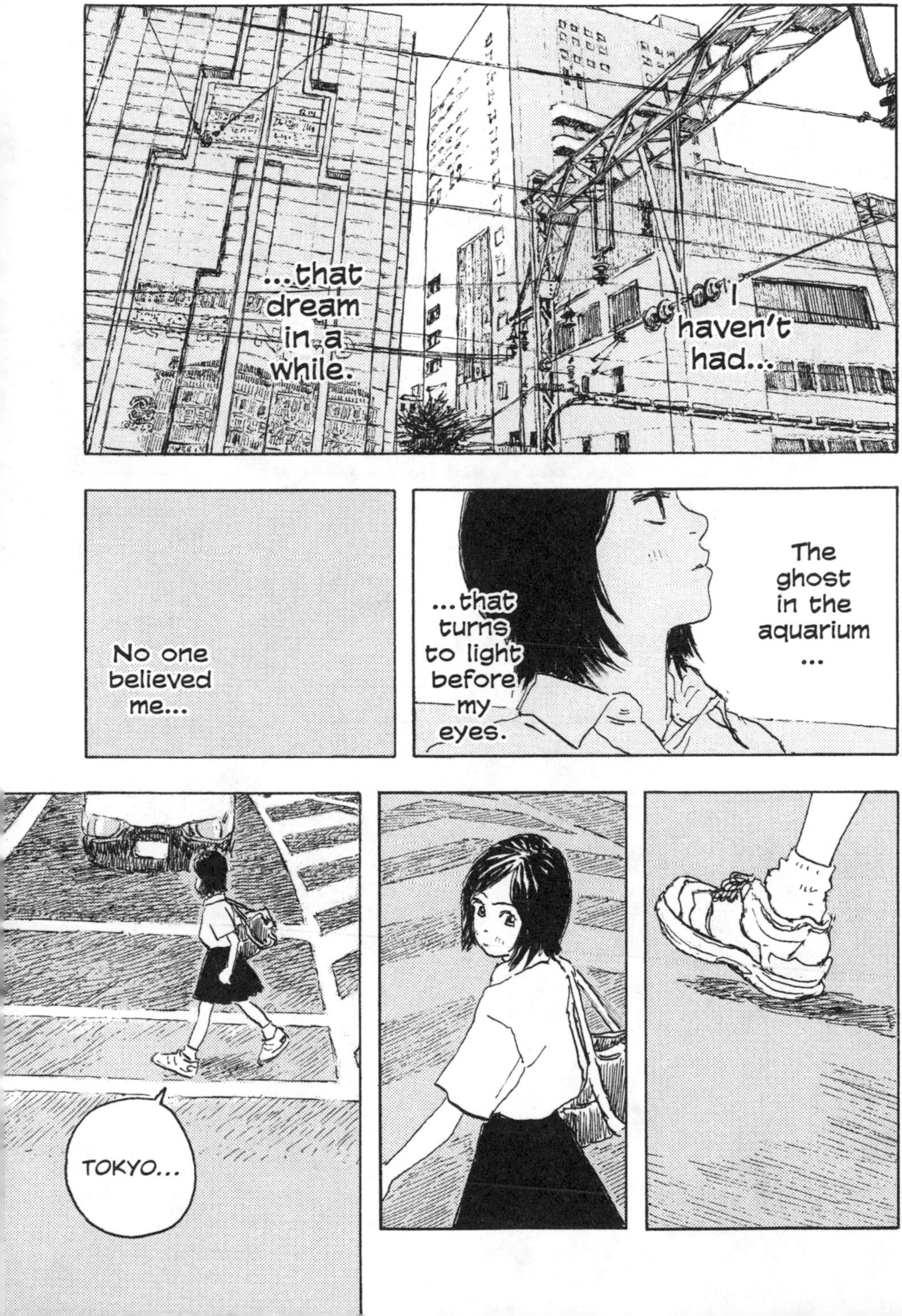
I haven't had...
...that dream in a while.
The ghost in the aquarium...
...that turns to light before my eyes.
No one believed me...
TOKYO...

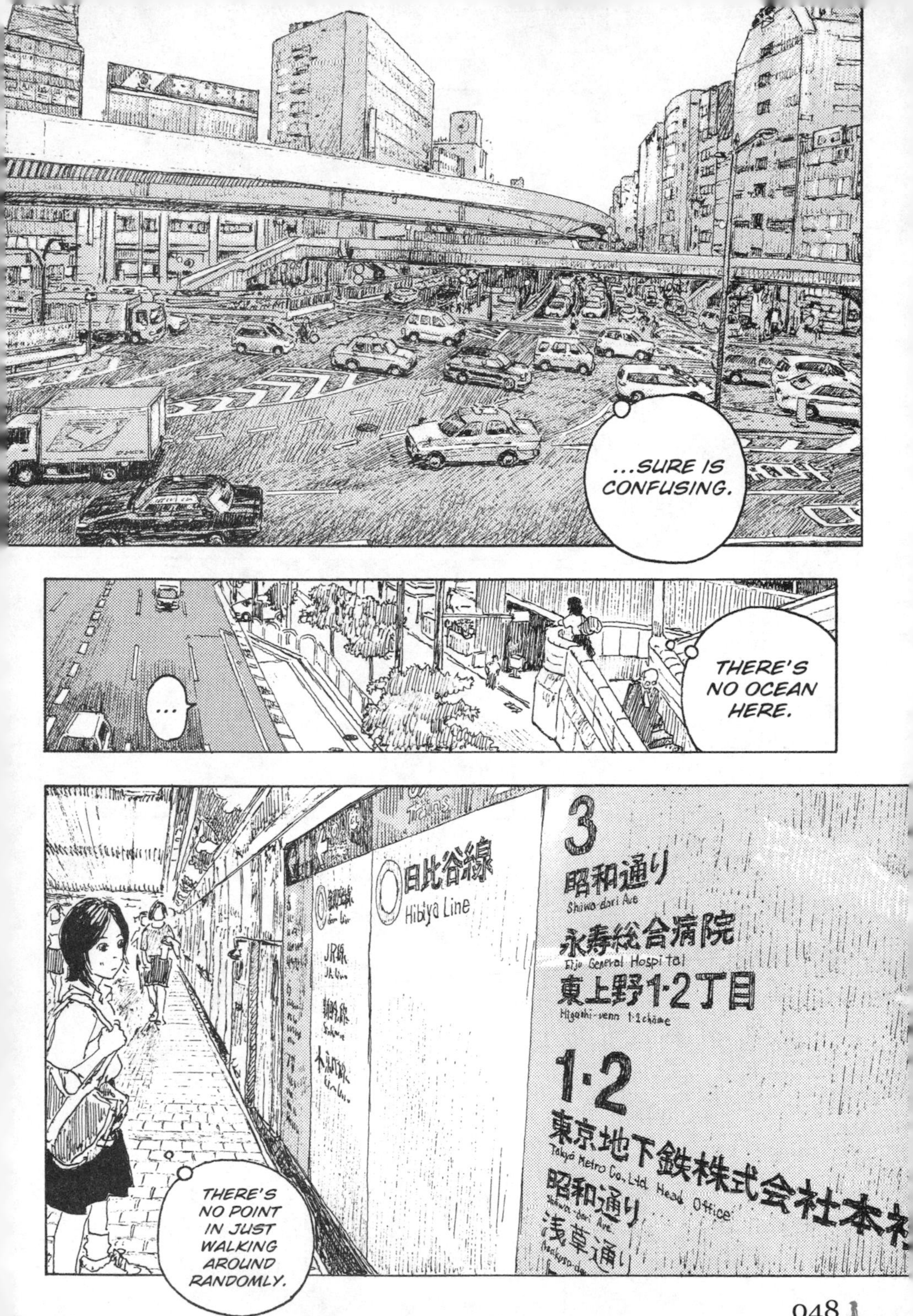
...SURE IS CONFUSING.
THERE'S NO OCEAN HERE.
...
日比谷線
Hibiya Line
3
昭和通り
永寿総合病院
Eiju General Hospital
東上野1·2丁目
1·2
東京地下鉄株式会社本
Tokyo Metro Co., Ltd. Head Office
昭和通り
浅草通り
THERE'S NO POINT IN JUST WALKING AROUND RANDOMLY.

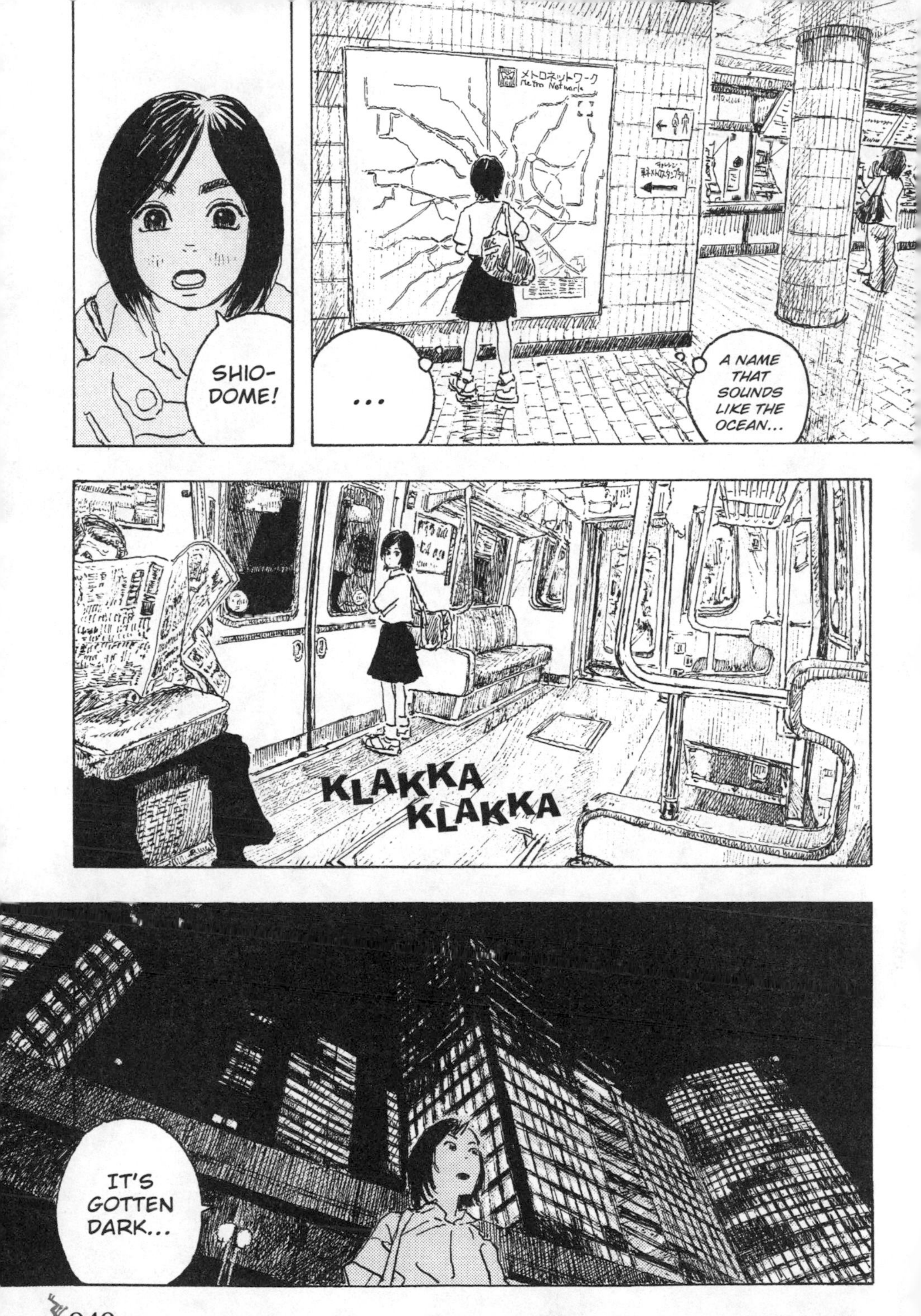
メトロネットワーク
A NAME THAT SOUNDS LIKE THE OCEAN...
...
SHIO-DOME!
KLAKKA KLAKKA
IT'S GOTTEN DARK...

SO THERE'S NO OCEAN HERE AFTER ALL.

MY FEET HURT ...

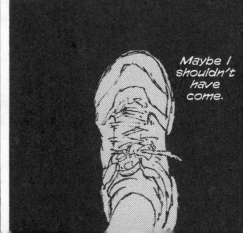

Maybe I shouldn't have come.

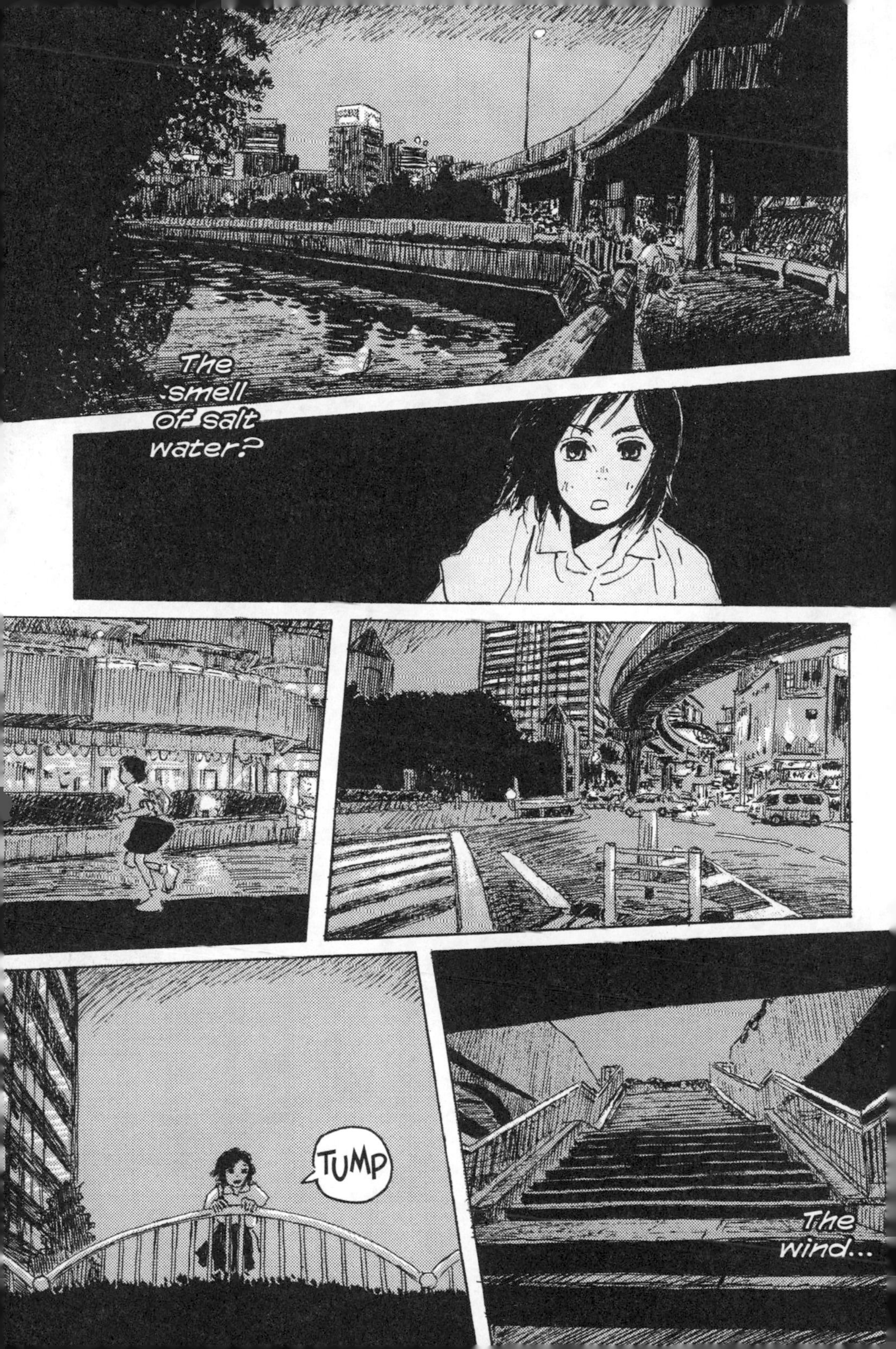
The smell of salt water?
The wind...
TUMP

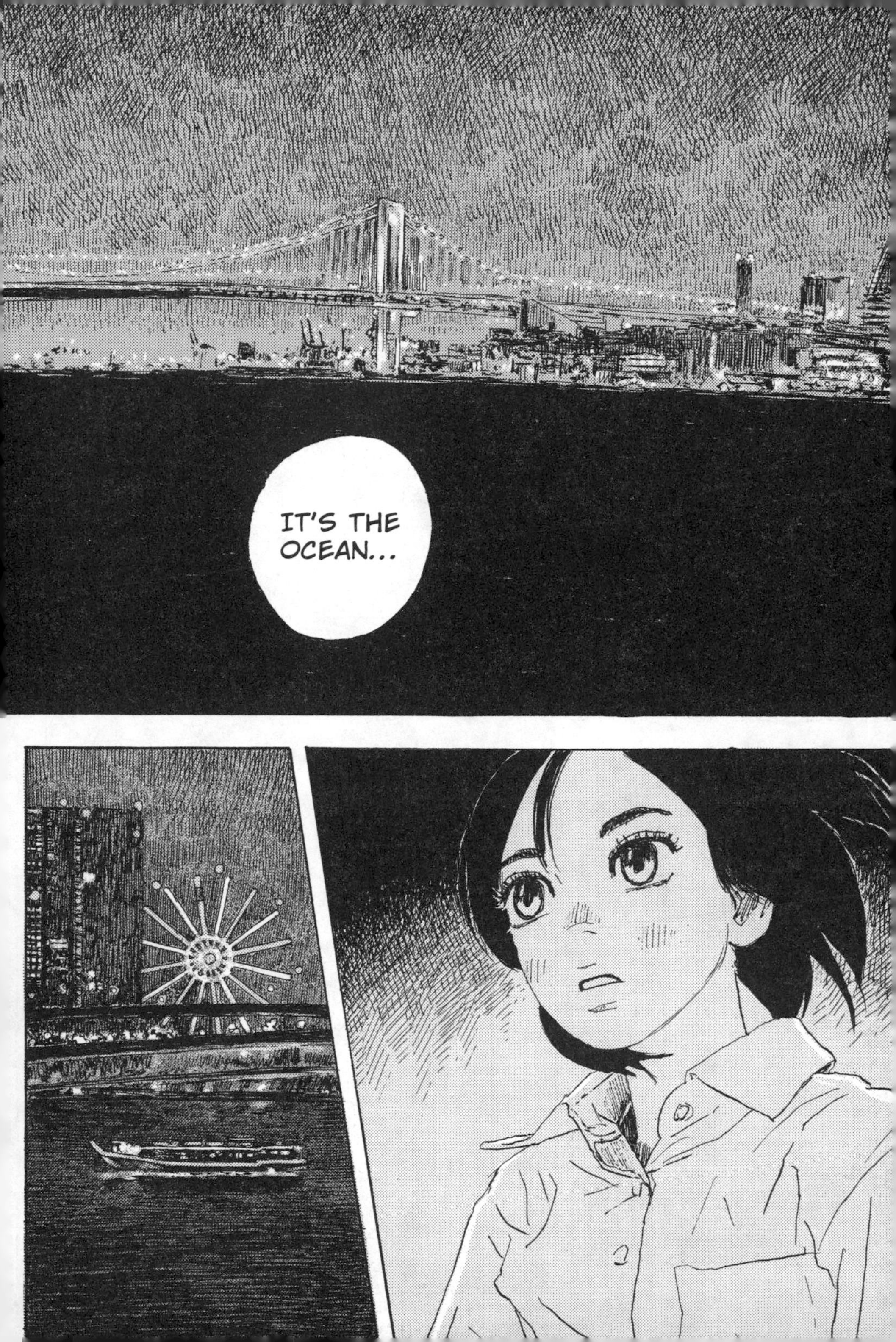
IT'S THE OCEAN...

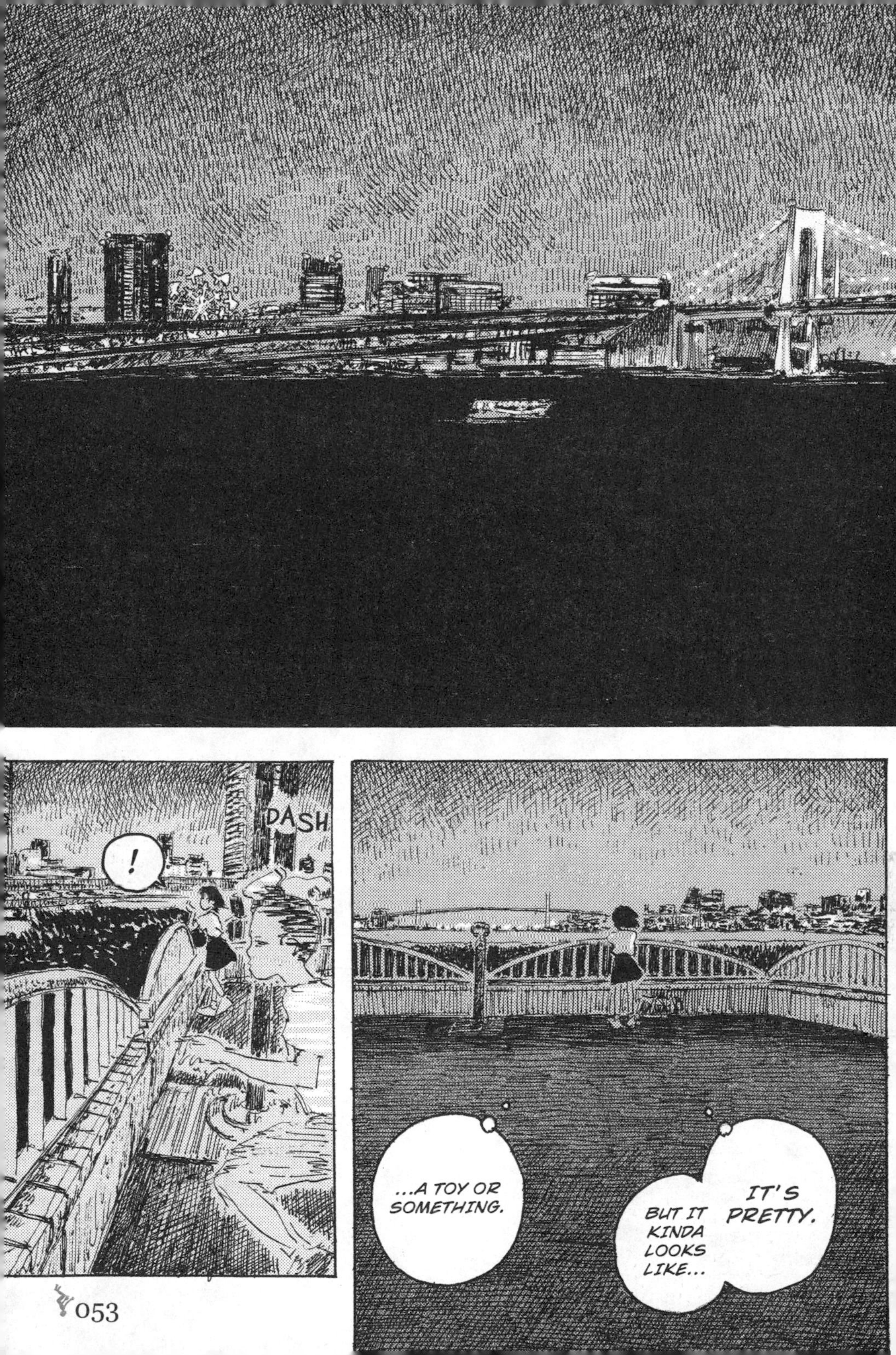
IT'S PRETTY.
BUT IT KINDA LOOKS LIKE...
...A TOY OR SOMETHING.
DASH
!

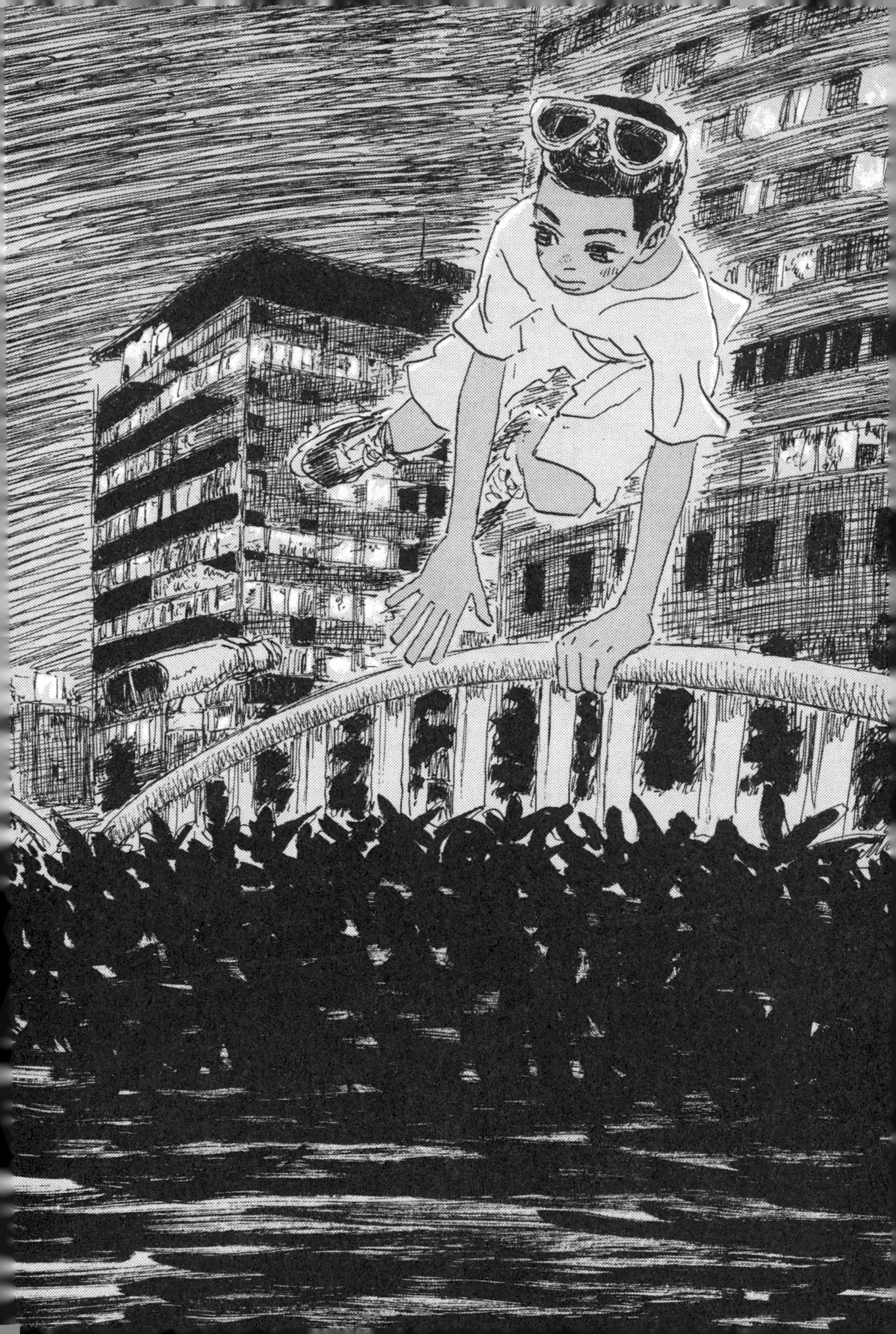

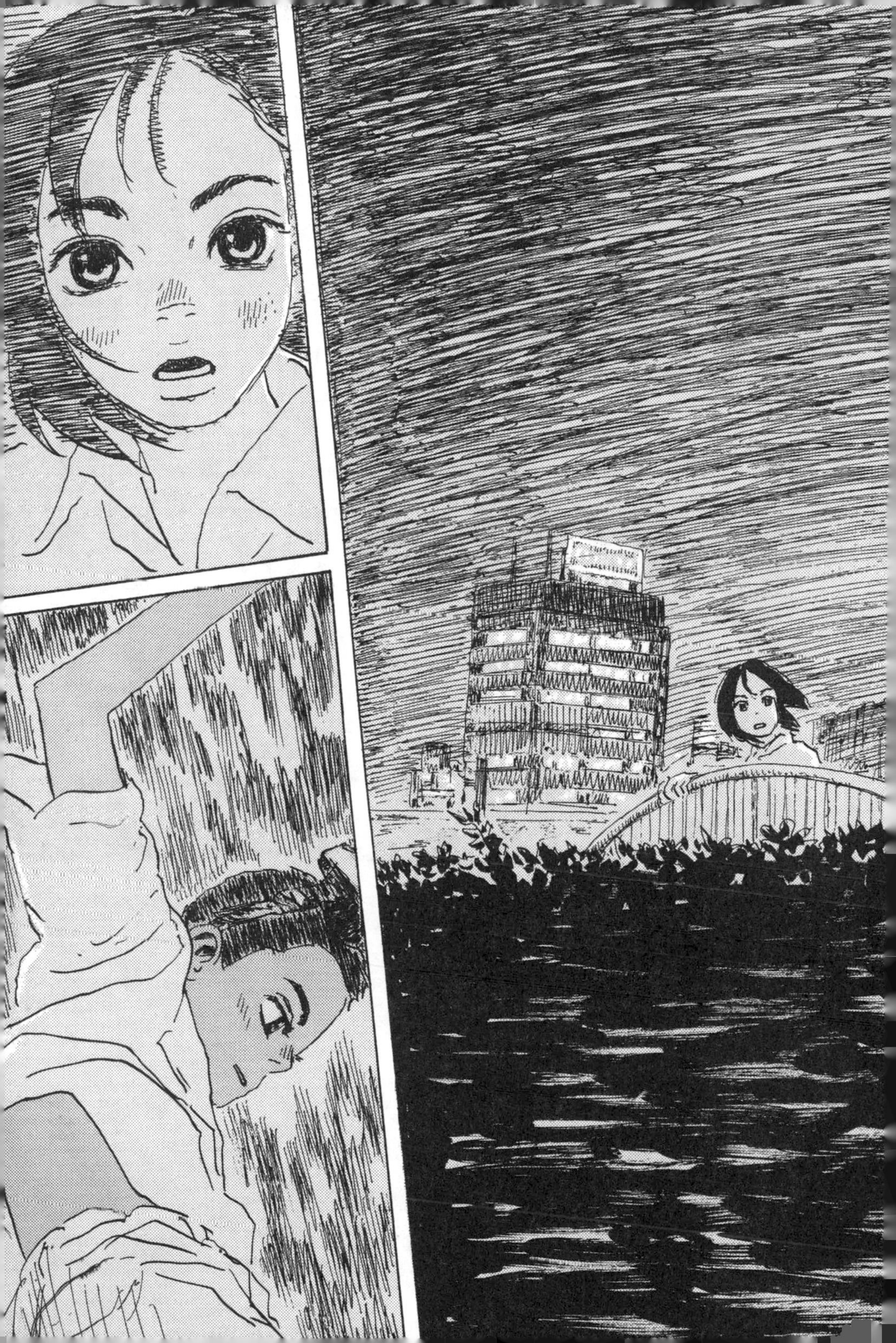

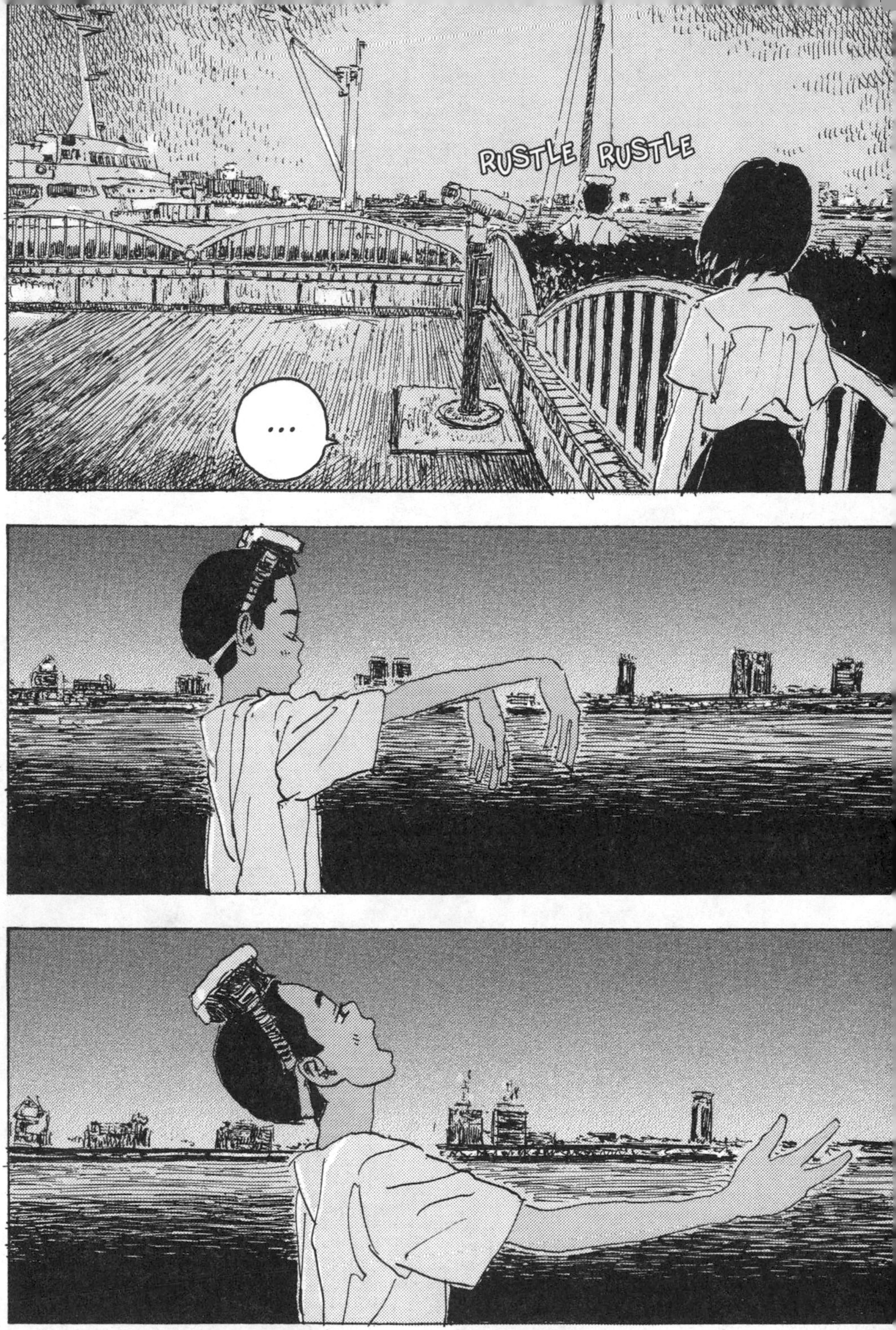
RUSTLE RUSTLE
...

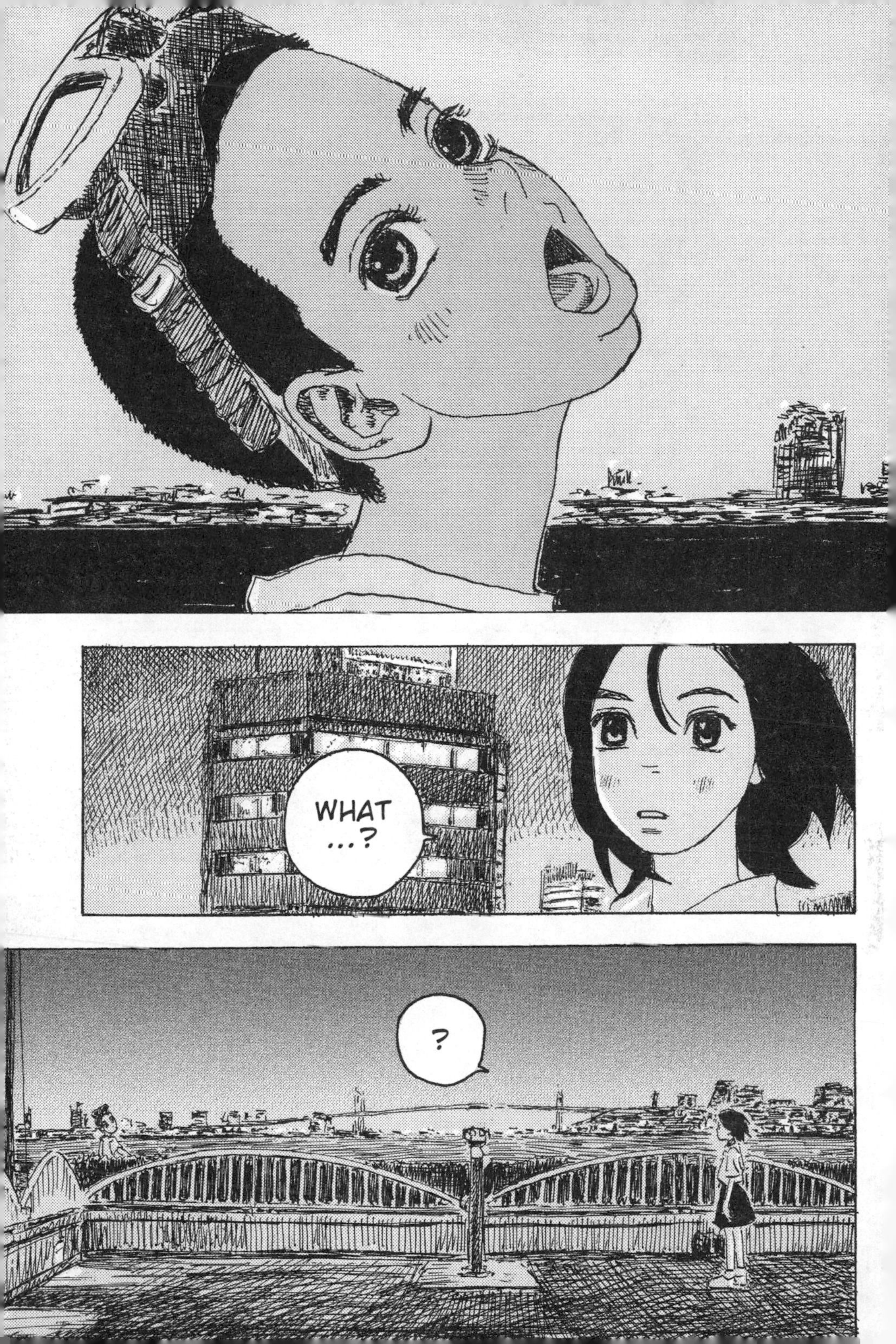
WHAT ...?
?

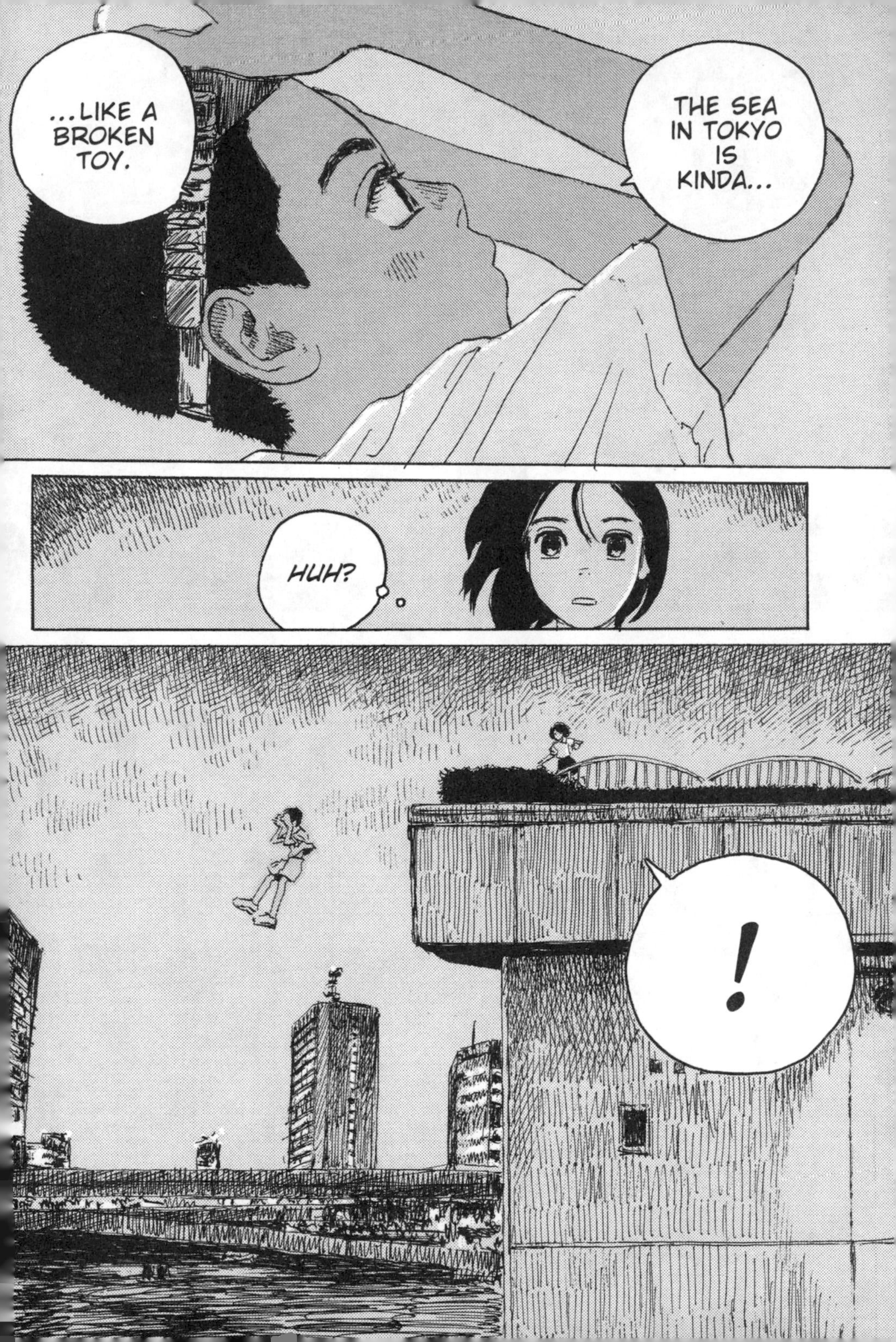
THE SEA IN TOKYO IS KINDA...
...LIKE A BROKEN TOY.
HUH?
!

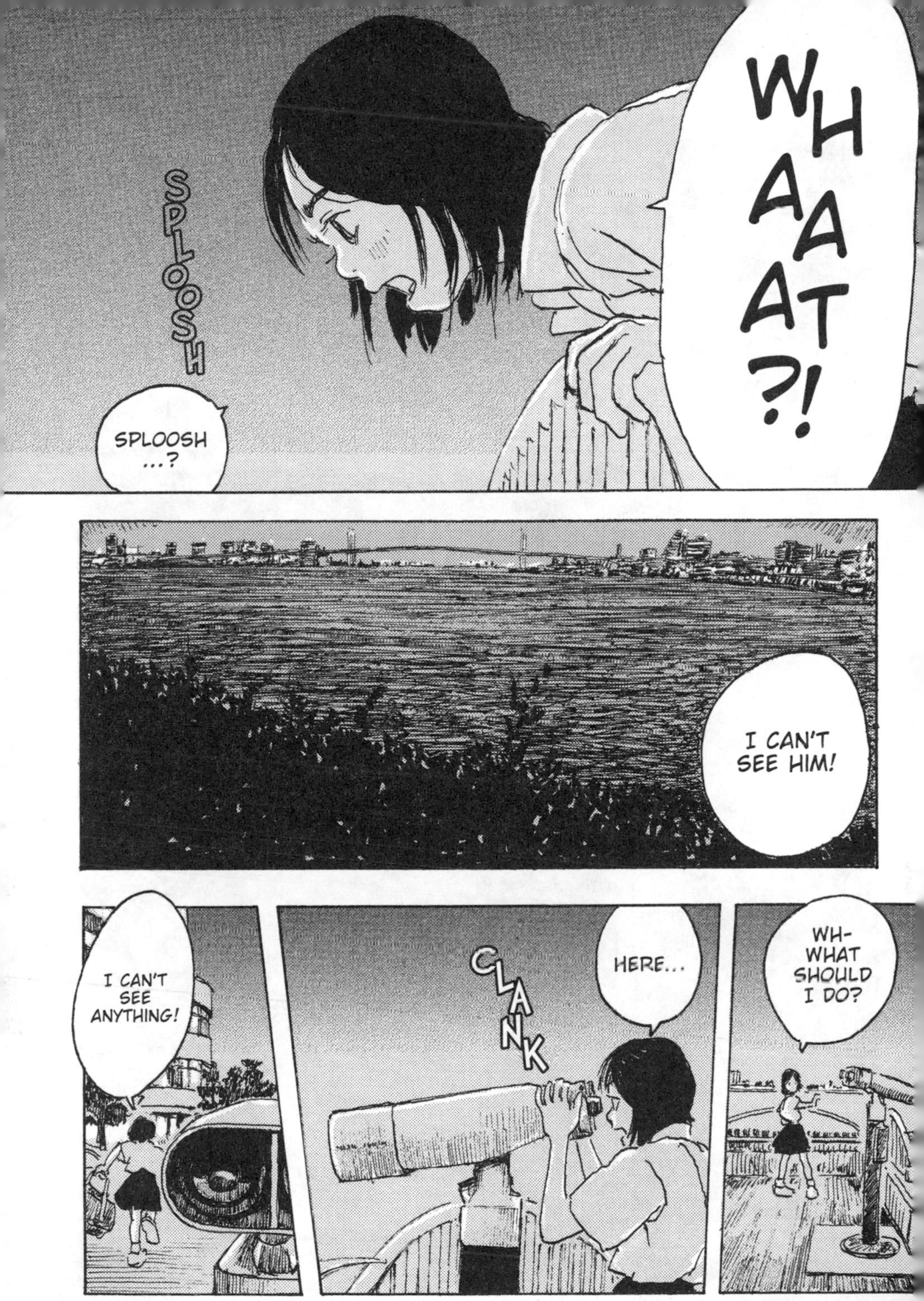
WHAAAT?!
SPLOOSH
SPLOOSH ...?
I CAN'T SEE HIM!
WH-WHAT SHOULD I DO?
HERE...
CLANK
I CAN'T SEE ANYTHING!

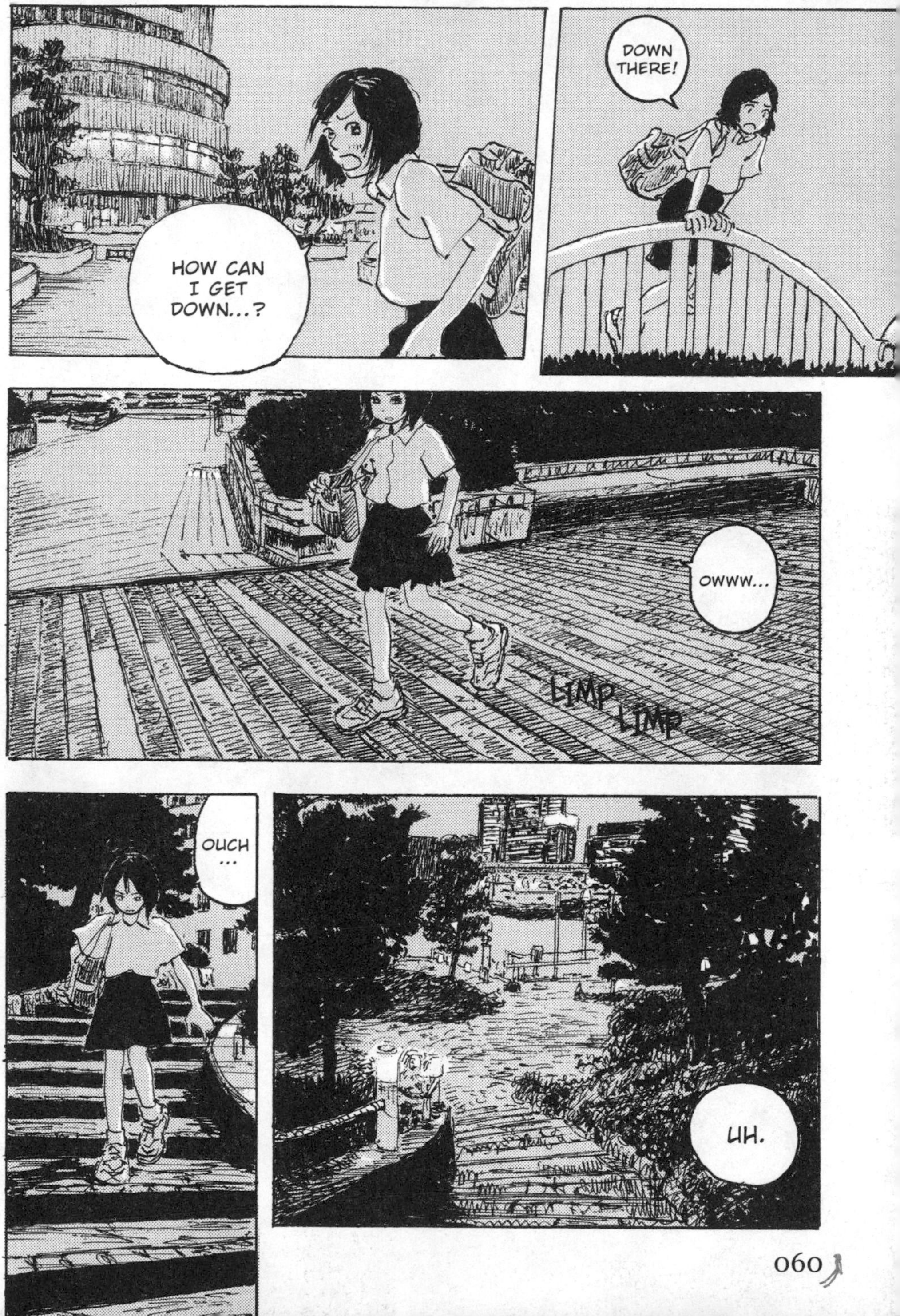
DOWN THERE!
HOW CAN I GET DOWN...?
OWWW...
LIMP LIMP
UH.
OUCH ...

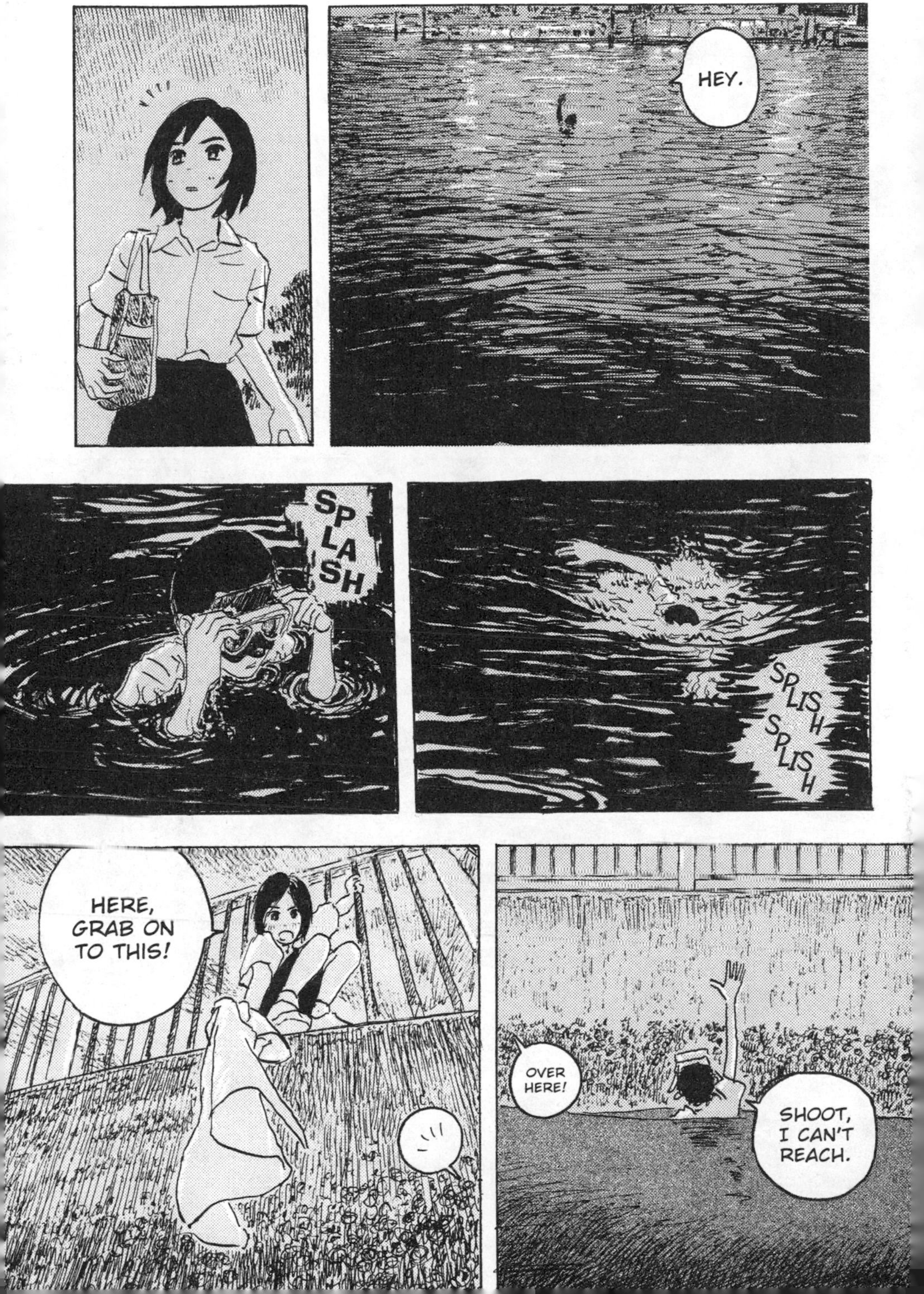
HEY.
SPLISH SPLISH
SPLASH
OVER HERE!
SHOOT, I CAN'T REACH.
HERE, GRAB ON TO THIS!

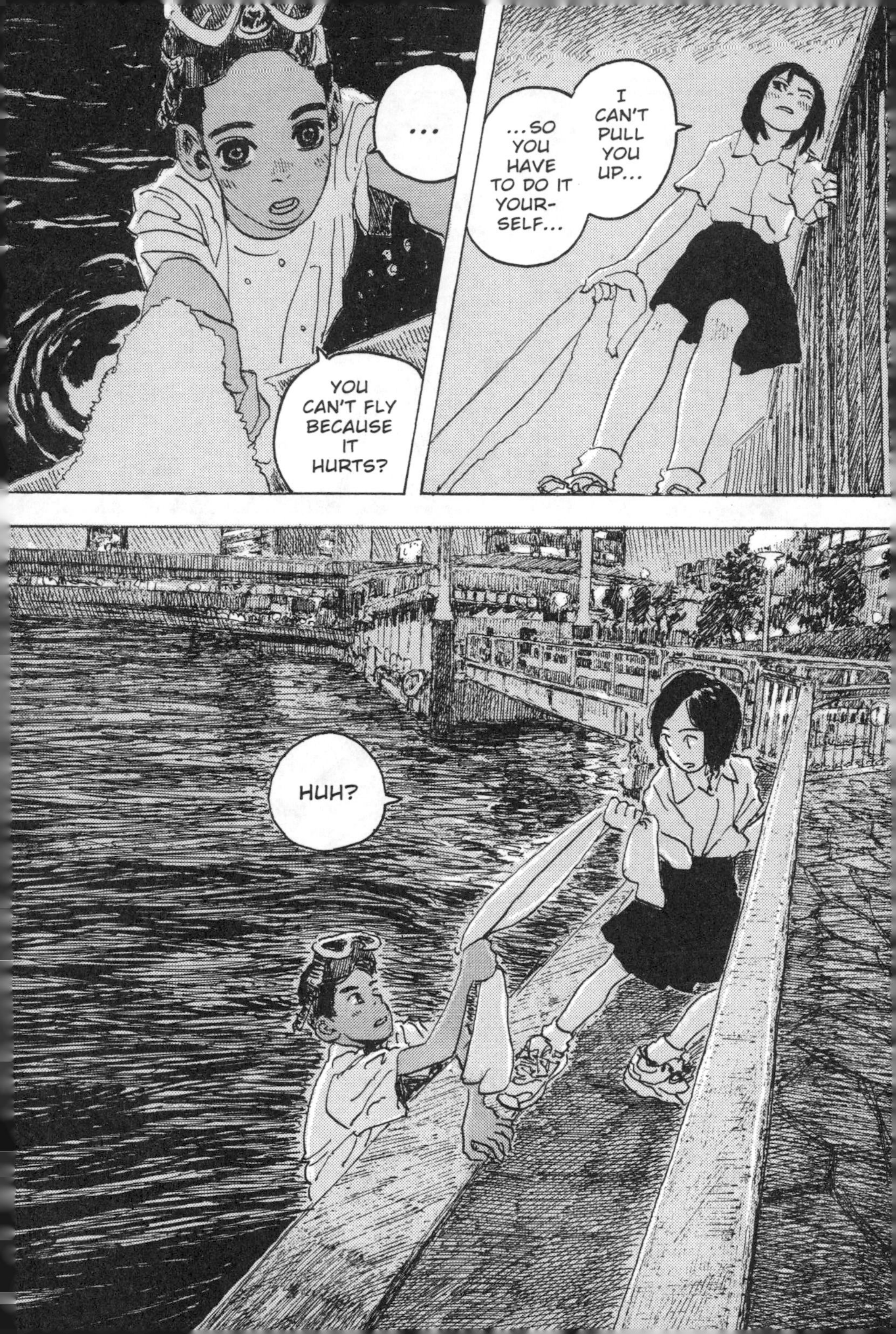
I CAN'T PULL YOU UP...
...SO YOU HAVE TO DO IT YOURSELF...
...
YOU CAN'T FLY BECAUSE IT HURTS?
HUH?

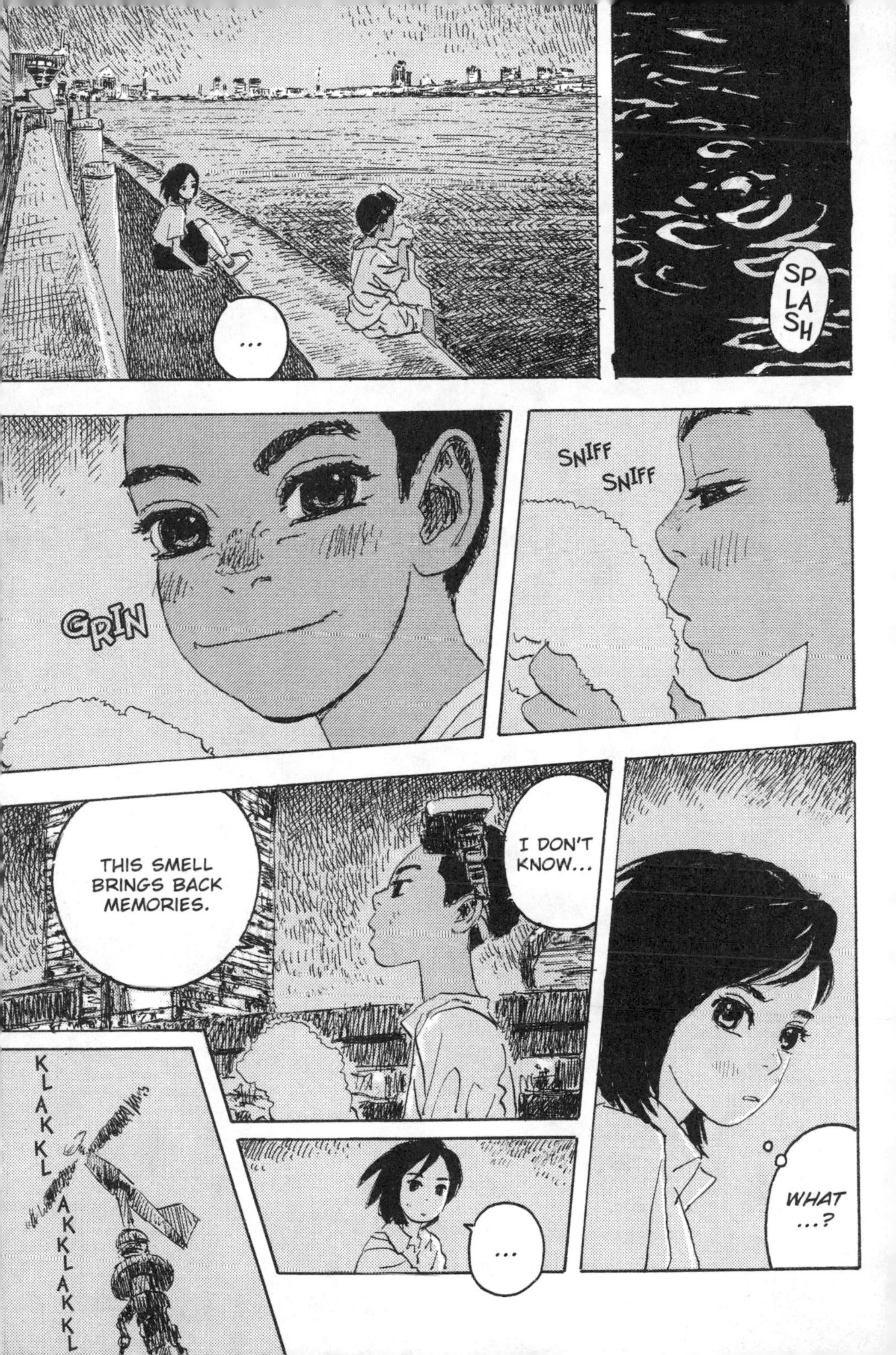
SPLASH
...
SNIFF SNIFF
GRIN
I DON'T KNOW...
THIS SMELL BRINGS BACK MEMORIES.
WHAT ...?
...
KLAKKLAKKLAKKL

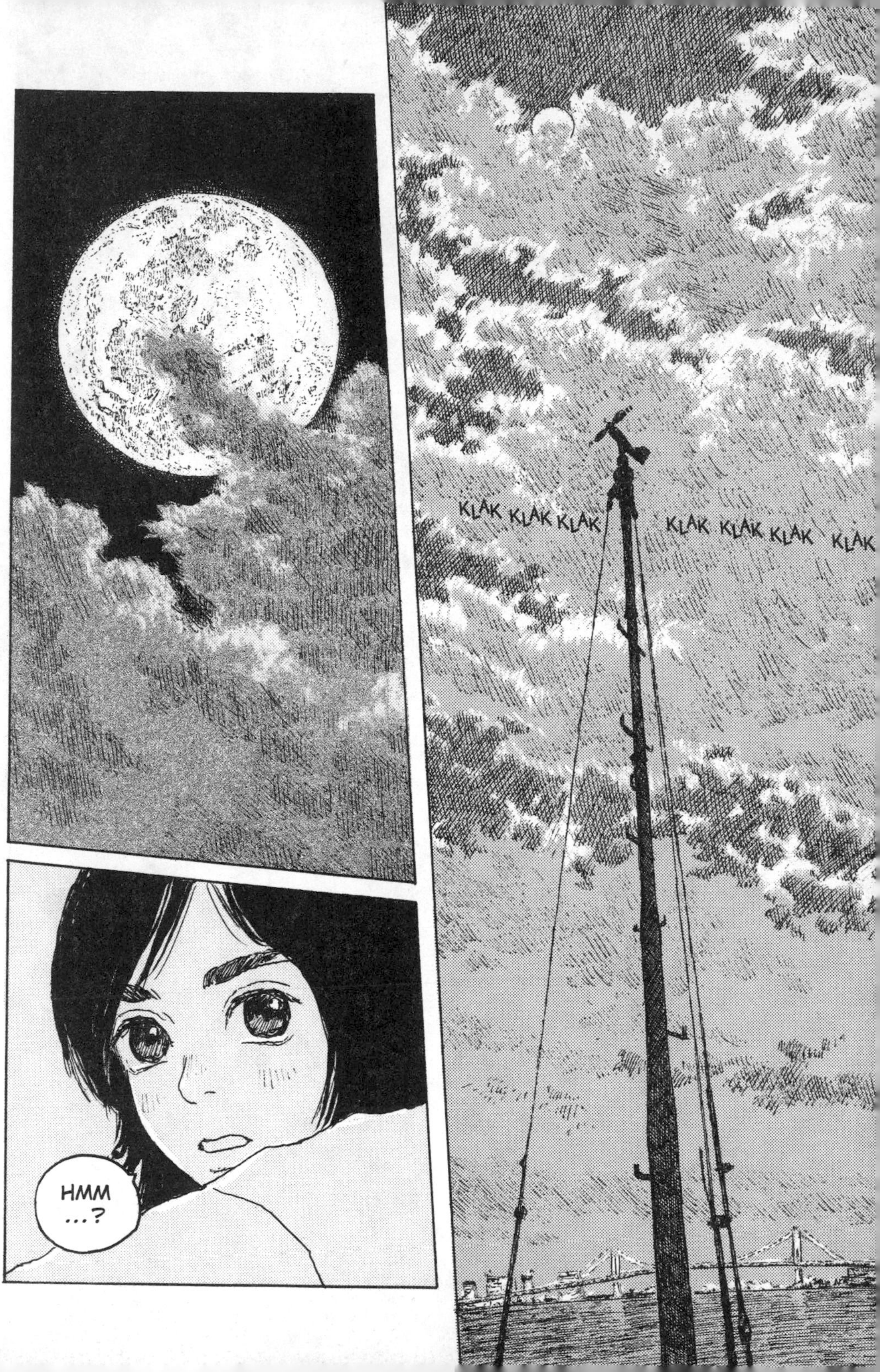
KLAK KLAK KLAK
KLAK KLAK KLAK KLAK
HMM ...?

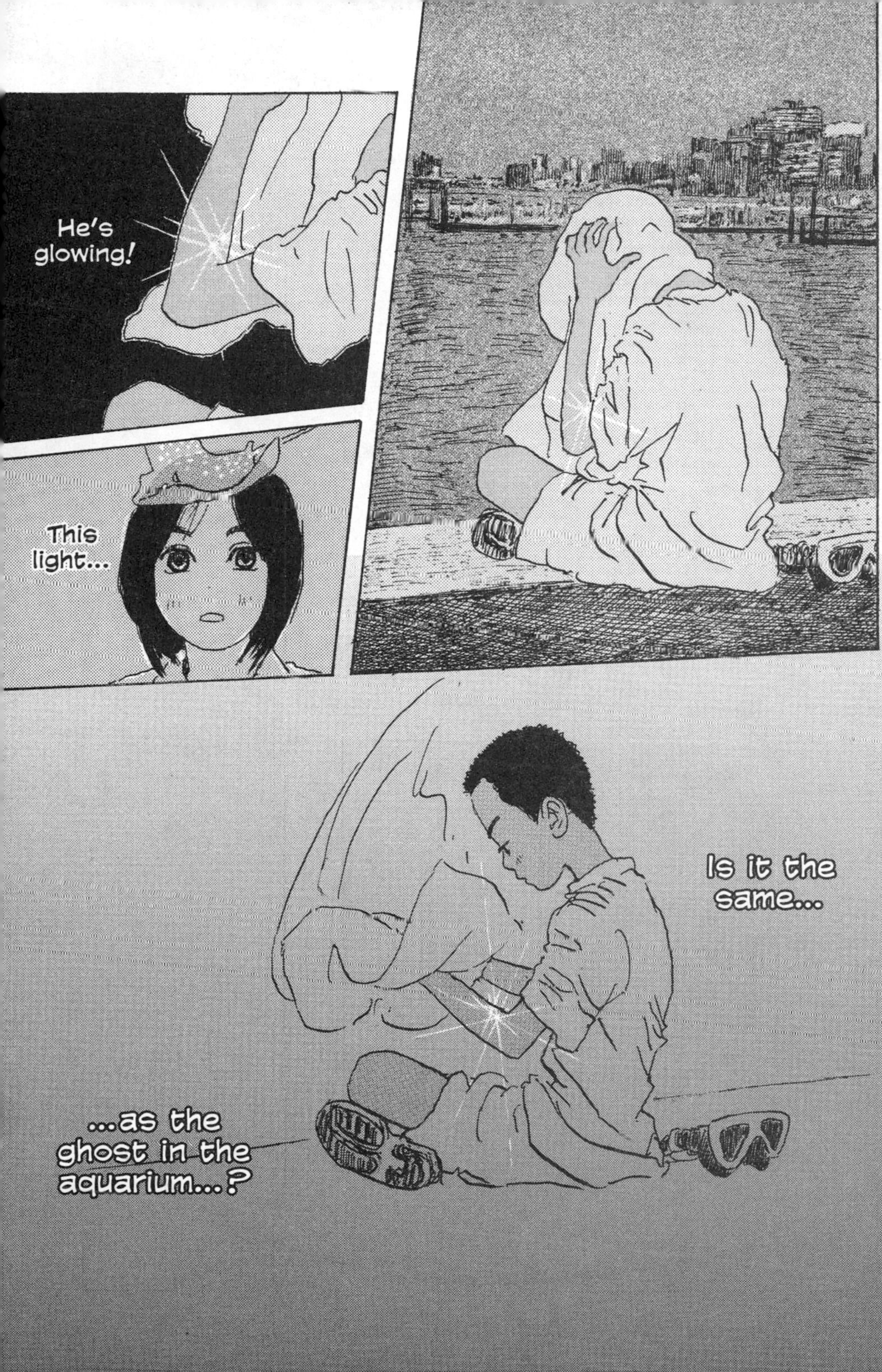
He's glowing!
This light...
Is it the same...
...as the ghost in the aquarium...?

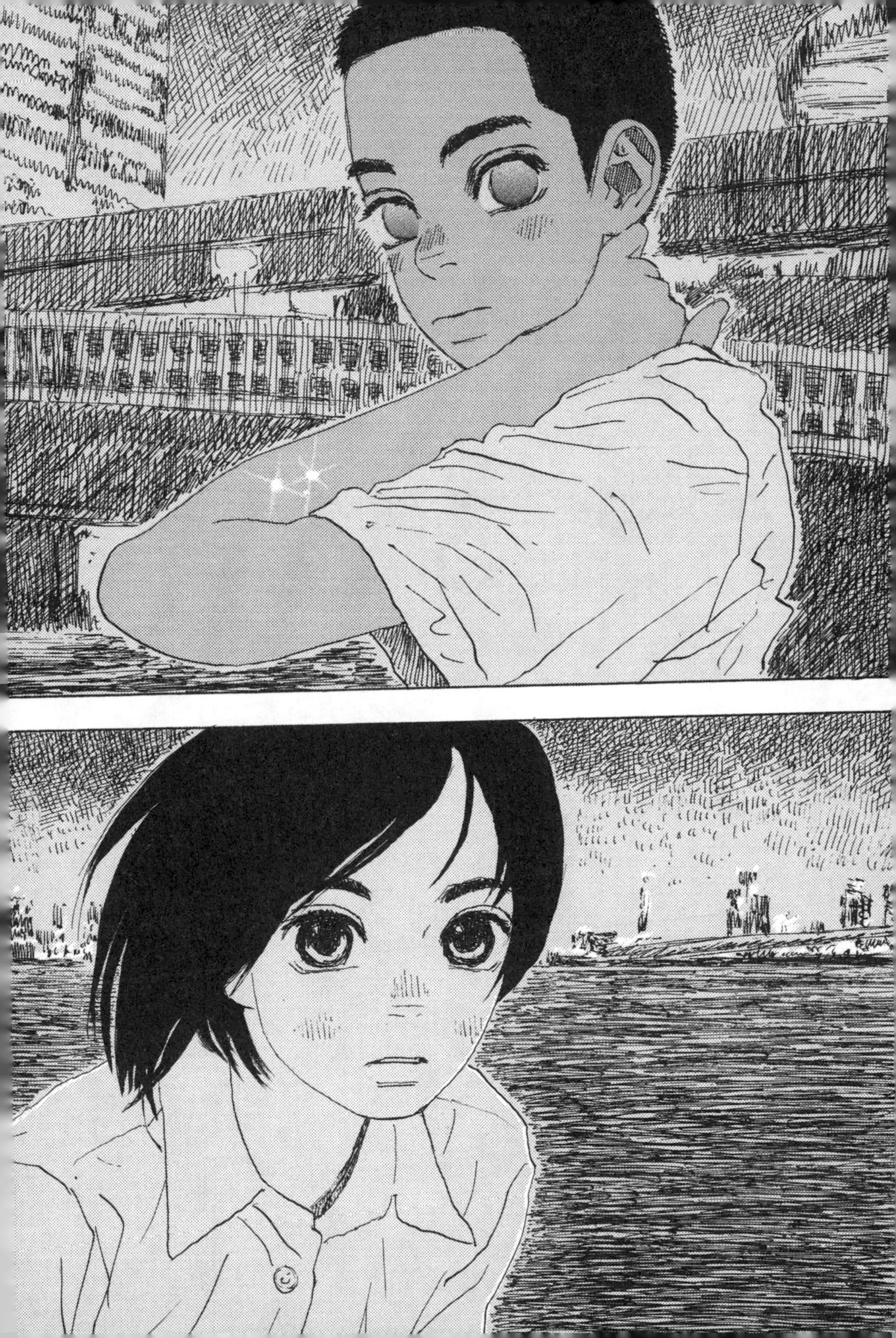

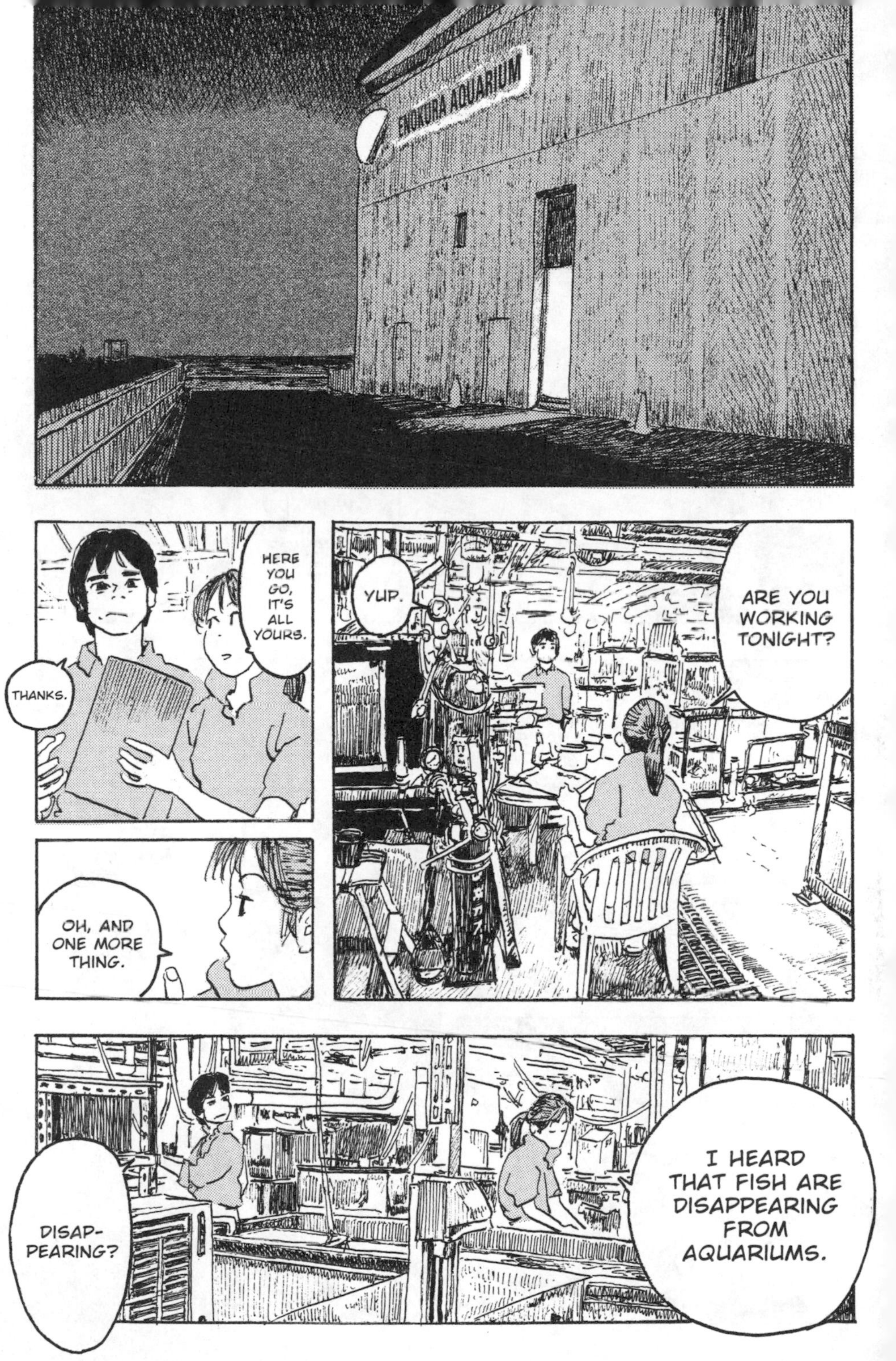
ENOKURA AQUARIUM
ARE YOU WORKING TONIGHT?
YUP.
HERE YOU GO, IT'S ALL YOURS.
THANKS.
OH, AND ONE MORE THING.
I HEARD THAT FISH ARE DISAPPEARING FROM AQUARIUMS.
DISAP-PEARING?

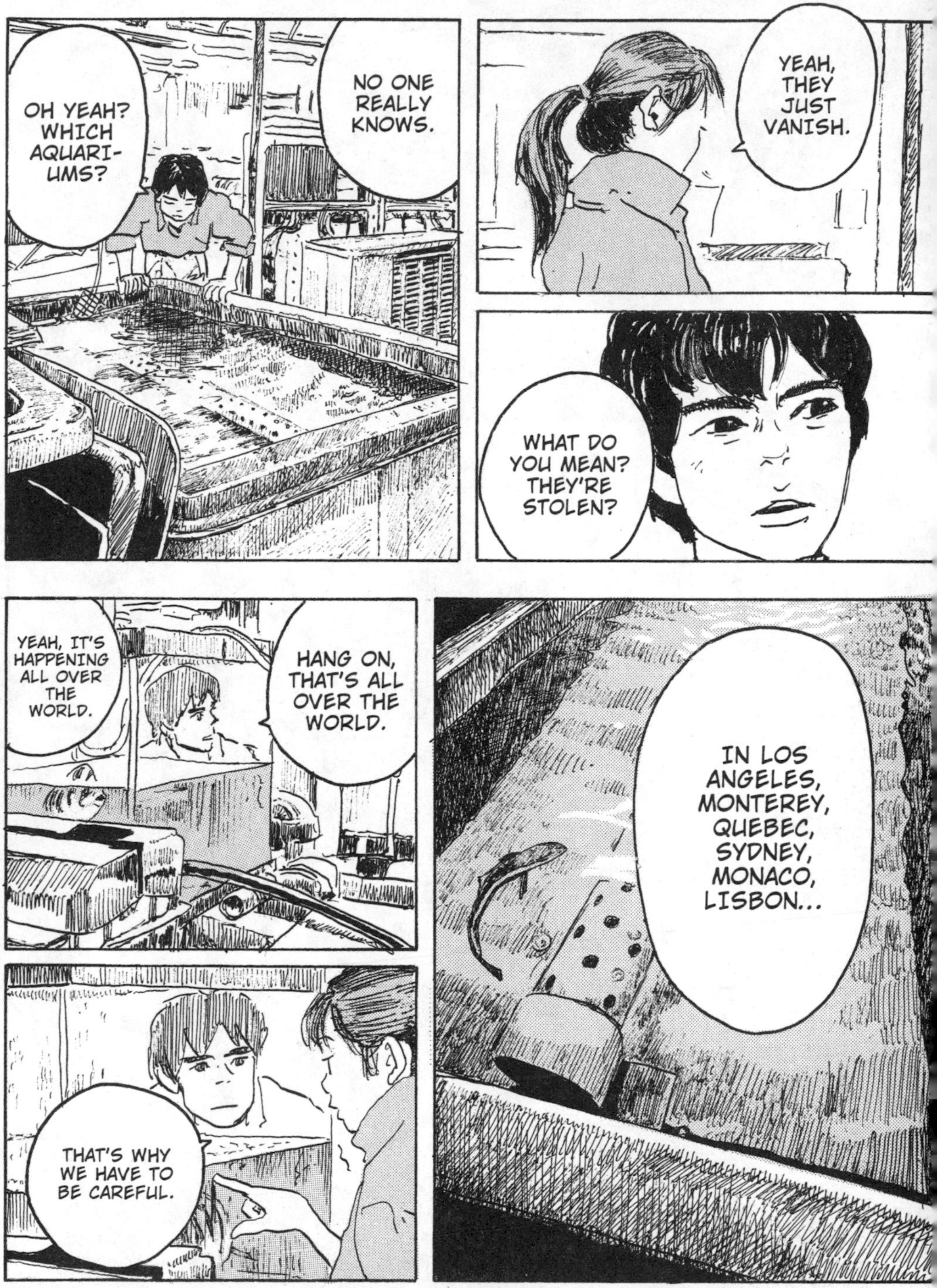
YEAH, THEY JUST VANISH.
WHAT DO YOU MEAN? THEY'RE STOLEN?
NO ONE REALLY KNOWS.
OH YEAH? WHICH AQUARI-UMS?
IN LOS ANGELES, MONTEREY, QUEBEC, SYDNEY, MONACO, LISBON...
HANG ON, THAT'S ALL OVER THE WORLD.
YEAH, IT'S HAPPENING ALL OVER THE WORLD.
THAT'S WHY WE HAVE TO BE CAREFUL.

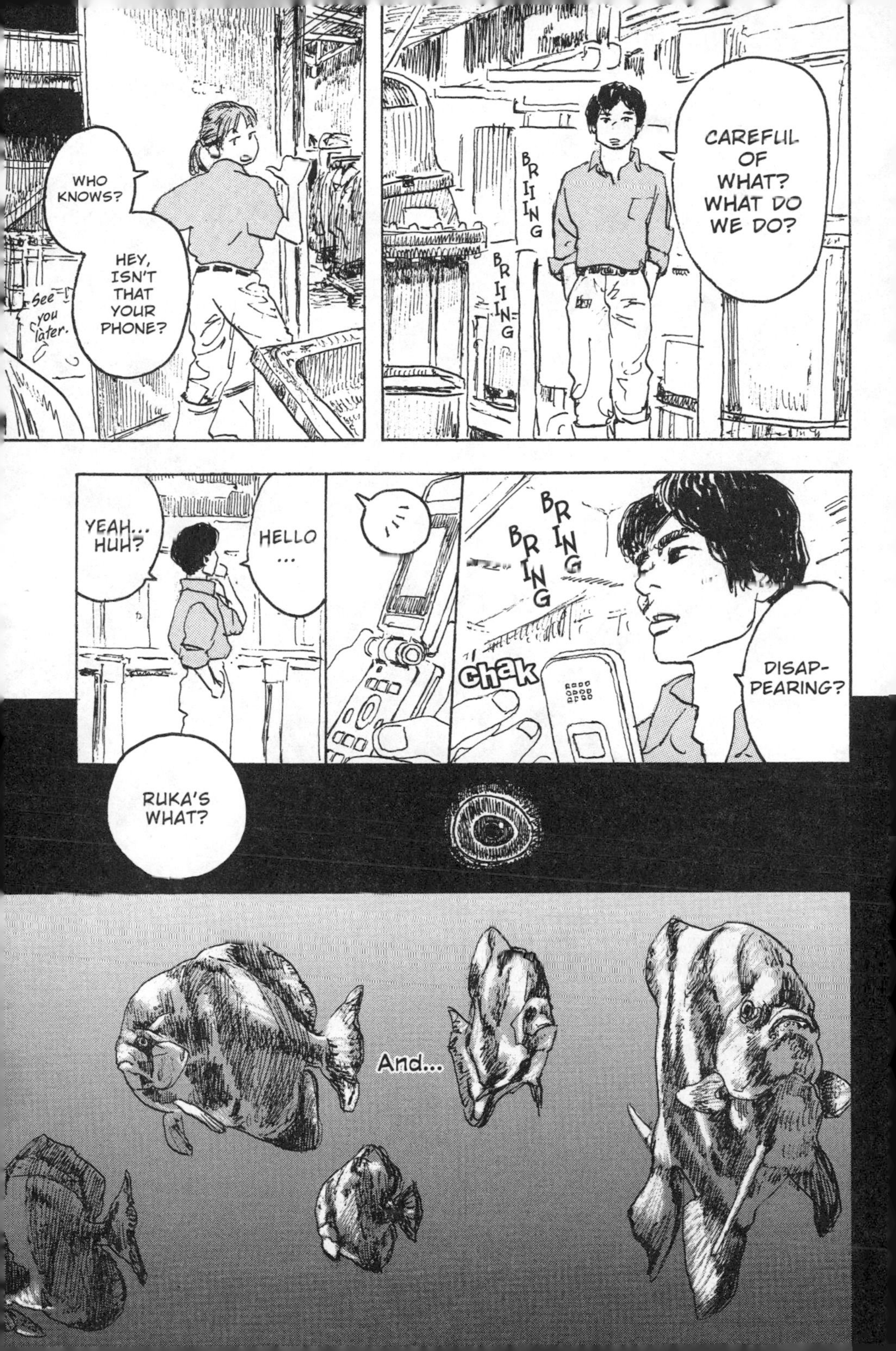
CAREFUL OF WHAT? WHAT DO WE DO?
BRIIING
BRIIING
WHO KNOWS?
HEY, ISN'T THAT YOUR PHONE?
See you later.
BRING
BRING
DISAP-PEARING?
chak
HELLO...
YEAH... HUH?
RUKA'S WHAT?
And...

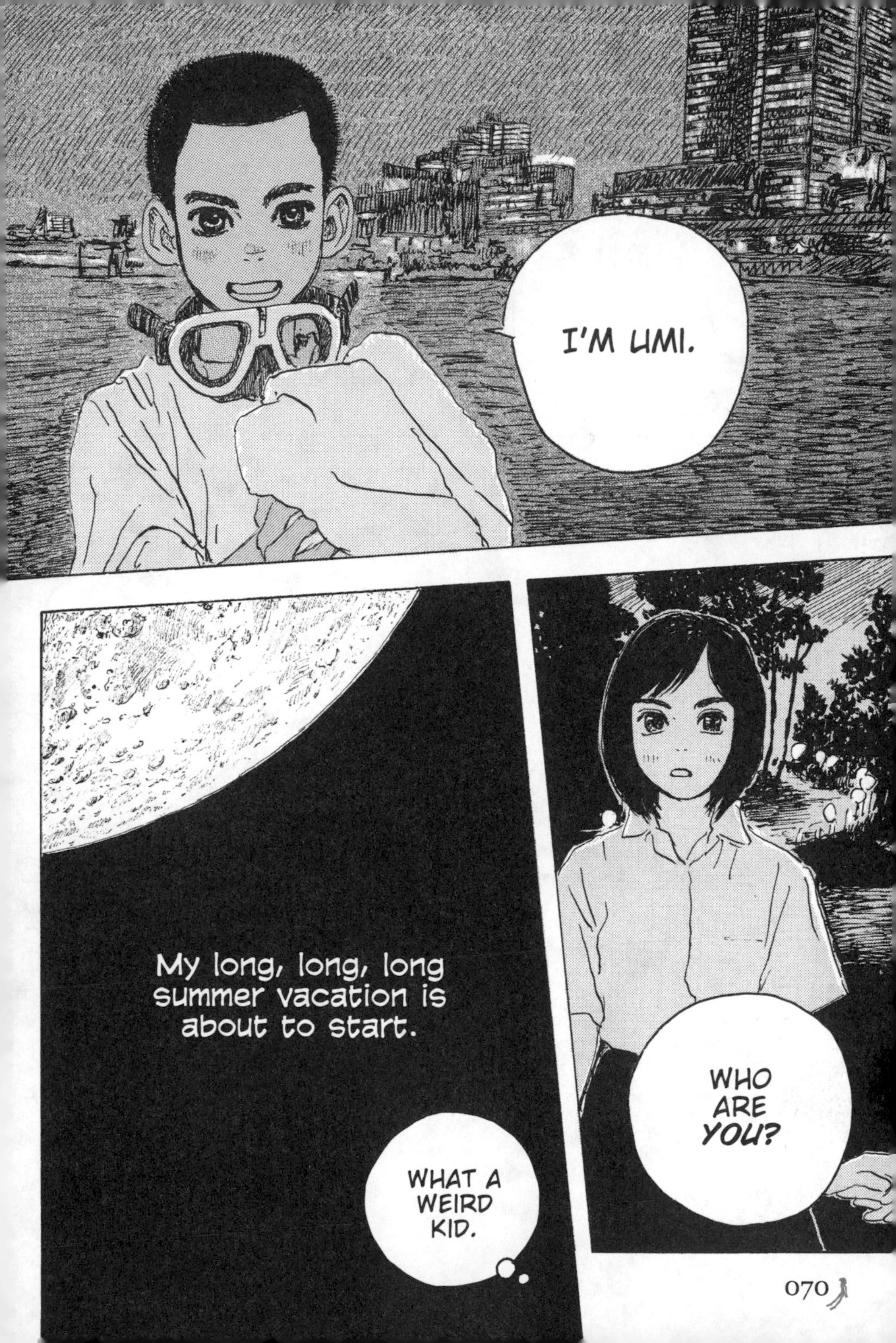

I'M UMI.
WHO ARE *YOU?*
My long, long, long summer vacation is about to start.
WHAT A WEIRD KID.

Chapter 2:
The Day of Thunder

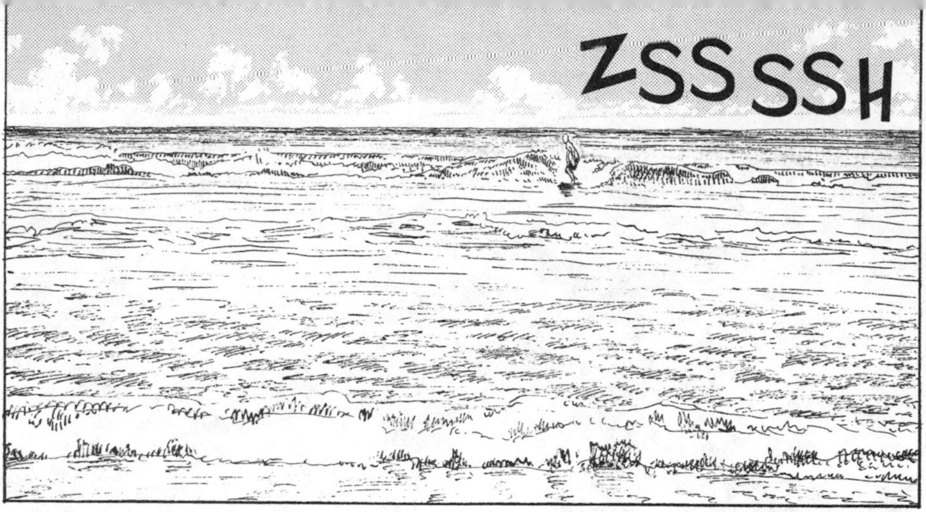
ZSS SSH
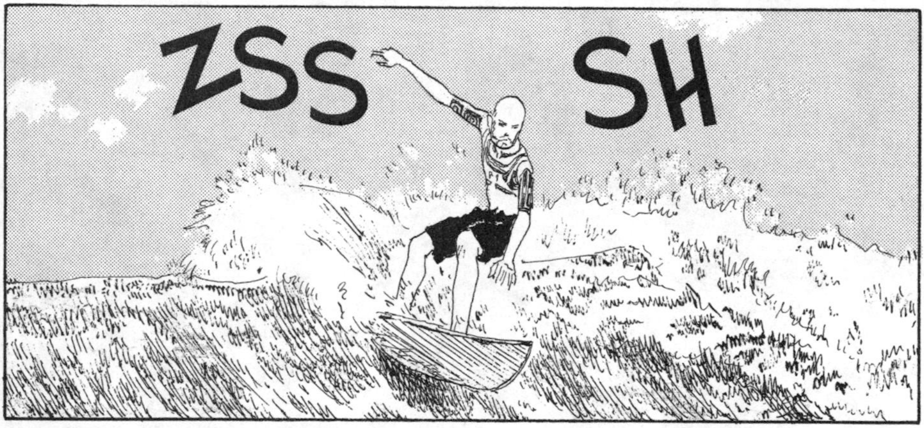
ZSS SH
2
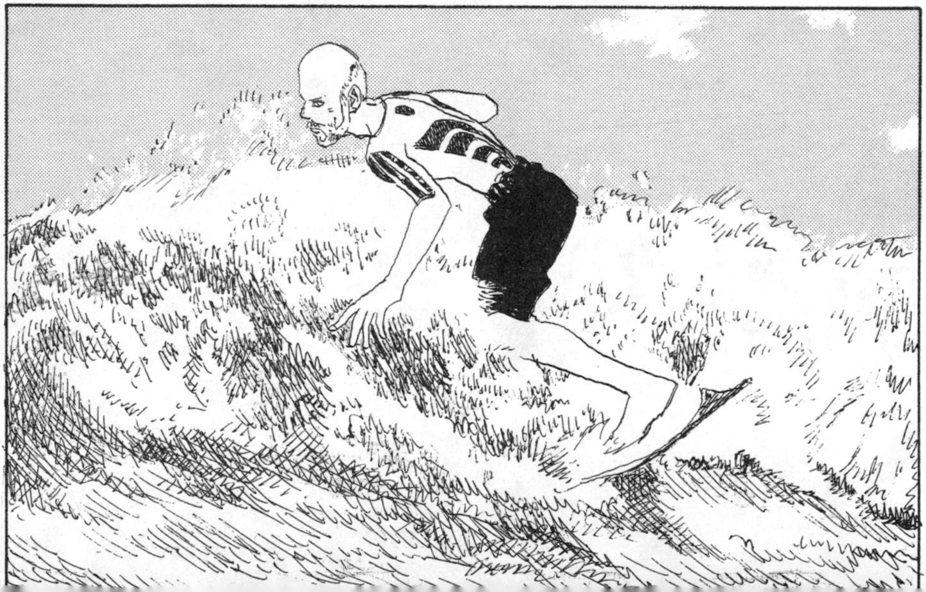

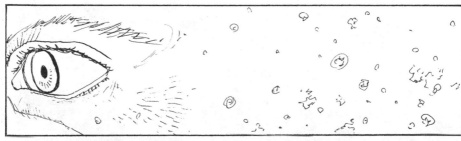

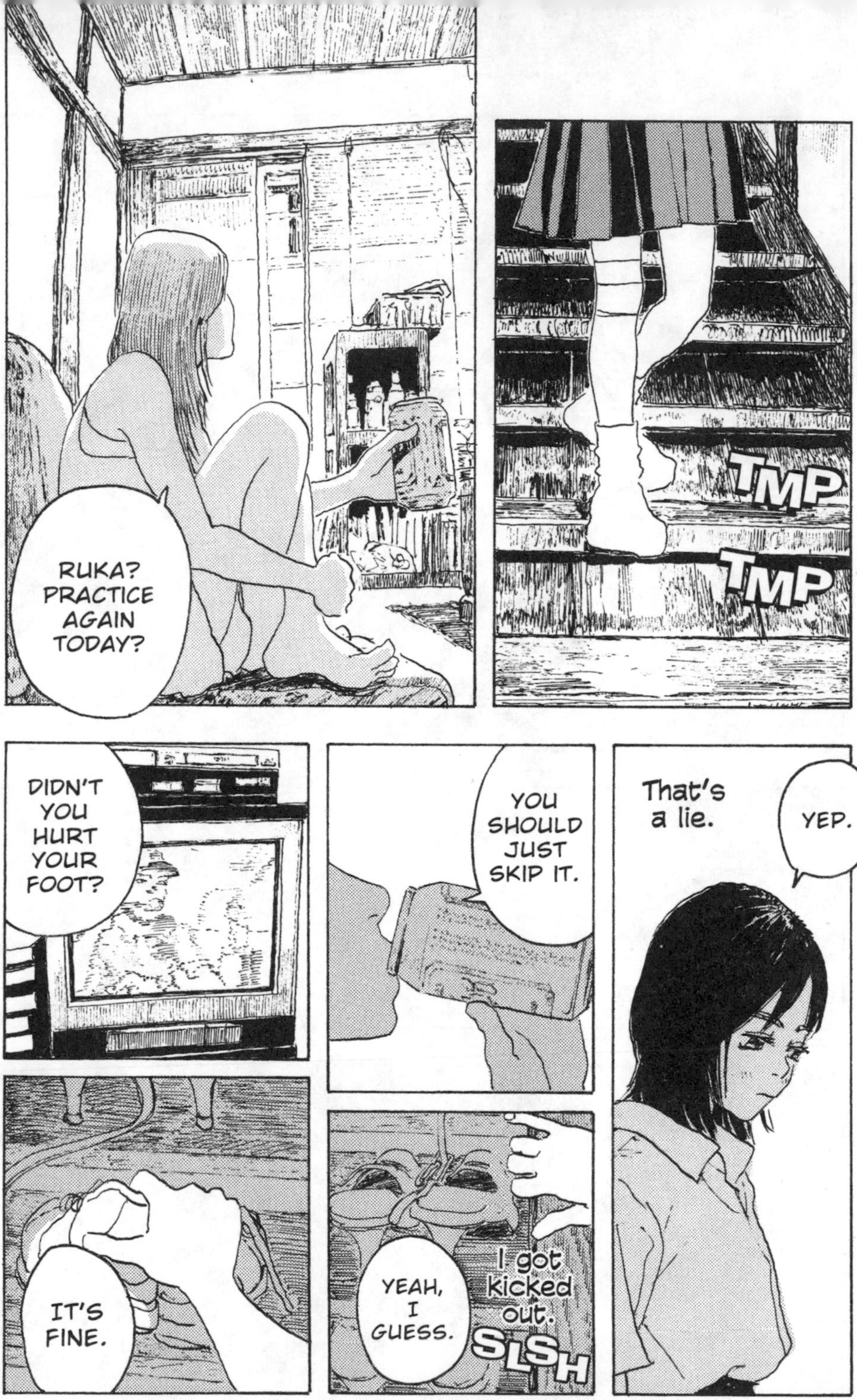
TMP
TMP
RUKA? PRACTICE AGAIN TODAY?
YEP.
That's a lie.
YOU SHOULD JUST SKIP IT.
DIDN'T YOU HURT YOUR FOOT?
I got kicked out.
YEAH, I GUESS.
SLSH
IT'S FINE.

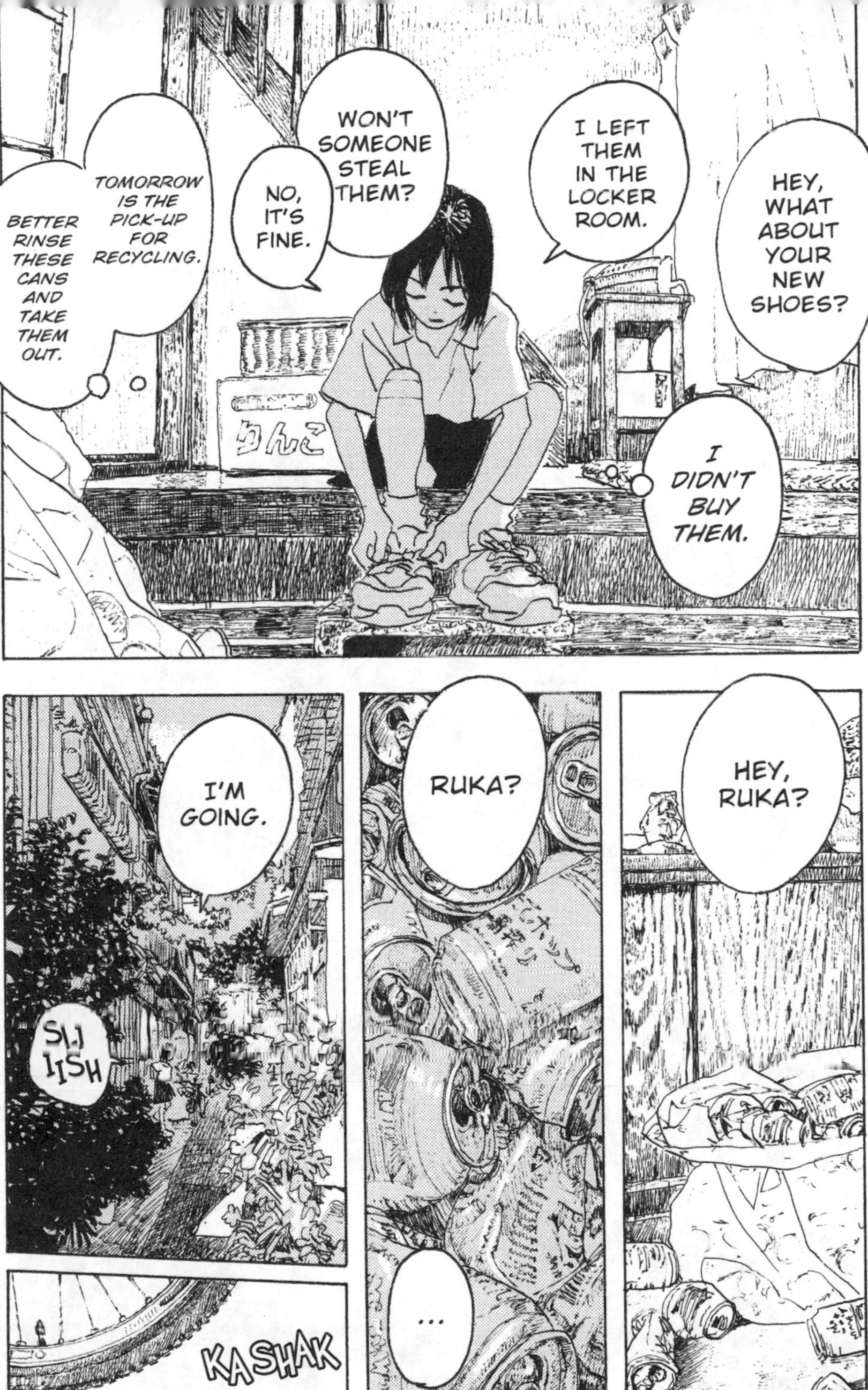
HEY, WHAT ABOUT YOUR NEW SHOES?
I LEFT THEM IN THE LOCKER ROOM.
I DIDN'T BUY THEM.
WON'T SOMEONE STEAL THEM?
NO, IT'S FINE.
TOMORROW IS THE PICK-UP FOR RECYCLING.
BETTER RINSE THESE CANS AND TAKE THEM OUT.
HEY, RUKA?
RUKA?
...
I'M GOING.
SHIISH
KASHAK

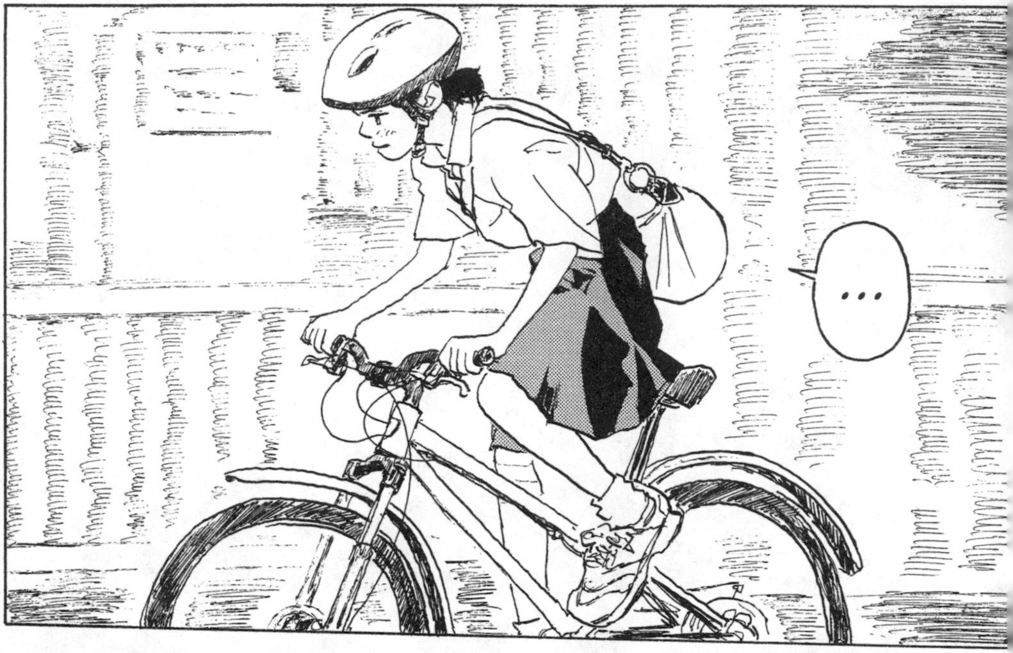
...

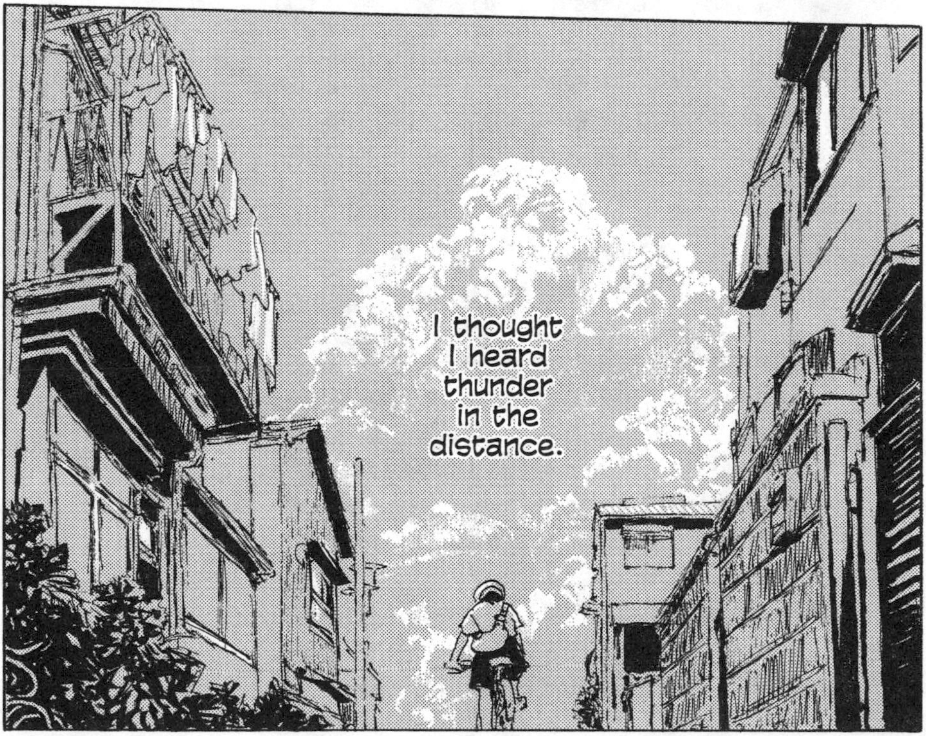
I thought I heard thunder in the distance.

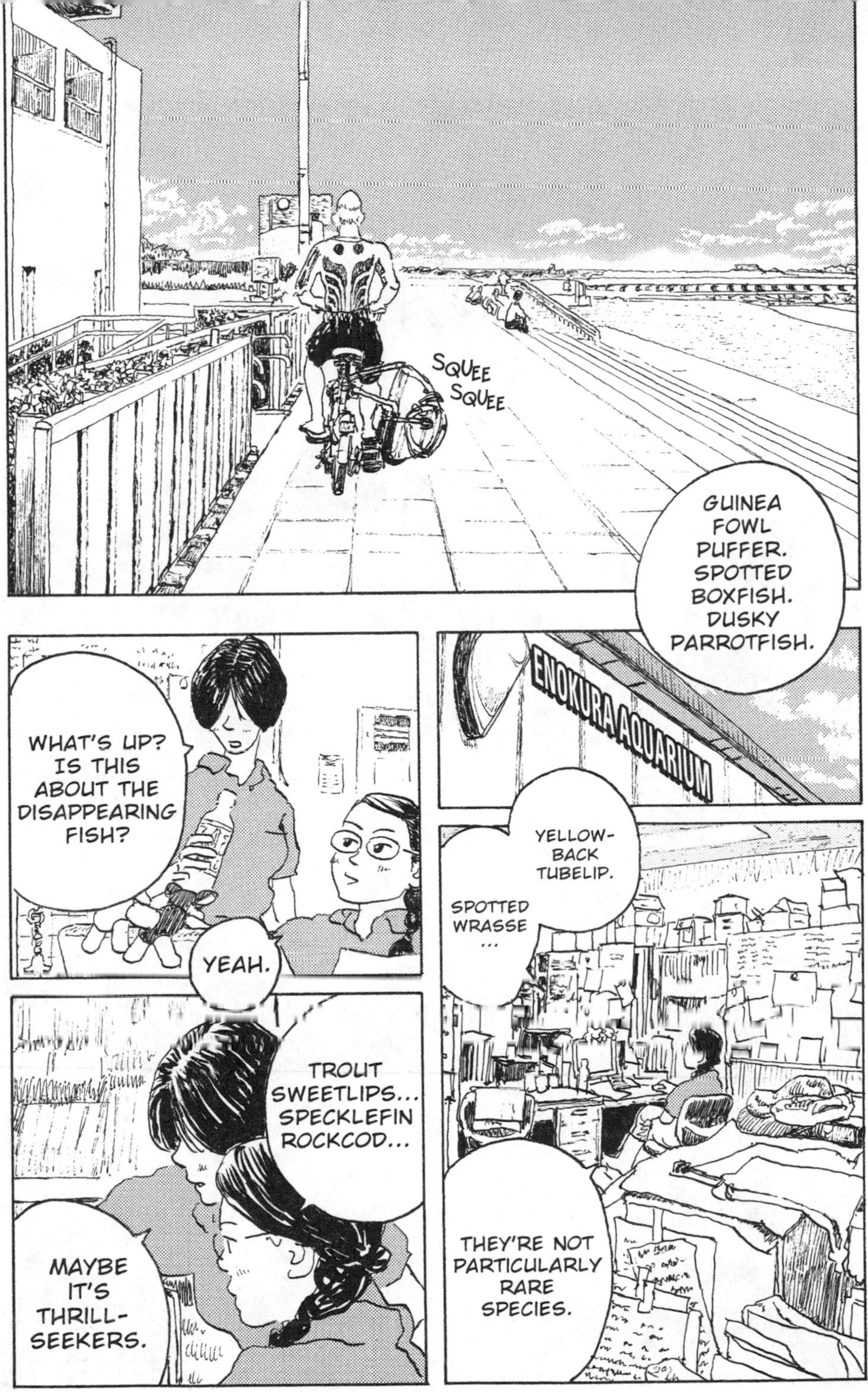
SQUEE SQUEE
GUINEA FOWL PUFFER. SPOTTED BOXFISH. DUSKY PARROTFISH.
ENOKURA AQUARIUM
WHAT'S UP? IS THIS ABOUT THE DISAPPEARING FISH?
YEAH.
YELLOW-BACK TUBELIP.
SPOTTED WRASSE ...
THEY'RE NOT PARTICULARLY RARE SPECIES.
TROUT SWEETLIPS... SPECKLEFIN ROCKCOD...
MAYBE IT'S THRILL-SEEKERS.

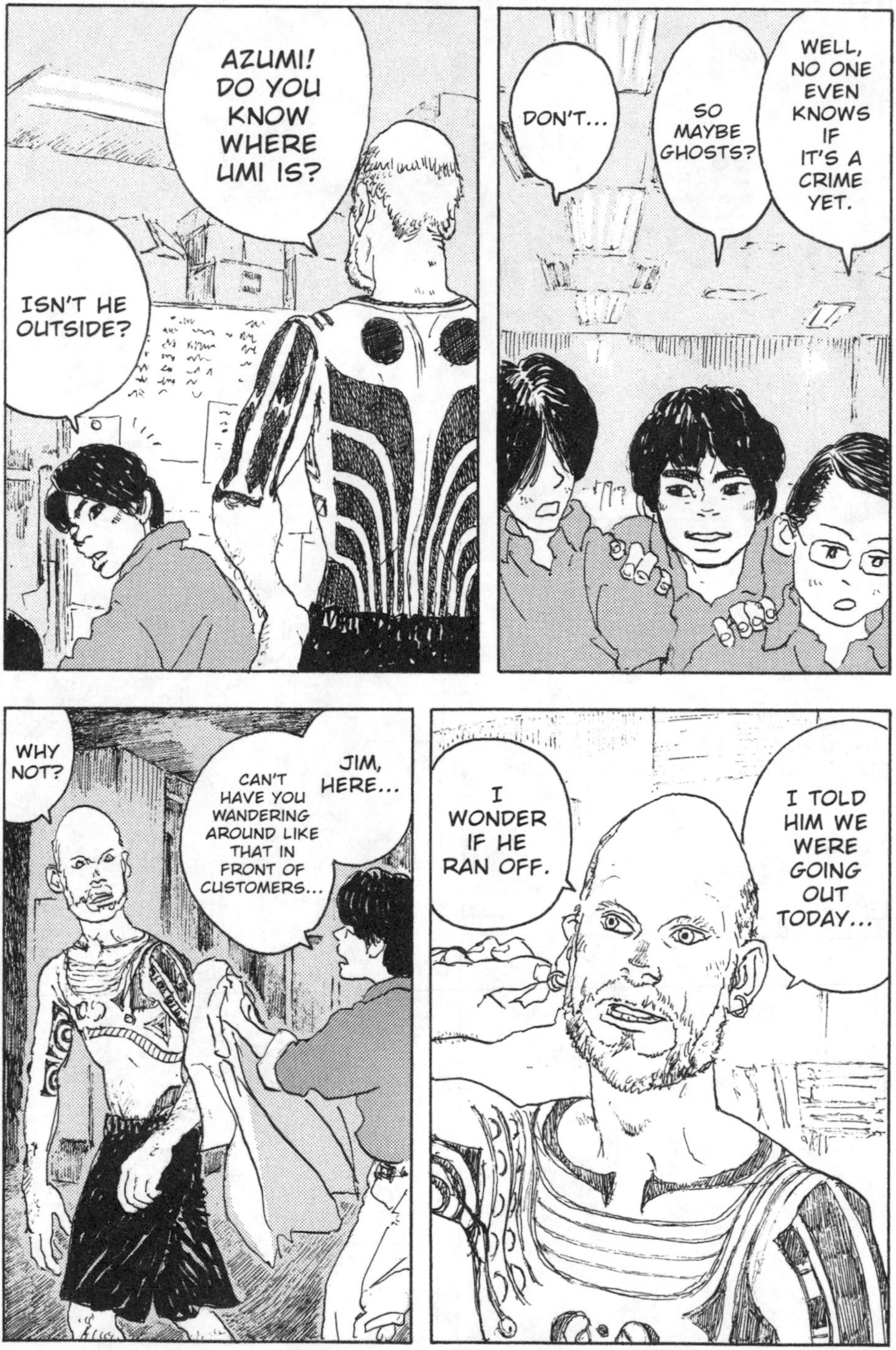
WELL, NO ONE EVEN KNOWS IF IT'S A CRIME YET.
SO MAYBE GHOSTS?
DON'T...
AZUMI! DO YOU KNOW WHERE UMI IS?
ISN'T HE OUTSIDE?
I TOLD HIM WE WERE GOING OUT TODAY...
I WONDER IF HE RAN OFF.
JIM, HERE...
CAN'T HAVE YOU WANDERING AROUND LIKE THAT IN FRONT OF CUSTOMERS...
WHY NOT?

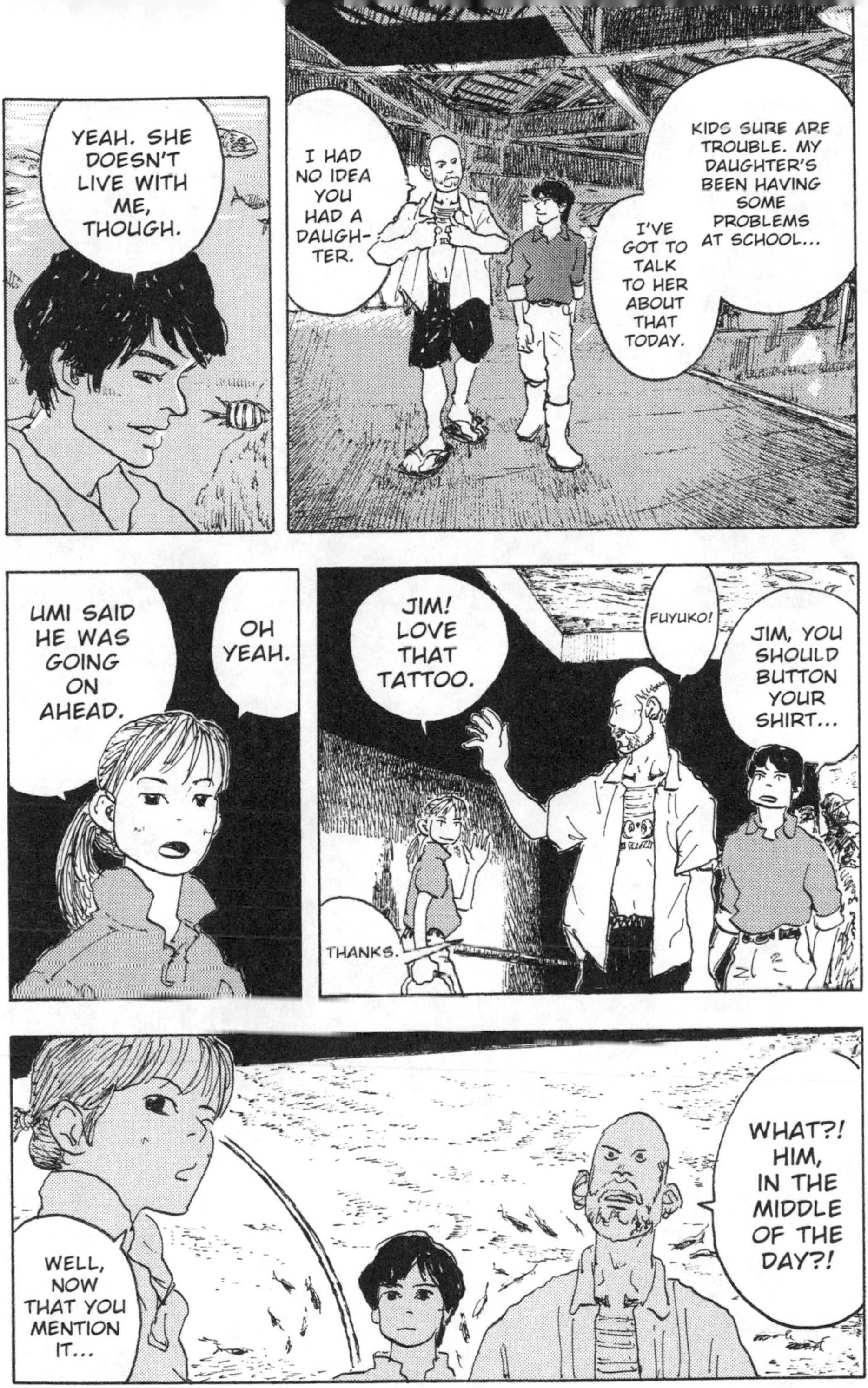
KIDS SURE ARE TROUBLE. MY DAUGHTER'S BEEN HAVING SOME PROBLEMS AT SCHOOL...
I'VE GOT TO TALK TO HER ABOUT THAT TODAY.
I HAD NO IDEA YOU HAD A DAUGH-TER.
YEAH. SHE DOESN'T LIVE WITH ME, THOUGH.
JIM, YOU SHOULD BUTTON YOUR SHIRT...
FUYUKO!
JIM! LOVE THAT TATTOO.
THANKS.
OH YEAH.
UMI SAID HE WAS GOING ON AHEAD.
WHAT?! HIM, IN THE MIDDLE OF THE DAY?!
WELL, NOW THAT YOU MENTION IT...

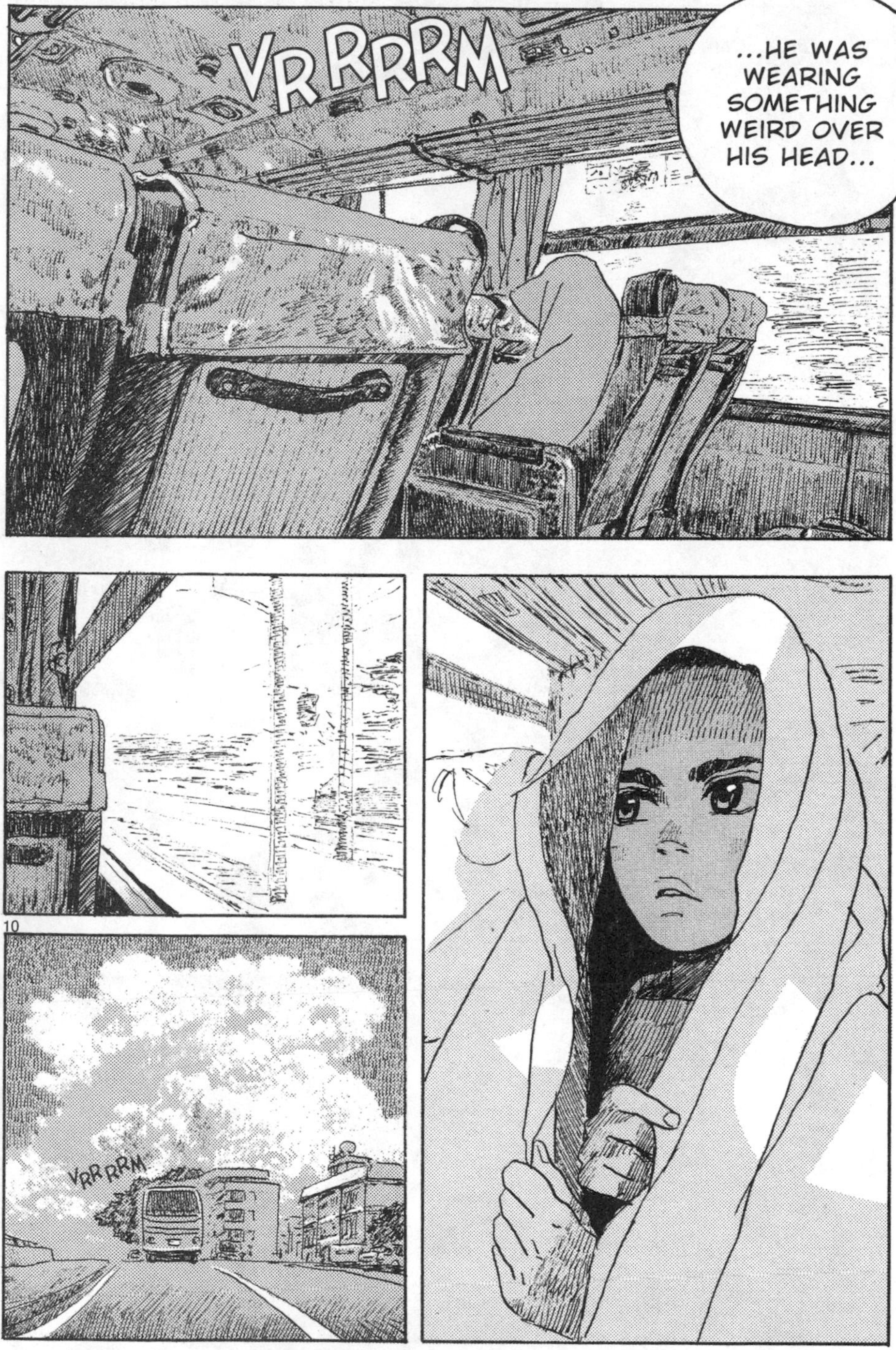
...HE WAS WEARING SOMETHING WEIRD OVER HIS HEAD...
VRRRRM
VRRRRM

10

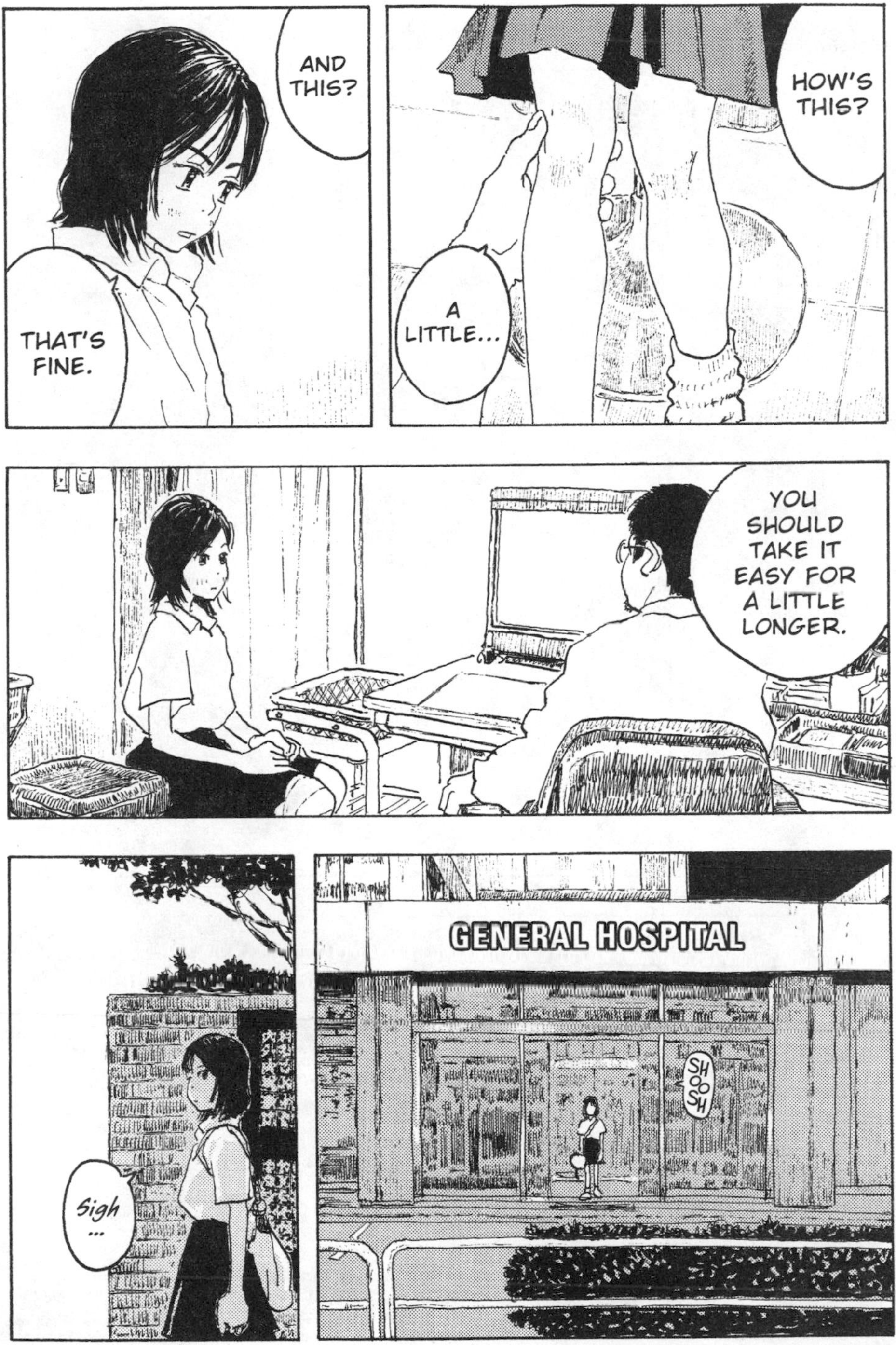
HOW'S THIS?
A LITTLE...
AND THIS?
THAT'S FINE.
YOU SHOULD TAKE IT EASY FOR A LITTLE LONGER.
GENERAL HOSPITAL
SHOOSH
Sigh...

...

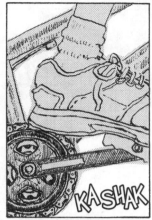

KASHAK

FWIP

GENERAL HOSPITAL

RAL HOSPITAL
SHOOSH
REGISTRATION
CHAK
SORA.

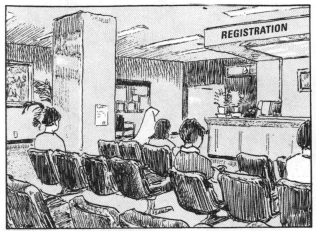

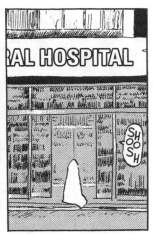

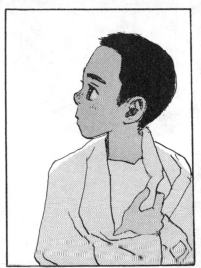

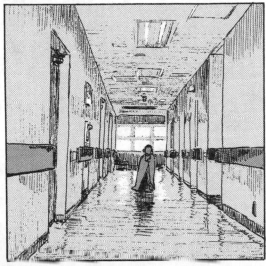

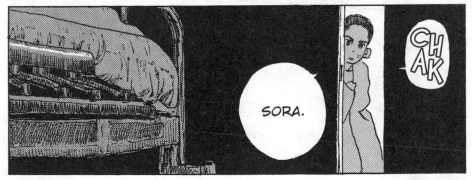

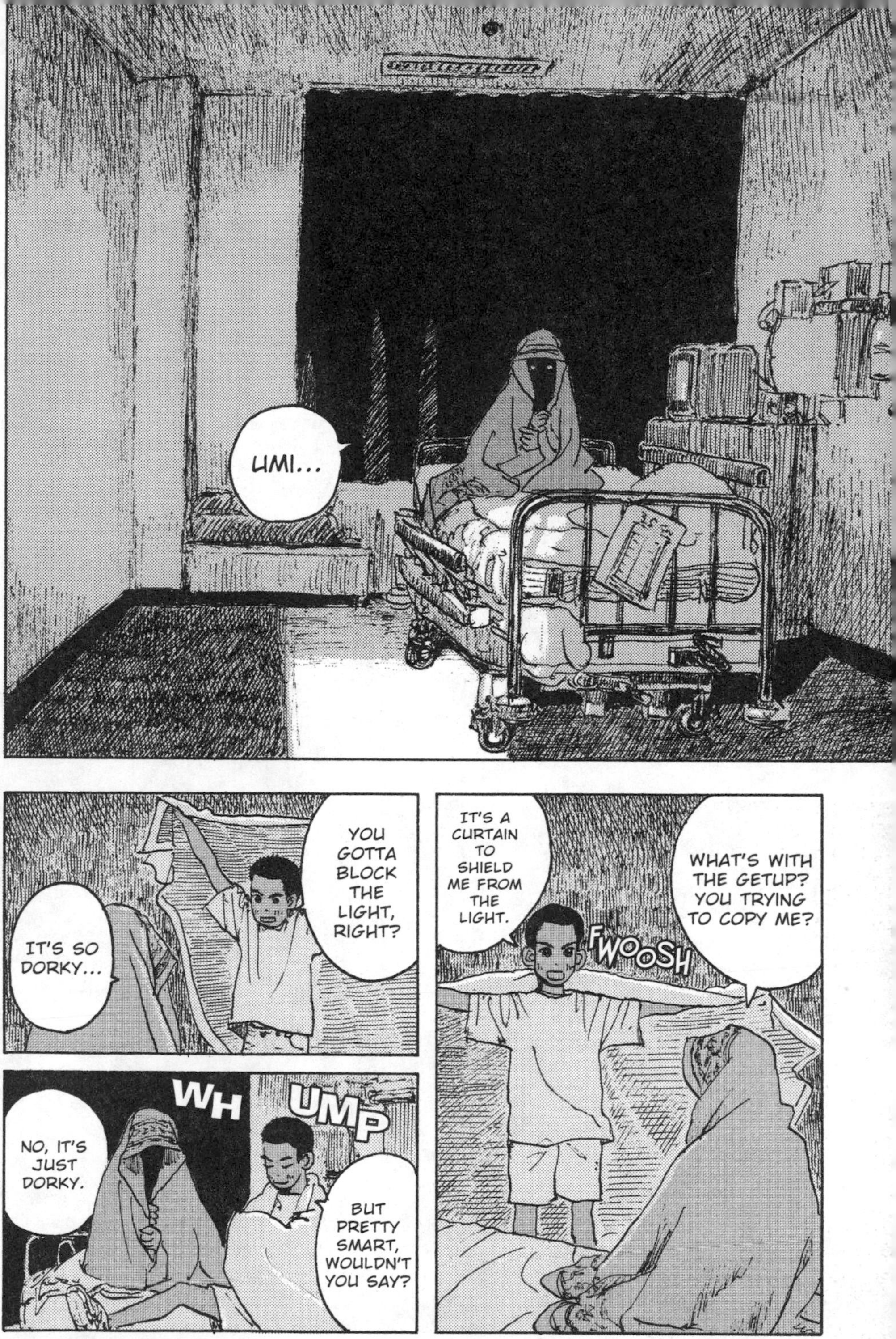
UMI...
WHAT'S WITH THE GETUP? YOU TRYING TO COPY ME?
FWOOSH
IT'S A CURTAIN TO SHIELD ME FROM THE LIGHT.
YOU GOTTA BLOCK THE LIGHT, RIGHT?
IT'S SO DORKY...
WHUMP
BUT PRETTY SMART, WOULDN'T YOU SAY?
NO, IT'S JUST DORKY.

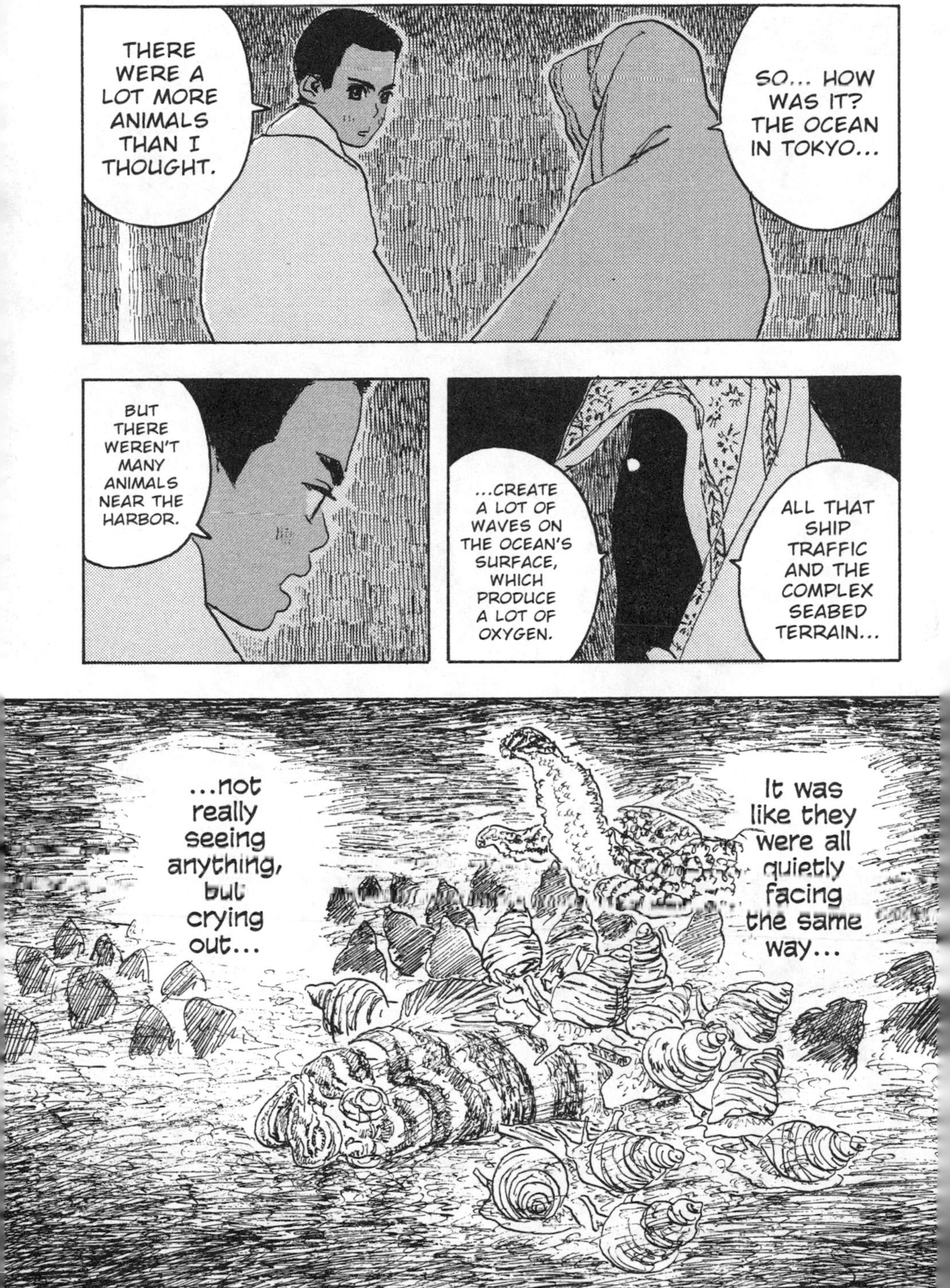
SO... HOW WAS IT? THE OCEAN IN TOKYO...
THERE WERE A LOT MORE ANIMALS THAN I THOUGHT.
ALL THAT SHIP TRAFFIC AND THE COMPLEX SEABED TERRAIN...
...CREATE A LOT OF WAVES ON THE OCEAN'S SURFACE, WHICH PRODUCE A LOT OF OXYGEN.
BUT THERE WEREN'T MANY ANIMALS NEAR THE HARBOR.
It was like they were all quietly facing the same way...
...not really seeing anything, but crying out...

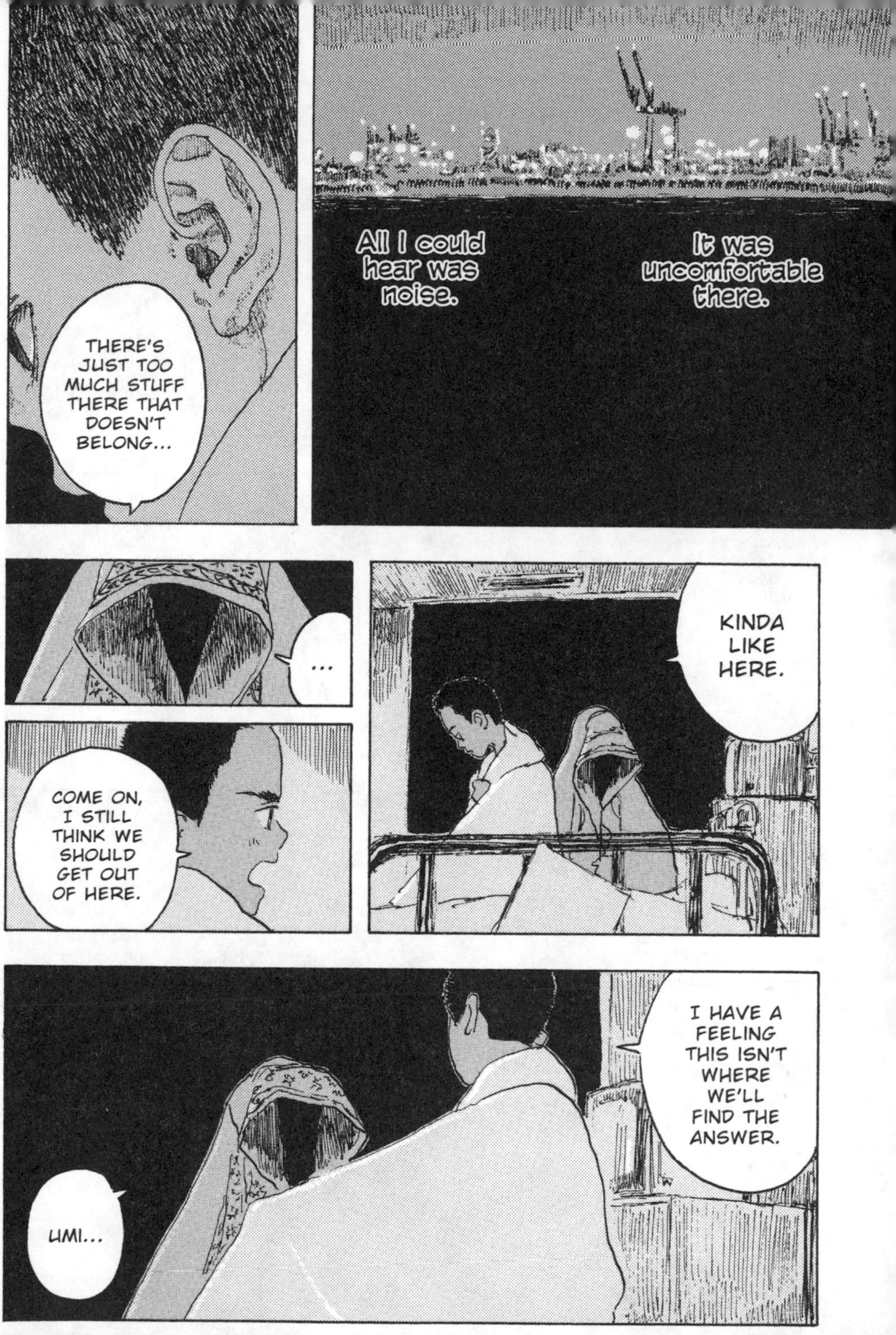
It was uncomfortable there.
All I could hear was noise.
THERE'S JUST TOO MUCH STUFF THERE THAT DOESN'T BELONG...
KINDA LIKE HERE.
...
COME ON, I STILL THINK WE SHOULD GET OUT OF HERE.
I HAVE A FEELING THIS ISN'T WHERE WE'LL FIND THE ANSWER.
UMI...

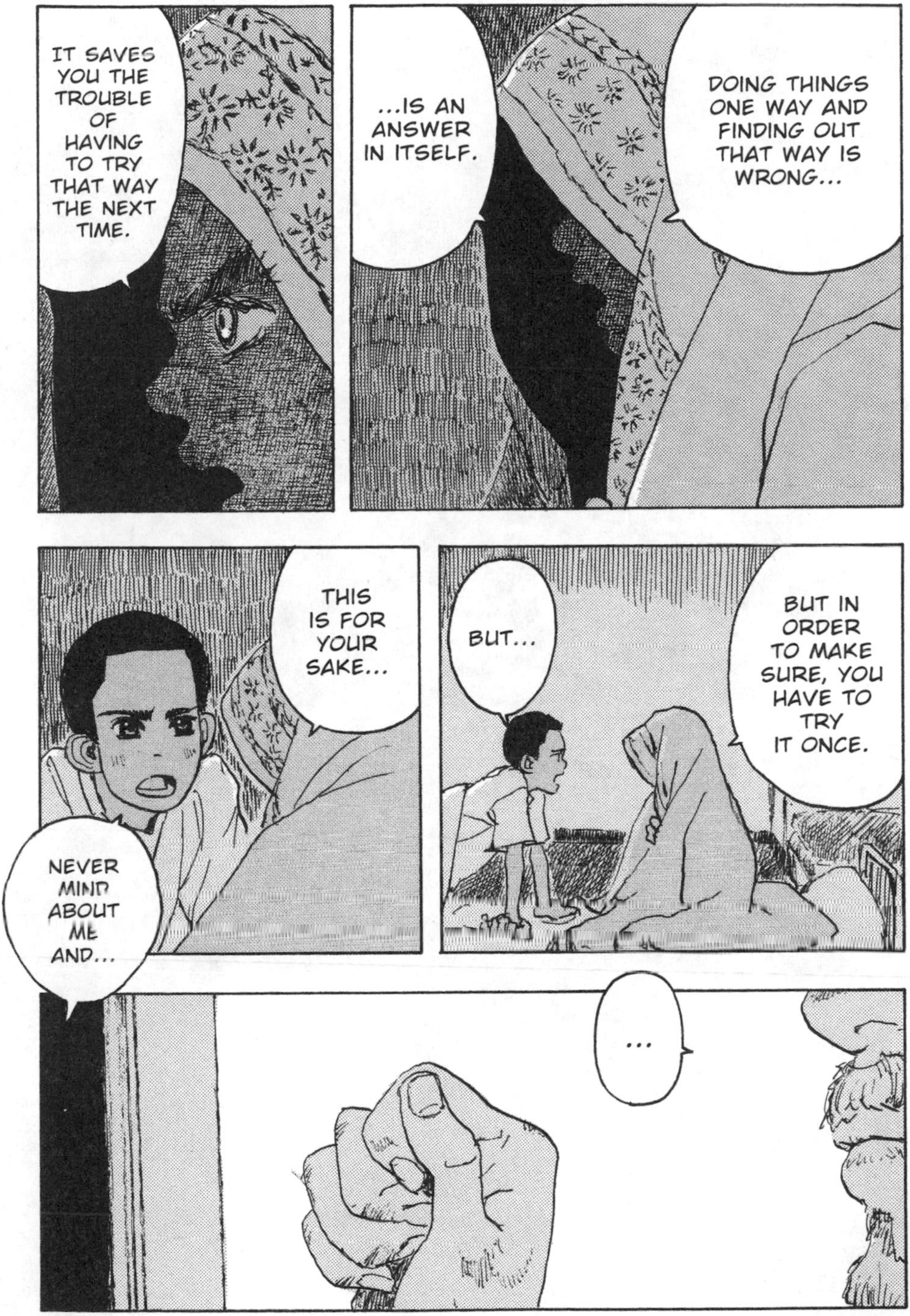
DOING THINGS ONE WAY AND FINDING OUT THAT WAY IS WRONG...
...IS AN ANSWER IN ITSELF.
IT SAVES YOU THE TROUBLE OF HAVING TO TRY THAT WAY THE NEXT TIME.
BUT IN ORDER TO MAKE SURE, YOU HAVE TO TRY IT ONCE.
BUT...
THIS IS FOR YOUR SAKE...
NEVER MIND ABOUT ME AND...
...

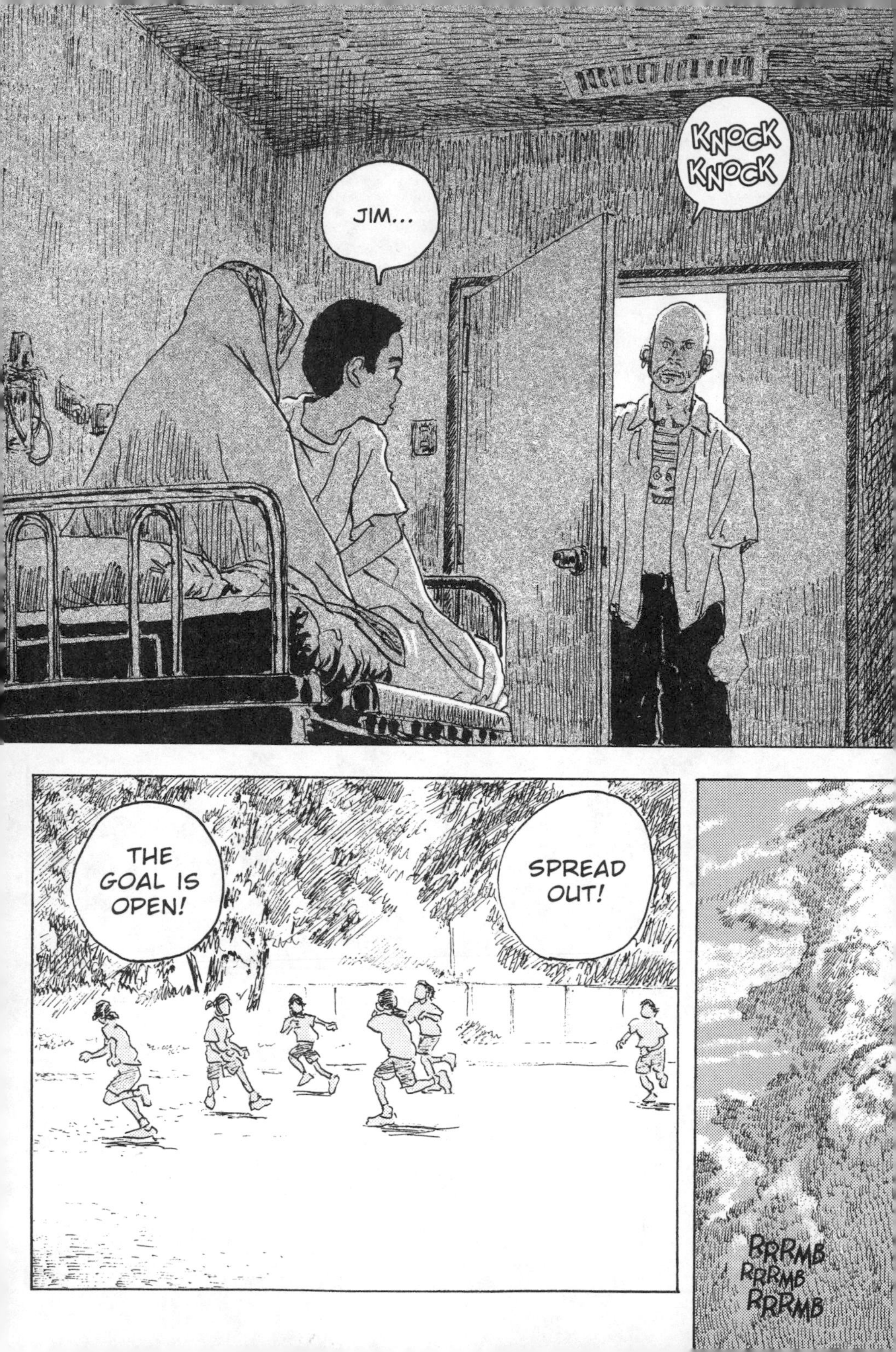
KNOCK KNOCK
JIM...
RRRMB RRRMB RRRMB
SPREAD OUT!
THE GOAL IS OPEN!

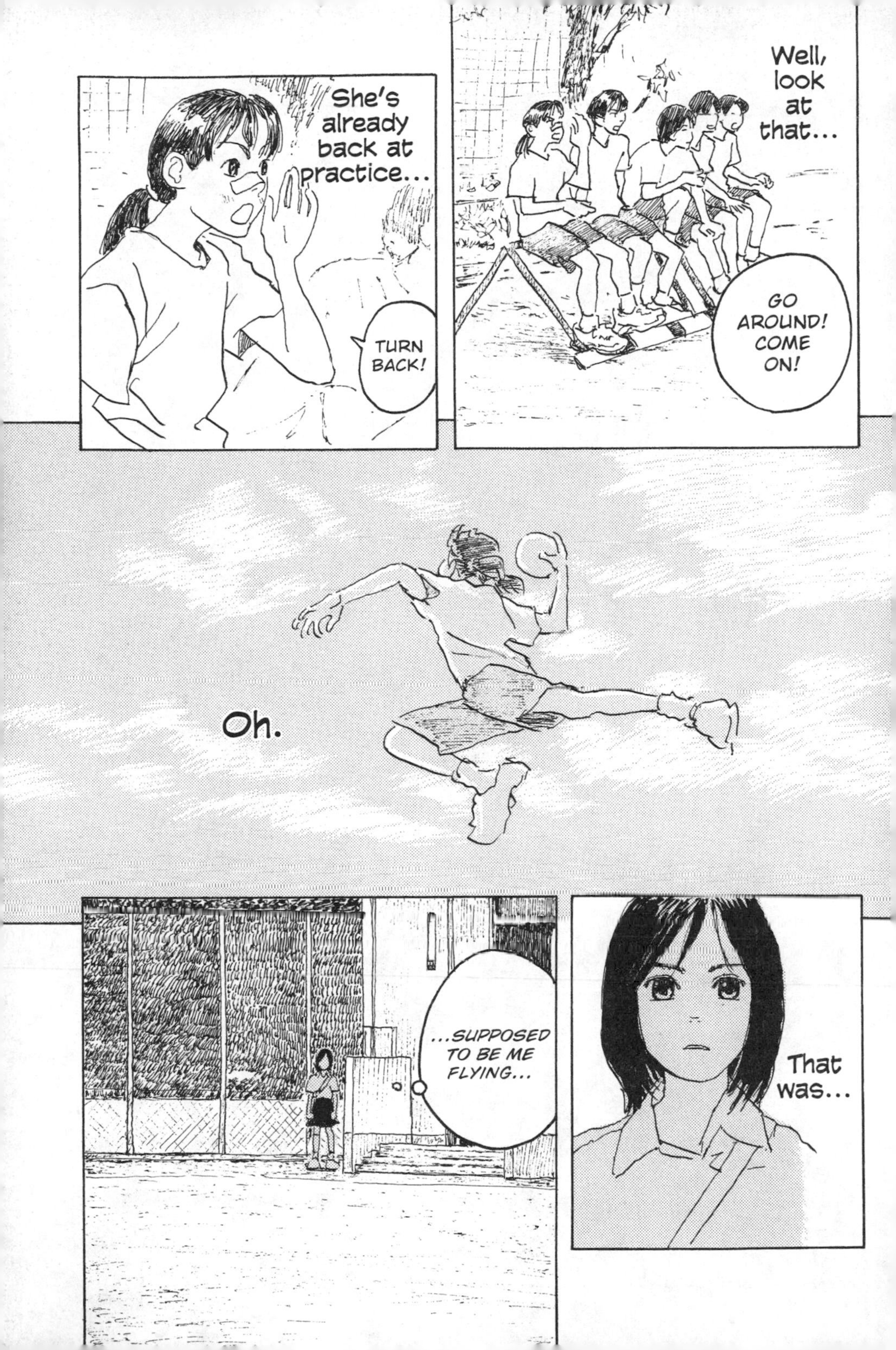
Well, look at that...
GO AROUND! COME ON!
She's already back at practice...
TURN BACK!
Oh.
That was...
...SUPPOSED TO BE ME FLYING...

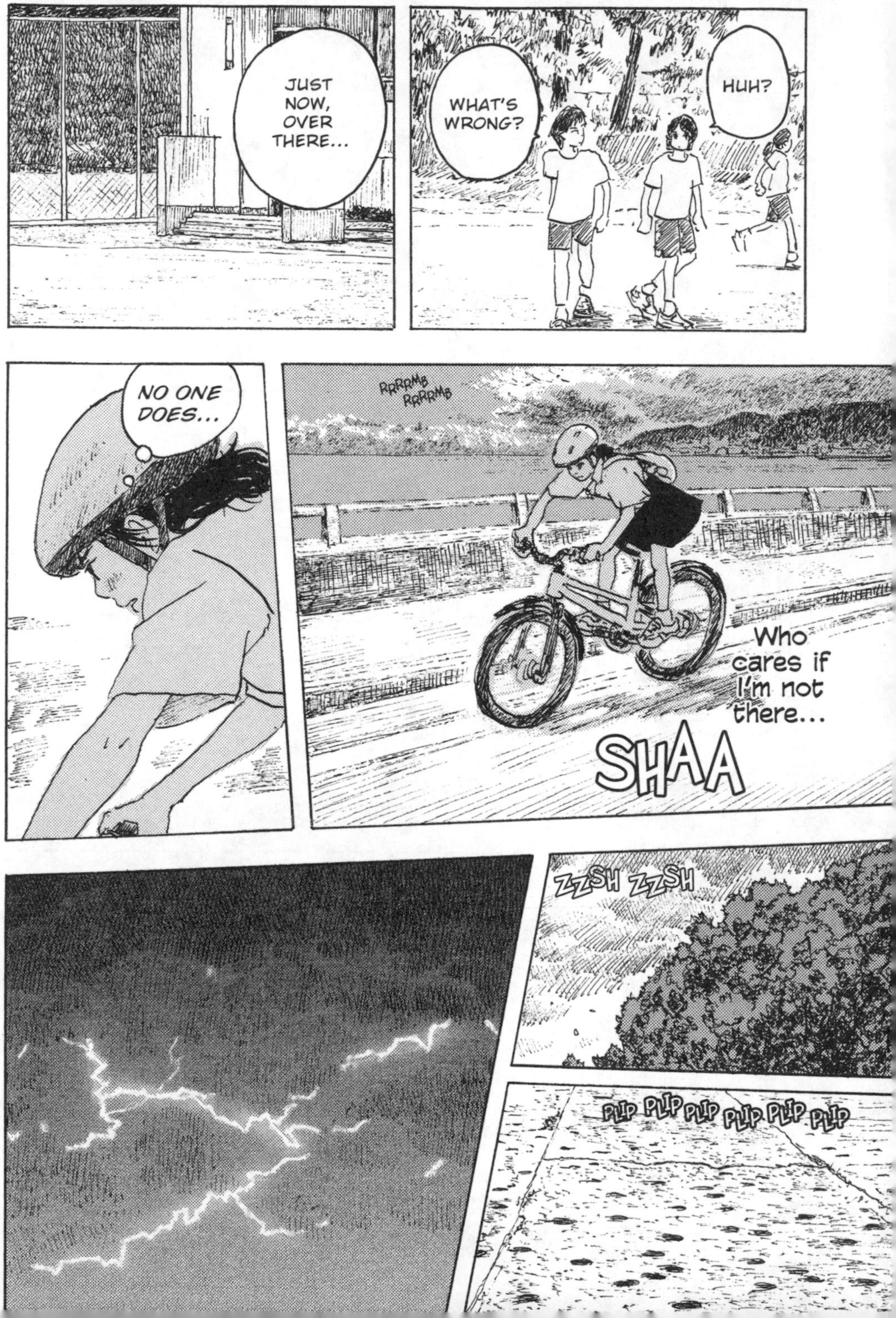
HUH?
WHAT'S WRONG?
JUST NOW, OVER THERE...
RRRRMB RRRRMB
Who cares if I'm not there...
SHAA
NO ONE DOES...
ZZSH ZZSH
PLIP PLIP PLIP PLIP PLIP PLIP

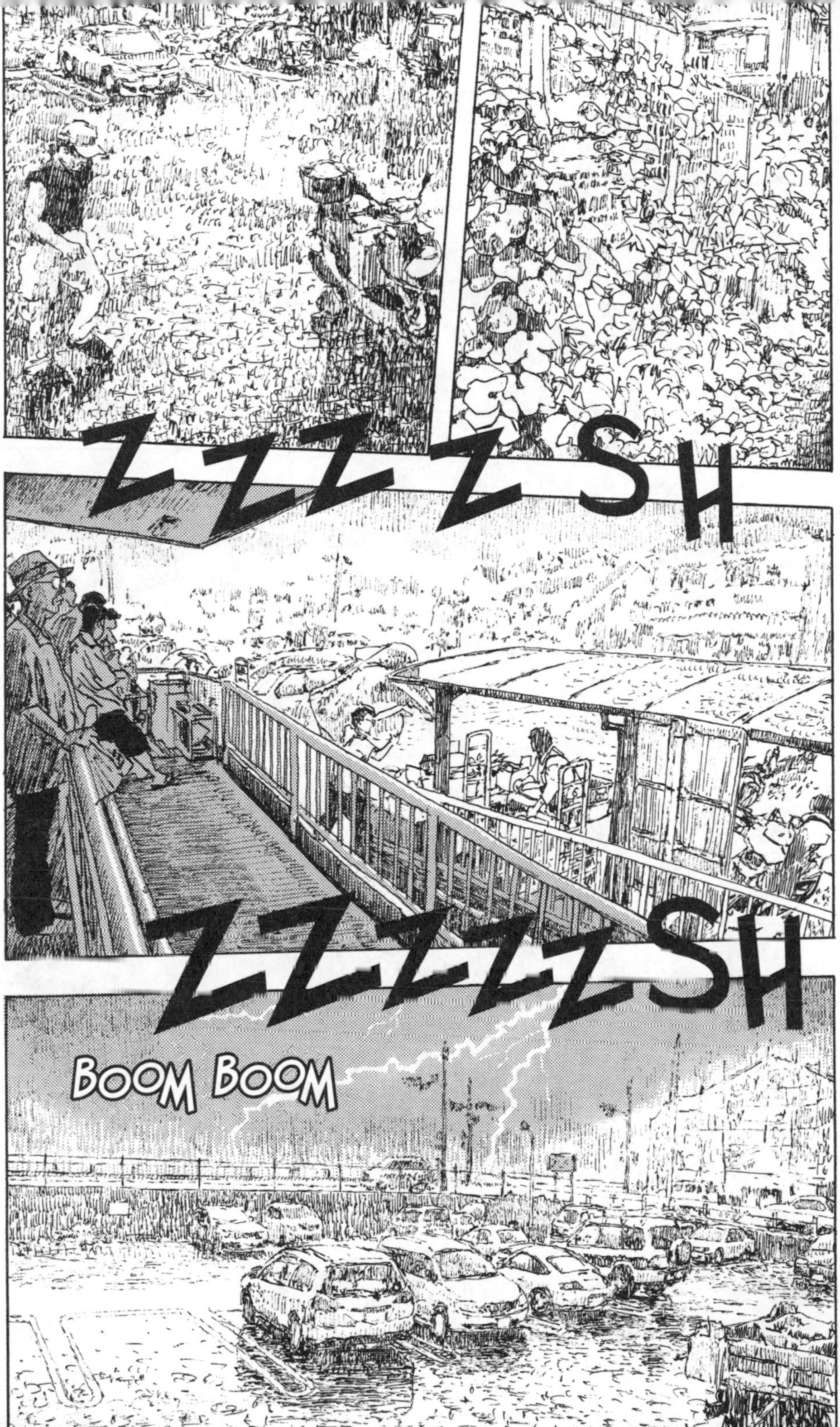
ZZZZSH
ZZZZZSH
BOOM BOOM

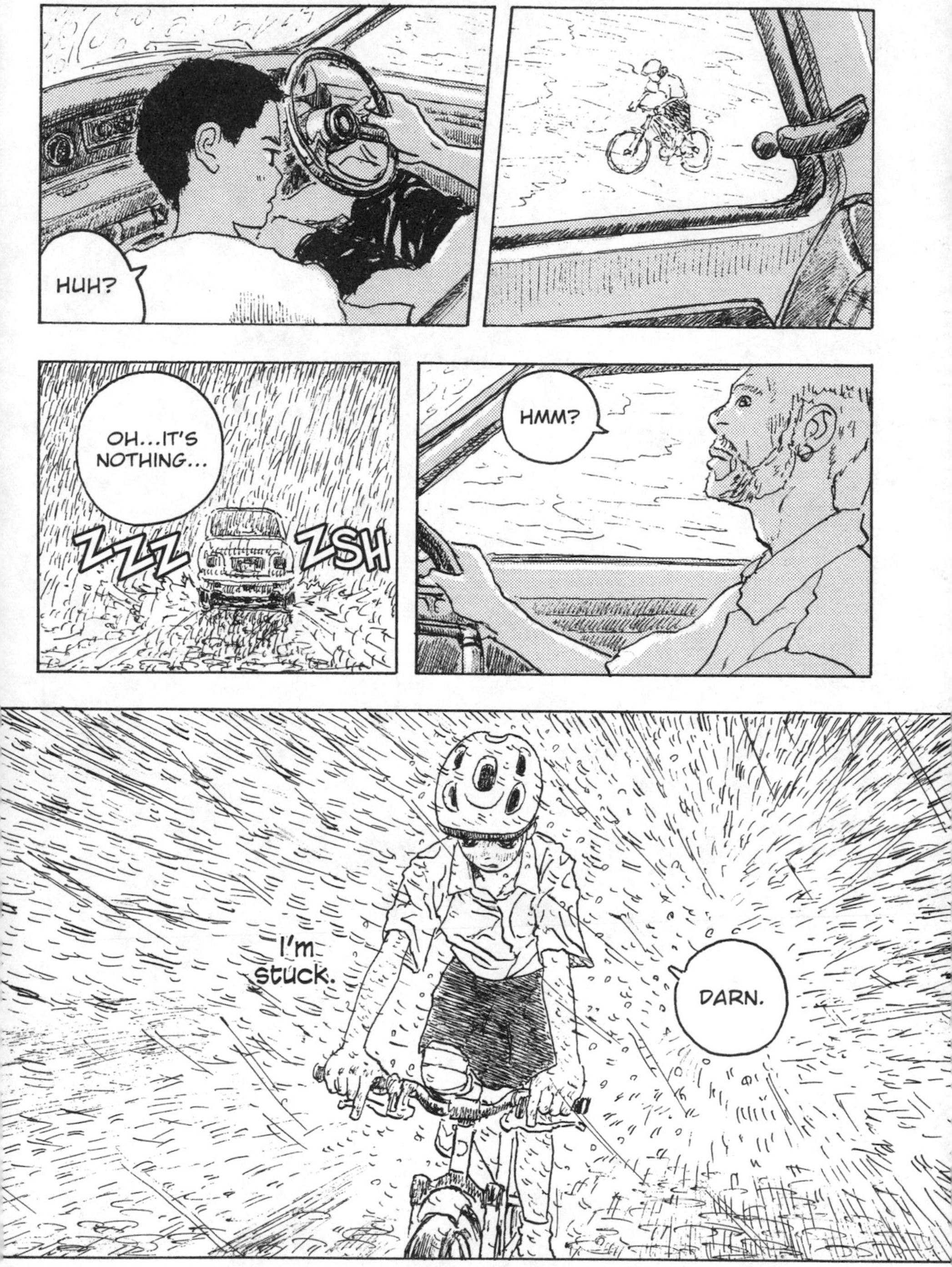
HUH?
HMM?
OH...IT'S NOTHING...
ZZZ ZSH
DARN.
I'm stuck.

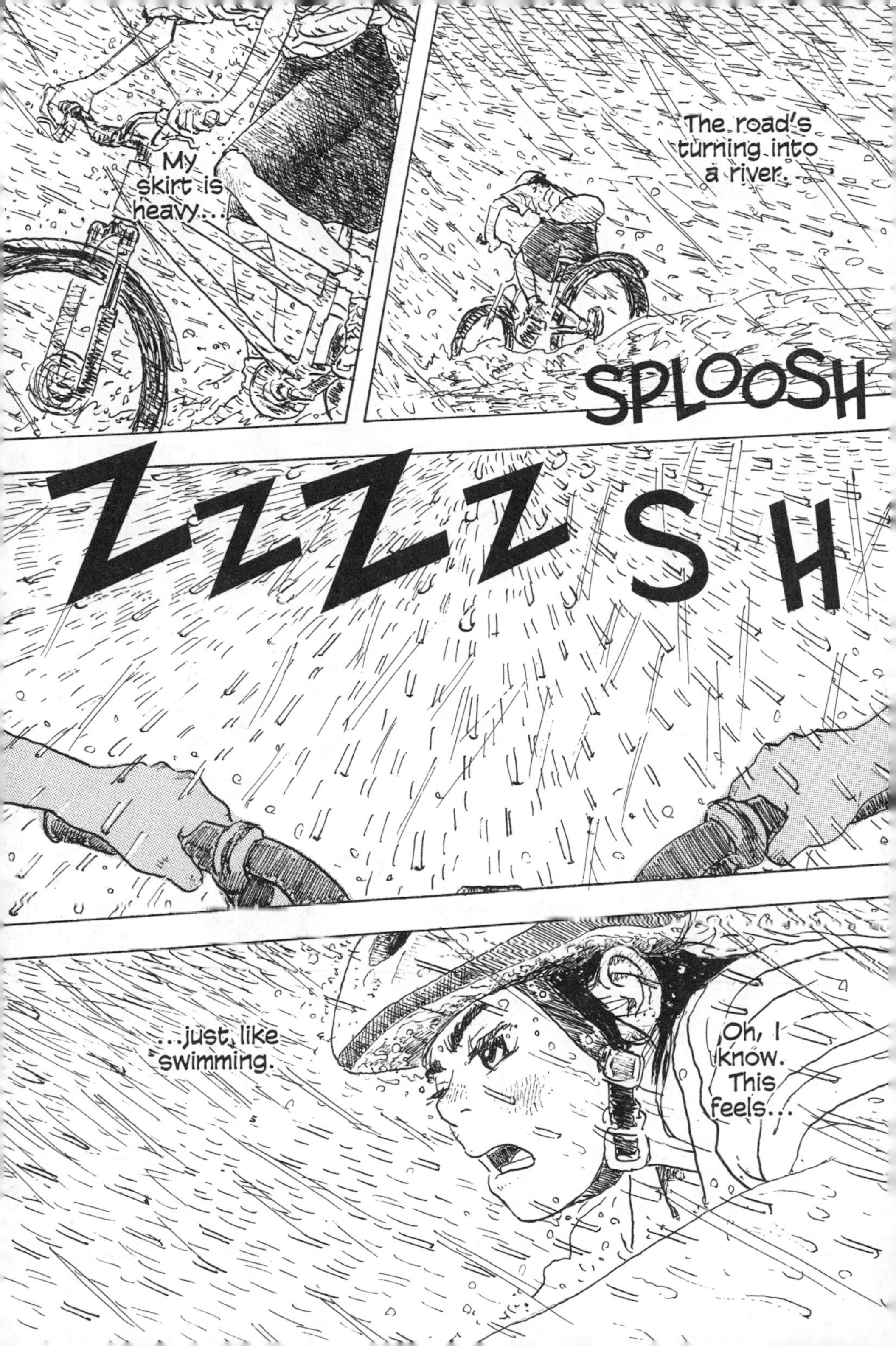
The road's turning into a river.
SPLOOSH
My skirt is heavy...
ZZZZSH
Oh, I know. This feels...
...just like swimming.

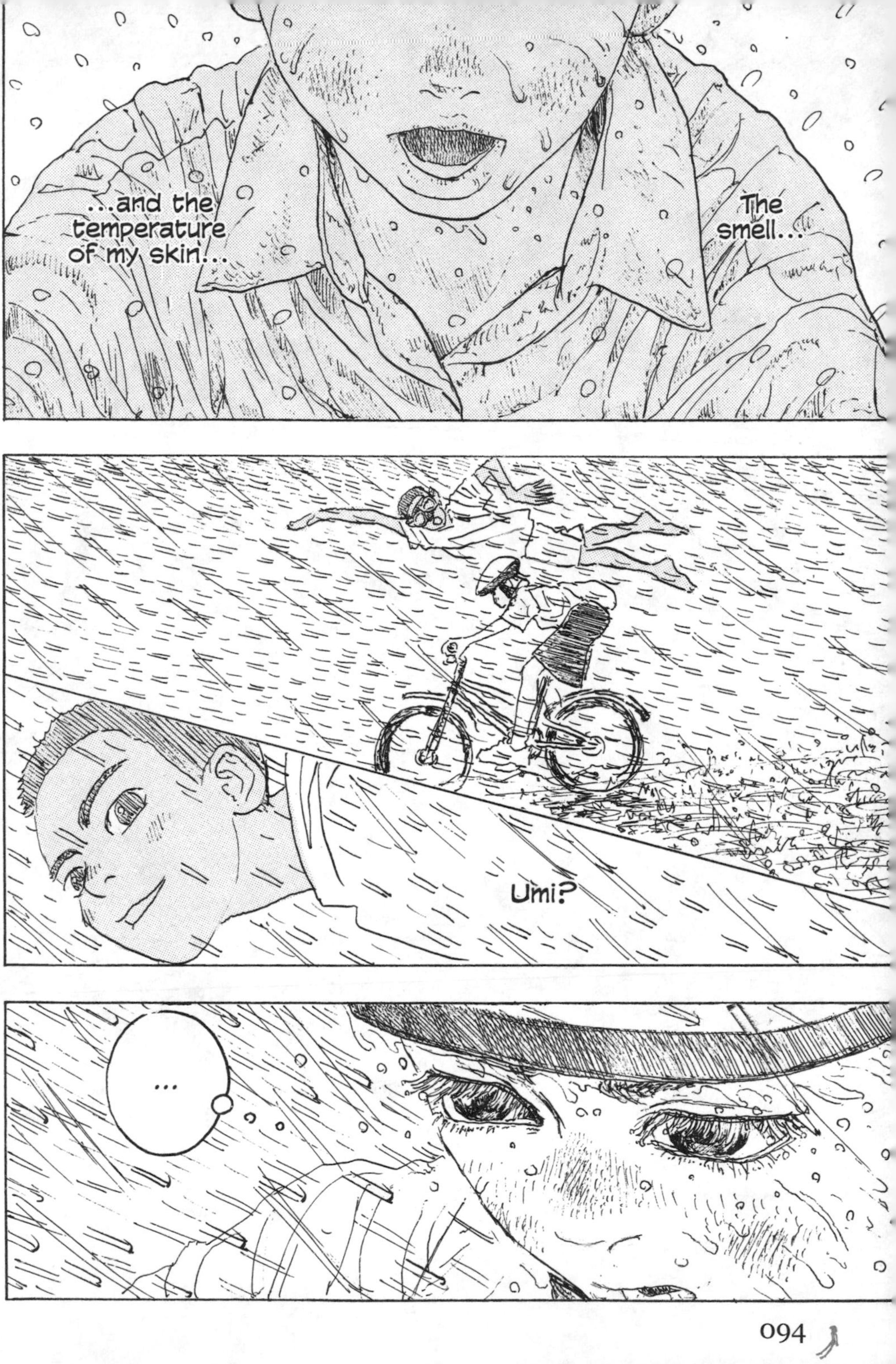
The smell...
...and the temperature of my skin...
Umi?
...

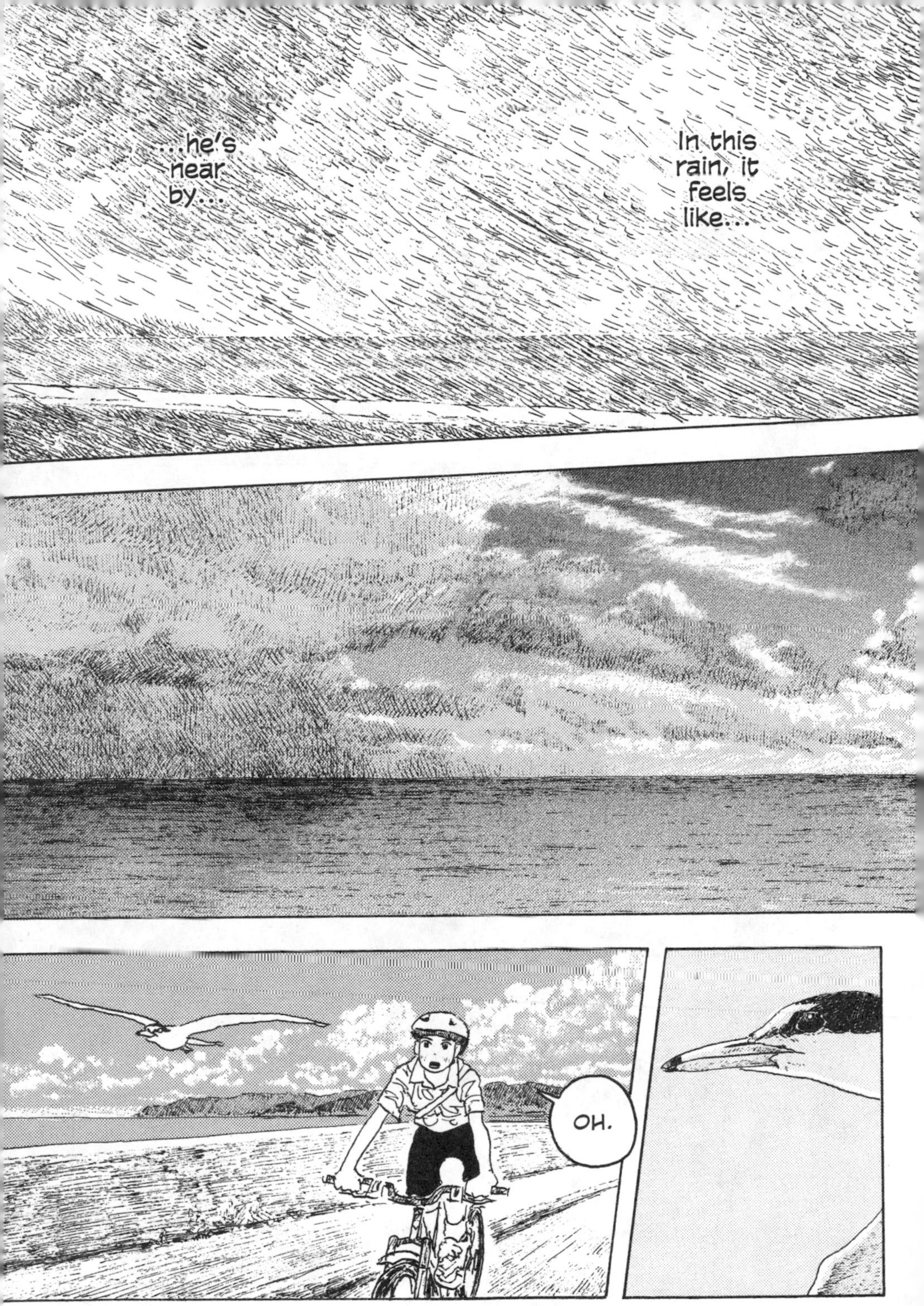
In this rain, it feels like...
...he's near by...
OH.

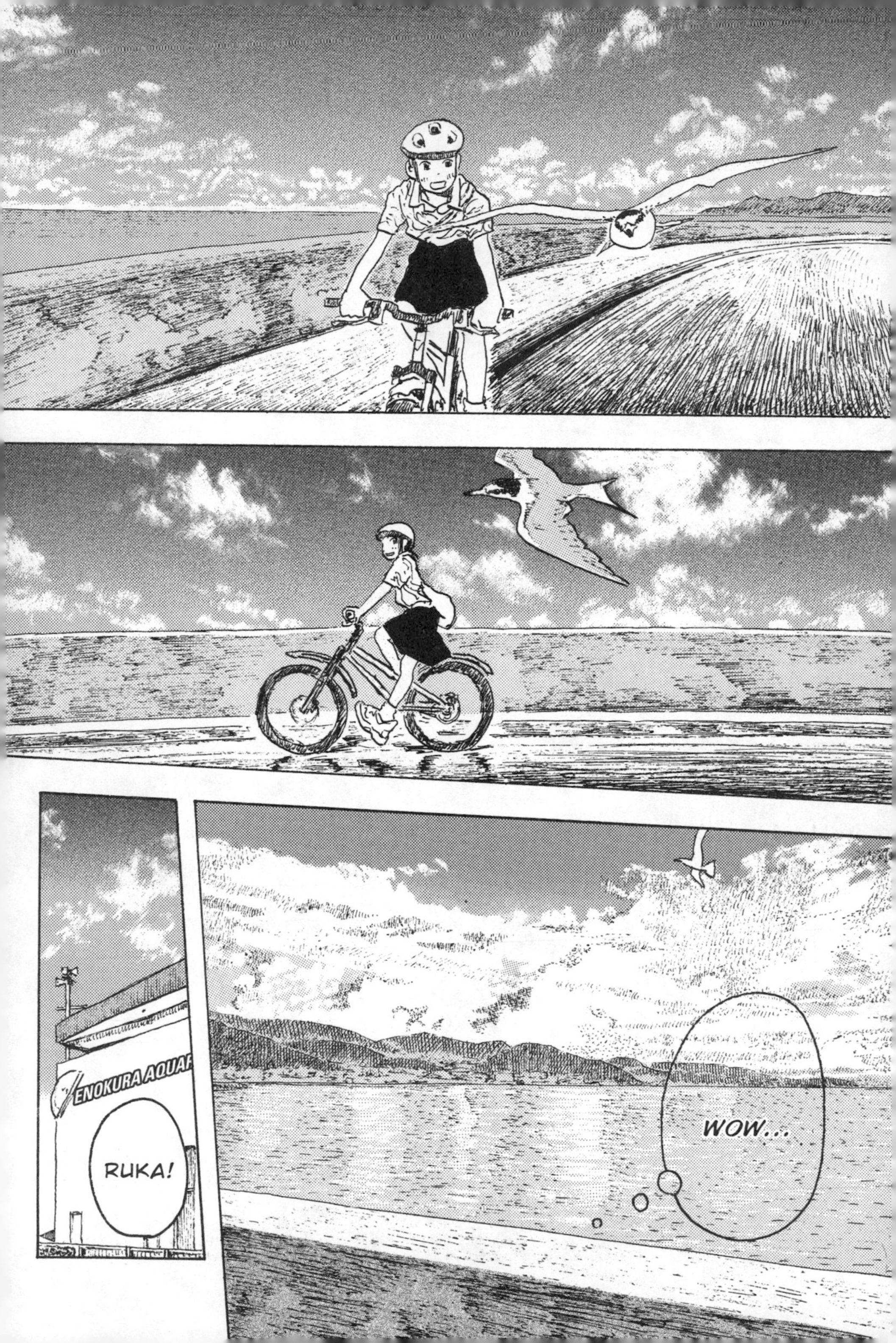
WOW...
ENOKURA AQUAR
RUKA!

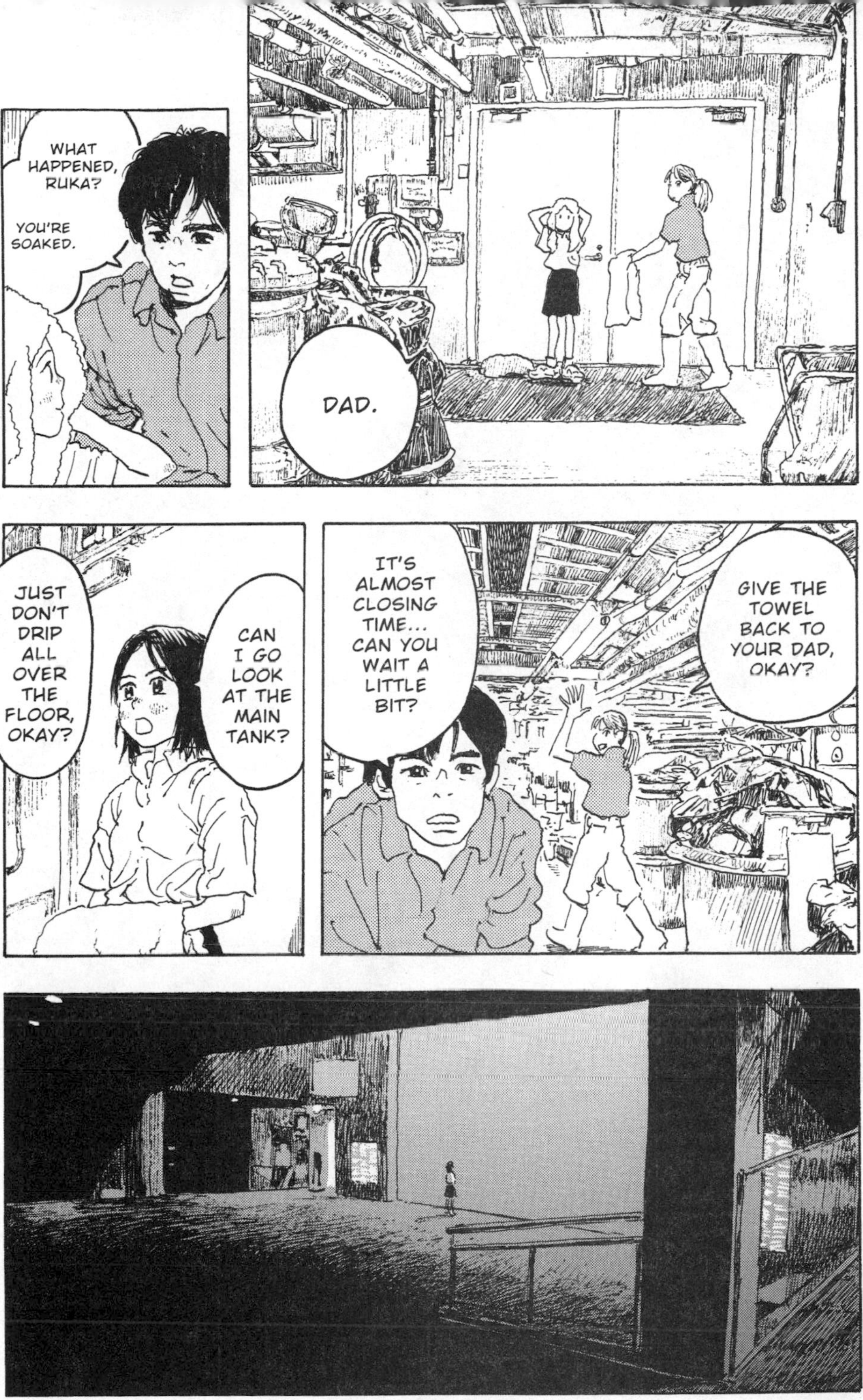
DAD.
WHAT HAPPENED, RUKA?
YOU'RE SOAKED.
GIVE THE TOWEL BACK TO YOUR DAD, OKAY?
IT'S ALMOST CLOSING TIME... CAN YOU WAIT A LITTLE BIT?
CAN I GO LOOK AT THE MAIN TANK?
JUST DON'T DRIP ALL OVER THE FLOOR, OKAY?

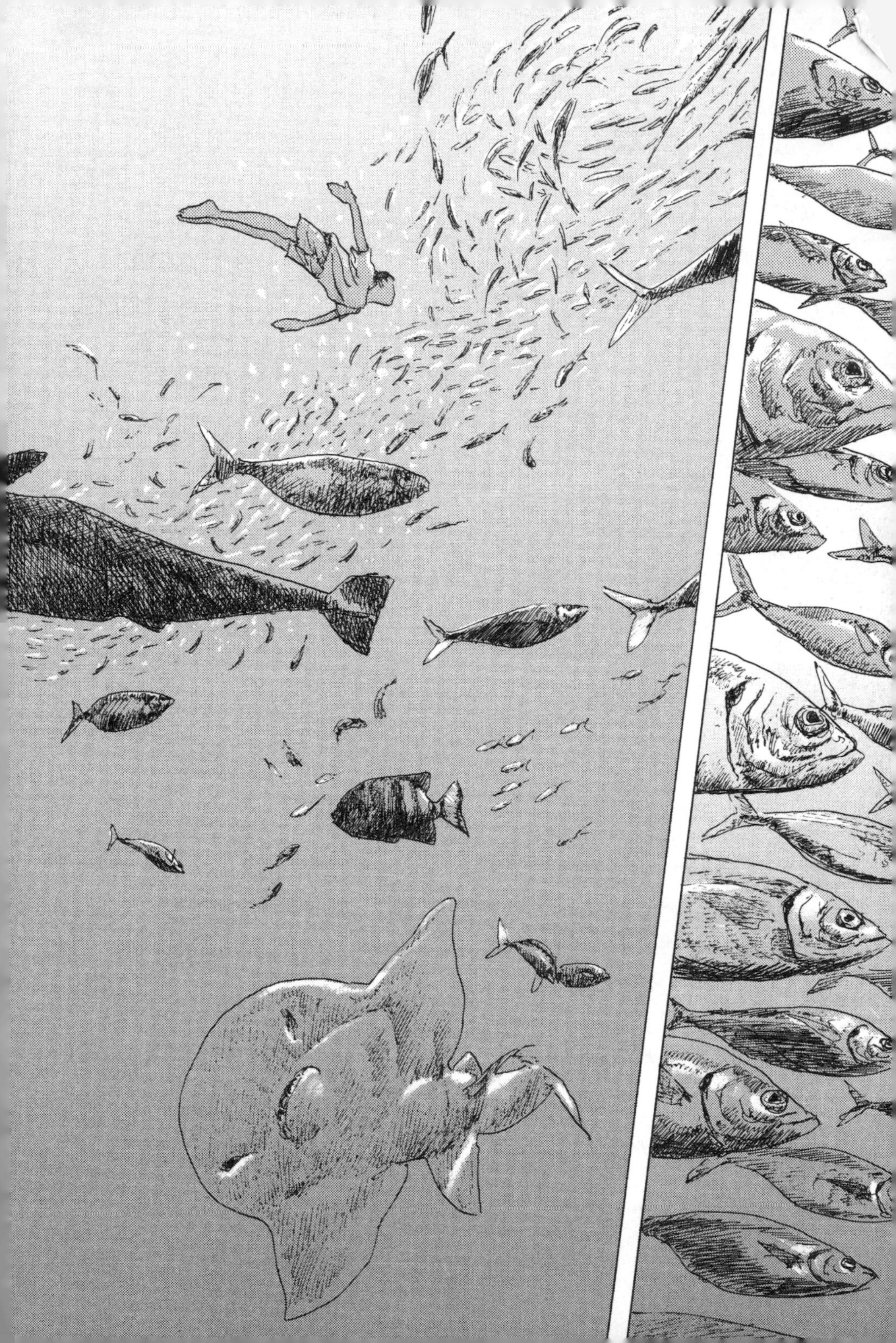

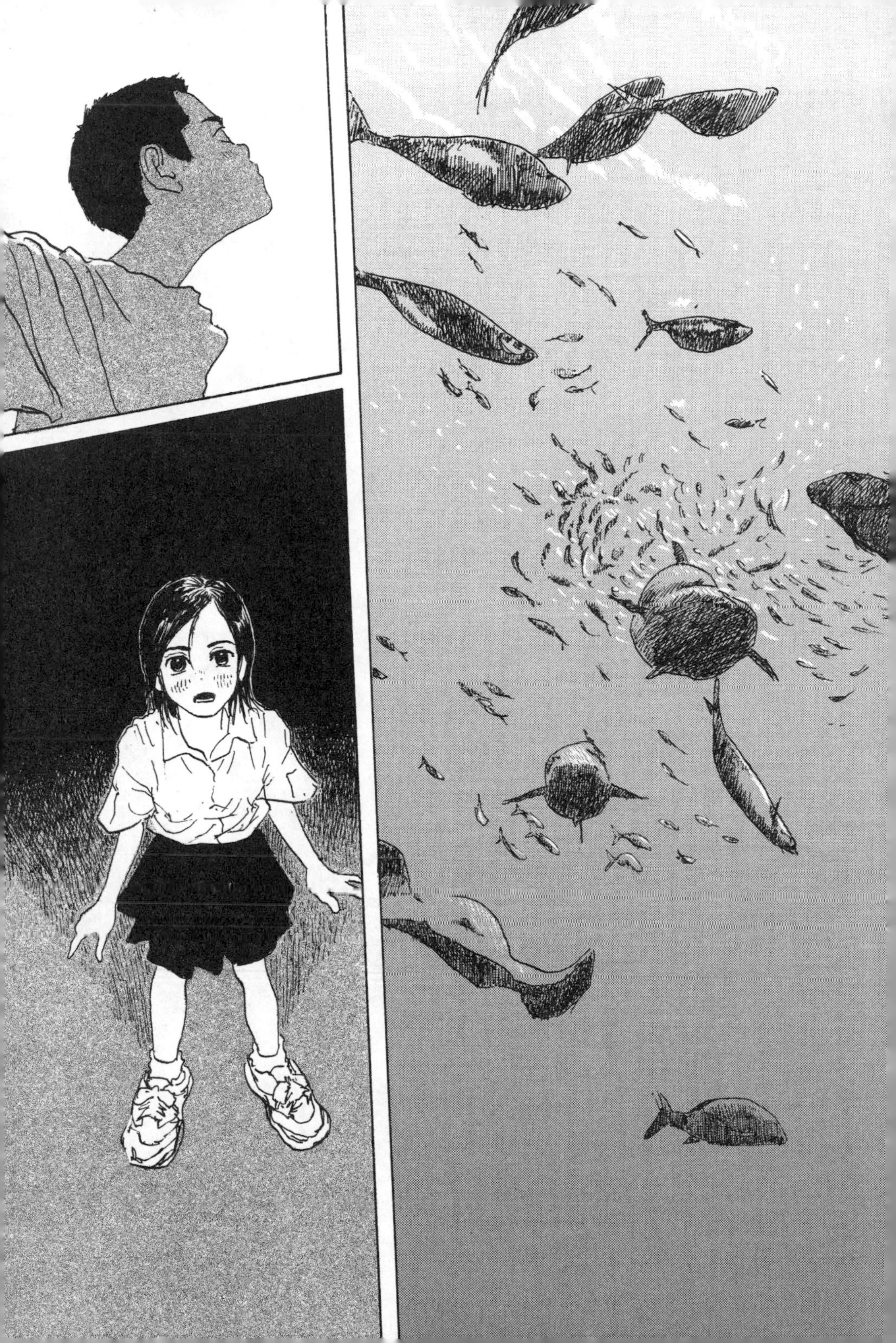

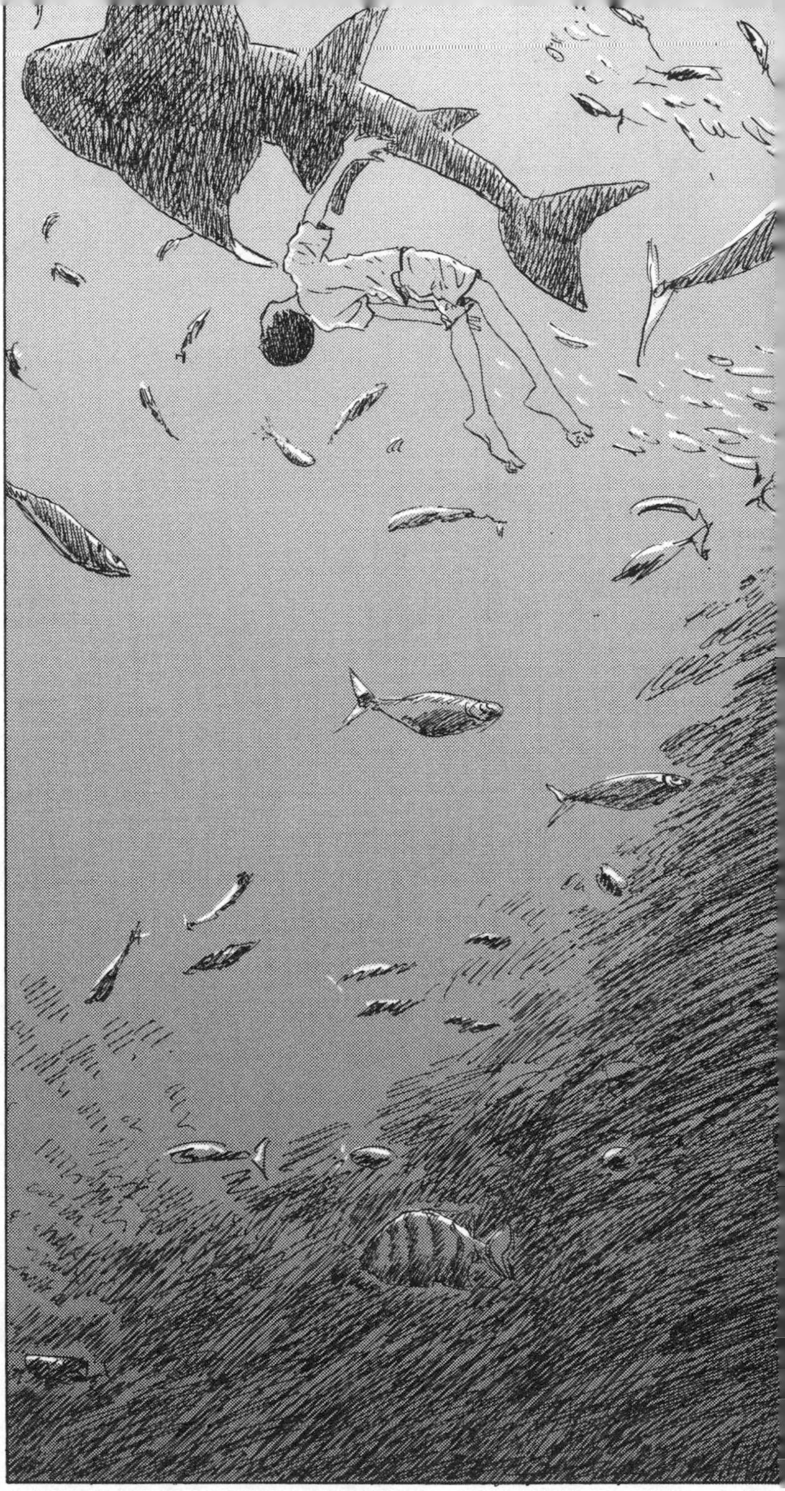
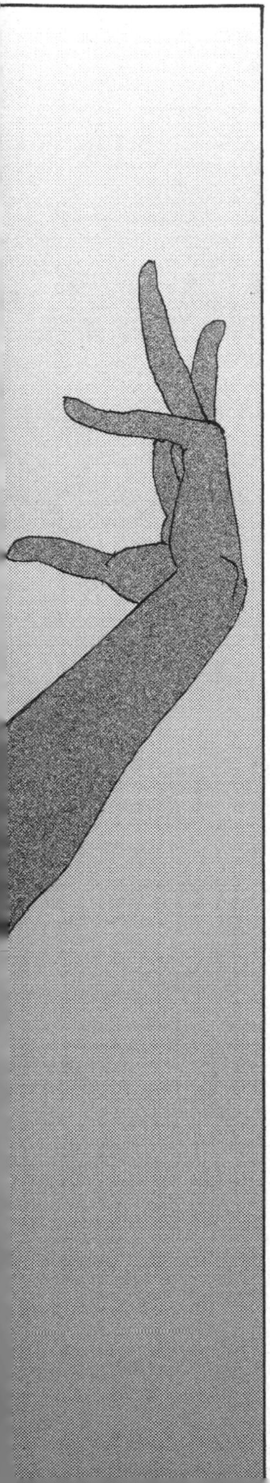

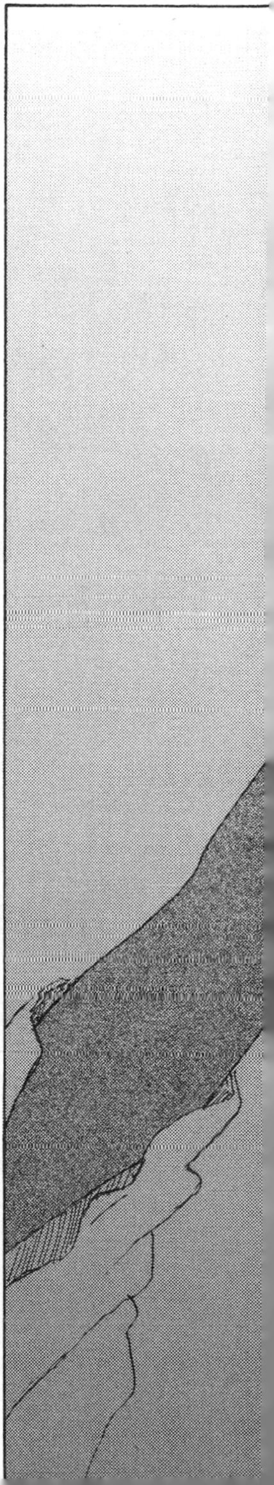
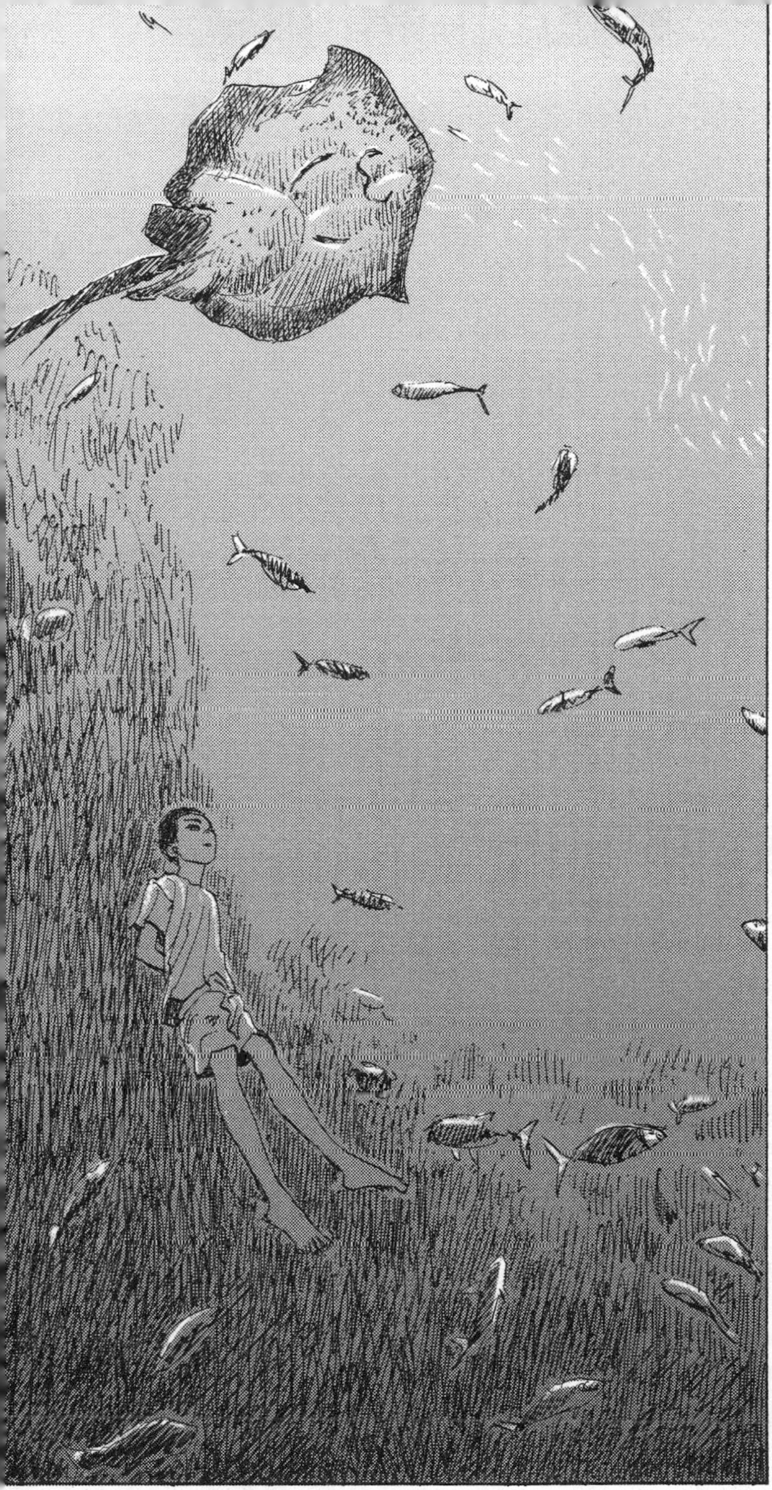

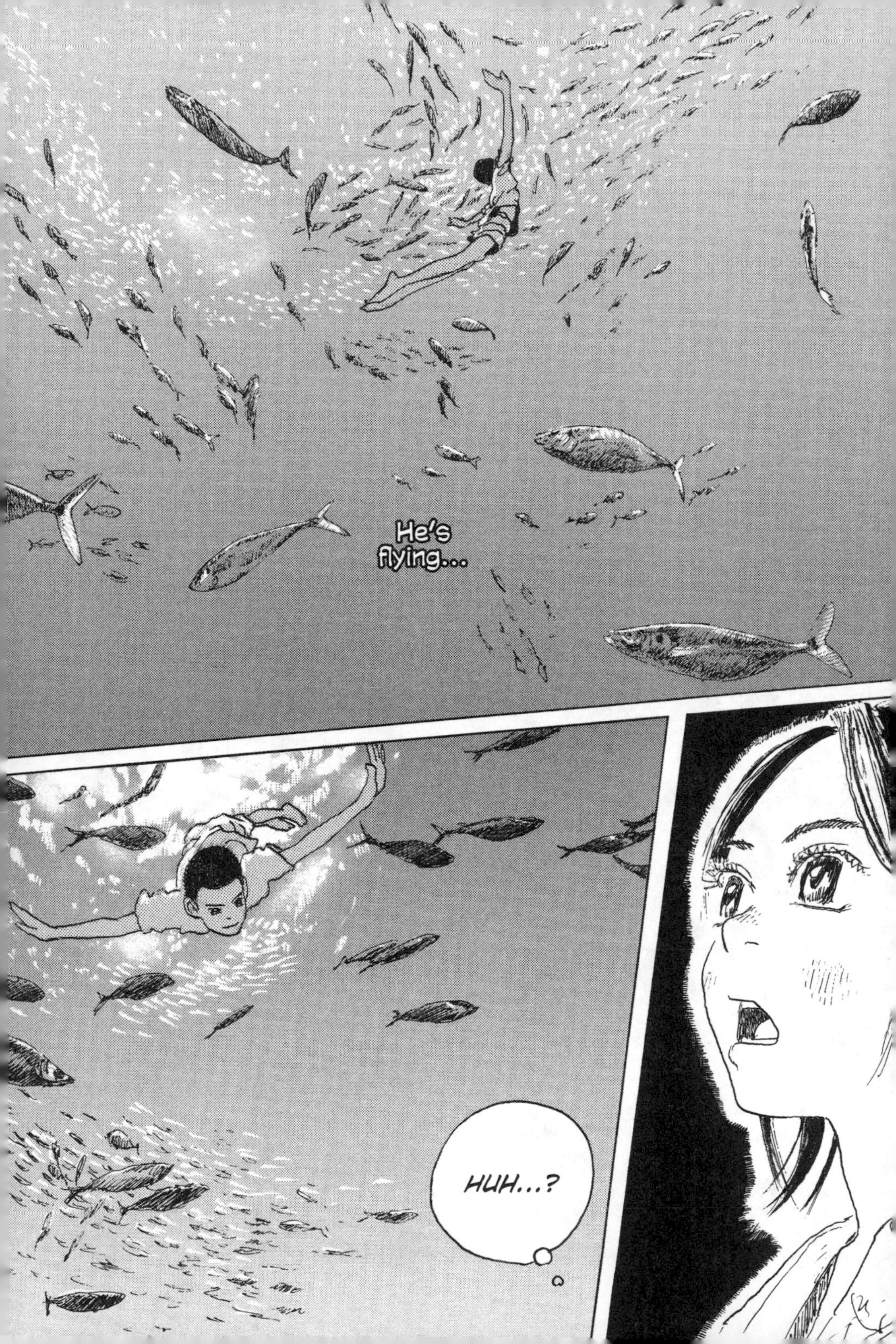
He's flying...
HUH...?

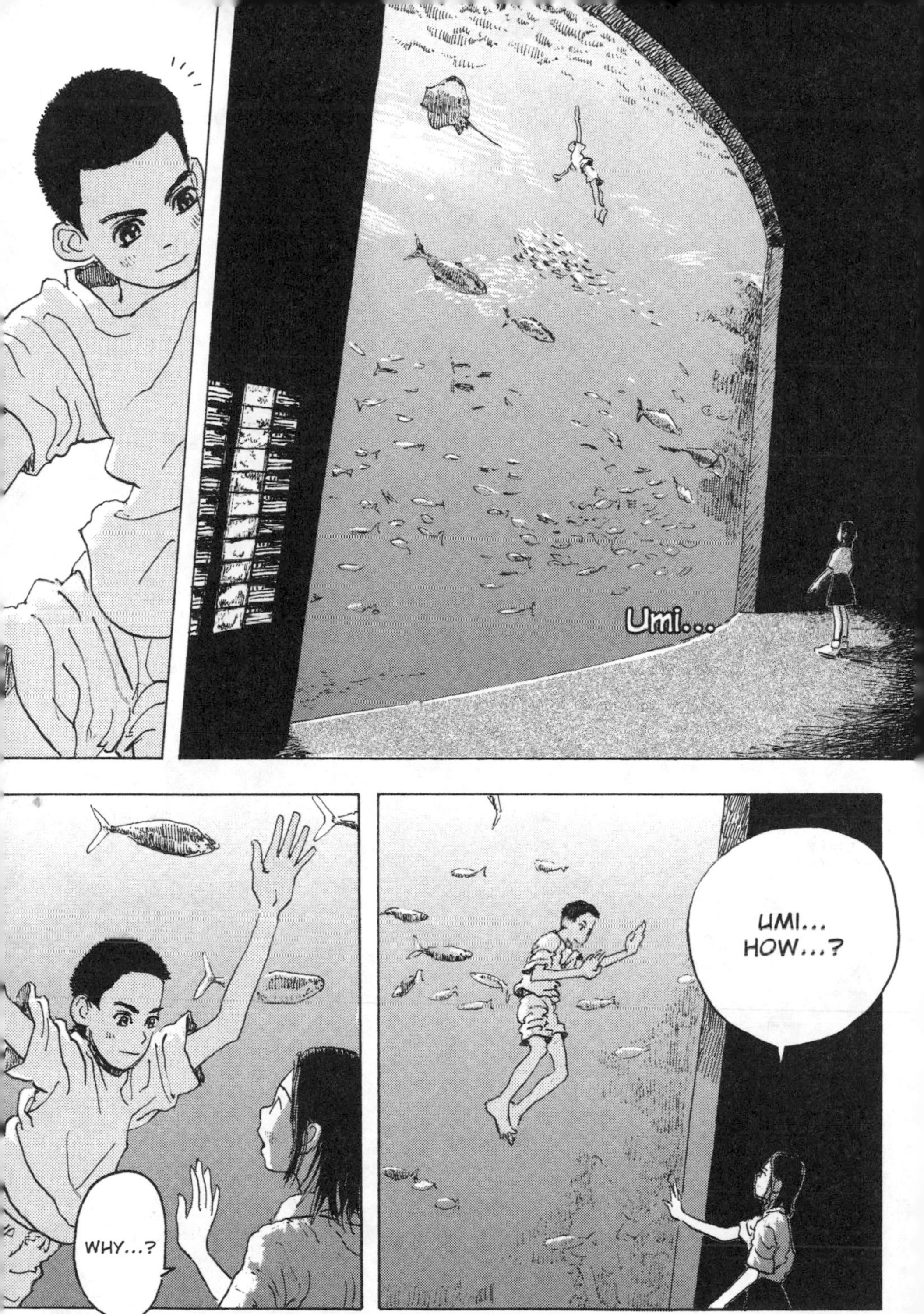
Umi...
UMI... HOW...?
WHY...?

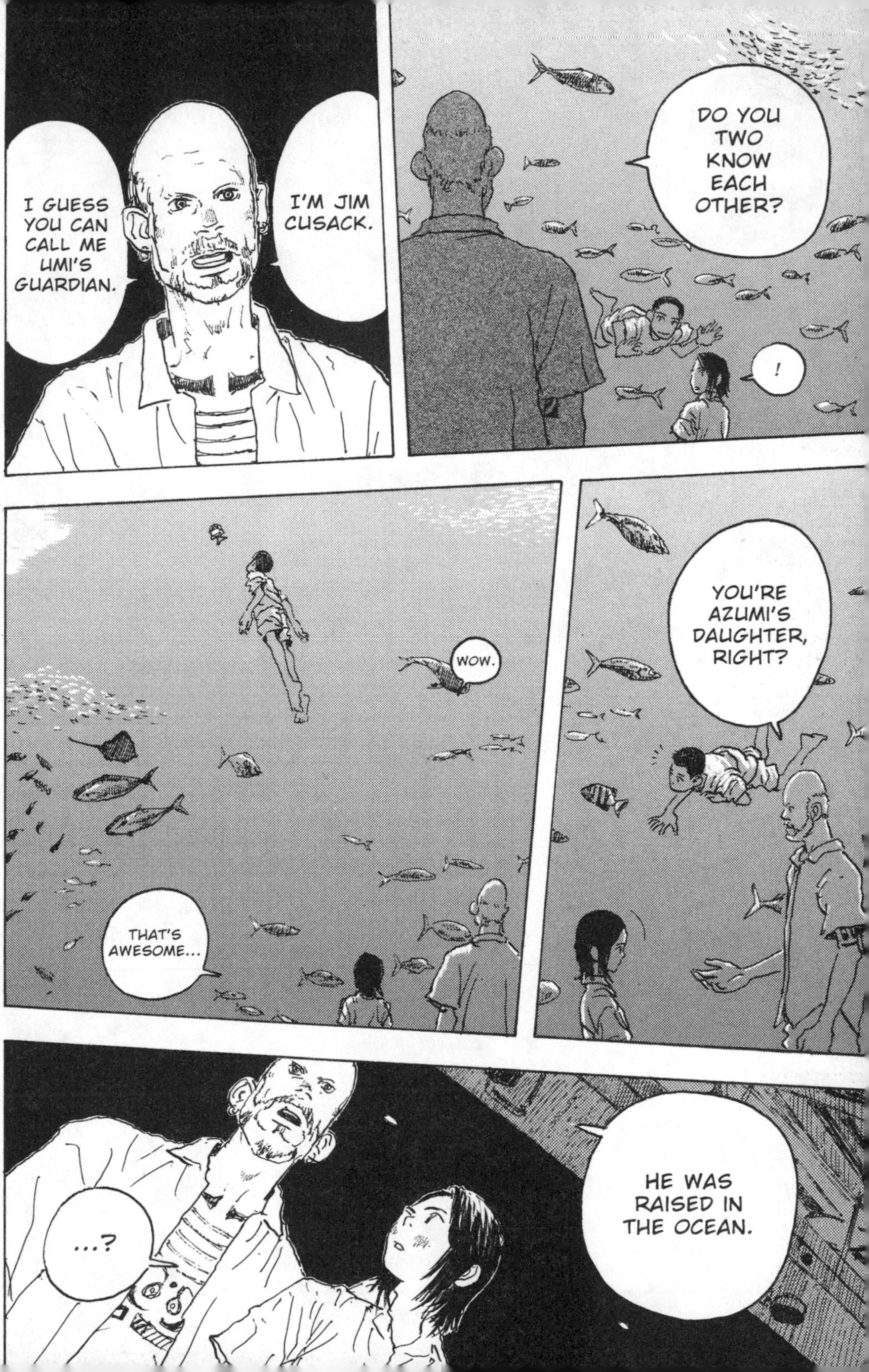
DO YOU TWO KNOW EACH OTHER?
!
I'M JIM CUSACK.
I GUESS YOU CAN CALL ME UMI'S GUARDIAN.
YOU'RE AZUMI'S DAUGHTER, RIGHT?
WOW.
THAT'S AWESOME...
HE WAS RAISED IN THE OCEAN.
...?

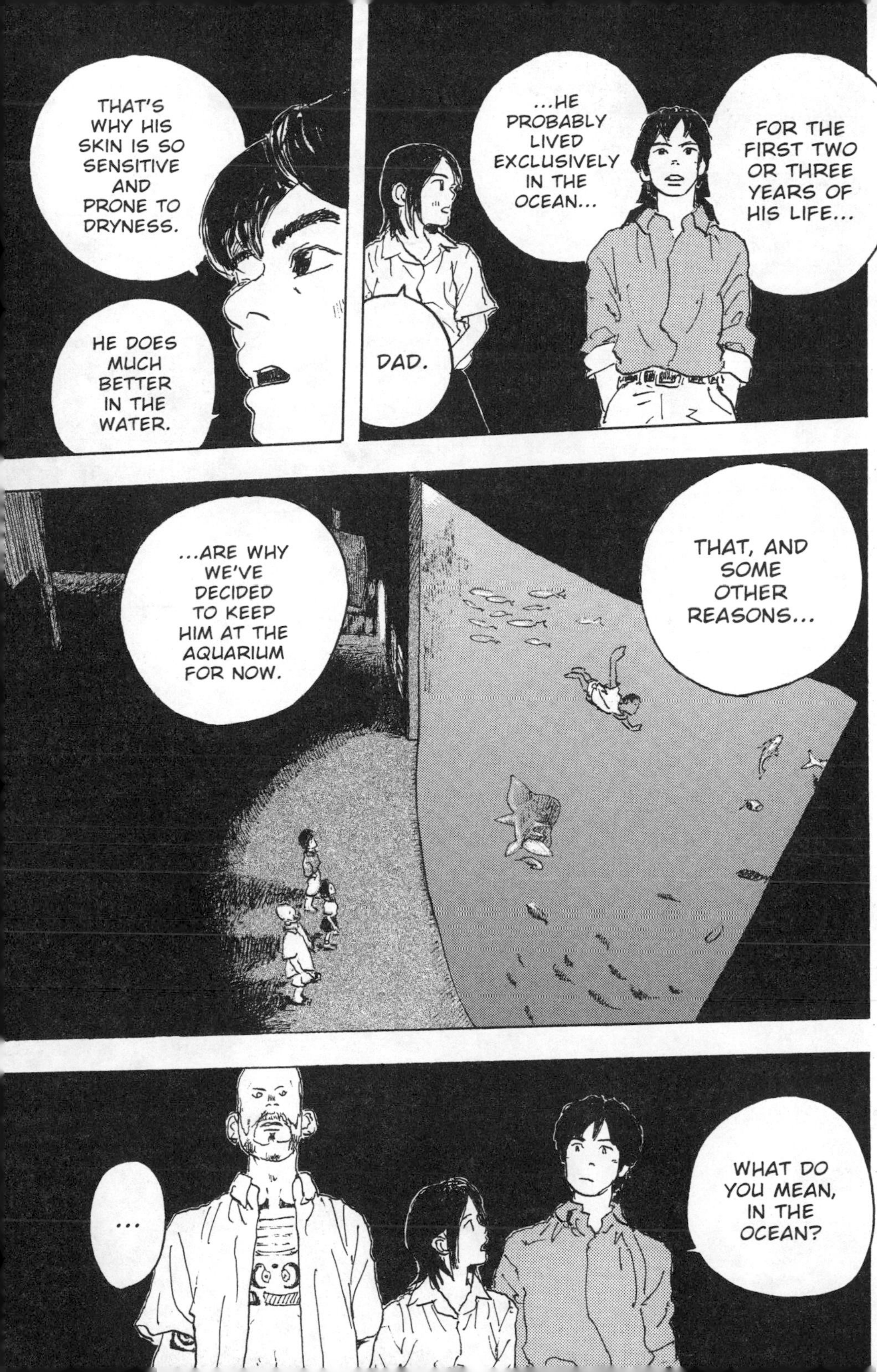
FOR THE FIRST TWO OR THREE YEARS OF HIS LIFE...
...HE PROBABLY LIVED EXCLUSIVELY IN THE OCEAN...
DAD.
THAT'S WHY HIS SKIN IS SO SENSITIVE AND PRONE TO DRYNESS.
HE DOES MUCH BETTER IN THE WATER.
THAT, AND SOME OTHER REASONS...
...ARE WHY WE'VE DECIDED TO KEEP HIM AT THE AQUARIUM FOR NOW.
WHAT DO YOU MEAN, IN THE OCEAN?
...

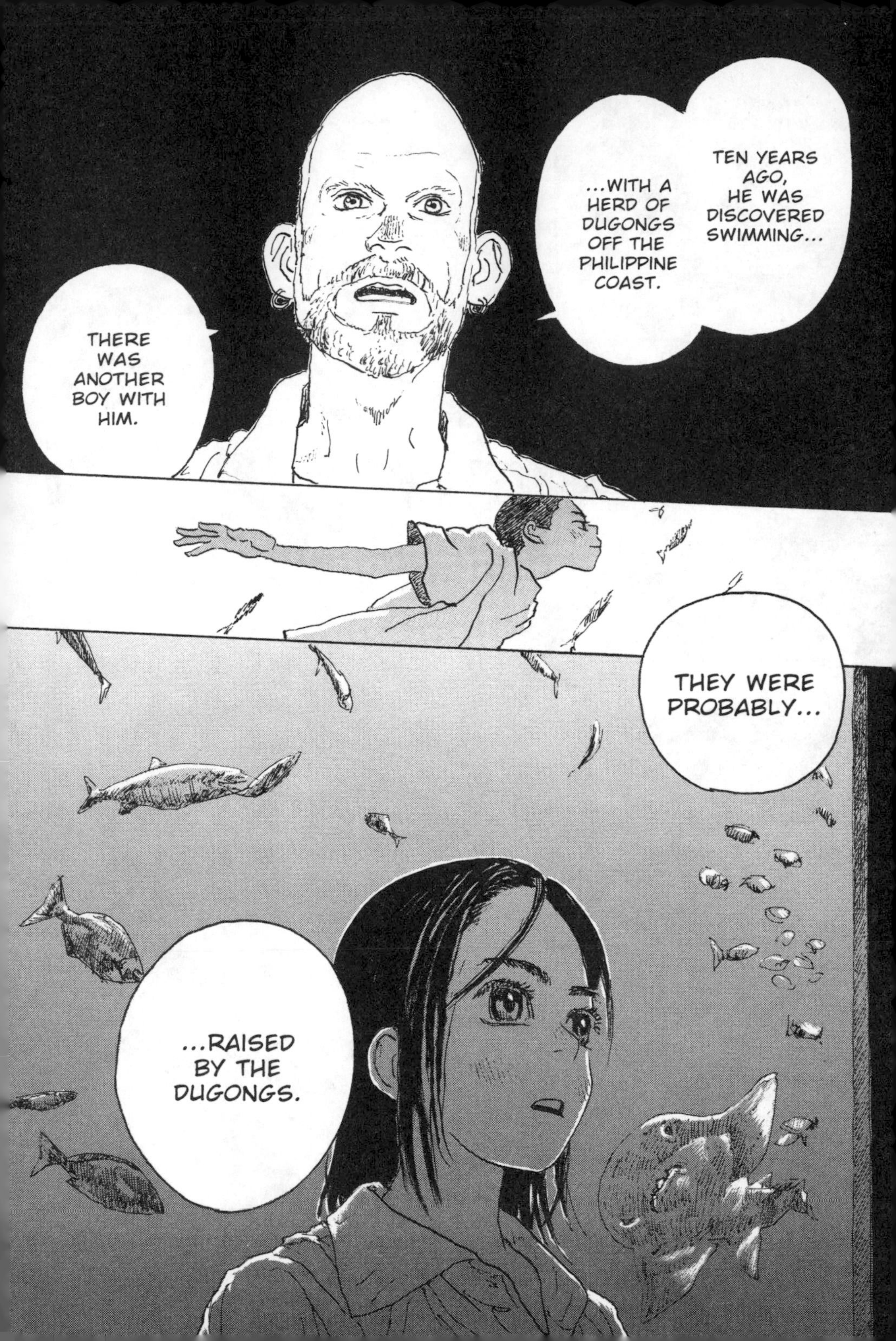
TEN YEARS AGO, HE WAS DISCOVERED SWIMMING...
...WITH A HERD OF DUGONGS OFF THE PHILIPPINE COAST.
THERE WAS ANOTHER BOY WITH HIM.
THEY WERE PROBABLY...
...RAISED BY THE DUGONGS.

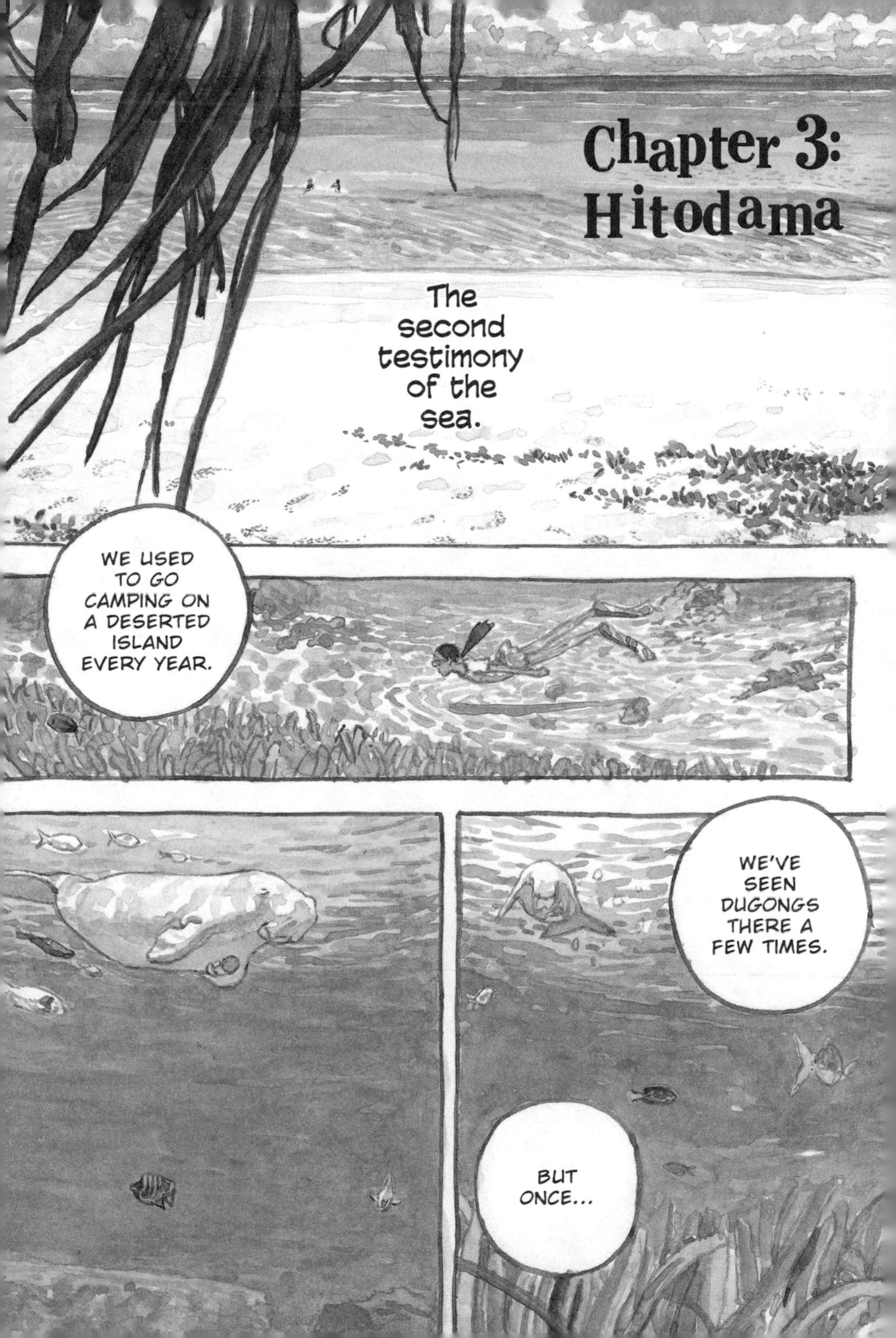
Chapter 3: Hitodama
The second testimony of the sea.
WE USED TO GO CAMPING ON A DESERTED ISLAND EVERY YEAR.
WE'VE SEEN DUGONGS THERE A FEW TIMES.
BUT ONCE...

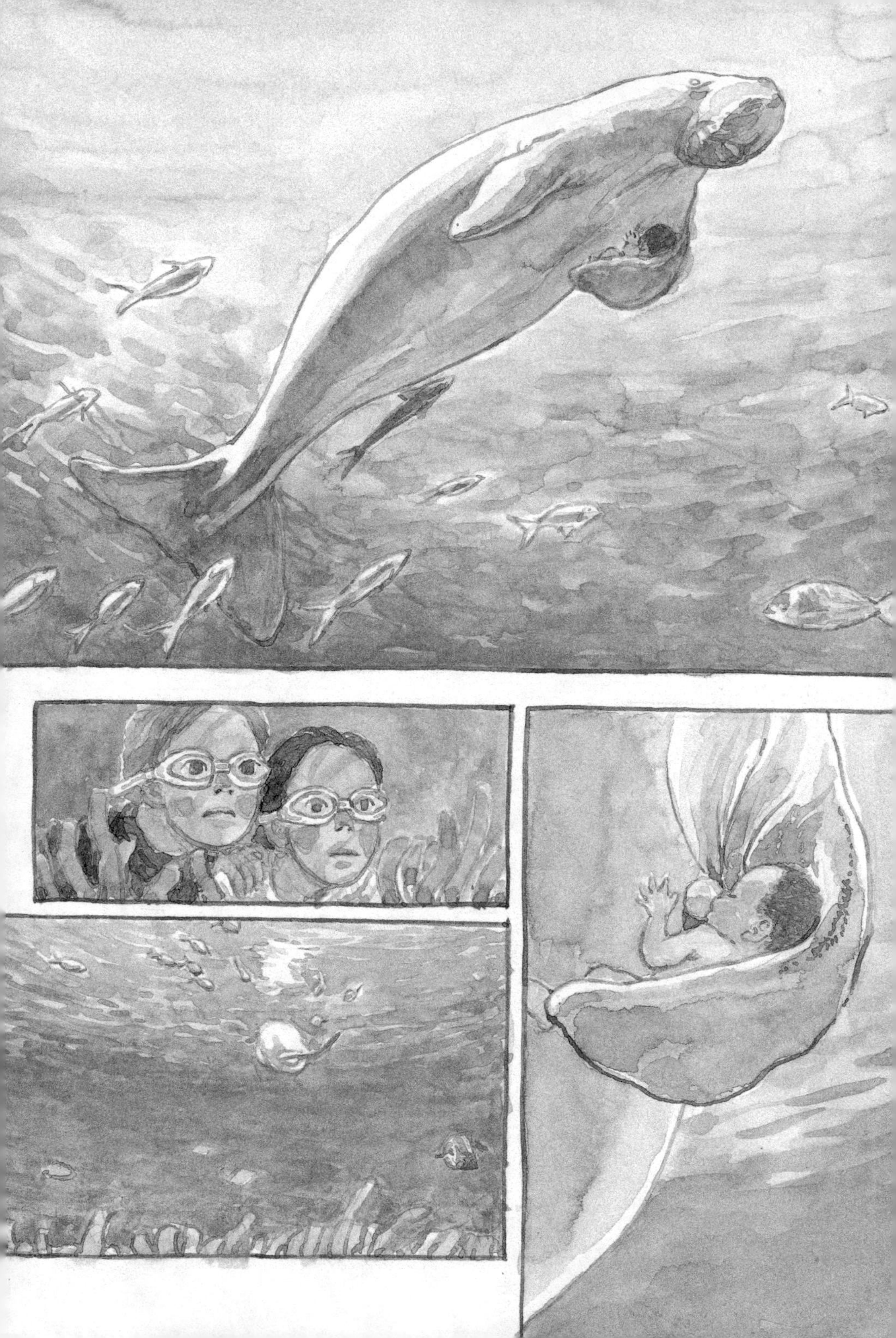

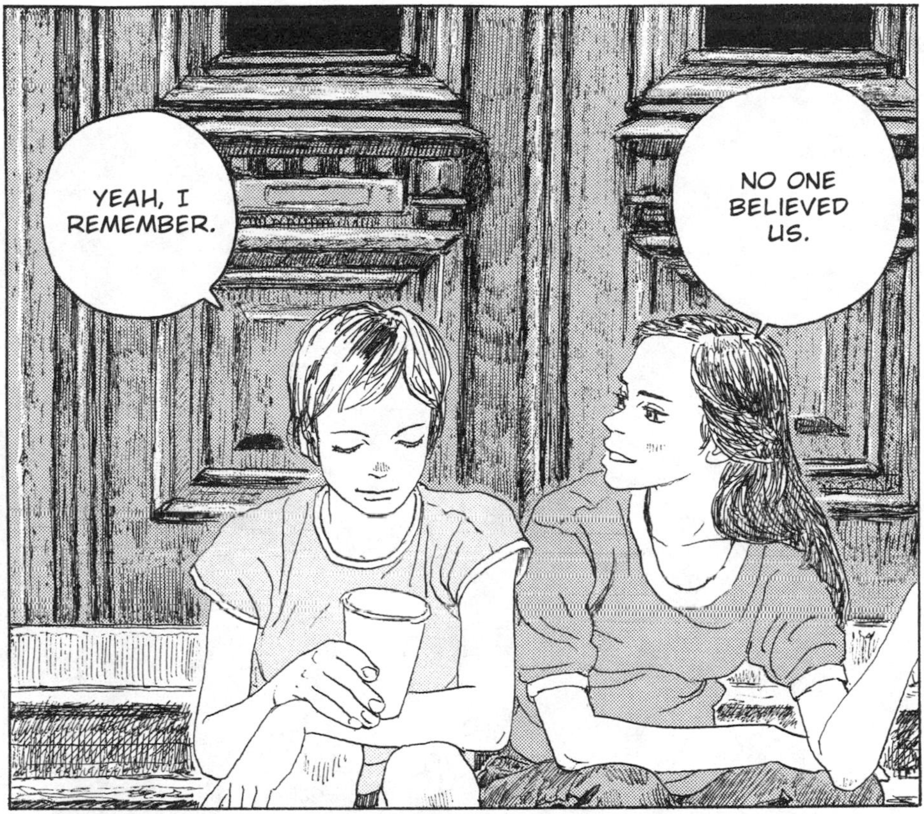
NO ONE BELIEVED US.
YEAH, I REMEMBER.

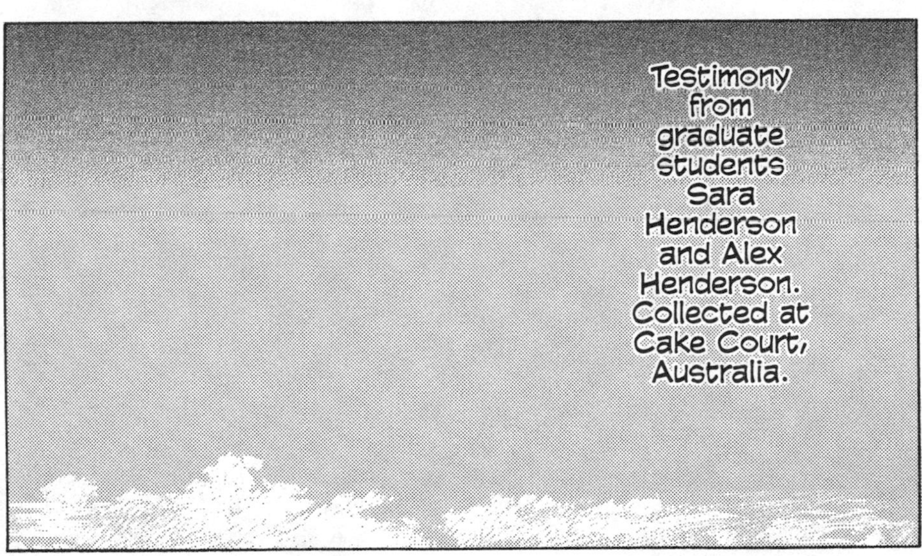
Testimony from graduate students Sara Henderson and Alex Henderson. Collected at Cake Court, Australia.

Chapter 3: Hitodama

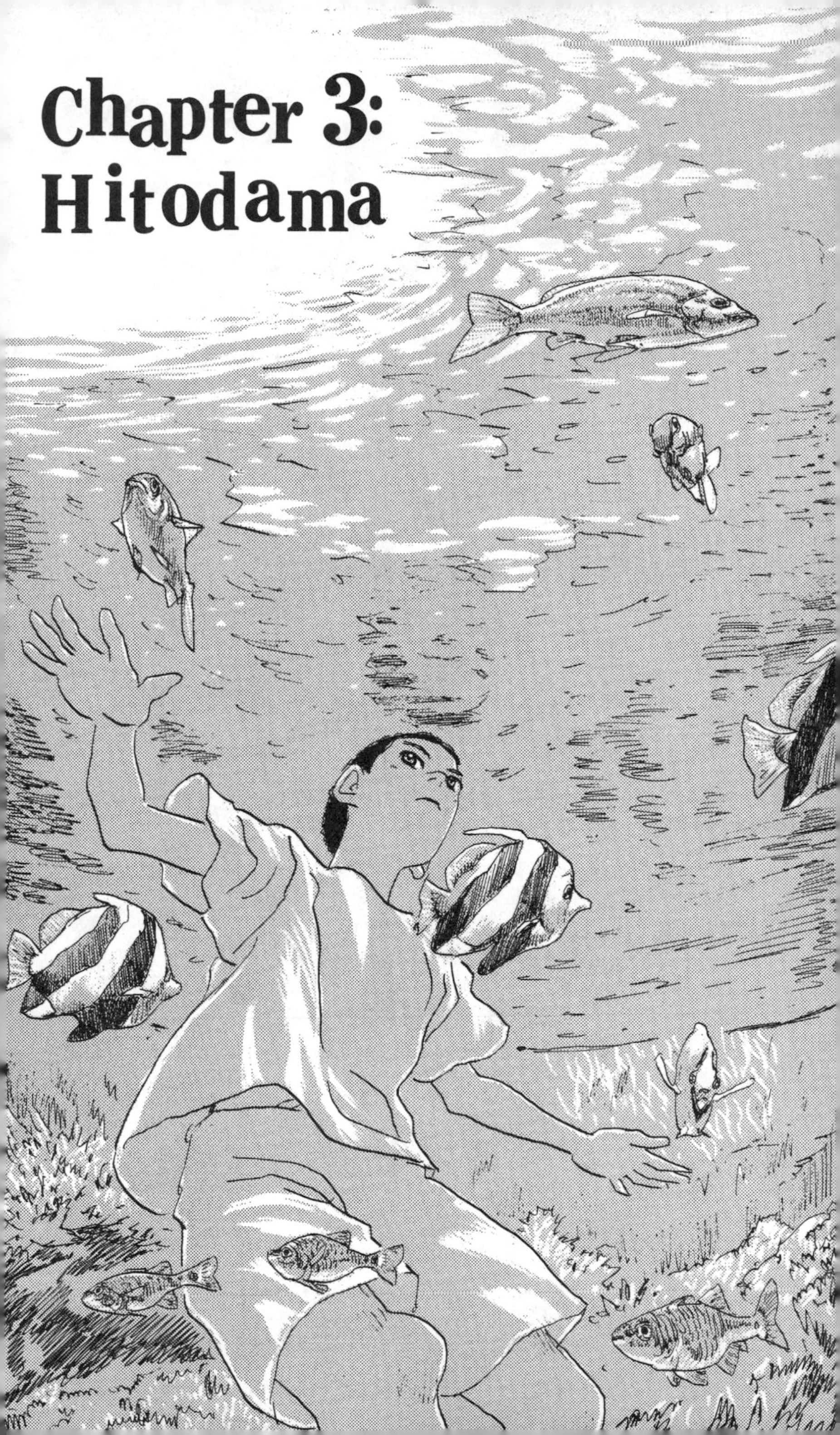

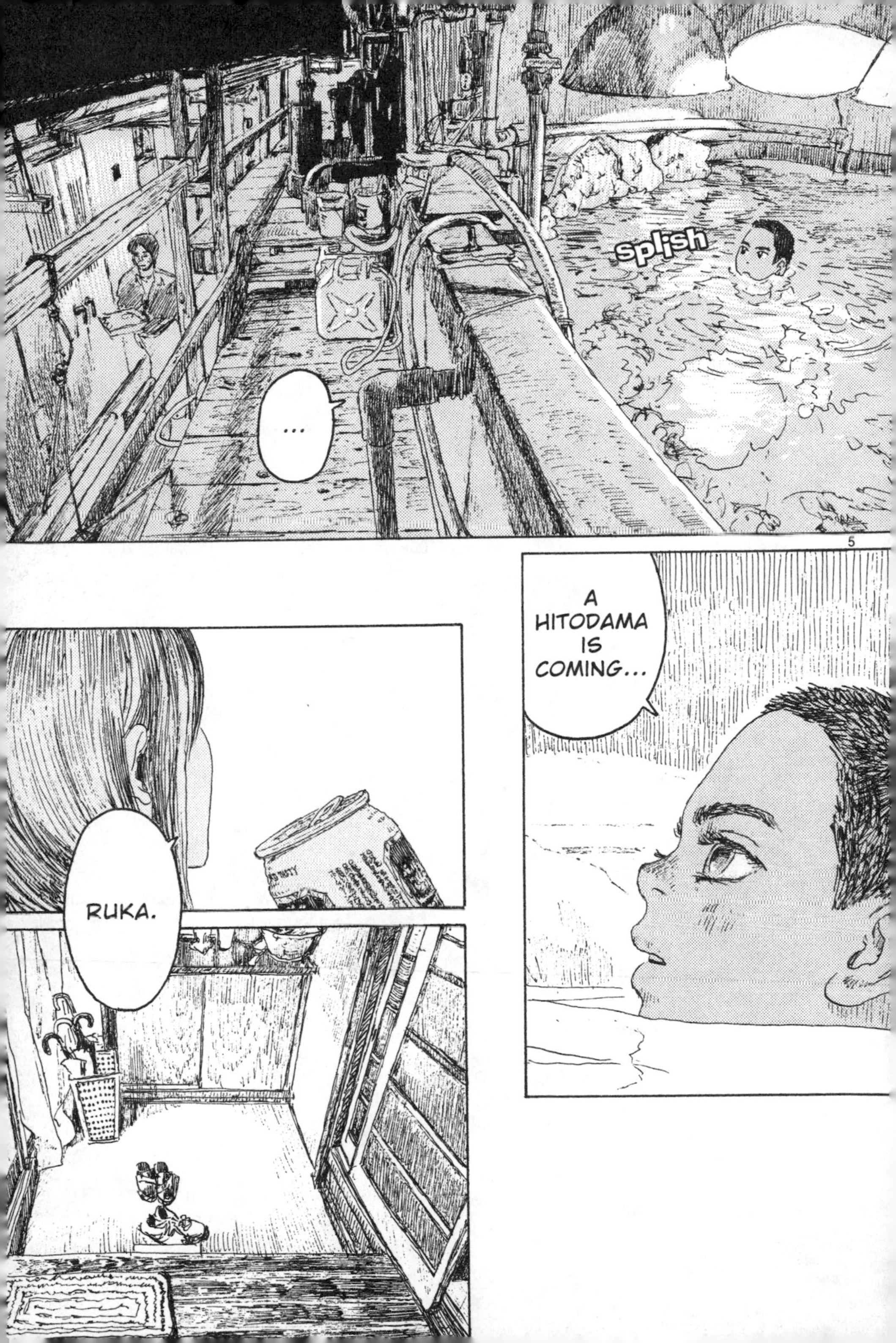
splish
...
A HITODAMA IS COMING...
RUKA.

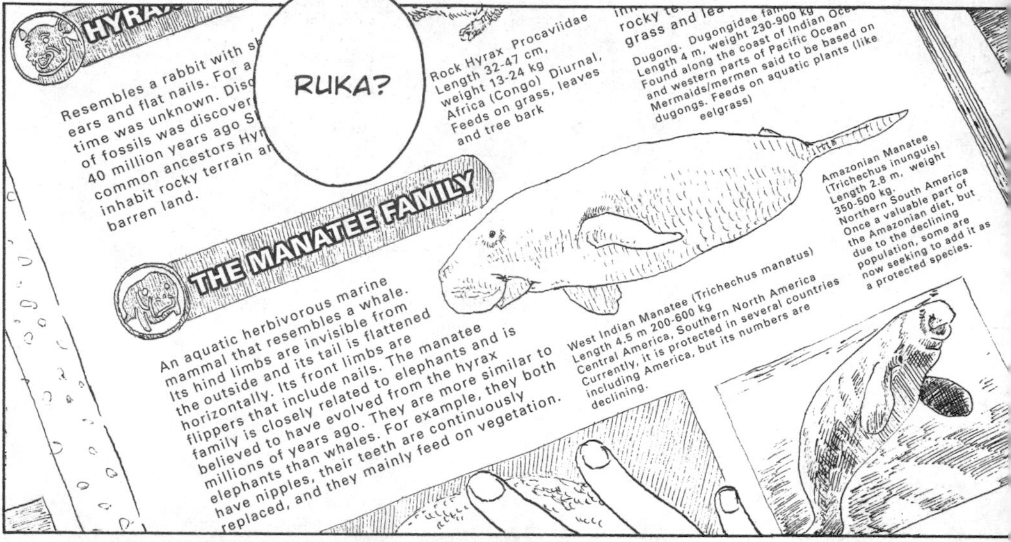
RUKA?
Dugong. Dugongidae family. Length 4 m, weight 230-900 kg
Found along the coast of Indian Oce
and western parts of Pacific Ocean
Mermaids/mermen said to be based on dugongs. Feeds on aquatic plants (like eelgrass)
Rock Hyrax Procaviidae
Length 32-47 cm, weight 13-24 kg
Africa (Congo) Diurnal,
Feeds on grass, leaves and tree bark
Resembles a rabbit with s
ears and flat nails. For a
time was unknown. Disc
of fossils was discover
40 million years ago S
common ancestors Hy
inhabit rocky terrain a
barren land.
THE MANATEE FAMILY
Amazonian Manatee (Trichechus inunguis) Length 2.8 m, weight 350-500 kg. Northern South America
Once a valuable part of the Amazonian diet, but due to the declining population, some are now seeking to add it as a protected species.
West Indian Manatee (Trichechus manatus) Length 4.5 m 200-600 kg
Central America, Southern North America
Currently, it is protected in several countries including America, but its numbers are declining.
An aquatic herbivorous marine mammal that resembles a whale. Its hind limbs are invisible from the outside and its tail is flattened horizontally. Its front limbs are flippers that include nails. The manatee family is closely related to elephants and is believed to have evolved from the hyrax millions of years ago. They are more similar to elephants than whales. For example, they both have nipples, their teeth are continuously replaced, and they mainly feed on vegetation.

From New Wide Gakken Zukan, Doubutsu (New Wide Pictorial Encyclopedia – Animals). Published by Gakushu Kenkyusha Kan

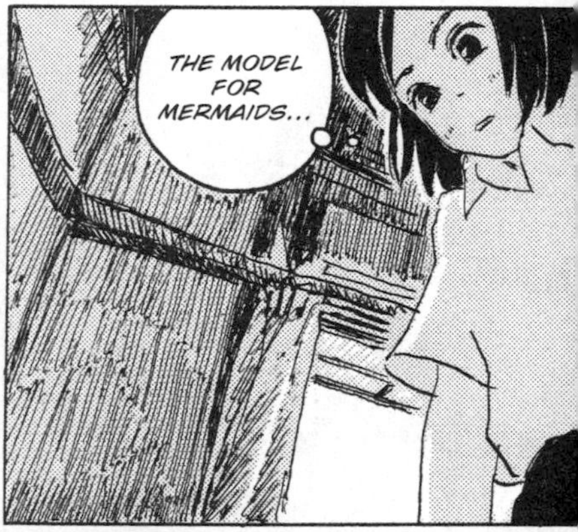
THE MODEL FOR MERMAIDS...

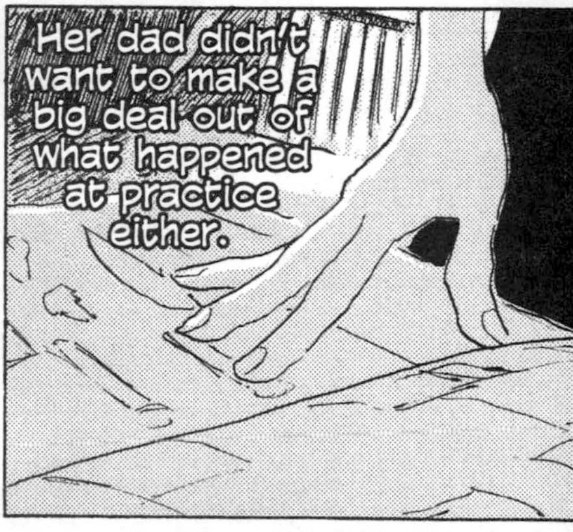
Her dad didn't want to make a big deal out of what happened at practice either.

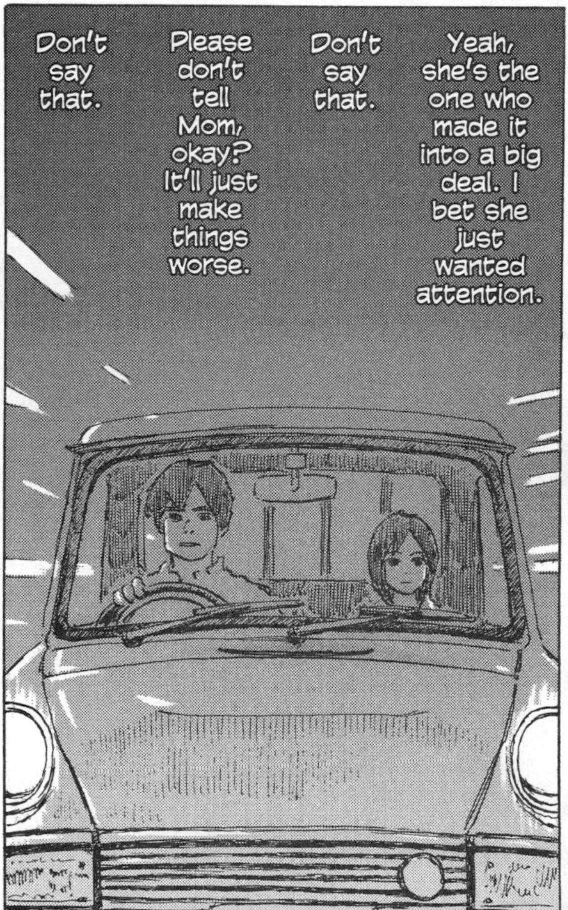
Yeah, she's the one who made it into a big deal. I bet she just wanted attention.
Don't say that.
Please don't tell Mom, okay? It'll just make things worse.
Don't say that.

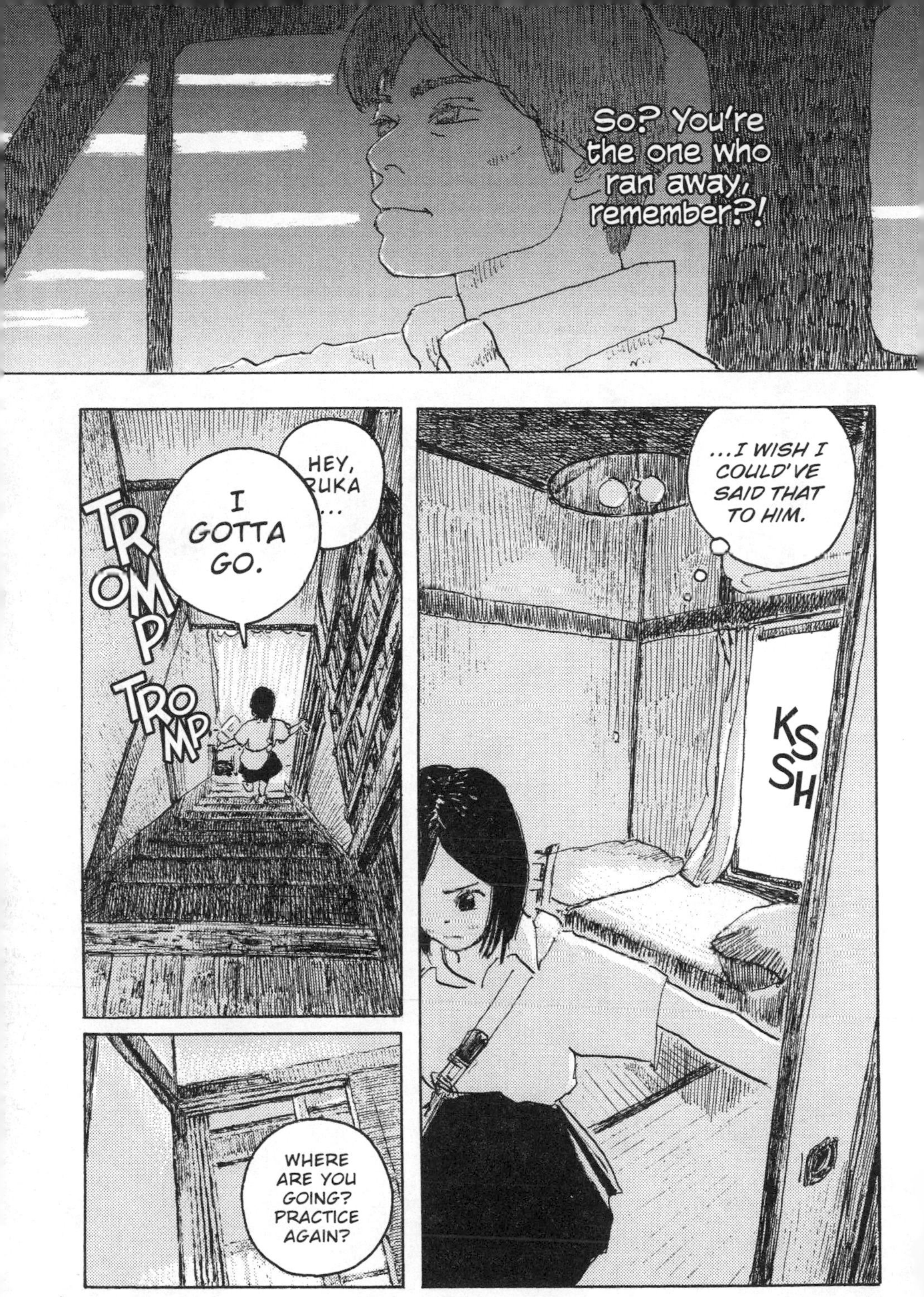
So? You're the one who ran away, remember?!
...I WISH I COULD'VE SAID THAT TO HIM.
KSSH
HEY, RUKA...
I GOTTA GO.
TROMP
TROMP
WHERE ARE YOU GOING? PRACTICE AGAIN?

Icchu...

OH! ICCHU!
GO! GO!

TMP TMP TMP TMP

...

Go, oh,
go, oh,
go, oh,
go, oh...

OH, IT'S
OPEN...

KSSH

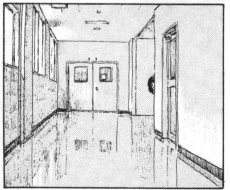

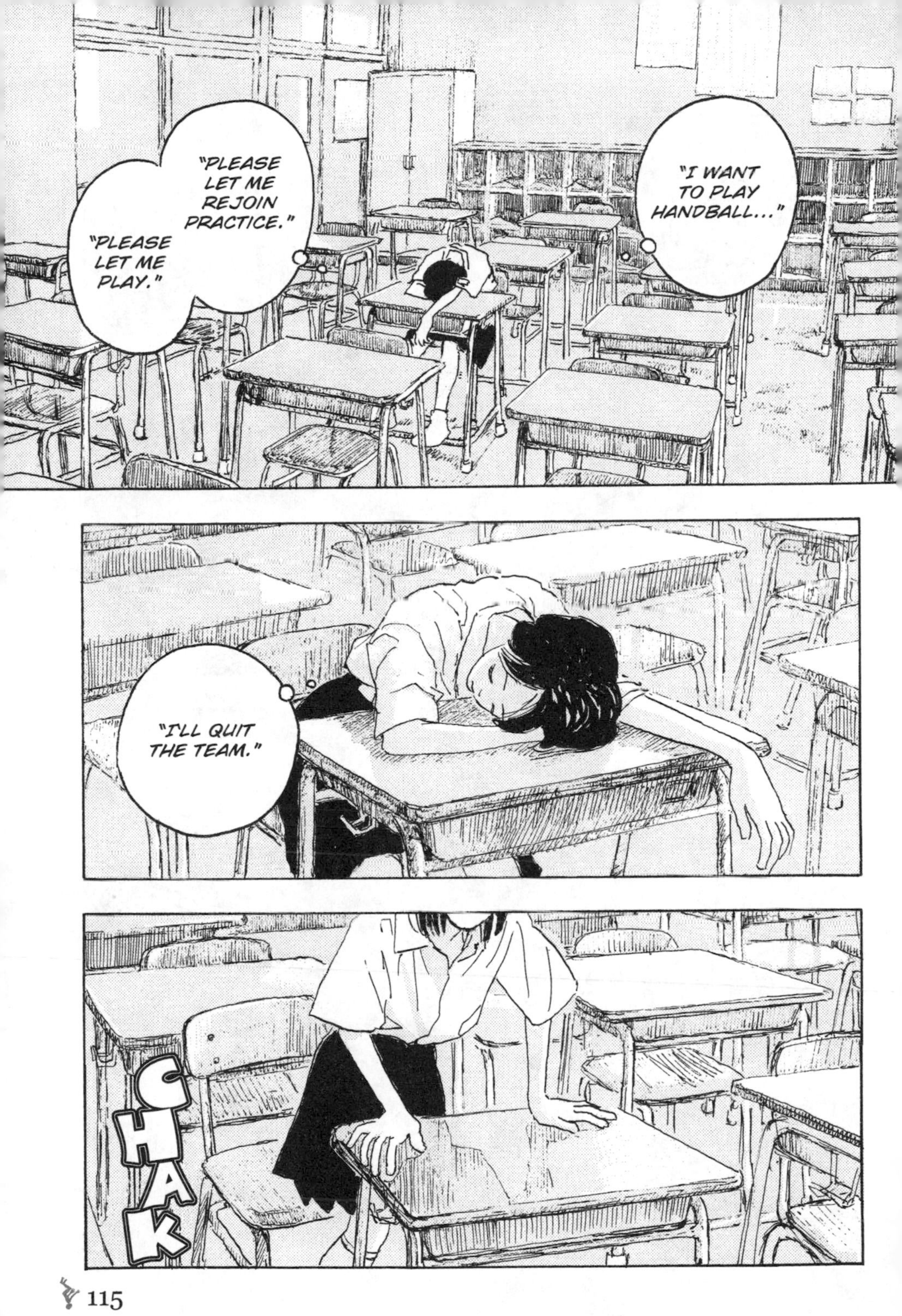
"I WANT TO PLAY HANDBALL..."
"PLEASE LET ME REJOIN PRACTICE."
"PLEASE LET ME PLAY."
"I'LL QUIT THE TEAM."
CHAK

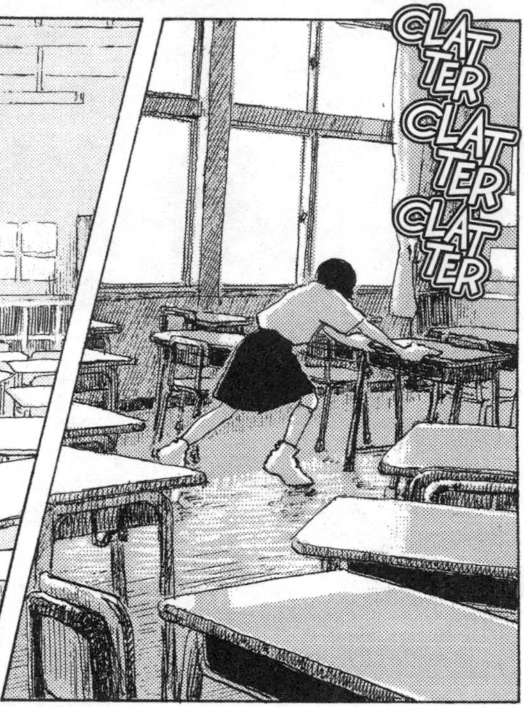
CLAT
TER
CLAT
TER
CLAT
TER
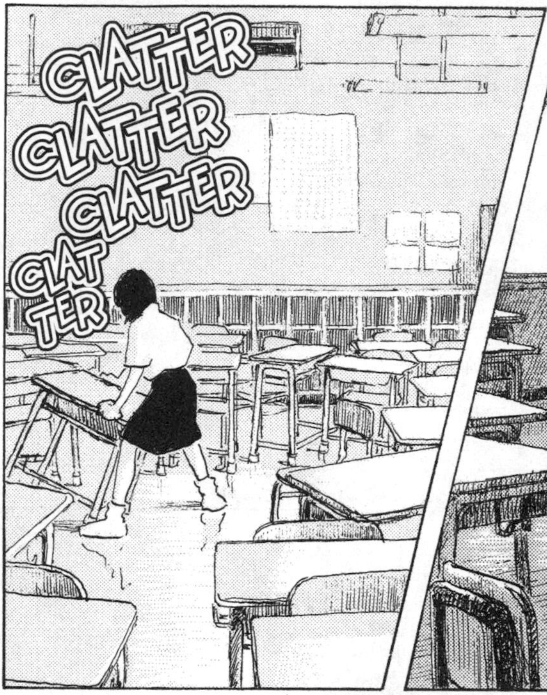
CLATTER
CLATTER
CLATTER
CLAT
TER
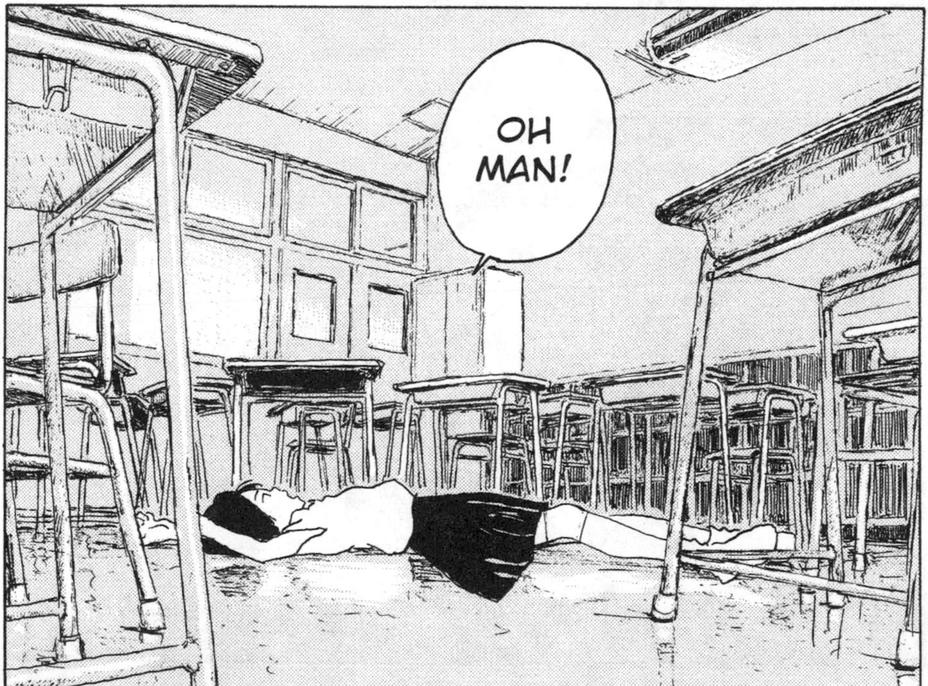
OH MAN!

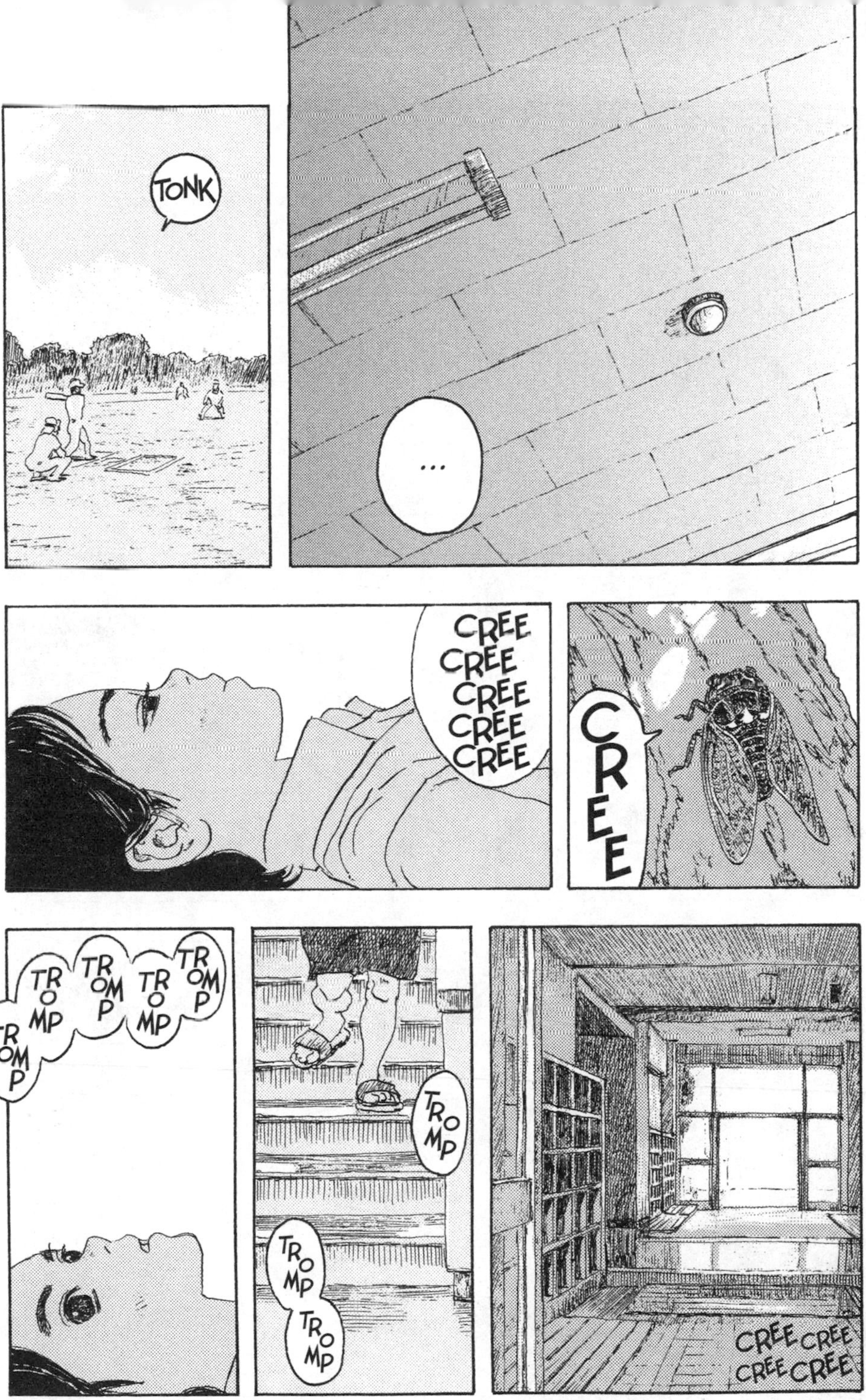
...
TONK
CREE
CREE CREE CREE CREE CREE
CREE CREE CREE CREE
TROMP
TROMP
TROMP
TROMP
TROMP
TROMP
TROMP
TROMP

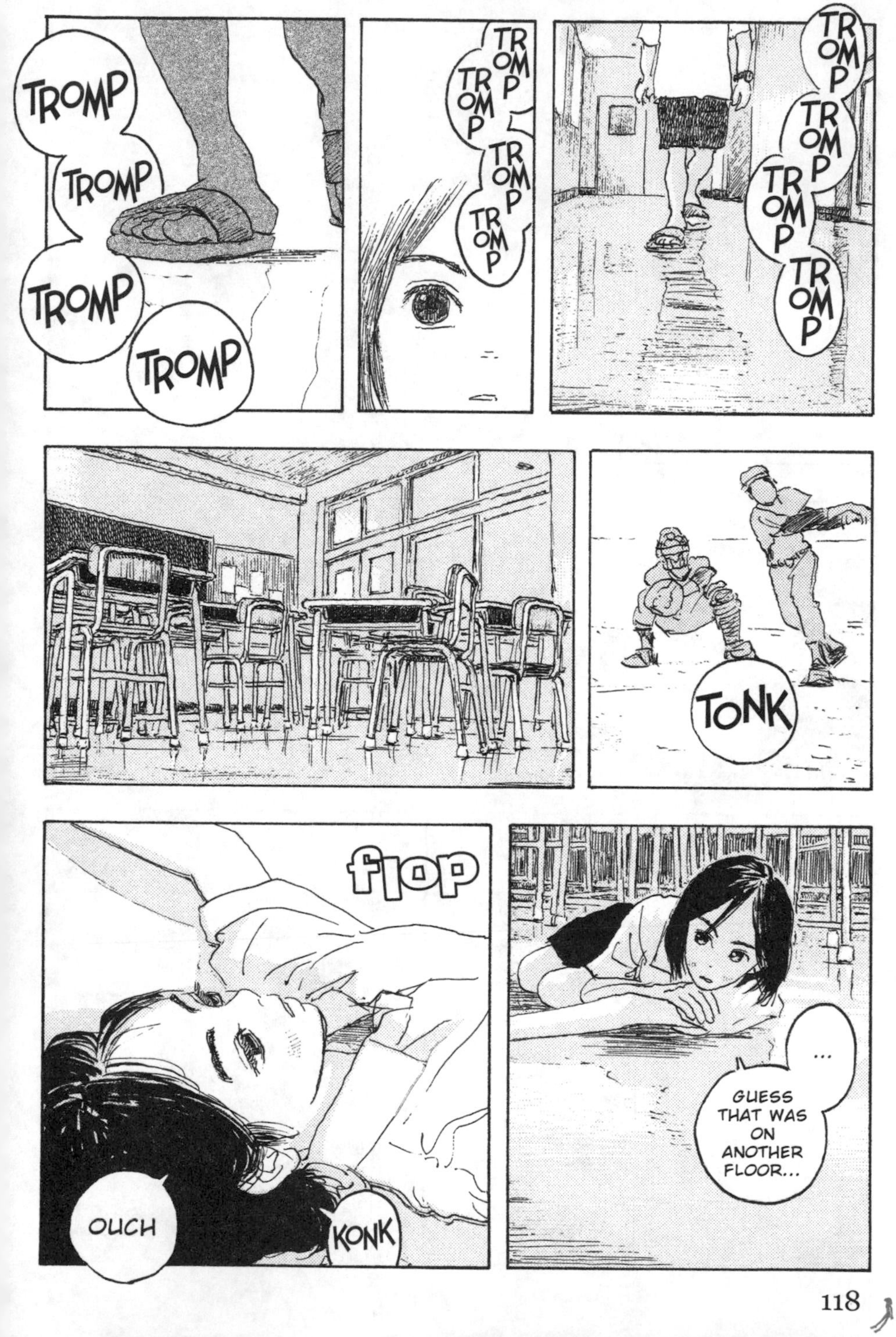
TROMP
TROMP
TROMP
TROMP
TROMP
TROMP
TROMP
TROMP
TROMP
TROMP
TROMP
TROMP
TONK
...
GUESS THAT WAS ON ANOTHER FLOOR...
flop
KONK
OUCH

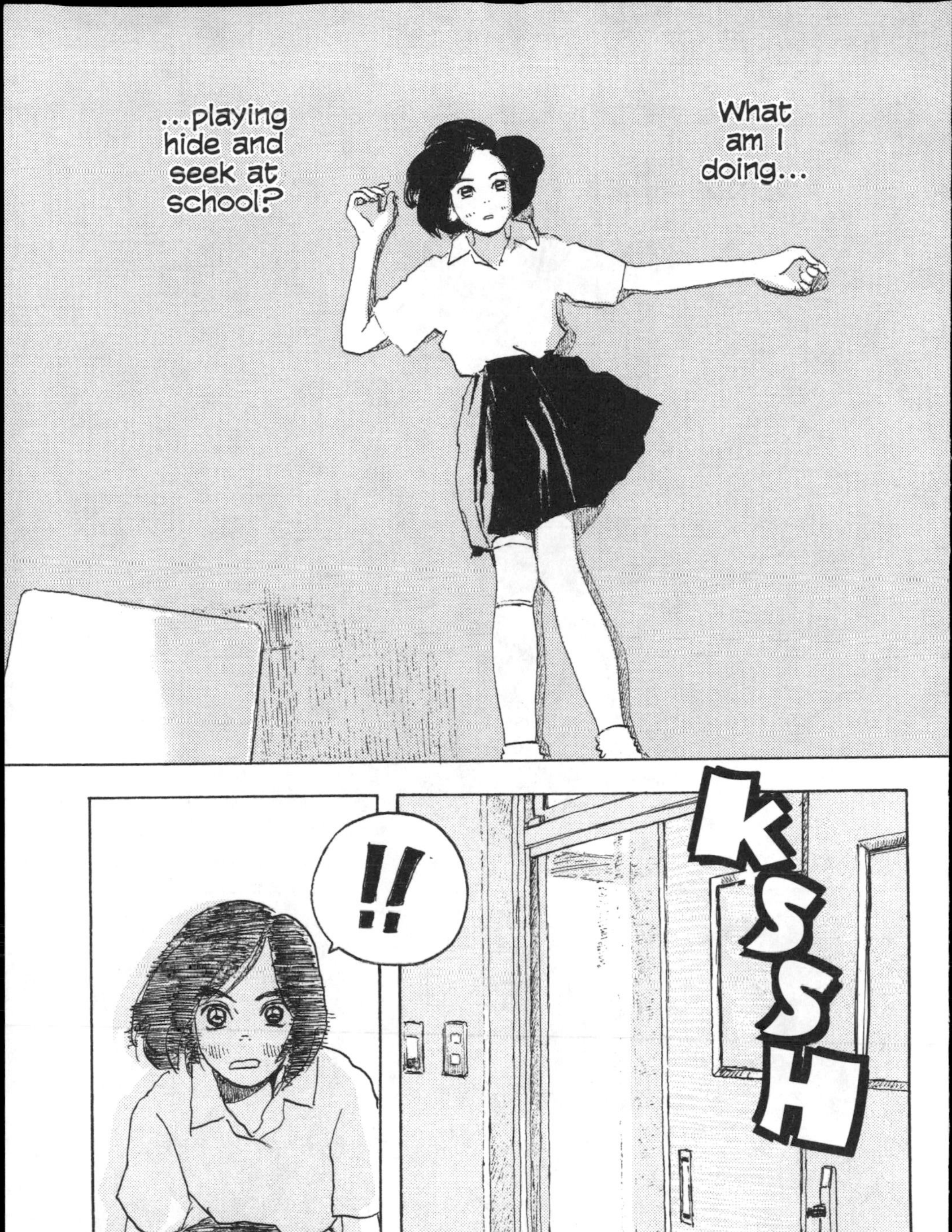
What am I doing...
...playing hide and seek at school?
KSSH
!!

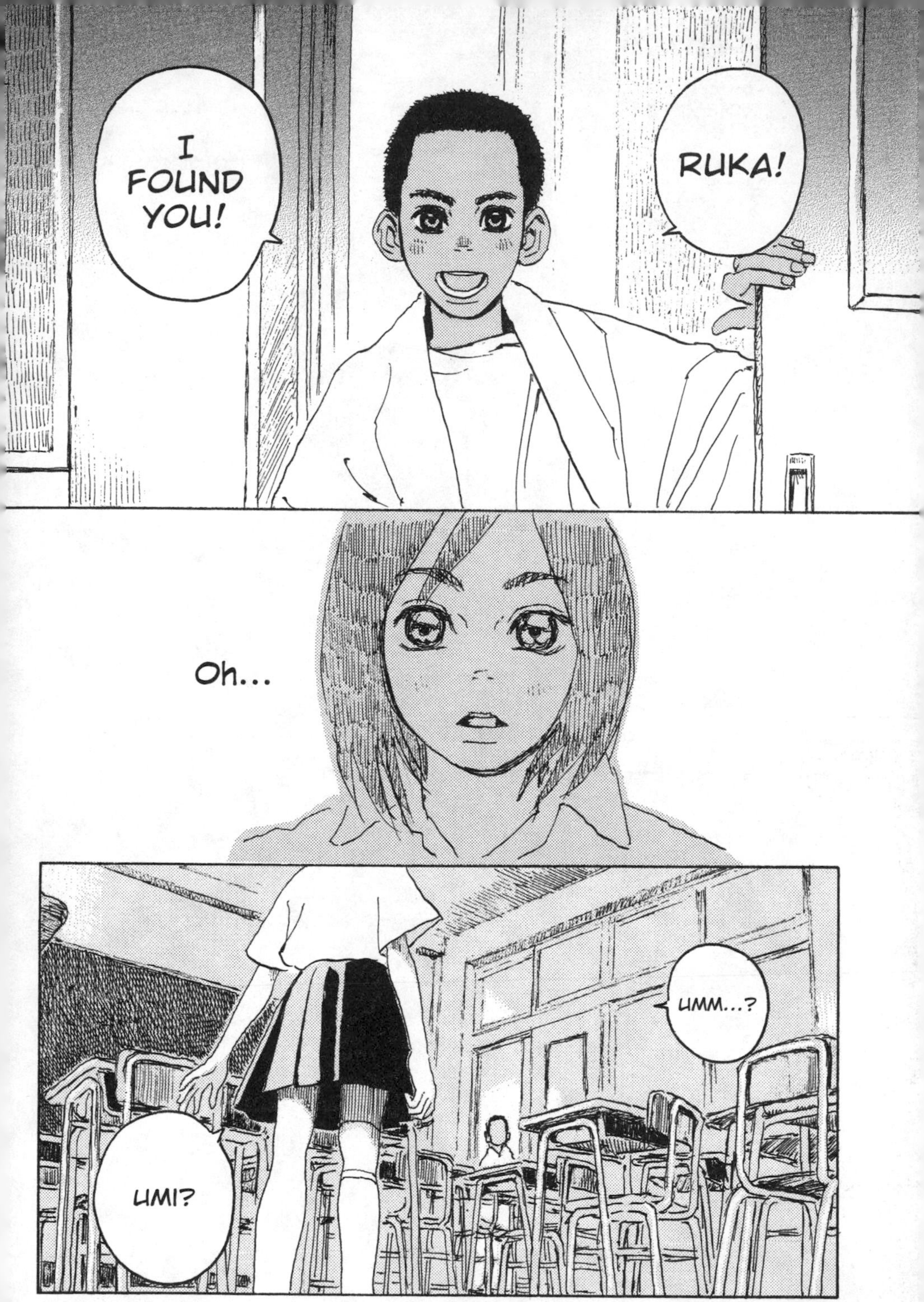
RUKA!
I FOUND YOU!
Oh...
UMM...?
UMI?

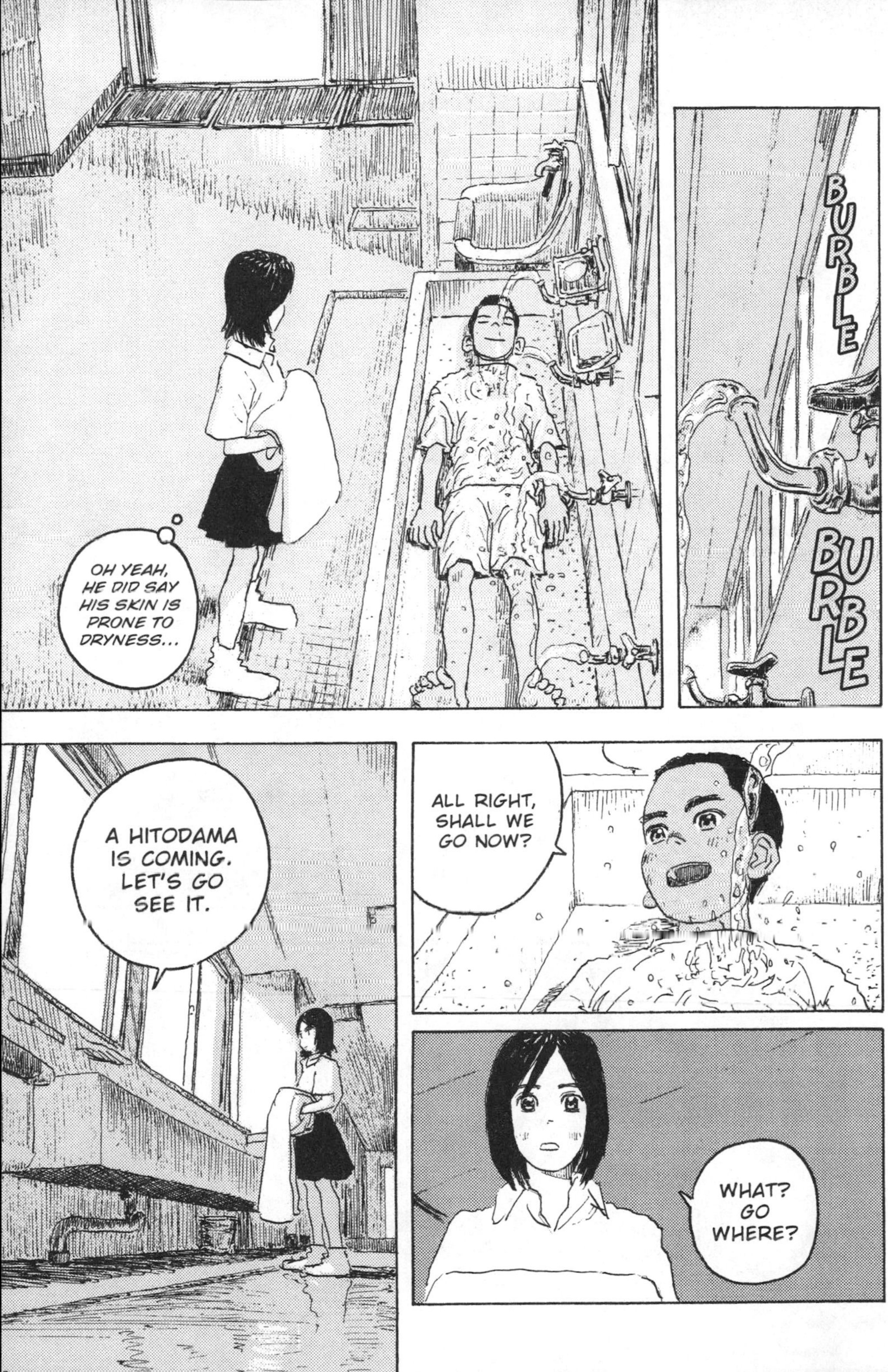
BURBLE
BURBLE
OH YEAH, HE DID SAY HIS SKIN IS PRONE TO DRYNESS...
ALL RIGHT, SHALL WE GO NOW?
WHAT? GO WHERE?
A HITODAMA IS COMING. LET'S GO SEE IT.

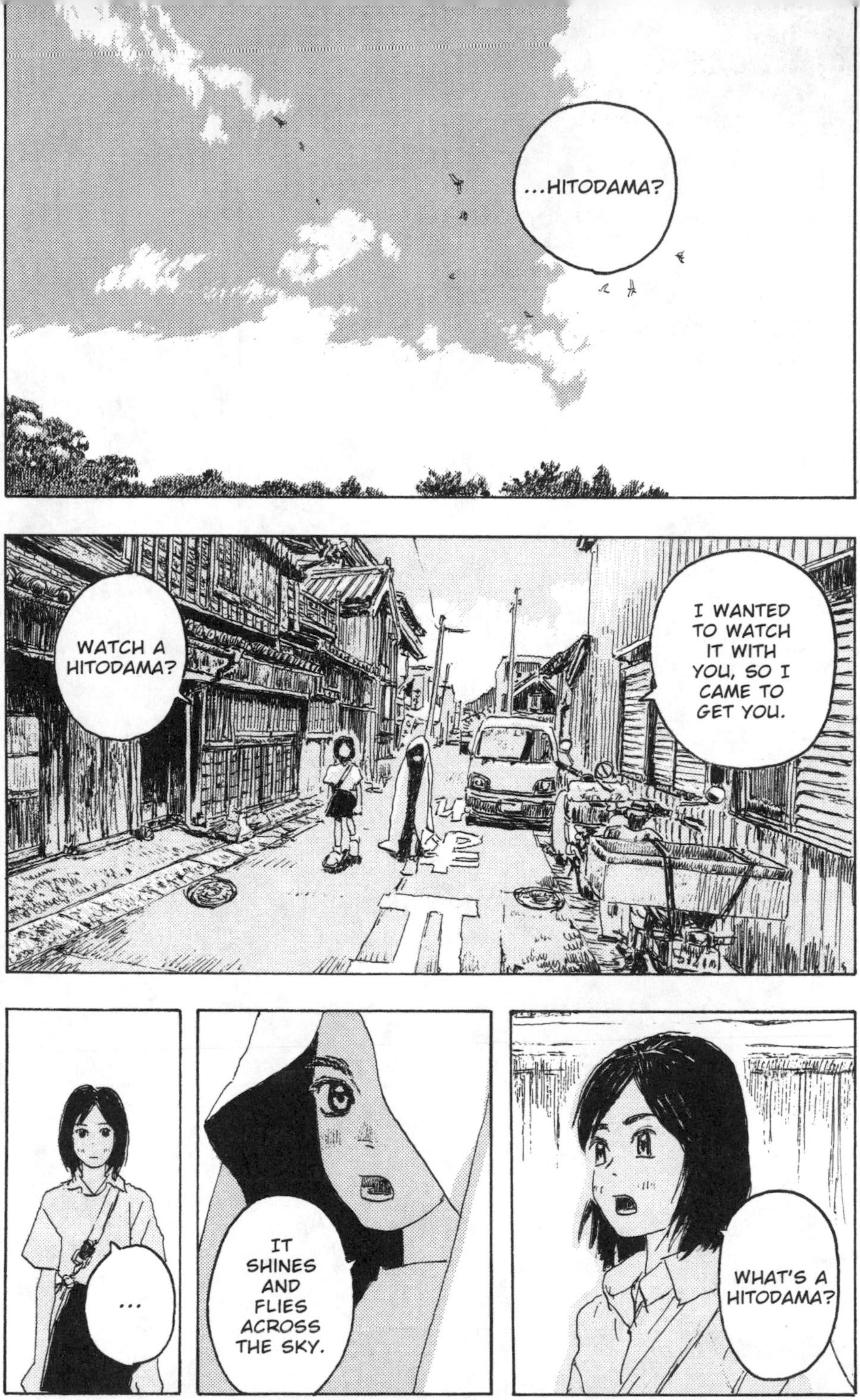
...HITODAMA?
I WANTED TO WATCH IT WITH YOU, SO I CAME TO GET YOU.
WATCH A HITODAMA?
WHAT'S A HITODAMA?
IT SHINES AND FLIES ACROSS THE SKY.
...

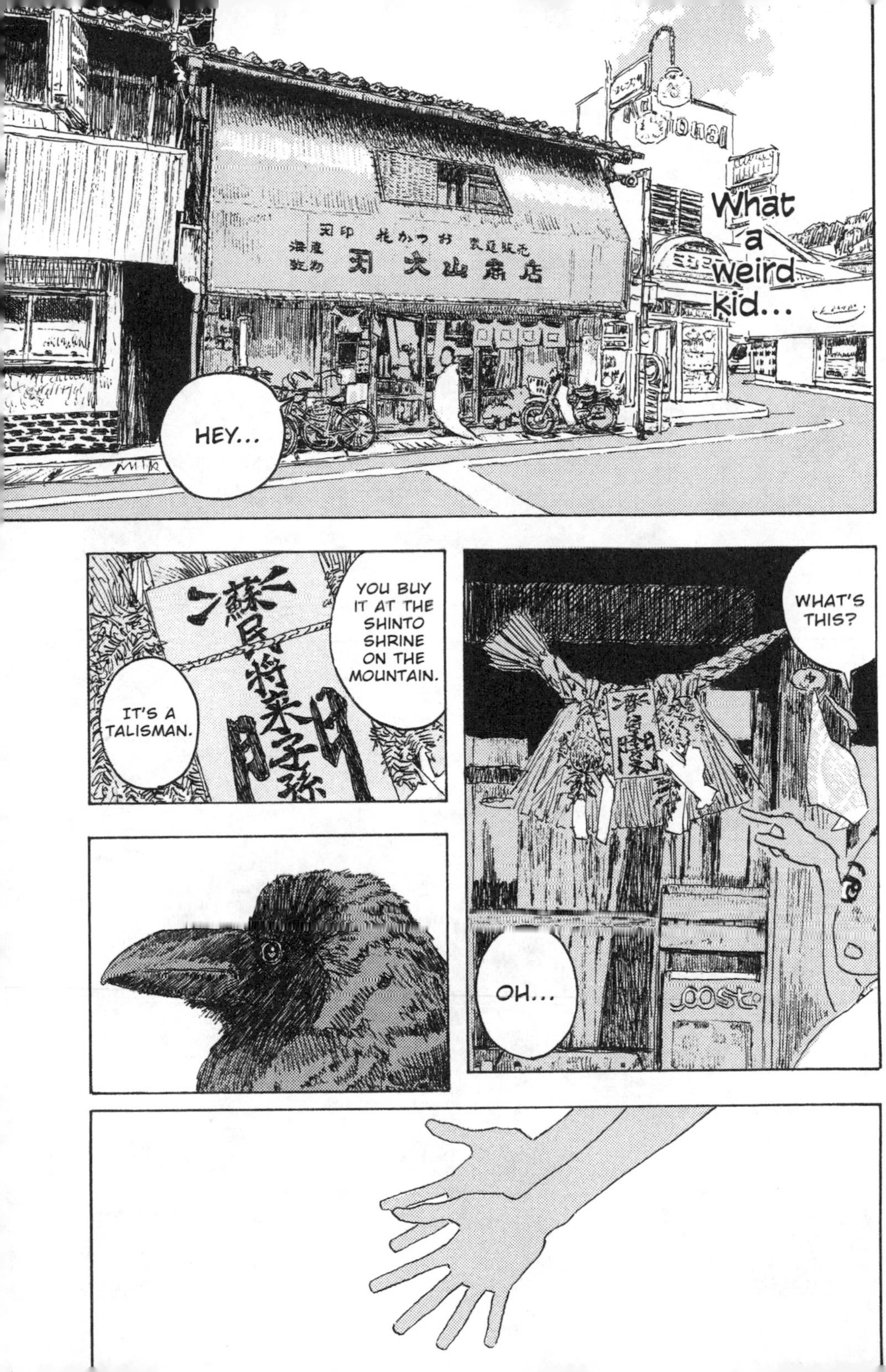
What a weird kid...
HEY...
WHAT'S THIS?
OH...
YOU BUY IT AT THE SHINTO SHRINE ON THE MOUNTAIN.
IT'S A TALISMAN.

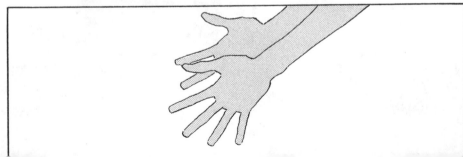

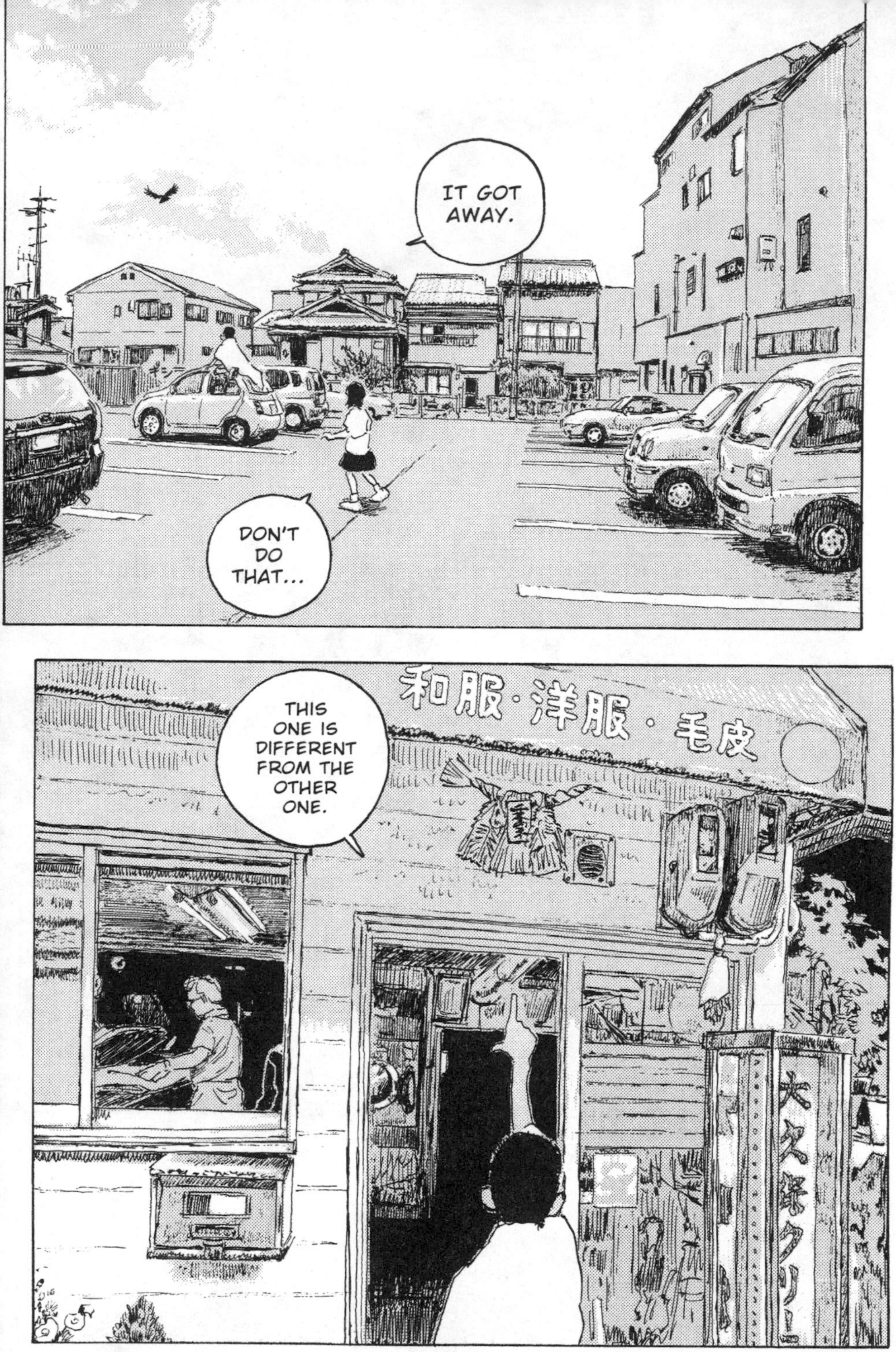
IT GOT AWAY.
DON'T DO THAT...
和服・洋服・毛皮
THIS ONE IS DIFFERENT FROM THE OTHER ONE.

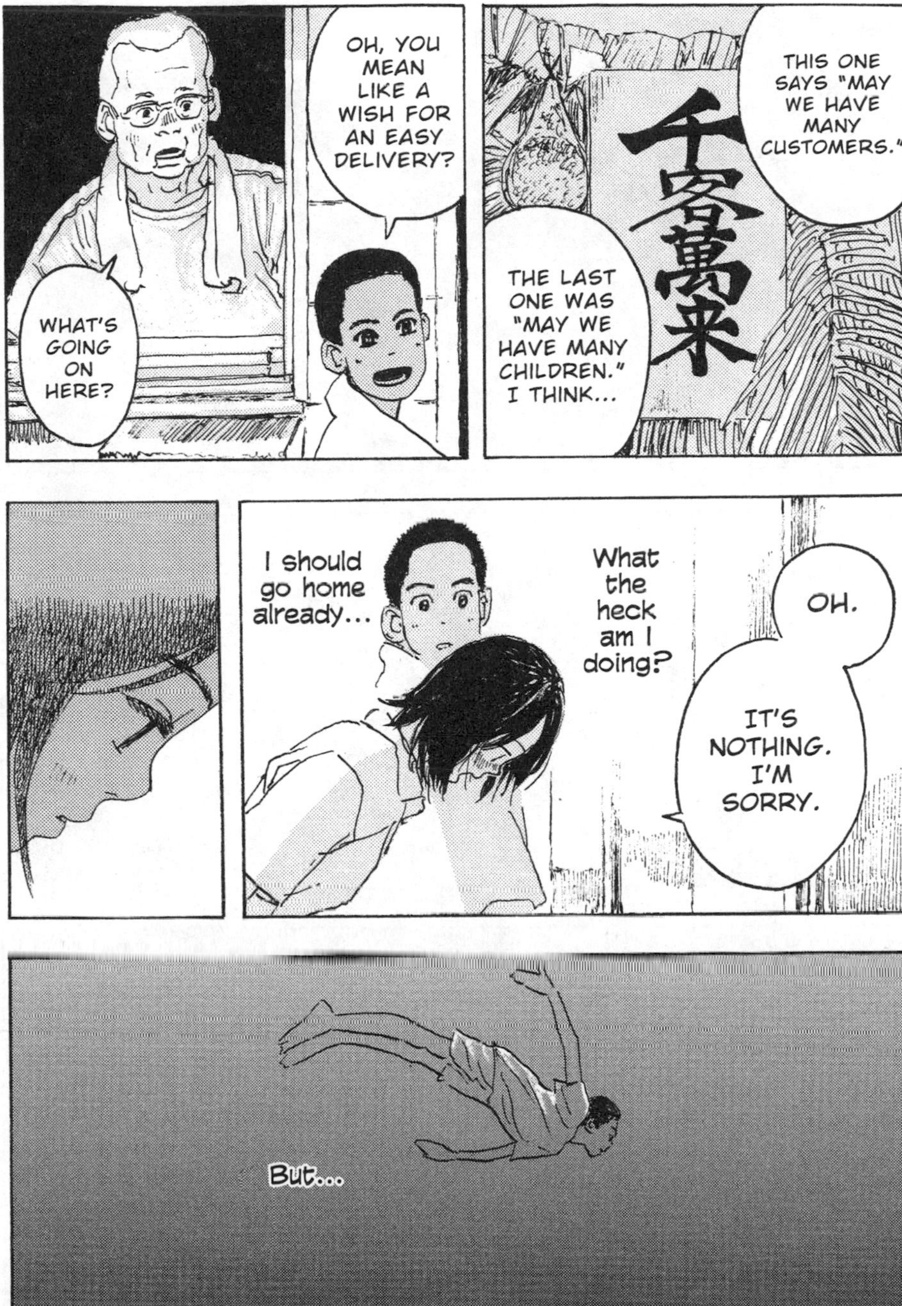
THIS ONE SAYS "MAY WE HAVE MANY CUSTOMERS."
千客萬来
THE LAST ONE WAS "MAY WE HAVE MANY CHILDREN." I THINK...
OH, YOU MEAN LIKE A WISH FOR AN EASY DELIVERY?
WHAT'S GOING ON HERE?
OH.
IT'S NOTHING. I'M SORRY.
What the heck am I doing?
I should go home already...
But...

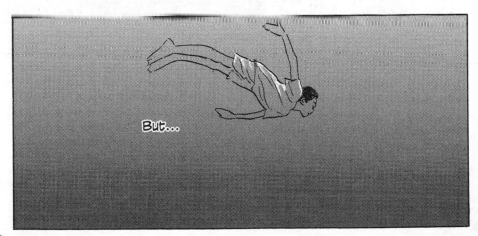

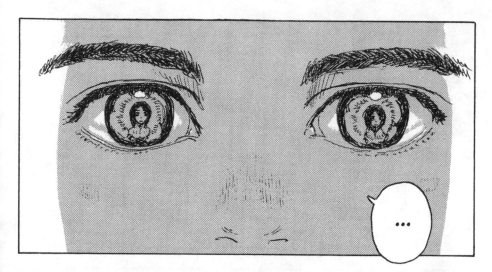

...

HMM?

UM, THAT...

YEOW!

RUKA.

SOFT SERVE

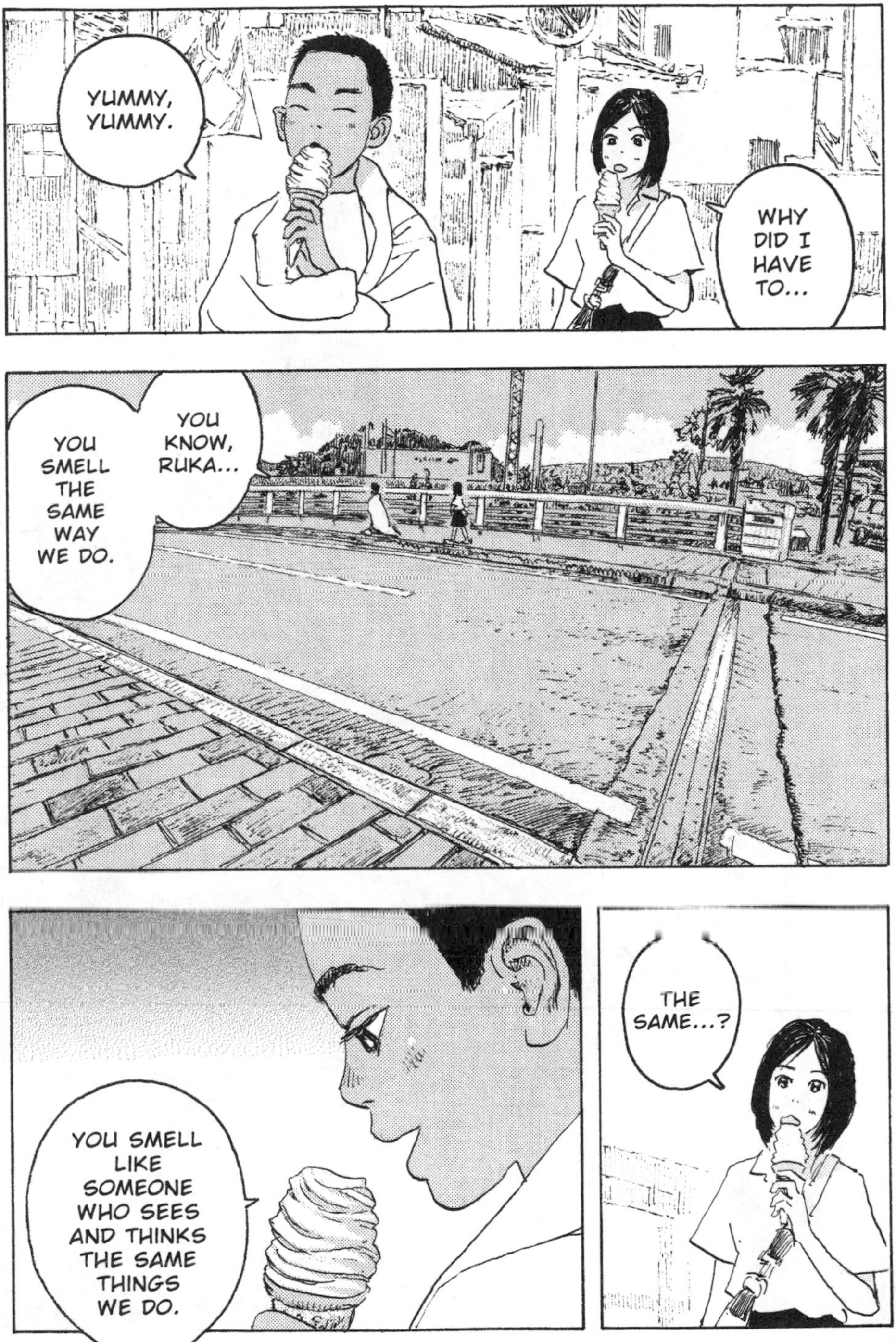
WHY DID I HAVE TO...
YUMMY, YUMMY.
YOU KNOW, RUKA...
YOU SMELL THE SAME WAY WE DO.
THE SAME...?
YOU SMELL LIKE SOMEONE WHO SEES AND THINKS THE SAME THINGS WE DO.

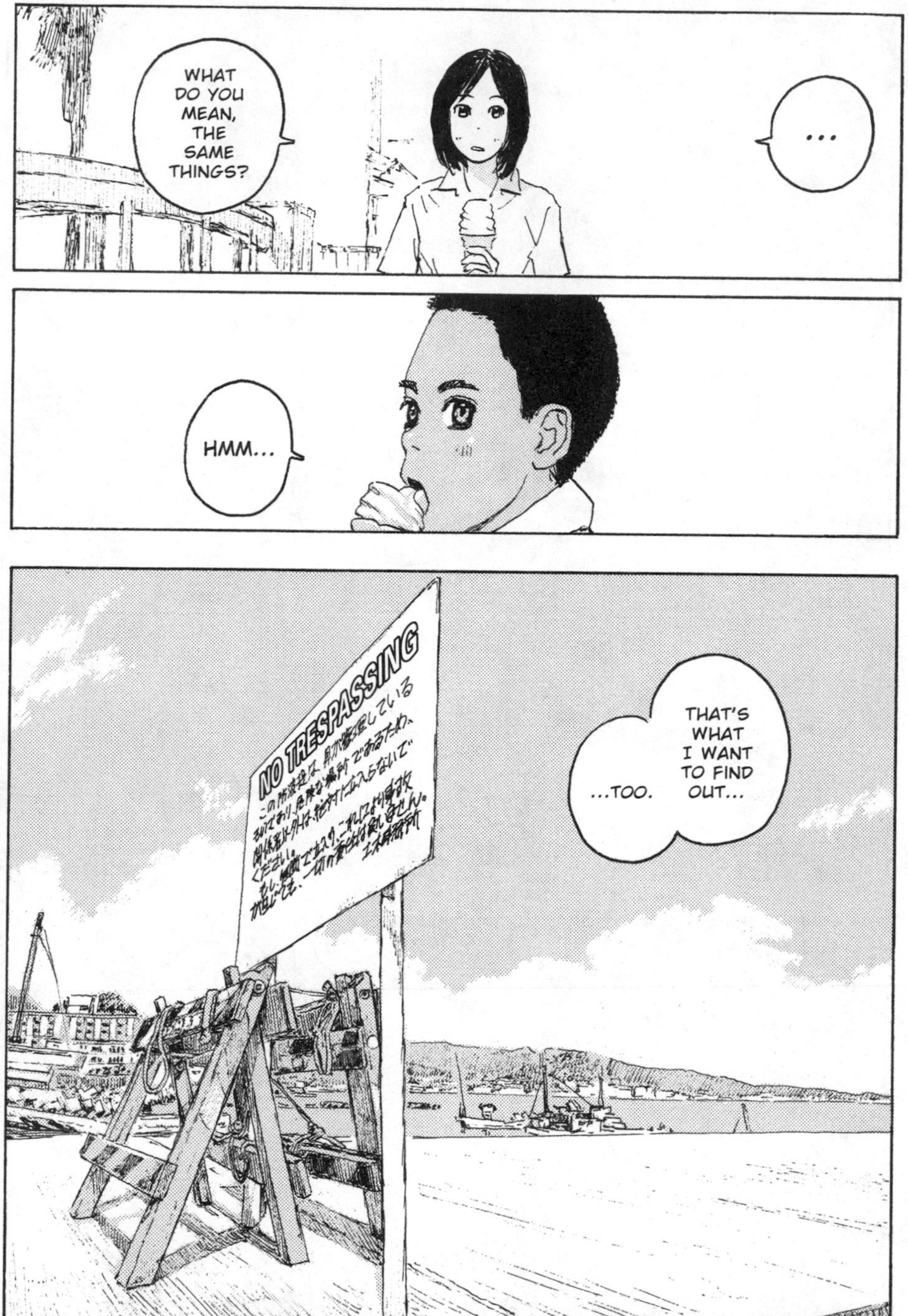
...
WHAT DO YOU MEAN, THE SAME THINGS?
HMM...
NO TRESPASSING
THAT'S WHAT I WANT TO FIND OUT...
...TOO.

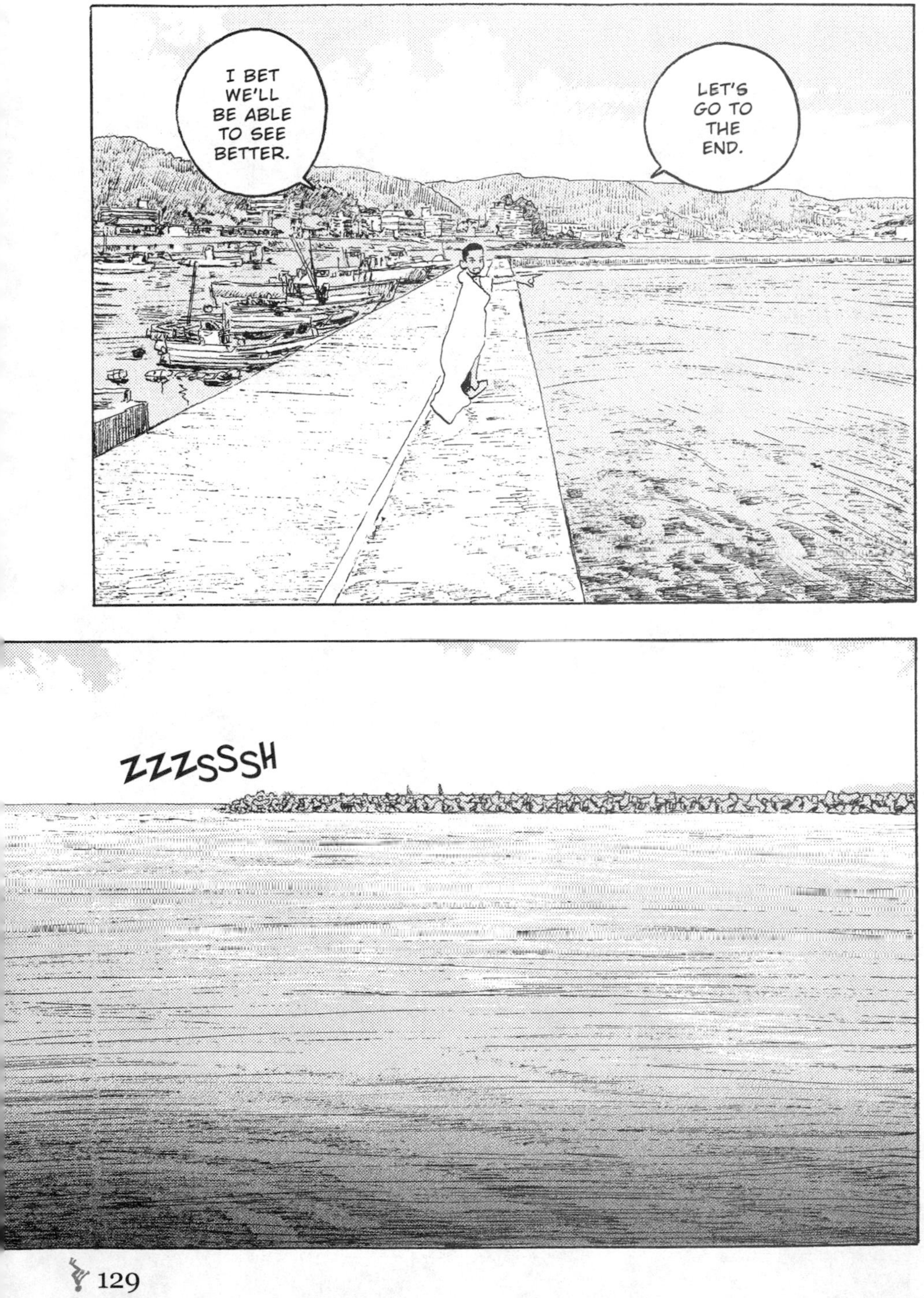
LET'S GO TO THE END.
I BET WE'LL BE ABLE TO SEE BETTER.
ZZZSSSH

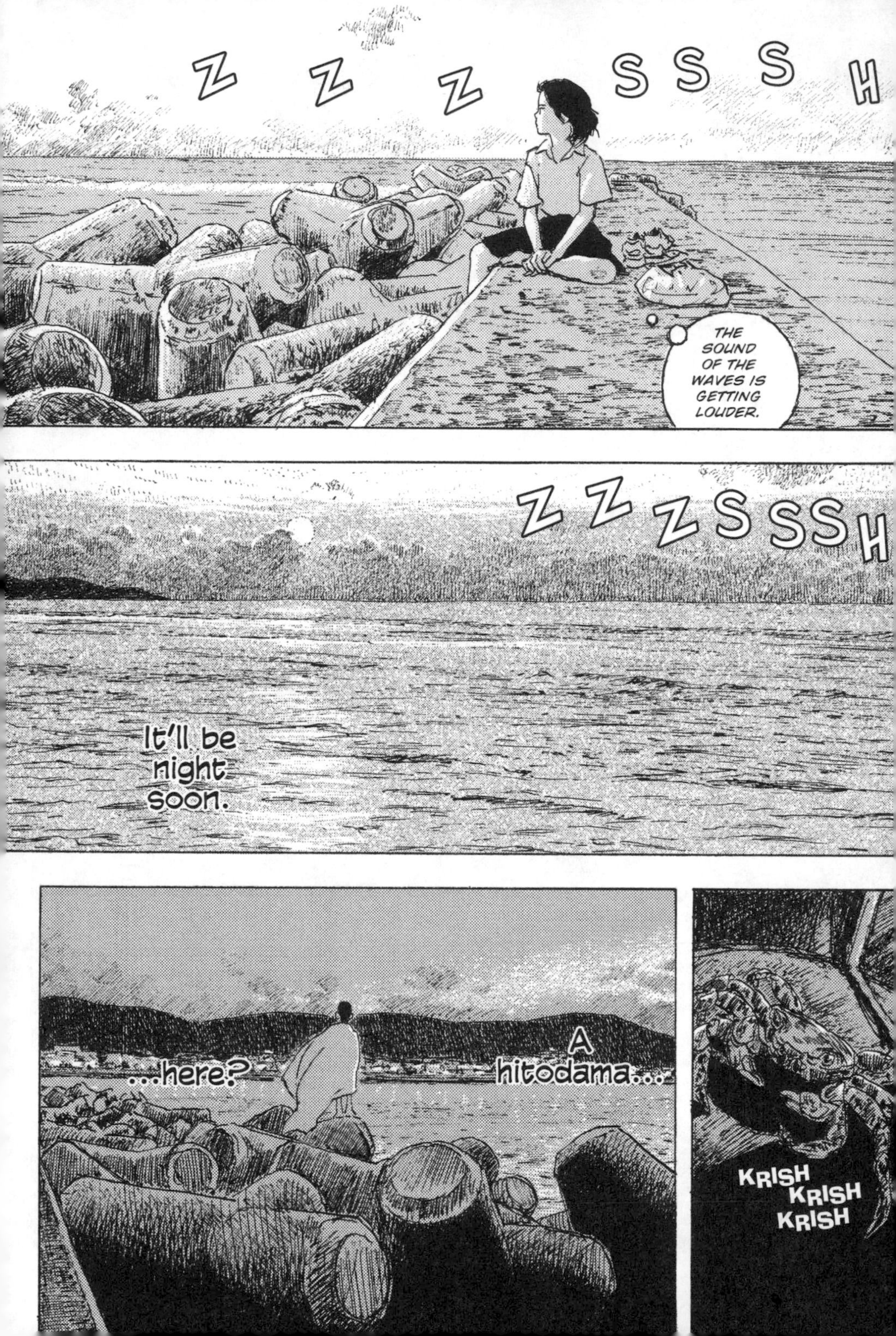
ZZZSSSH
THE SOUND OF THE WAVES IS GETTING LOUDER.
ZZZSSSH
It'll be night soon.
KRISH KRISH KRISH
A hitodama...
...here?

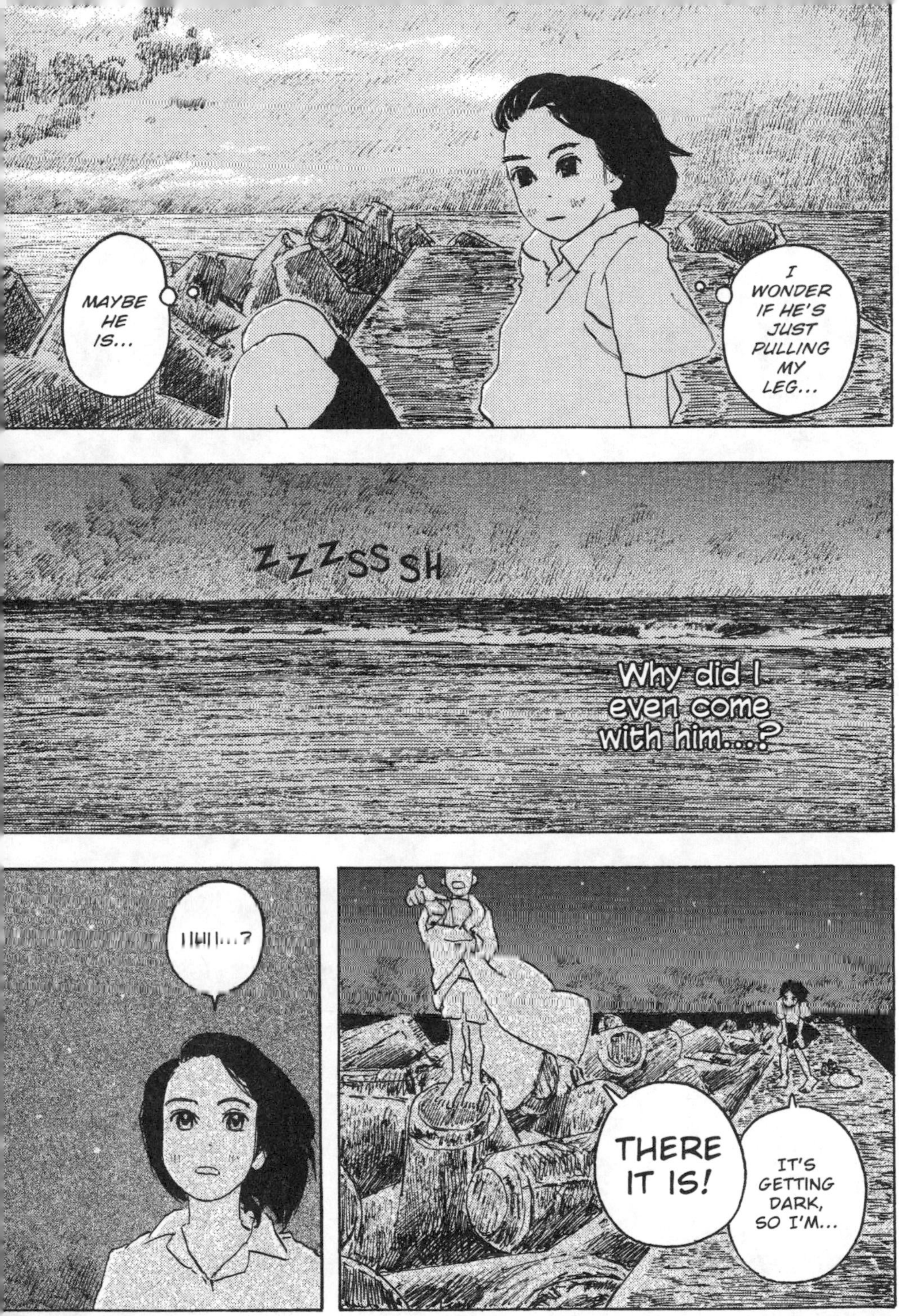

I WONDER IF HE'S JUST PULLING MY LEG...
MAYBE HE IS...
ZZZSSSH
Why did I even come with him...?
IT'S GETTING DARK, SO I'M...
THERE IT IS!

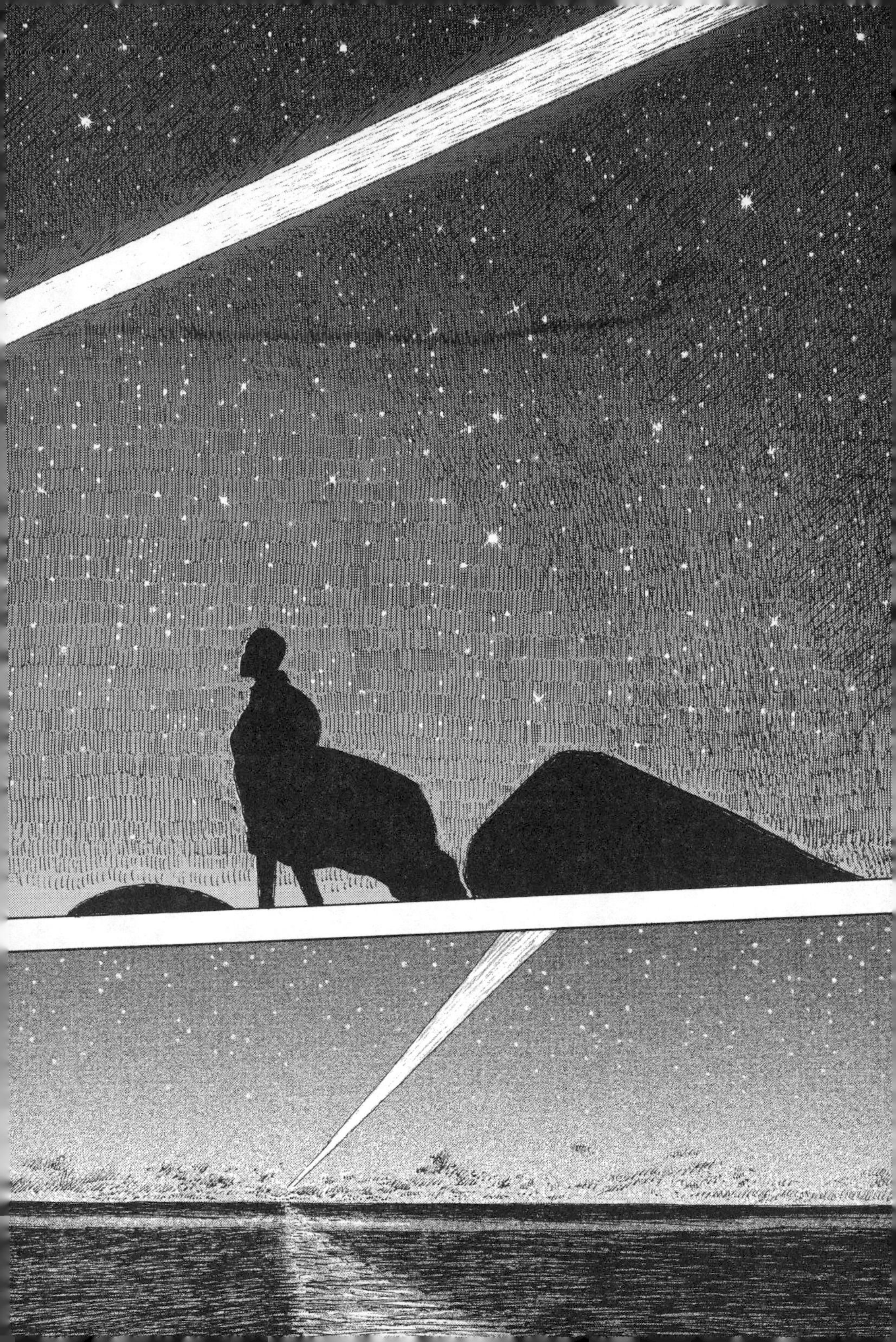

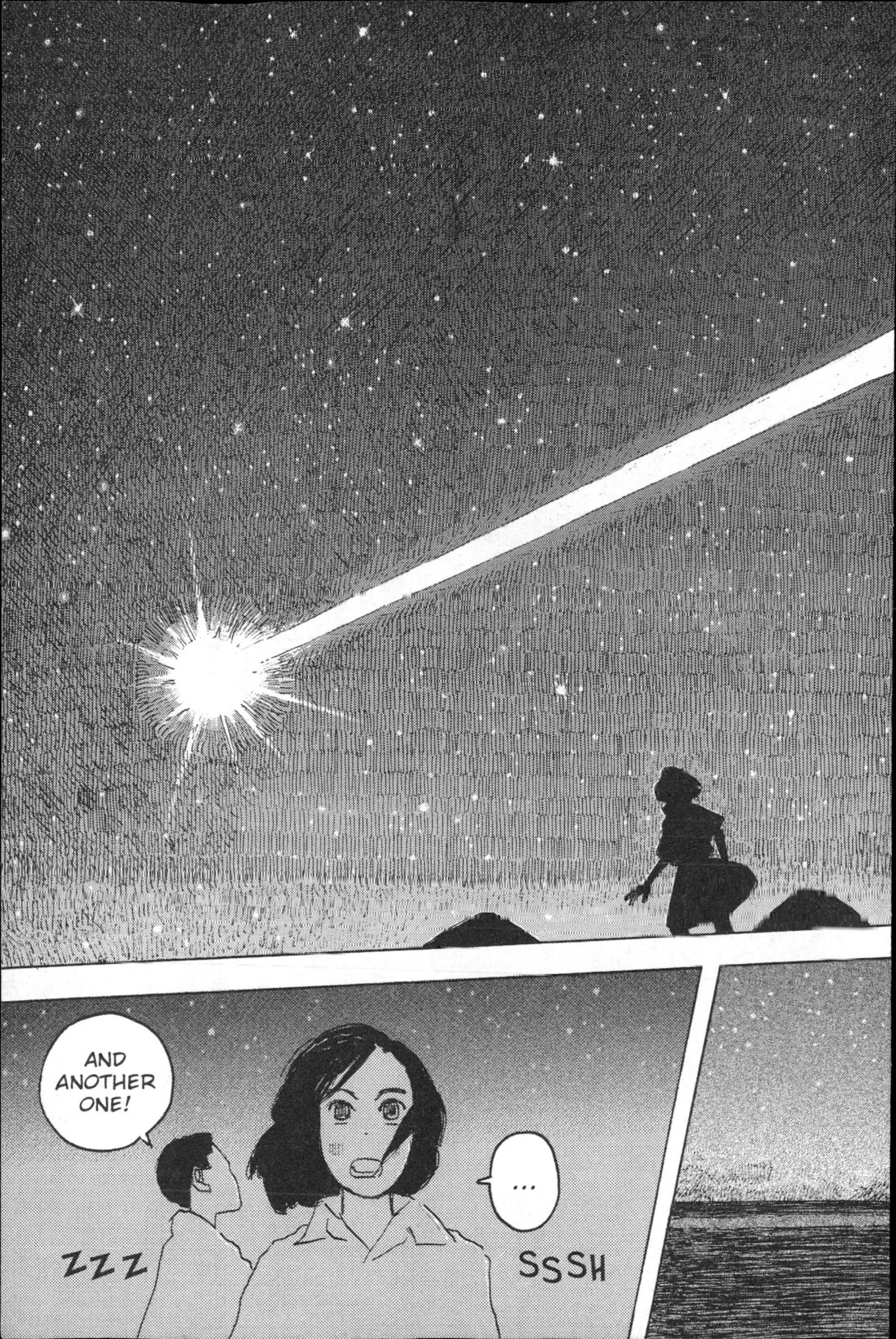
AND ANOTHER ONE!
...
SSSH
ZZZ

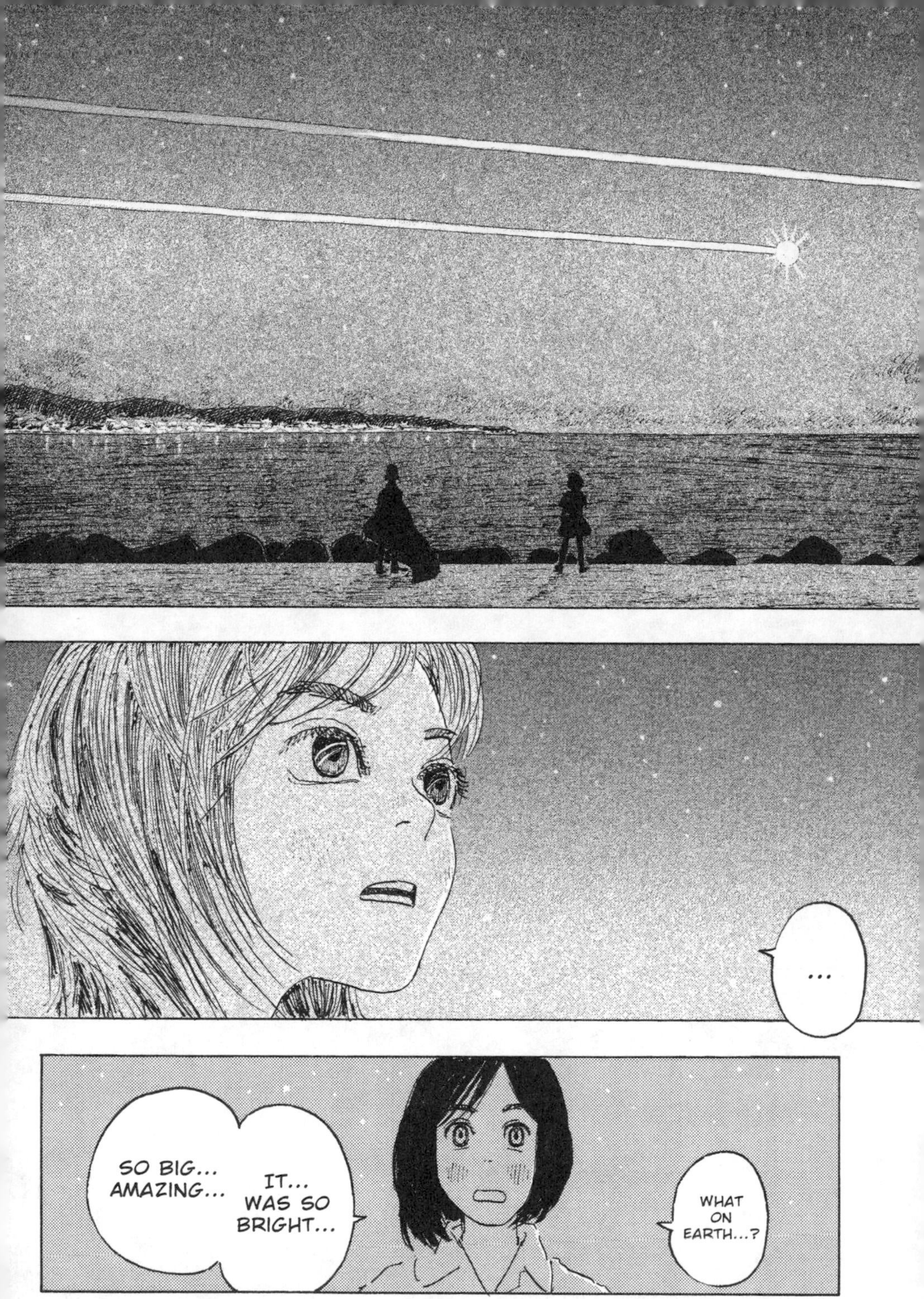
...
WHAT ON EARTH...?
IT... WAS SO BRIGHT...
SO BIG... AMAZING...

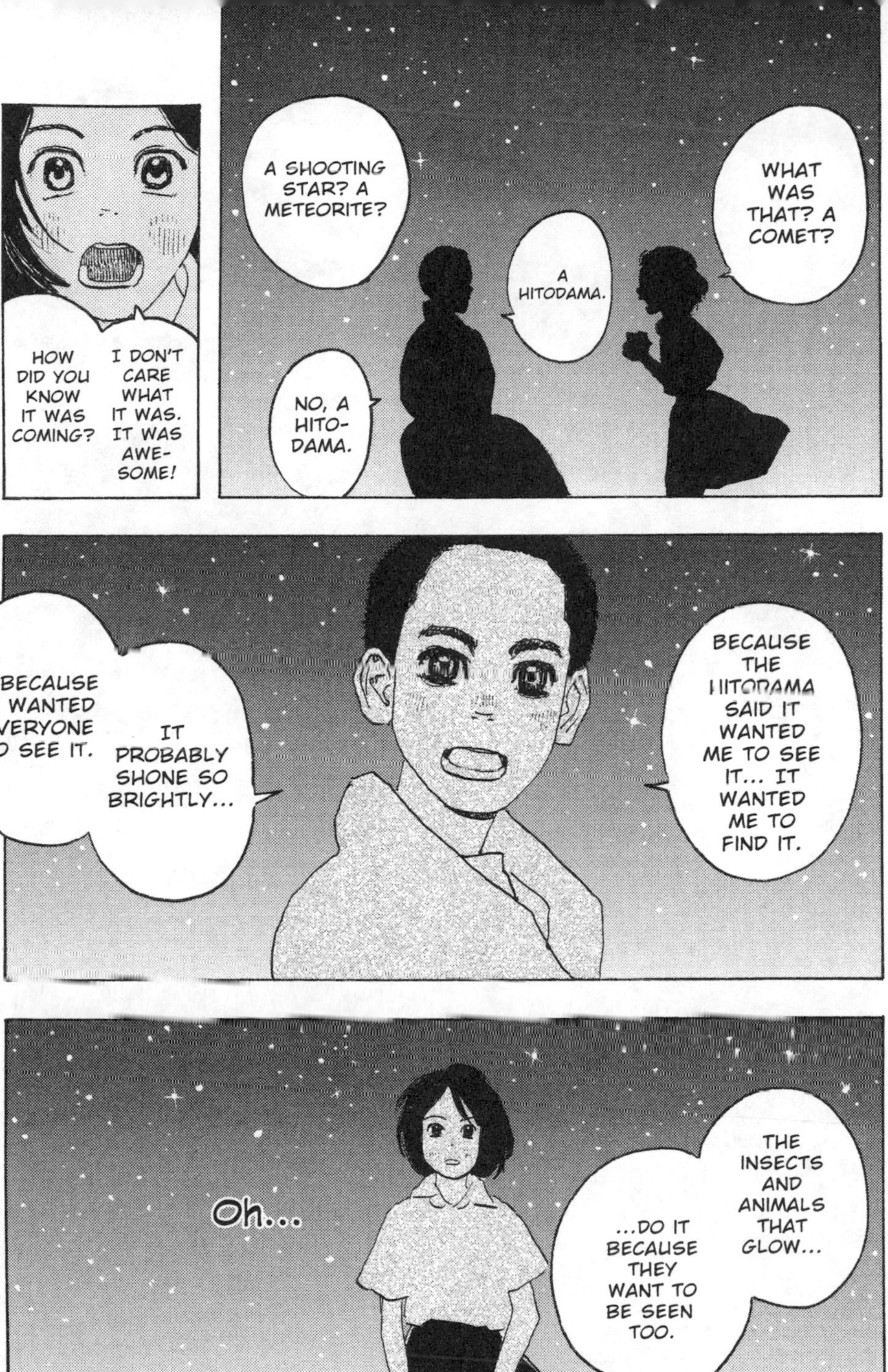
WHAT WAS THAT? A COMET?
A HITODAMA.
A SHOOTING STAR? A METEORITE?
NO, A HITO-DAMA.
I DON'T CARE WHAT IT WAS. IT WAS AWE-SOME!
HOW DID YOU KNOW IT WAS COMING?
BECAUSE THE HITODAMA SAID IT WANTED ME TO SEE IT... IT WANTED ME TO FIND IT.
IT PROBABLY SHONE SO BRIGHTLY...
...BECAUSE IT WANTED EVERYONE TO SEE IT.
THE INSECTS AND ANIMALS THAT GLOW...
...DO IT BECAUSE THEY WANT TO BE SEEN TOO.
Oh...

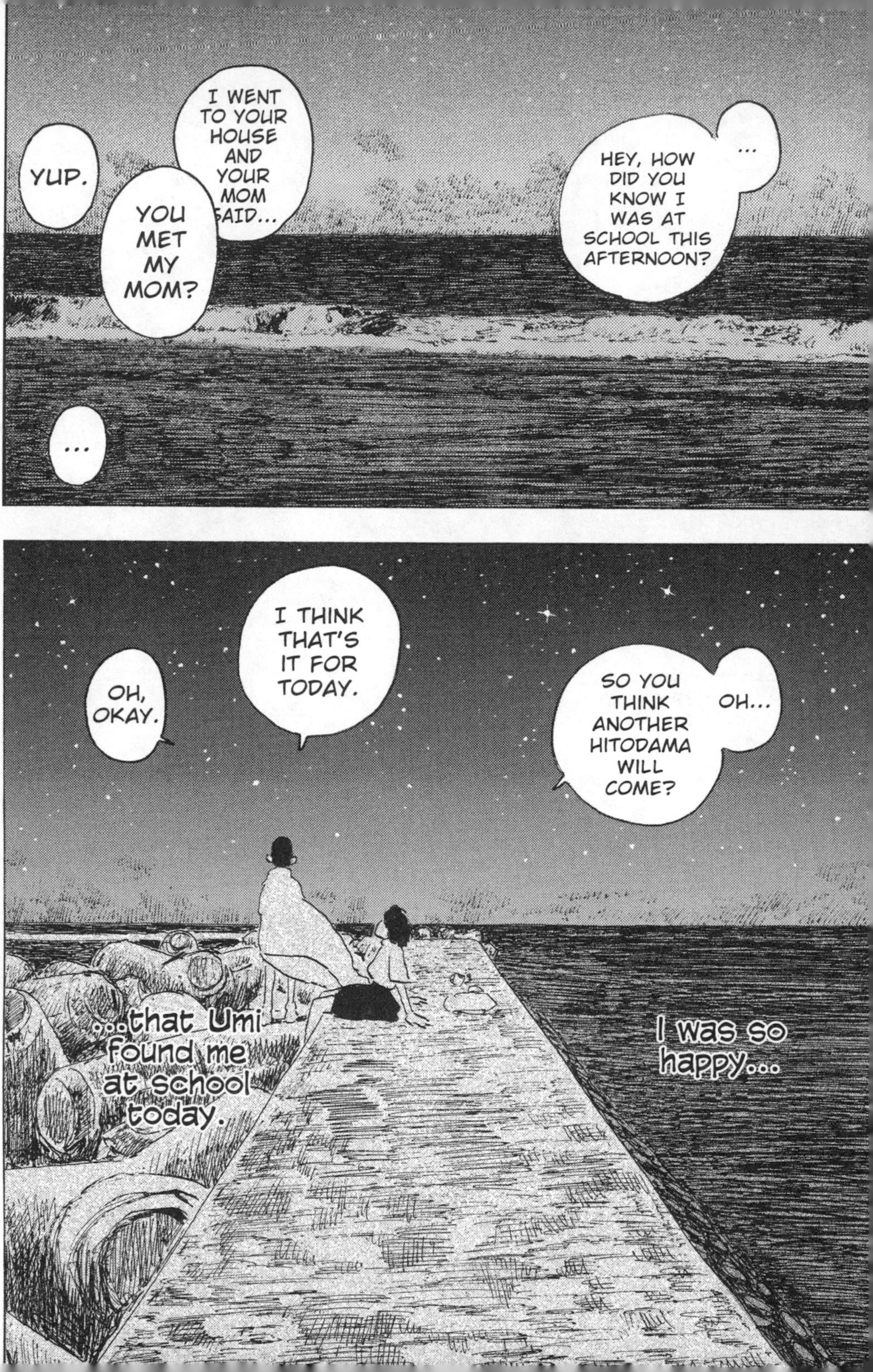
...
HEY, HOW DID YOU KNOW I WAS AT SCHOOL THIS AFTERNOON?
I WENT TO YOUR HOUSE AND YOUR MOM SAID...
YOU MET MY MOM?
YUP.
...
OH...
SO YOU THINK ANOTHER HITODAMA WILL COME?
I THINK THAT'S IT FOR TODAY.
OH, OKAY.
I was so happy...
...that Umi found me at school today.

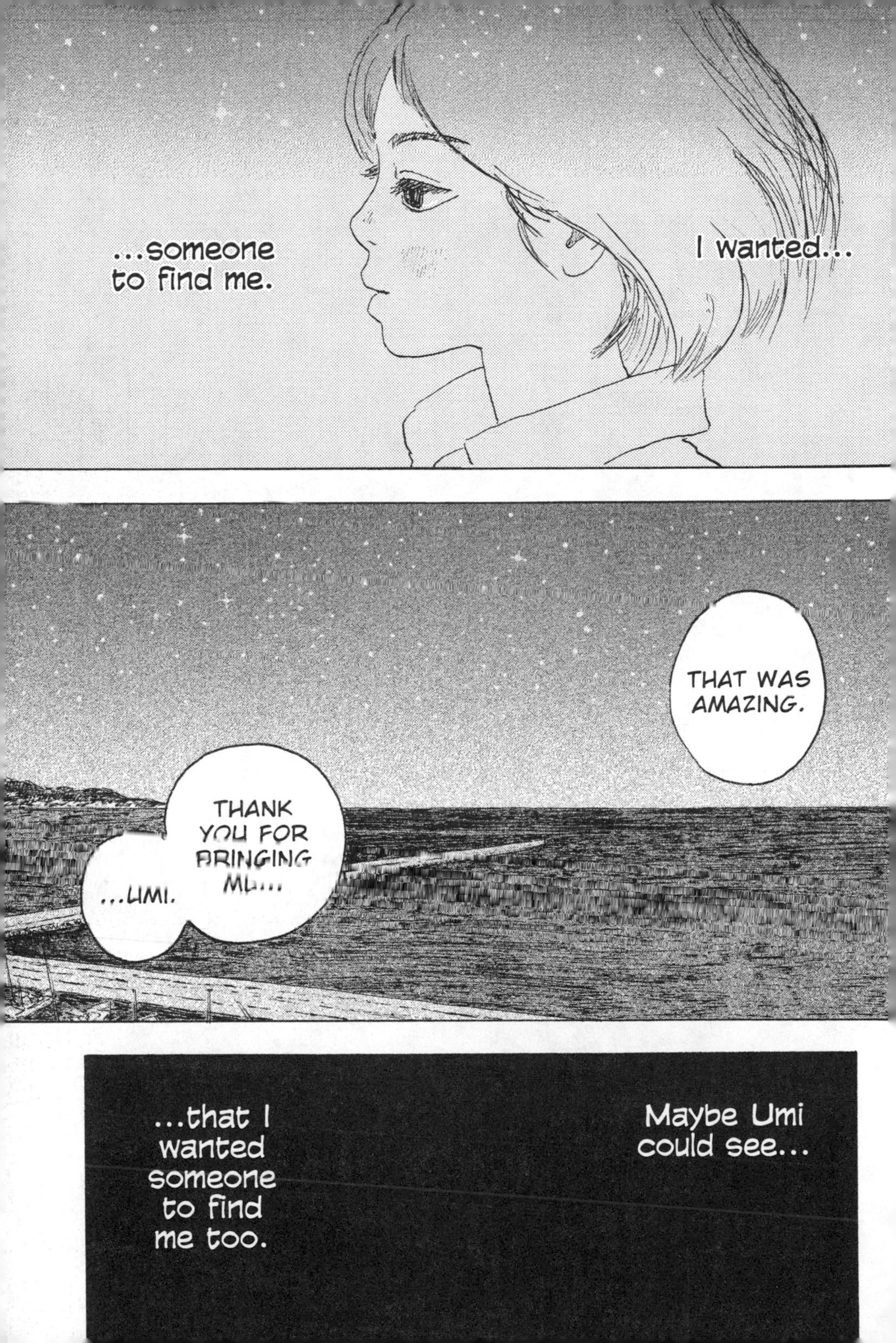
I wanted...
...someone to find me.
THAT WAS AMAZING.
THANK YOU FOR BRINGING ME...
...UMI.
Maybe Umi could see...
...that I wanted someone to find me too.

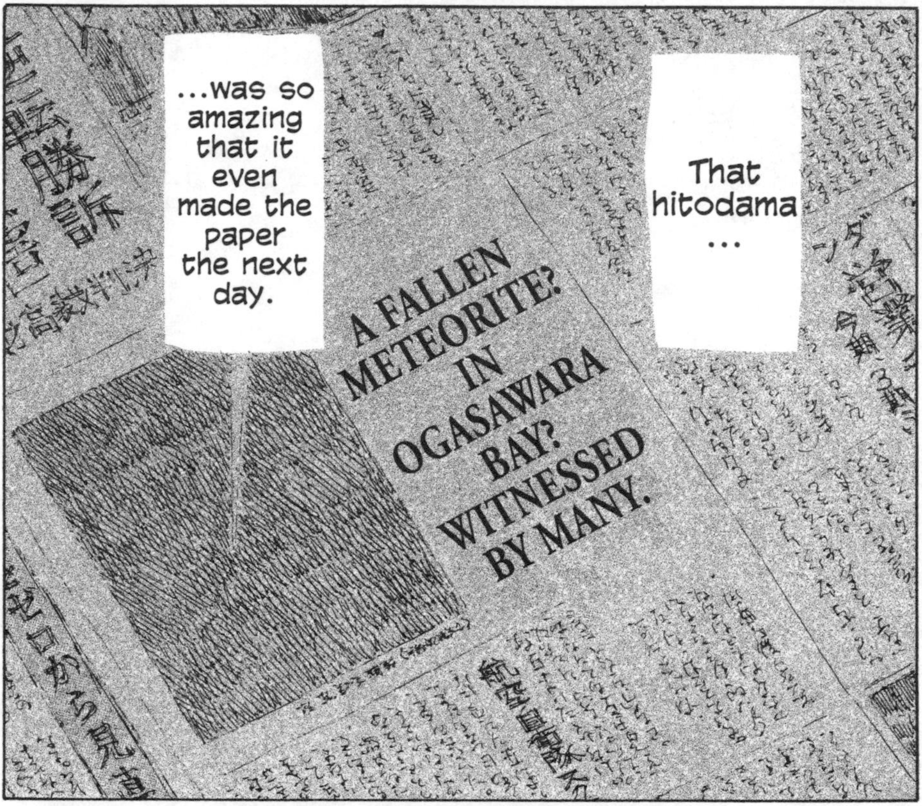
That hitodama ...
...was so amazing that it even made the paper the next day.
A FALLEN METEORITE? IN OGASAWARA BAY? WITNESSED BY MANY.

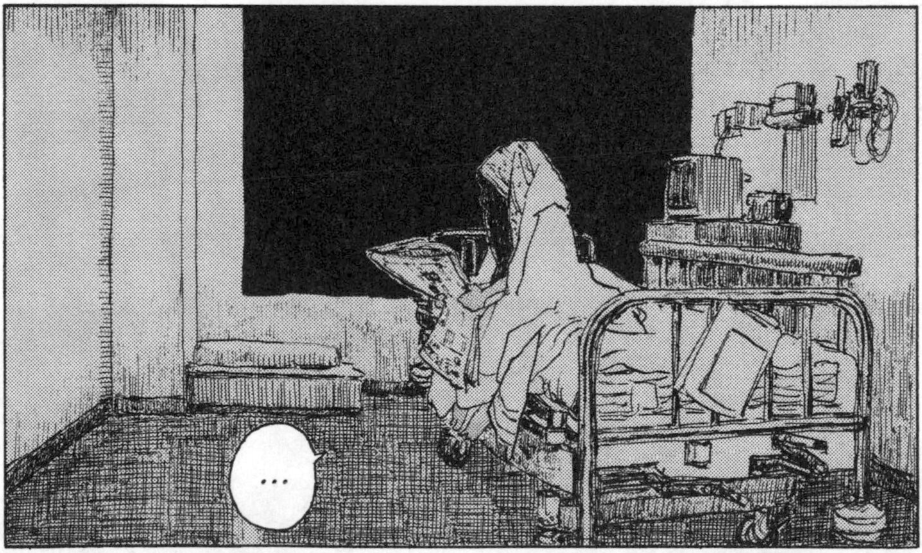
...

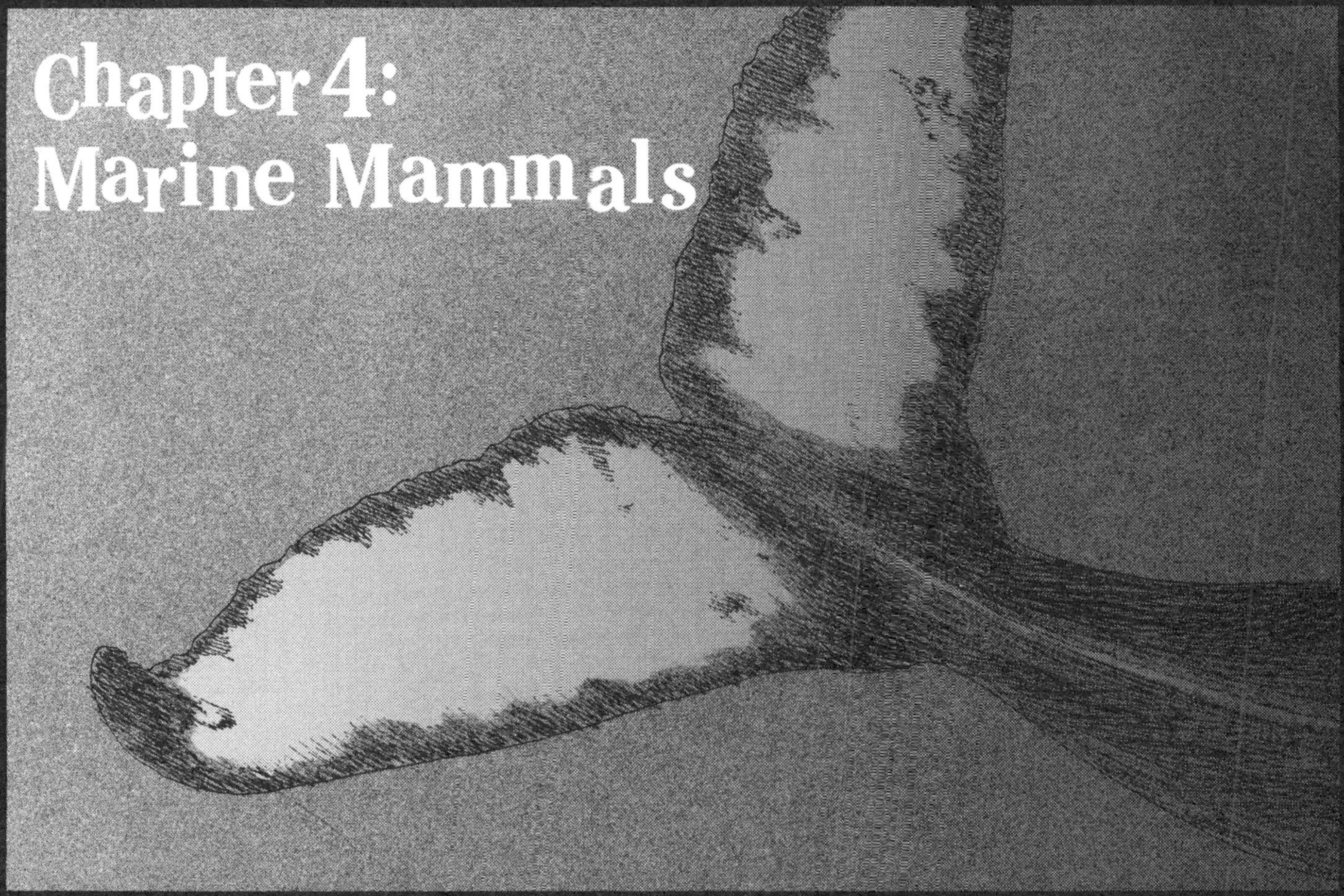
Chapter 4:
Marine Mammals

ZZzSSSH

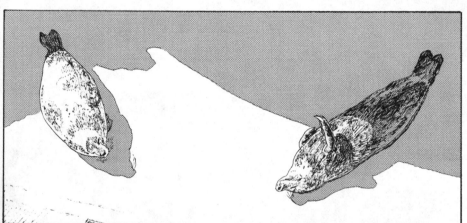

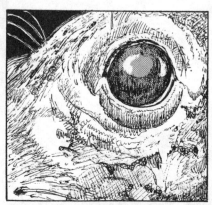

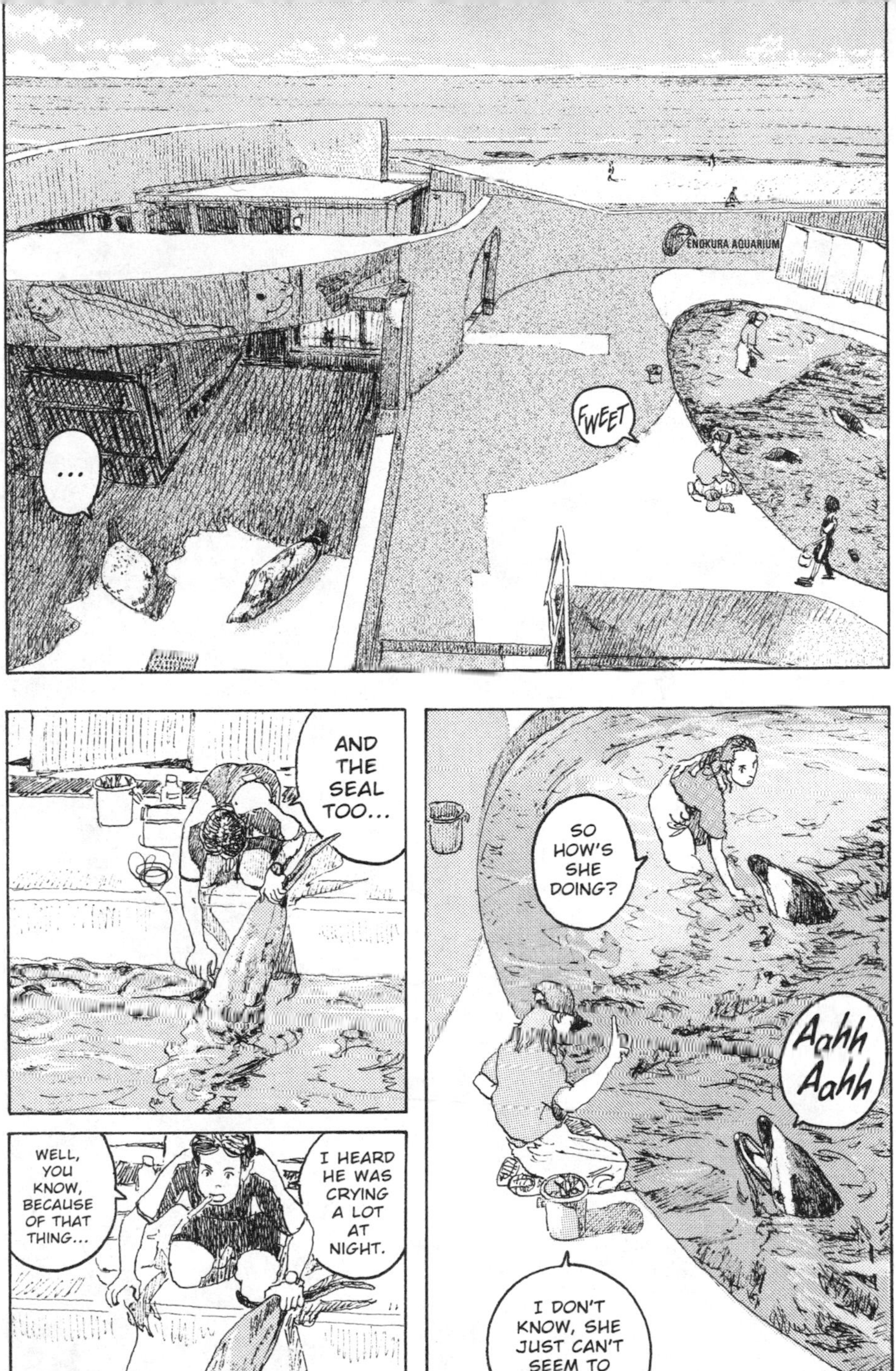
ENOKURA AQUARIUM
FWEET
...
SO HOW'S SHE DOING?
Aahh Aahh
I DON'T KNOW, SHE JUST CAN'T SEEM TO FOCUS.
AND THE SEAL TOO...
I HEARD HE WAS CRYING A LOT AT NIGHT.
WELL, YOU KNOW, BECAUSE OF THAT THING...

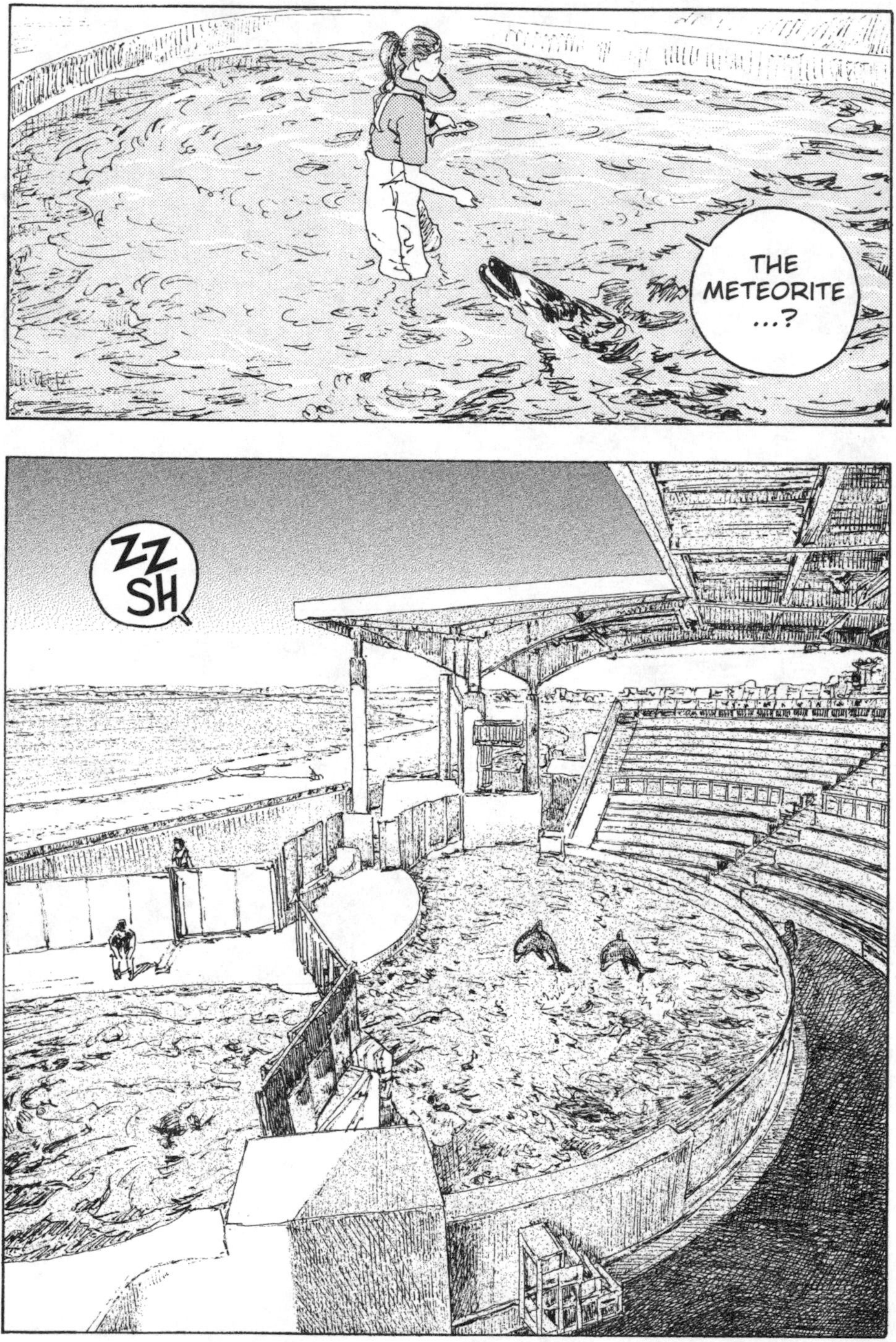
THE METEORITE ...?
ZZSH

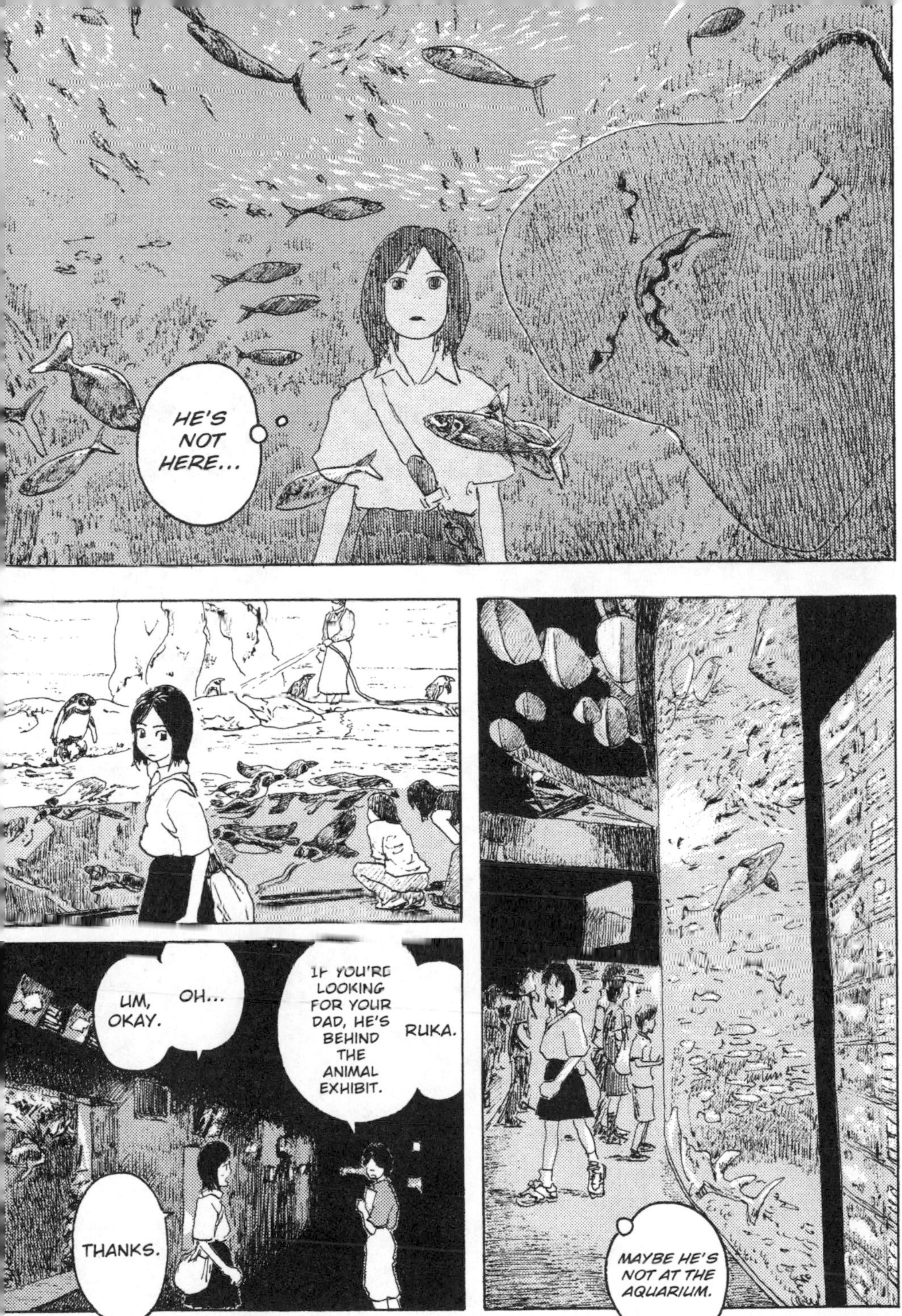
HE'S NOT HERE...
MAYBE HE'S NOT AT THE AQUARIUM.
RUKA.
IF YOU'RE LOOKING FOR YOUR DAD, HE'S BEHIND THE ANIMAL EXHIBIT.
OH...
UM, OKAY.
THANKS.

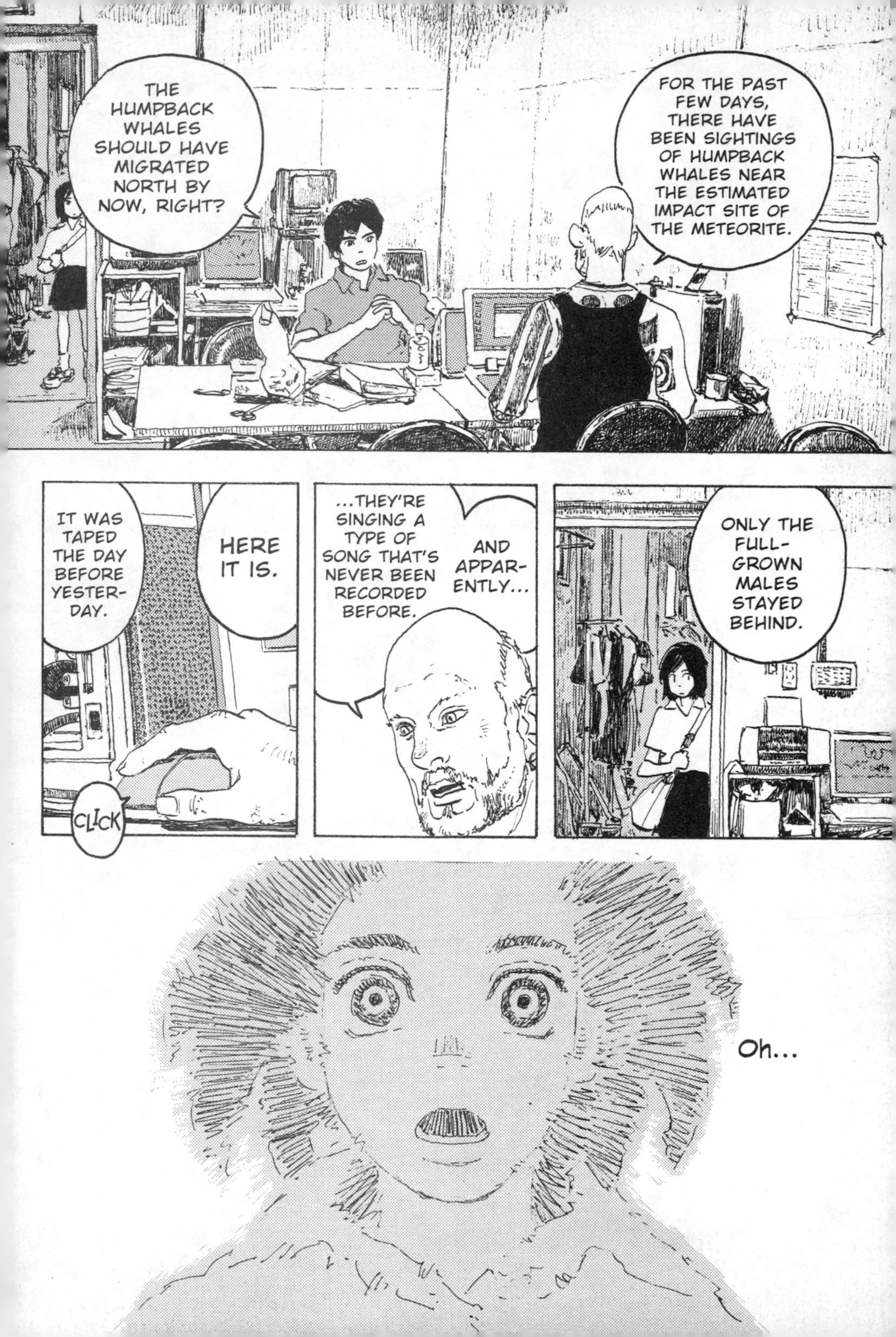
FOR THE PAST FEW DAYS, THERE HAVE BEEN SIGHTINGS OF HUMPBACK WHALES NEAR THE ESTIMATED IMPACT SITE OF THE METEORITE.
THE HUMPBACK WHALES SHOULD HAVE MIGRATED NORTH BY NOW, RIGHT?
ONLY THE FULL-GROWN MALES STAYED BEHIND.
AND APPARENTLY...
...THEY'RE SINGING A TYPE OF SONG THAT'S NEVER BEEN RECORDED BEFORE.
HERE IT IS.
IT WAS TAPED THE DAY BEFORE YESTERDAY.
CLICK
Oh...

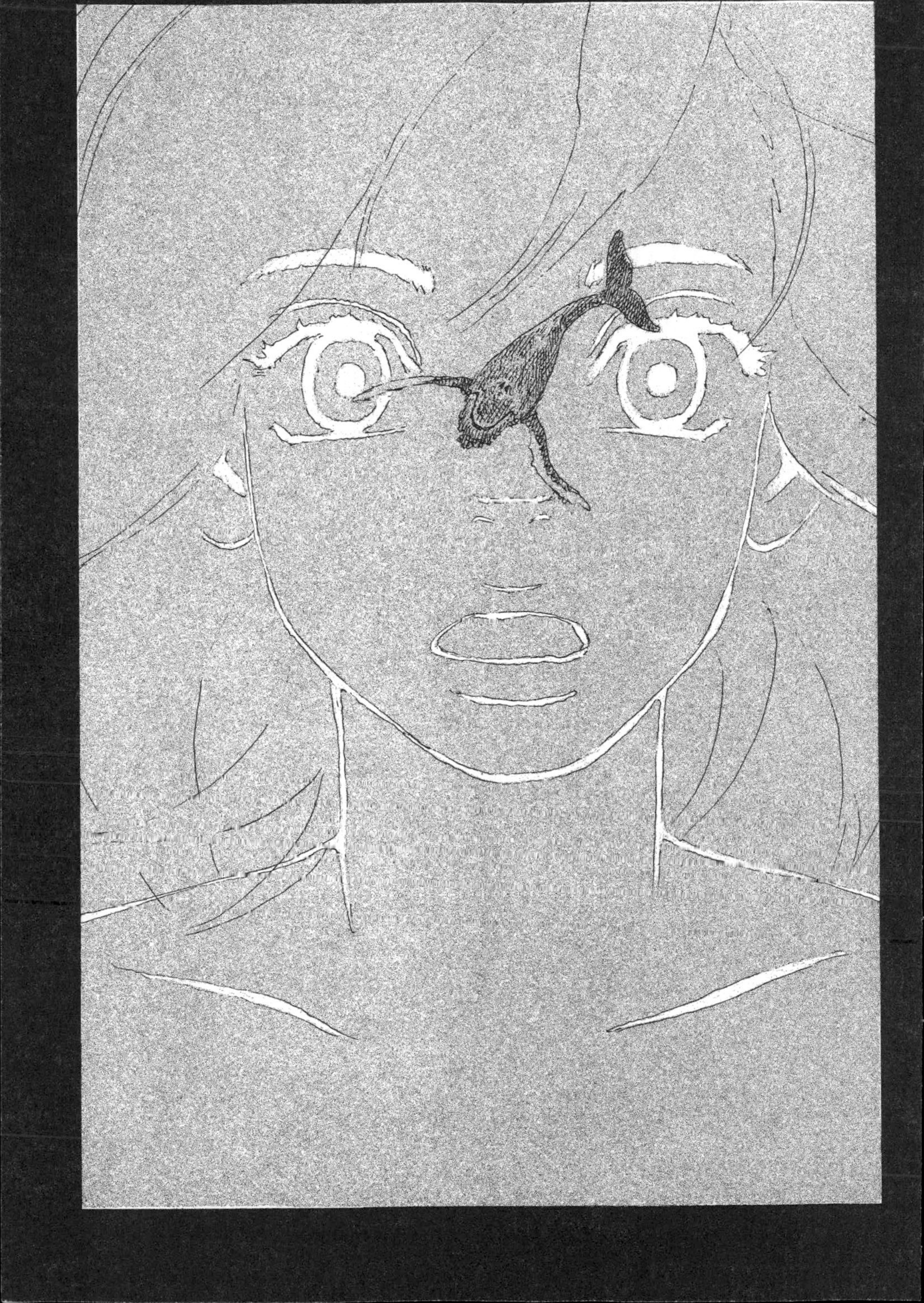

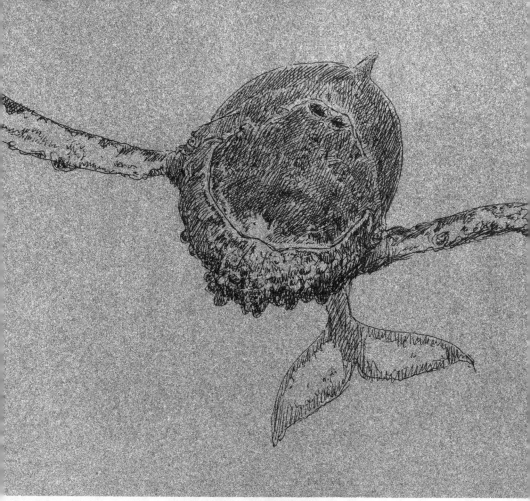

YEAH...

NOW THAT YOU MENTION IT, UMI WAS GOING ON ABOUT THE WHALES TOO.

...

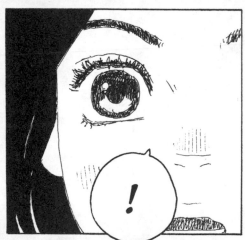

!

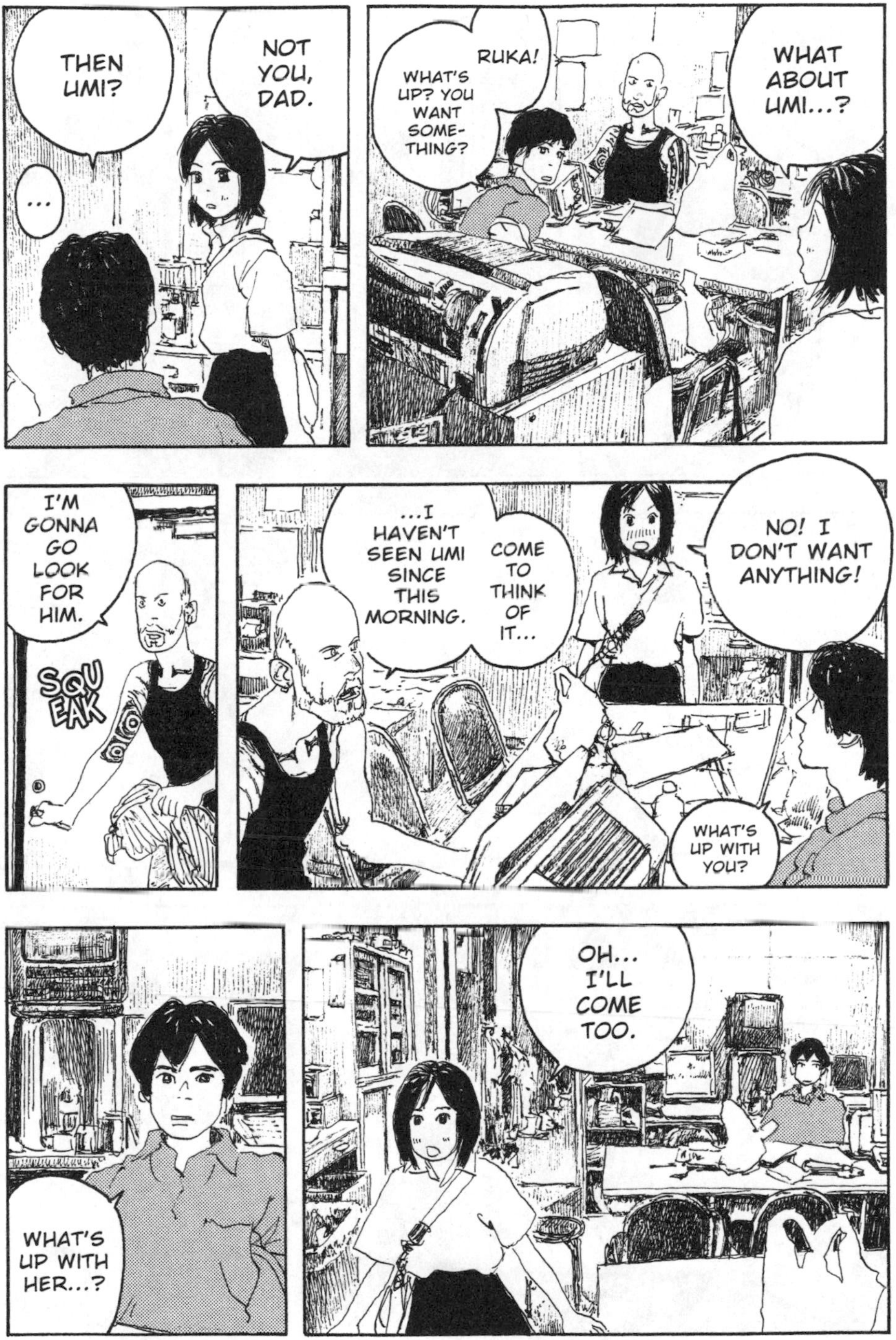
WHAT ABOUT UMI...?
RUKA!
WHAT'S UP? YOU WANT SOME-THING?
NOT YOU, DAD.
THEN UMI?
...
NO! I DON'T WANT ANYTHING!
COME TO THINK OF IT...
...I HAVEN'T SEEN UMI SINCE THIS MORNING.
WHAT'S UP WITH YOU?
I'M GONNA GO LOOK FOR HIM.
SQUEAK
OH... I'LL COME TOO.
WHAT'S UP WITH HER...?

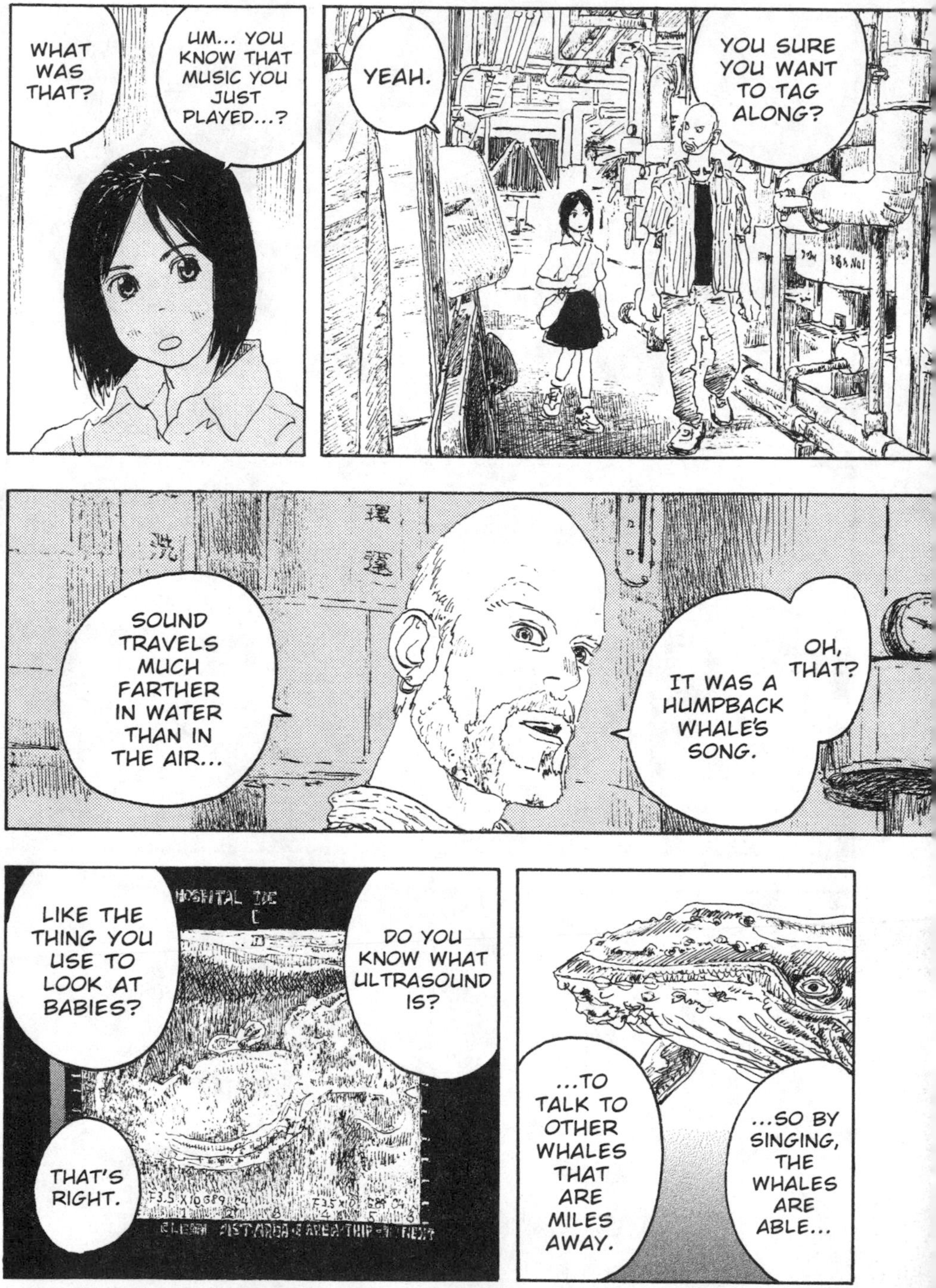
YOU SURE YOU WANT TO TAG ALONG?
YEAH.
UM... YOU KNOW THAT MUSIC YOU JUST PLAYED...?
WHAT WAS THAT?
OH, THAT?
IT WAS A HUMPBACK WHALE'S SONG.
SOUND TRAVELS MUCH FARTHER IN WATER THAN IN THE AIR...
...SO BY SINGING, THE WHALES ARE ABLE...
...TO TALK TO OTHER WHALES THAT ARE MILES AWAY.
DO YOU KNOW WHAT ULTRASOUND IS?
LIKE THE THING YOU USE TO LOOK AT BABIES?
THAT'S RIGHT.

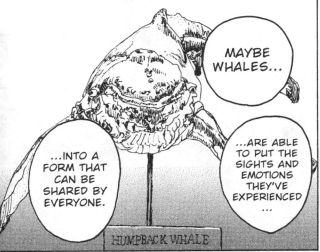

A WHALE'S SONG...
...IS A VERY COMPLEX WAVE OF INFORMATION.
MAYBE WHALES...
...ARE ABLE TO PUT THE SIGHTS AND EMOTIONS THEY'VE EXPERIENCED ...
...INTO A FORM THAT CAN BE SHARED BY EVERYONE.
HUMPBACK WHALE
HAVE YOU EVER BEEN ABLE TO COMMUNICATE...
...EVEN HALF OF WHAT YOU WERE THINKING, RUKA?
PERHAPS WHALES ...
...ARE ABLE TO DO THAT.
APPARENTLY HE HASN'T BEEN TO THE HOSPITAL.

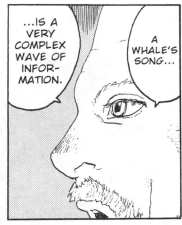

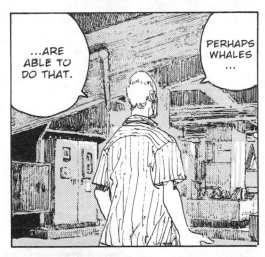

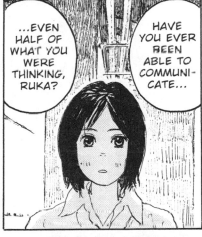

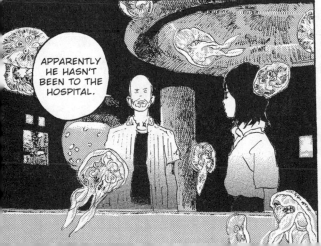

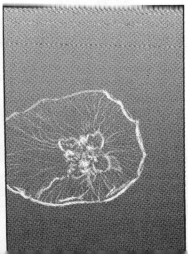

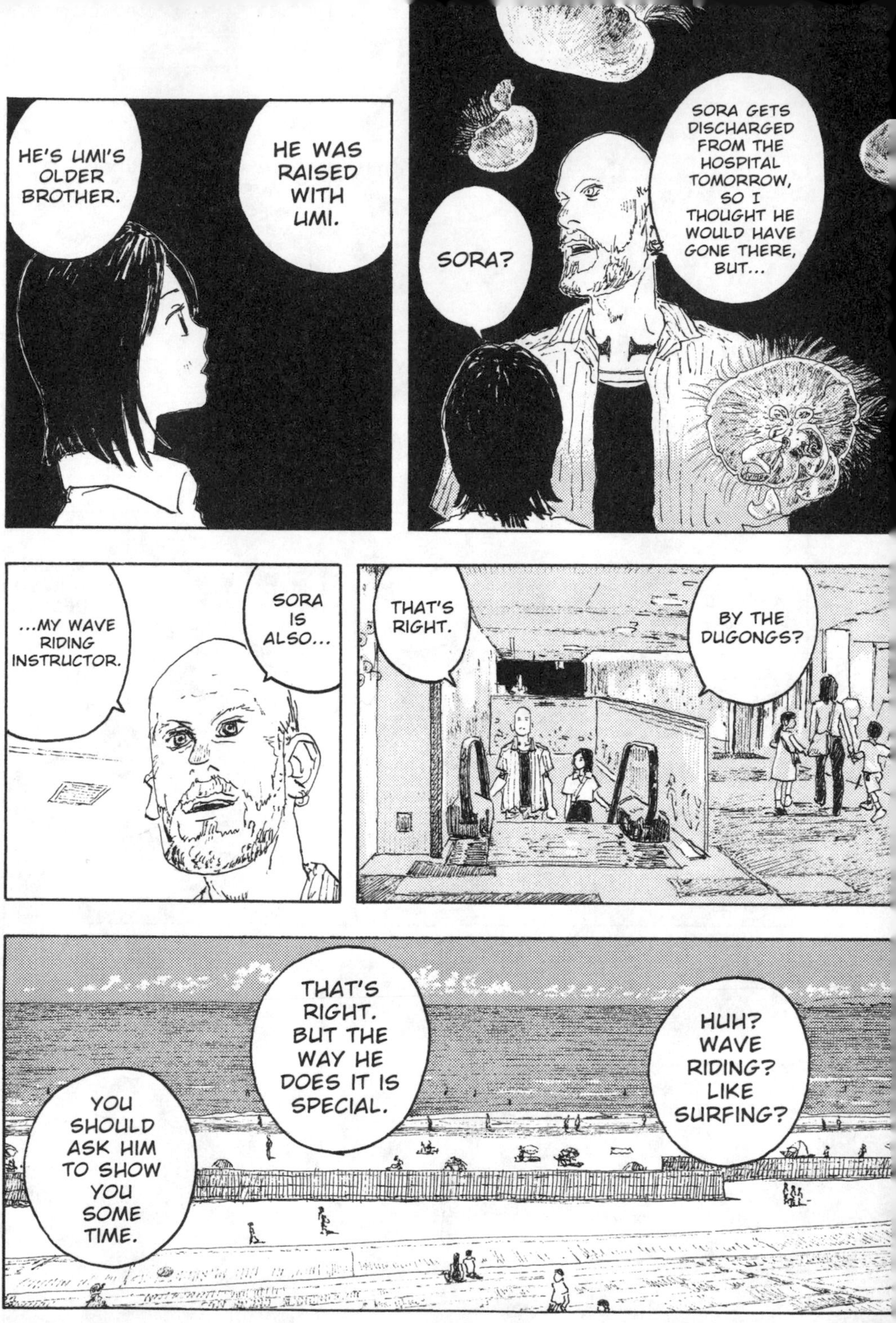
SORA GETS DISCHARGED FROM THE HOSPITAL TOMORROW, SO I THOUGHT HE WOULD HAVE GONE THERE, BUT...
SORA?
HE WAS RAISED WITH UMI.
HE'S UMI'S OLDER BROTHER.
BY THE DUGONGS?
THAT'S RIGHT.
SORA IS ALSO...
...MY WAVE RIDING INSTRUCTOR.
HUH? WAVE RIDING? LIKE SURFING?
THAT'S RIGHT. BUT THE WAY HE DOES IT IS SPECIAL.
YOU SHOULD ASK HIM TO SHOW YOU SOME TIME.

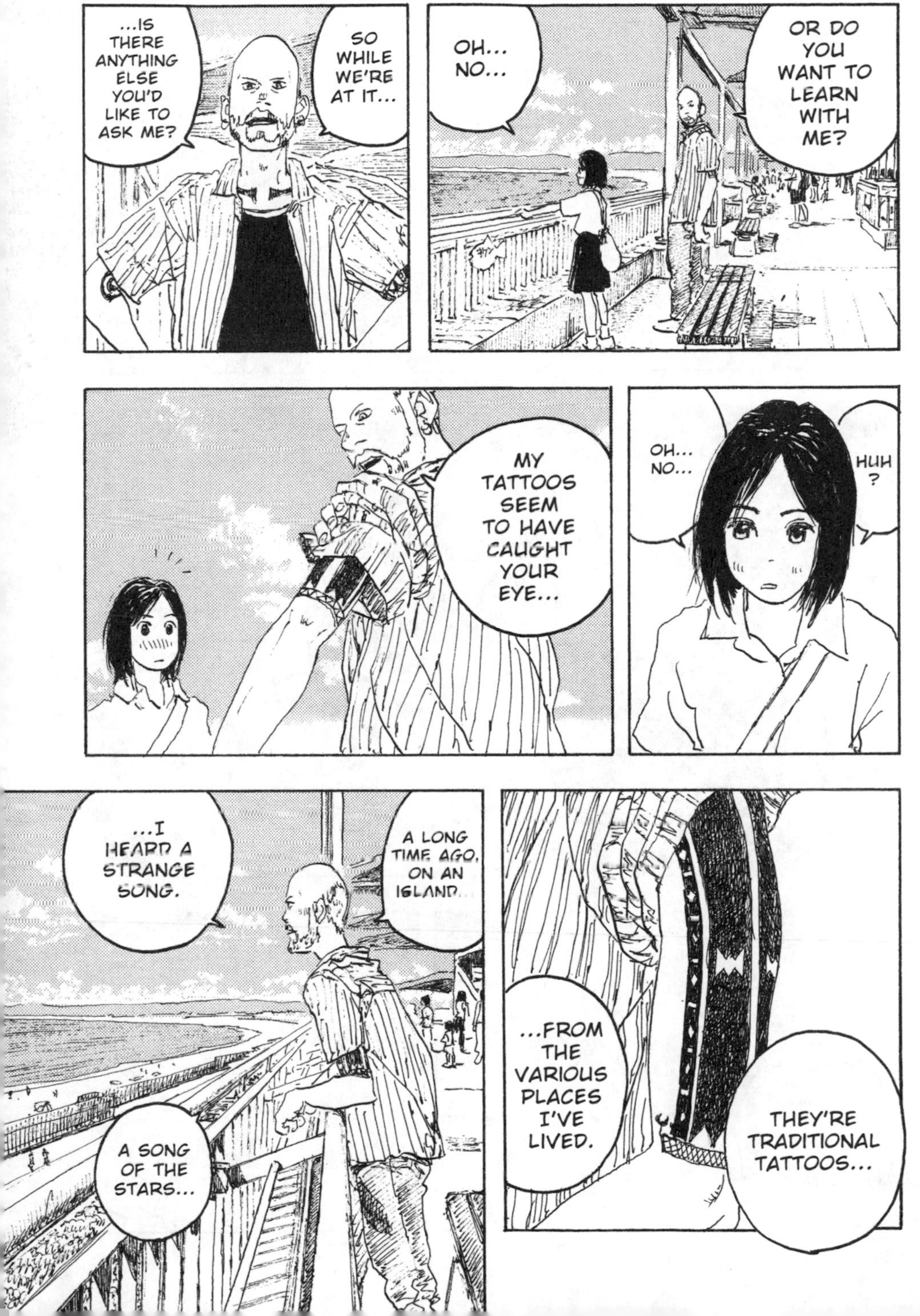
OR DO YOU WANT TO LEARN WITH ME?
OH... NO...
SO WHILE WE'RE AT IT...
...IS THERE ANYTHING ELSE YOU'D LIKE TO ASK ME?
HUH?
OH... NO...
MY TATTOOS SEEM TO HAVE CAUGHT YOUR EYE...
THEY'RE TRADITIONAL TATTOOS...
...FROM THE VARIOUS PLACES I'VE LIVED.
A LONG TIME AGO, ON AN ISLAND...
...I HEARD A STRANGE SONG.
A SONG OF THE STARS...

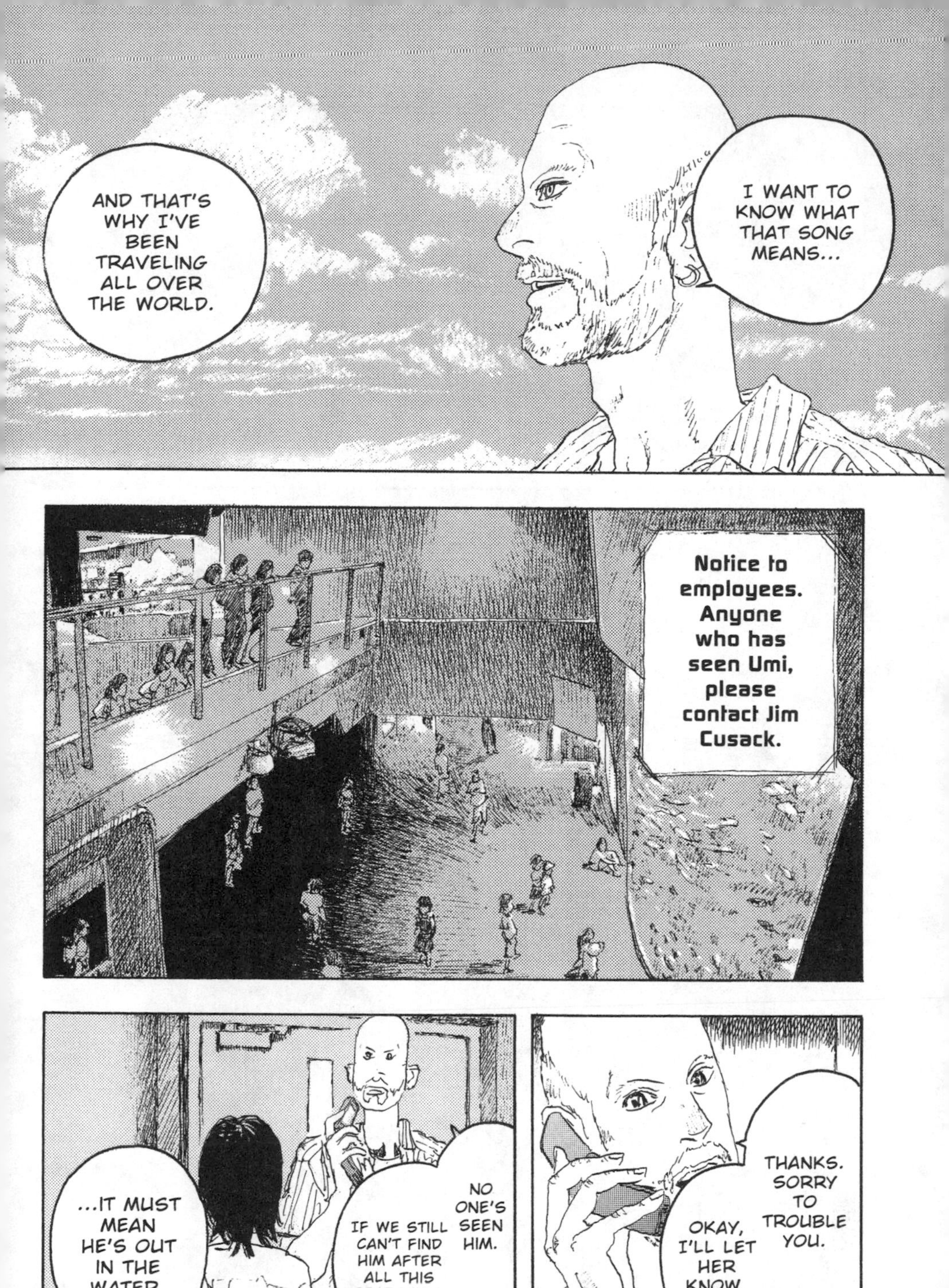
I WANT TO KNOW WHAT THAT SONG MEANS...
AND THAT'S WHY I'VE BEEN TRAVELING ALL OVER THE WORLD.
Notice to employees. Anyone who has seen Umi, please contact Jim Cusack.
THANKS. SORRY TO TROUBLE YOU.
OKAY, I'LL LET HER KNOW.
NO ONE'S SEEN HIM.
IF WE STILL CAN'T FIND HIM AFTER ALL THIS SEARCHING...
...IT MUST MEAN HE'S OUT IN THE WATER.

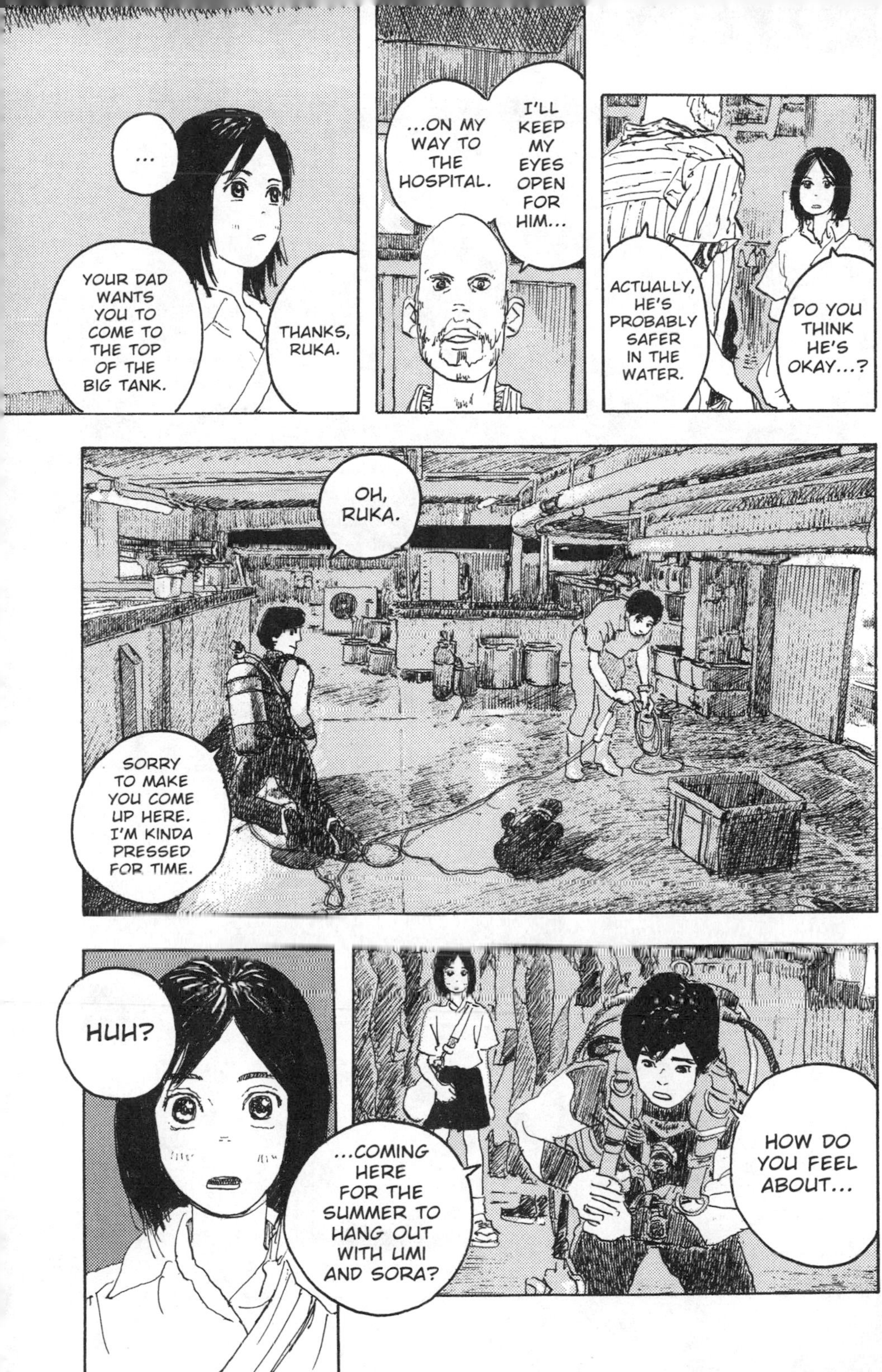
DO YOU THINK HE'S OKAY...?
ACTUALLY, HE'S PROBABLY SAFER IN THE WATER.
I'LL KEEP MY EYES OPEN FOR HIM...
...ON MY WAY TO THE HOSPITAL.
...
THANKS, RUKA.
YOUR DAD WANTS YOU TO COME TO THE TOP OF THE BIG TANK.
OH, RUKA.
SORRY TO MAKE YOU COME UP HERE. I'M KINDA PRESSED FOR TIME.
HOW DO YOU FEEL ABOUT...
...COMING HERE FOR THE SUMMER TO HANG OUT WITH UMI AND SORA?
HUH?

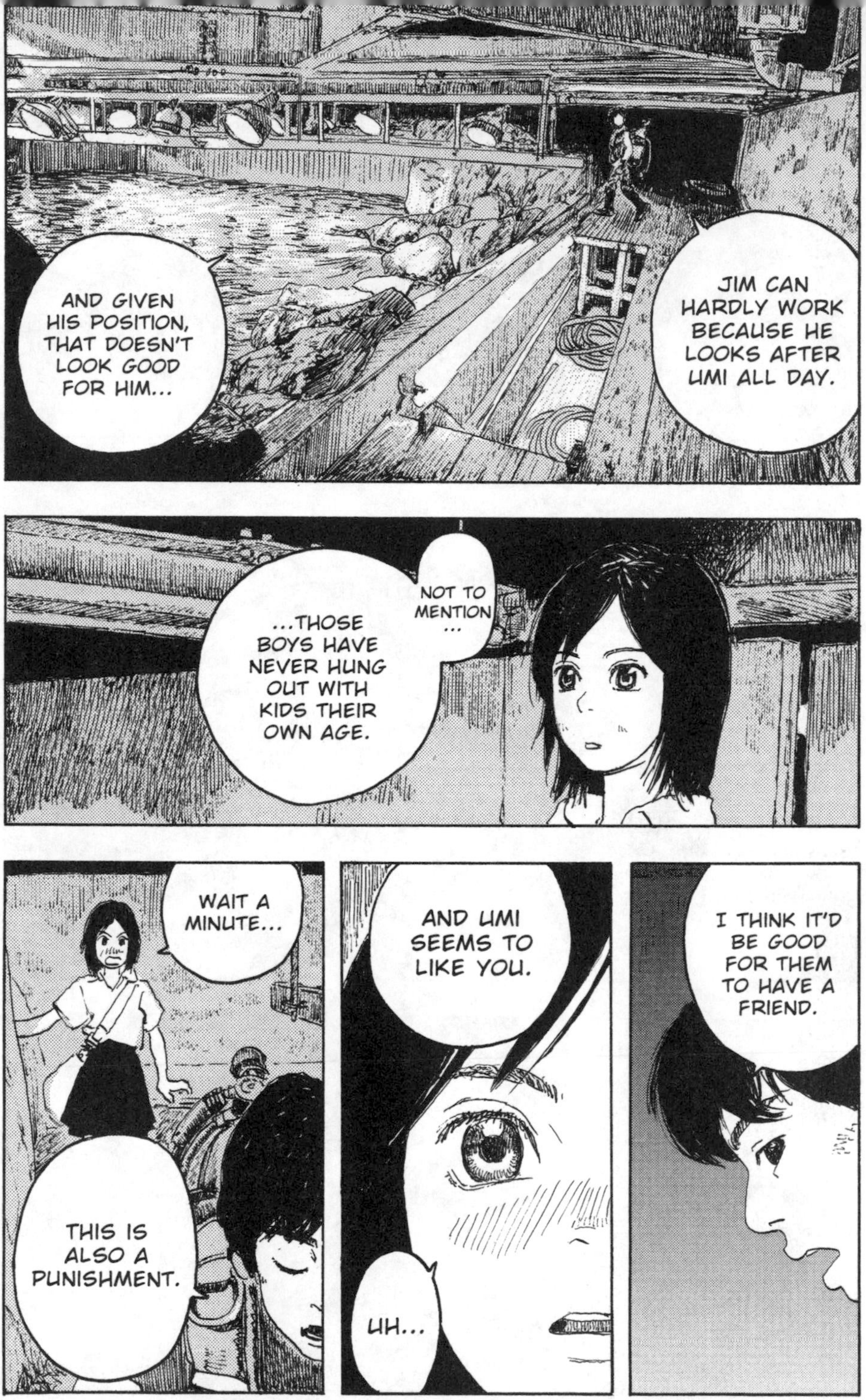
JIM CAN HARDLY WORK BECAUSE HE LOOKS AFTER UMI ALL DAY.
AND GIVEN HIS POSITION, THAT DOESN'T LOOK GOOD FOR HIM...
NOT TO MENTION ...
...THOSE BOYS HAVE NEVER HUNG OUT WITH KIDS THEIR OWN AGE.
I THINK IT'D BE GOOD FOR THEM TO HAVE A FRIEND.
AND UMI SEEMS TO LIKE YOU.
UH...
WAIT A MINUTE...
THIS IS ALSO A PUNISHMENT.

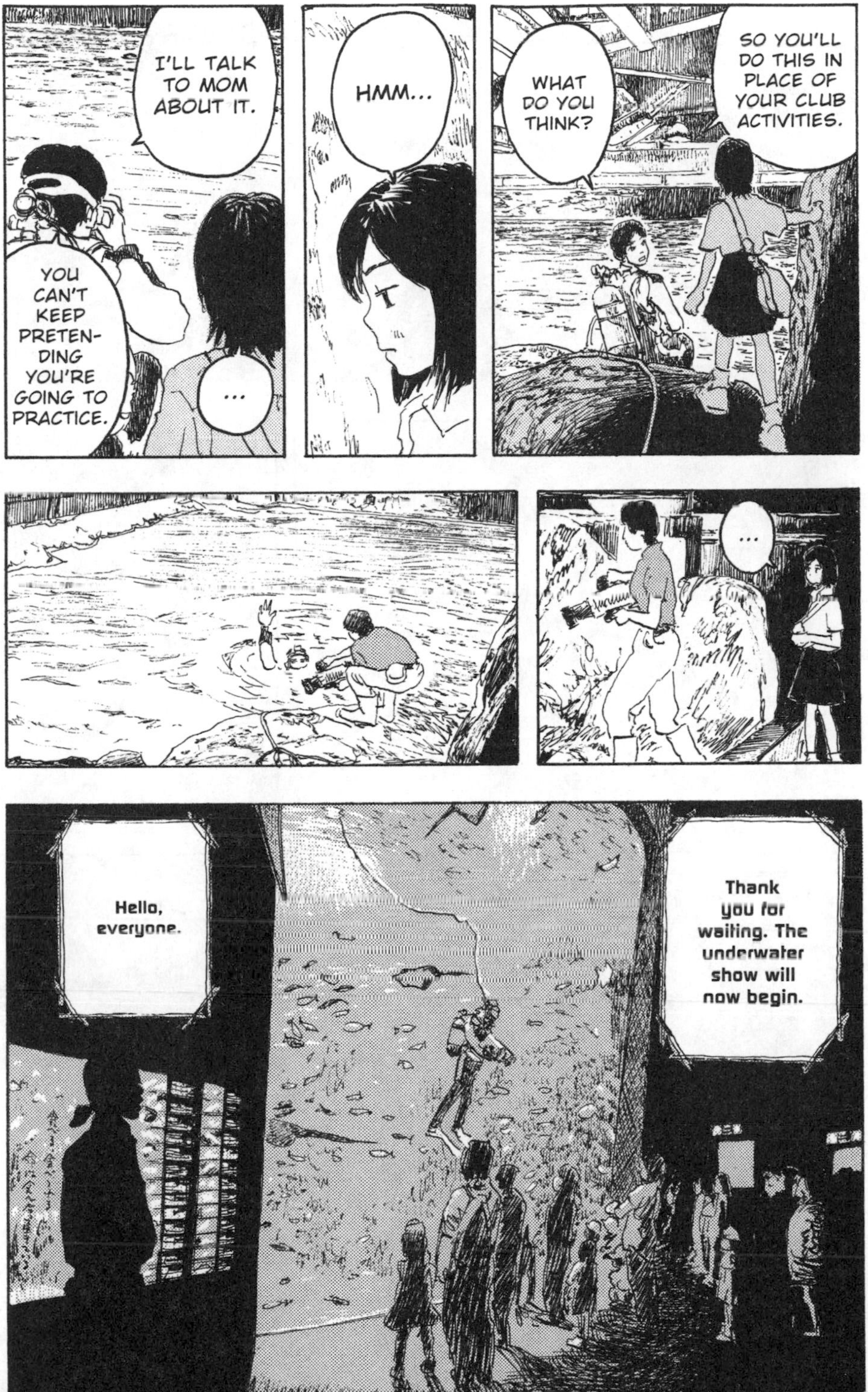
SO YOU'LL DO THIS IN PLACE OF YOUR CLUB ACTIVITIES.
WHAT DO YOU THINK?
HMM...
I'LL TALK TO MOM ABOUT IT.
YOU CAN'T KEEP PRETEN-DING YOU'RE GOING TO PRACTICE.
...
...
Thank you for waiting. The underwater show will now begin.
Hello, everyone.

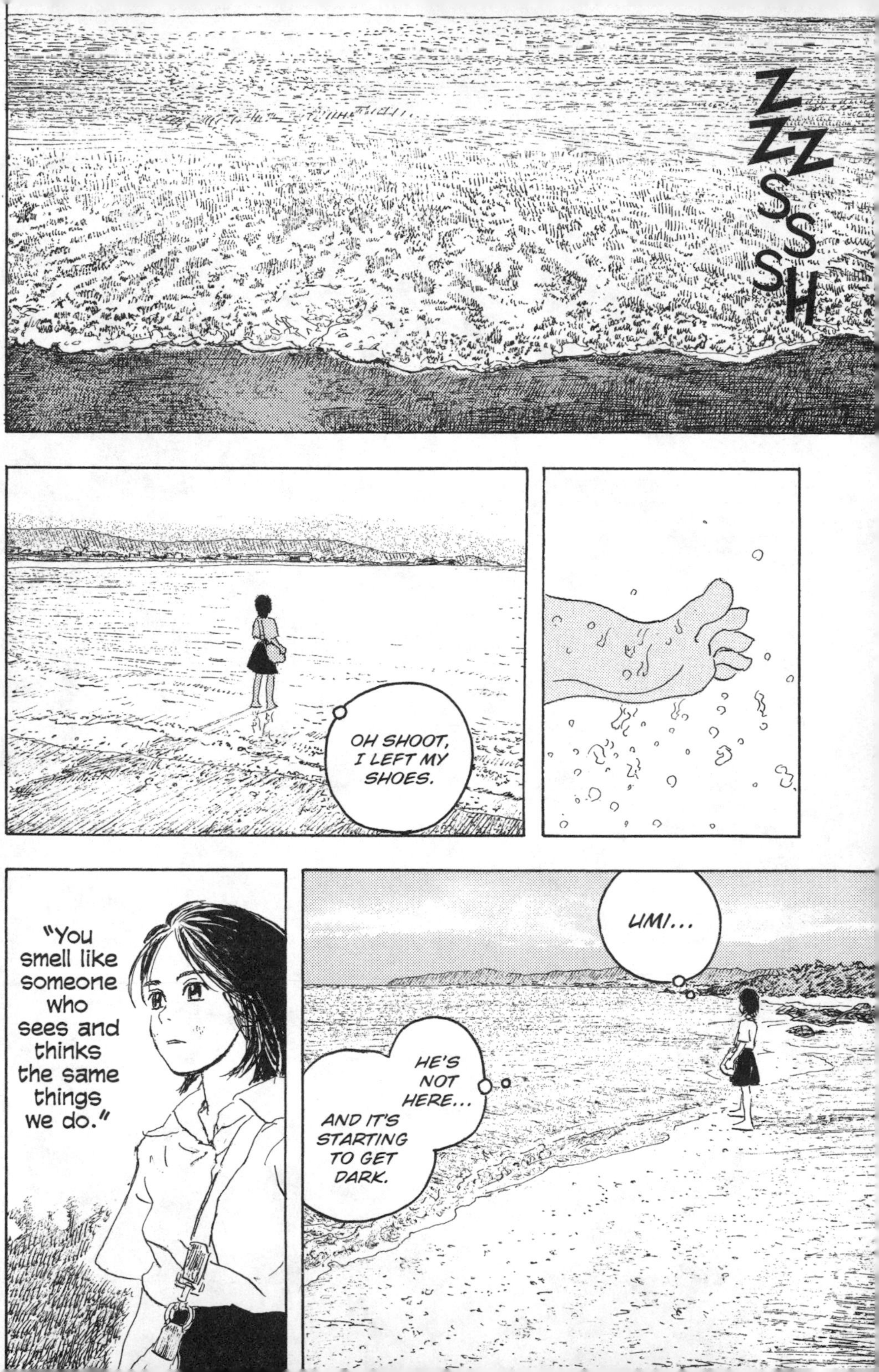
ZZZSSSH
OH SHOOT, I LEFT MY SHOES.
UMI...
HE'S NOT HERE... AND IT'S STARTING TO GET DARK.
"You smell like someone who sees and thinks the same things we do."

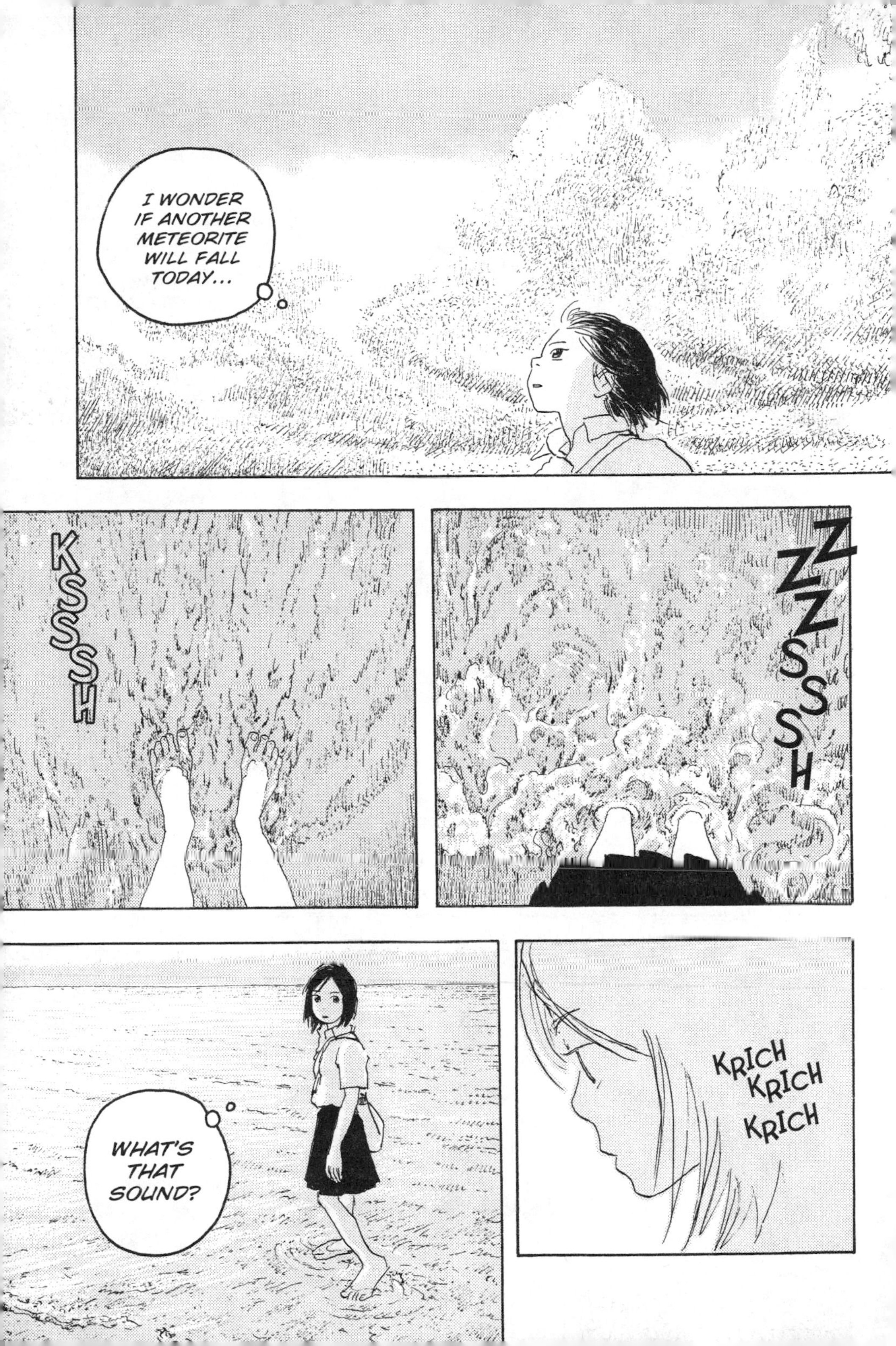
I WONDER IF ANOTHER METEORITE WILL FALL TODAY...
ZZZSSSH
KSSSH
KRICH KRICH KRICH
WHAT'S THAT SOUND?

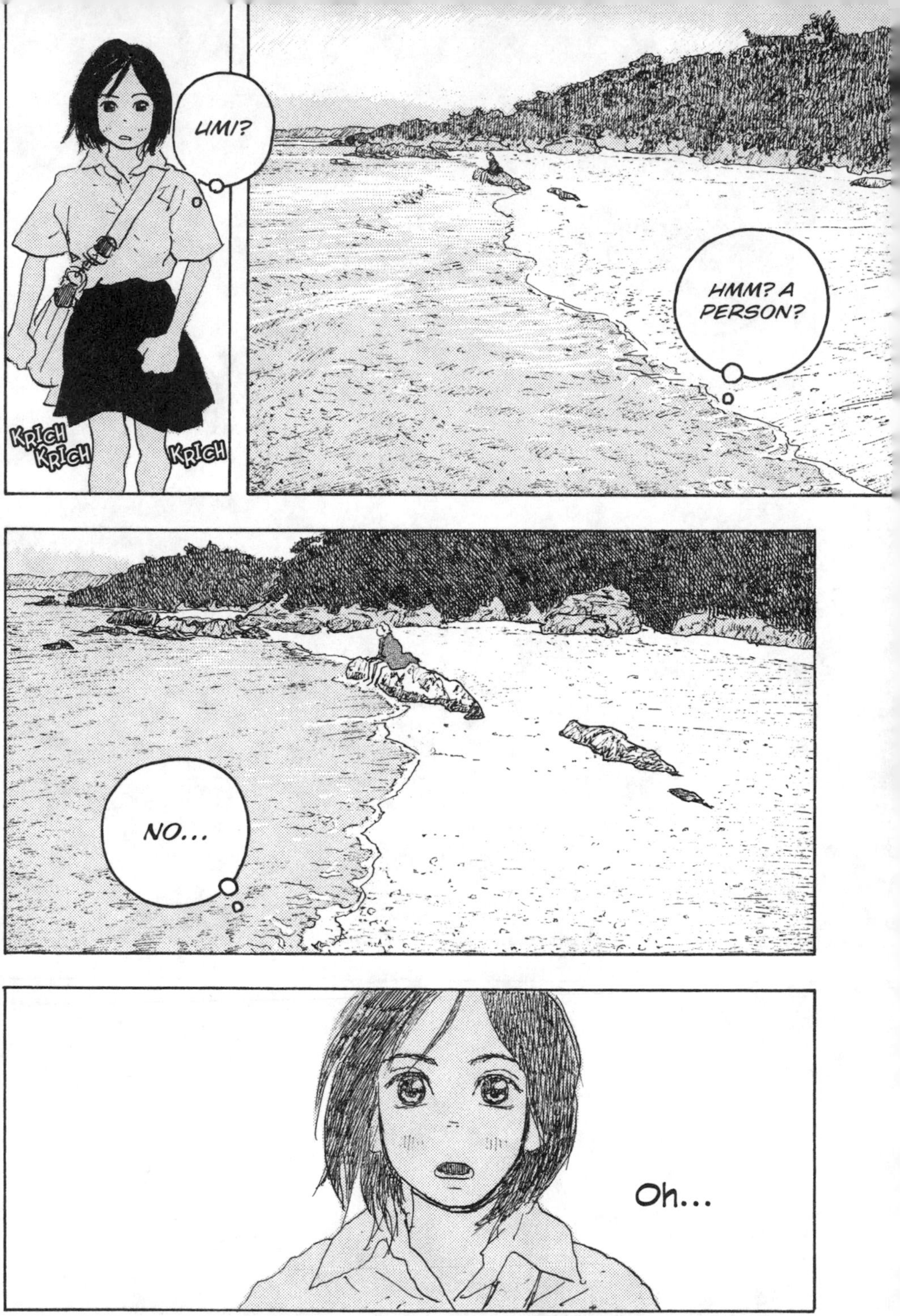
HMM? A PERSON?
UMI?
KRICH
KRICH KRICH
NO...
Oh...

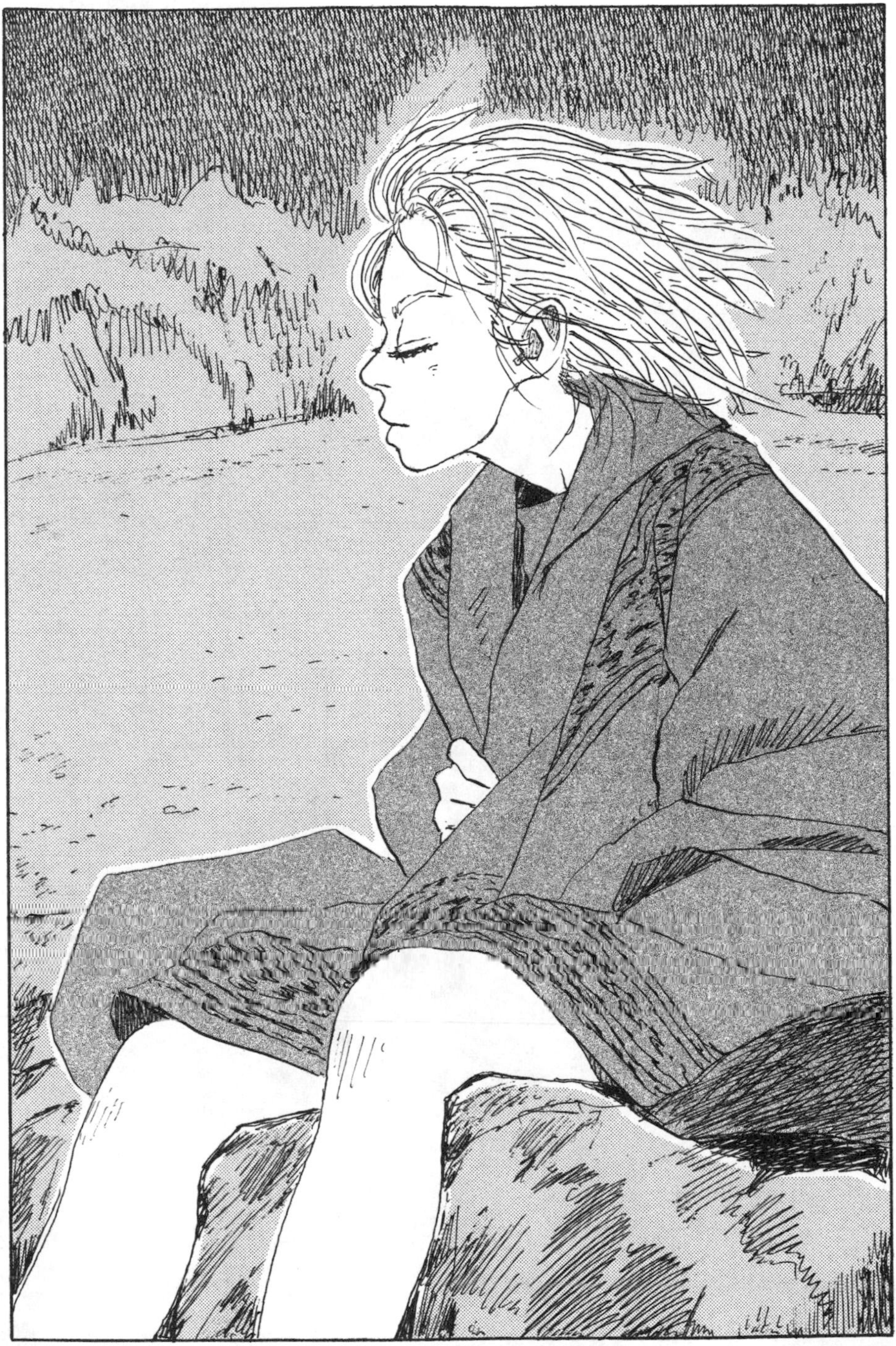

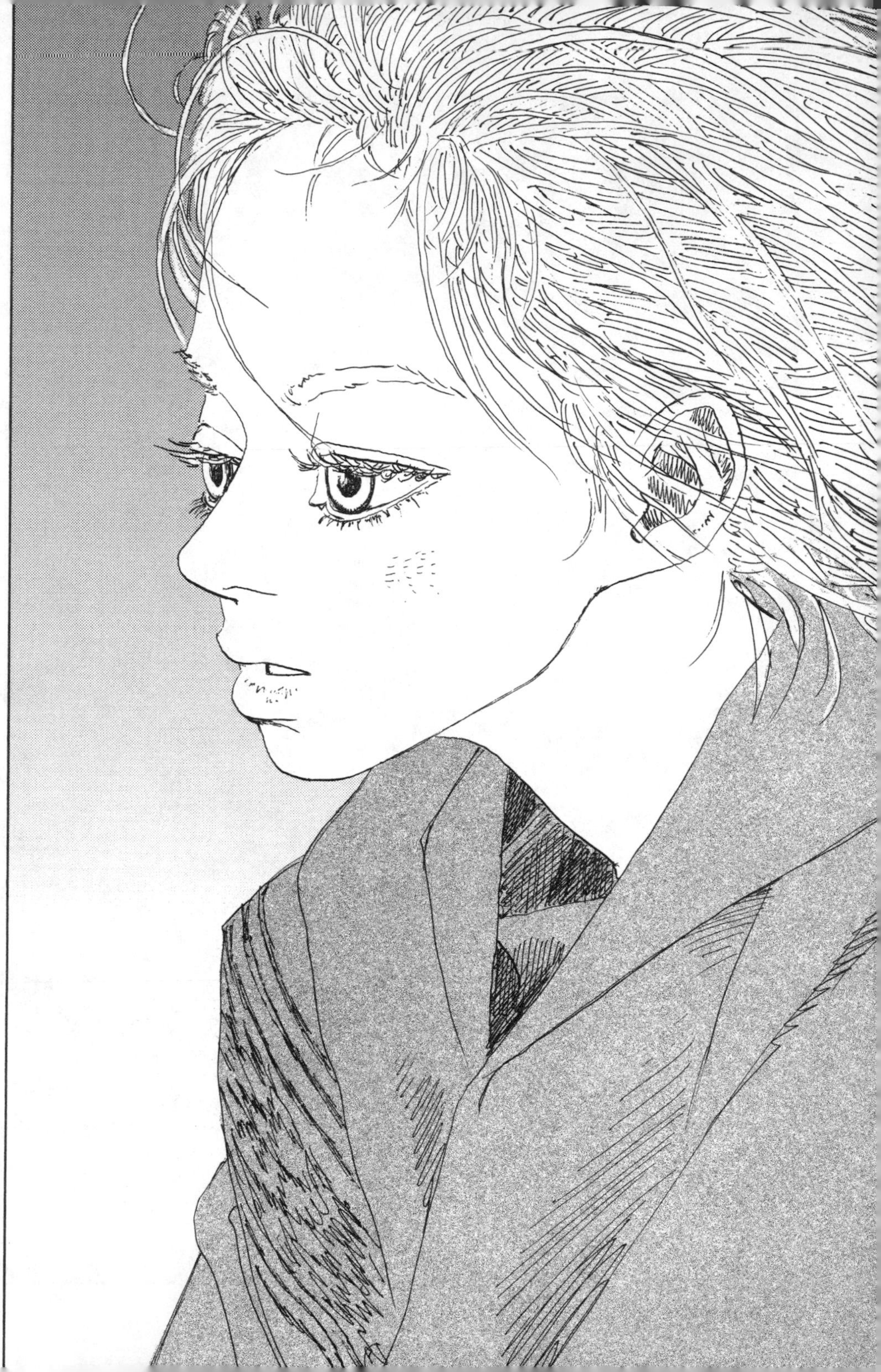

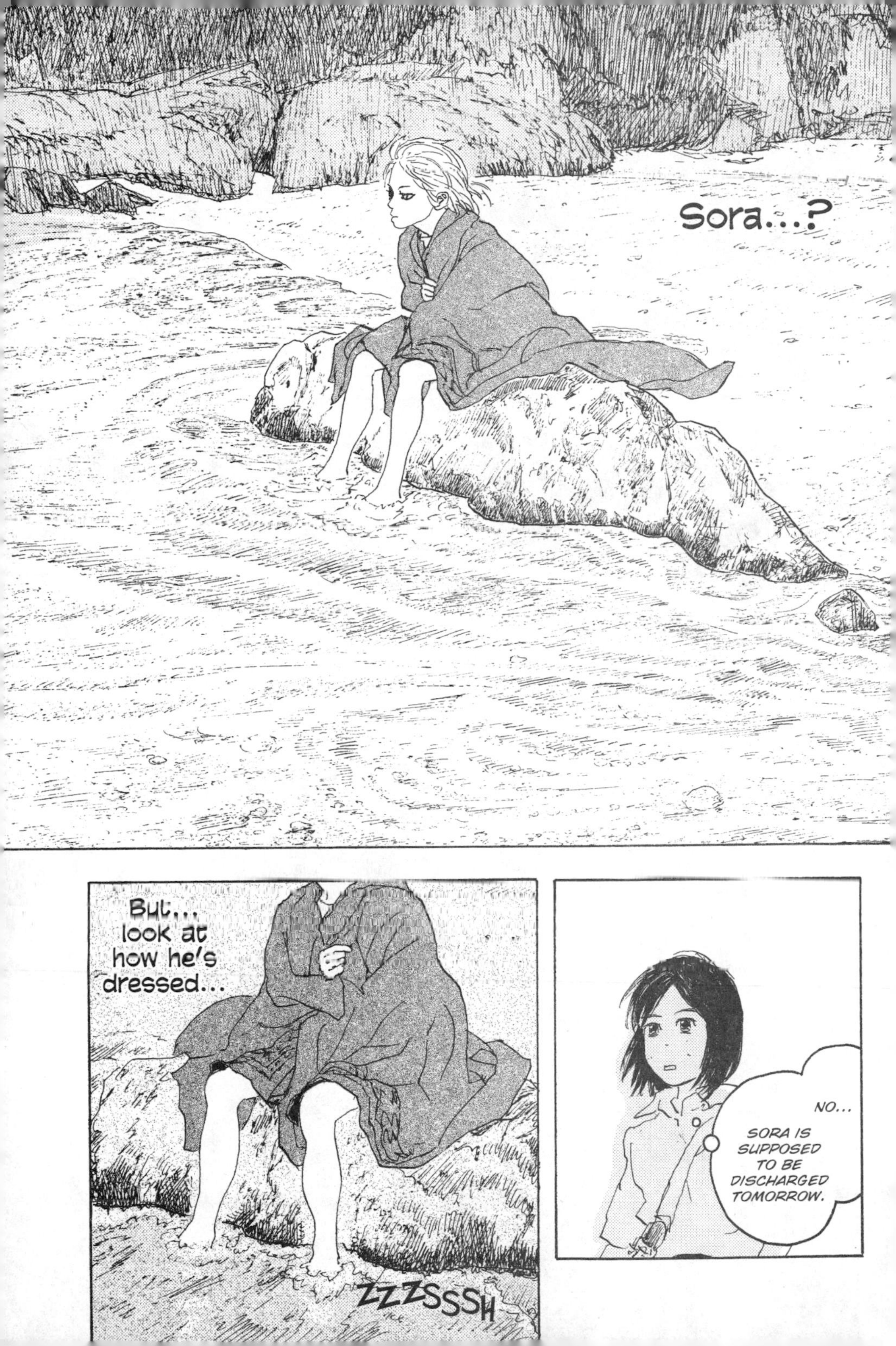
Sora...?
NO...
SORA IS SUPPOSED TO BE DISCHARGED TOMORROW.
But... look at how he's dressed...
ZZZSSSH

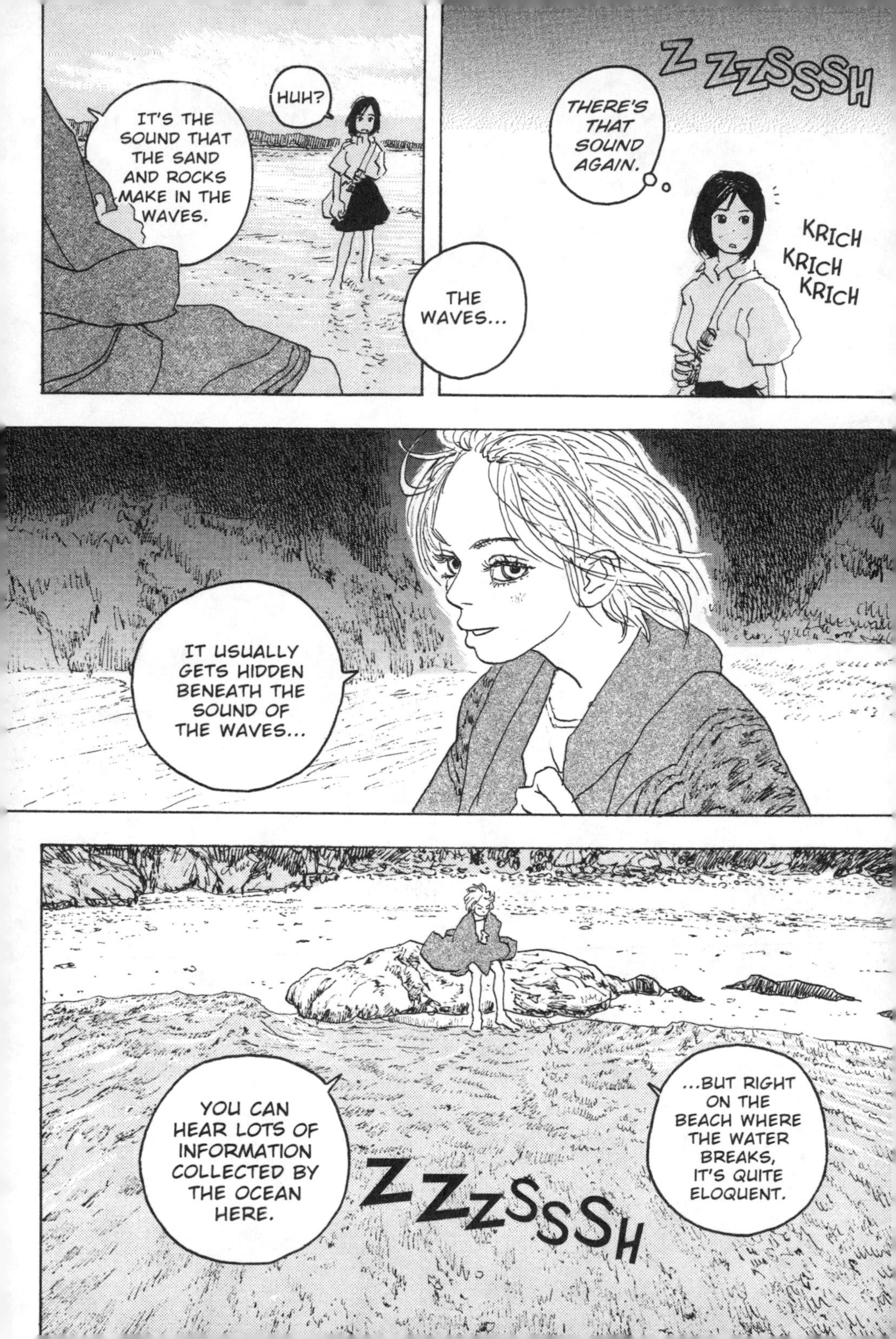
Z ZZSSSH
THERE'S THAT SOUND AGAIN.
KRICH KRICH KRICH
THE WAVES...
HUH?
IT'S THE SOUND THAT THE SAND AND ROCKS MAKE IN THE WAVES.
IT USUALLY GETS HIDDEN BENEATH THE SOUND OF THE WAVES...
...BUT RIGHT ON THE BEACH WHERE THE WATER BREAKS, IT'S QUITE ELOQUENT.
ZZZSSSH
YOU CAN HEAR LOTS OF INFORMATION COLLECTED BY THE OCEAN HERE.

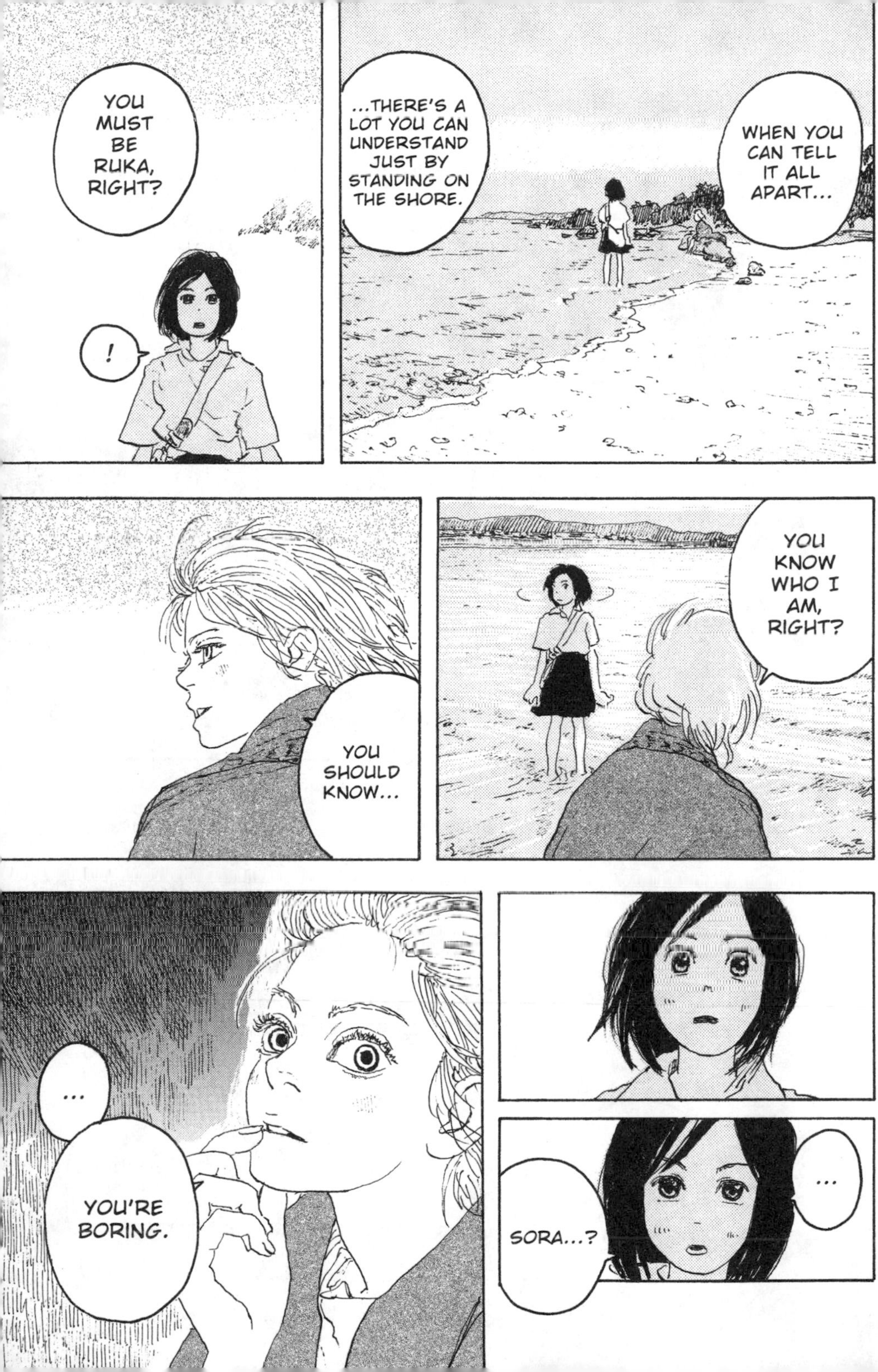
WHEN YOU CAN TELL IT ALL APART...
...THERE'S A LOT YOU CAN UNDERSTAND JUST BY STANDING ON THE SHORE.
YOU MUST BE RUKA, RIGHT?
!
YOU KNOW WHO I AM, RIGHT?
YOU SHOULD KNOW...
...
SORA...?
...
YOU'RE BORING.

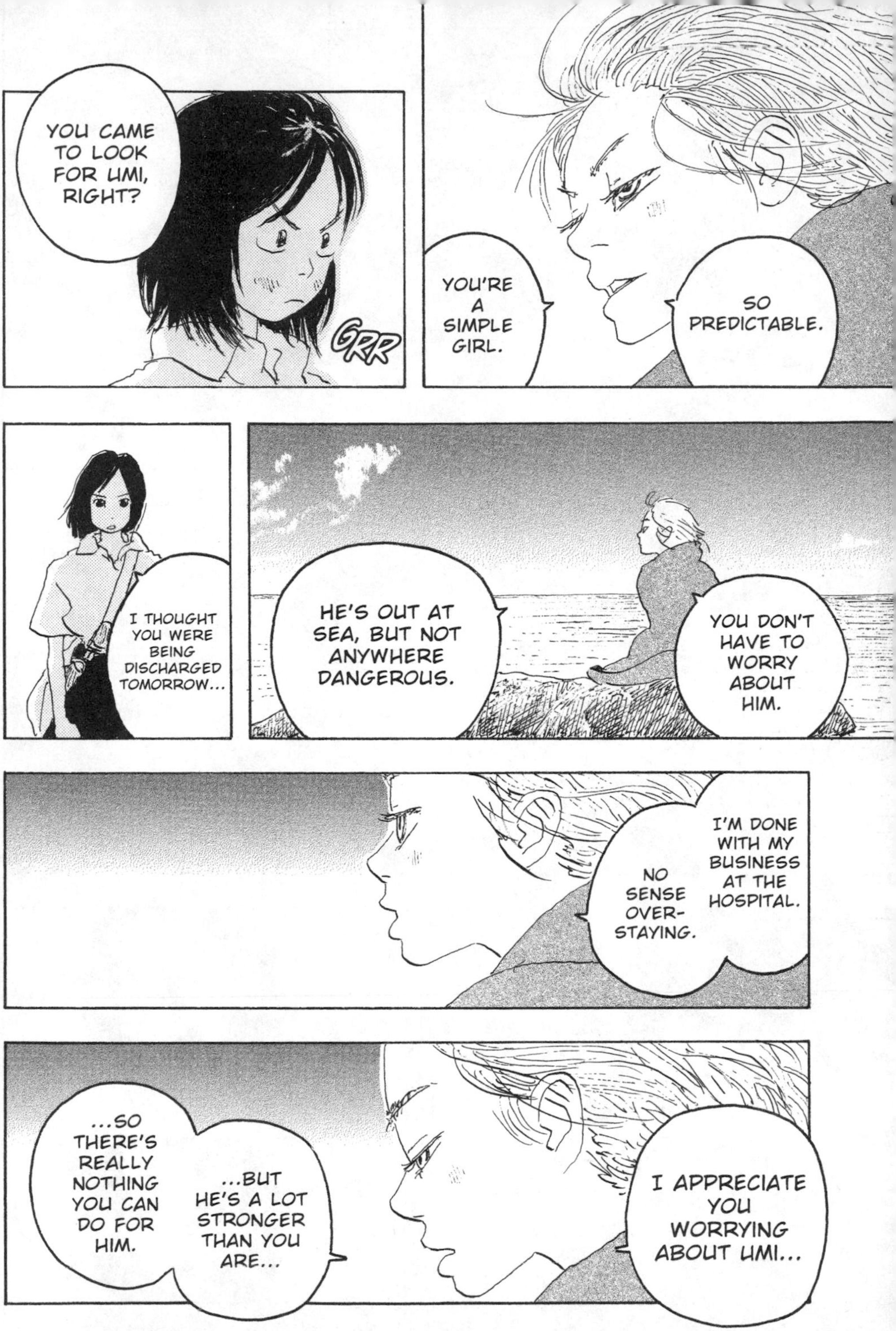
SO PREDICTABLE.
YOU'RE A SIMPLE GIRL.
YOU CAME TO LOOK FOR UMI, RIGHT?
GRR
YOU DON'T HAVE TO WORRY ABOUT HIM.
HE'S OUT AT SEA, BUT NOT ANYWHERE DANGEROUS.
I THOUGHT YOU WERE BEING DISCHARGED TOMORROW...
I'M DONE WITH MY BUSINESS AT THE HOSPITAL.
NO SENSE OVER-STAYING.
I APPRECIATE YOU WORRYING ABOUT UMI...
...BUT HE'S A LOT STRONGER THAN YOU ARE...
...SO THERE'S REALLY NOTHING YOU CAN DO FOR HIM.

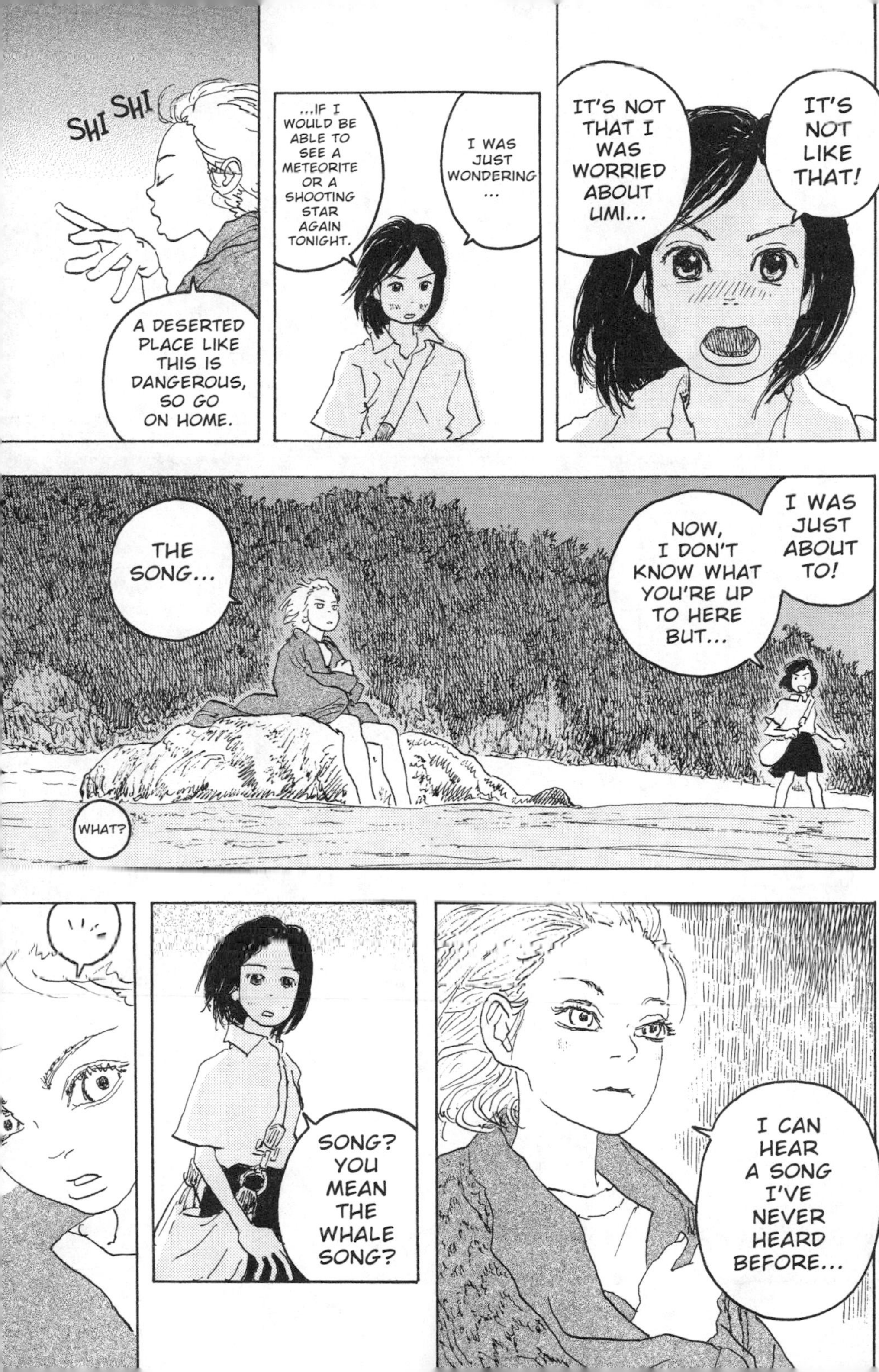
IT'S NOT LIKE THAT!
IT'S NOT THAT I WAS WORRIED ABOUT UMI...
I WAS JUST WONDERING...
...IF I WOULD BE ABLE TO SEE A METEORITE OR A SHOOTING STAR AGAIN TONIGHT.
SHI SHI
A DESERTED PLACE LIKE THIS IS DANGEROUS, SO GO ON HOME.
I WAS JUST ABOUT TO!
NOW, I DON'T KNOW WHAT YOU'RE UP TO HERE BUT...
THE SONG...
WHAT?
I CAN HEAR A SONG I'VE NEVER HEARD BEFORE...
SONG? YOU MEAN THE WHALE SONG?
!

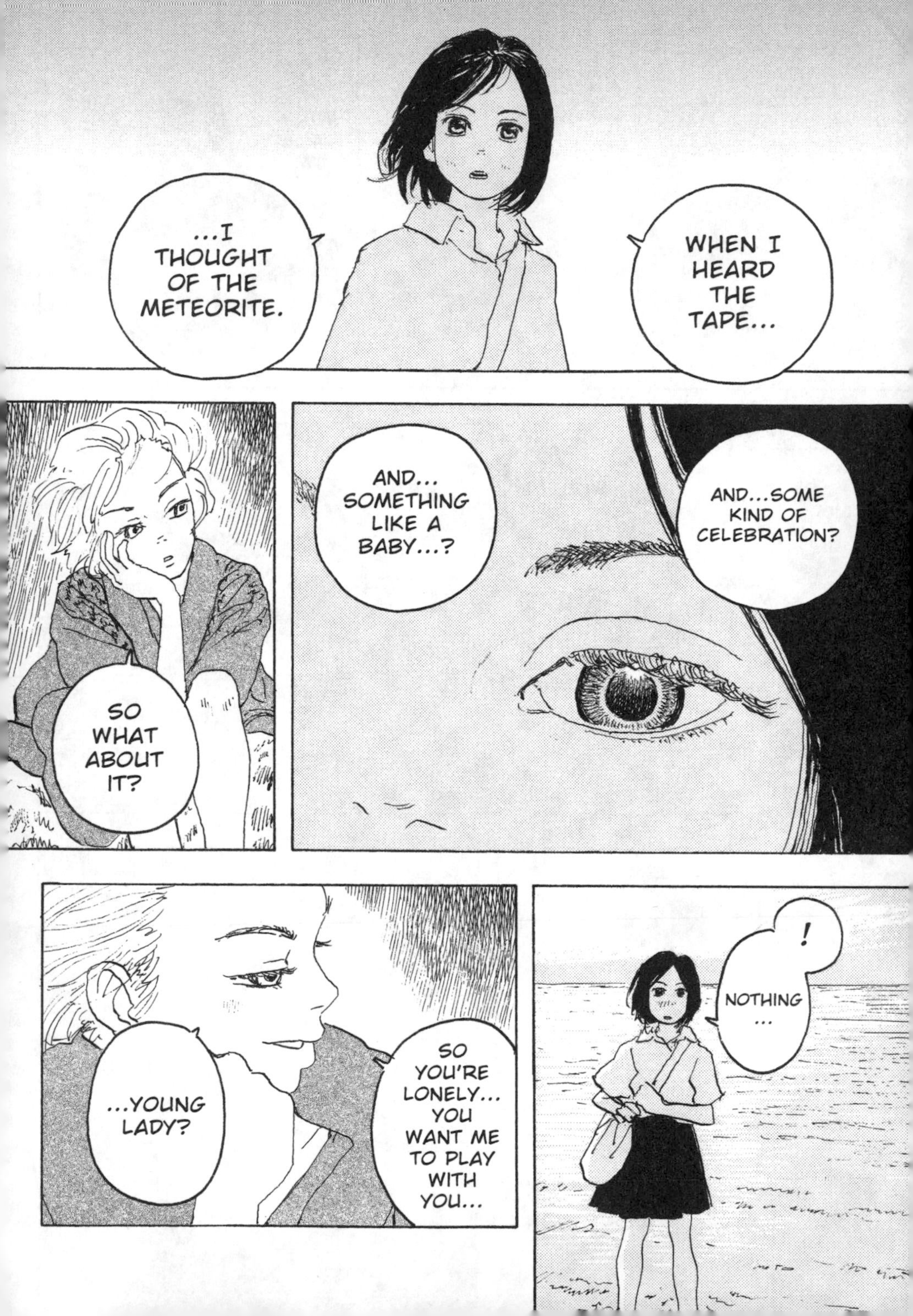
WHEN I HEARD THE TAPE...
...I THOUGHT OF THE METEORITE.
AND...SOME KIND OF CELEBRATION?
AND... SOMETHING LIKE A BABY...?
SO WHAT ABOUT IT?
!
NOTHING ...
SO YOU'RE LONELY... YOU WANT ME TO PLAY WITH YOU...
...YOUNG LADY?

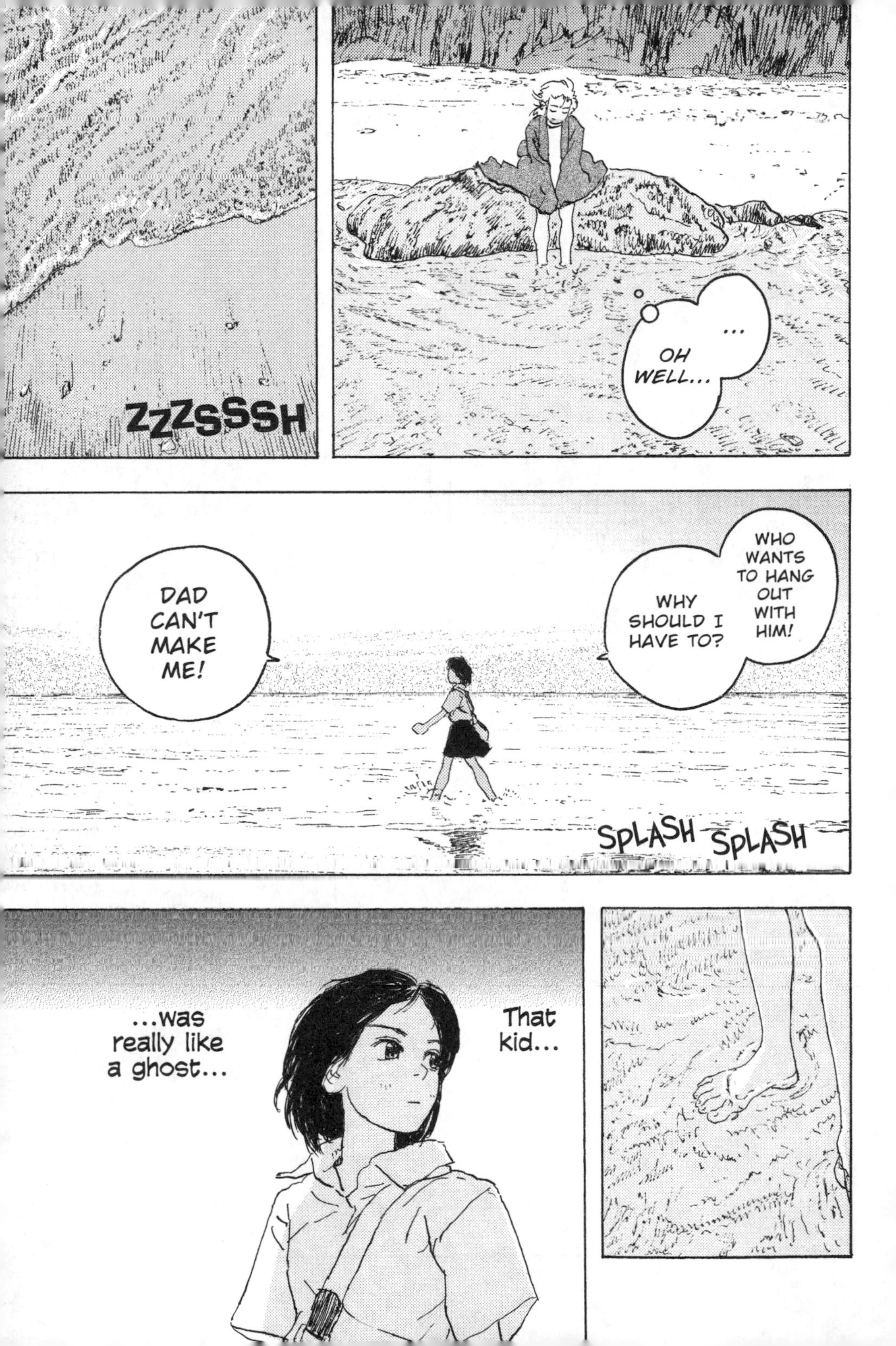
...
OH WELL...
ZZZSSSH
WHO WANTS TO HANG OUT WITH HIM!
WHY SHOULD I HAVE TO?
DAD CAN'T MAKE ME!
SPLASH SPLASH
That kid...
...was really like a ghost...

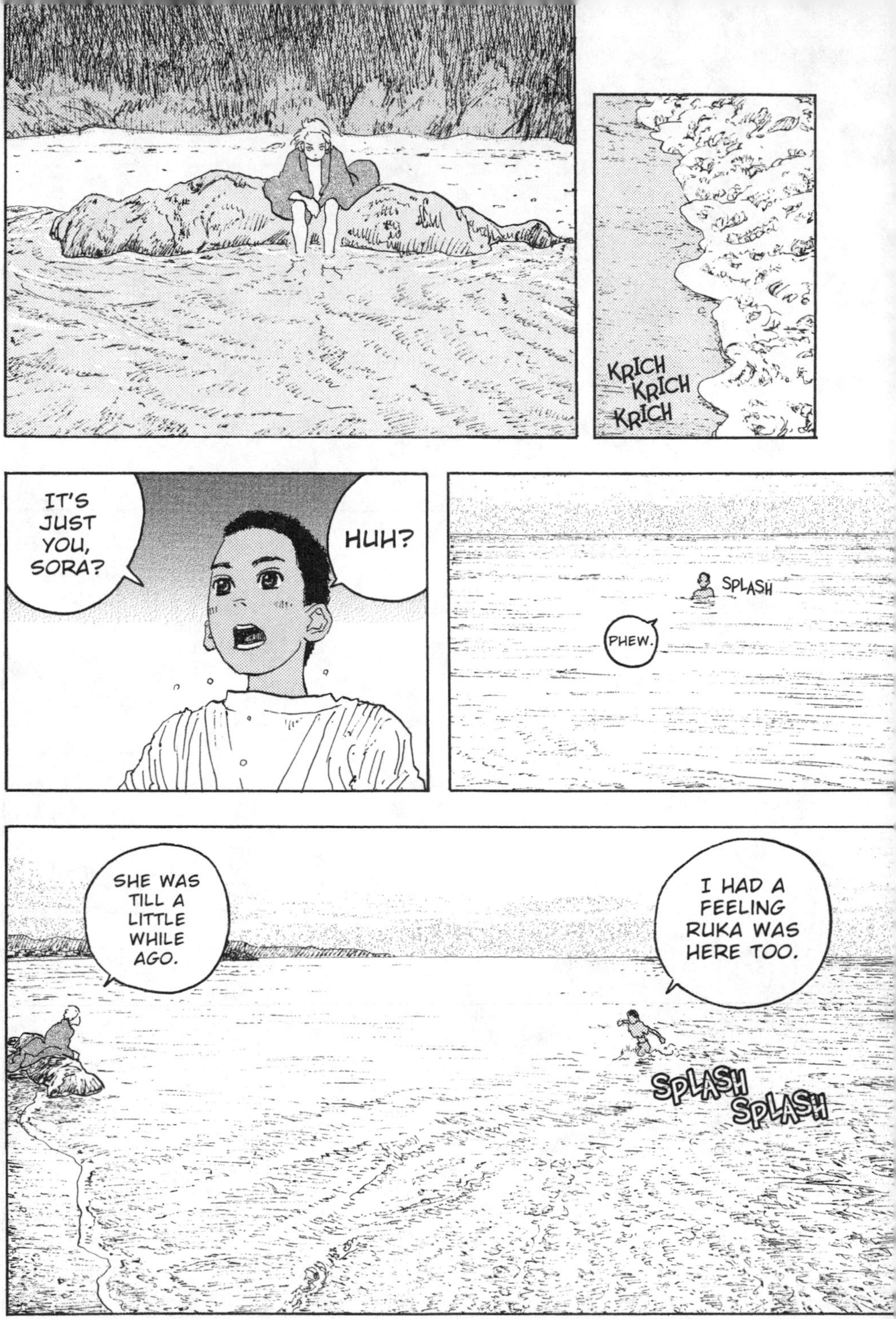
KRICH KRICH KRICH
SPLASH
PHEW.
HUH?
IT'S JUST YOU, SORA?
I HAD A FEELING RUKA WAS HERE TOO.
SHE WAS TILL A LITTLE WHILE AGO.
SPLASH SPLASH

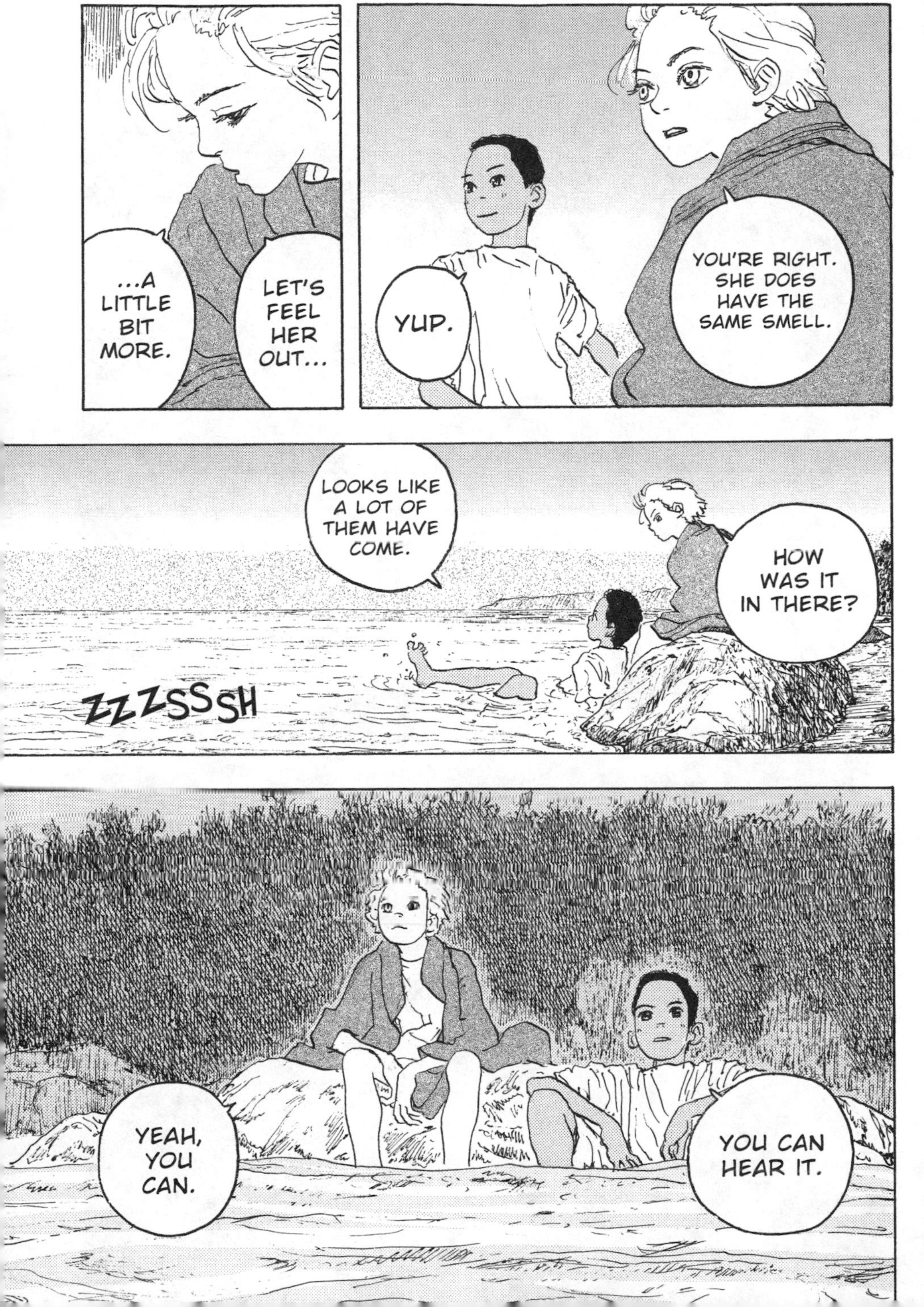
YOU'RE RIGHT. SHE DOES HAVE THE SAME SMELL.
YUP.
LET'S FEEL HER OUT...
...A LITTLE BIT MORE.
HOW WAS IT IN THERE?
LOOKS LIKE A LOT OF THEM HAVE COME.
ZZZSSSH
YOU CAN HEAR IT.
YEAH, YOU CAN.

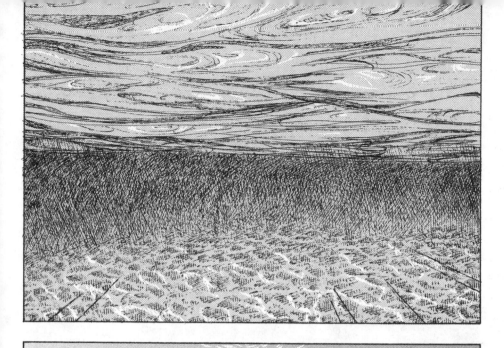

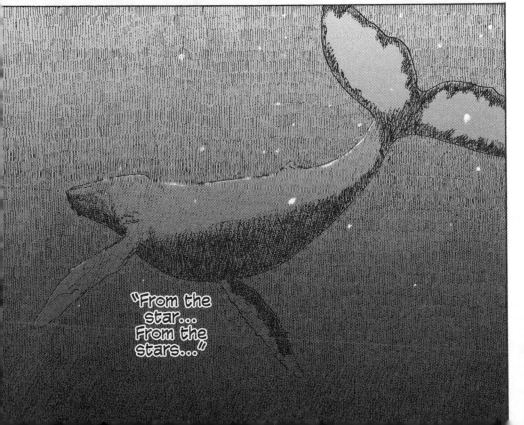

"From the star... From the stars..."

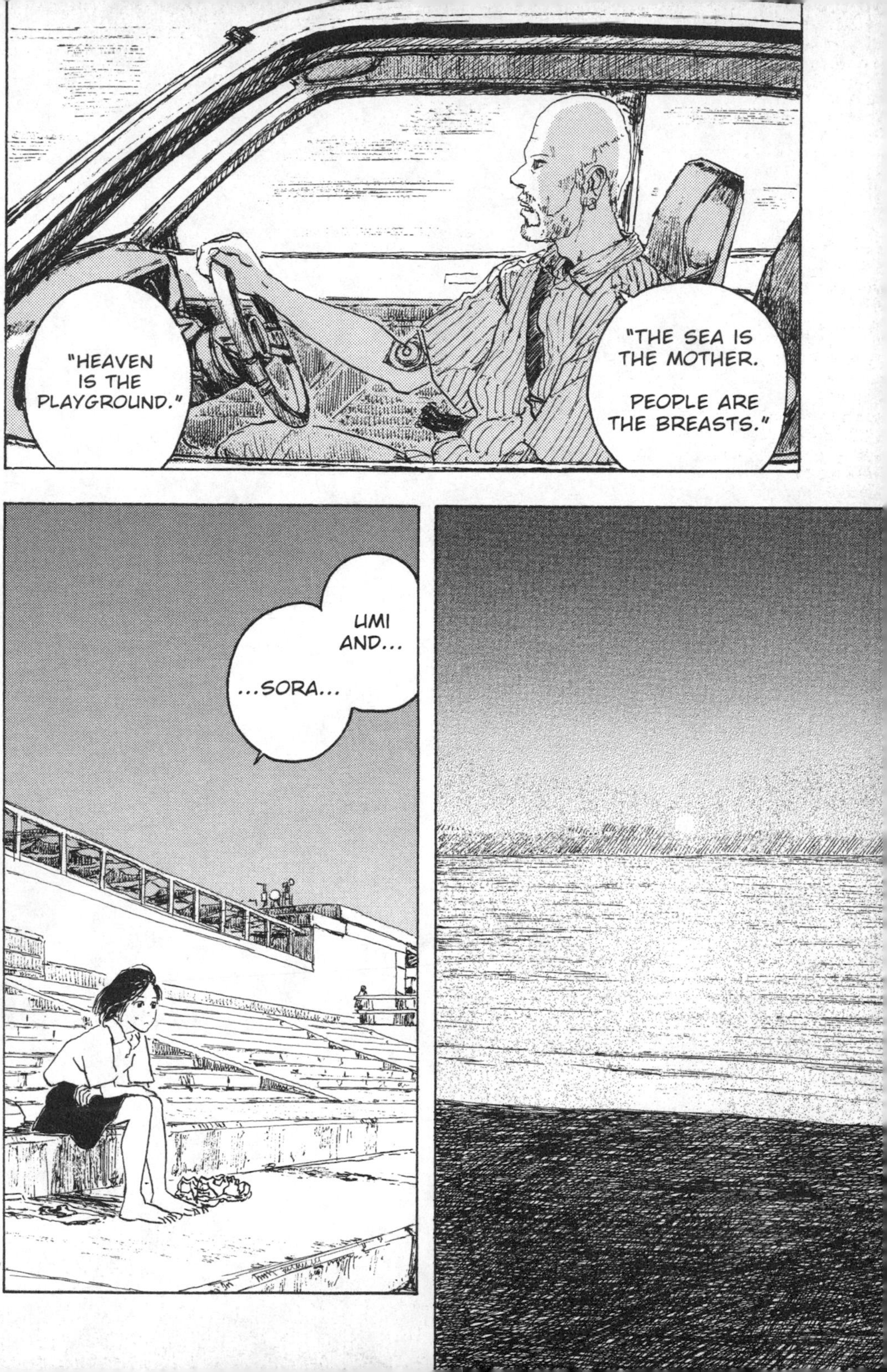
"THE SEA IS THE MOTHER.
PEOPLE ARE THE BREASTS."
"HEAVEN IS THE PLAYGROUND."
UMI AND...
...SORA...

Chapter 5: Patterns

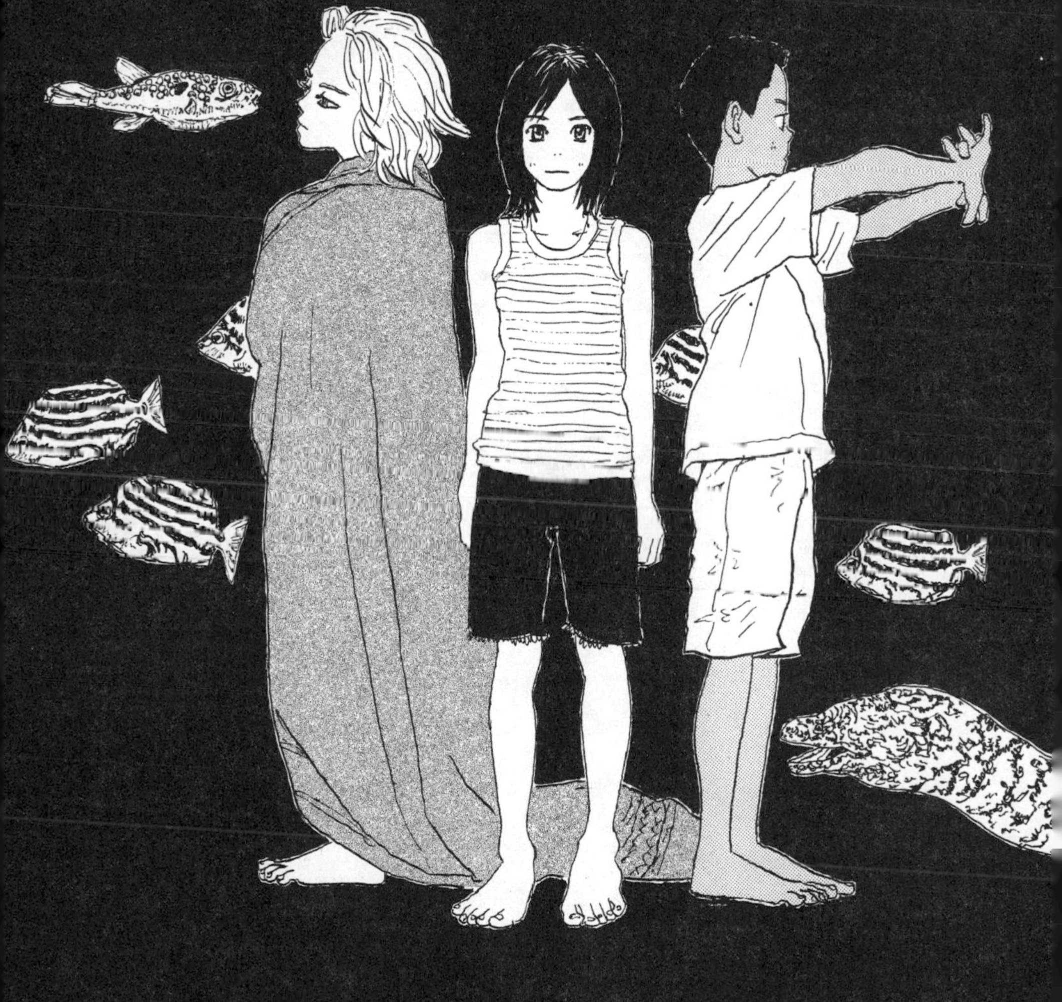

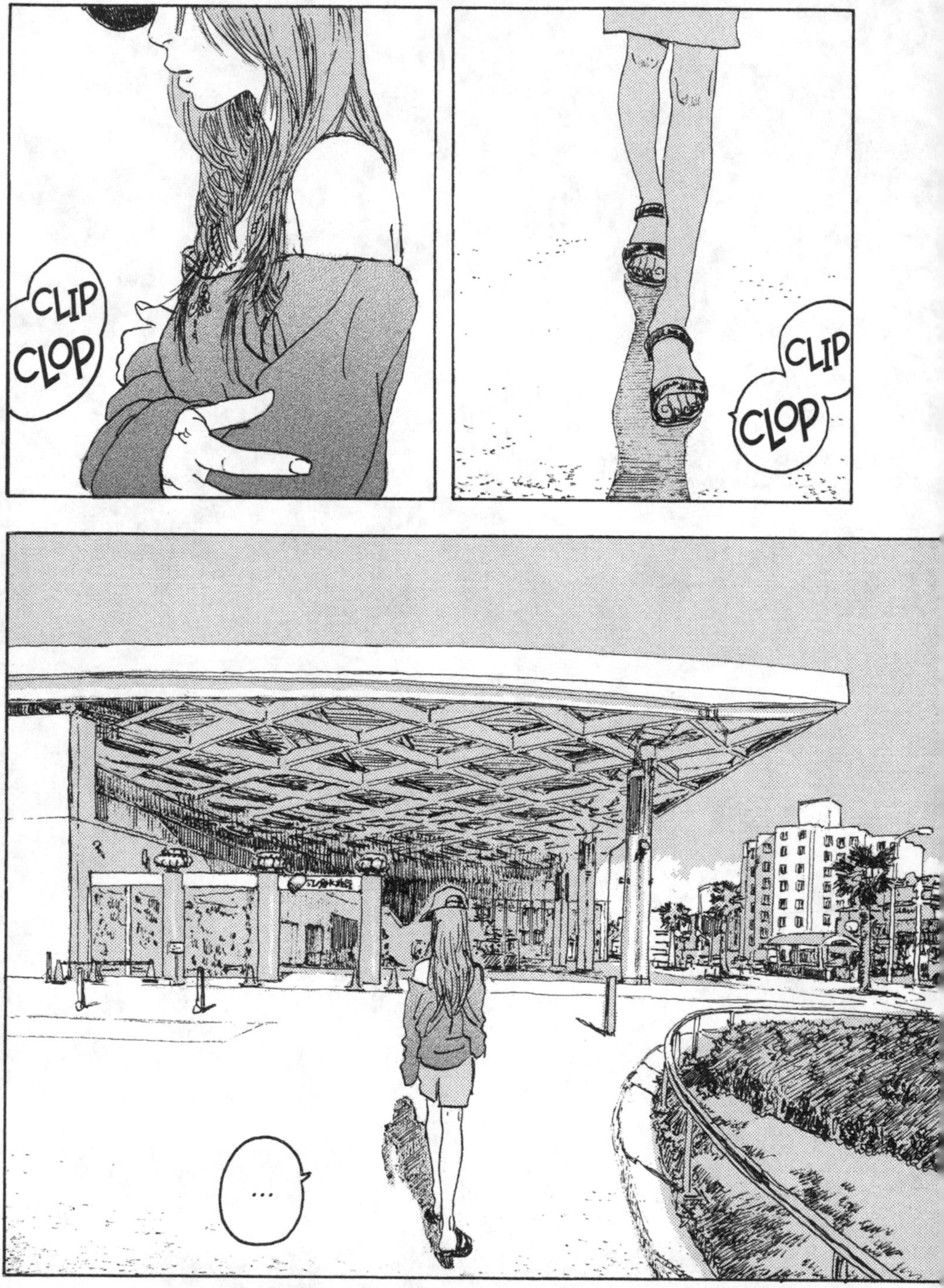
CLIP CLOP
CLIP CLOP
...

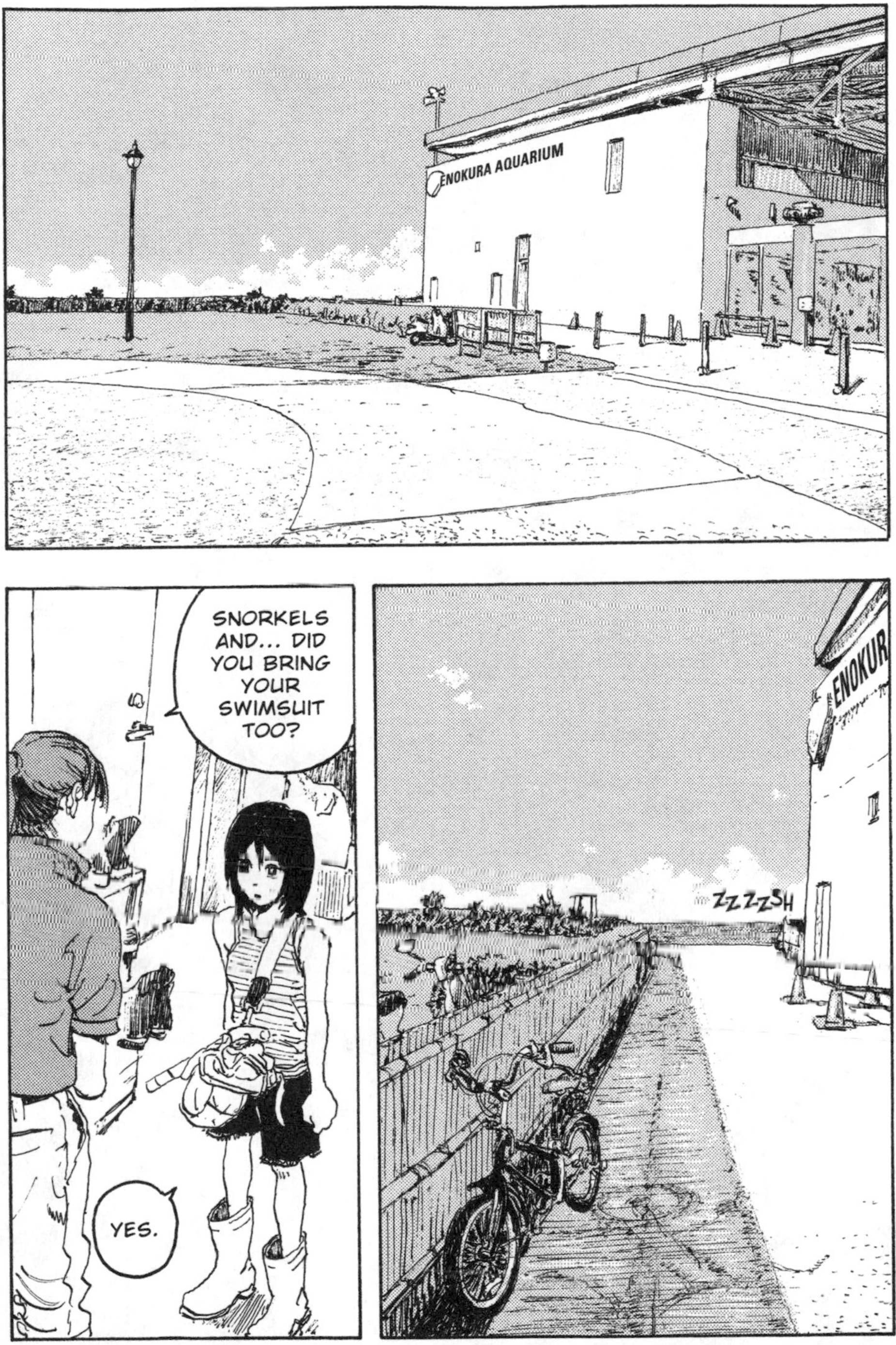
ENOKURA AQUARIUM
ENOKUR
ZZZ-ZSH
SNORKELS AND... DID YOU BRING YOUR SWIMSUIT TOO?
YES.

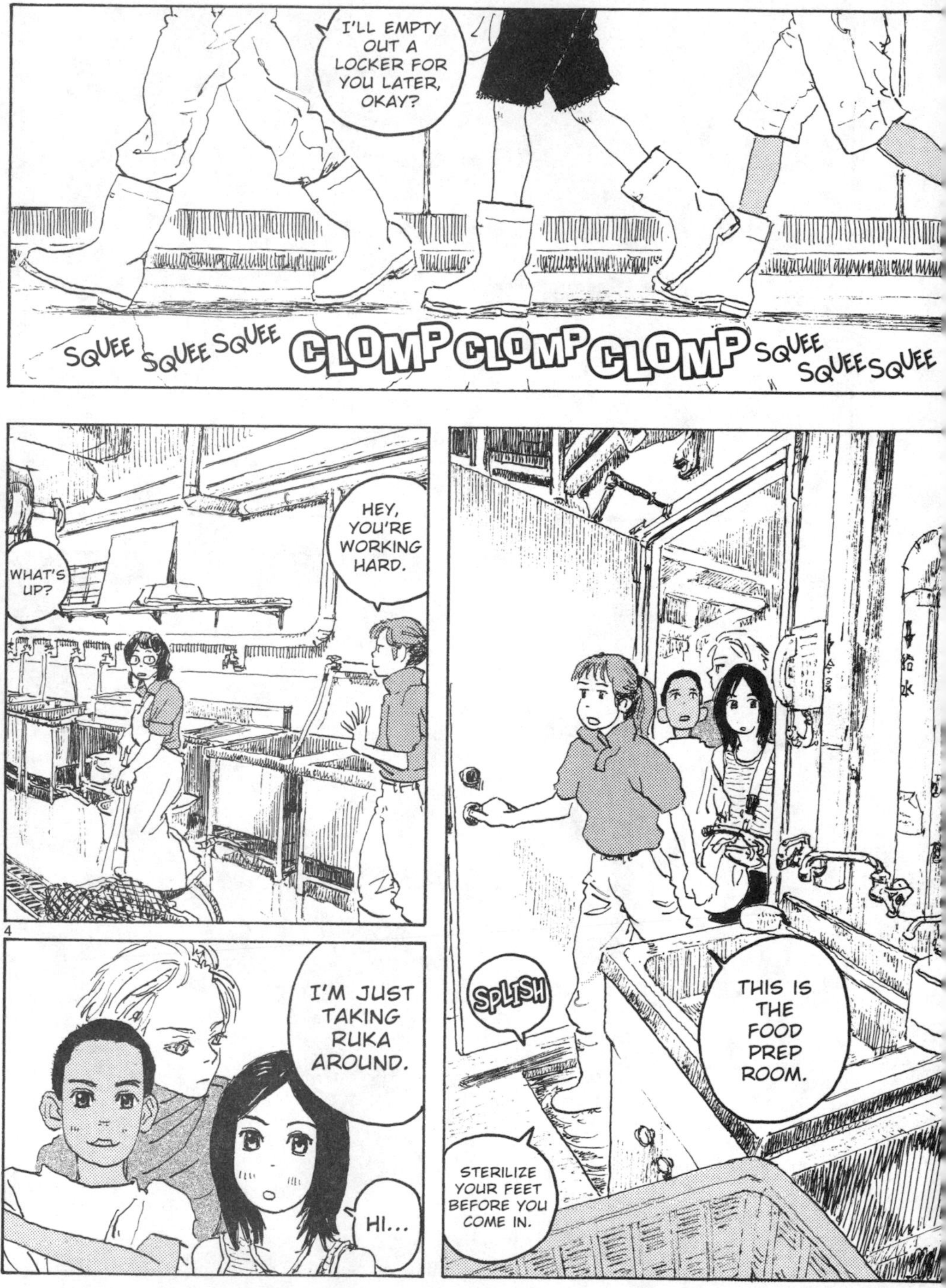
I'LL EMPTY OUT A LOCKER FOR YOU LATER, OKAY?
SQUEE SQUEE SQUEE
CLOMP CLOMP CLOMP
SQUEE SQUEE SQUEE
THIS IS THE FOOD PREP ROOM.
SPLISH
STERILIZE YOUR FEET BEFORE YOU COME IN.
HEY, YOU'RE WORKING HARD.
WHAT'S UP?
I'M JUST TAKING RUKA AROUND.
HI...

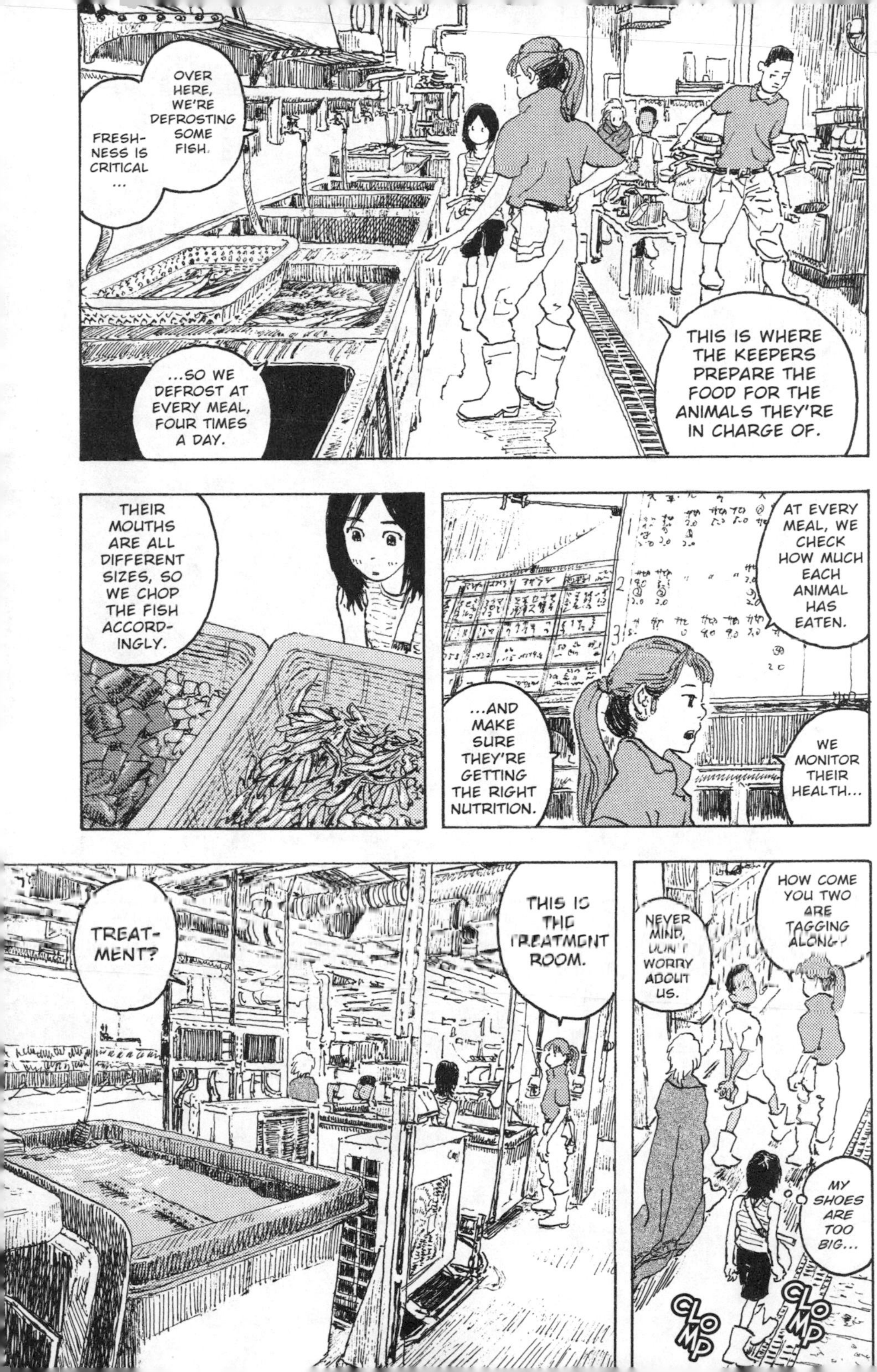
THIS IS WHERE THE KEEPERS PREPARE THE FOOD FOR THE ANIMALS THEY'RE IN CHARGE OF.
OVER HERE, WE'RE DEFROSTING SOME FISH.
FRESHNESS IS CRITICAL...
...SO WE DEFROST AT EVERY MEAL, FOUR TIMES A DAY.
AT EVERY MEAL, WE CHECK HOW MUCH EACH ANIMAL HAS EATEN.
WE MONITOR THEIR HEALTH...
...AND MAKE SURE THEY'RE GETTING THE RIGHT NUTRITION.
THEIR MOUTHS ARE ALL DIFFERENT SIZES, SO WE CHOP THE FISH ACCORDINGLY.
HOW COME YOU TWO ARE TAGGING ALONG?
NEVER MIND, DON'T WORRY ABOUT US.
MY SHOES ARE TOO BIG...
CLOMP
CLOMP
THIS IS THE TREATMENT ROOM.
TREATMENT?

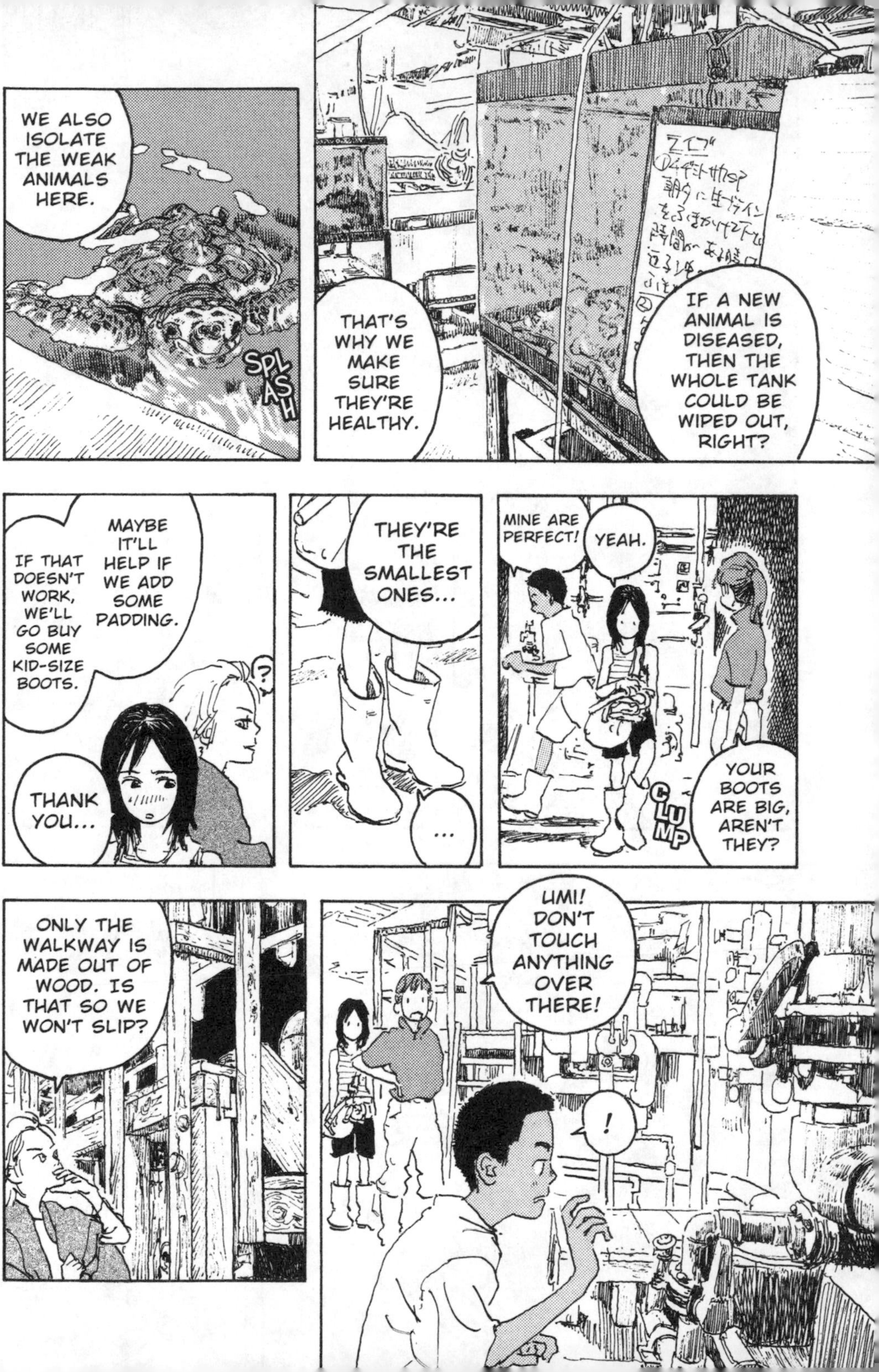
IF A NEW ANIMAL IS DISEASED, THEN THE WHOLE TANK COULD BE WIPED OUT, RIGHT?
THAT'S WHY WE MAKE SURE THEY'RE HEALTHY.
WE ALSO ISOLATE THE WEAK ANIMALS HERE.
SPLASH
YEAH.
MINE ARE PERFECT!
YOUR BOOTS ARE BIG, AREN'T THEY?
CLUMP
THEY'RE THE SMALLEST ONES...
...
MAYBE IT'LL HELP IF WE ADD SOME PADDING.
IF THAT DOESN'T WORK, WE'LL GO BUY SOME KID-SIZE BOOTS.
?
THANK YOU...
UMI! DON'T TOUCH ANYTHING OVER THERE!
!
ONLY THE WALKWAY IS MADE OUT OF WOOD. IS THAT SO WE WON'T SLIP?

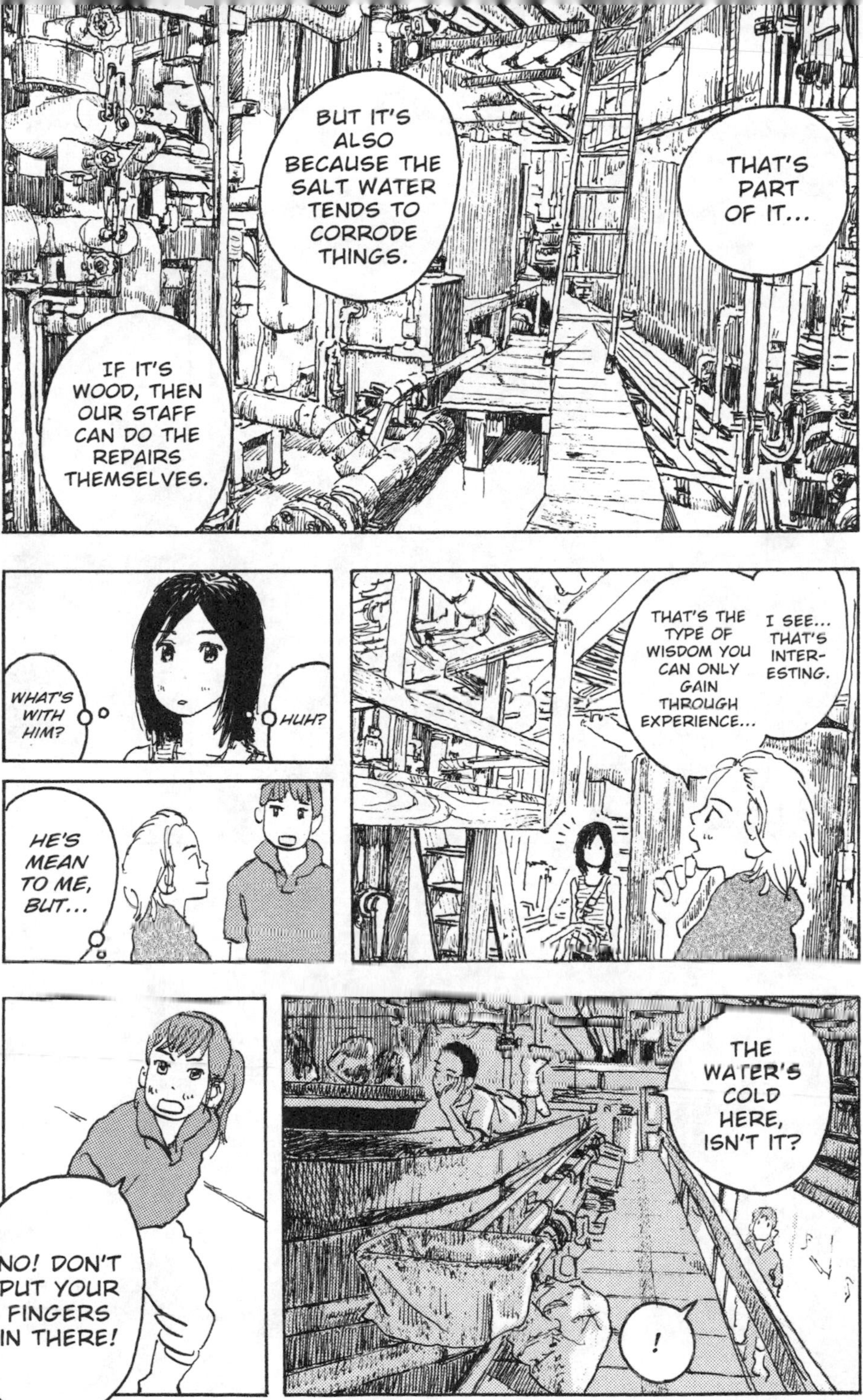
THAT'S PART OF IT...
BUT IT'S ALSO BECAUSE THE SALT WATER TENDS TO CORRODE THINGS.
IF IT'S WOOD, THEN OUR STAFF CAN DO THE REPAIRS THEMSELVES.
I SEE... THAT'S INTER-ESTING.
THAT'S THE TYPE OF WISDOM YOU CAN ONLY GAIN THROUGH EXPERIENCE...
HUH?
WHAT'S WITH HIM?
HE'S MEAN TO ME, BUT...
THE WATER'S COLD HERE, ISN'T IT?
!
NO! DON'T PUT YOUR FINGERS IN THERE!

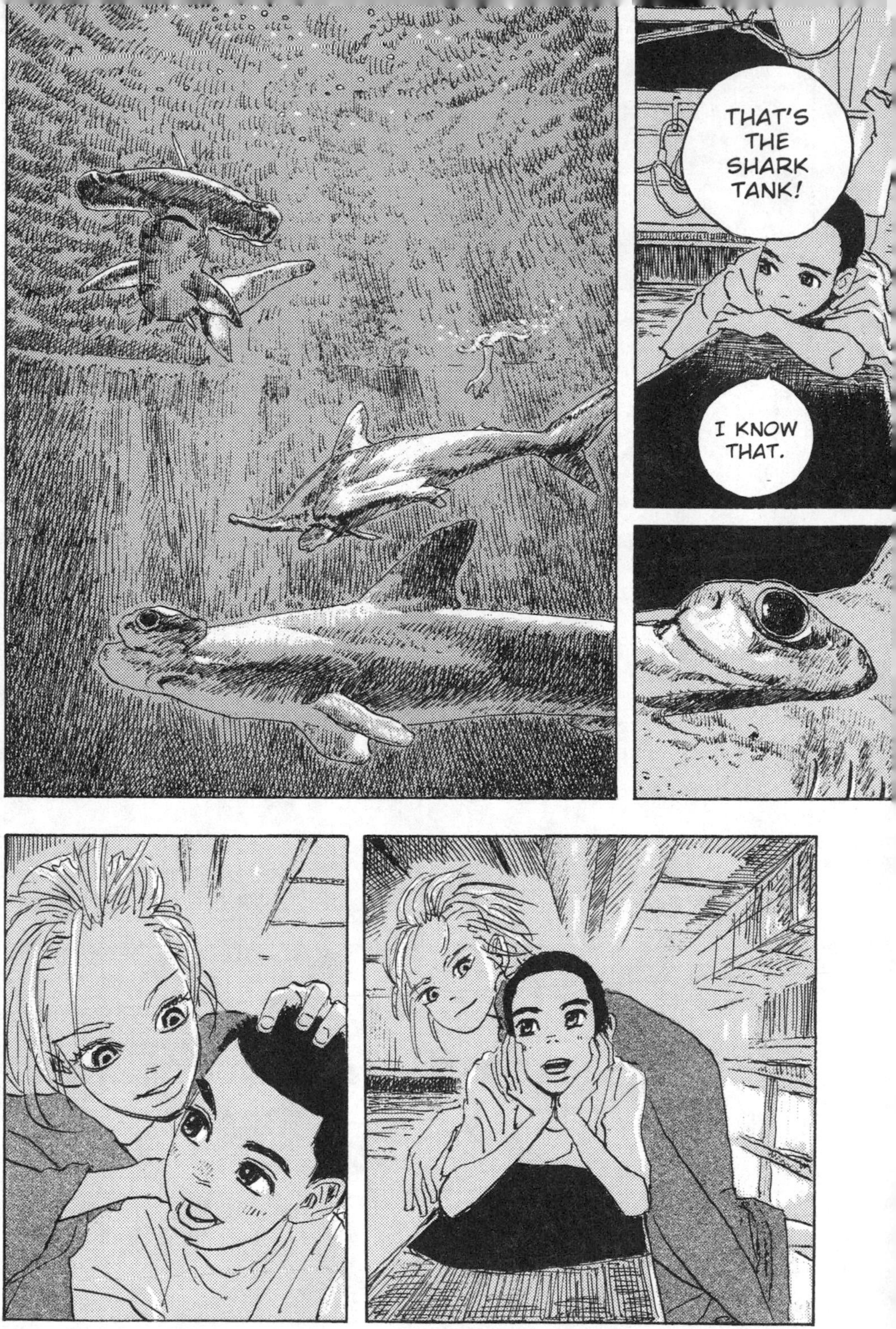
THAT'S THE SHARK TANK!
I KNOW THAT.

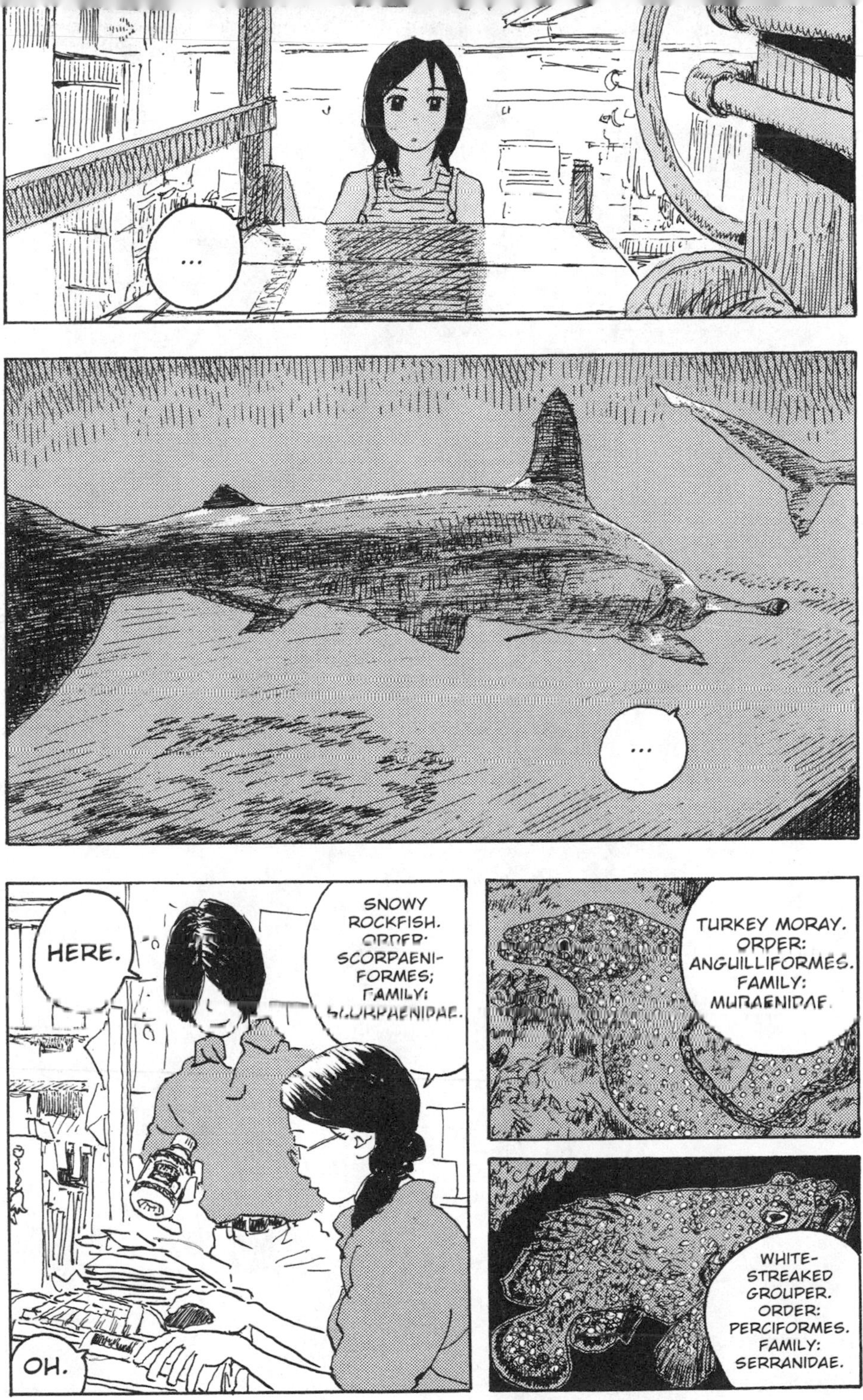
...
...
TURKEY MORAY. ORDER: ANGUILLIFORMES. FAMILY: MURAENIDAE.
WHITE-STREAKED GROUPER. ORDER: PERCIFORMES. FAMILY: SERRANIDAE.
SNOWY ROCKFISH. ORDER: SCORPAENIFORMES; FAMILY: SCORPAENIDAE.
HERE.
OH.

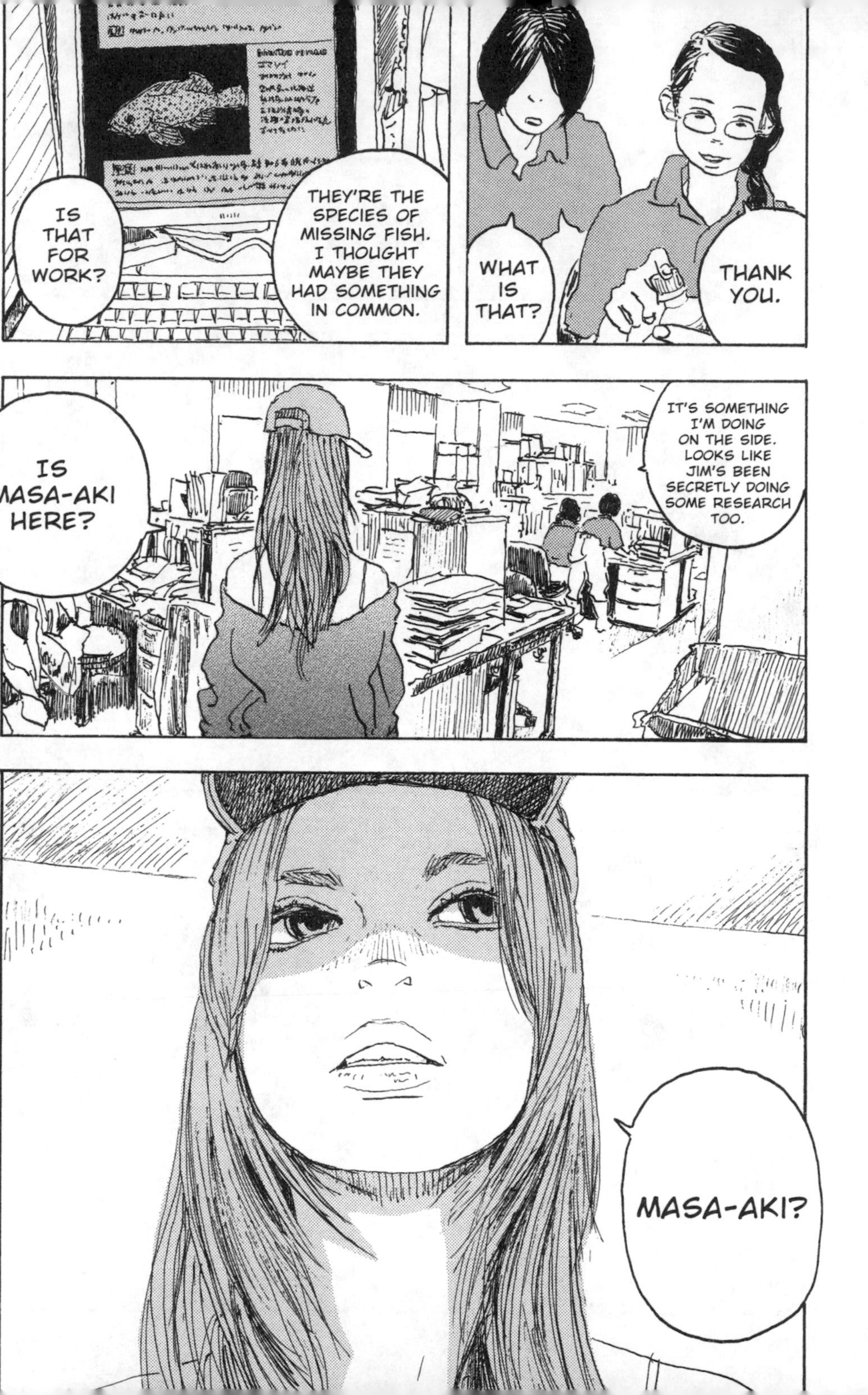
THANK YOU.
WHAT IS THAT?
THEY'RE THE SPECIES OF MISSING FISH. I THOUGHT MAYBE THEY HAD SOMETHING IN COMMON.
IS THAT FOR WORK?
IT'S SOMETHING I'M DOING ON THE SIDE. LOOKS LIKE JIM'S BEEN SECRETLY DOING SOME RESEARCH TOO.
IS MASA-AKI HERE?
MASA-AKI?

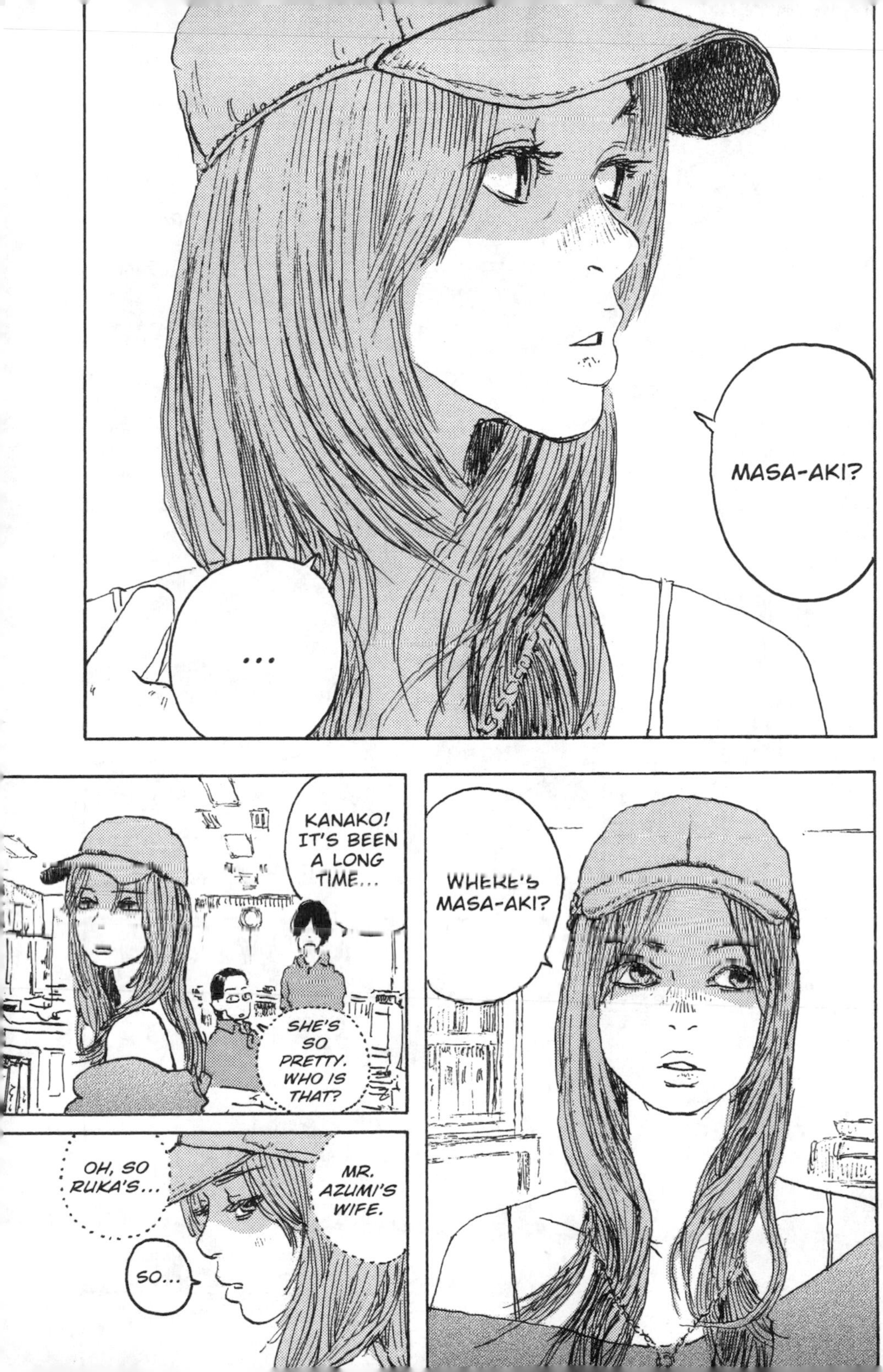
MASA-AKI?
...
WHERE'S MASA-AKI?
KANAKO! IT'S BEEN A LONG TIME...
SHE'S SO PRETTY. WHO IS THAT?
MR. AZUMI'S WIFE.
OH, SO RUKA'S...
SO...

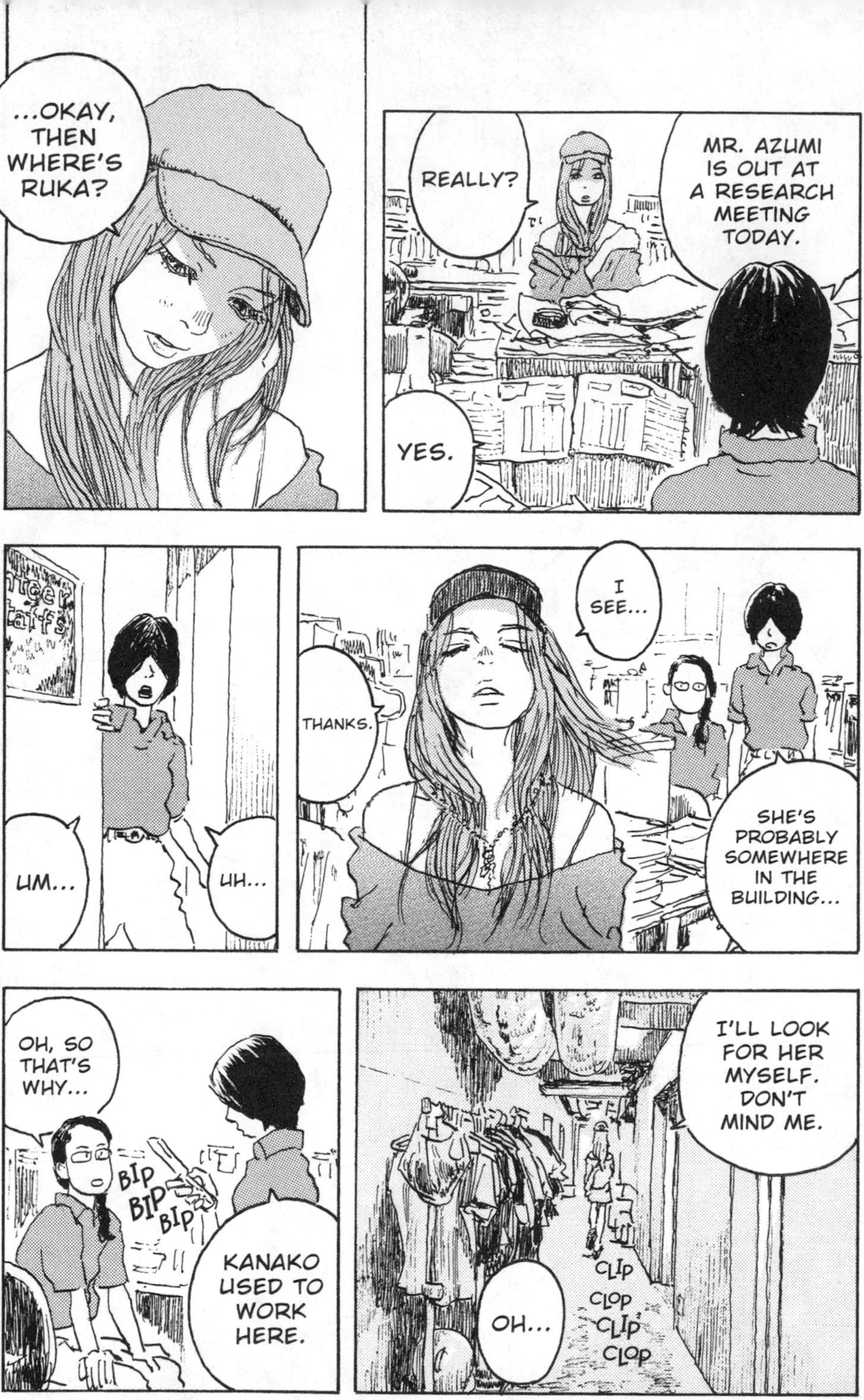
MR. AZUMI IS OUT AT A RESEARCH MEETING TODAY.
REALLY?
YES.
...OKAY, THEN WHERE'S RUKA?
I SEE...
SHE'S PROBABLY SOMEWHERE IN THE BUILDING...
THANKS.
UH...
UM...
I'LL LOOK FOR HER MYSELF. DON'T MIND ME.
CLIP CLOP CLIP CLOP
OH...
OH, SO THAT'S WHY...
BIP BIP BIP
KANAKO USED TO WORK HERE.

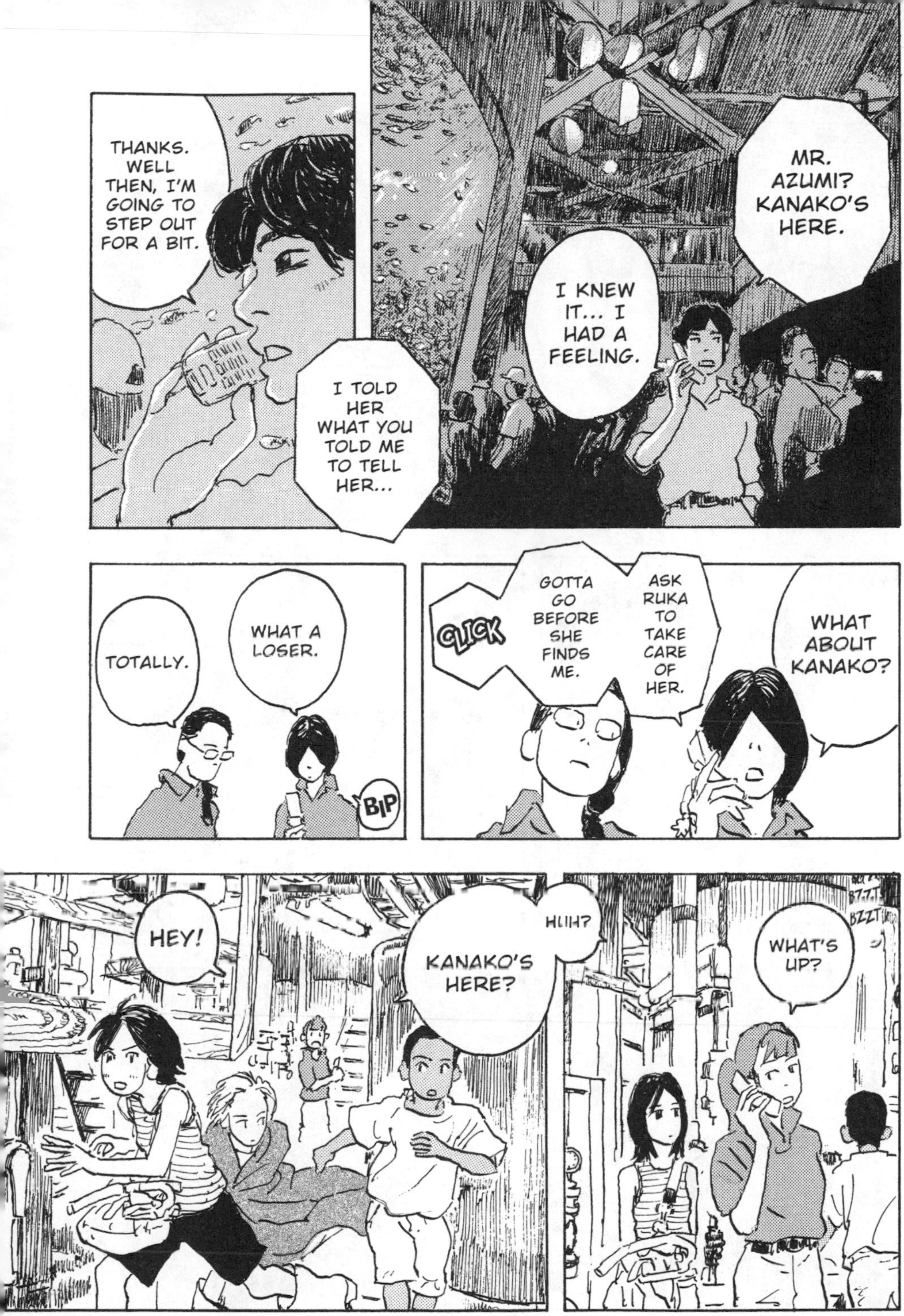
MR. AZUMI? KANAKO'S HERE.
I KNEW IT... I HAD A FEELING.
I TOLD HER WHAT YOU TOLD ME TO TELL HER...
THANKS. WELL THEN, I'M GOING TO STEP OUT FOR A BIT.
WHAT ABOUT KANAKO?
ASK RUKA TO TAKE CARE OF HER.
GOTTA GO BEFORE SHE FINDS ME.
CLICK
WHAT A LOSER.
TOTALLY.
BIP
BZZT
WHAT'S UP?
HUH?
KANAKO'S HERE?
HEY!

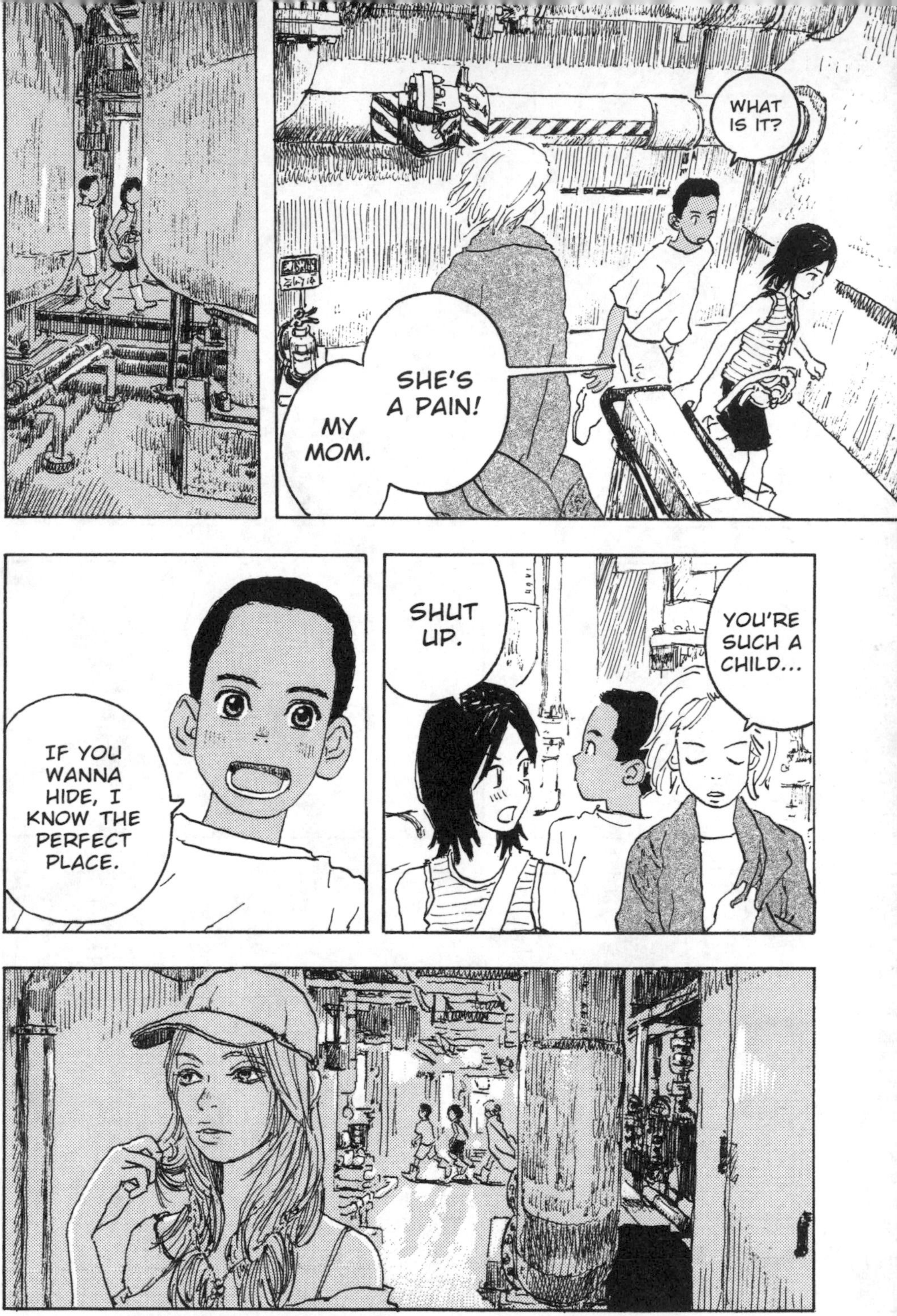
WHAT IS IT?
SHE'S A PAIN! MY MOM.
YOU'RE SUCH A CHILD...
SHUT UP.
IF YOU WANNA HIDE, I KNOW THE PERFECT PLACE.

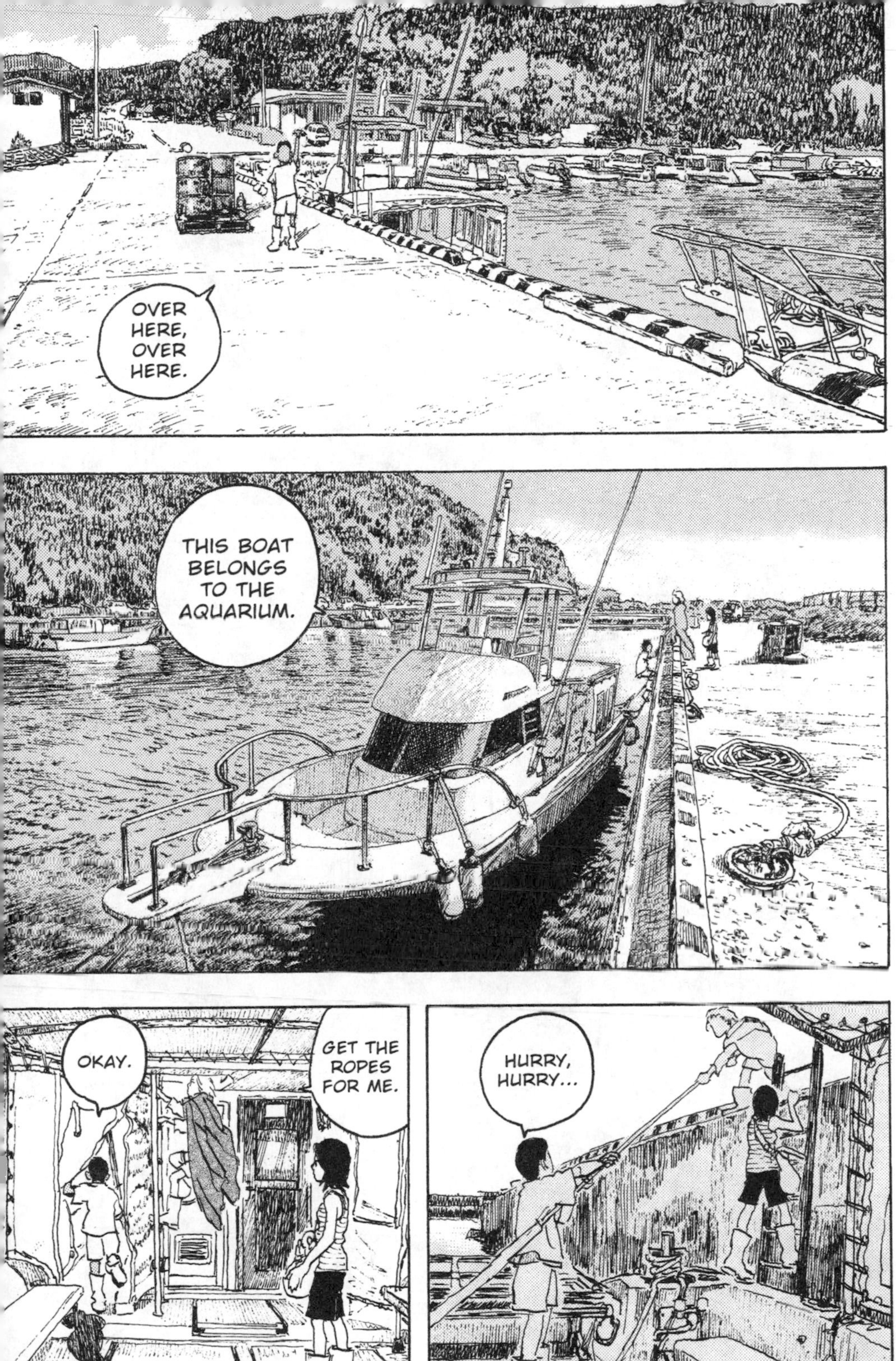
OVER HERE, OVER HERE.
THIS BOAT BELONGS TO THE AQUARIUM.
HURRY, HURRY...
GET THE ROPES FOR ME.
OKAY.

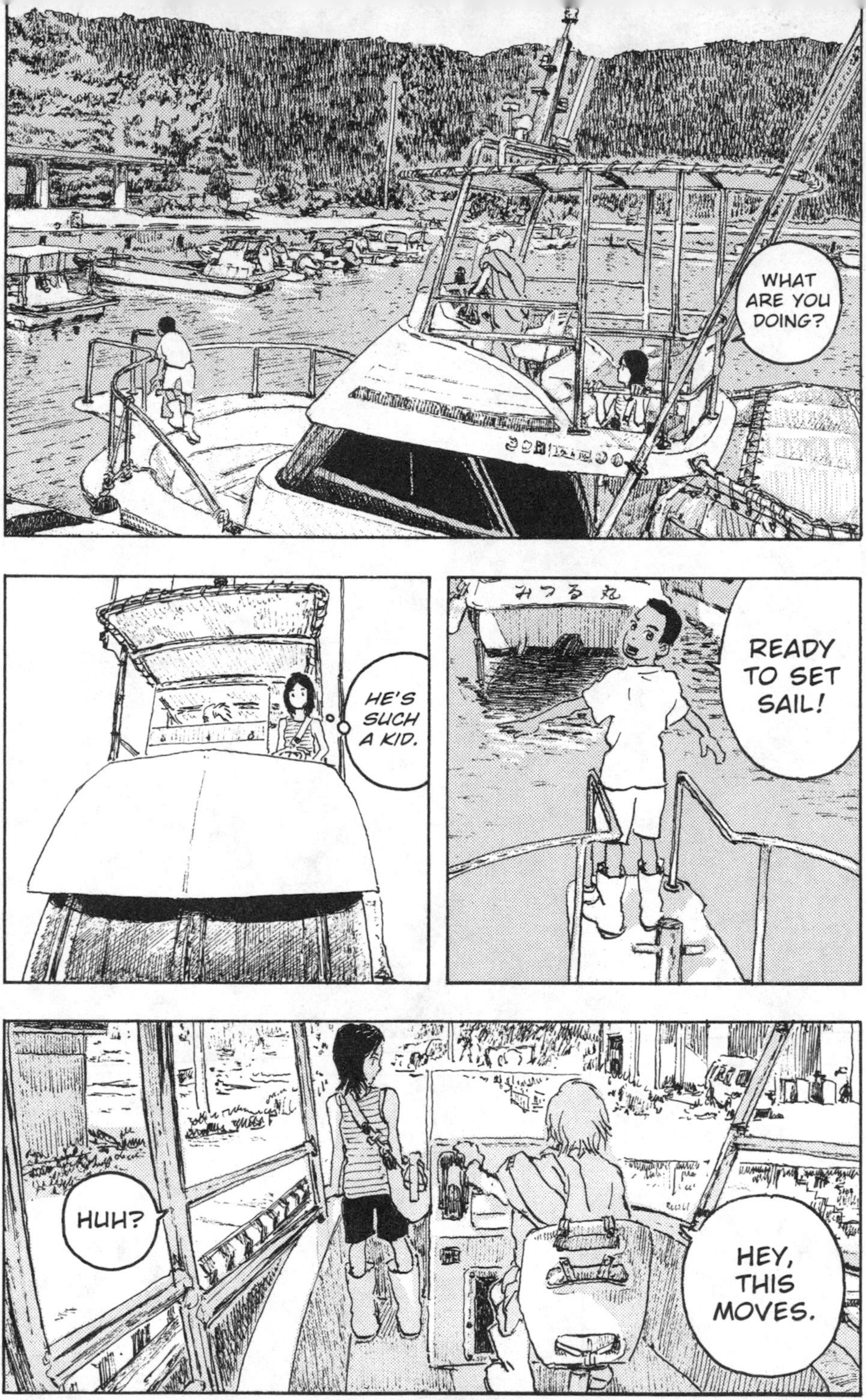
WHAT ARE YOU DOING?
READY TO SET SAIL!
みつる丸
HE'S SUCH A KID.
HEY, THIS MOVES.
HUH?

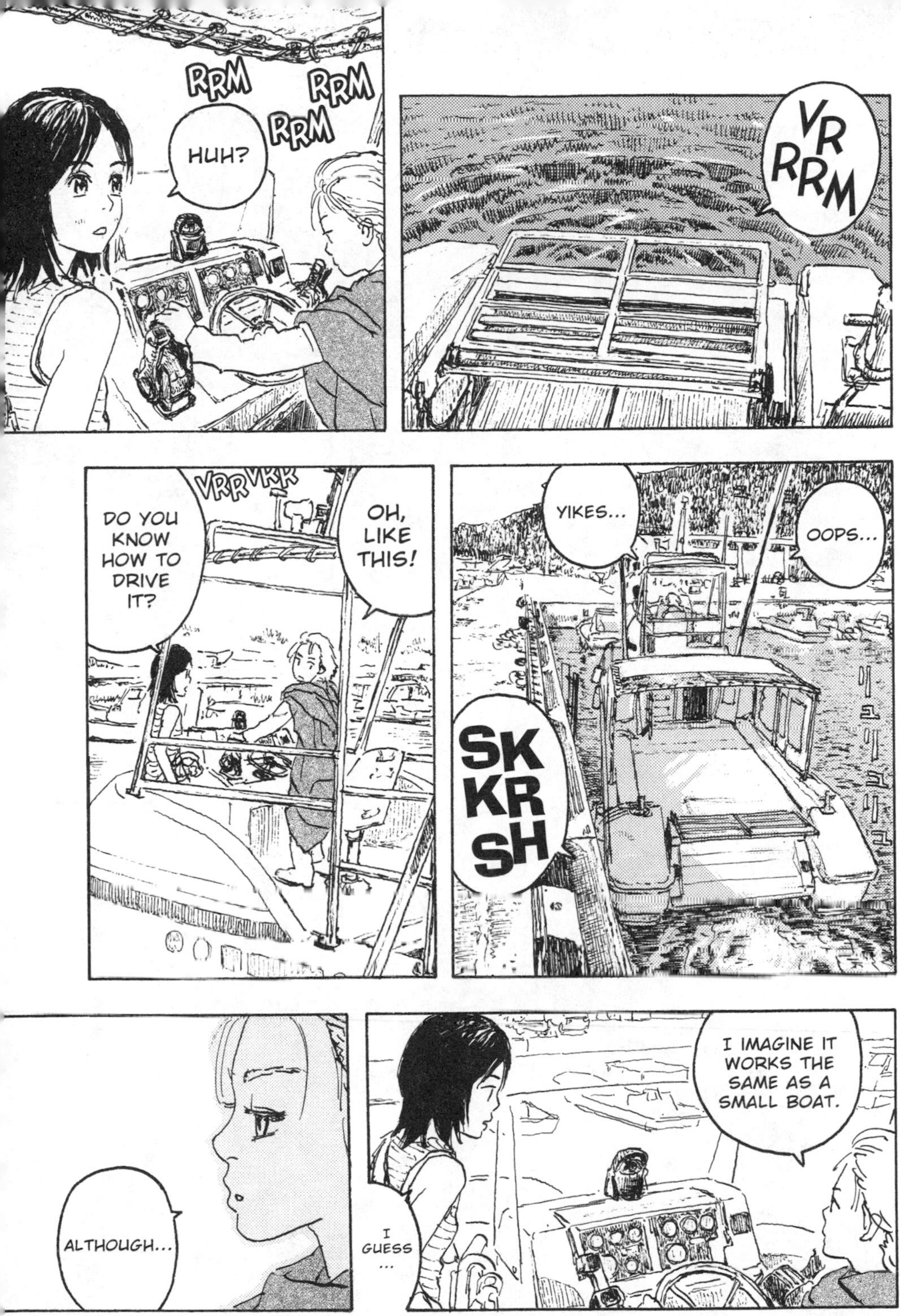
RRM
RRM
RRM
HUH?
VR RRM
VRRVKK
DO YOU KNOW HOW TO DRIVE IT?
OH, LIKE THIS!
YIKES...
OOPS...
SK KR SH
ALTHOUGH...
I IMAGINE IT WORKS THE SAME AS A SMALL BOAT.
I GUESS ...

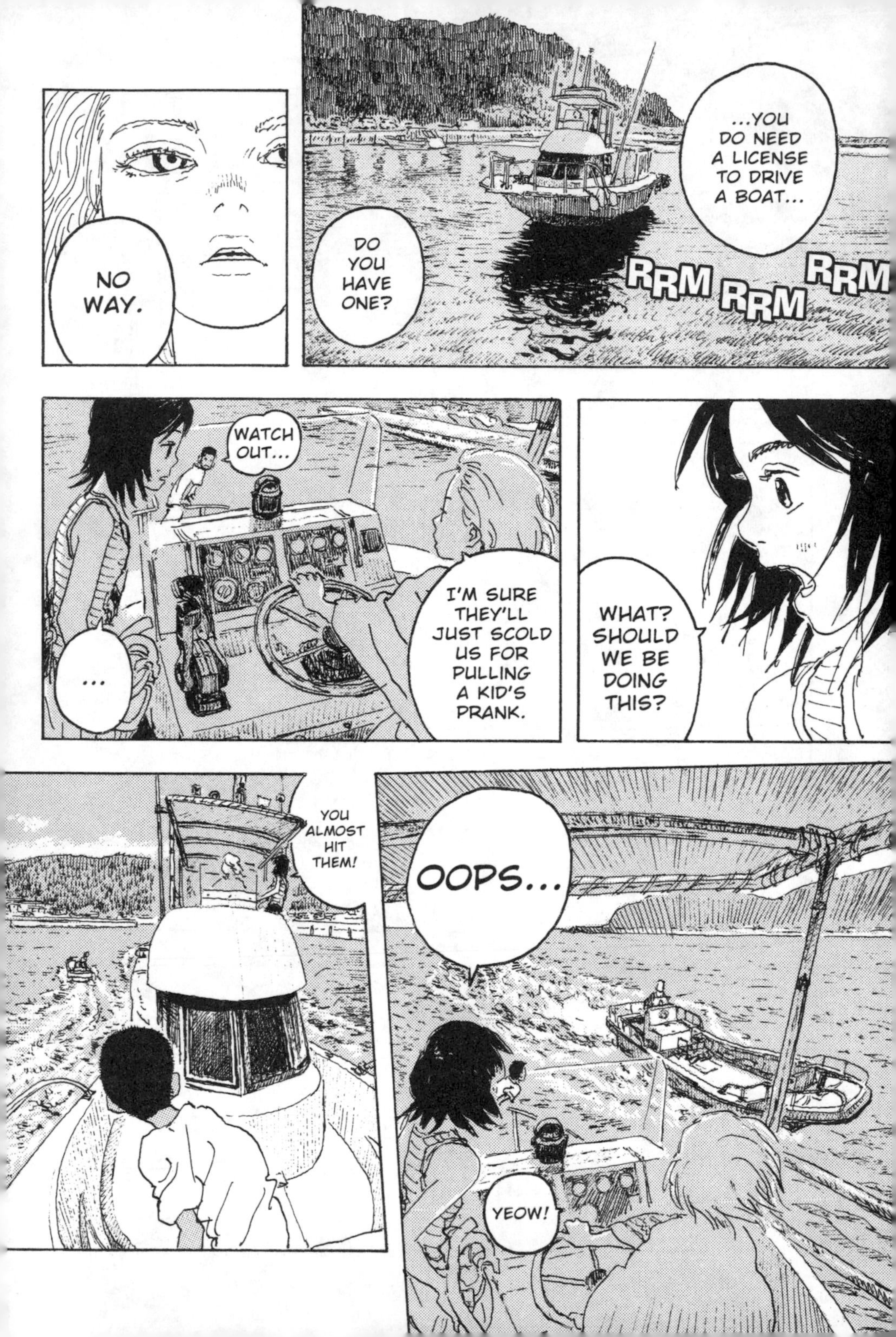
...YOU DO NEED A LICENSE TO DRIVE A BOAT...
RRM RRM RRM
DO YOU HAVE ONE?
NO WAY.
WHAT? SHOULD WE BE DOING THIS?
I'M SURE THEY'LL JUST SCOLD US FOR PULLING A KID'S PRANK.
WATCH OUT...
...
OOPS...
YEOW!
YOU ALMOST HIT THEM!

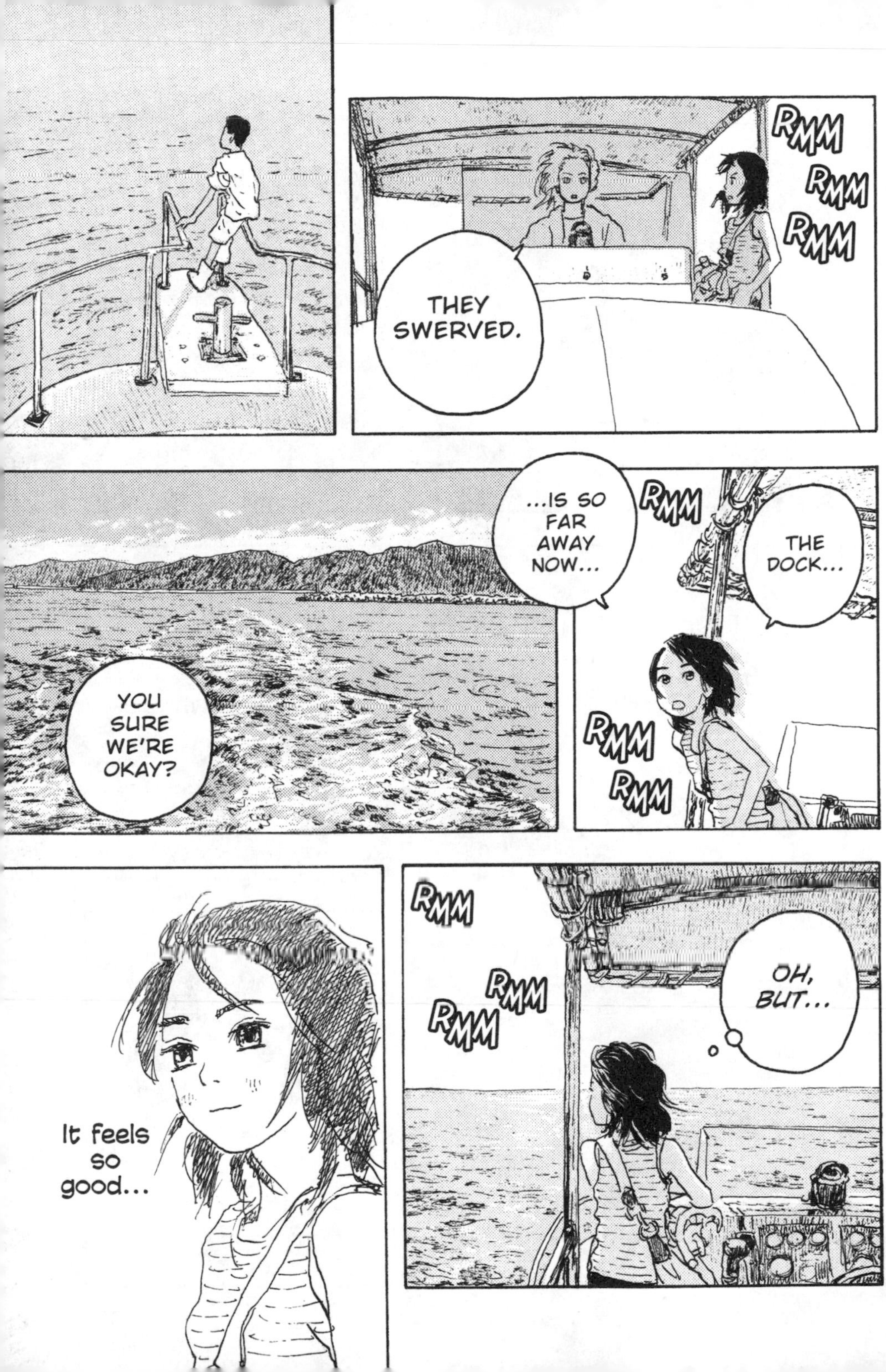
RMM
RMM
RMM
THEY SWERVED.
RMM
THE DOCK...
...IS SO FAR AWAY NOW...
RMM
RMM
YOU SURE WE'RE OKAY?
RMM
RMM
RMM
OH, BUT...
It feels so good...

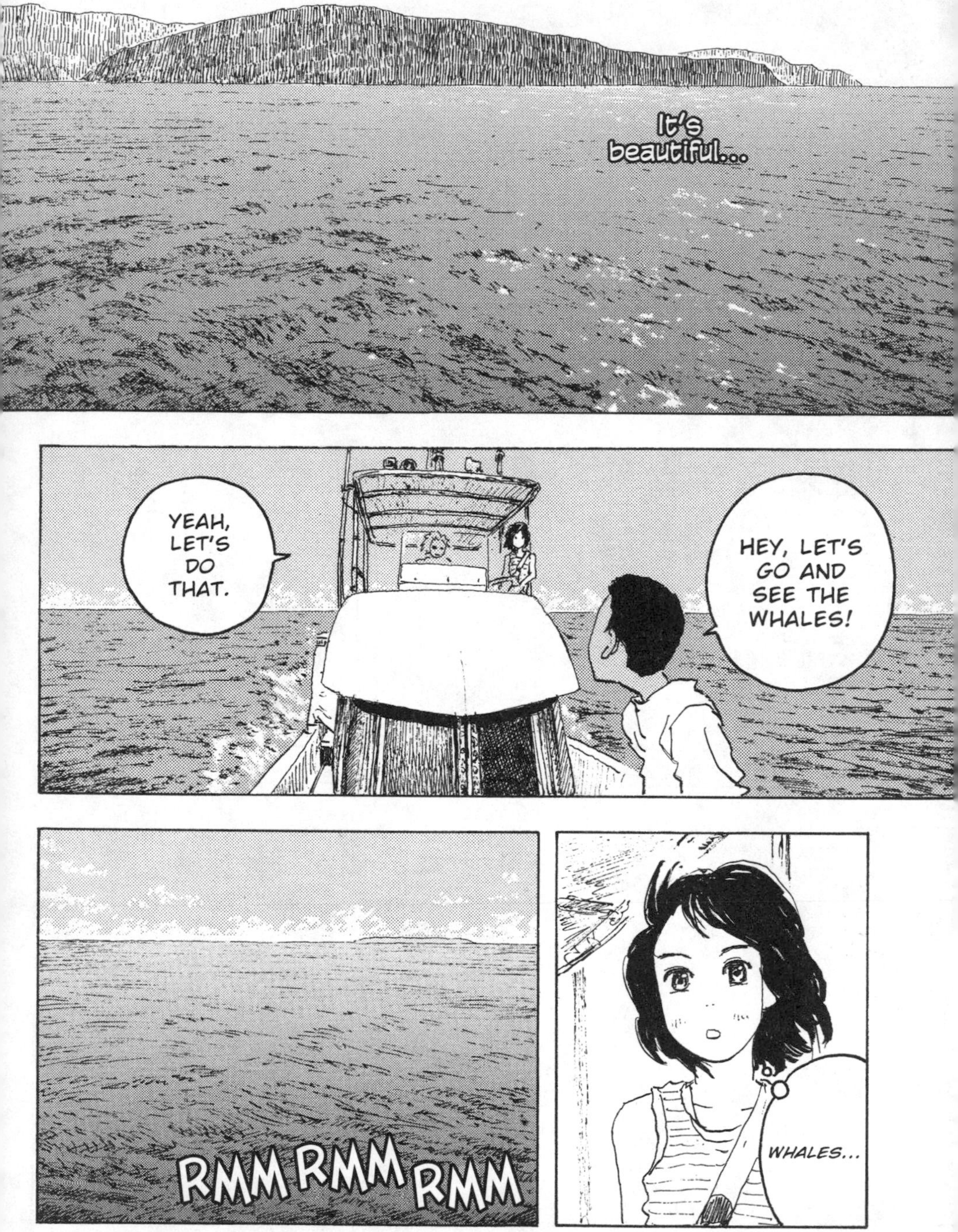
It's beautiful...
HEY, LET'S GO AND SEE THE WHALES!
YEAH, LET'S DO THAT.
WHALES...
RMM RMM RMM

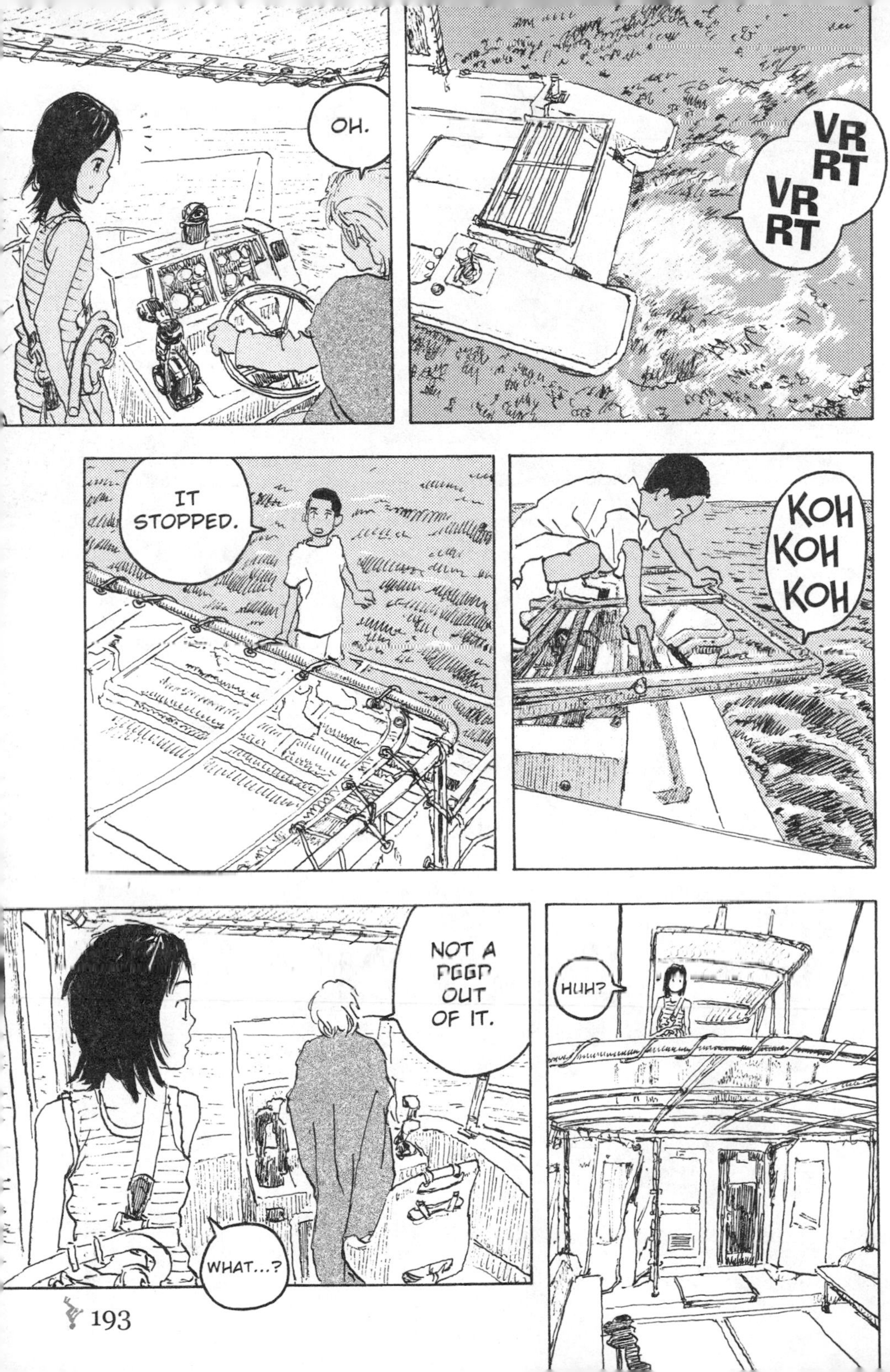
VRRT VRRT
OH.
KOH KOH KOH
IT STOPPED.
HUH?
NOT A PEEP OUT OF IT.
WHAT...?

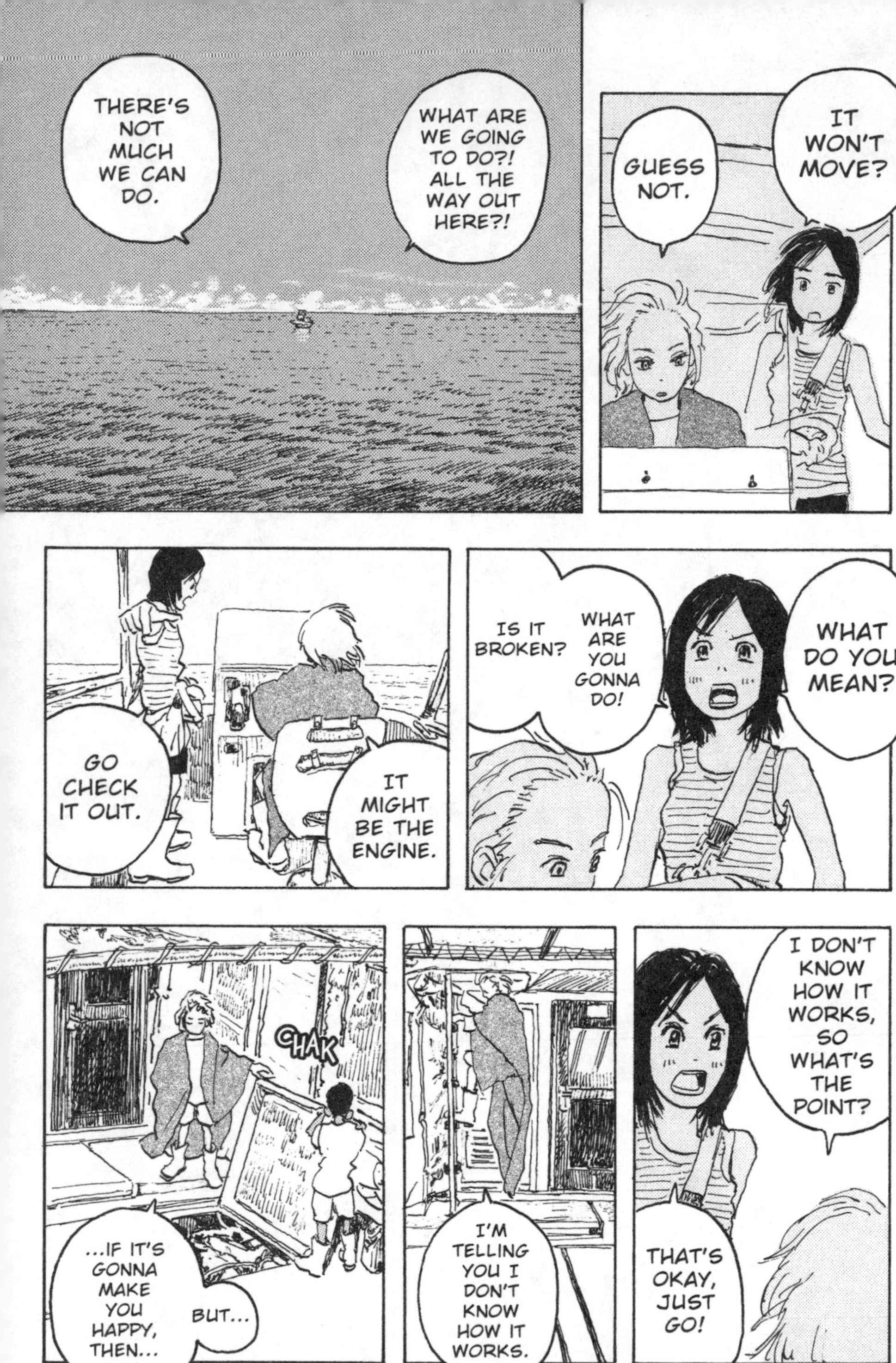
IT WON'T MOVE?
GUESS NOT.
WHAT ARE WE GOING TO DO?! ALL THE WAY OUT HERE?!
THERE'S NOT MUCH WE CAN DO.
WHAT DO YOU MEAN?
WHAT ARE YOU GONNA DO!
IS IT BROKEN?
IT MIGHT BE THE ENGINE.
GO CHECK IT OUT.
I DON'T KNOW HOW IT WORKS, SO WHAT'S THE POINT?
THAT'S OKAY, JUST GO!
I'M TELLING YOU I DON'T KNOW HOW IT WORKS.
CHAK
BUT...
...IF IT'S GONNA MAKE YOU HAPPY, THEN...

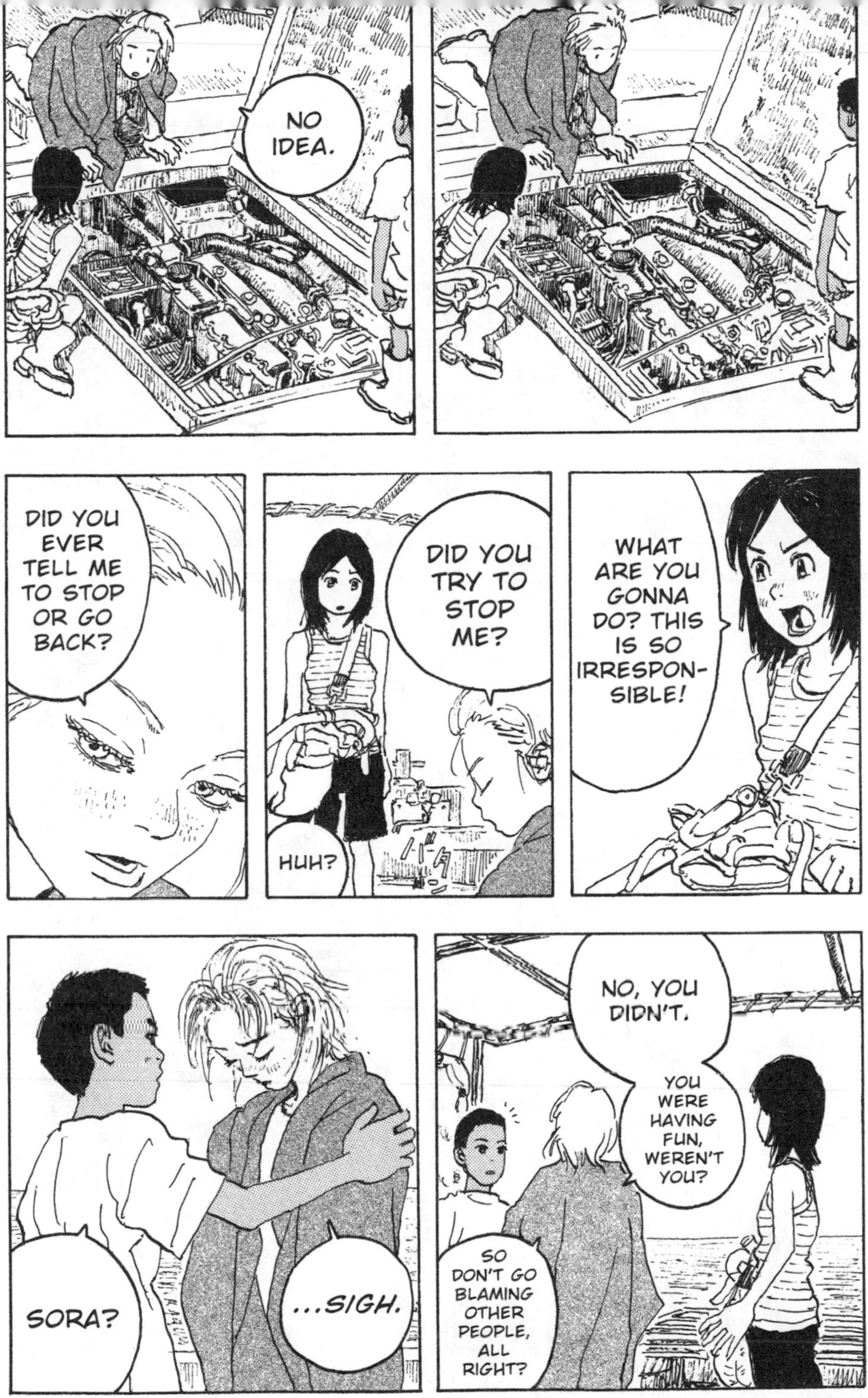
NO IDEA.
WHAT ARE YOU GONNA DO? THIS IS SO IRRESPON-SIBLE!
DID YOU TRY TO STOP ME?
HUH?
DID YOU EVER TELL ME TO STOP OR GO BACK?
NO, YOU DIDN'T.
YOU WERE HAVING FUN, WEREN'T YOU?
SO DON'T GO BLAMING OTHER PEOPLE, ALL RIGHT?
...SIGH.
SORA?

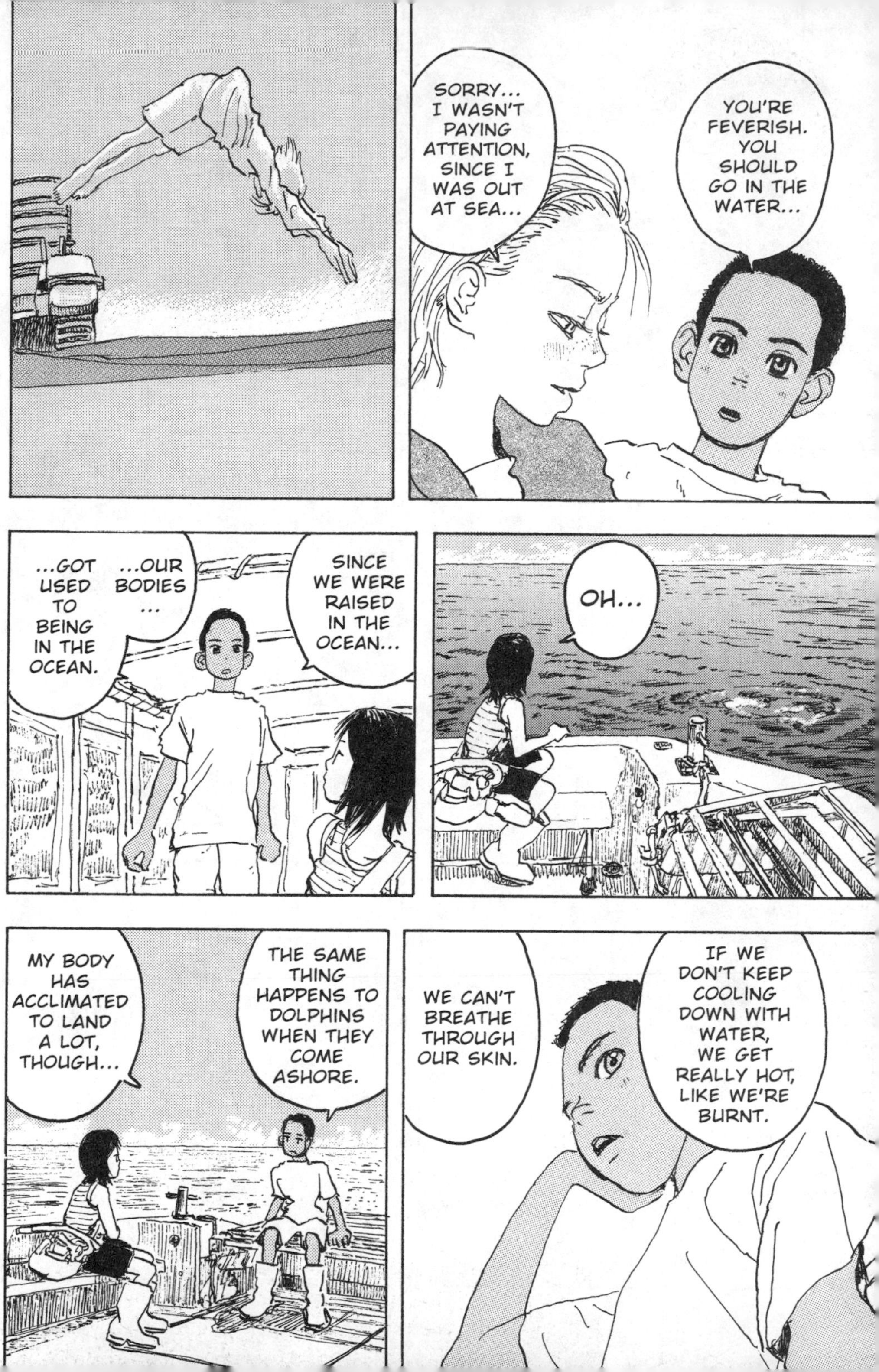
YOU'RE FEVERISH. YOU SHOULD GO IN THE WATER...
SORRY... I WASN'T PAYING ATTENTION, SINCE I WAS OUT AT SEA...
OH...
SINCE WE WERE RAISED IN THE OCEAN...
...OUR BODIES ...
...GOT USED TO BEING IN THE OCEAN.
IF WE DON'T KEEP COOLING DOWN WITH WATER, WE GET REALLY HOT, LIKE WE'RE BURNT.
WE CAN'T BREATHE THROUGH OUR SKIN.
THE SAME THING HAPPENS TO DOLPHINS WHEN THEY COME ASHORE.
MY BODY HAS ACCLIMATED TO LAND A LOT, THOUGH...

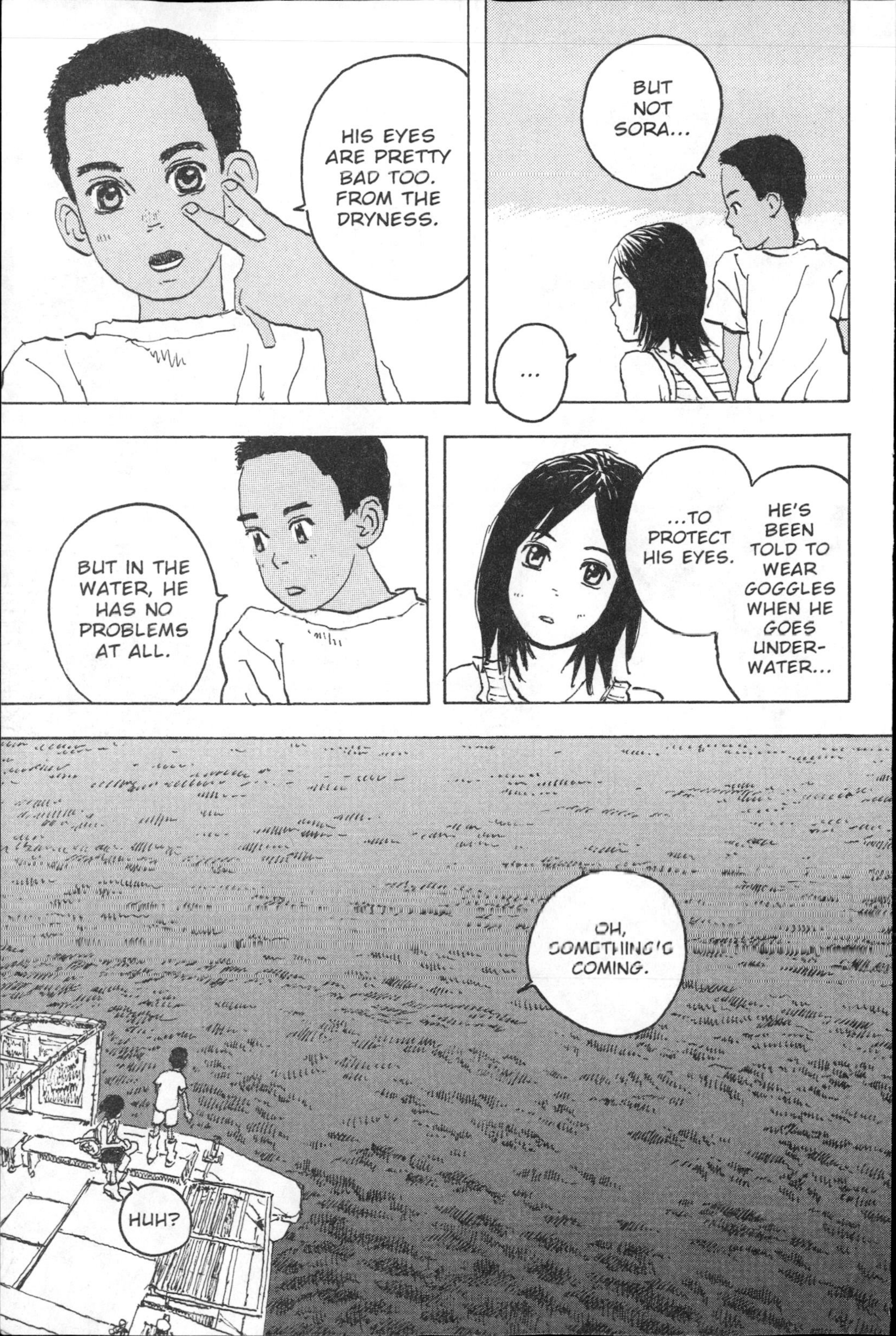
BUT NOT SORA...
...
HIS EYES ARE PRETTY BAD TOO. FROM THE DRYNESS.
HE'S BEEN TOLD TO WEAR GOGGLES WHEN HE GOES UNDER-WATER...
...TO PROTECT HIS EYES.
BUT IN THE WATER, HE HAS NO PROBLEMS AT ALL.
OH, SOMETHING'S COMING.
HUH?

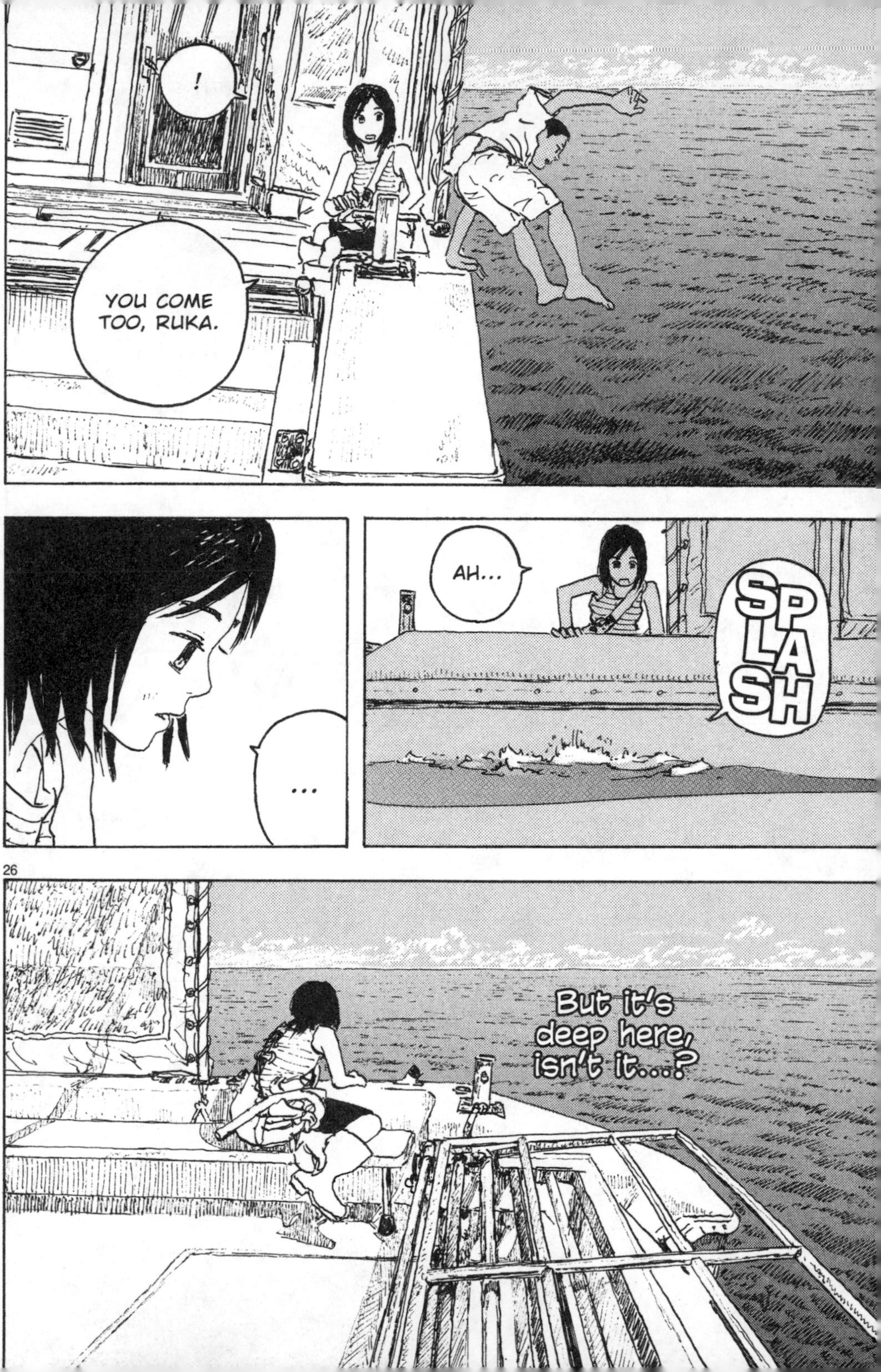
!
YOU COME TOO, RUKA.
AH...
SPLASH
...
But it's deep here, isn't it...?

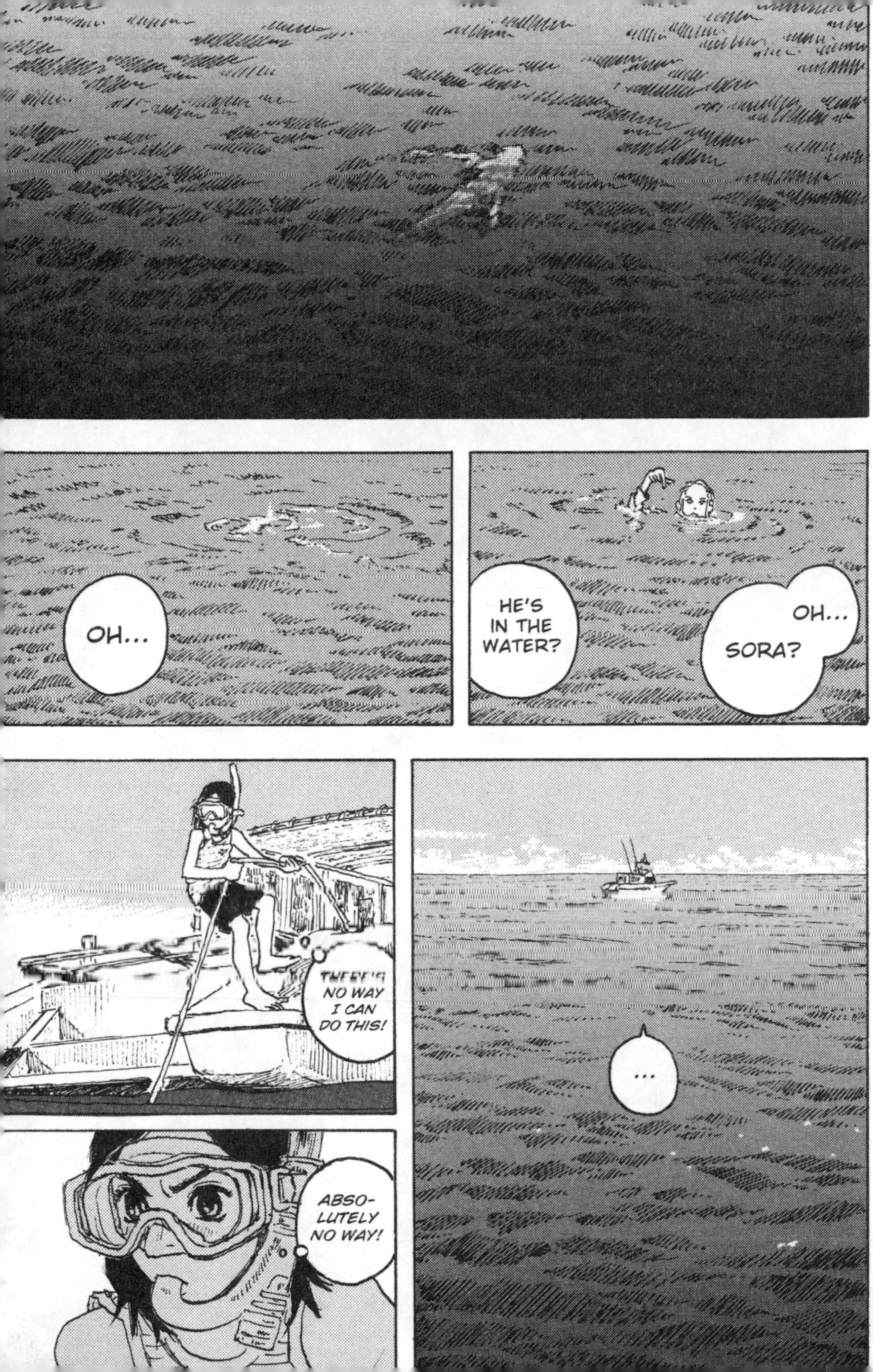
OH... SORA?
HE'S IN THE WATER?
OH...
...
NO WAY I CAN DO THIS!
ABSO-LUTELY NO WAY!

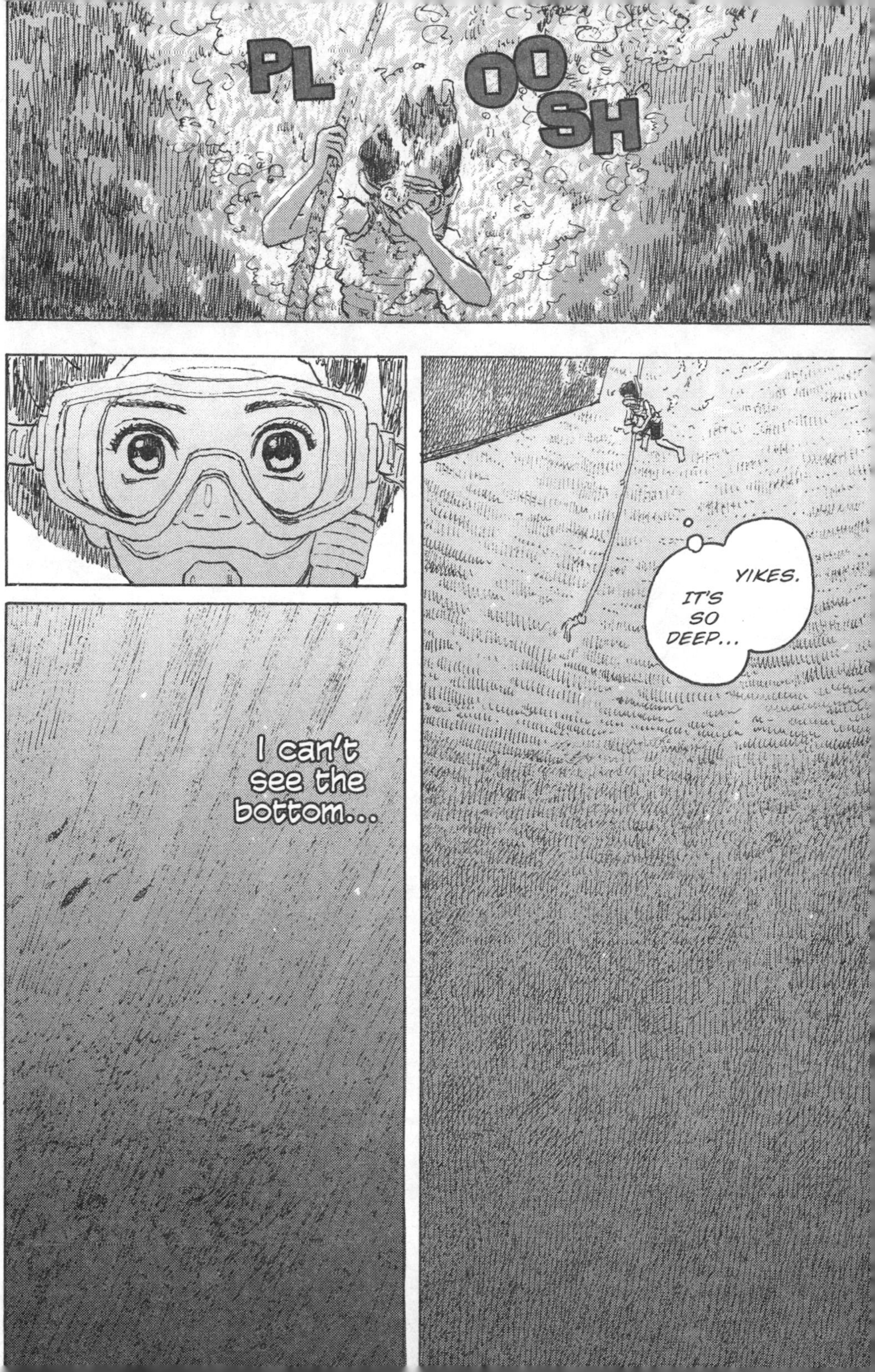
PLOOSH
YIKES. IT'S SO DEEP...
I can't see the bottom...

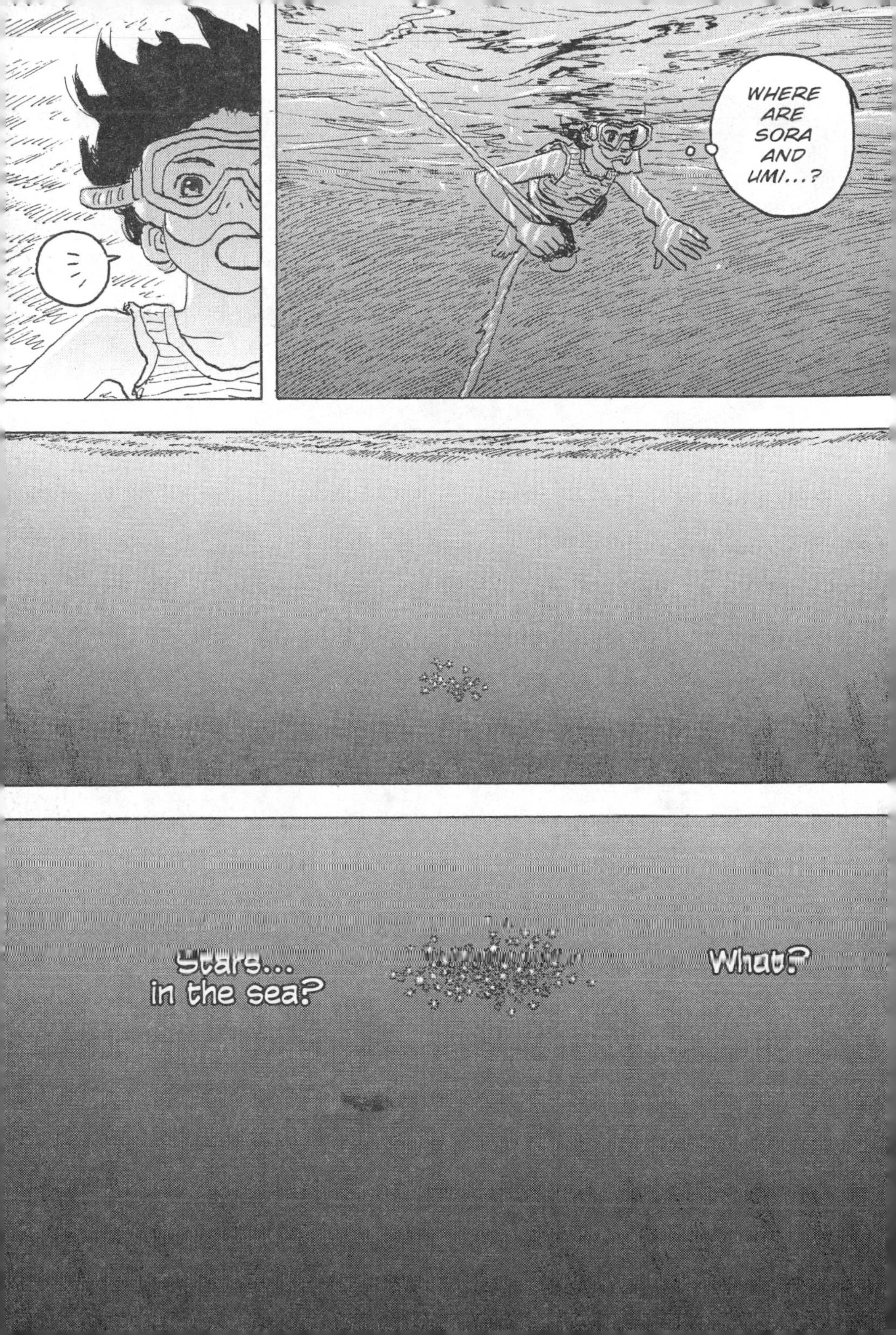
WHERE ARE SORA AND UMI...?
What?
Stars... in the sea?

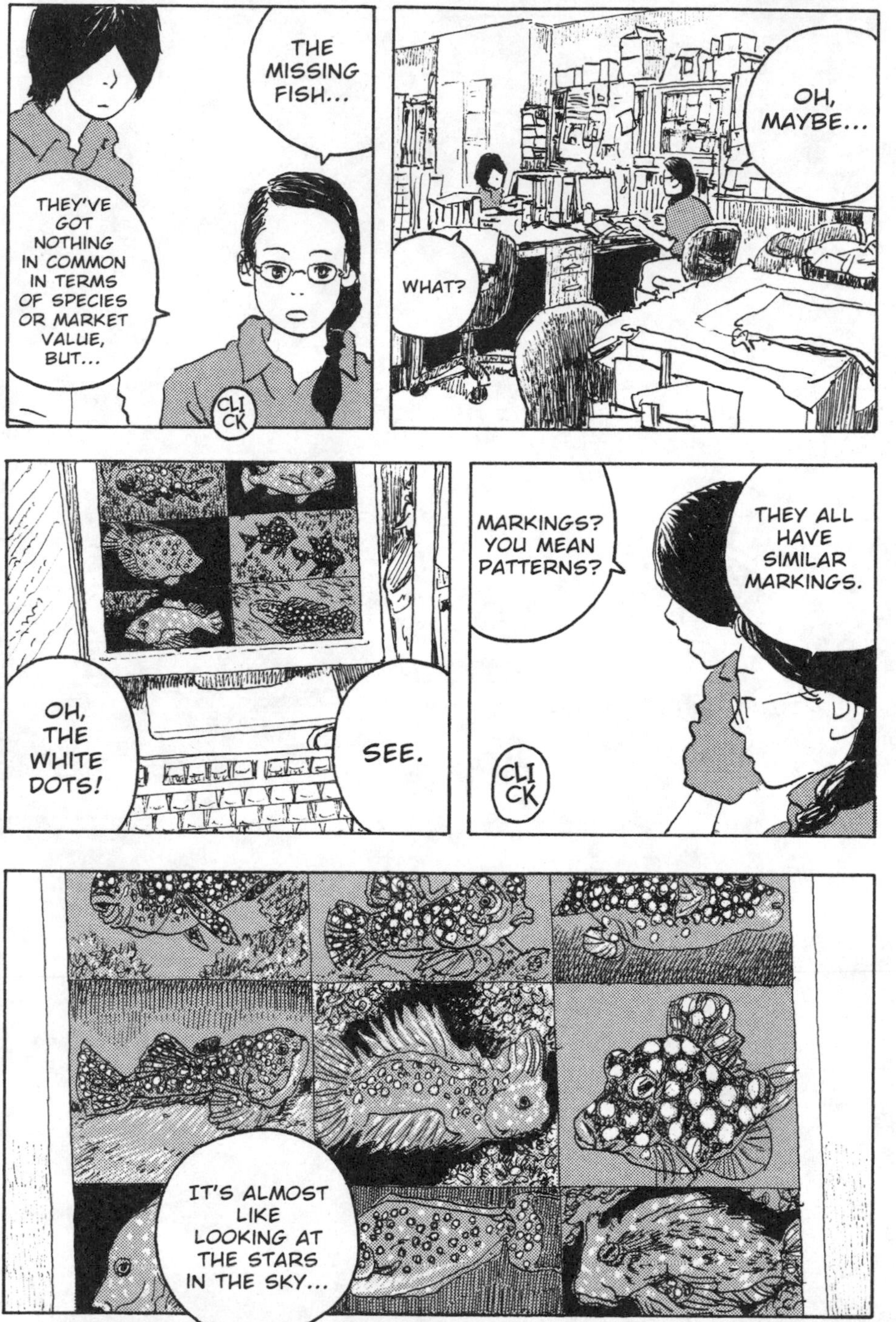
OH, MAYBE...
WHAT?
THE MISSING FISH...
THEY'VE GOT NOTHING IN COMMON IN TERMS OF SPECIES OR MARKET VALUE, BUT...
CLICK
THEY ALL HAVE SIMILAR MARKINGS.
MARKINGS? YOU MEAN PATTERNS?
CLICK
SEE.
OH, THE WHITE DOTS!
IT'S ALMOST LIKE LOOKING AT THE STARS IN THE SKY...

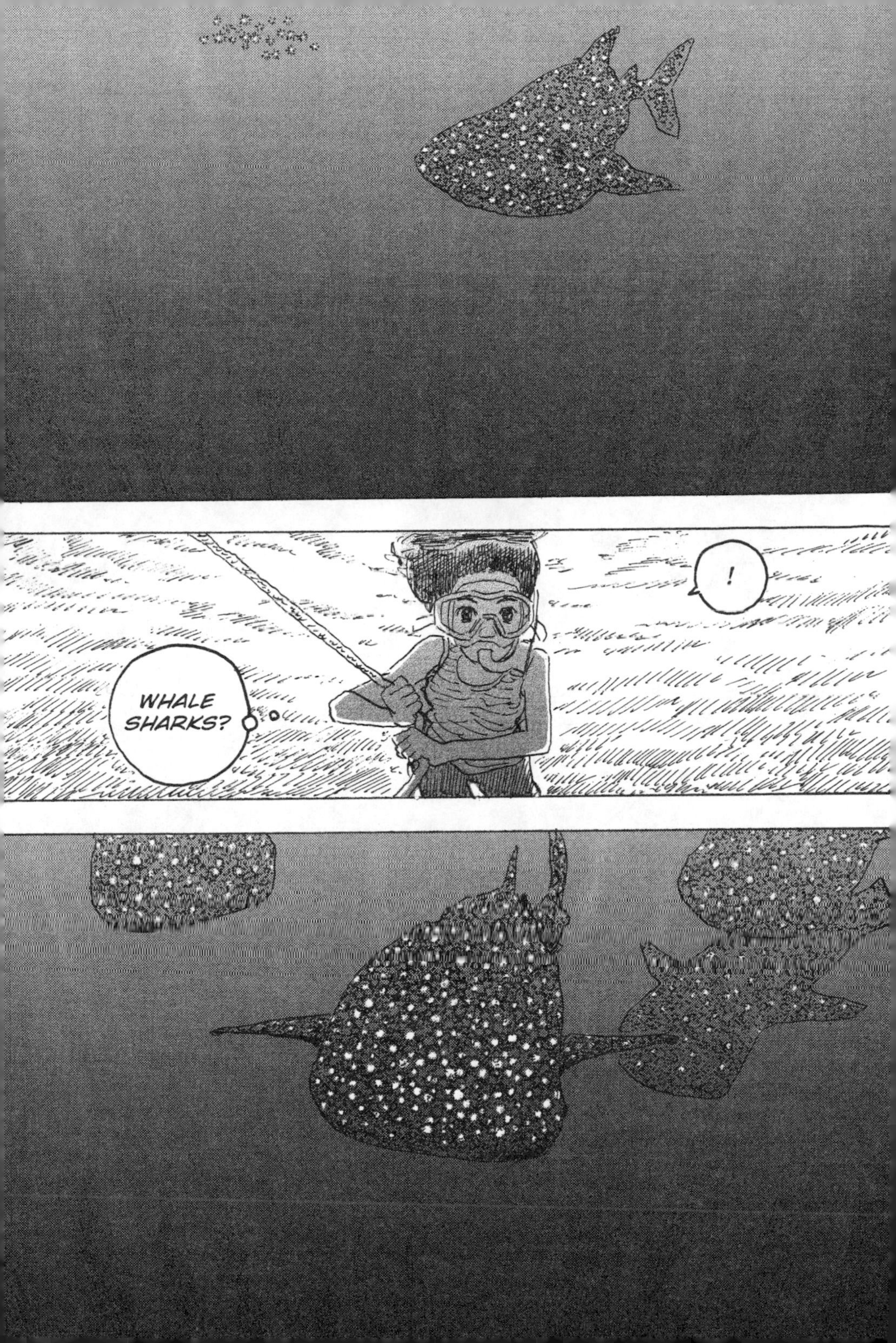
!
WHALE SHARKS?

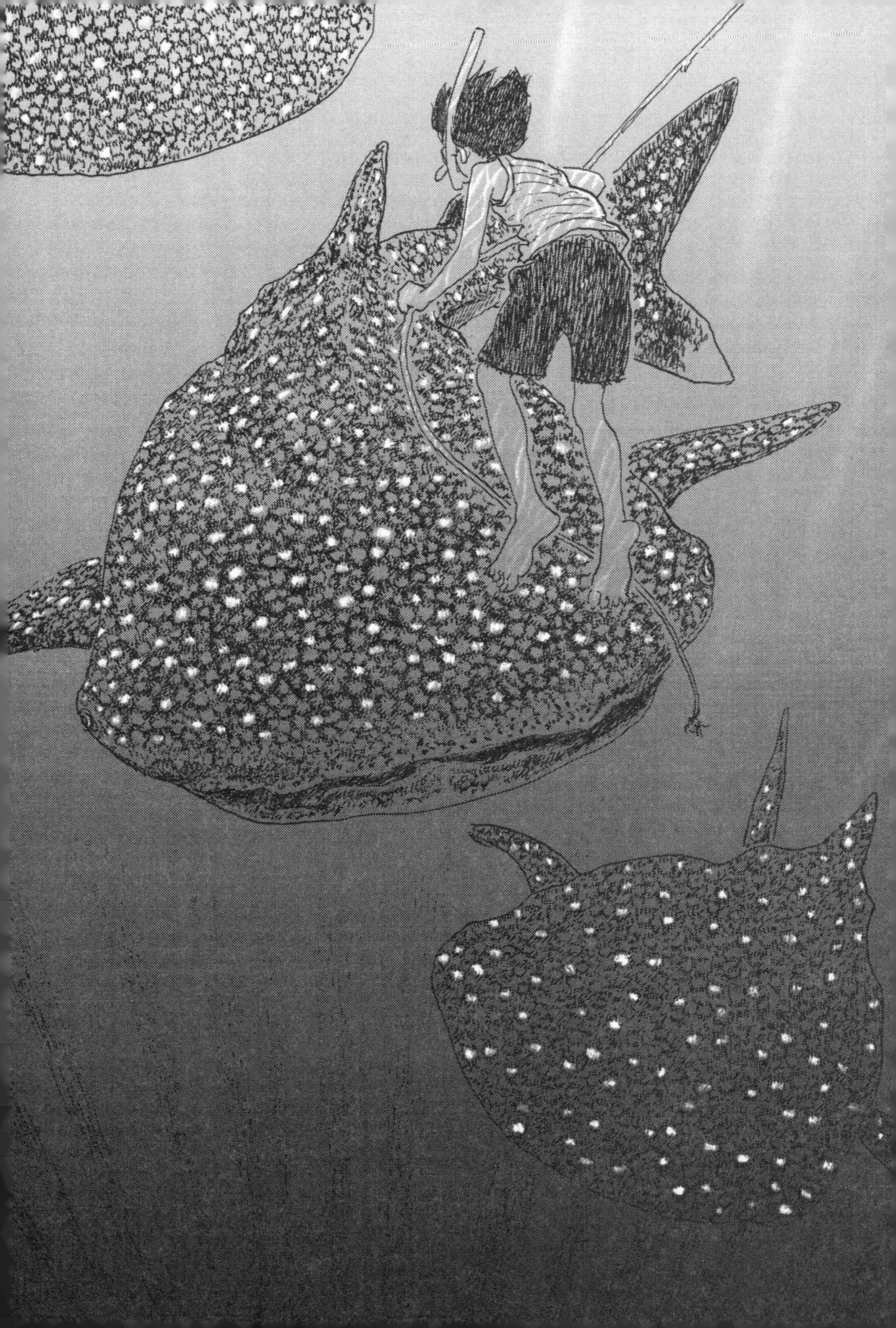

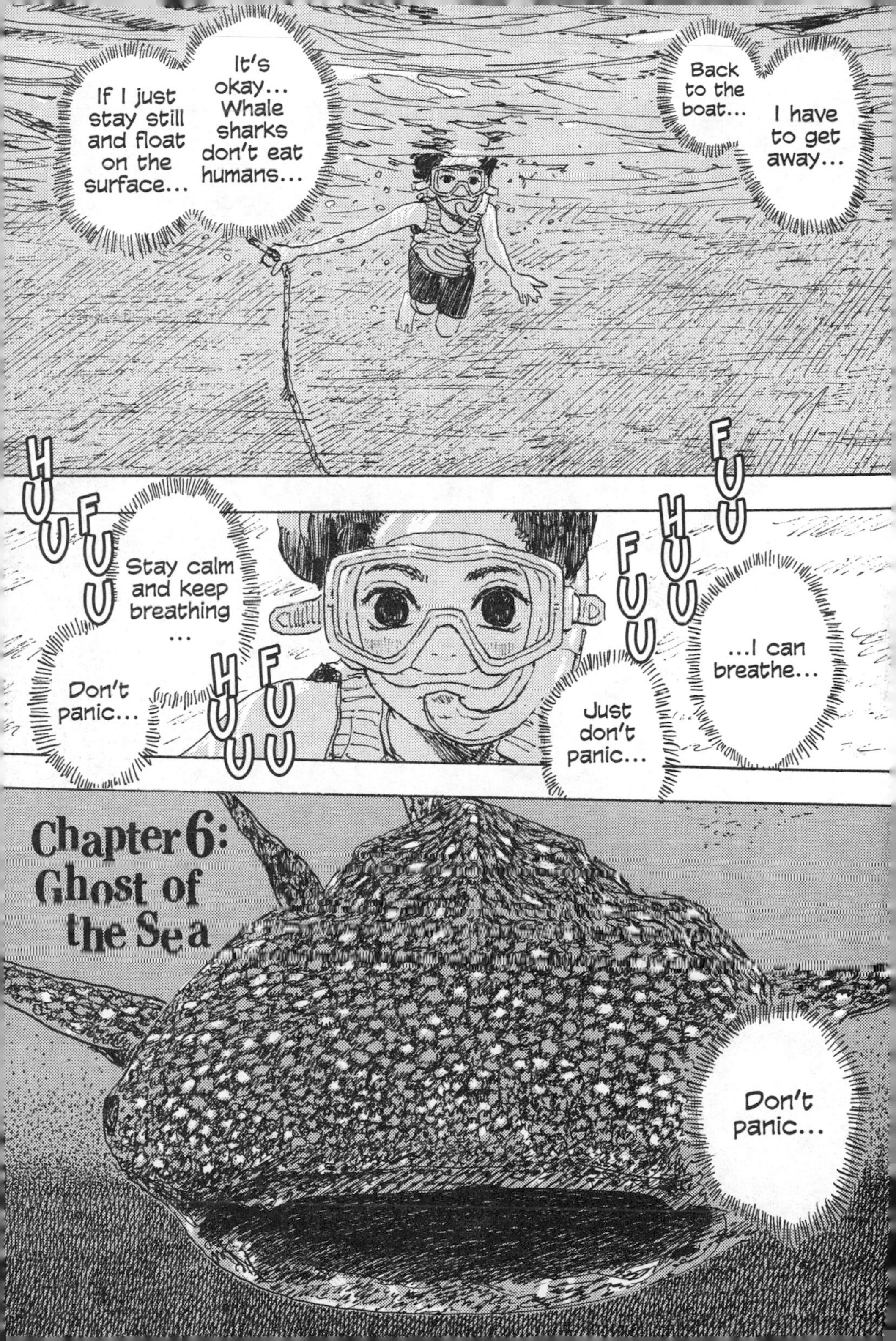
I have to get away...
Back to the boat...
It's okay... Whale sharks don't eat humans...
If I just stay still and float on the surface...
FUU
HUU
...I can breathe...
FUU
Just don't panic...
FUU
HUU
Stay calm and keep breathing...
FUU
HUU
Don't panic...
Chapter 6: Ghost of the Sea
Don't panic...

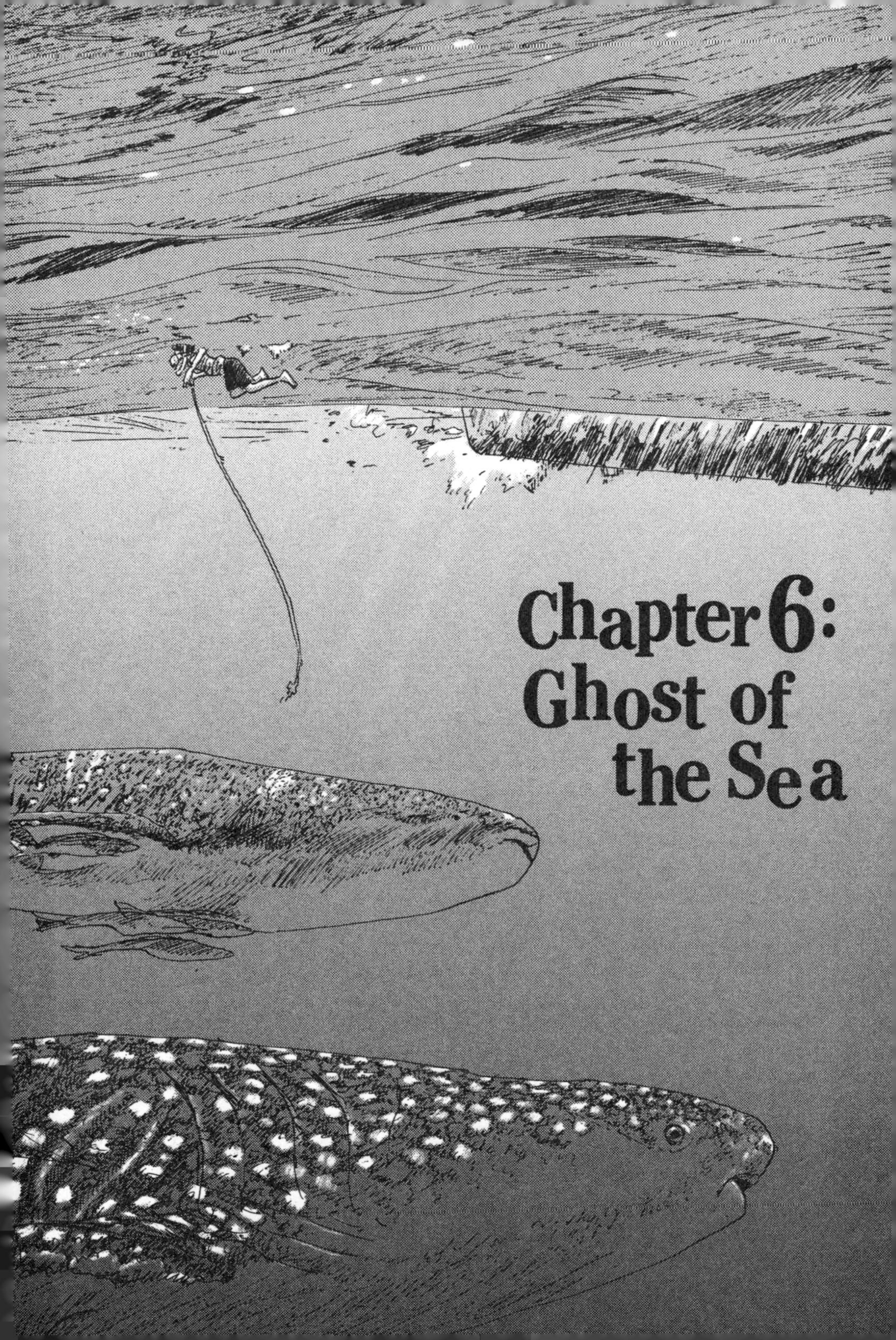
Chapter 6:
Ghost of
the Sea

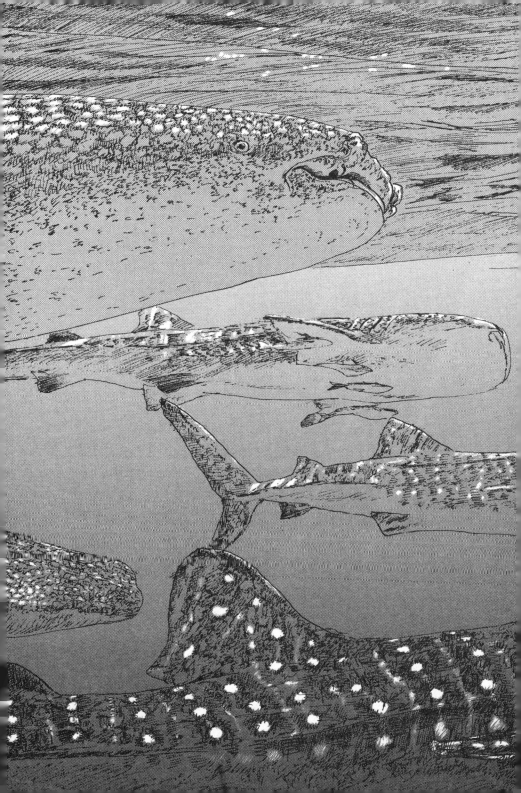

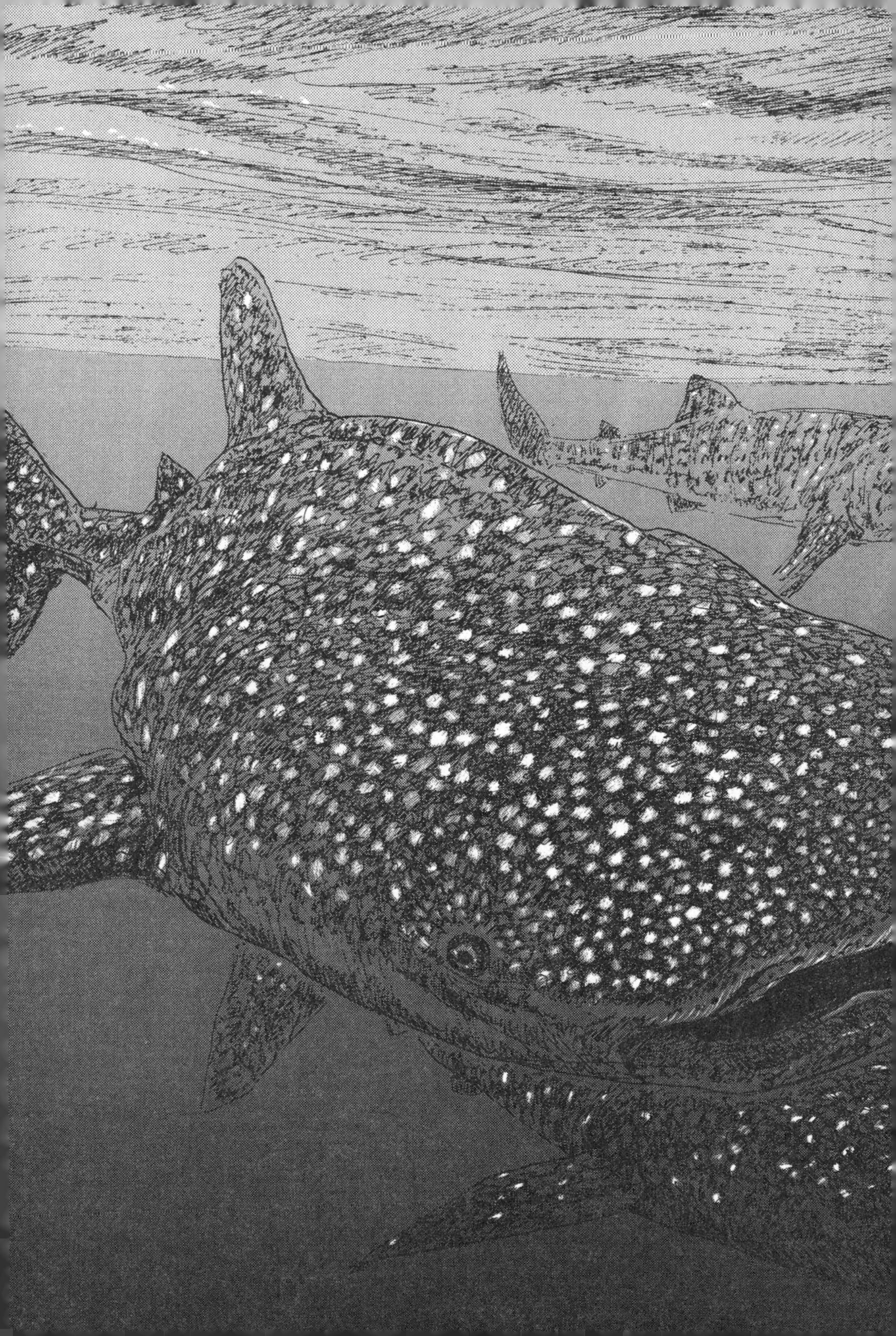

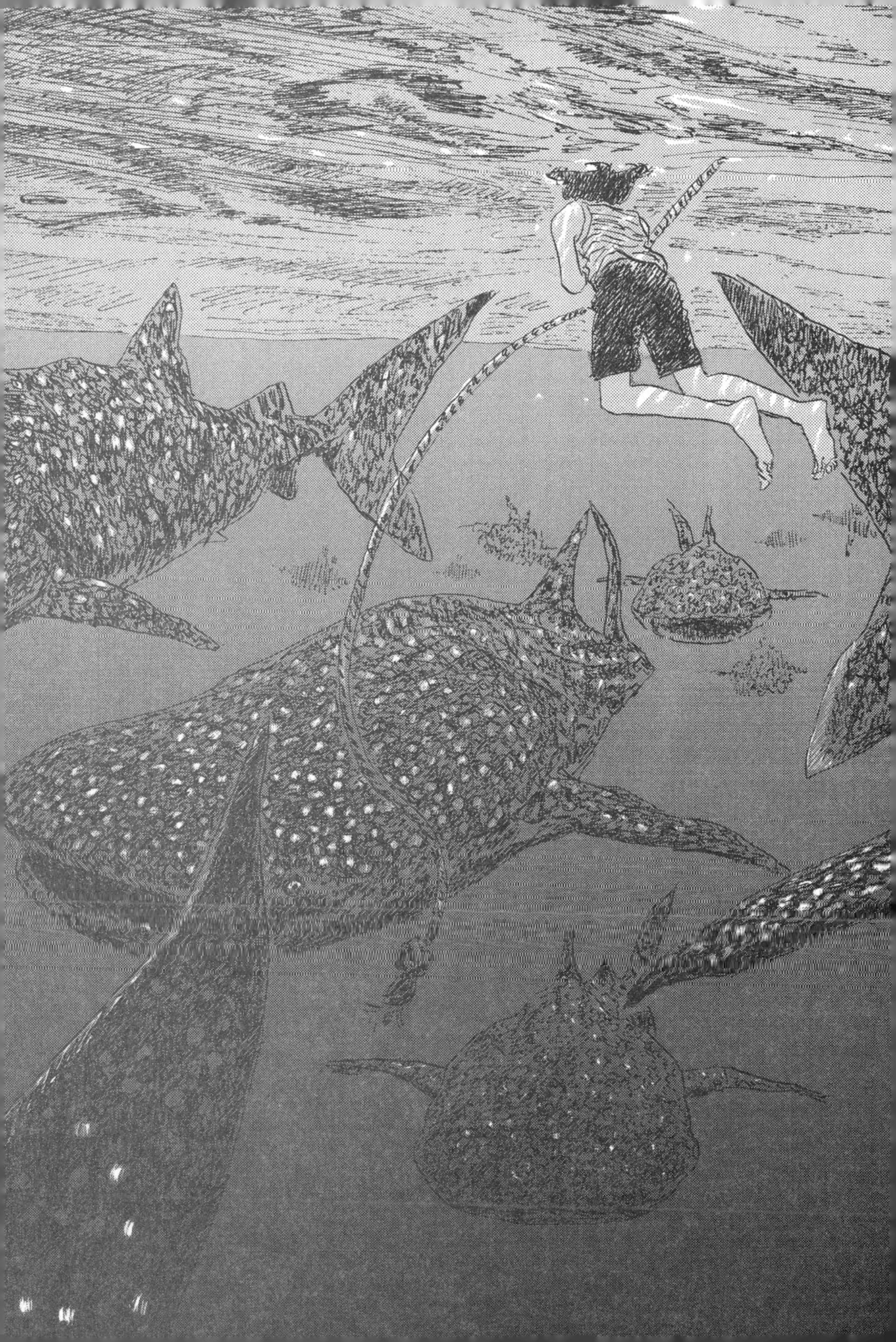

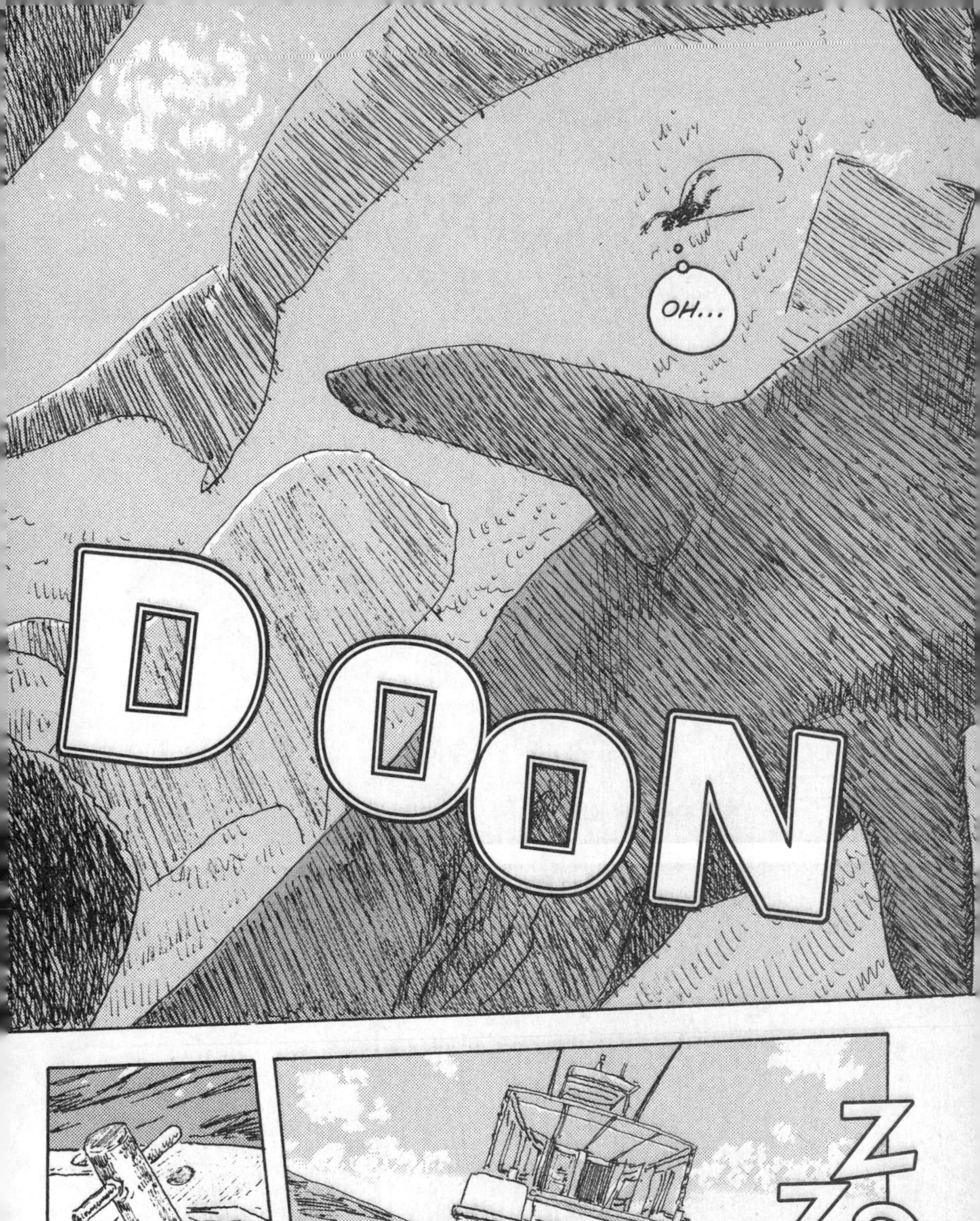
OH...
DOON
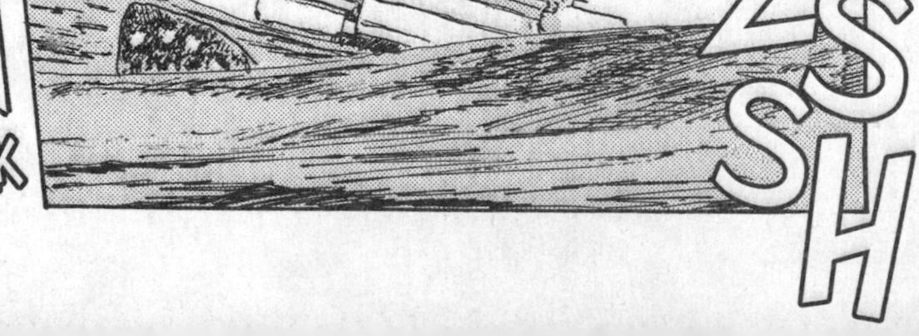
ZZSSH
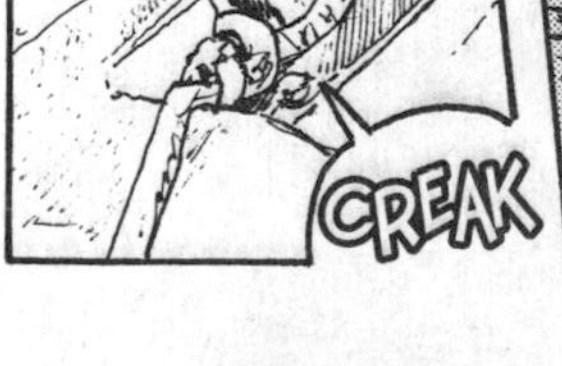
CREAK

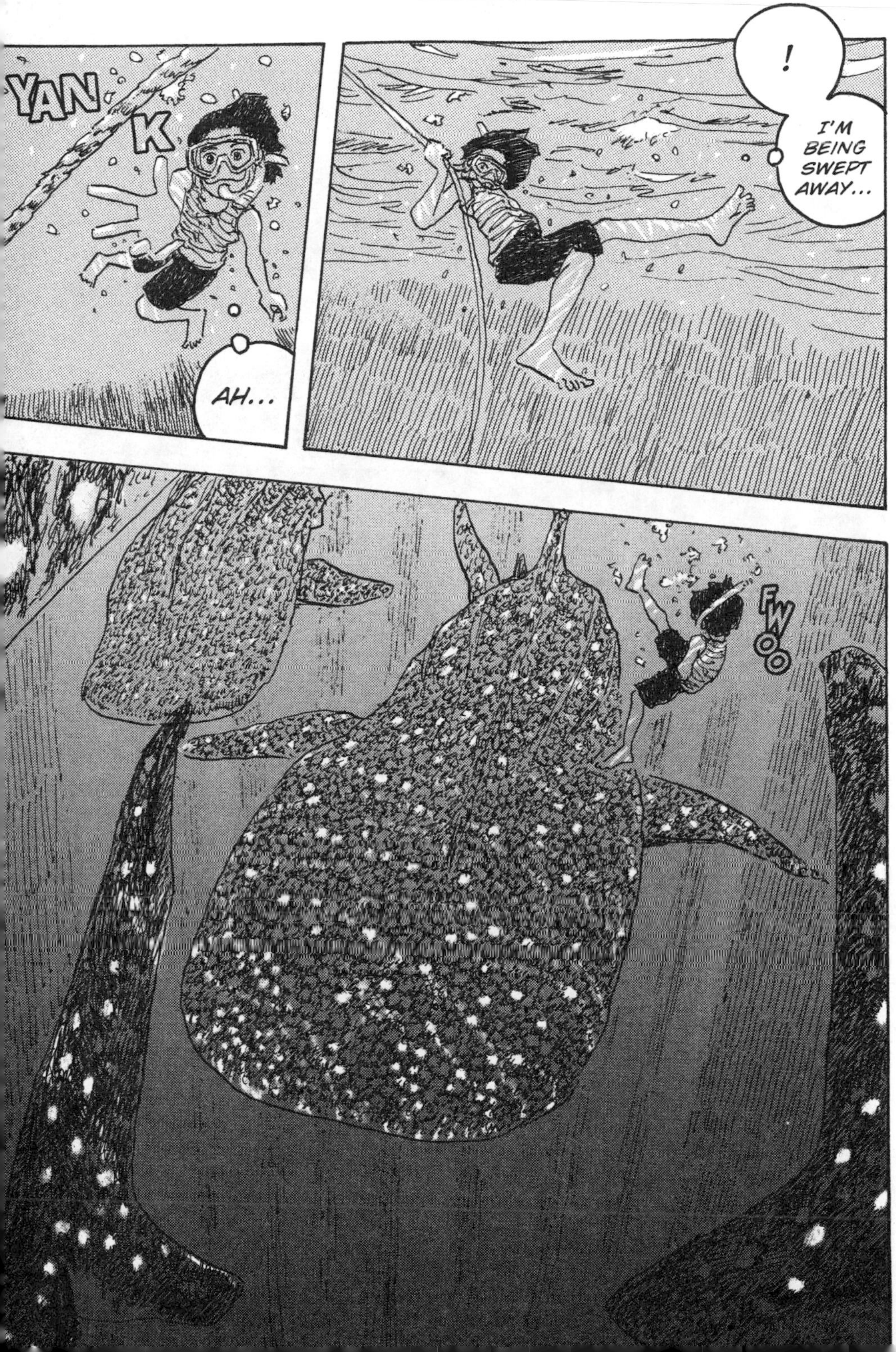
!
I'M BEING SWEPT AWAY...
YANK
AH...
FWOO

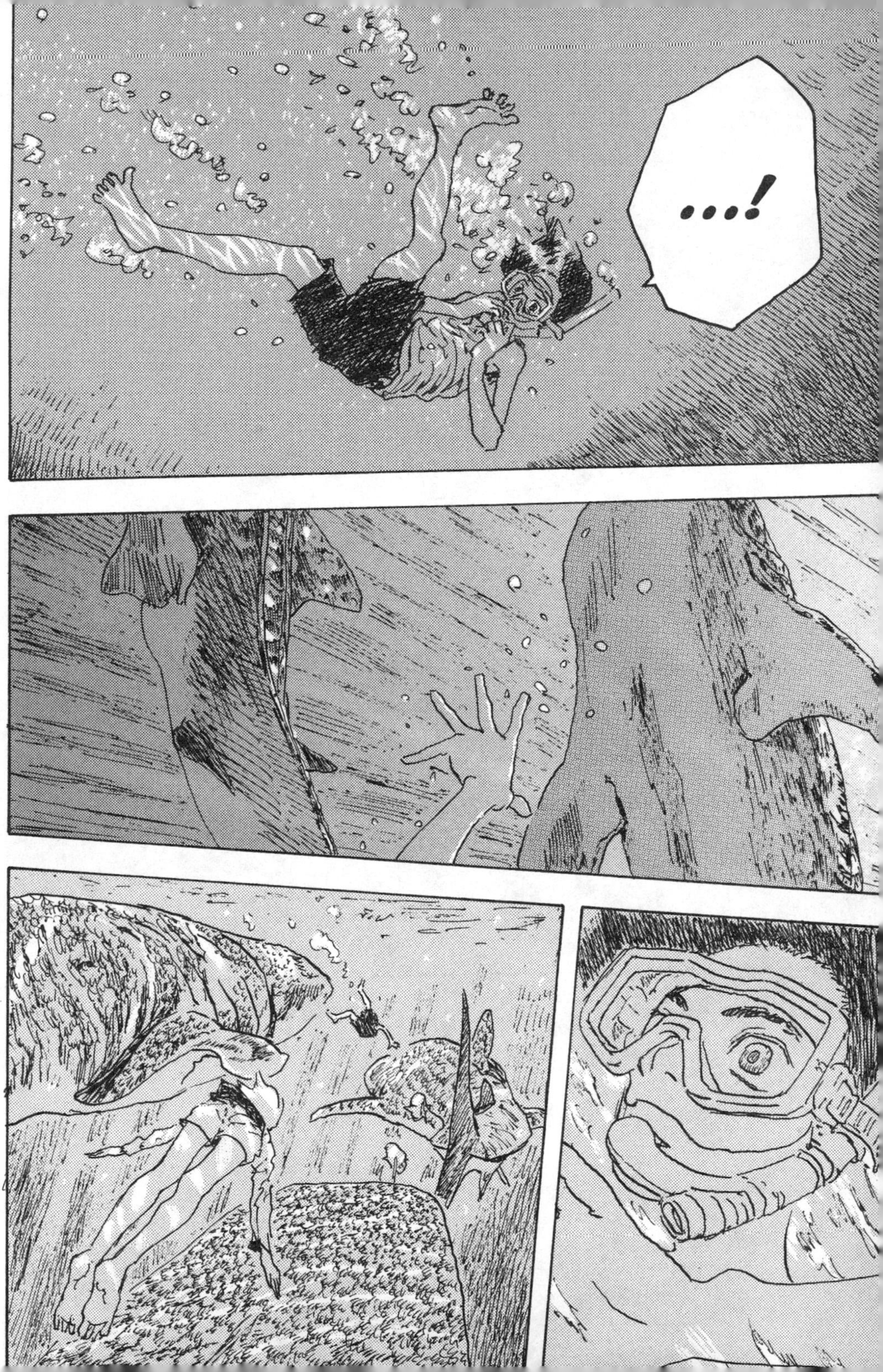
...!

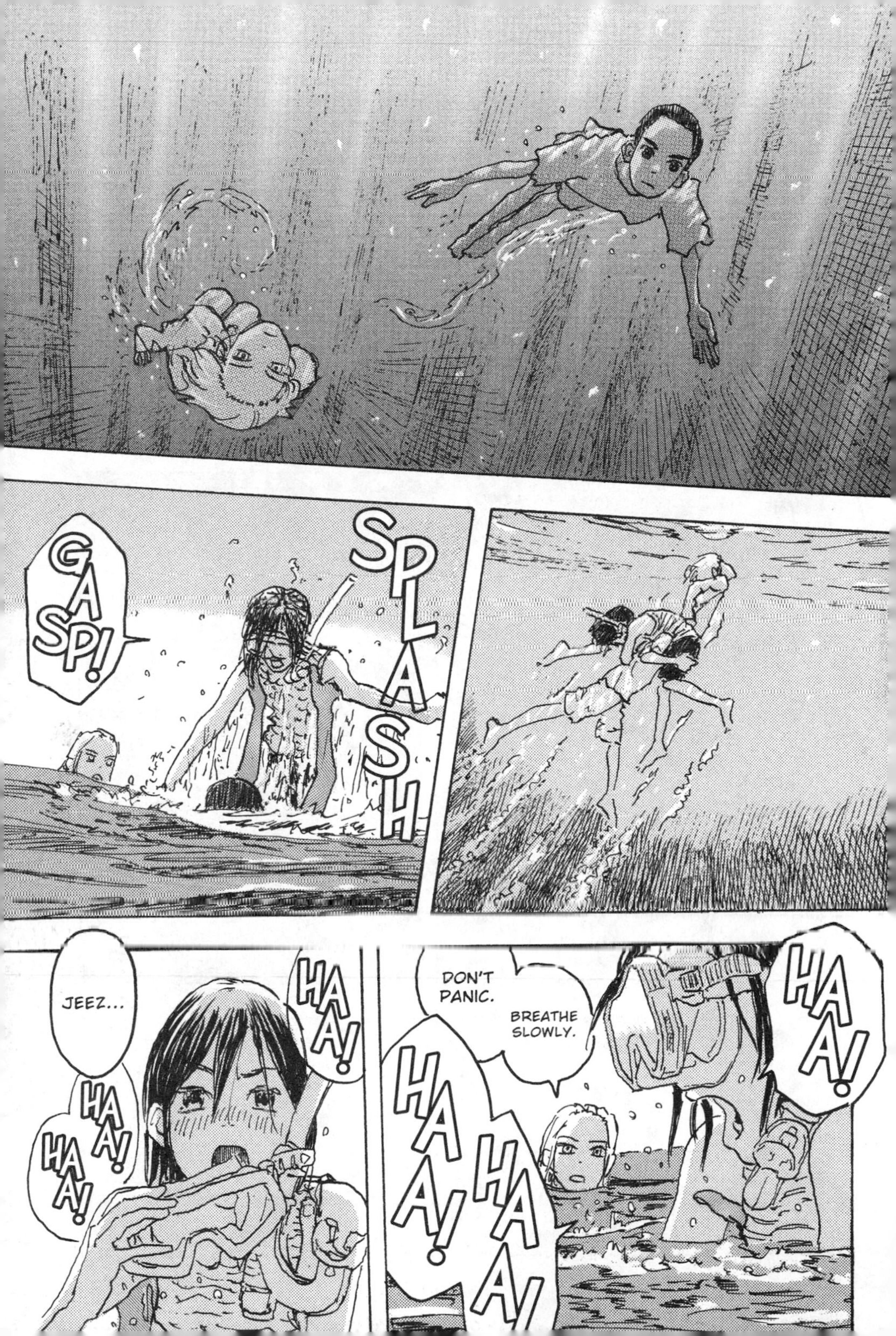
SPLASH
GASP!
HAA!
DON'T PANIC.
BREATHE SLOWLY.
HAHAA!
HAHAA!
HAA!
JEEZ...
HAA!
HAA!

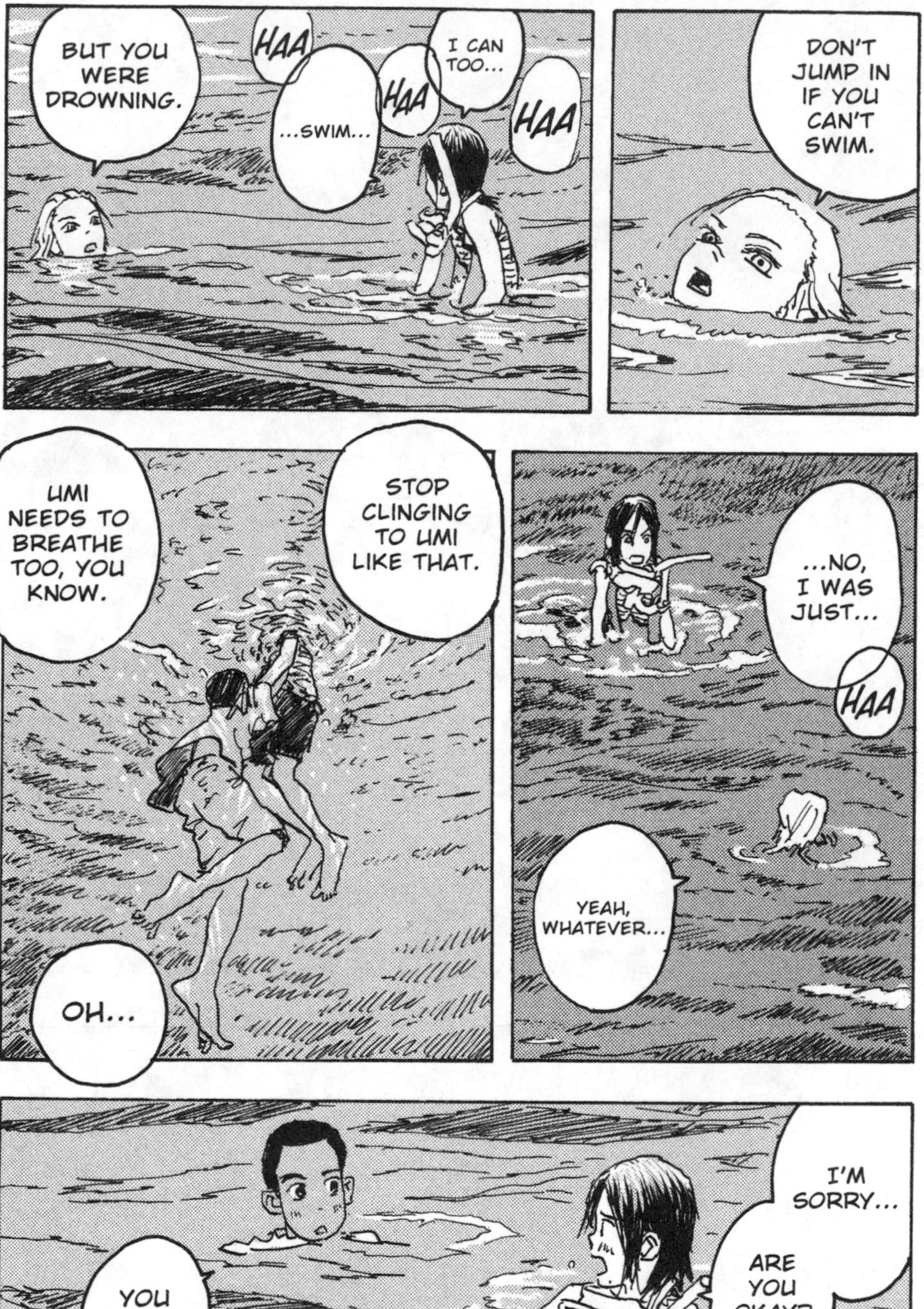
DON'T JUMP IN IF YOU CAN'T SWIM.
I CAN TOO...
HAA
HAA
...SWIM...
HAA
BUT YOU WERE DROWNING.
...NO, I WAS JUST...
HAA
YEAH, WHATEVER...
STOP CLINGING TO UMI LIKE THAT.
UMI NEEDS TO BREATHE TOO, YOU KNOW.
OH...
I'M SORRY...
ARE YOU OKAY?
YOU OKAY?

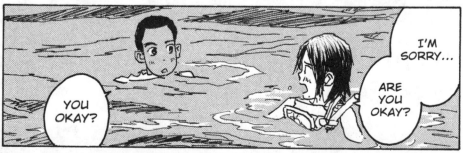

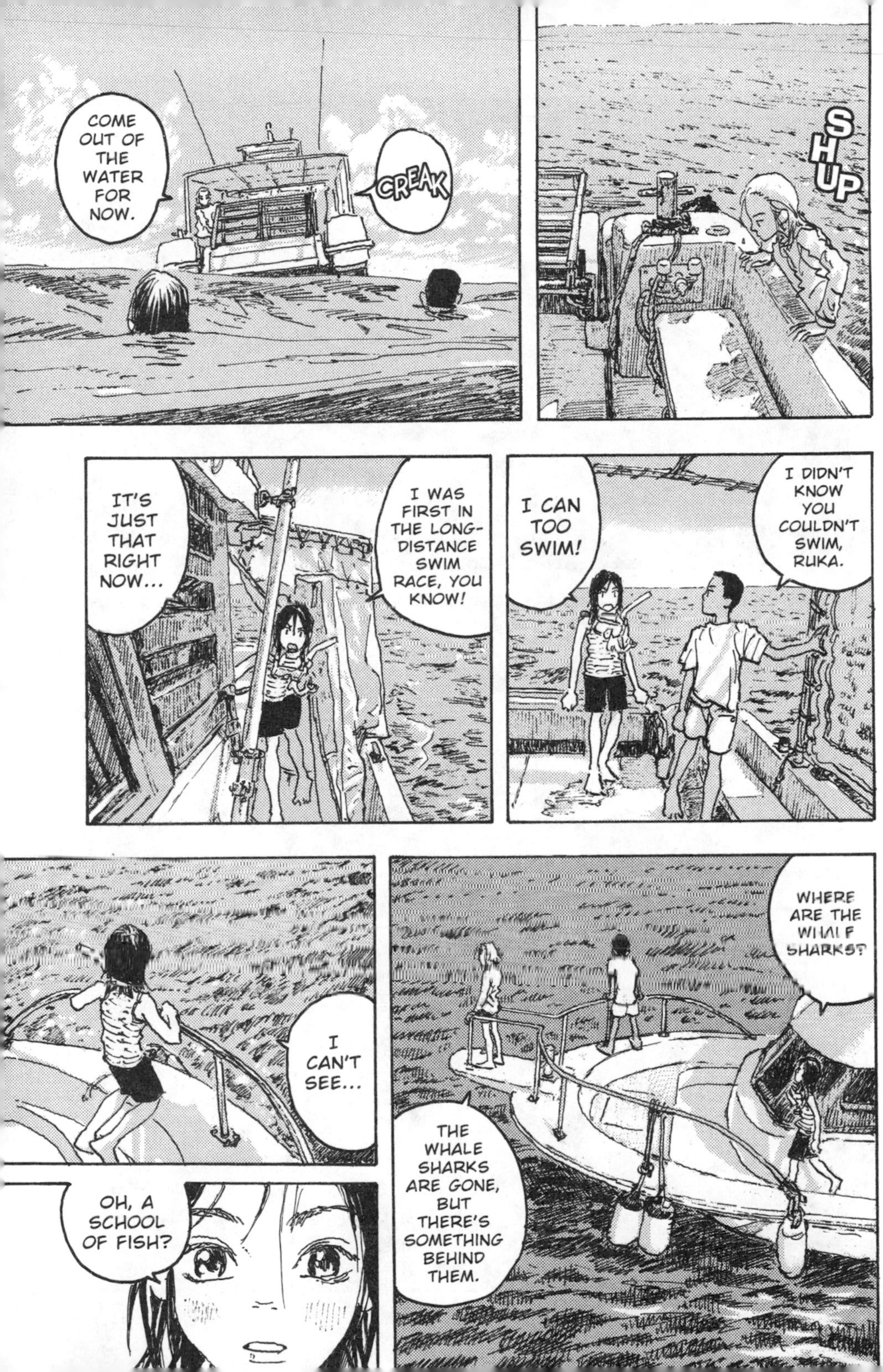
SHUP
CREAK
COME OUT OF THE WATER FOR NOW.
I DIDN'T KNOW YOU COULDN'T SWIM, RUKA.
I CAN TOO SWIM!
I WAS FIRST IN THE LONG-DISTANCE SWIM RACE, YOU KNOW!
IT'S JUST THAT RIGHT NOW...
WHERE ARE THE WHALE SHARKS?
THE WHALE SHARKS ARE GONE, BUT THERE'S SOMETHING BEHIND THEM.
I CAN'T SEE...
OH, A SCHOOL OF FISH?

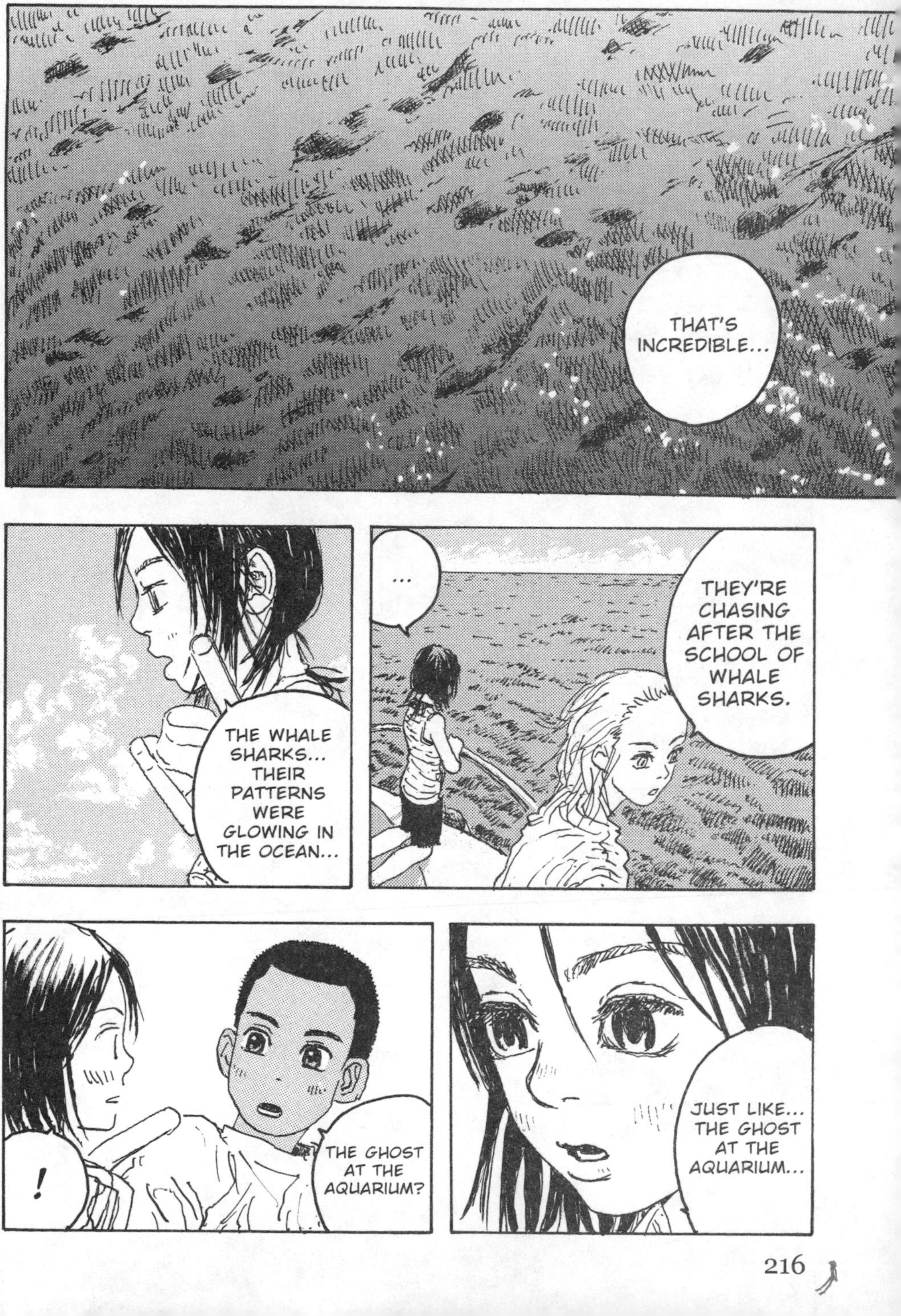
THAT'S INCREDIBLE...
THEY'RE CHASING AFTER THE SCHOOL OF WHALE SHARKS.
...
THE WHALE SHARKS... THEIR PATTERNS WERE GLOWING IN THE OCEAN...
JUST LIKE... THE GHOST AT THE AQUARIUM...
THE GHOST AT THE AQUARIUM?
!

...

WHAT?

WHAT?

YEAH...

A LONG TIME AGO... I SAW IT.

THE FISH TURNED INTO LIGHT AND DISAPPEARED...

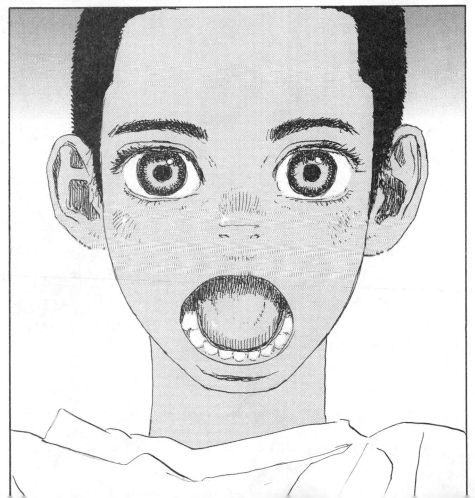

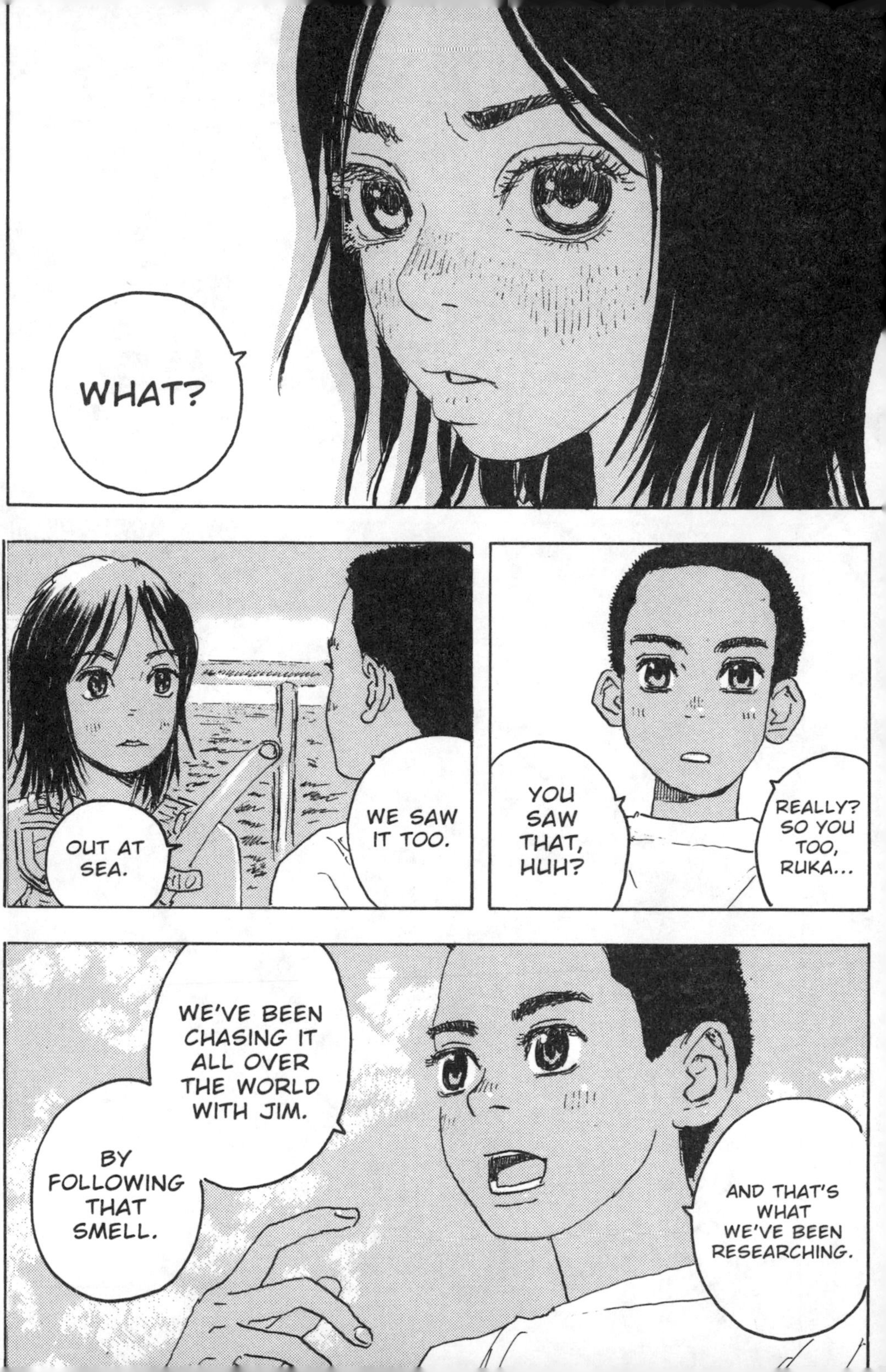
WHAT?
REALLY? SO YOU TOO, RUKA...
YOU SAW THAT, HUH?
WE SAW IT TOO.
OUT AT SEA.
WE'VE BEEN CHASING IT ALL OVER THE WORLD WITH JIM.
BY FOLLOWING THAT SMELL.
AND THAT'S WHAT WE'VE BEEN RESEARCHING.

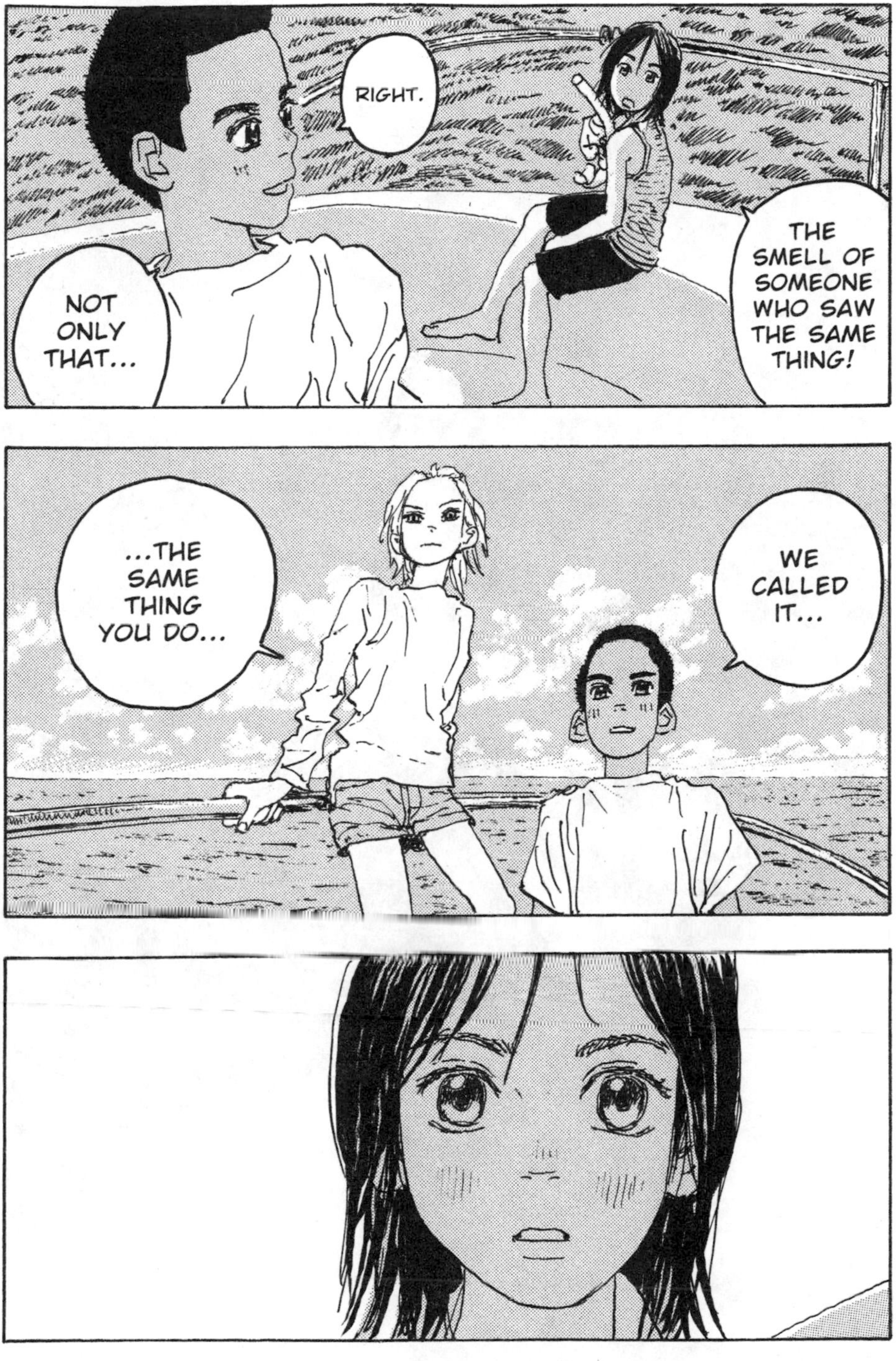
THE SMELL OF SOMEONE WHO SAW THE SAME THING!
RIGHT.
NOT ONLY THAT...
WE CALLED IT...
...THE SAME THING YOU DO...

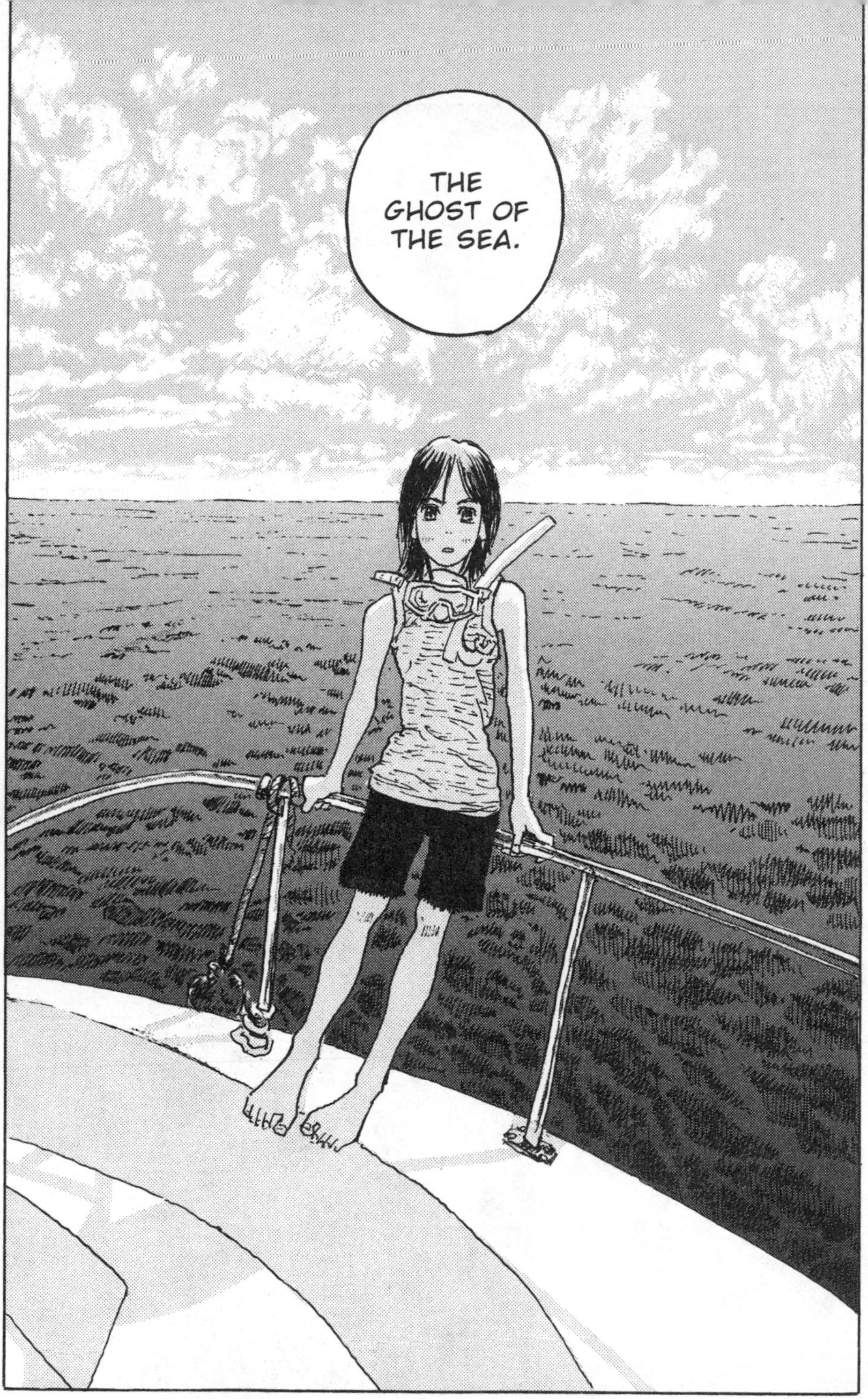
THE GHOST OF THE SEA.

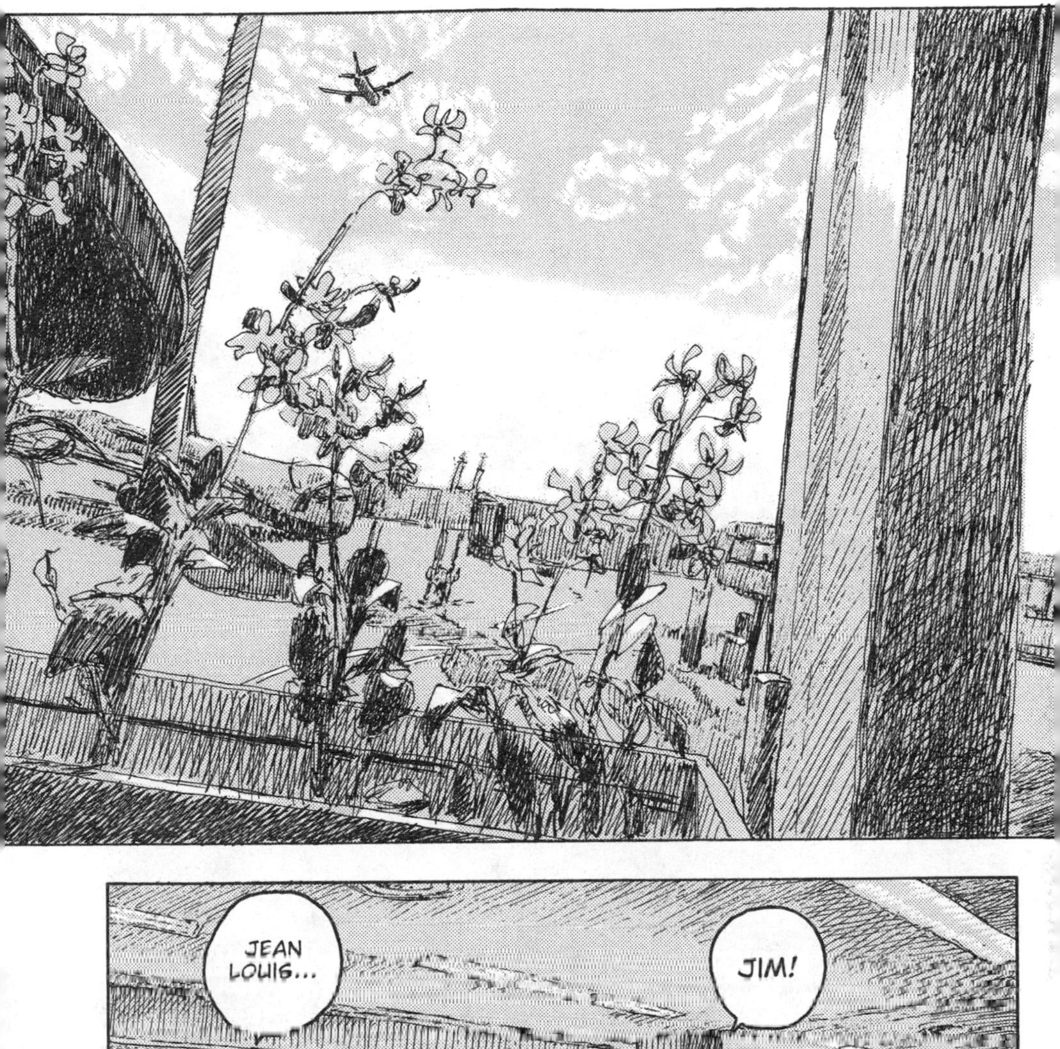

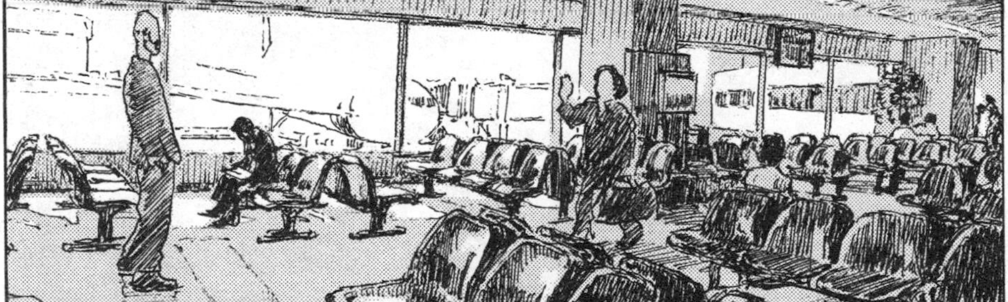
JIM!
JEAN LOUIS...

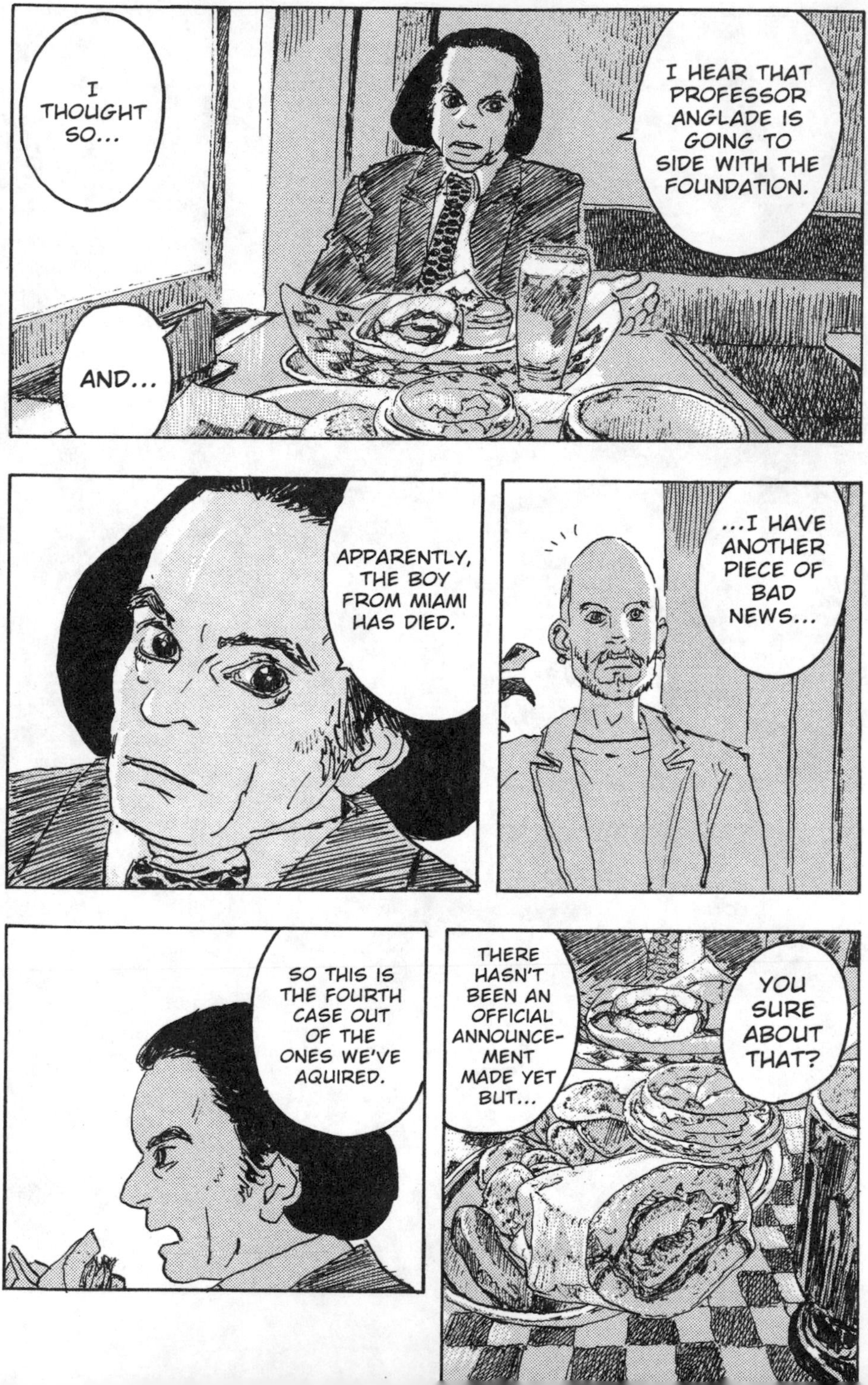
I HEAR THAT PROFESSOR ANGLADE IS GOING TO SIDE WITH THE FOUNDATION.
I THOUGHT SO...
AND...
...I HAVE ANOTHER PIECE OF BAD NEWS...
APPARENTLY, THE BOY FROM MIAMI HAS DIED.
YOU SURE ABOUT THAT?
THERE HASN'T BEEN AN OFFICIAL ANNOUNCE-MENT MADE YET BUT...
SO THIS IS THE FOURTH CASE OUT OF THE ONES WE'VE AQUIRED.

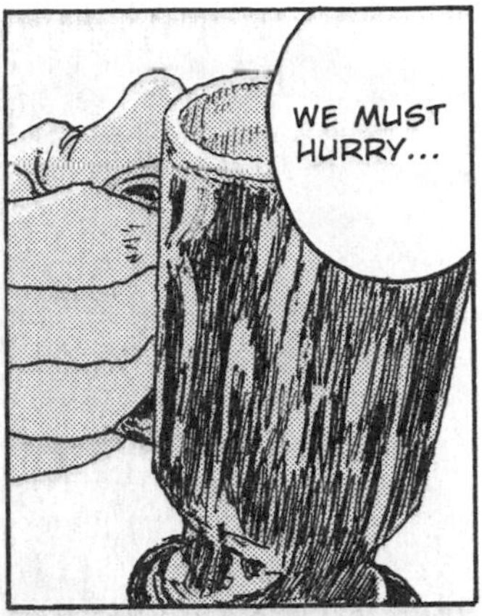
WE MUST HURRY...

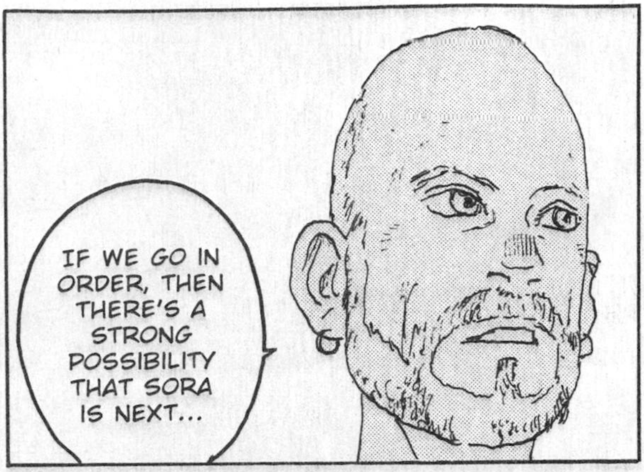
IF WE GO IN ORDER, THEN THERE'S A STRONG POSSIBILITY THAT SORA IS NEXT...

※ CHONDRITE: STONY METEORITES

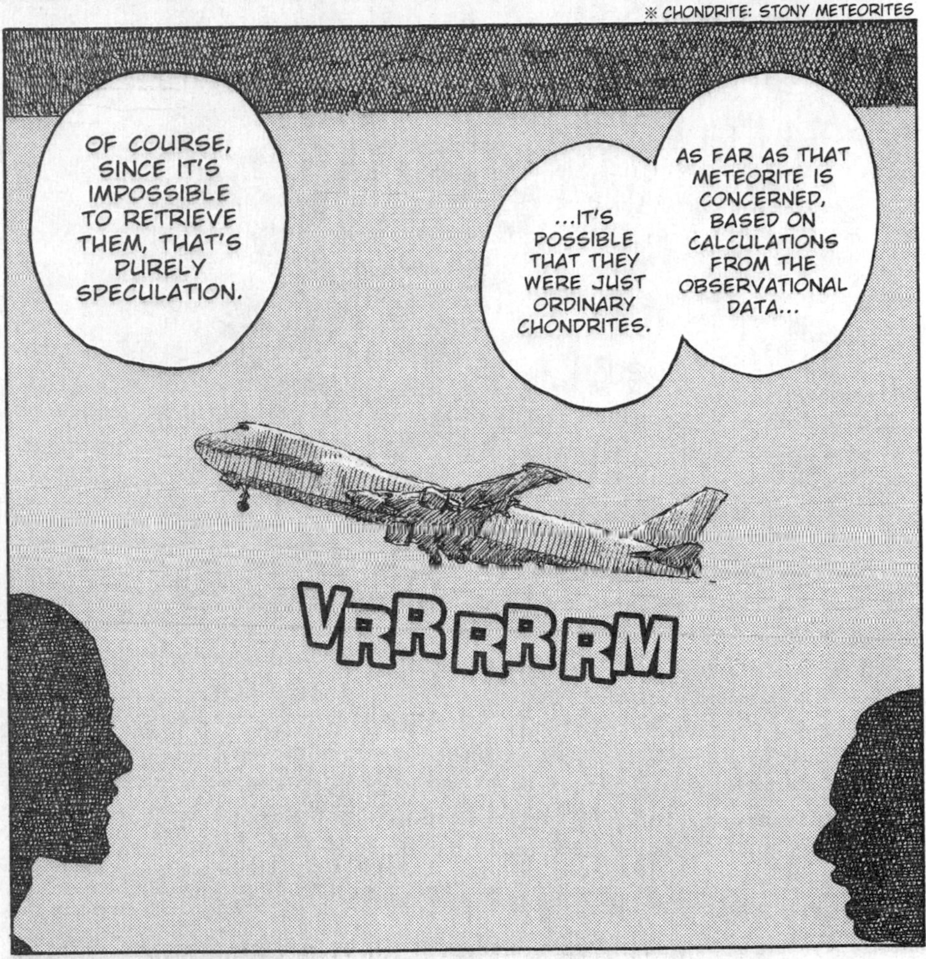
AS FAR AS THAT METEORITE IS CONCERNED, BASED ON CALCULATIONS FROM THE OBSERVATIONAL DATA...
...IT'S POSSIBLE THAT THEY WERE JUST ORDINARY CHONDRITES.
OF COURSE, SINCE IT'S IMPOSSIBLE TO RETRIEVE THEM, THAT'S PURELY SPECULATION.
VRRRRRM

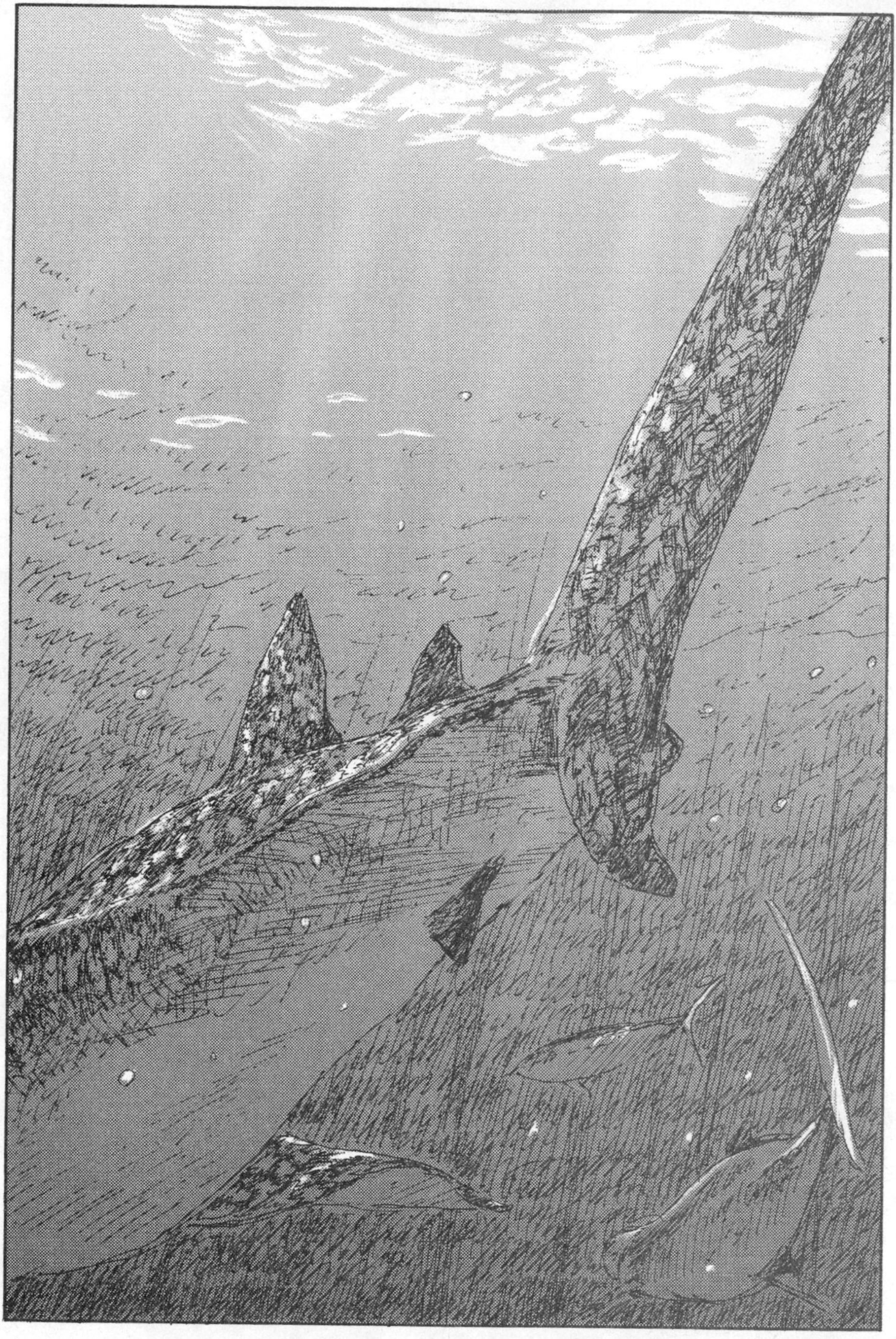

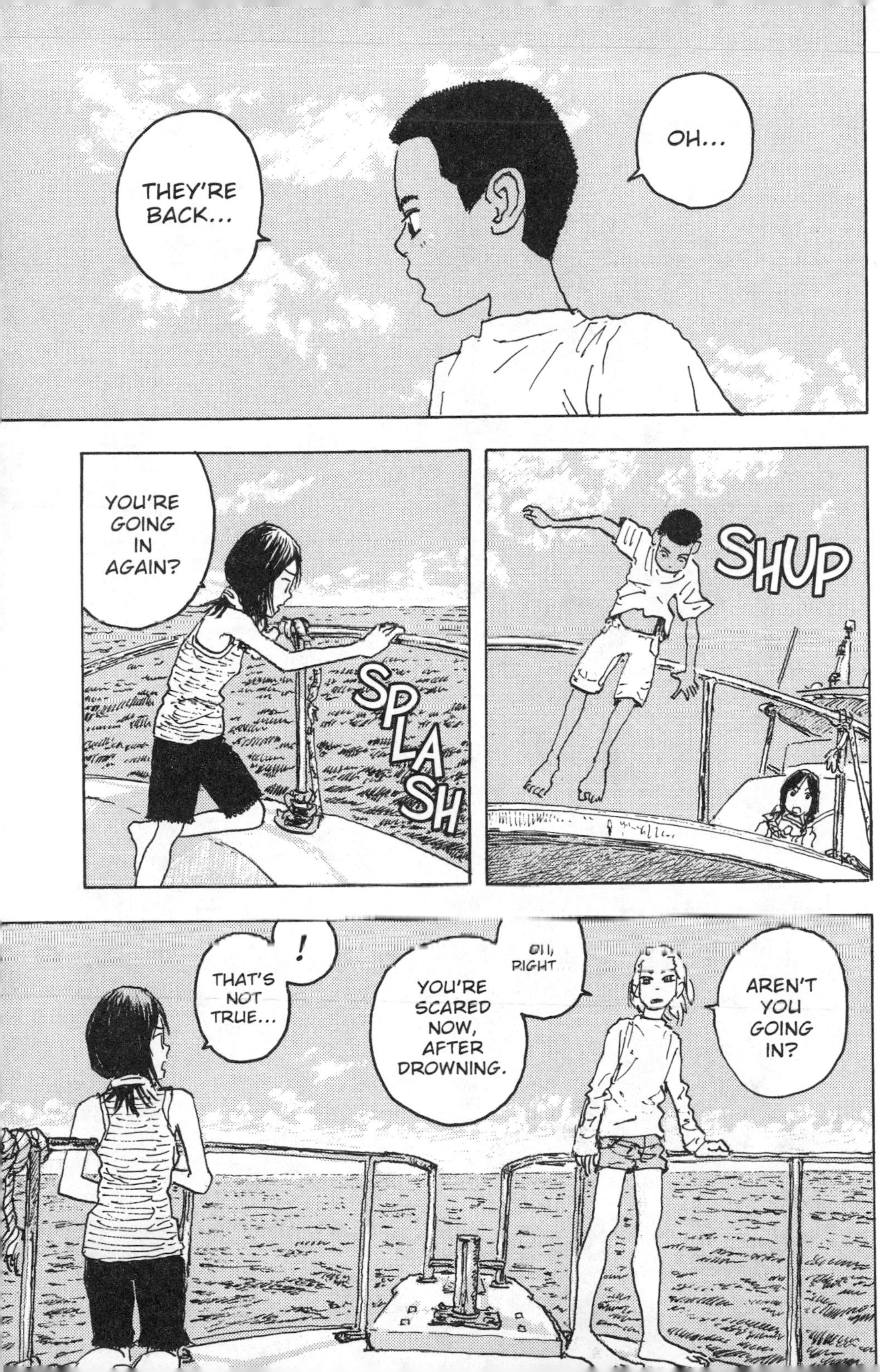
OH...
THEY'RE BACK...
SHUP
YOU'RE GOING IN AGAIN?
SPLASH
AREN'T YOU GOING IN?
OH, RIGHT
YOU'RE SCARED NOW, AFTER DROWNING.
!
THAT'S NOT TRUE...

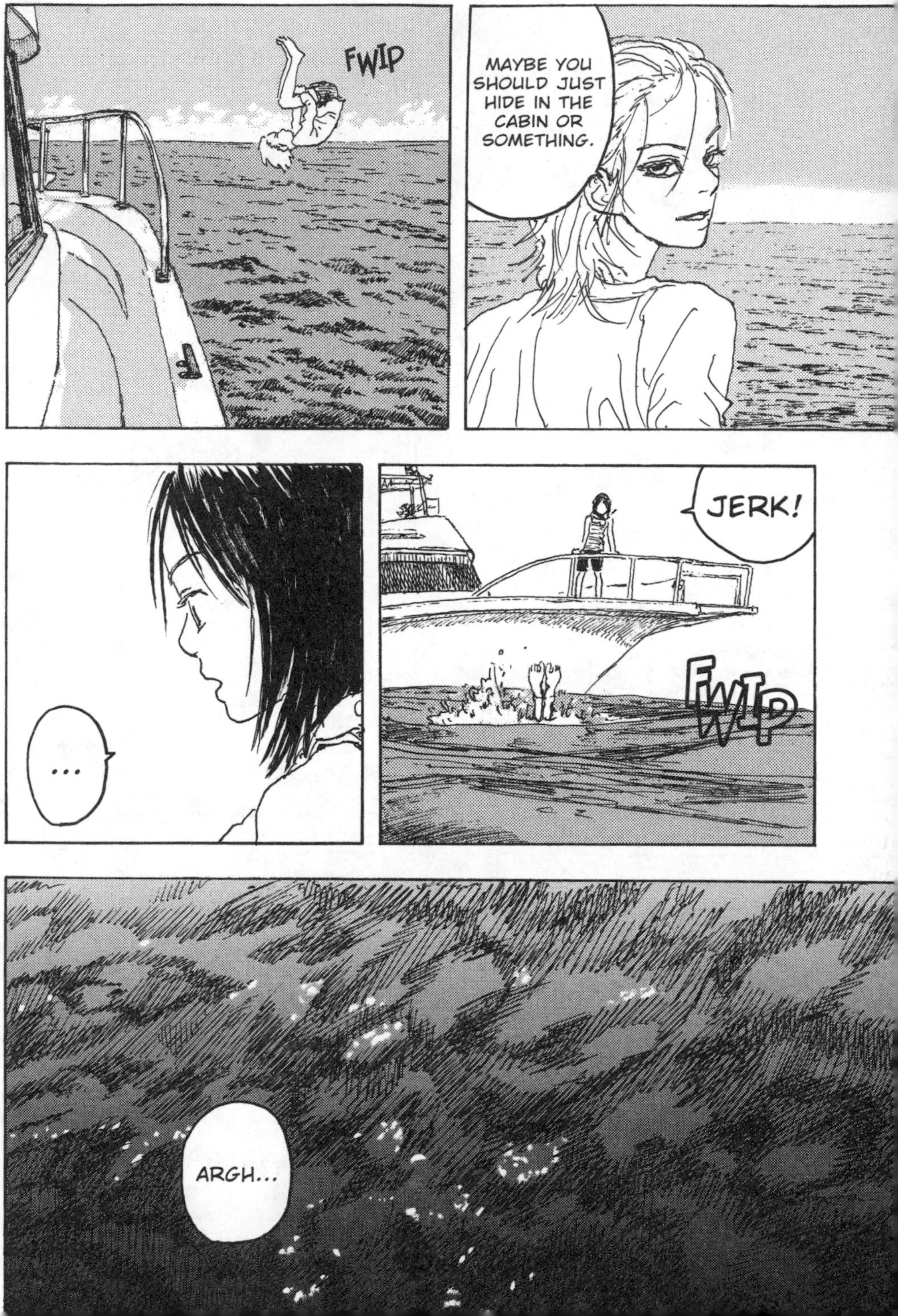
MAYBE YOU SHOULD JUST HIDE IN THE CABIN OR SOMETHING.
FWIP
JERK!
FWIP
...
ARGH...

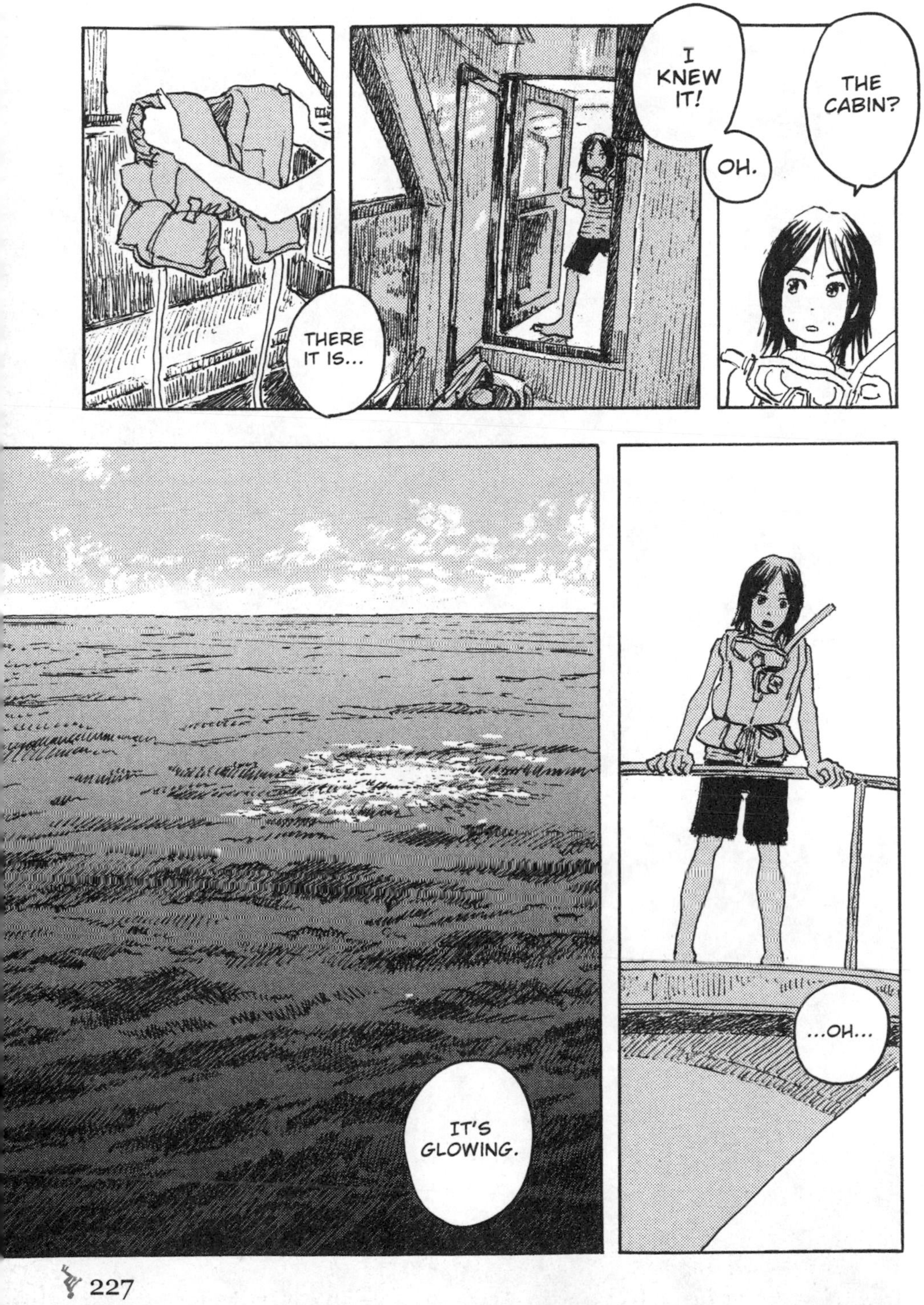
THE CABIN?
OH.
I KNEW IT!
THERE IT IS...
...OH...
IT'S GLOWING.

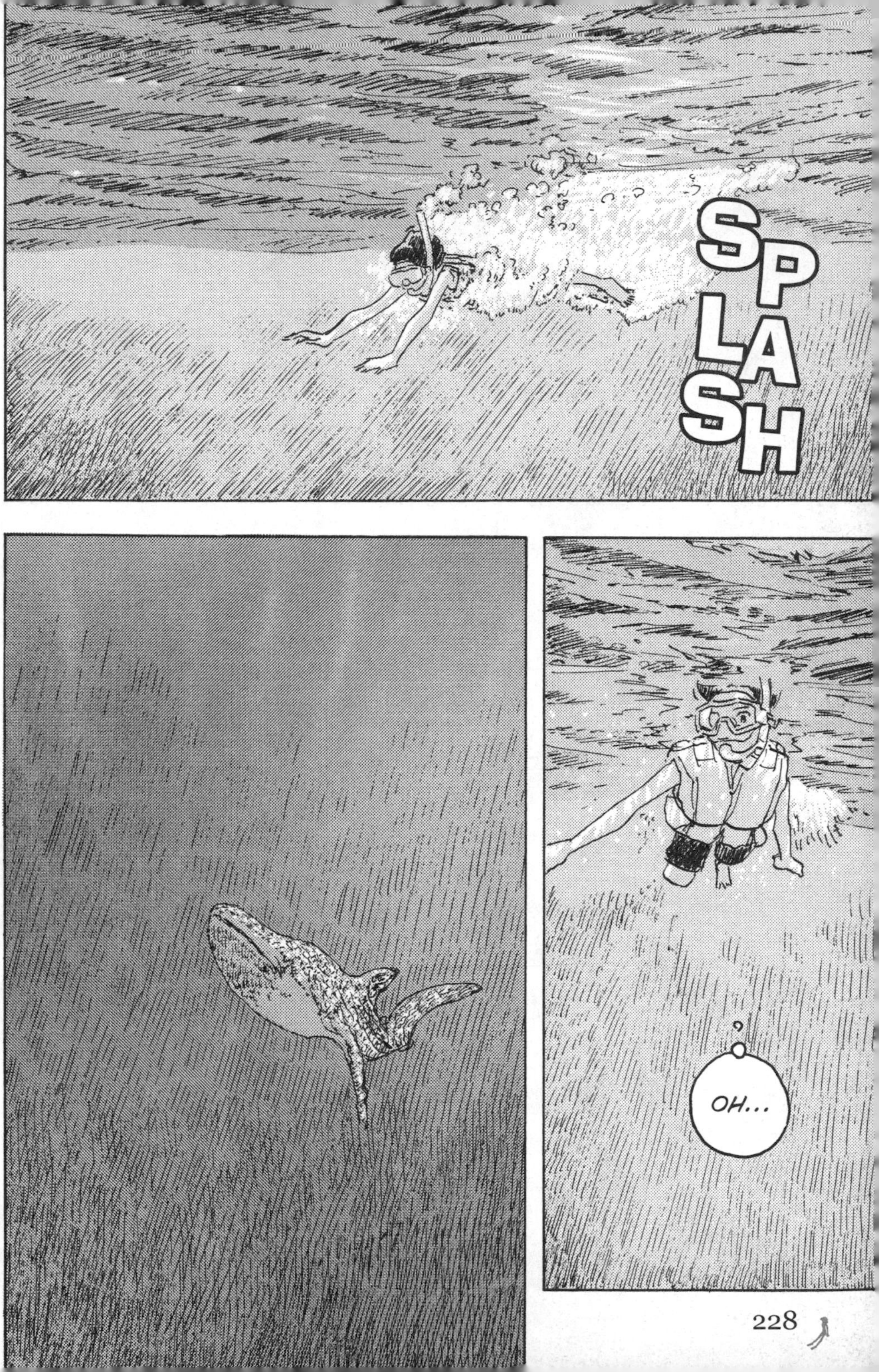
SPLASH
OH...

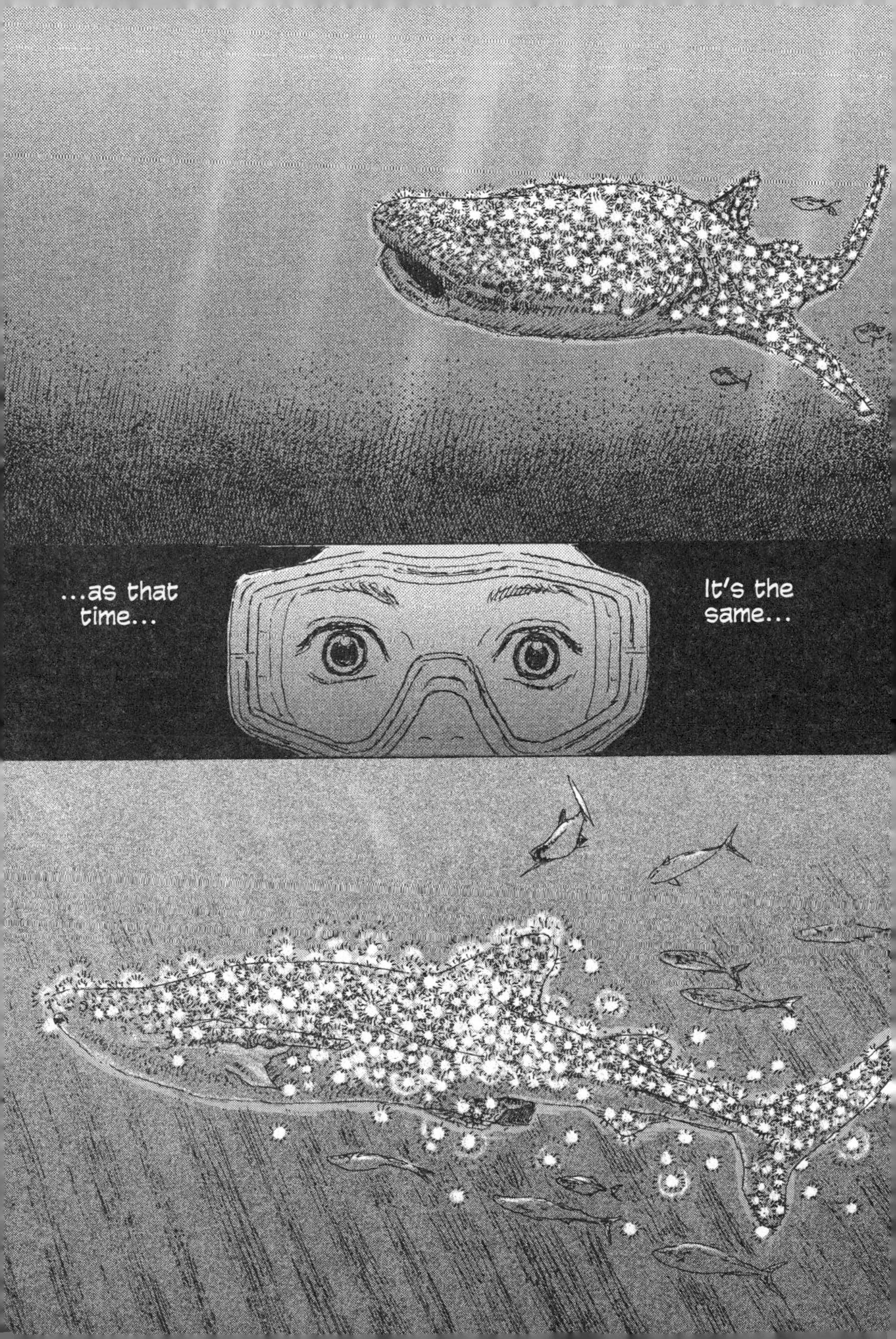
It's the same...
...as that time...

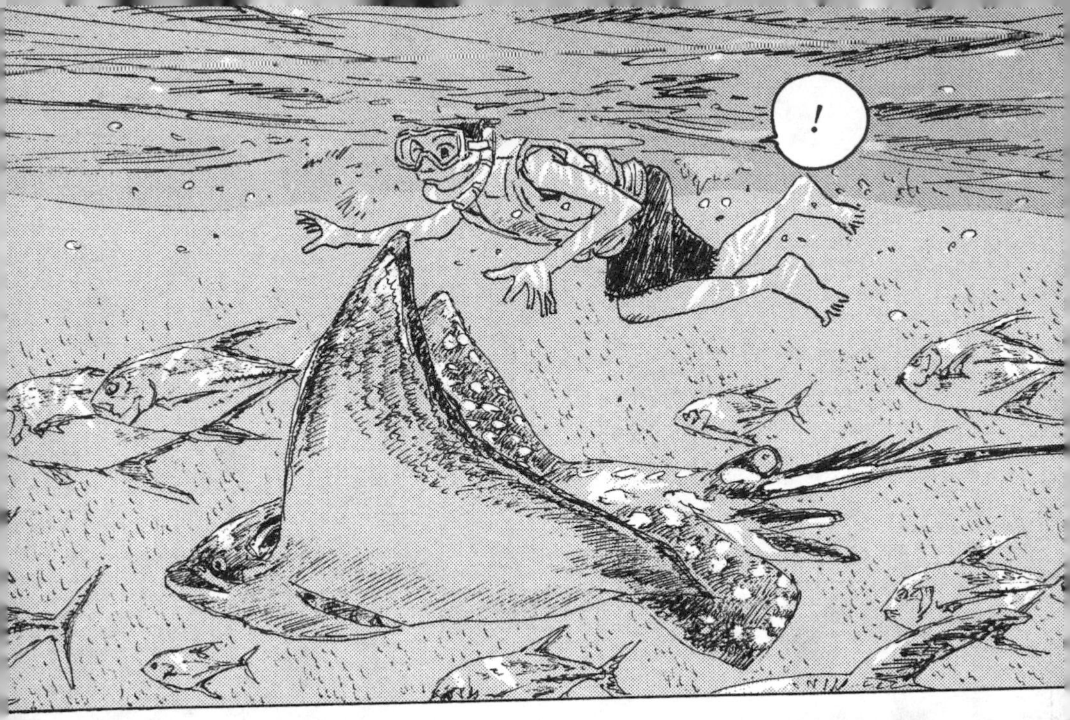
!
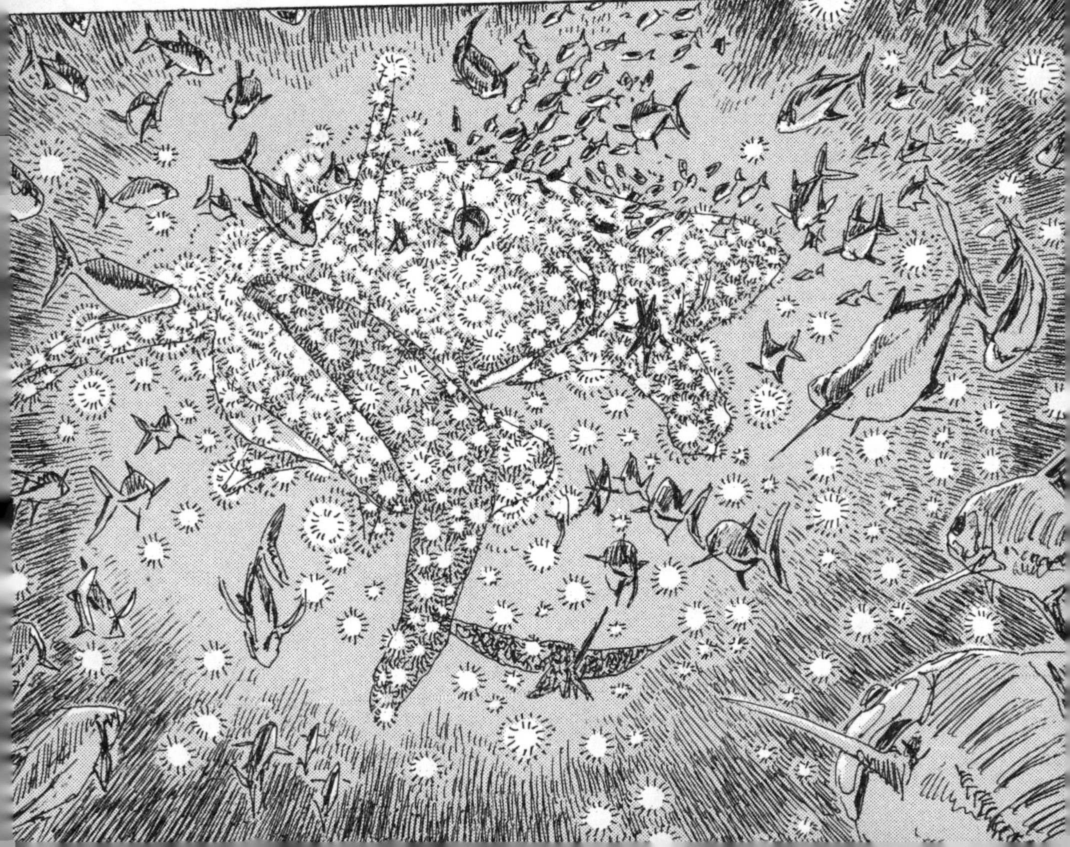

They're eating...

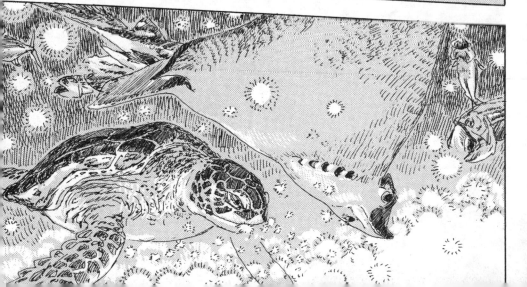

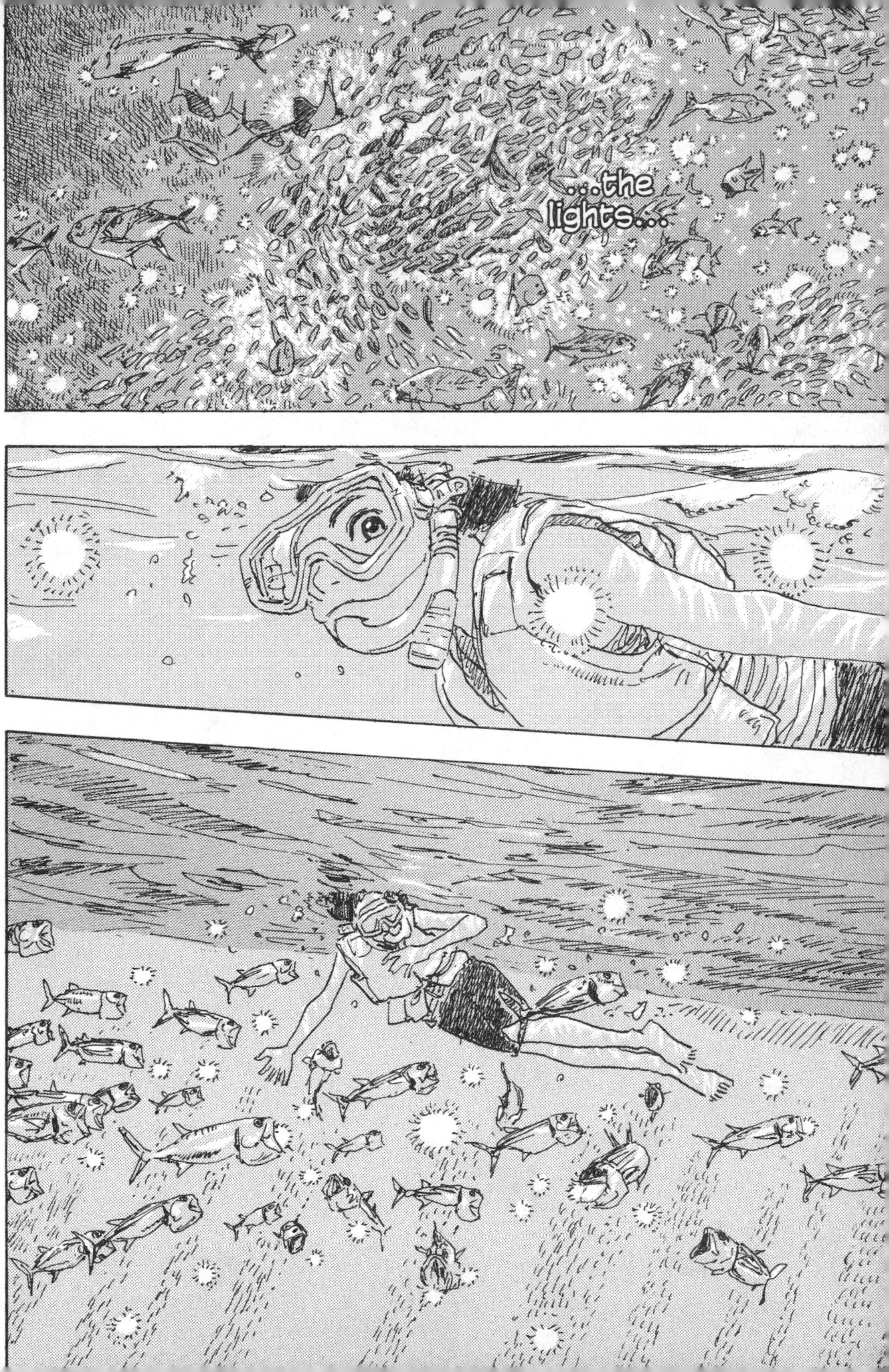
...the lights...

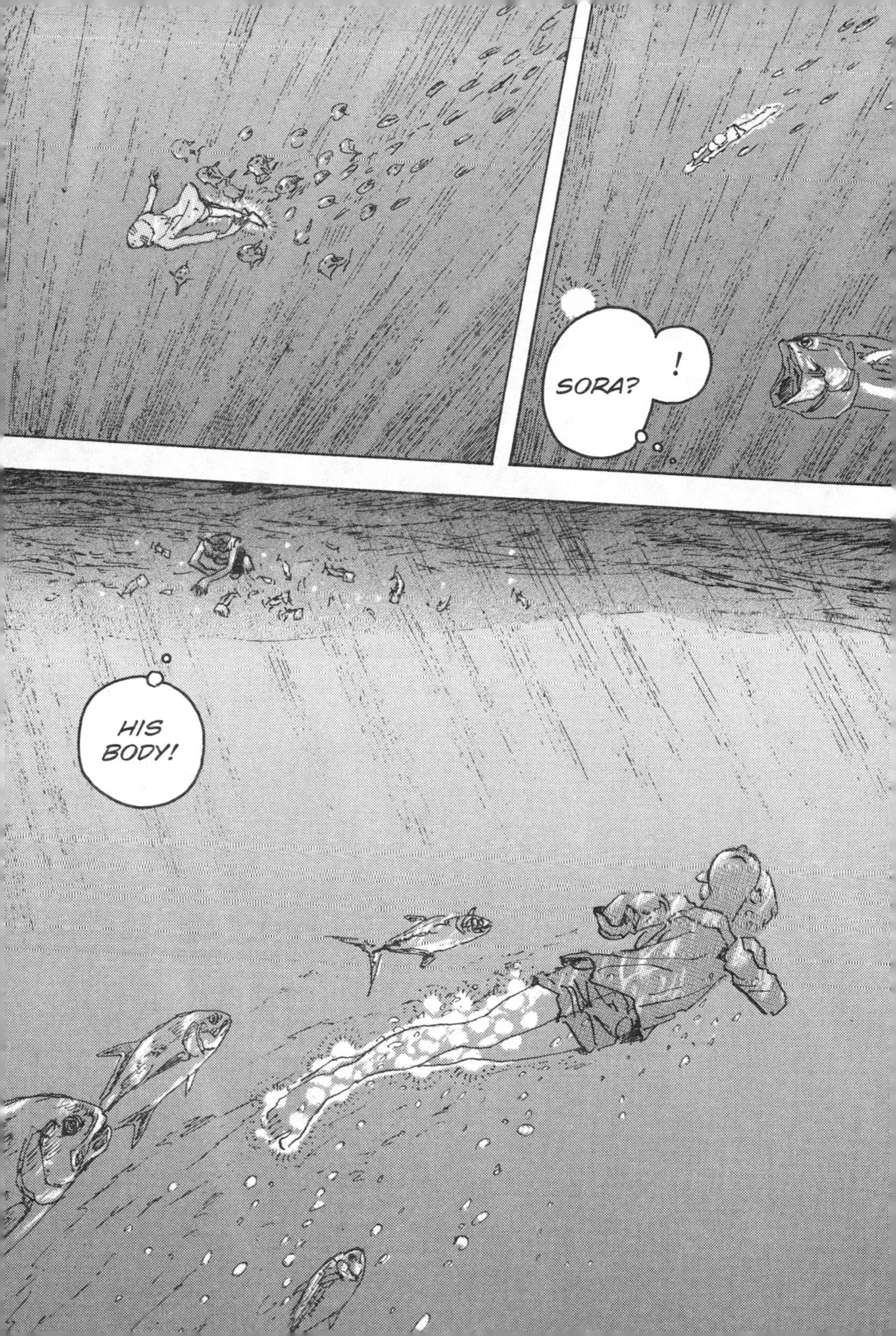
!
SORA?
HIS BODY!

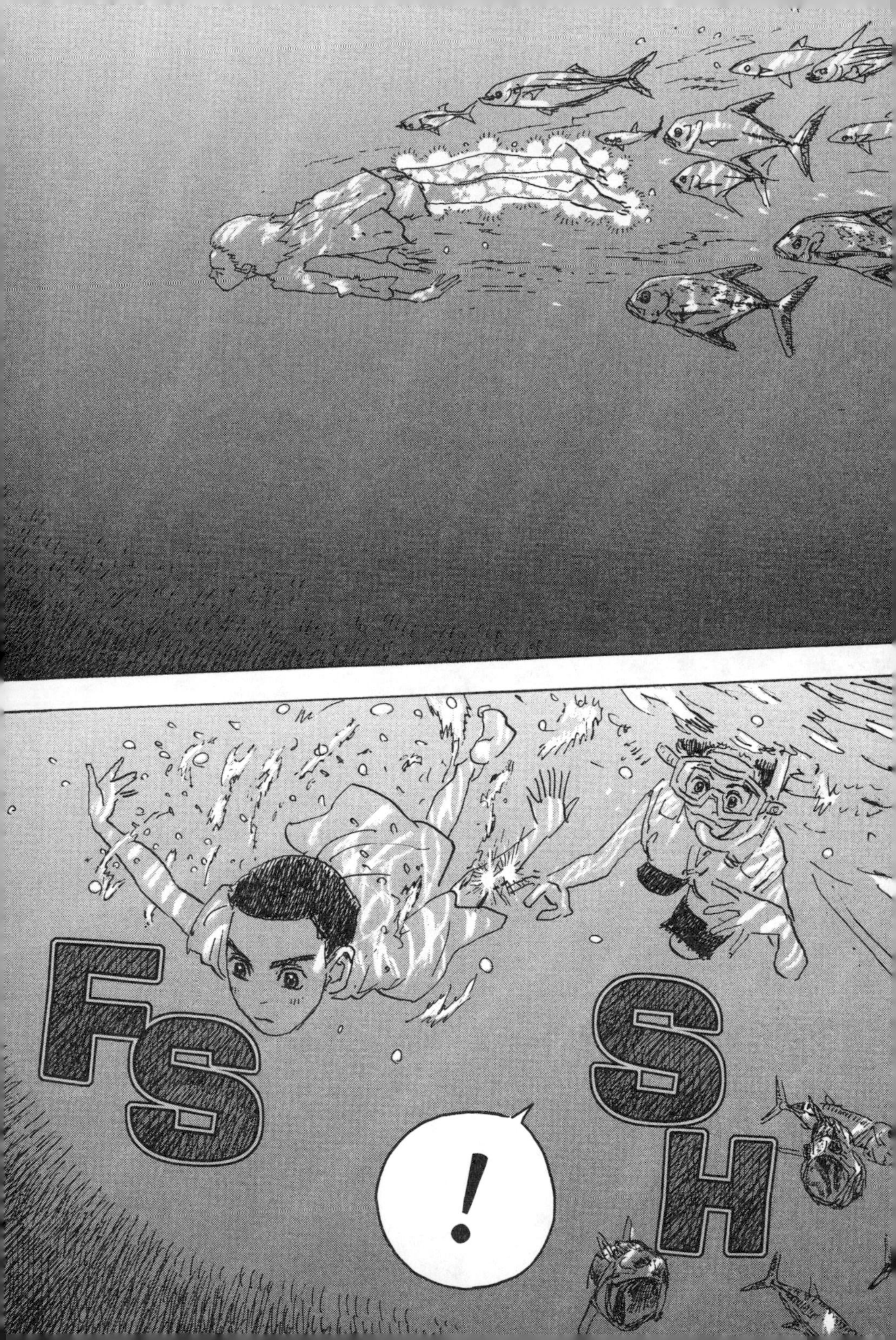
FSSH
!

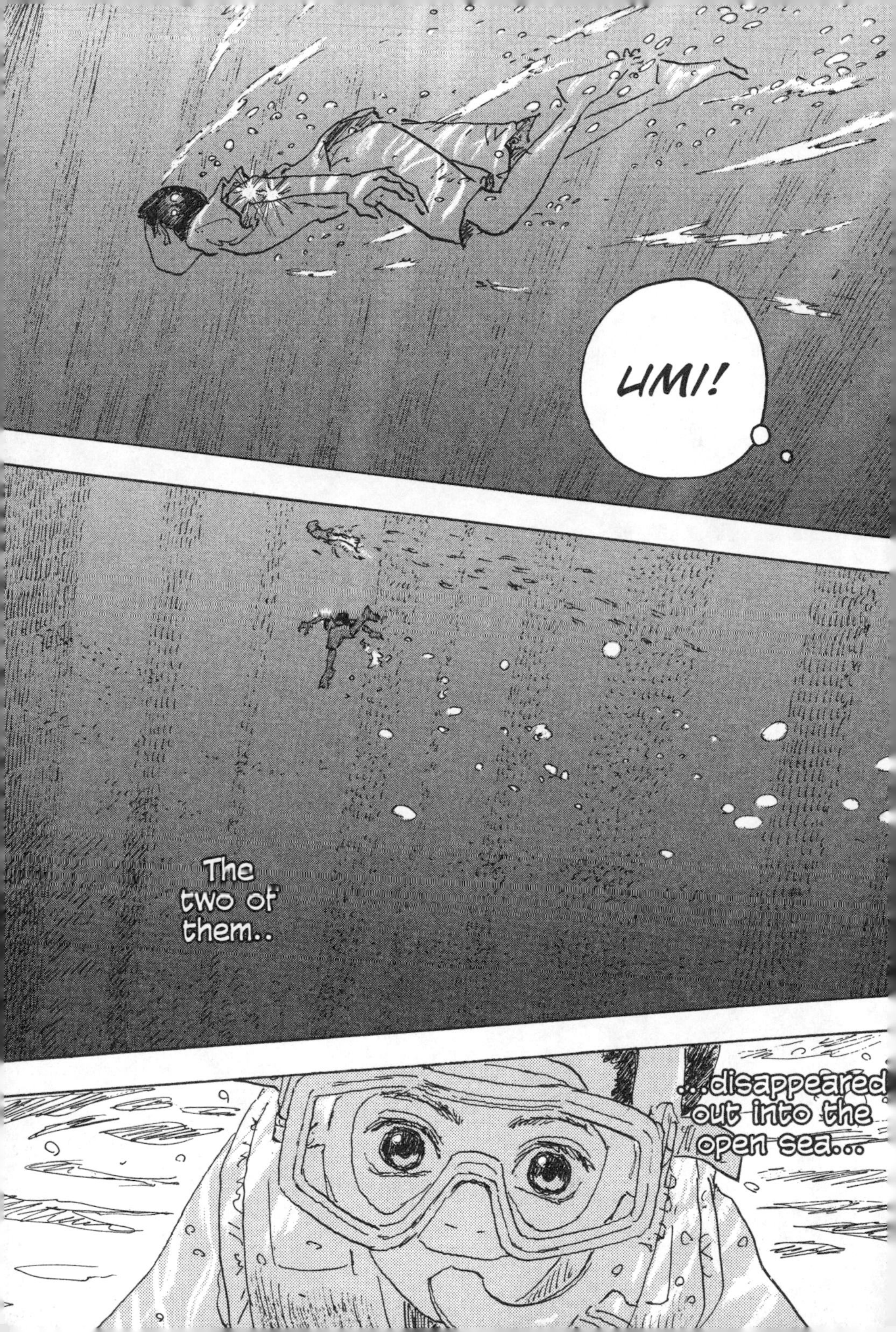
UMI!
The two of them..
...disappeared out into the open sea...

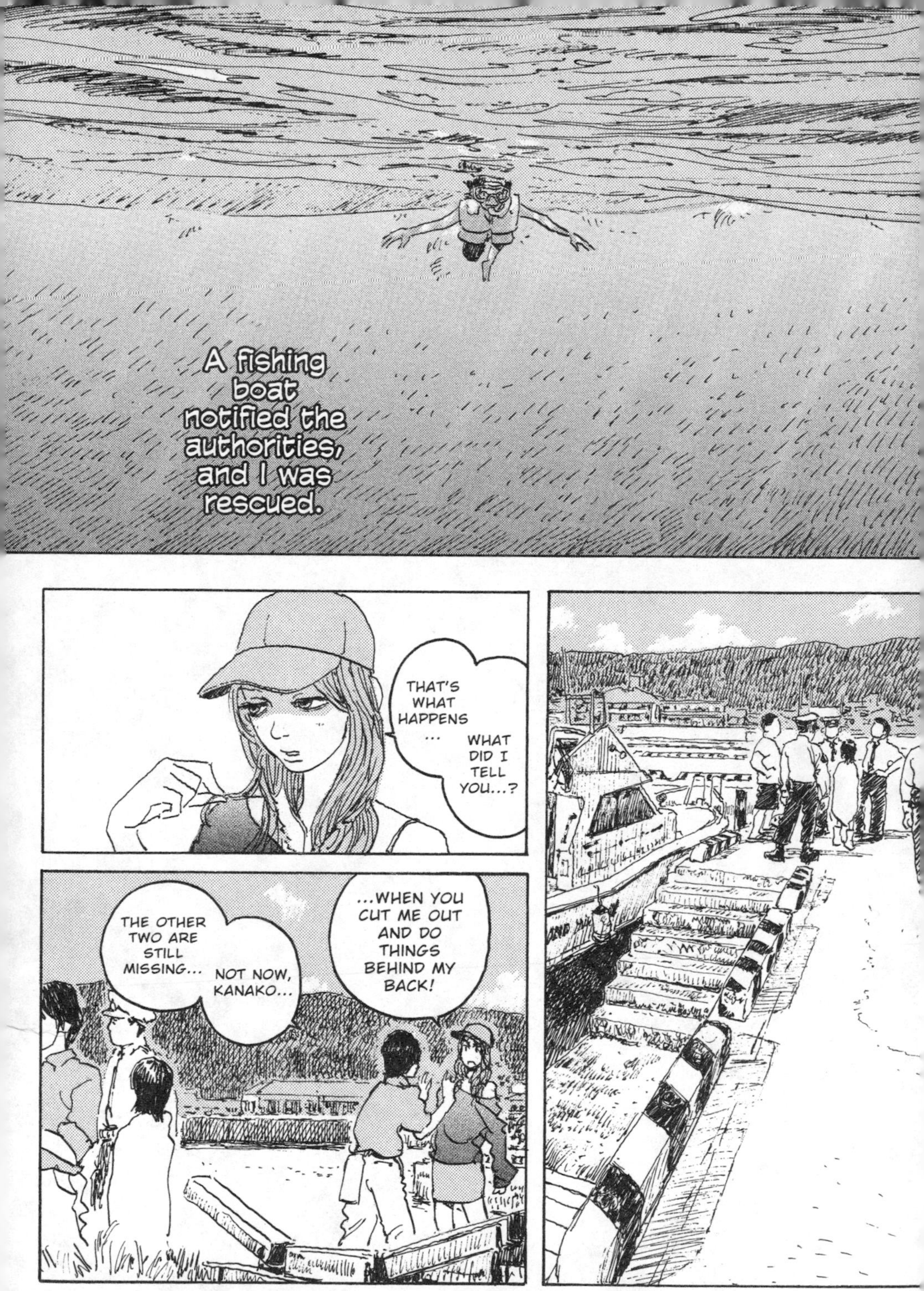
A fishing boat notified the authorities, and I was rescued.
THAT'S WHAT HAPPENS ...
WHAT DID I TELL YOU...?
...WHEN YOU CUT ME OUT AND DO THINGS BEHIND MY BACK!
NOT NOW, KANAKO...
THE OTHER TWO ARE STILL MISSING...

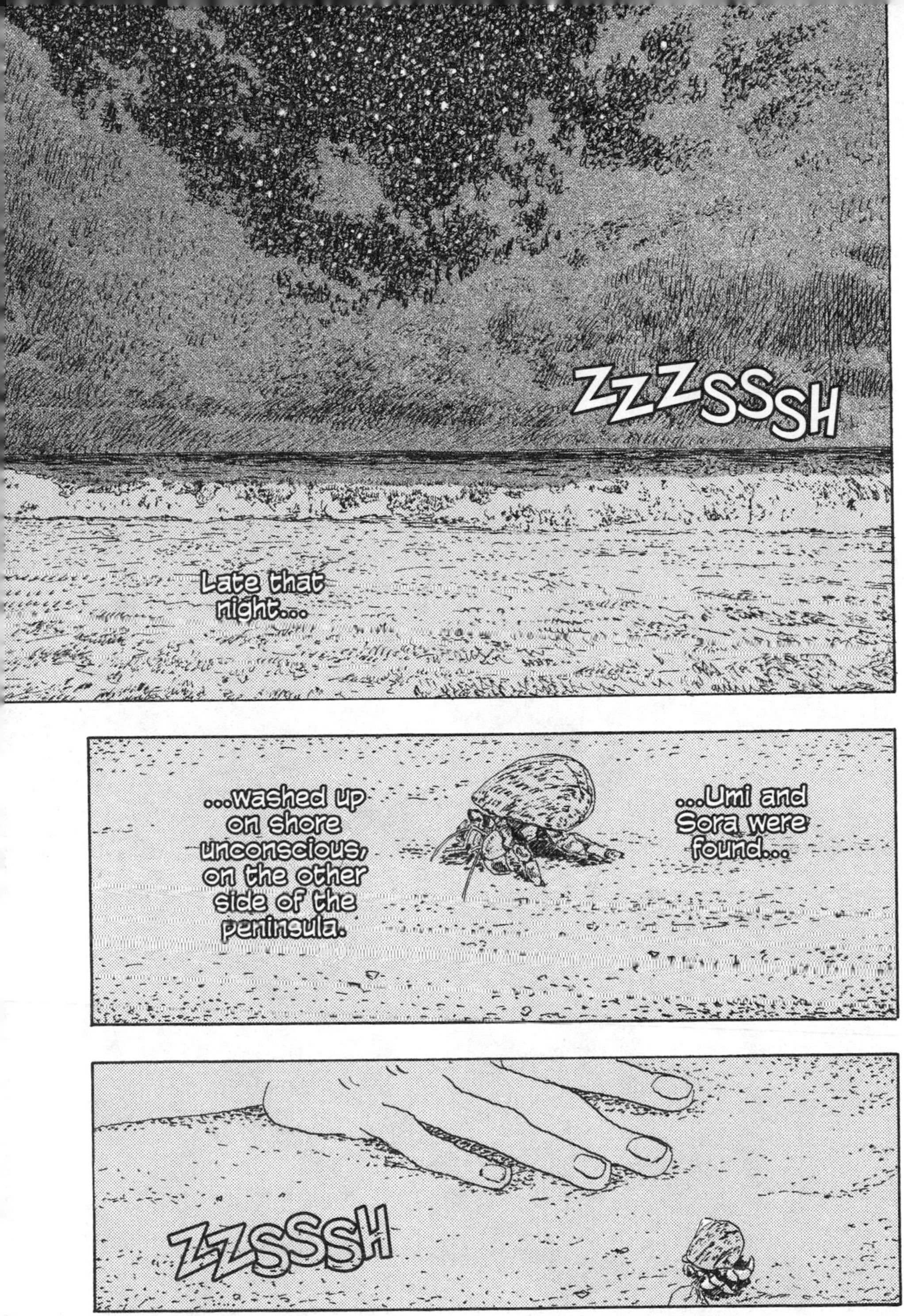
ZZZSSSH
Late that night...
...Umi and Sora were found...
...washed up on shore unconscious, on the other side of the peninsula.
ZZSSSH

ZZSSSH

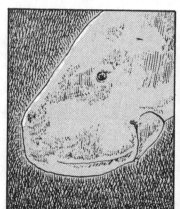

It was the seventh consecutive night that the temperature didn't fall below 77°F.

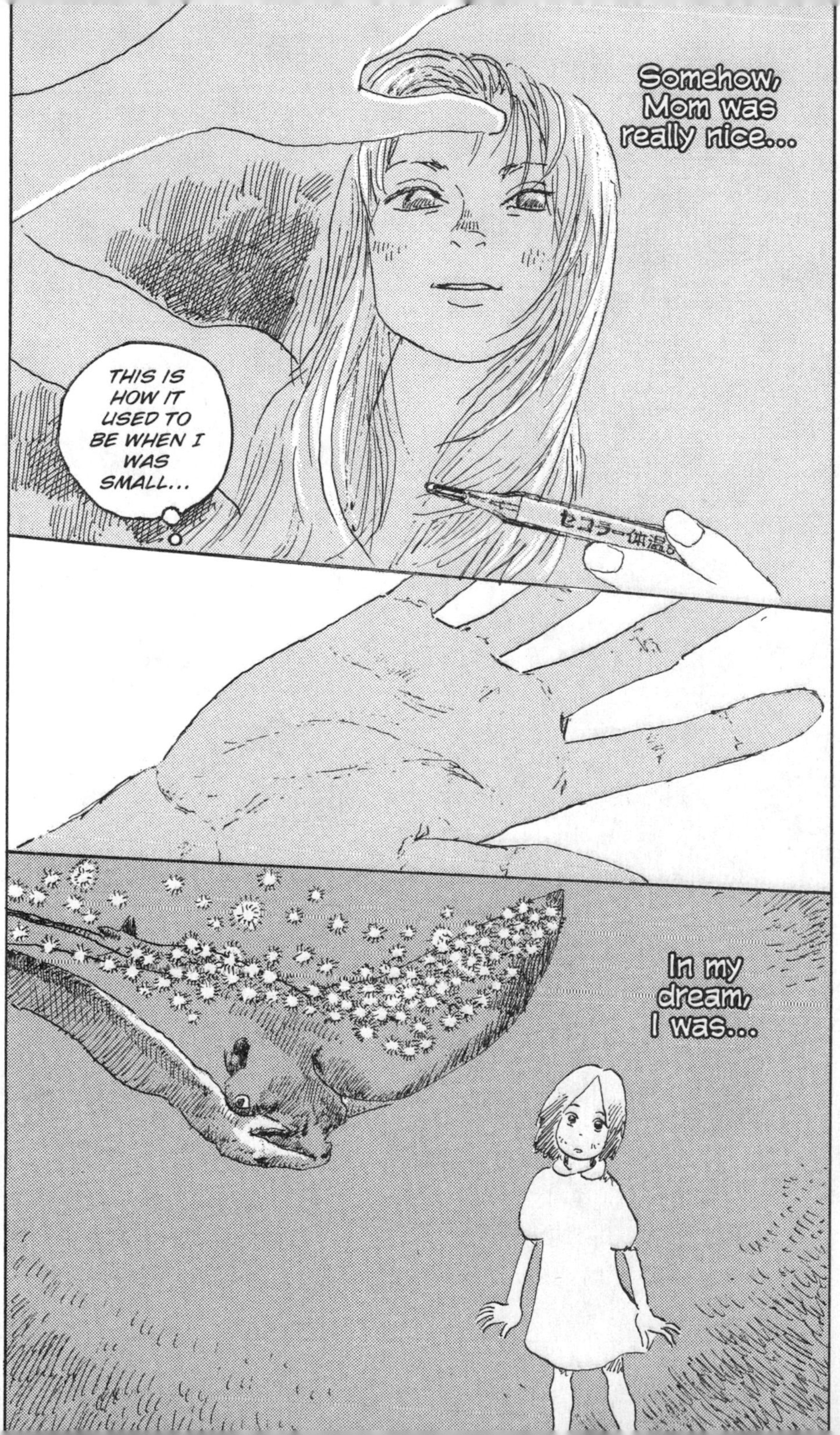
Somehow, Mom was really nice...
THIS IS HOW IT USED TO BE WHEN I WAS SMALL...
In my dream, I was...

Chapter 7: Chair

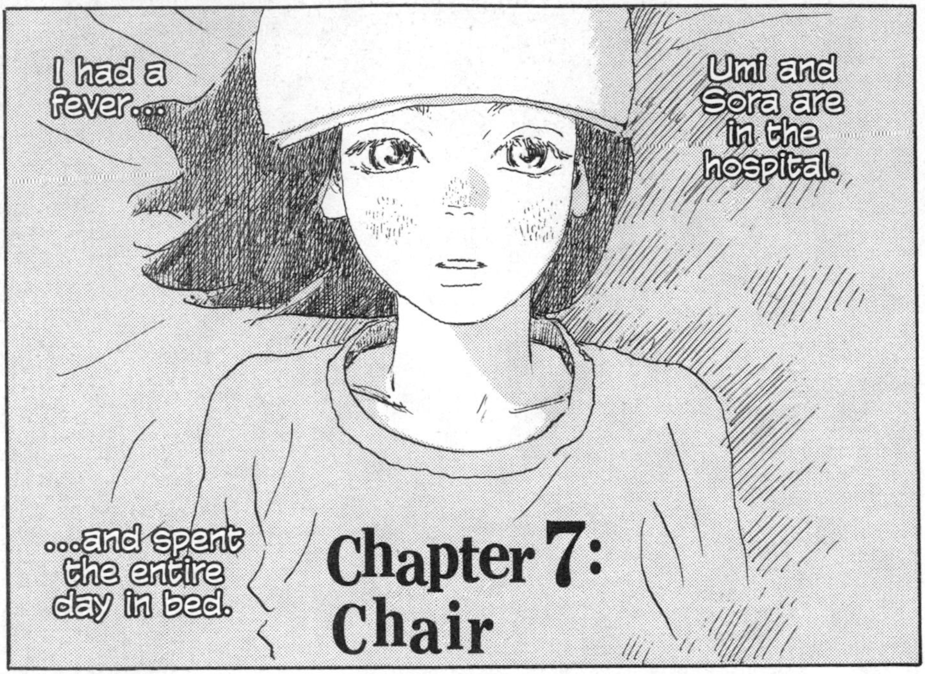
Umi and Sora are in the hospital.
I had a fever...
...and spent the entire day in bed.

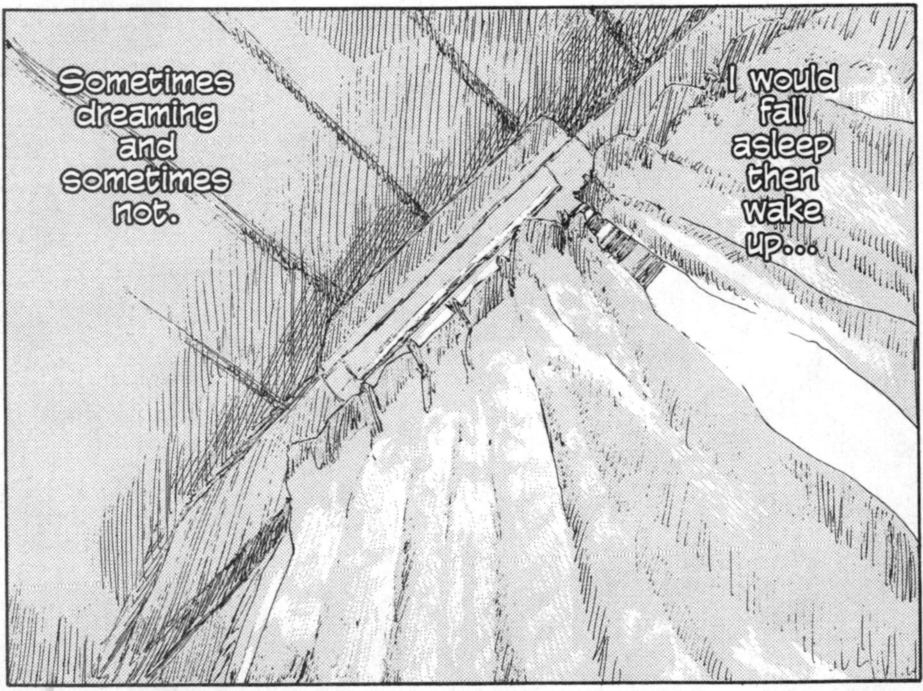
I would fall asleep then wake up...
Sometimes dreaming and sometimes not.

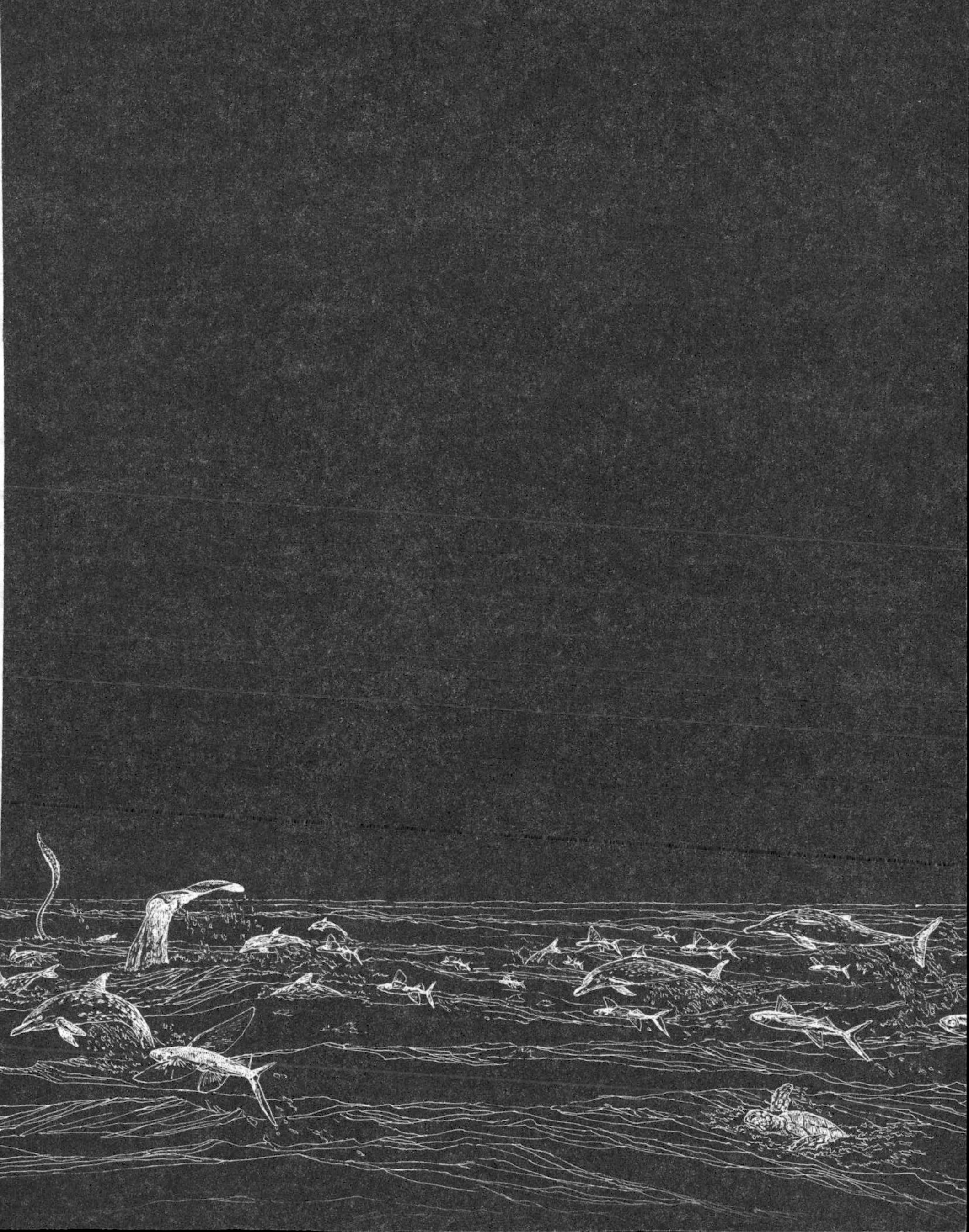

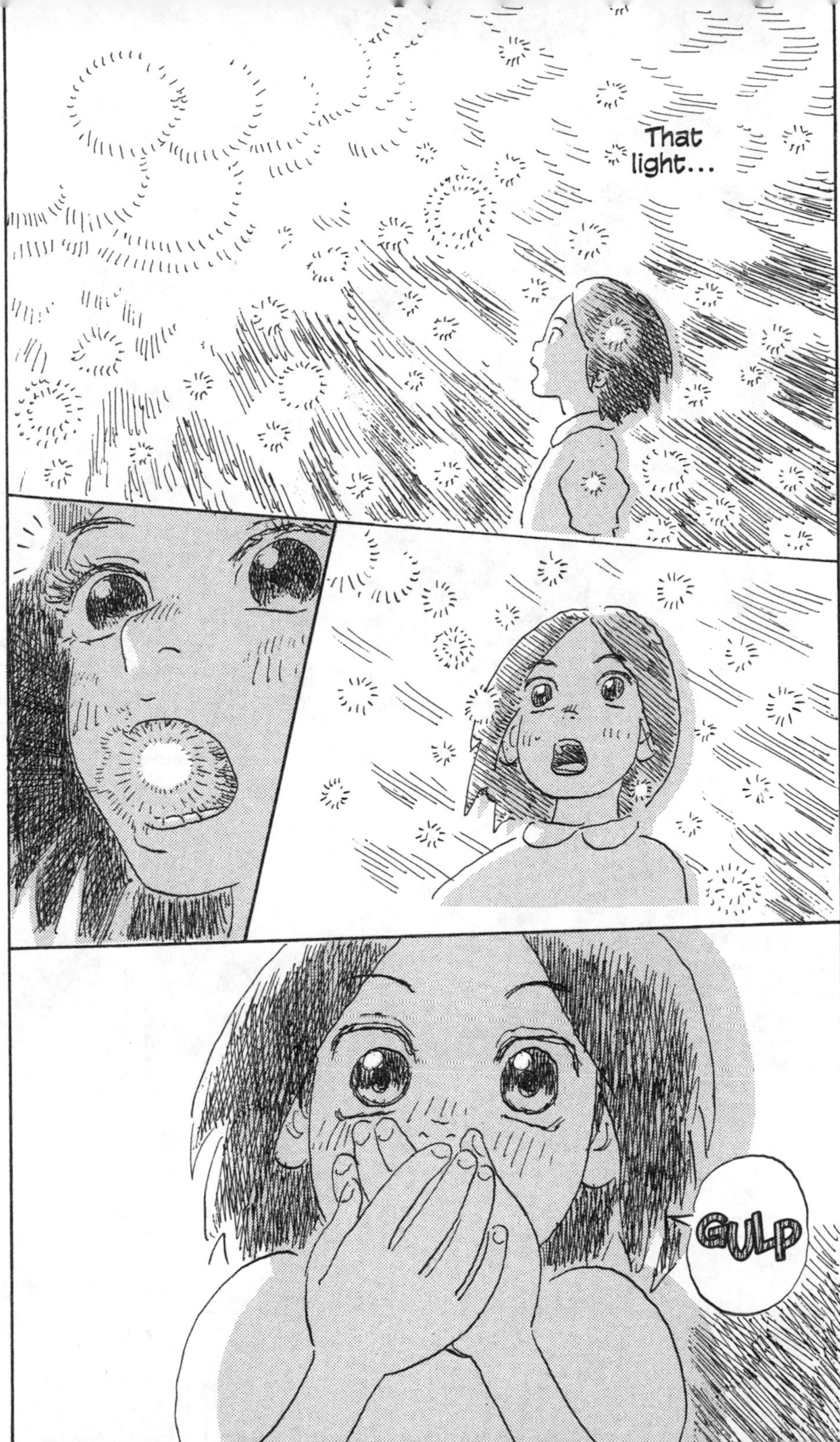
That light...
GULP

Chapter 7: Chair

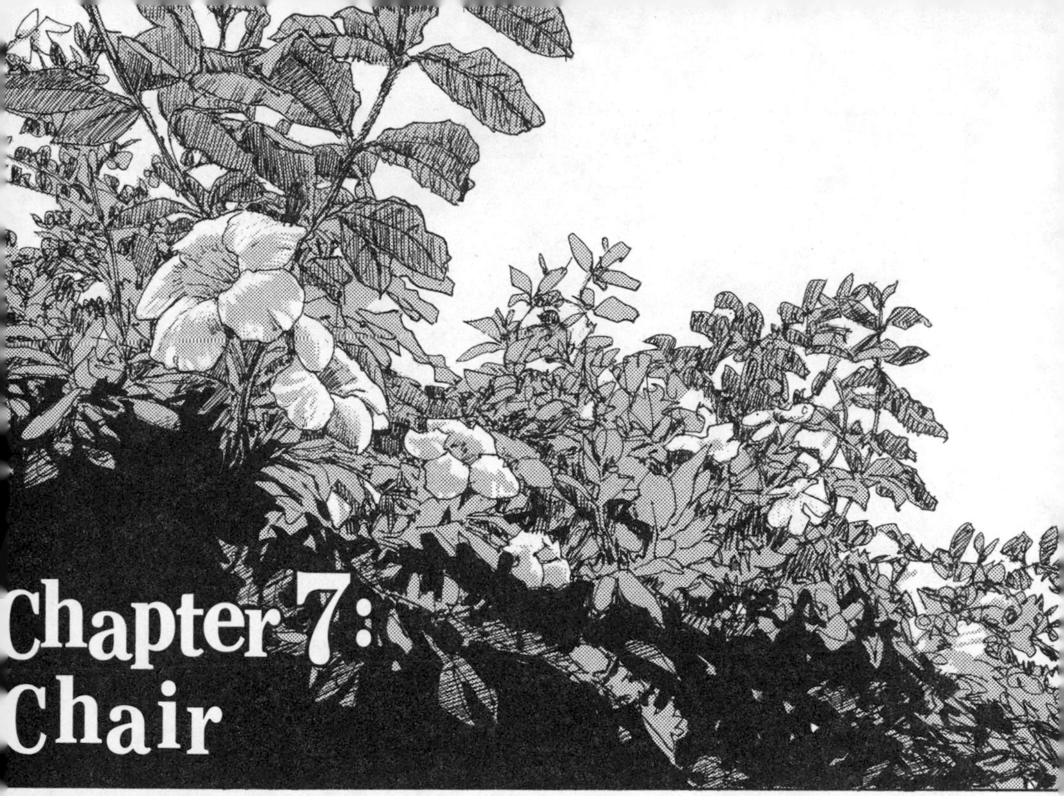

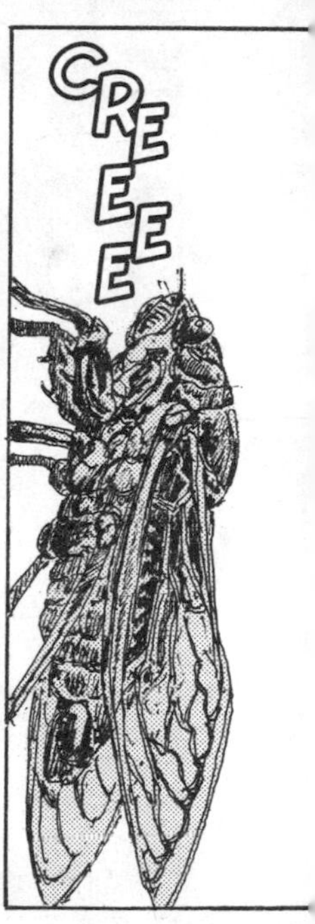
CREEEEE

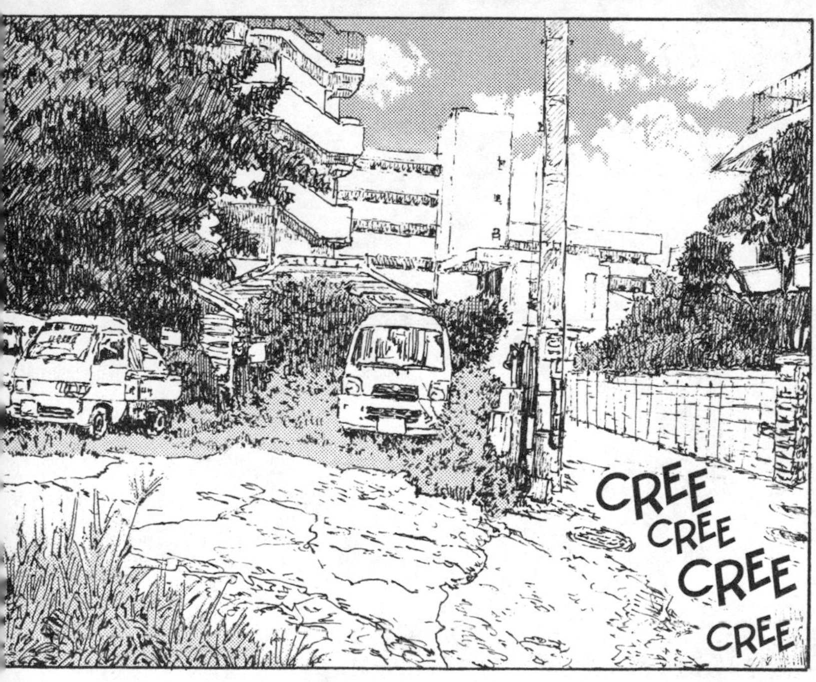
CREE
CREE
CREE
CREE

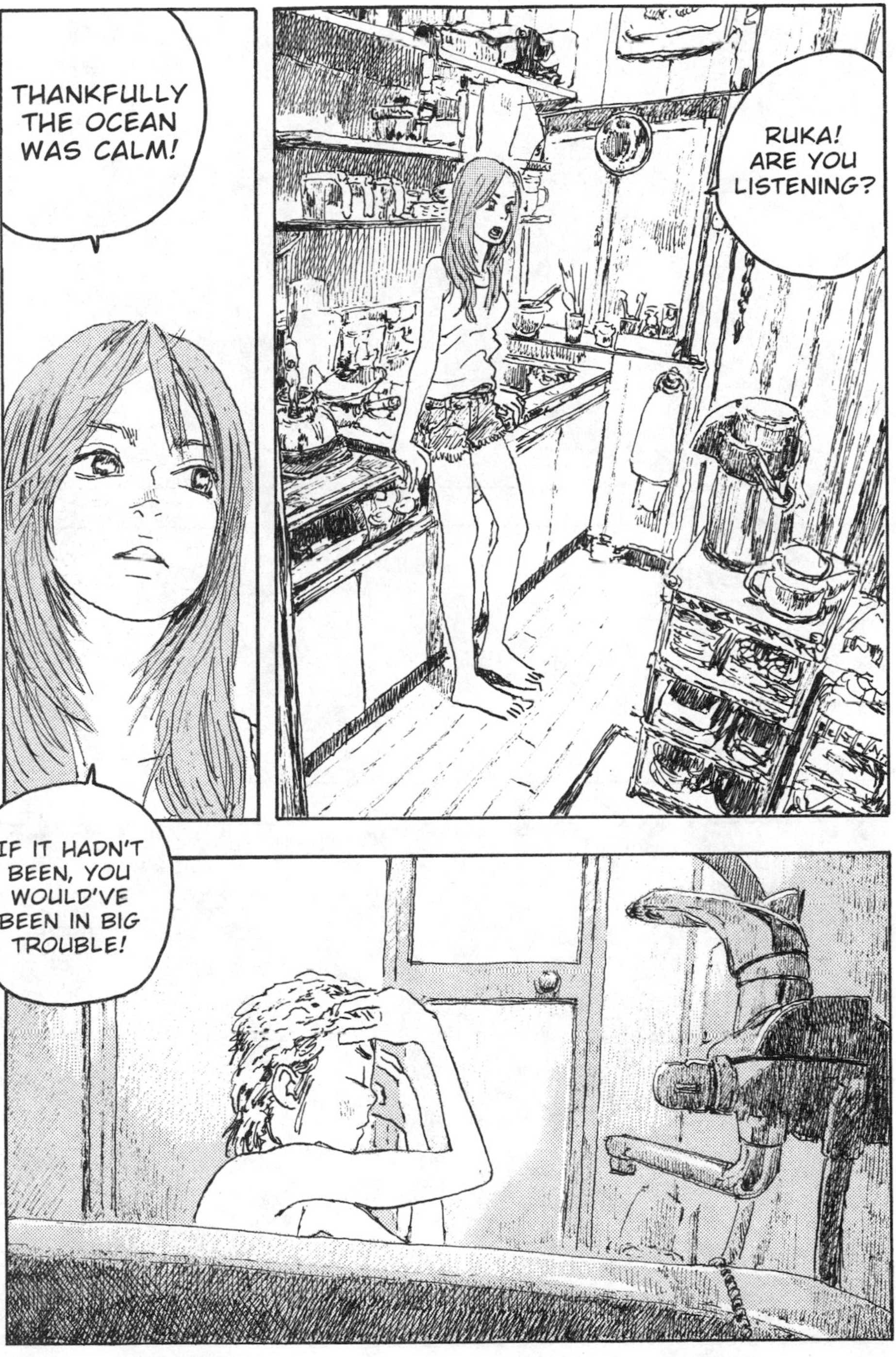
RUKA! ARE YOU LISTENING?
THANKFULLY THE OCEAN WAS CALM!
IF IT HADN'T BEEN, YOU WOULD'VE BEEN IN BIG TROUBLE!

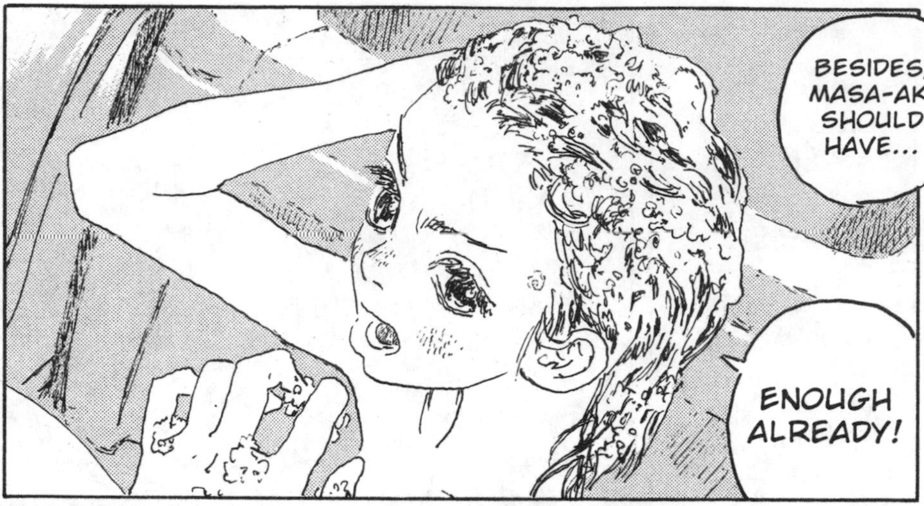
BESIDES, MASA-AKI SHOULD HAVE...
ENOUGH ALREADY!
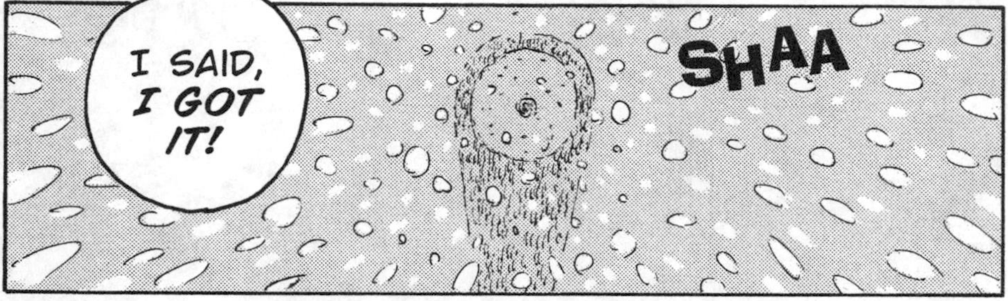
SHAA
I SAID, *I GOT IT!*
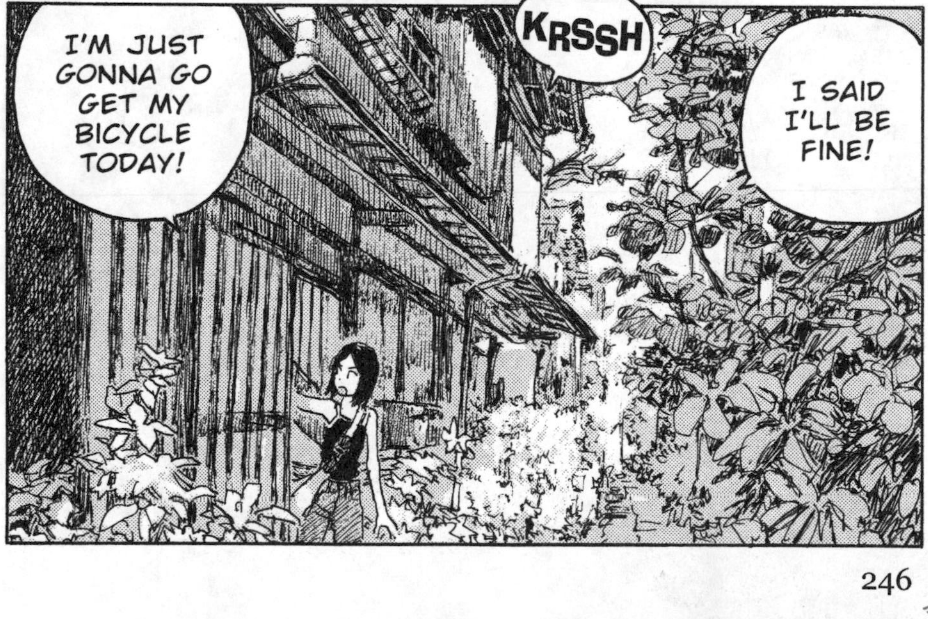
I SAID I'LL BE FINE!
KRSSH
I'M JUST GONNA GO GET MY BICYCLE TODAY!

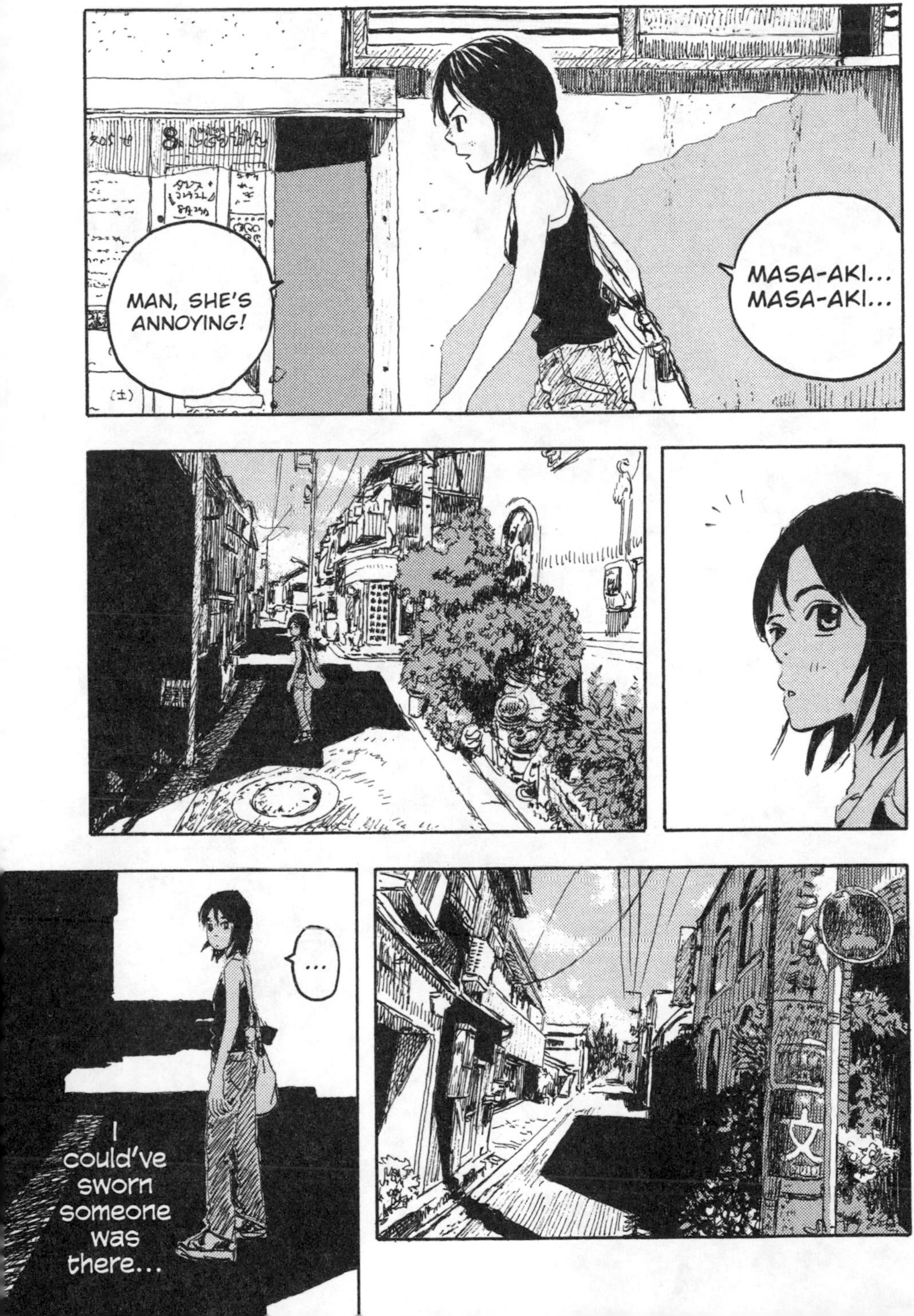
MASA-AKI... MASA-AKI...
MAN, SHE'S ANNOYING!
...
I could've sworn someone was there...

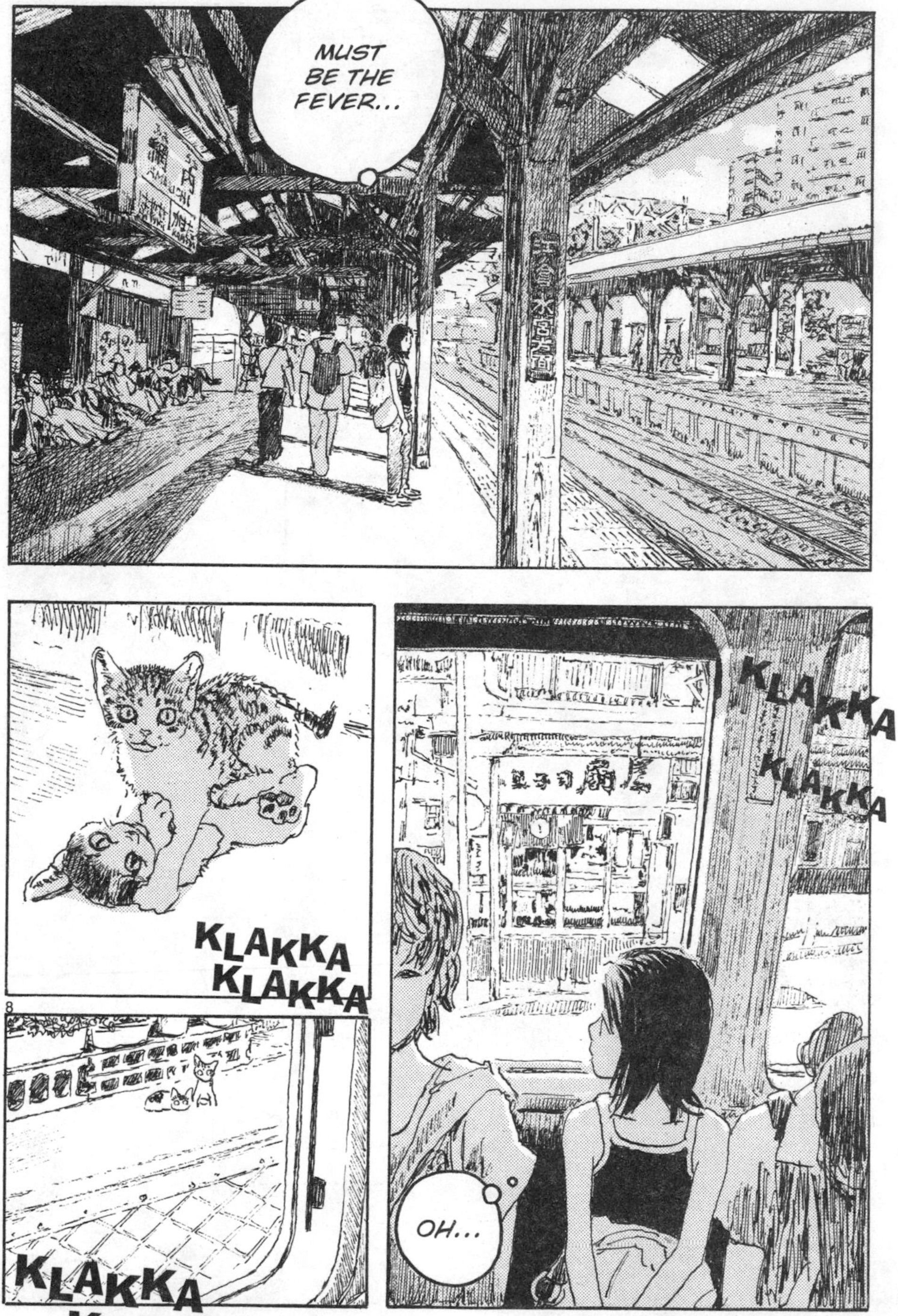
MUST BE THE FEVER...
KLAKKA KLAKKA
OH...
KLAKKA KLAKKA
KLAKKA KLAKKA

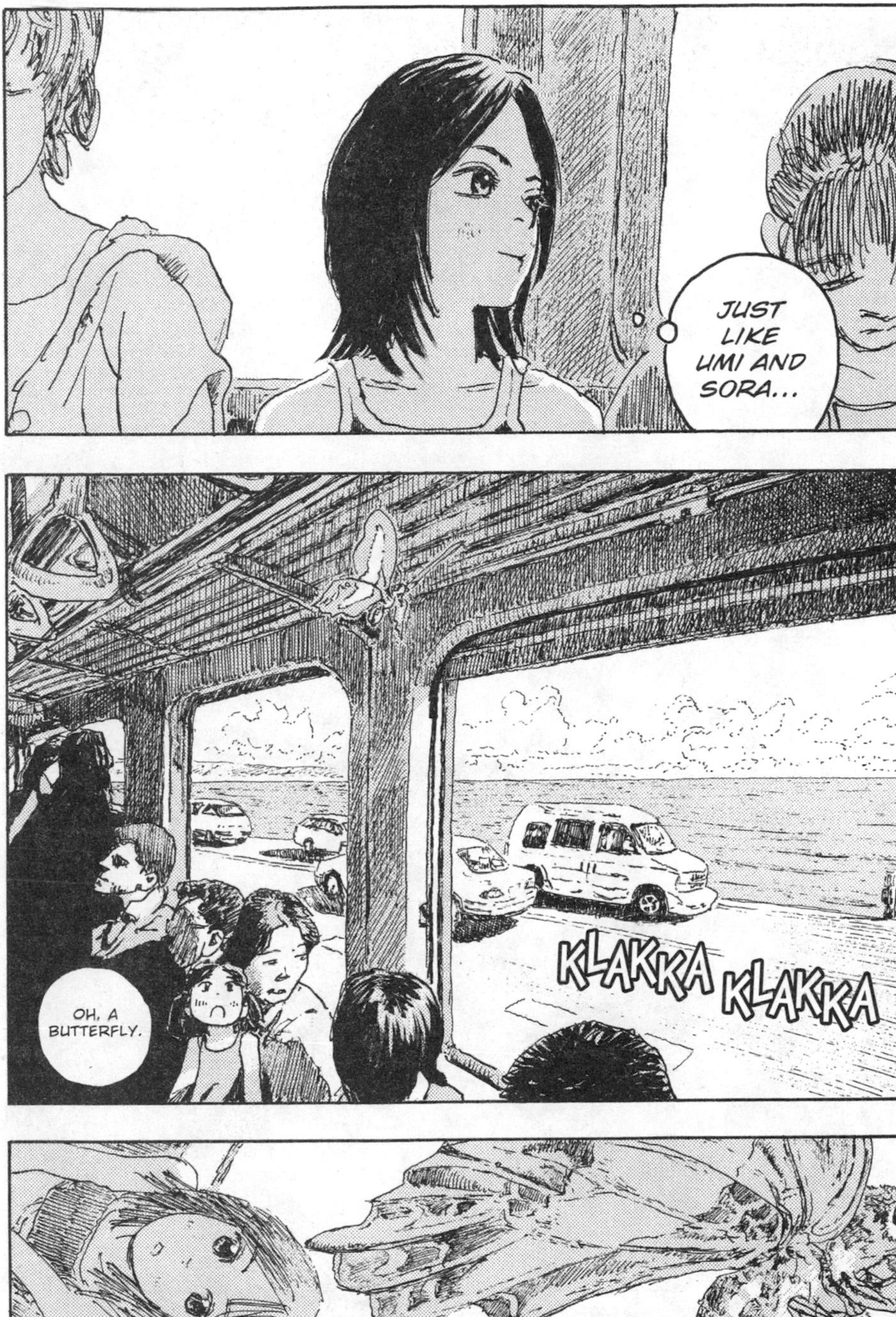
JUST LIKE UMI AND SORA...
KLAKKA KLAKKA
OH, A BUTTERFLY.
...

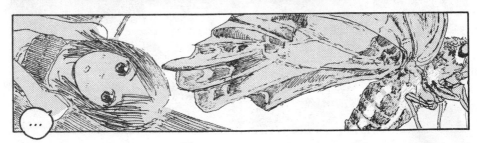

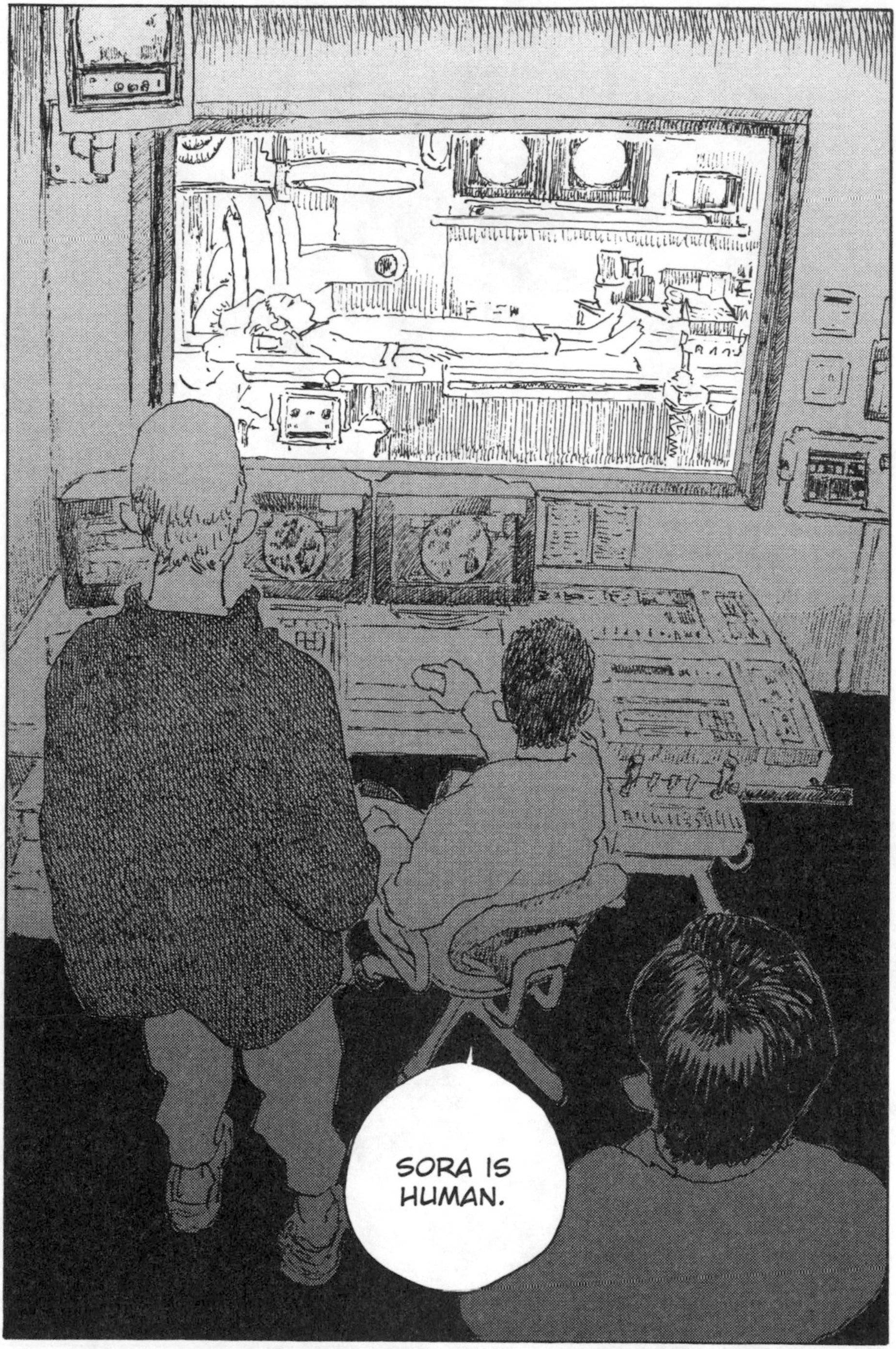
SORA IS HUMAN.

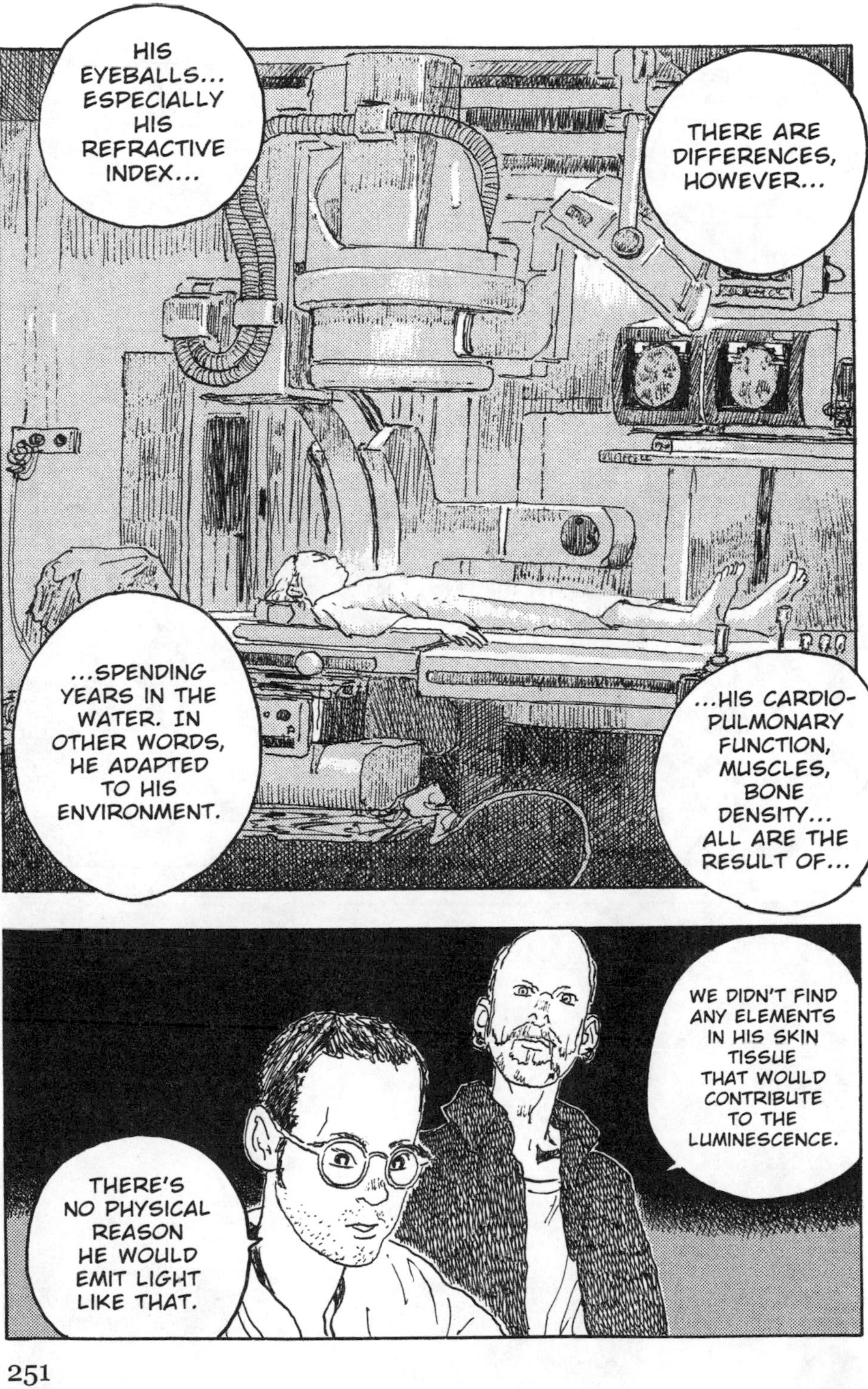
THERE ARE DIFFERENCES, HOWEVER...
HIS EYEBALLS... ESPECIALLY HIS REFRACTIVE INDEX...
...HIS CARDIO-PULMONARY FUNCTION, MUSCLES, BONE DENSITY... ALL ARE THE RESULT OF...
...SPENDING YEARS IN THE WATER. IN OTHER WORDS, HE ADAPTED TO HIS ENVIRONMENT.
WE DIDN'T FIND ANY ELEMENTS IN HIS SKIN TISSUE THAT WOULD CONTRIBUTE TO THE LUMINESCENCE.
THERE'S NO PHYSICAL REASON HE WOULD EMIT LIGHT LIKE THAT.

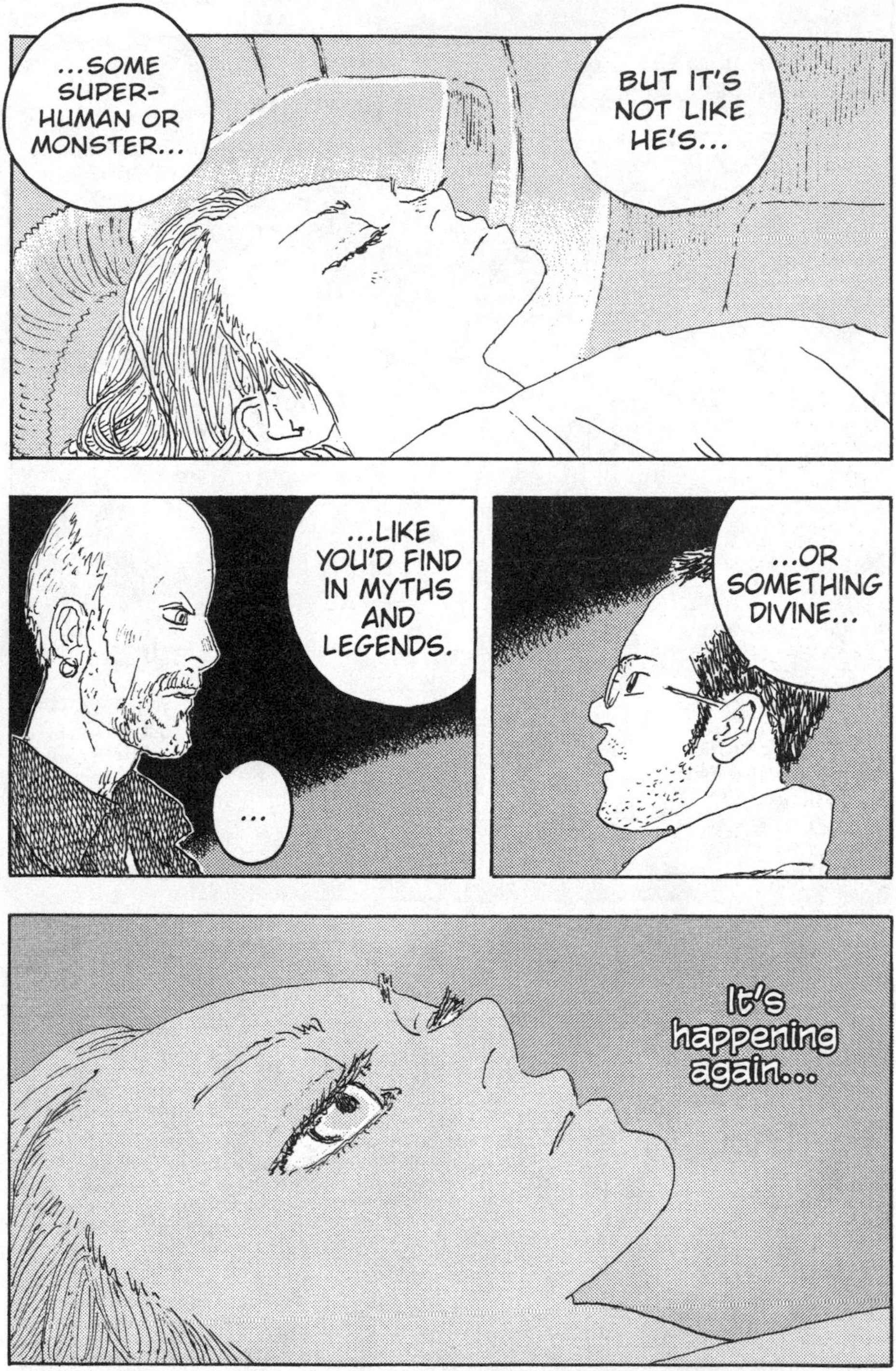
BUT IT'S NOT LIKE HE'S...
...SOME SUPER-HUMAN OR MONSTER...
...OR SOMETHING DIVINE...
...LIKE YOU'D FIND IN MYTHS AND LEGENDS.
...
It's happening again...

I'M SINKING INSIDE MY BODY...

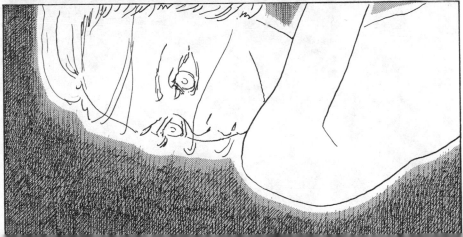

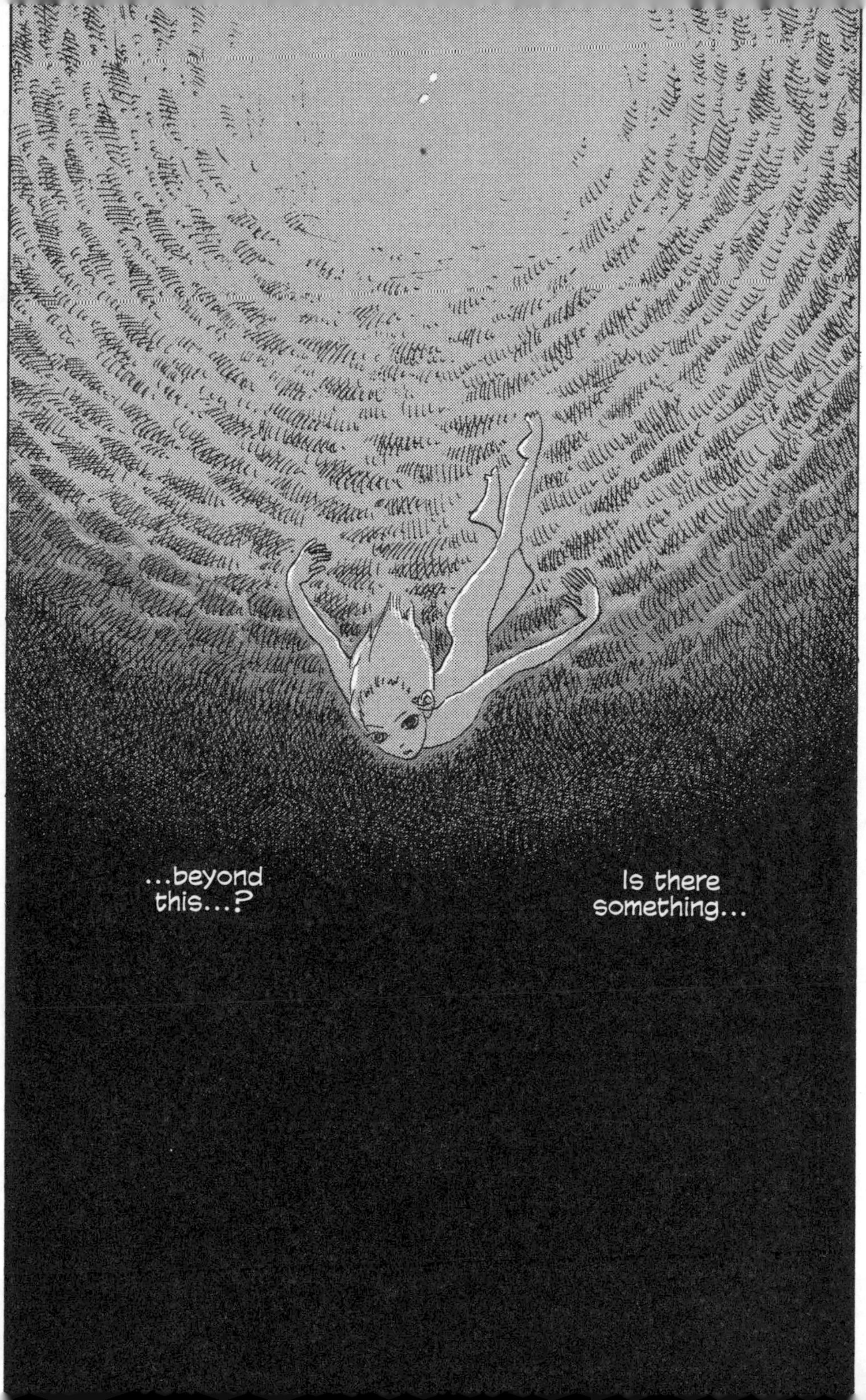
Is there something...
...beyond this...?

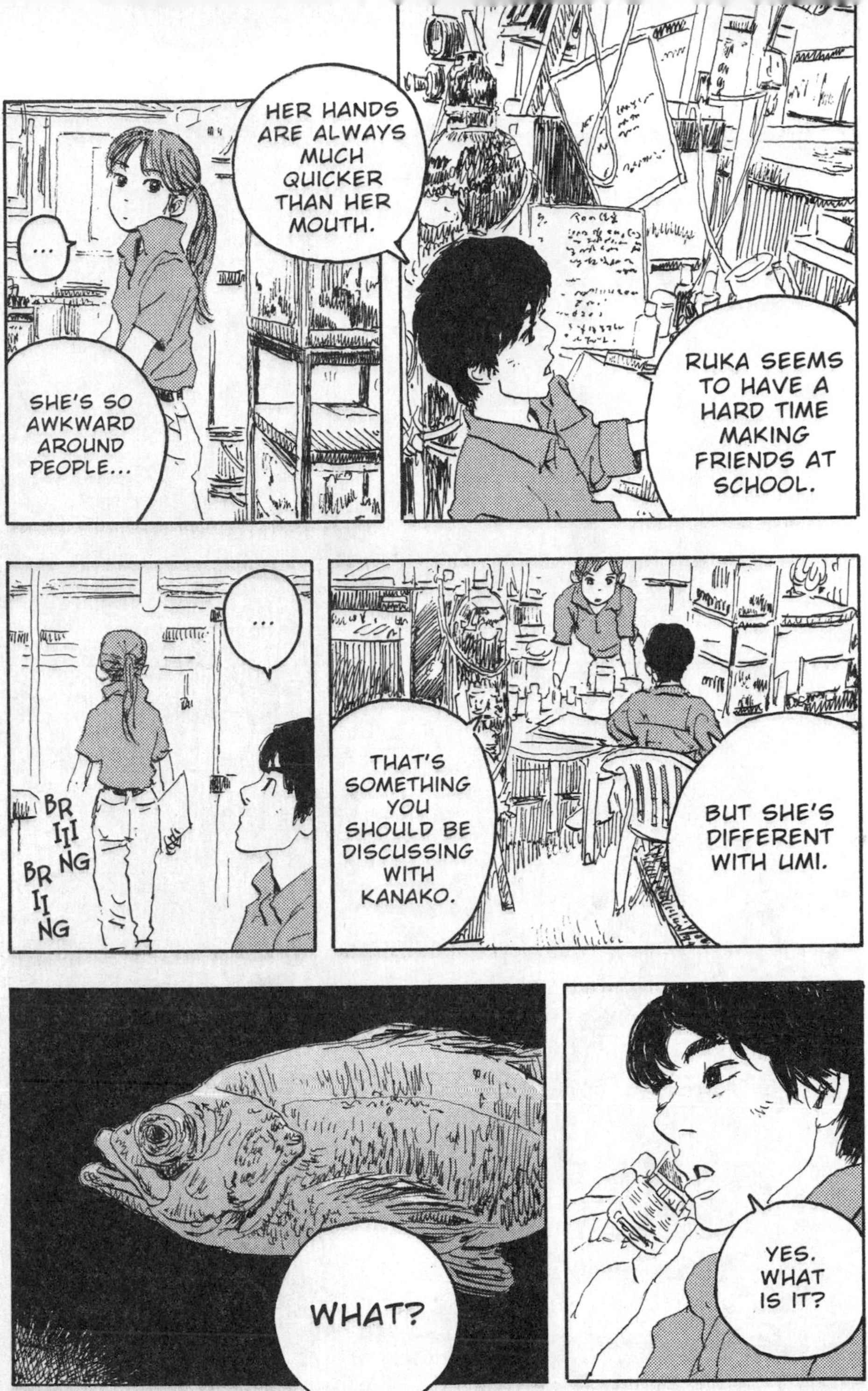
HER HANDS ARE ALWAYS MUCH QUICKER THAN HER MOUTH.
RUKA SEEMS TO HAVE A HARD TIME MAKING FRIENDS AT SCHOOL.
...
SHE'S SO AWKWARD AROUND PEOPLE...
BUT SHE'S DIFFERENT WITH UMI.
THAT'S SOMETHING YOU SHOULD BE DISCUSSING WITH KANAKO.
...
BRIIING
BRIIING
YES. WHAT IS IT?
WHAT?

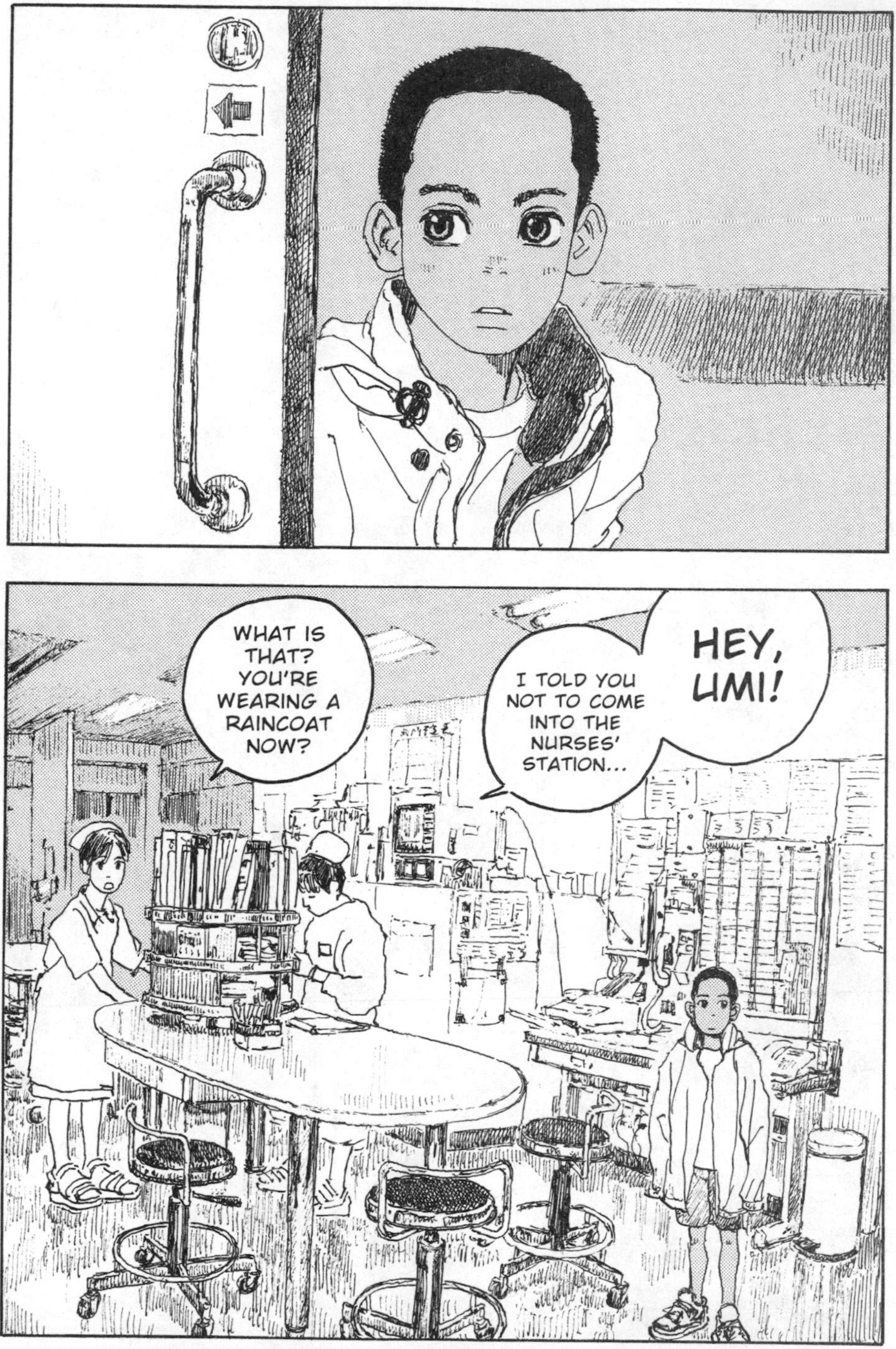
HEY, UMI!
I TOLD YOU NOT TO COME INTO THE NURSES' STATION...
WHAT IS THAT? YOU'RE WEARING A RAINCOAT NOW?

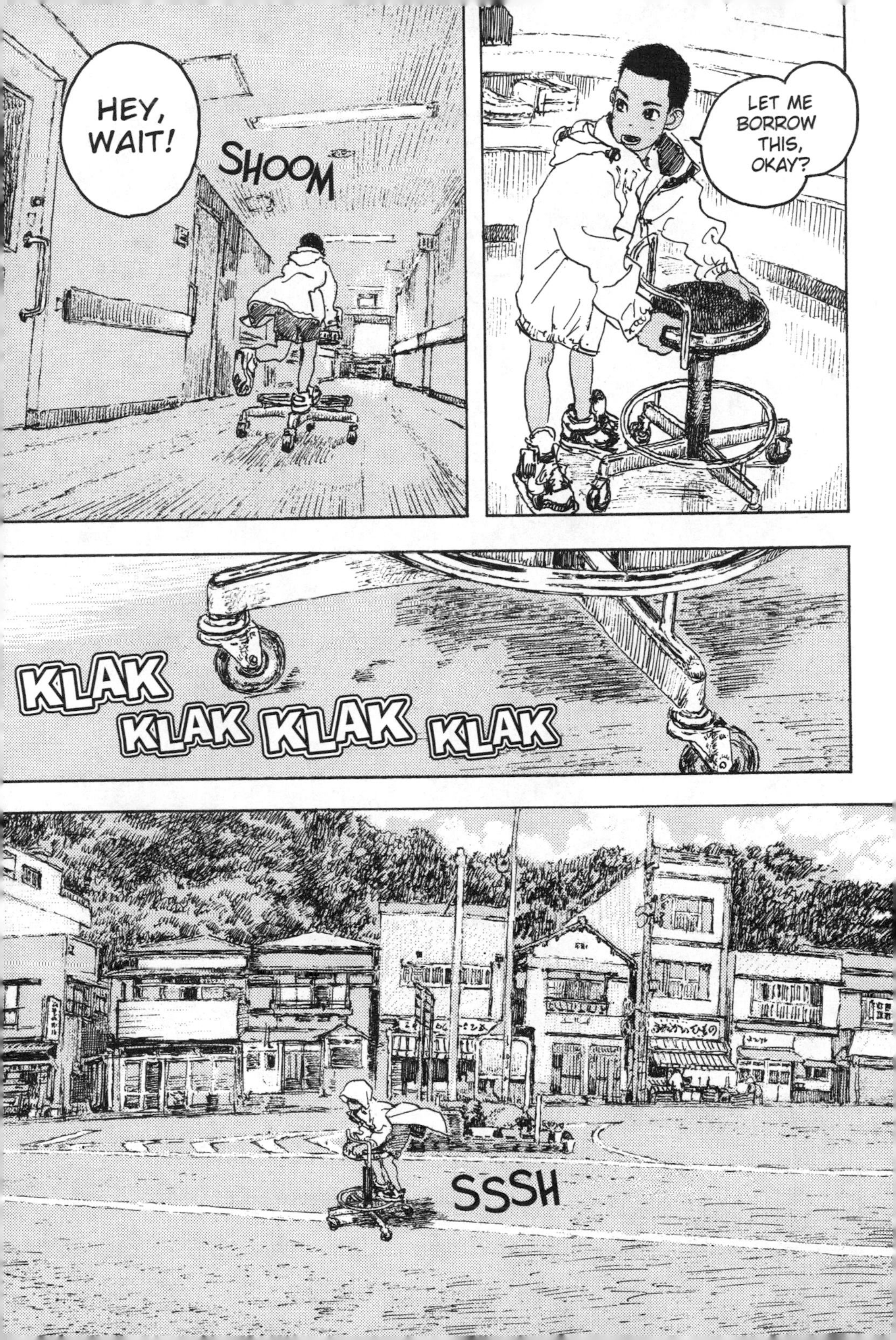
LET ME BORROW THIS, OKAY?
HEY, WAIT!
SHOOM
KLAK KLAK KLAK KLAK
SSSH

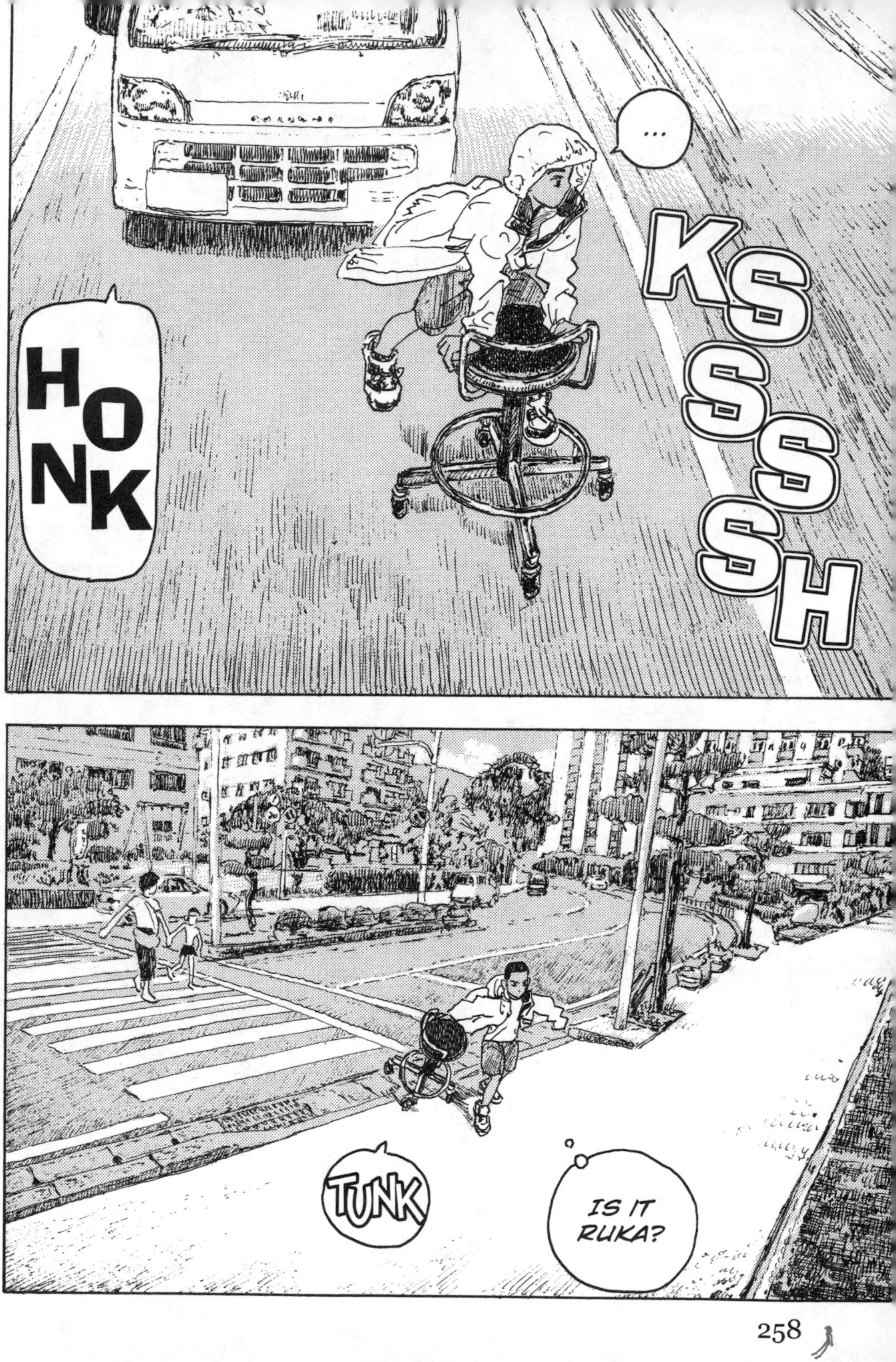
...
KSSSSH
HONK
IS IT RUKA?
TUNK

TONK
WHAT'S THE MATTER?
WHAT THE HECK IS IT?
SMELLS FISHY, DOESN'T IT?
IS IT A WHALE?
CAREFUL!

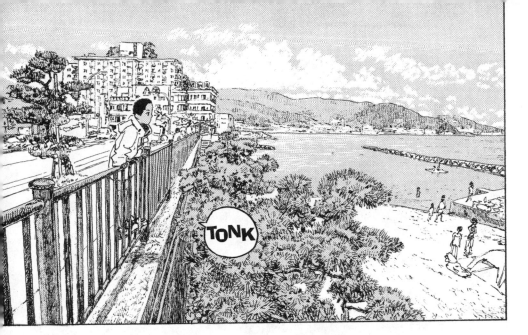

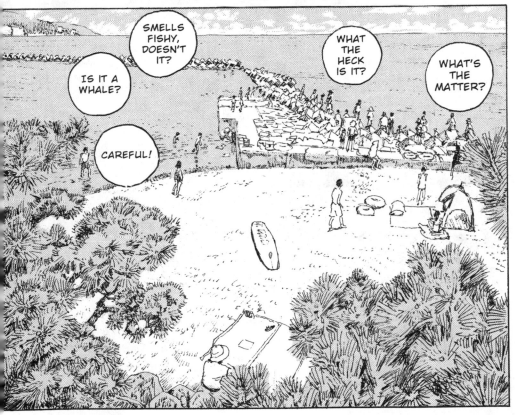

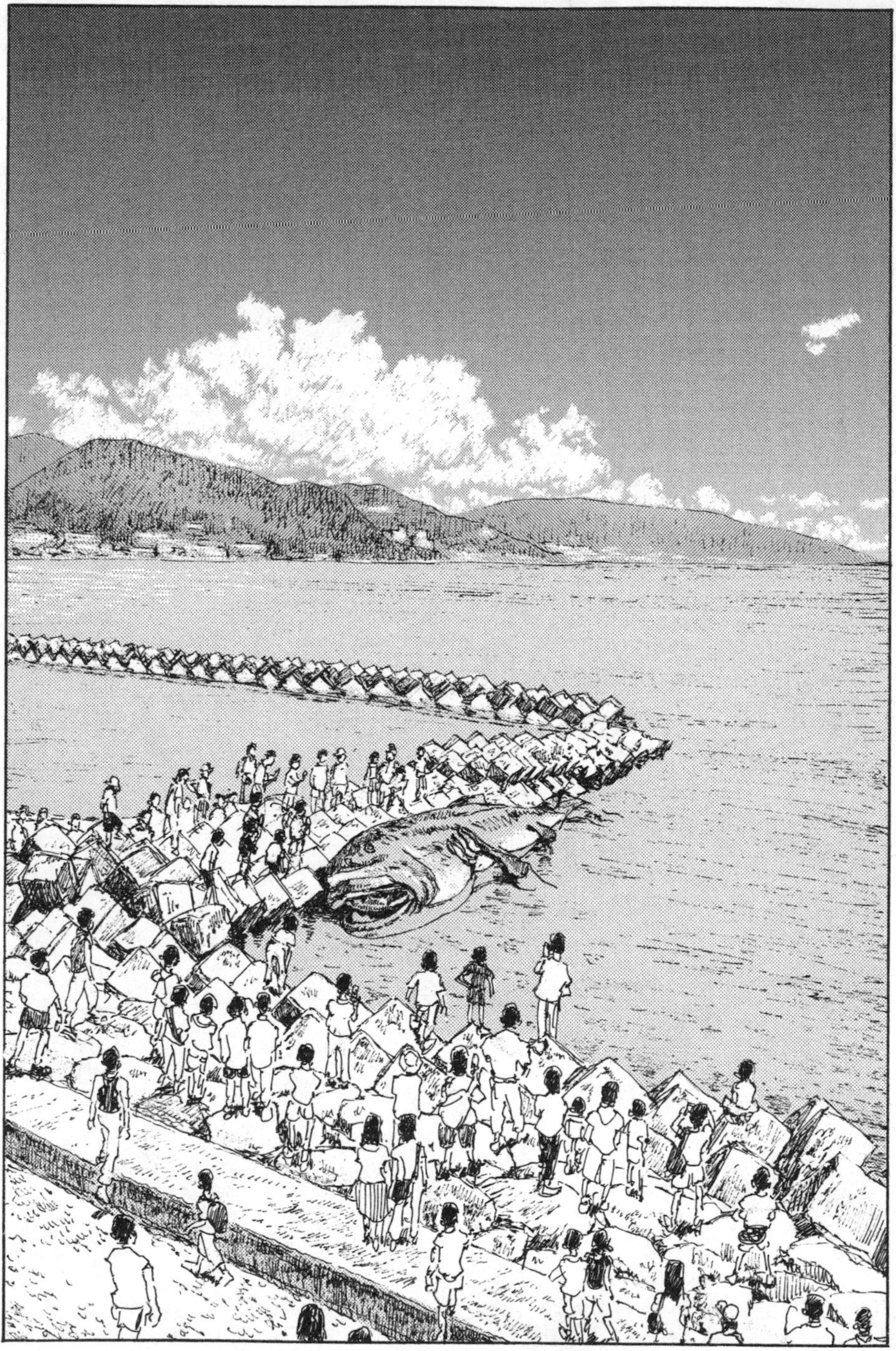

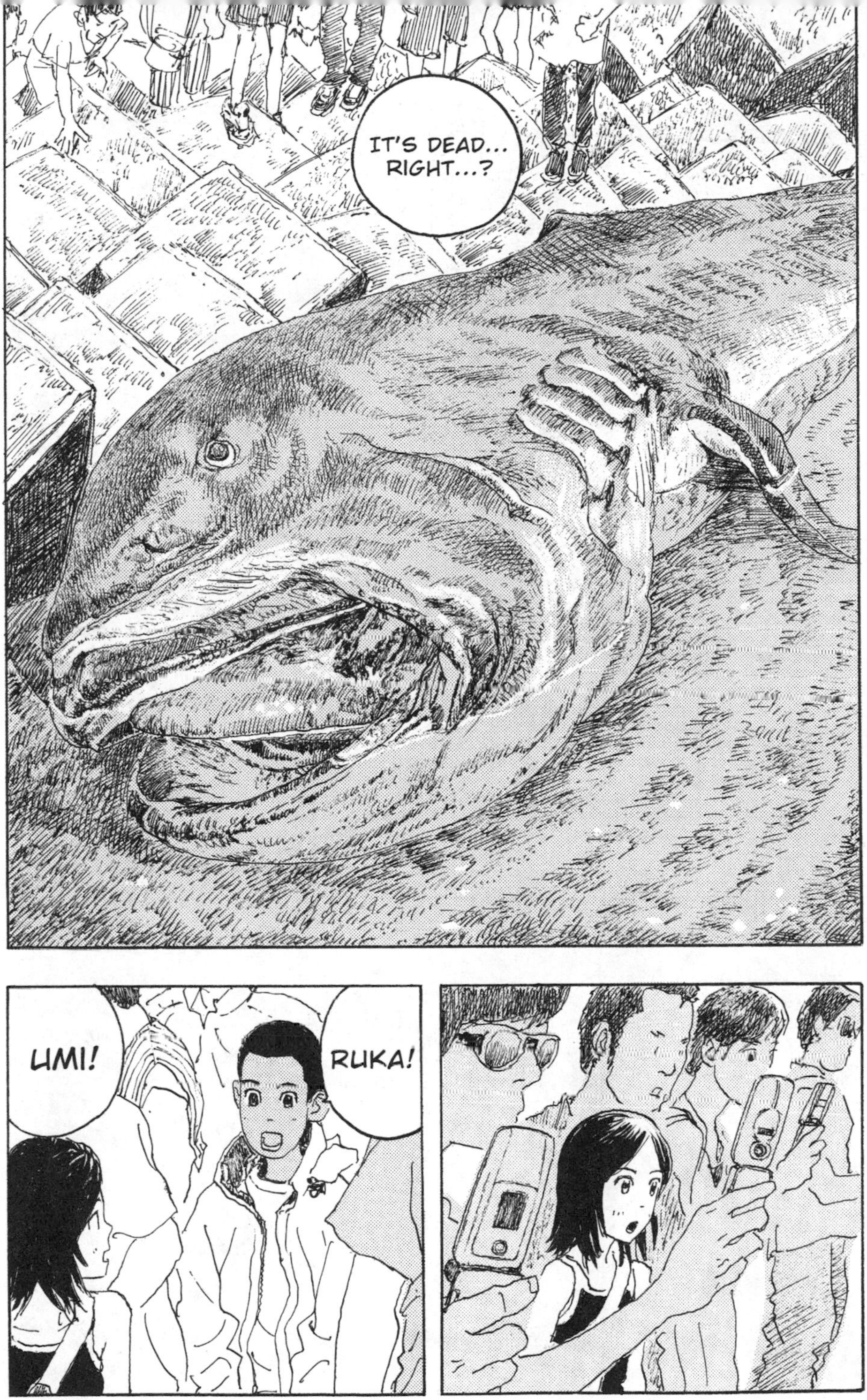
IT'S DEAD... RIGHT...?
RUKA!
UMI!

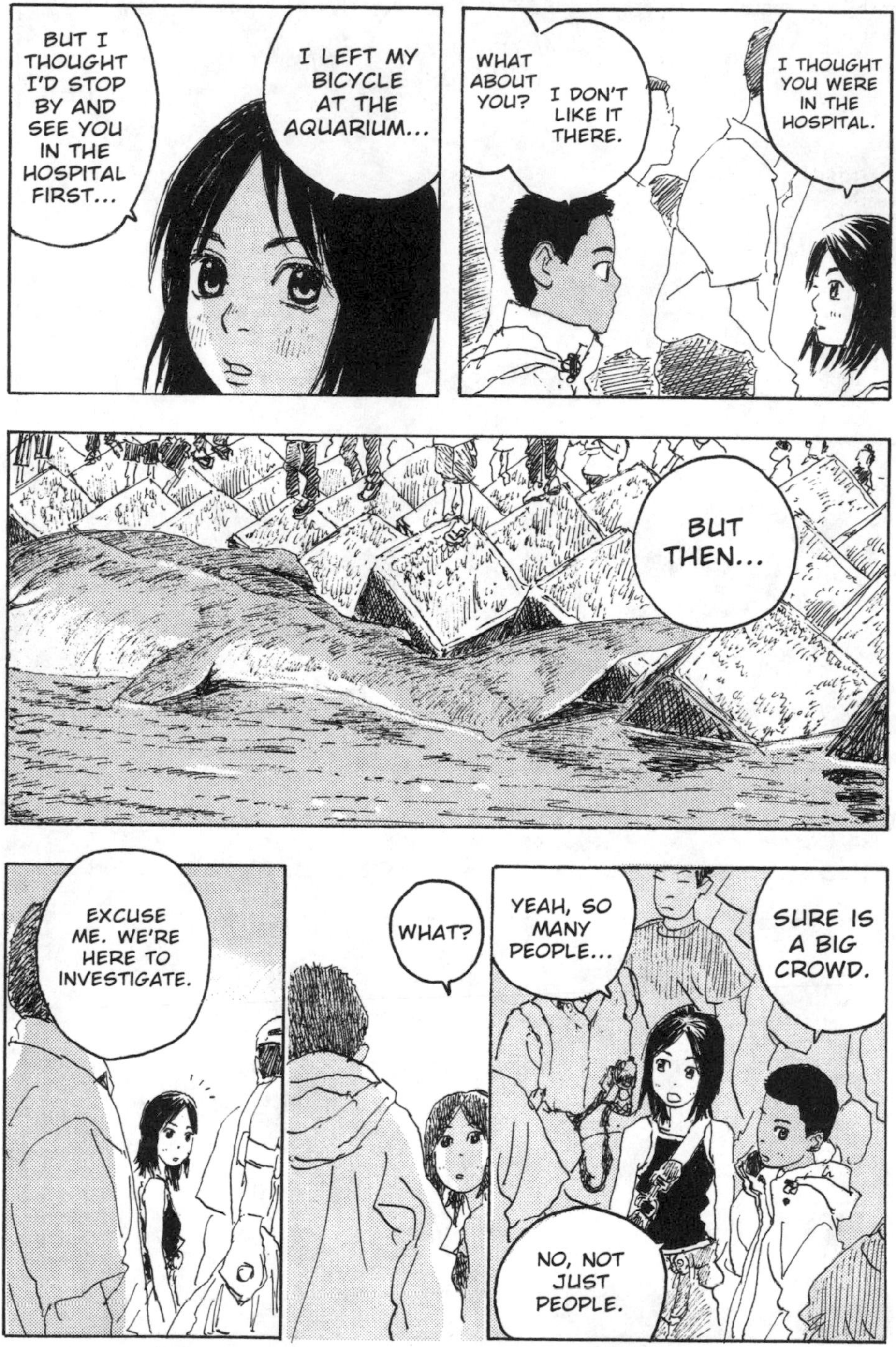
I THOUGHT YOU WERE IN THE HOSPITAL.
I DON'T LIKE IT THERE.
WHAT ABOUT YOU?
I LEFT MY BICYCLE AT THE AQUARIUM...
BUT I THOUGHT I'D STOP BY AND SEE YOU IN THE HOSPITAL FIRST...
BUT THEN...
SURE IS A BIG CROWD.
YEAH, SO MANY PEOPLE...
NO, NOT JUST PEOPLE.
WHAT?
EXCUSE ME. WE'RE HERE TO INVESTIGATE.

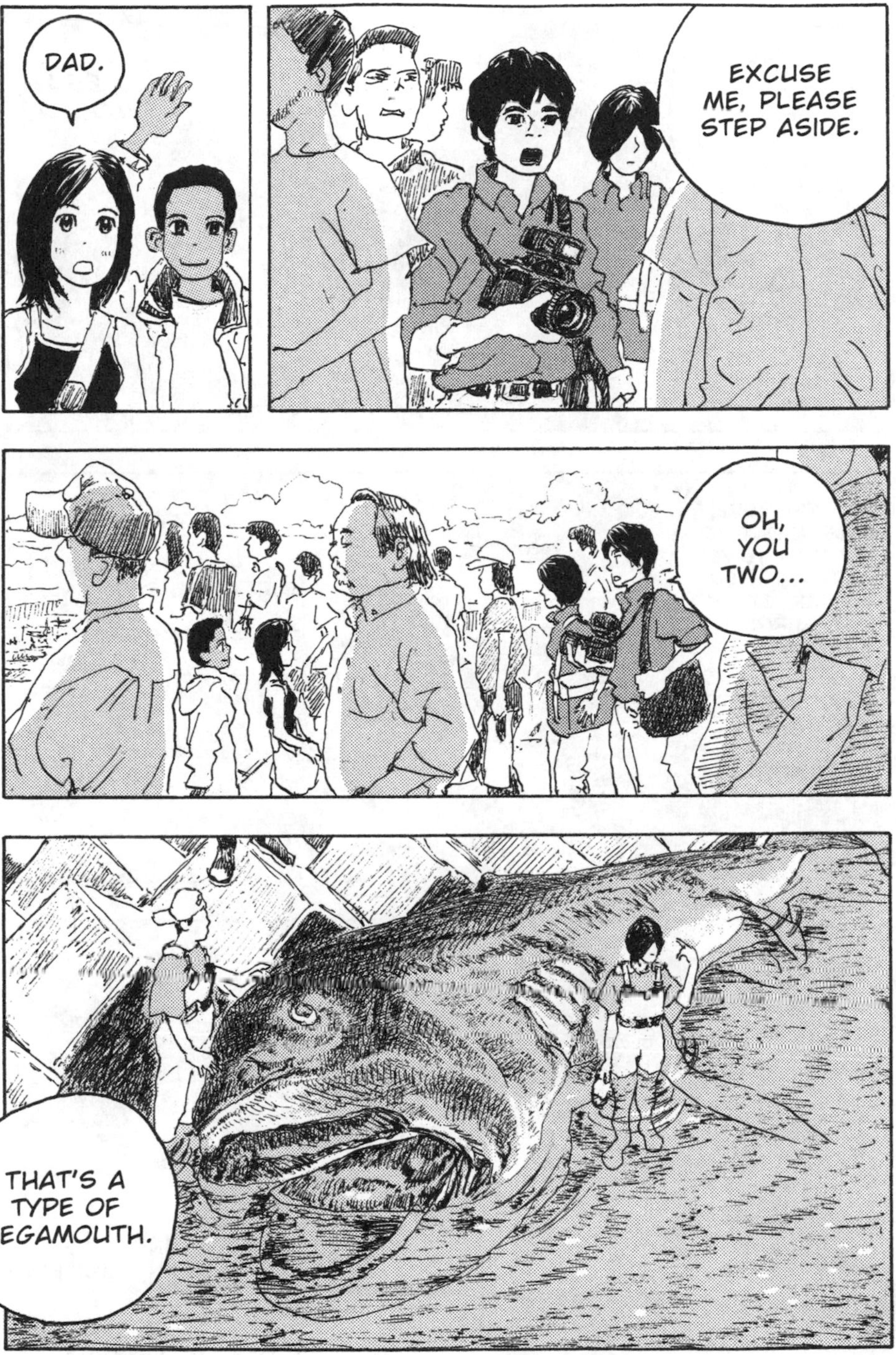
EXCUSE ME, PLEASE STEP ASIDE.
DAD.
OH, YOU TWO...
THAT'S A TYPE OF MEGAMOUTH.

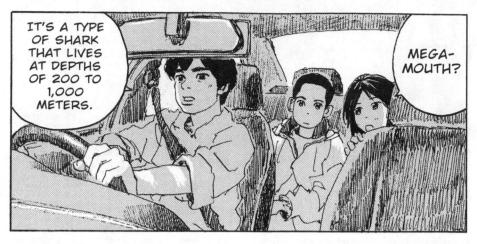

MEGA-MOUTH?
IT'S A TYPE OF SHARK THAT LIVES AT DEPTHS OF 200 TO 1,000 METERS.
THEY CAN GROW UP TO 5 METERS IN LENGTH, BUT THEY'VE ONLY BEEN DISCOVERED RECENTLY.
WHAT'S MORE, ONLY ABOUT 20 OF THEM HAVE BEEN SIGHTED SO FAR. IT'S A FISH SHROUDED IN MYSTERY.
IT CAME FROM SUCH DEEP WATERS ...
DID IT DIE AND THEN FLOAT UP?
IT'S NOT ONLY THE MEGAMOUTHS.

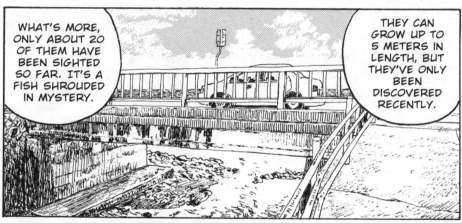

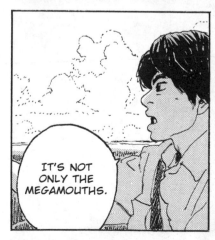

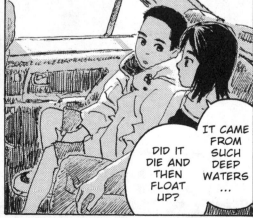

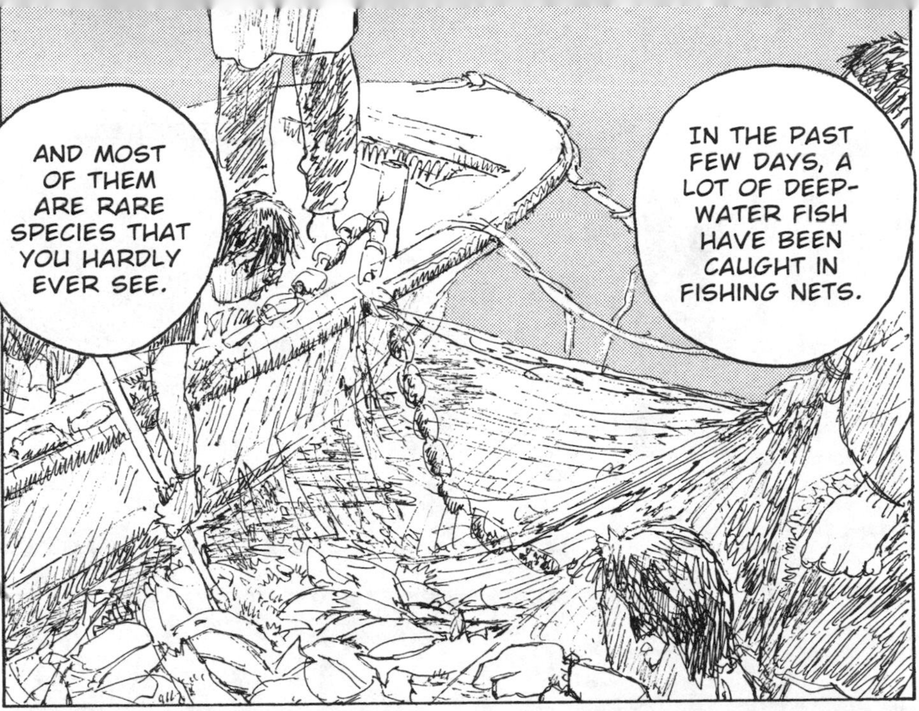
IN THE PAST FEW DAYS, A LOT OF DEEP-WATER FISH HAVE BEEN CAUGHT IN FISHING NETS.
AND MOST OF THEM ARE RARE SPECIES THAT YOU HARDLY EVER SEE.
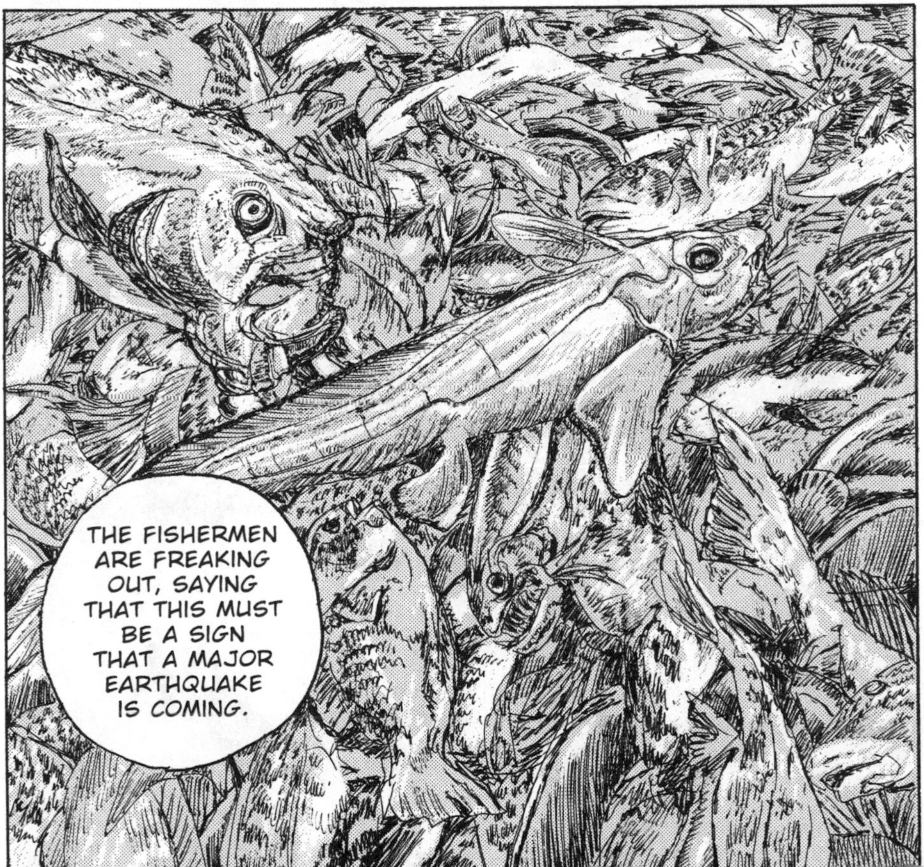
THE FISHERMEN ARE FREAKING OUT, SAYING THAT THIS MUST BE A SIGN THAT A MAJOR EARTHQUAKE IS COMING.

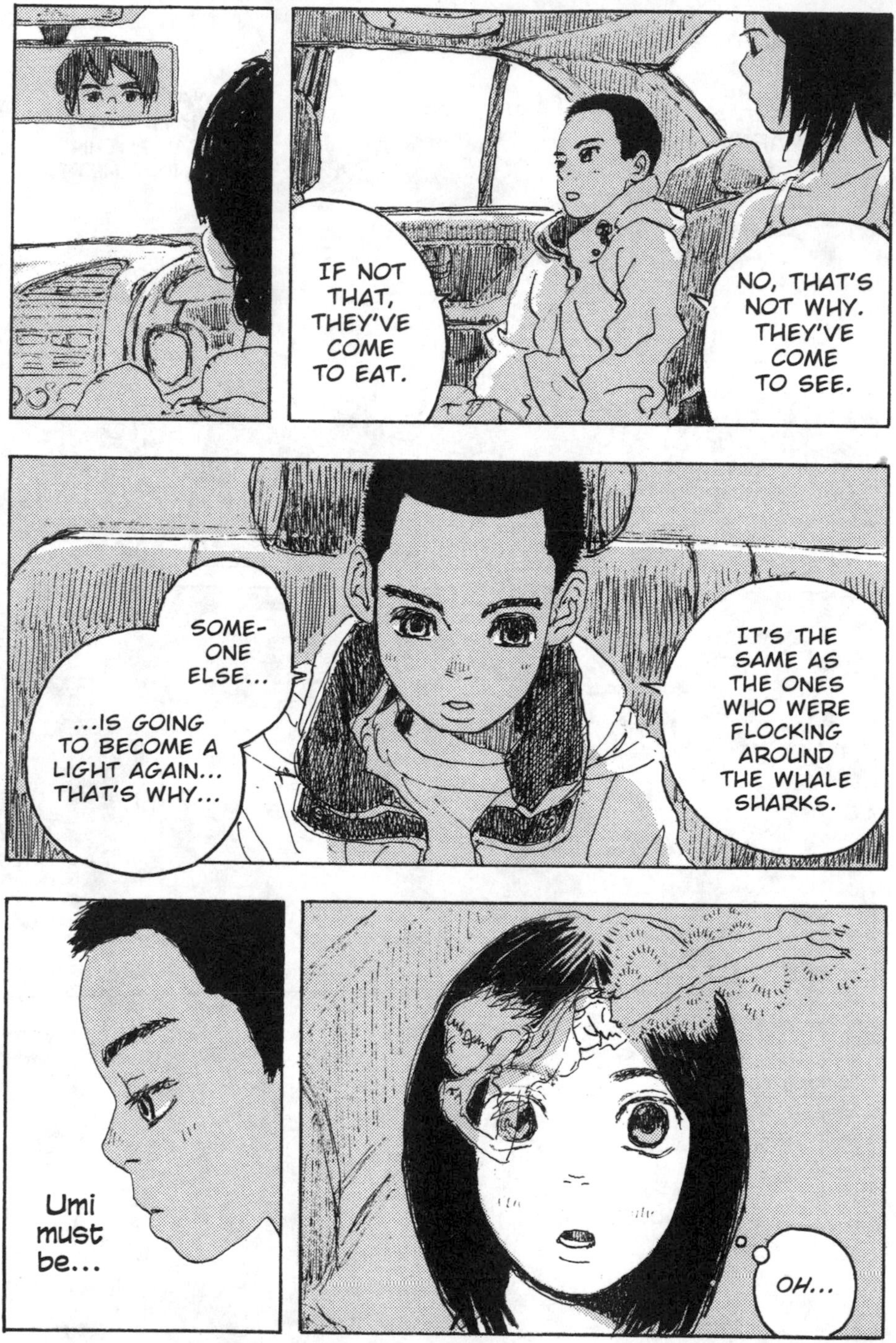
NO, THAT'S NOT WHY. THEY'VE COME TO SEE.
IF NOT THAT, THEY'VE COME TO EAT.
IT'S THE SAME AS THE ONES WHO WERE FLOCKING AROUND THE WHALE SHARKS.
SOME-ONE ELSE...
...IS GOING TO BECOME A LIGHT AGAIN... THAT'S WHY...
OH...
Umi must be...

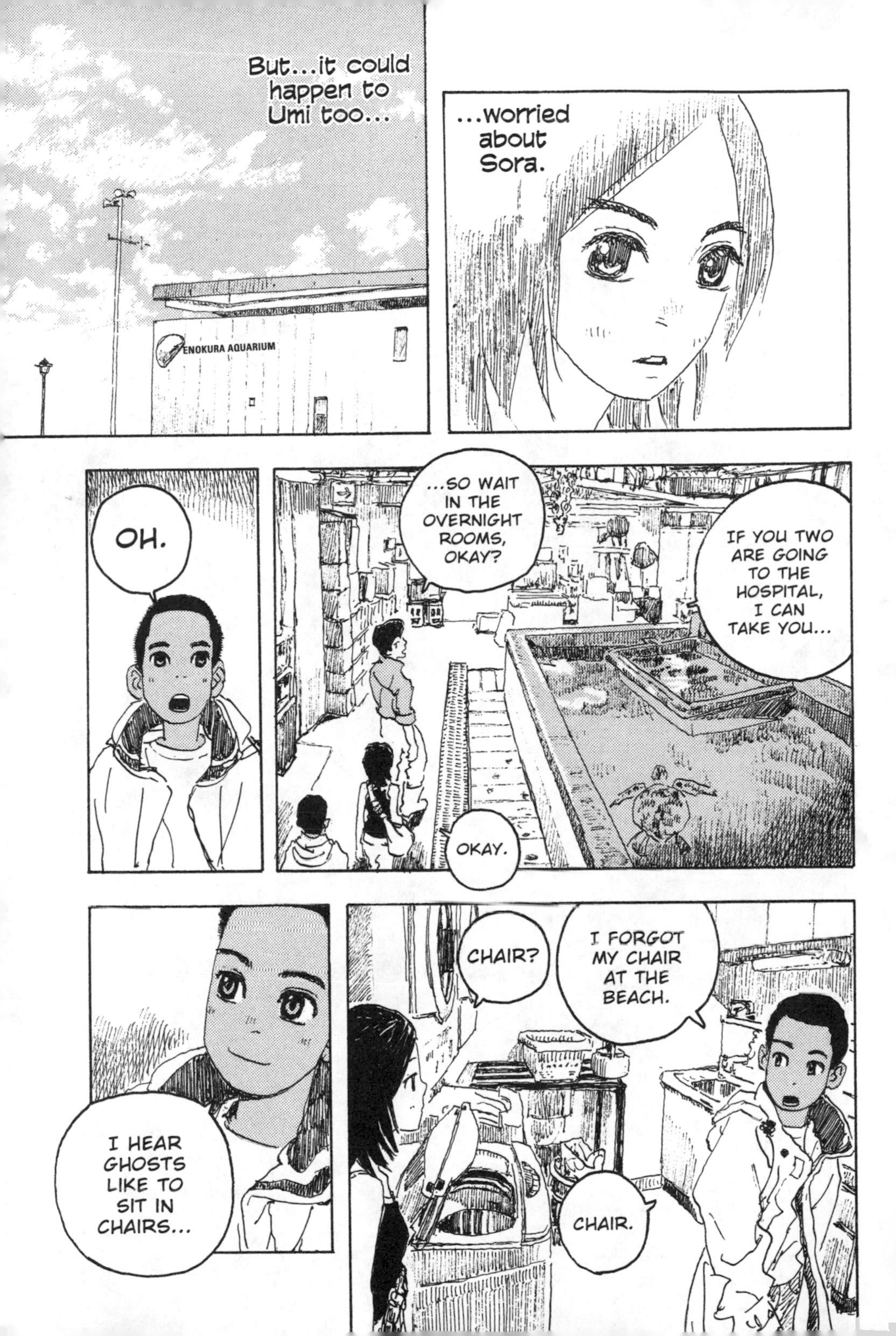
...worried about Sora.
But...it could happen to Umi too...
ENOKURA AQUARIUM
IF YOU TWO ARE GOING TO THE HOSPITAL, I CAN TAKE YOU...
...SO WAIT IN THE OVERNIGHT ROOMS, OKAY?
OKAY.
OH.
I FORGOT MY CHAIR AT THE BEACH.
CHAIR?
CHAIR.
I HEAR GHOSTS LIKE TO SIT IN CHAIRS...

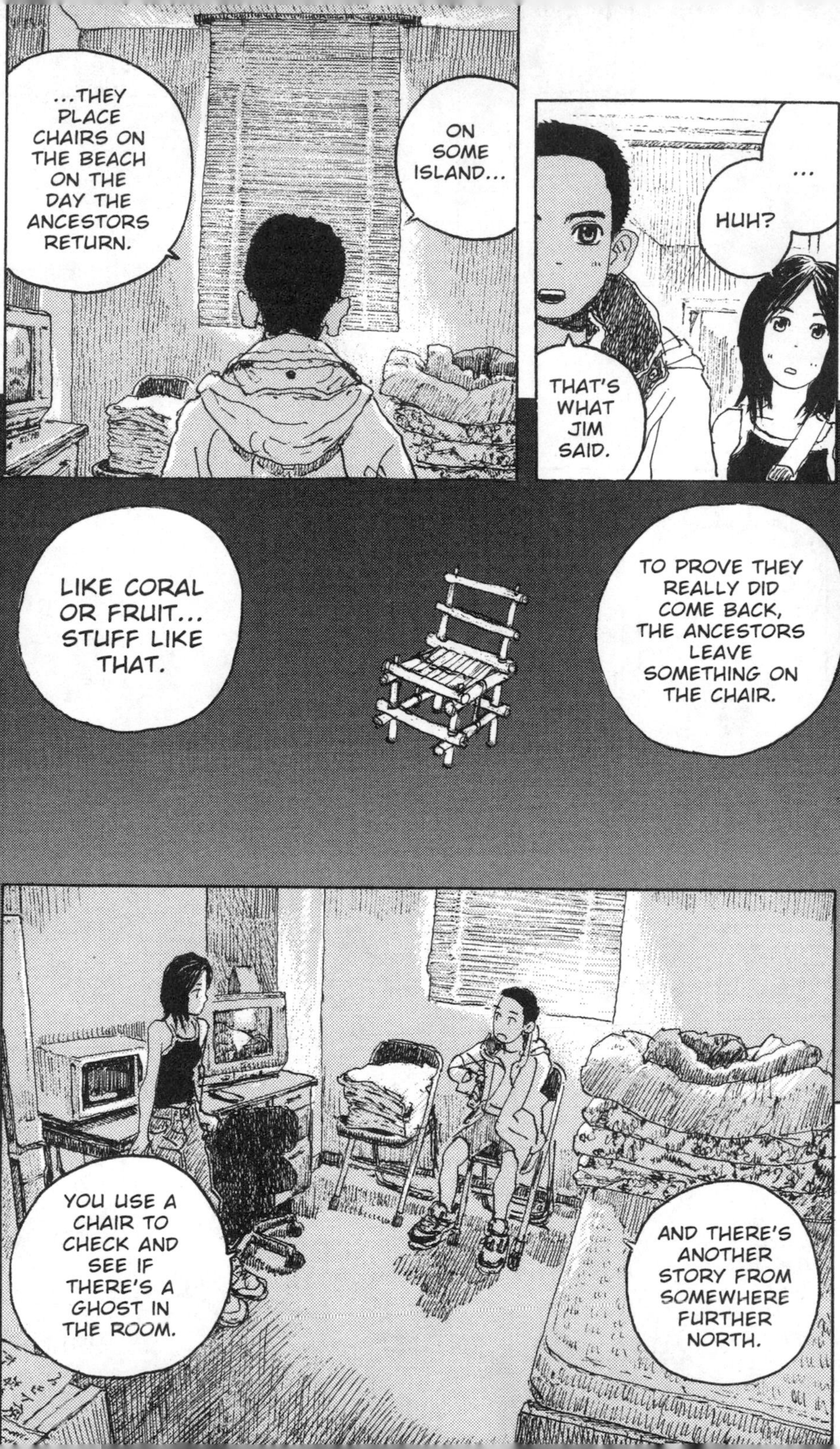
... HUH?
THAT'S WHAT JIM SAID.
ON SOME ISLAND...
...THEY PLACE CHAIRS ON THE BEACH ON THE DAY THE ANCESTORS RETURN.
TO PROVE THEY REALLY DID COME BACK, THE ANCESTORS LEAVE SOMETHING ON THE CHAIR.
LIKE CORAL OR FRUIT... STUFF LIKE THAT.
AND THERE'S ANOTHER STORY FROM SOMEWHERE FURTHER NORTH.
YOU USE A CHAIR TO CHECK AND SEE IF THERE'S A GHOST IN THE ROOM.

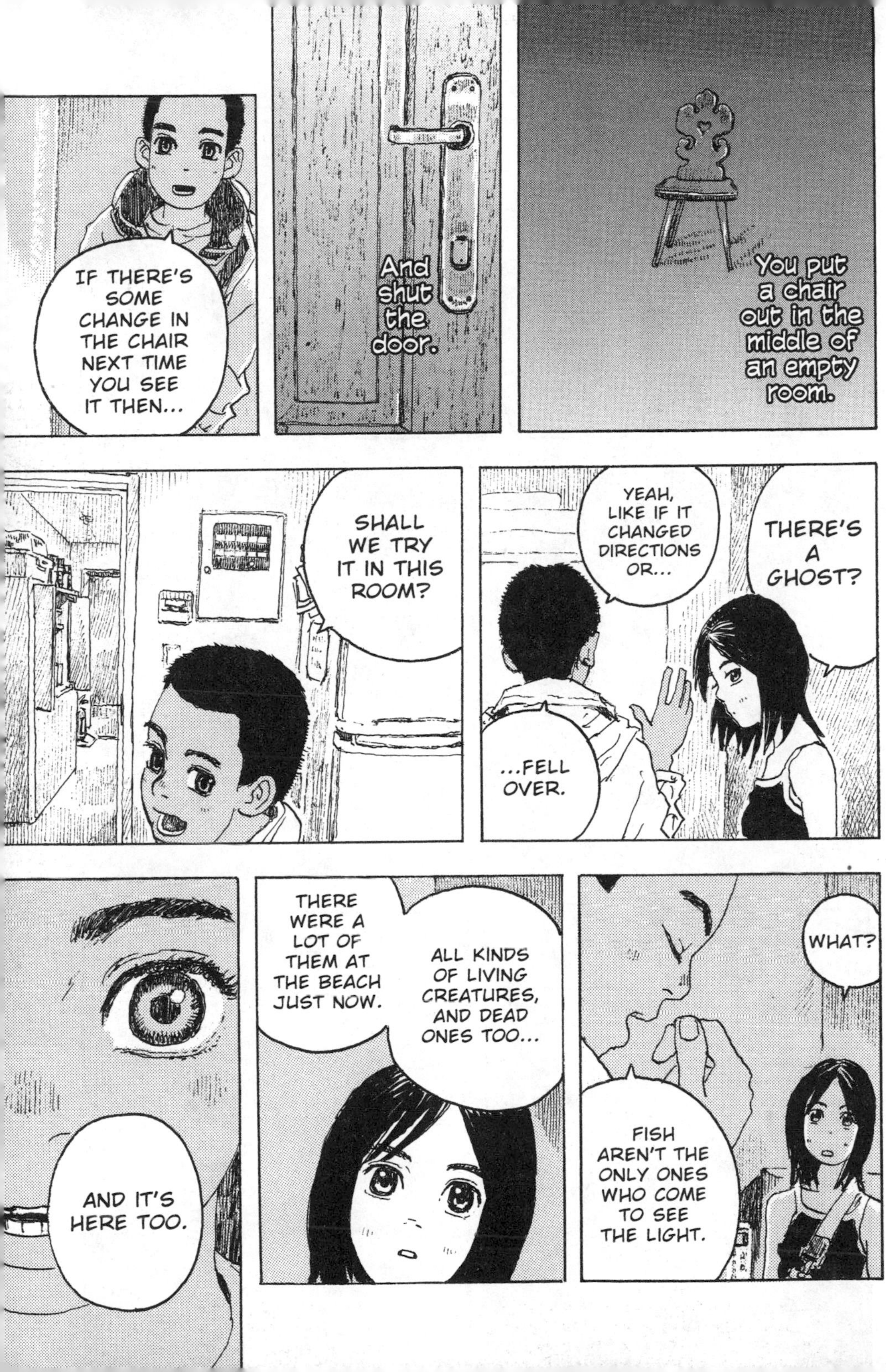
You put a chair out in the middle of an empty room.
And shut the door.
IF THERE'S SOME CHANGE IN THE CHAIR NEXT TIME YOU SEE IT THEN...
THERE'S A GHOST?
YEAH, LIKE IF IT CHANGED DIRECTIONS OR...
...FELL OVER.
SHALL WE TRY IT IN THIS ROOM?
WHAT?
FISH AREN'T THE ONLY ONES WHO COME TO SEE THE LIGHT.
ALL KINDS OF LIVING CREATURES, AND DEAD ONES TOO...
THERE WERE A LOT OF THEM AT THE BEACH JUST NOW.
AND IT'S HERE TOO.

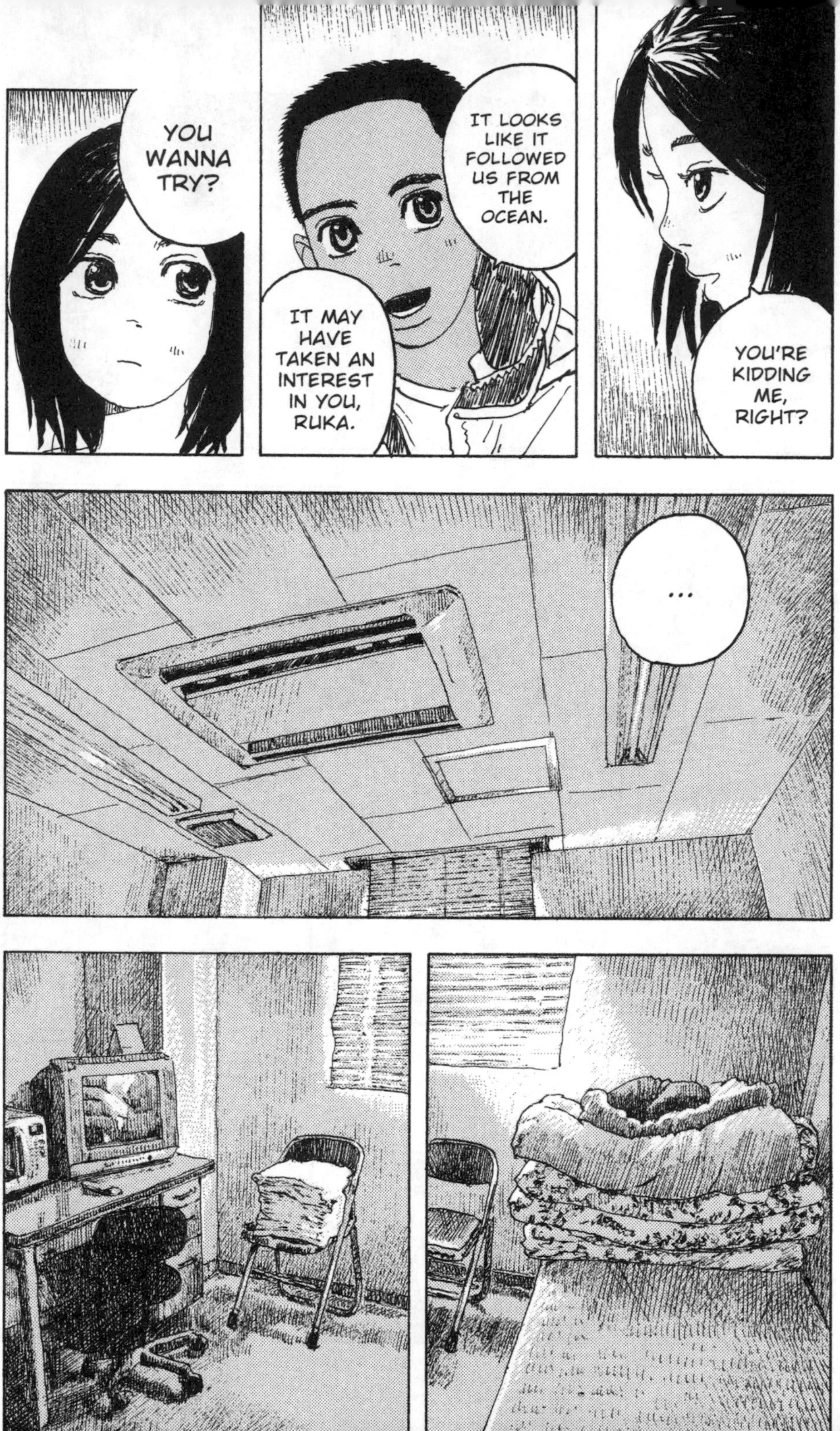
YOU'RE KIDDING ME, RIGHT?
IT LOOKS LIKE IT FOLLOWED US FROM THE OCEAN.
IT MAY HAVE TAKEN AN INTEREST IN YOU, RUKA.
YOU WANNA TRY?
...

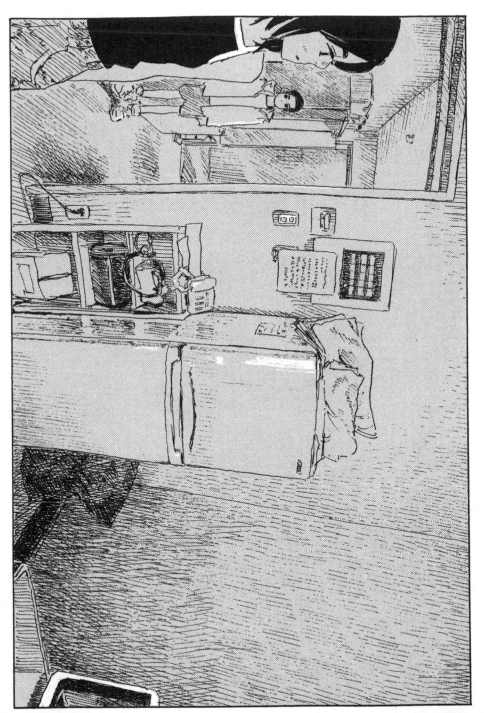

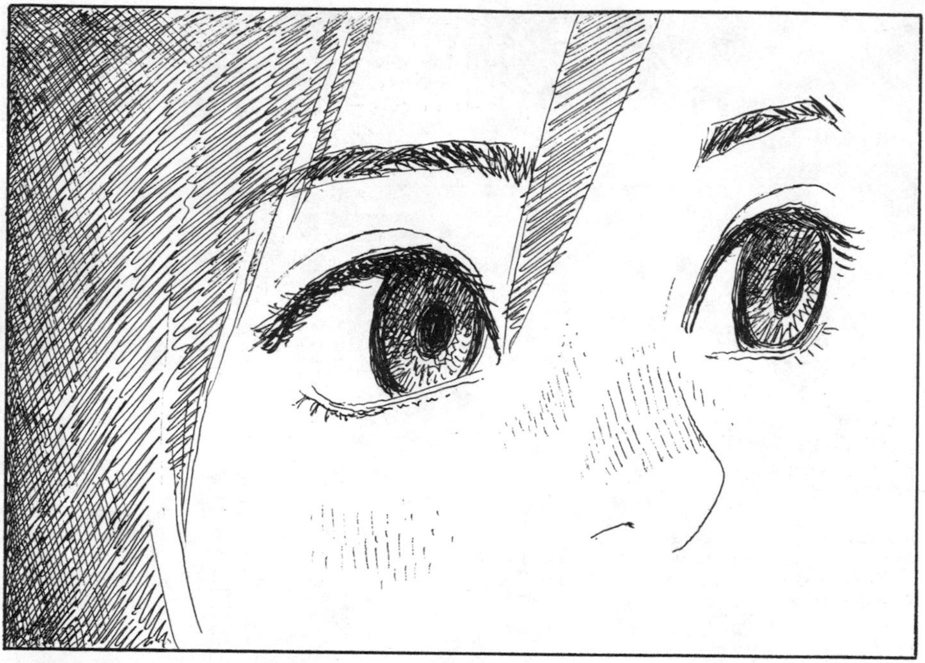

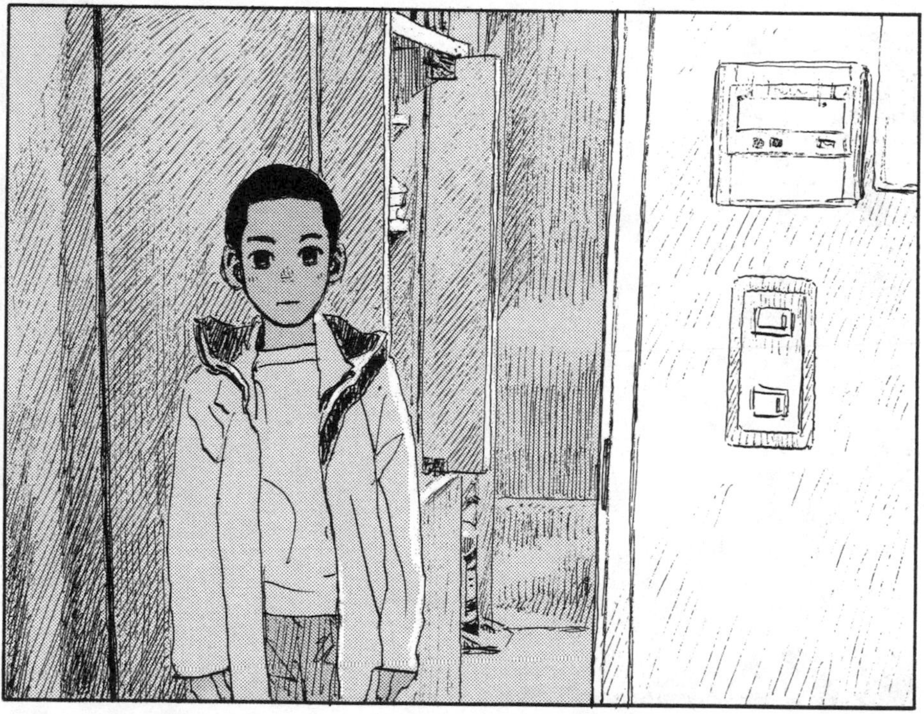

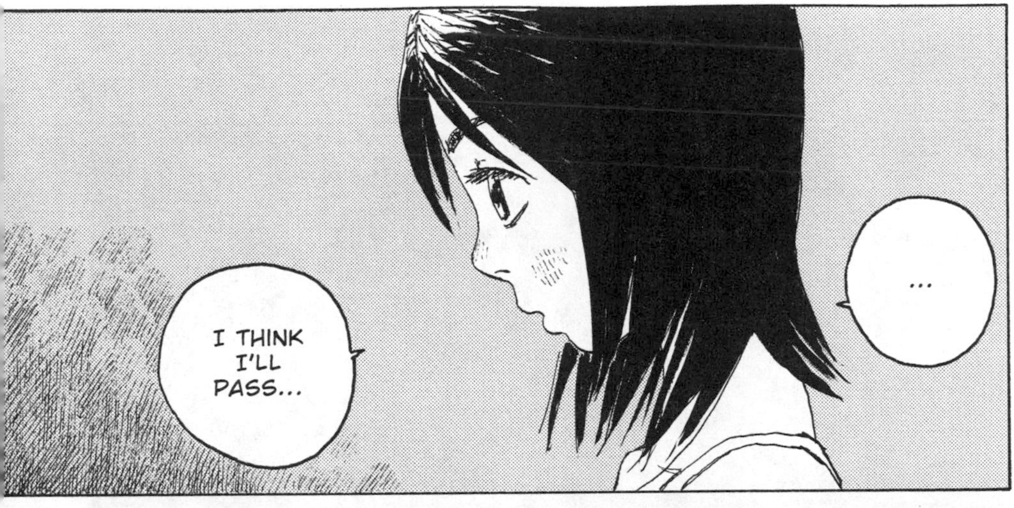
...
I THINK I'LL PASS...

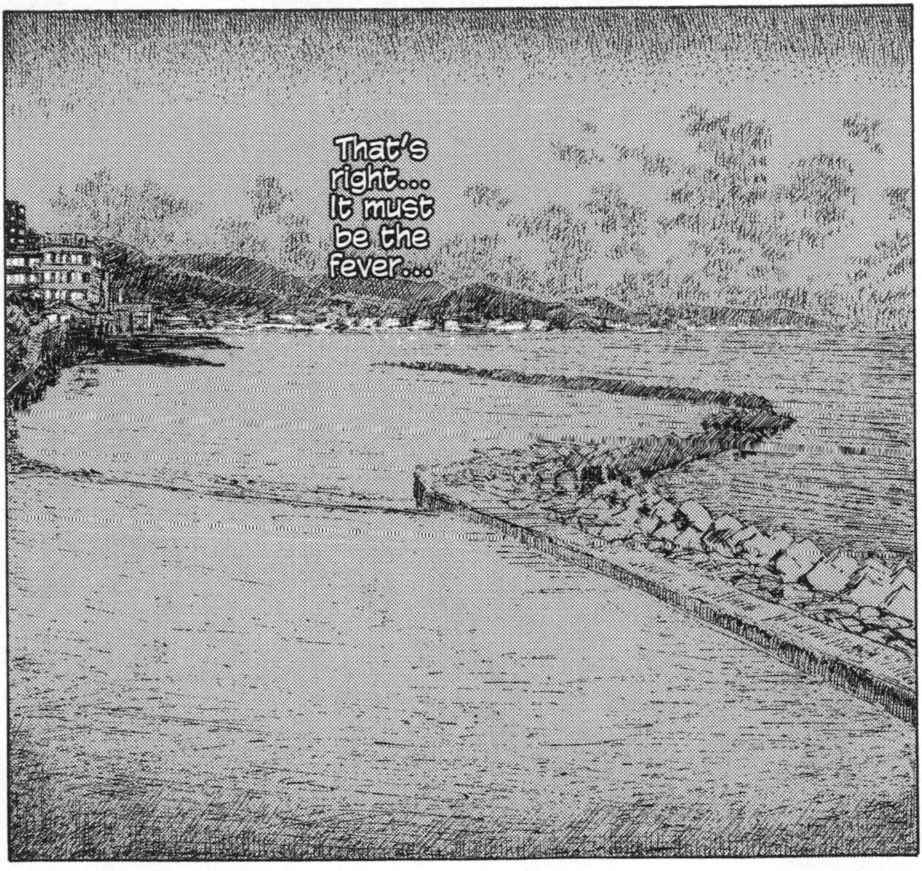
That's right... It must be the fever...

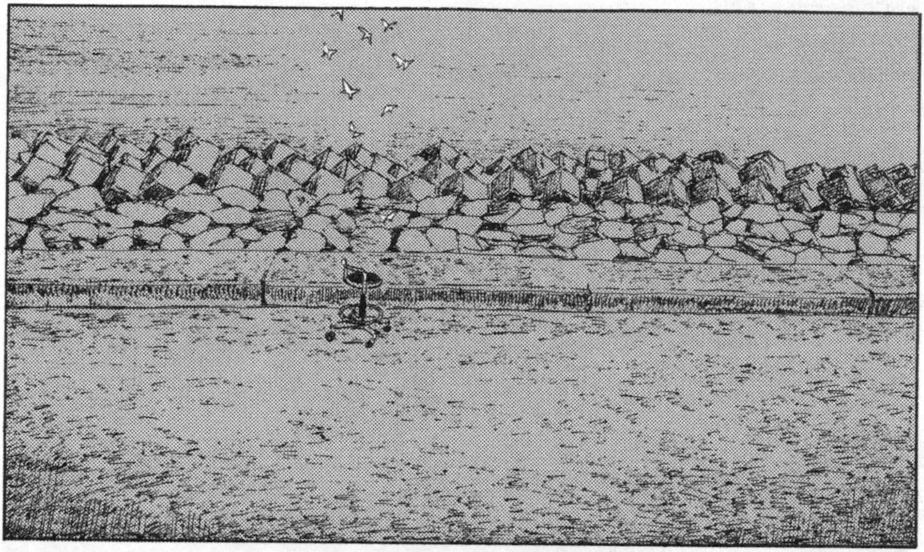

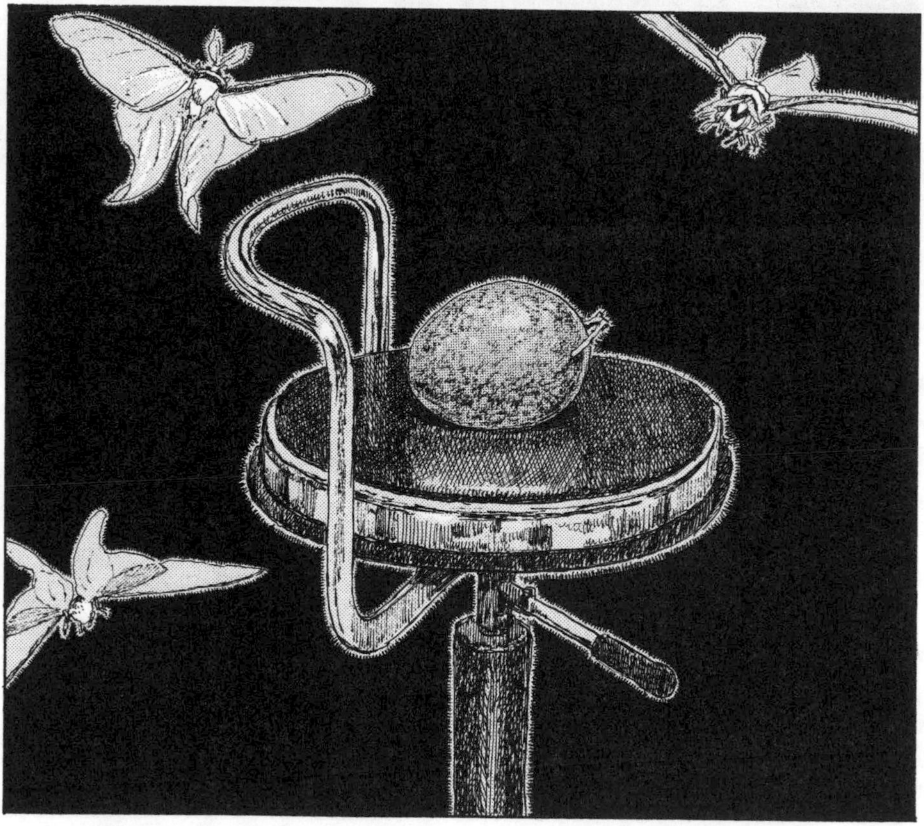

Chapter 8: The Realm of the Sea

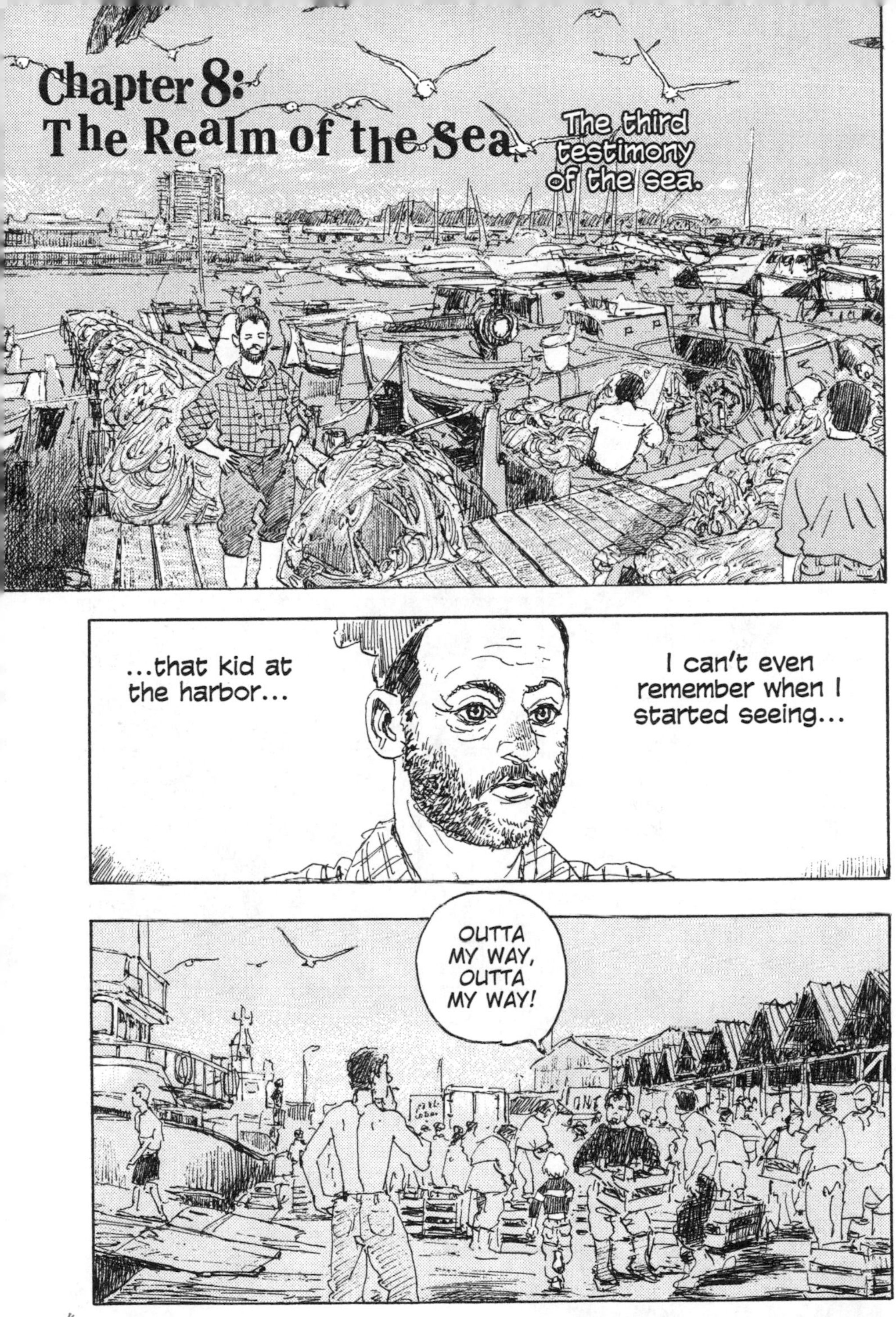
The third testimony of the sea.
I can't even remember when I started seeing...
...that kid at the harbor...
OUTTA MY WAY, OUTTA MY WAY!

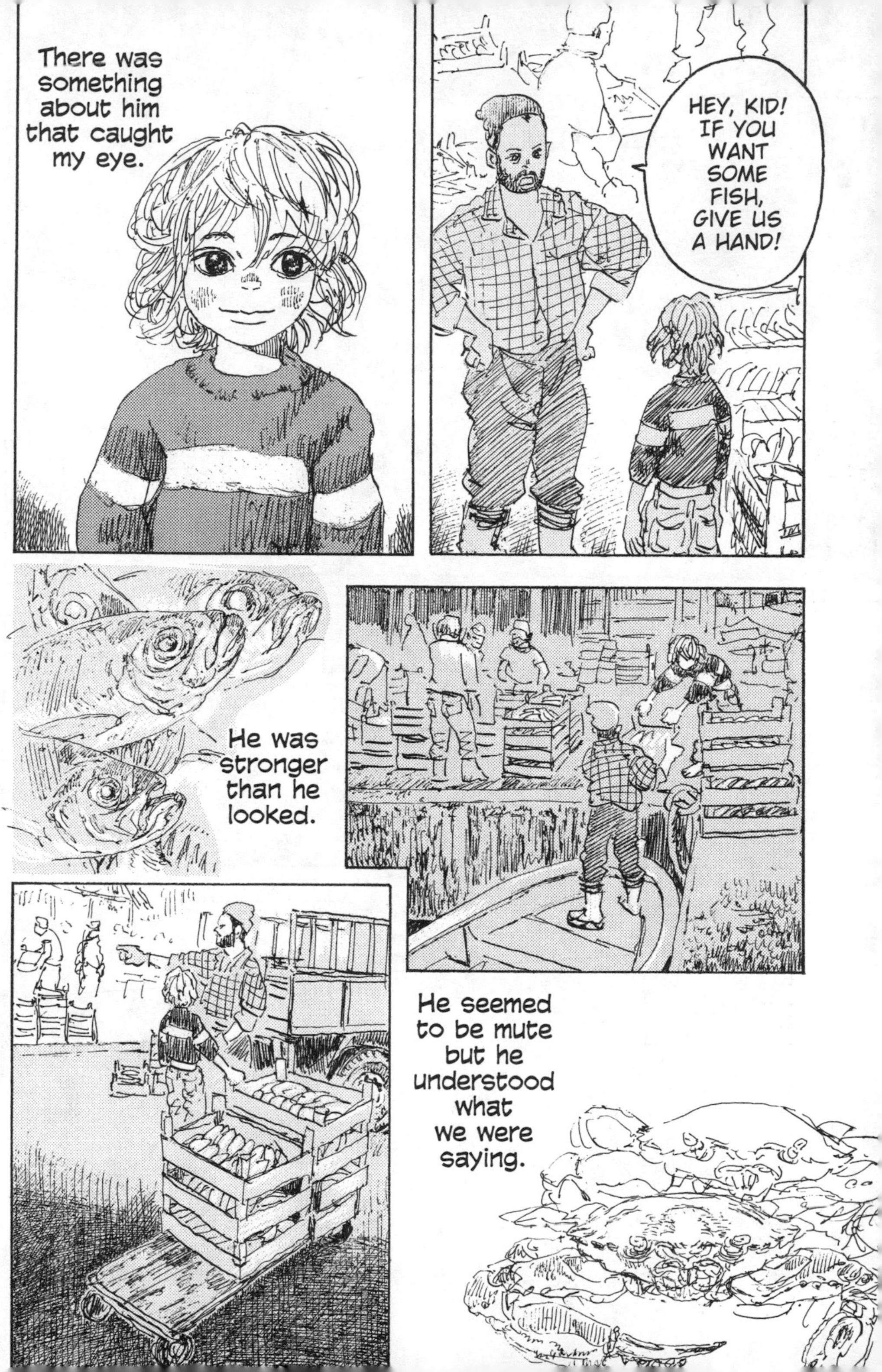
HEY, KID! IF YOU WANT SOME FISH, GIVE US A HAND!
There was something about him that caught my eye.
He was stronger than he looked.
He seemed to be mute but he understood what we were saying.

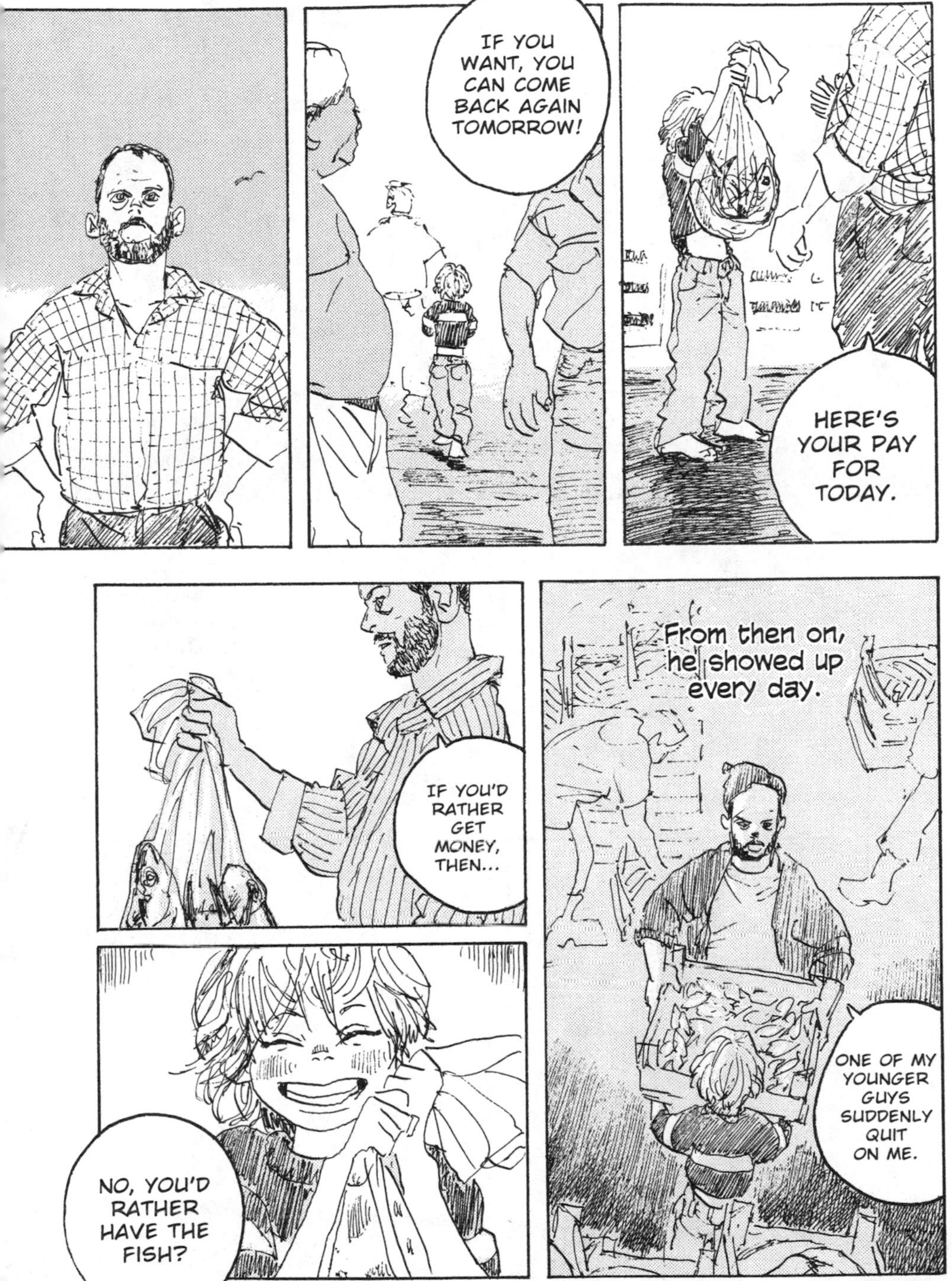
HERE'S YOUR PAY FOR TODAY.
IF YOU WANT, YOU CAN COME BACK AGAIN TOMORROW!
From then on, he showed up every day.
ONE OF MY YOUNGER GUYS SUDDENLY QUIT ON ME.
IF YOU'D RATHER GET MONEY, THEN...
NO, YOU'D RATHER HAVE THE FISH?

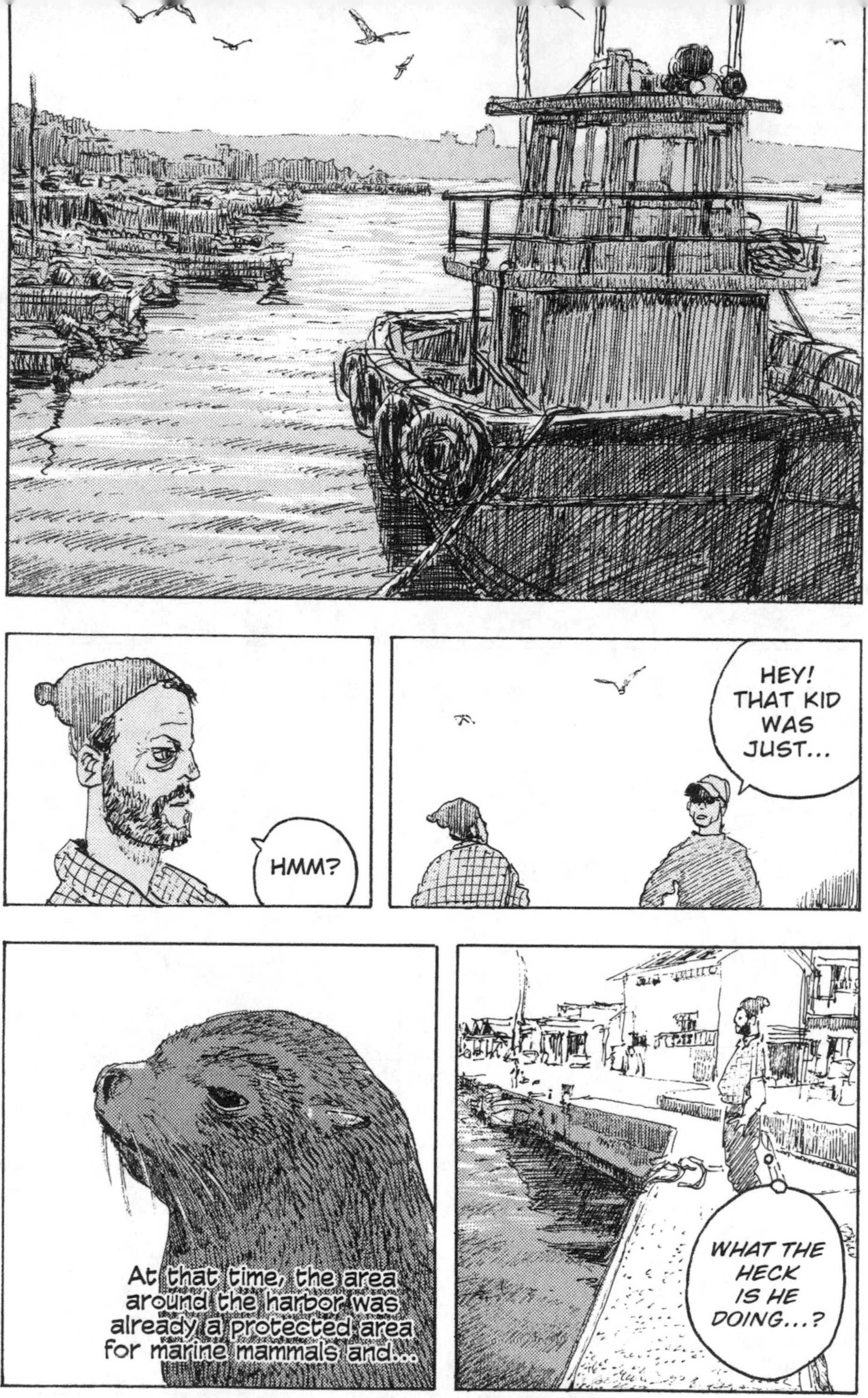
HEY! THAT KID WAS JUST...
HMM?
WHAT THE HECK IS HE DOING...?
At that time, the area around the harbor was already a protected area for marine mammals and...

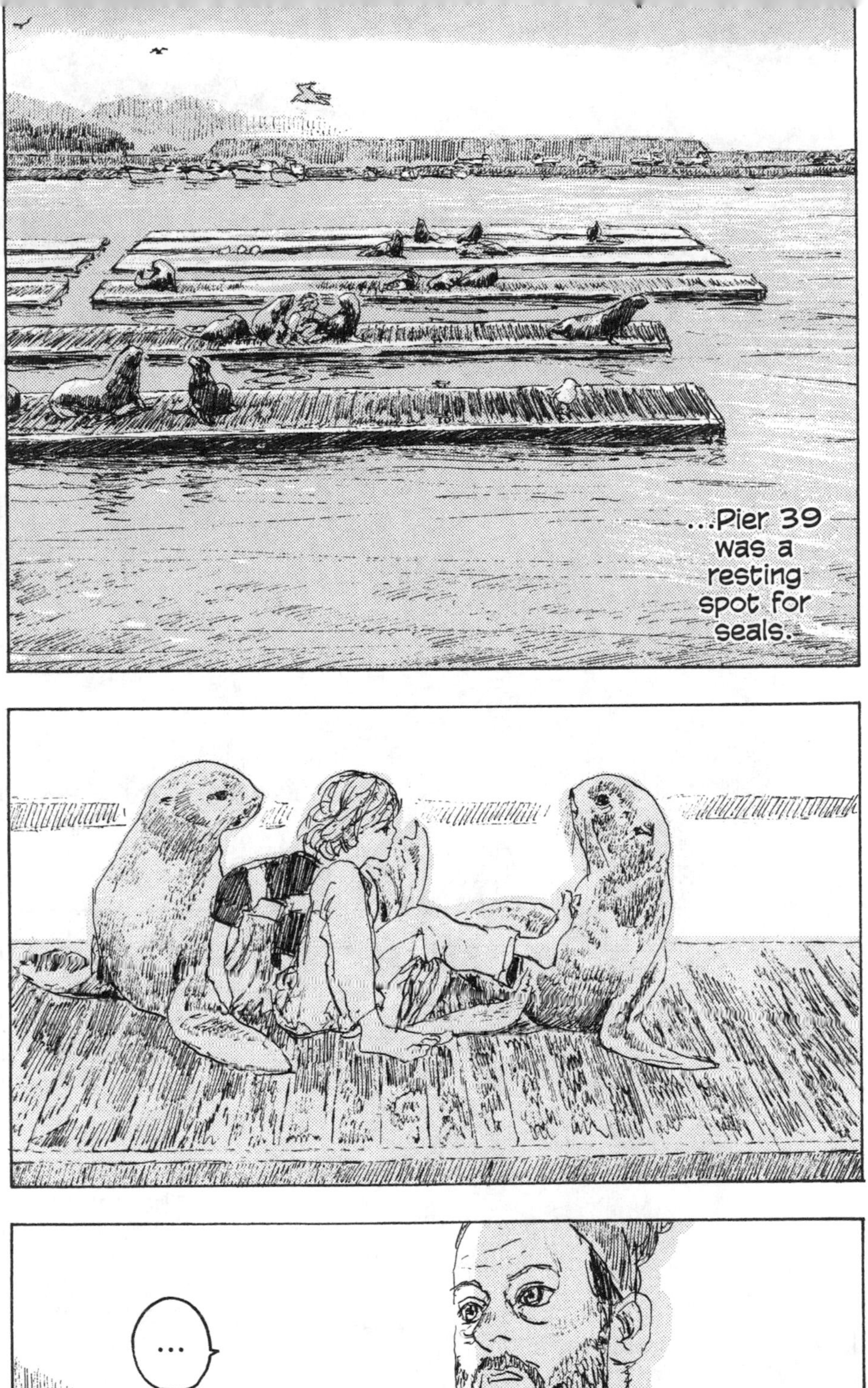
...Pier 39 was a resting spot for seals.
...

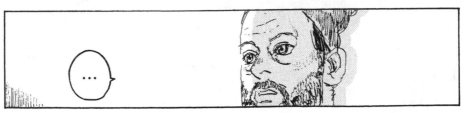

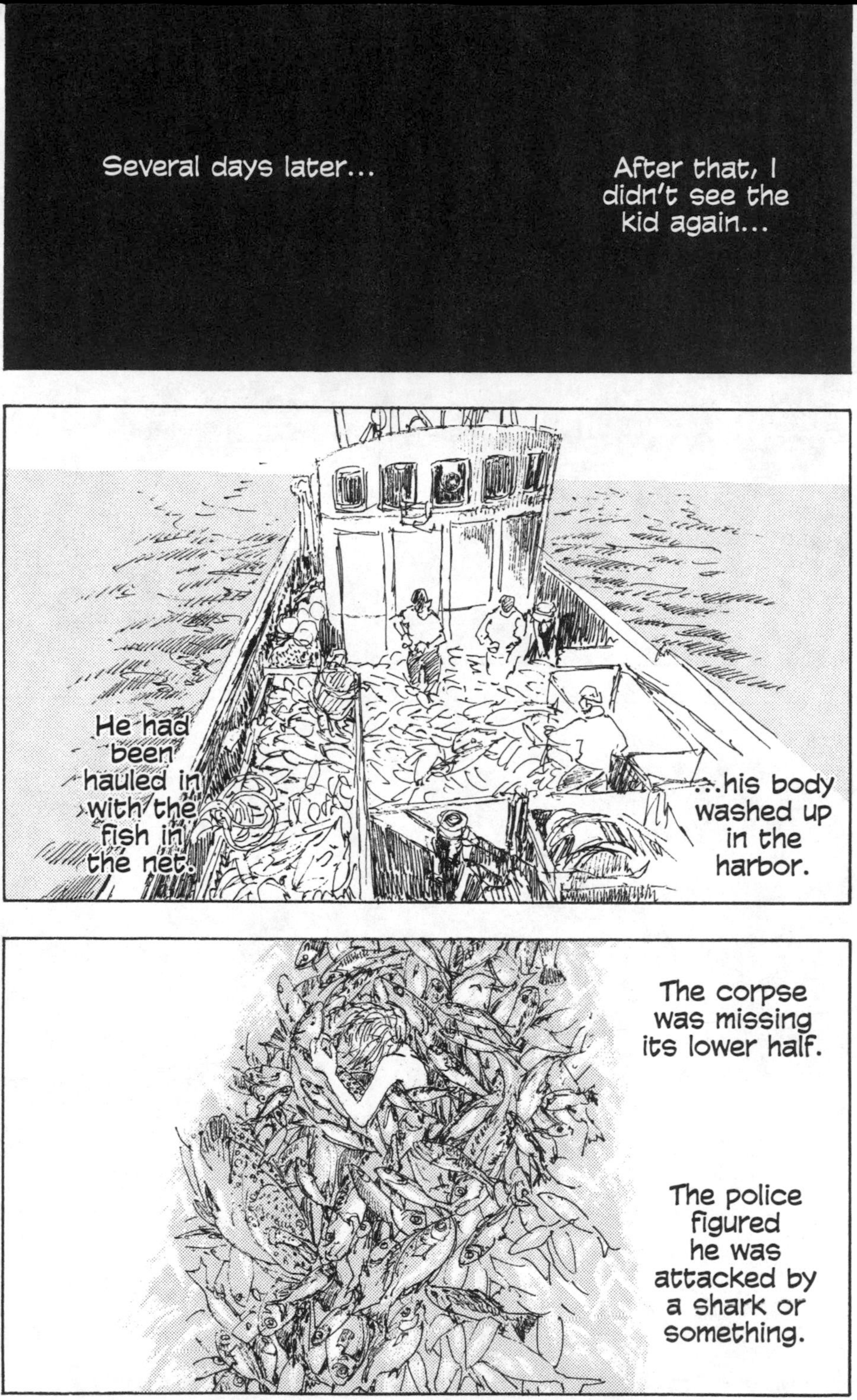
After that, I didn't see the kid again...
Several days later...
...his body washed up in the harbor.
He had been hauled in with the fish in the net.
The corpse was missing its lower half.
The police figured he was attacked by a shark or something.

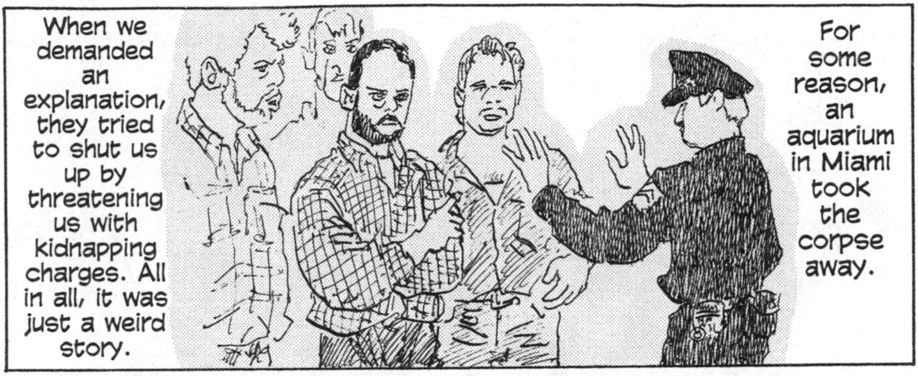
For some reason, an aquarium in Miami took the corpse away.
When we demanded an explanation, they tried to shut us up by threatening us with kidnapping charges. All in all, it was just a weird story.

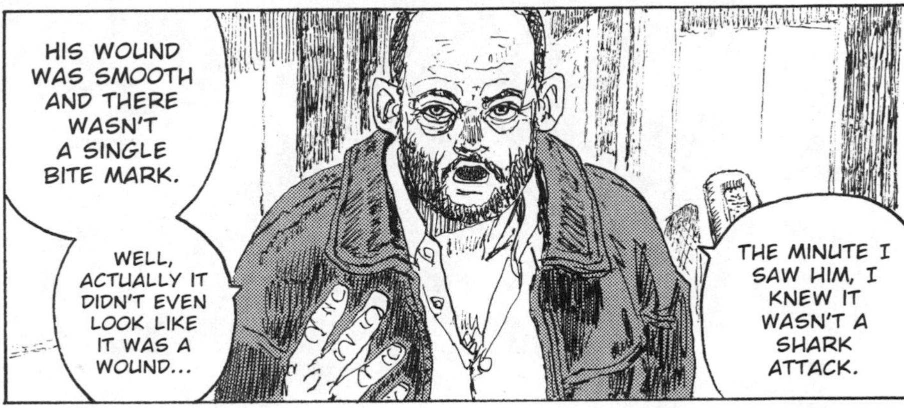
THE MINUTE I SAW HIM, I KNEW IT WASN'T A SHARK ATTACK.
HIS WOUND WAS SMOOTH AND THERE WASN'T A SINGLE BITE MARK.
WELL, ACTUALLY IT DIDN'T EVEN LOOK LIKE IT WAS A WOUND...

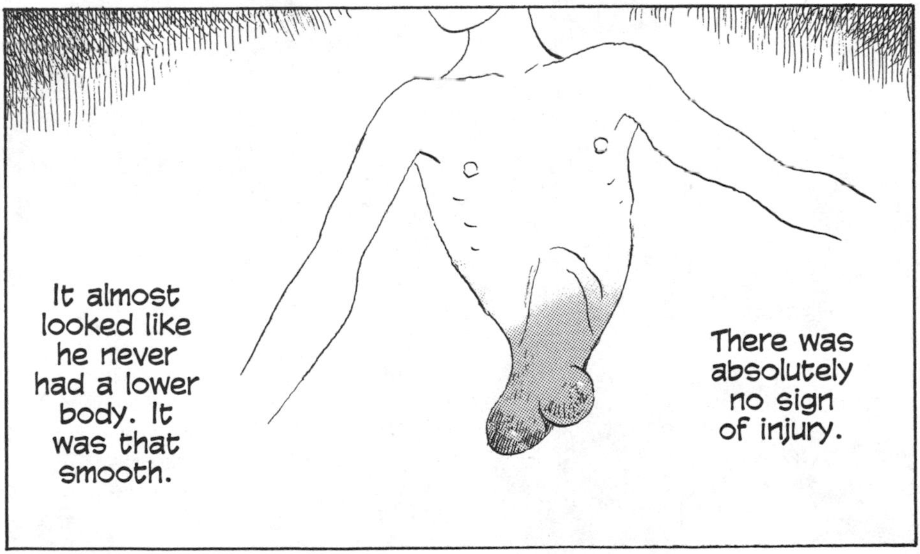
There was absolutely no sign of injury.
It almost looked like he never had a lower body. It was that smooth.

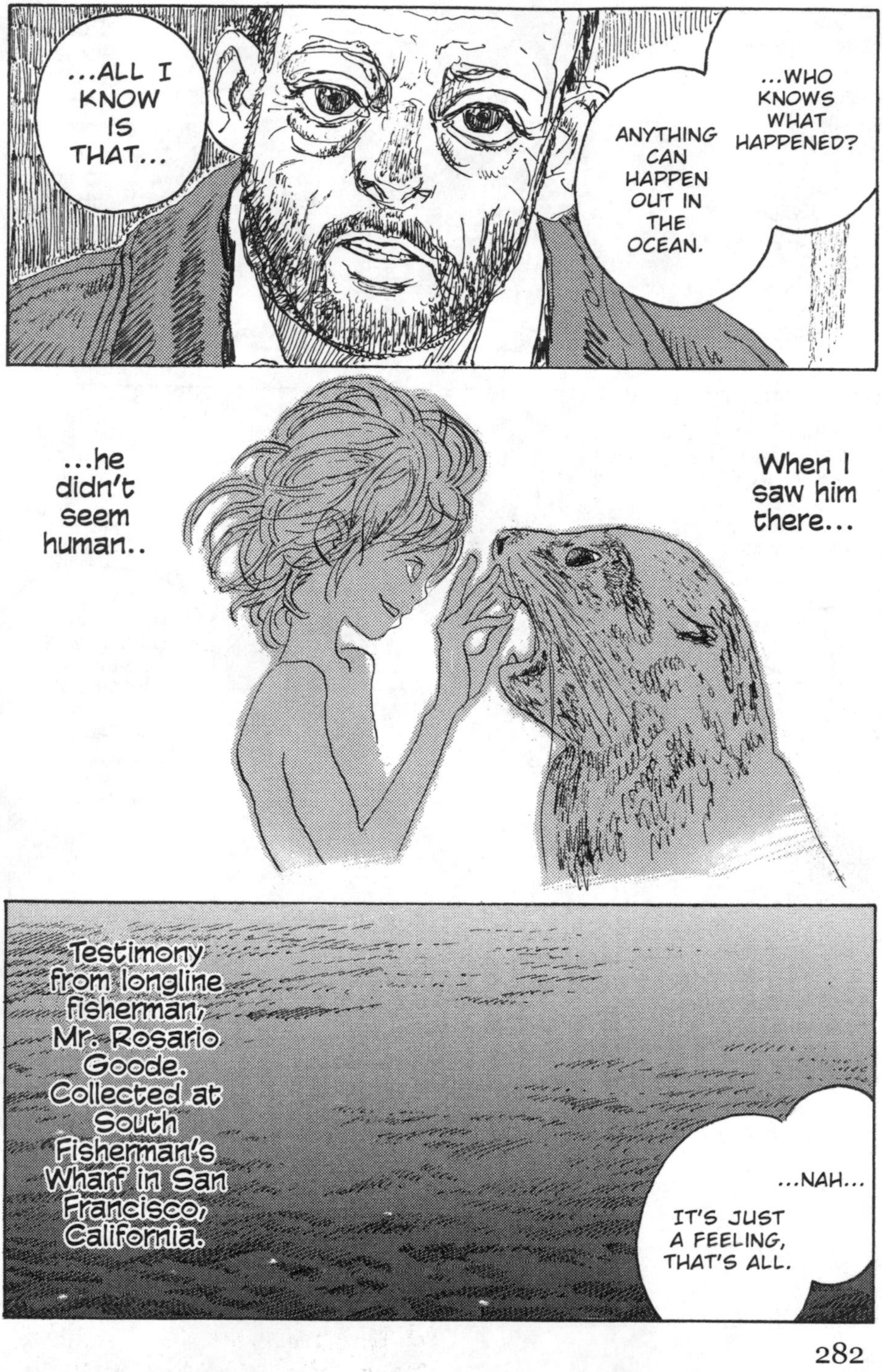
...WHO KNOWS WHAT HAPPENED?
ANYTHING CAN HAPPEN OUT IN THE OCEAN.
...ALL I KNOW IS THAT...
When I saw him there...
...he didn't seem human..
...NAH...
IT'S JUST A FEELING, THAT'S ALL.
Testimony from longline fisherman, Mr. Rosario Goode. Collected at South Fisherman's Wharf in San Francisco, California.

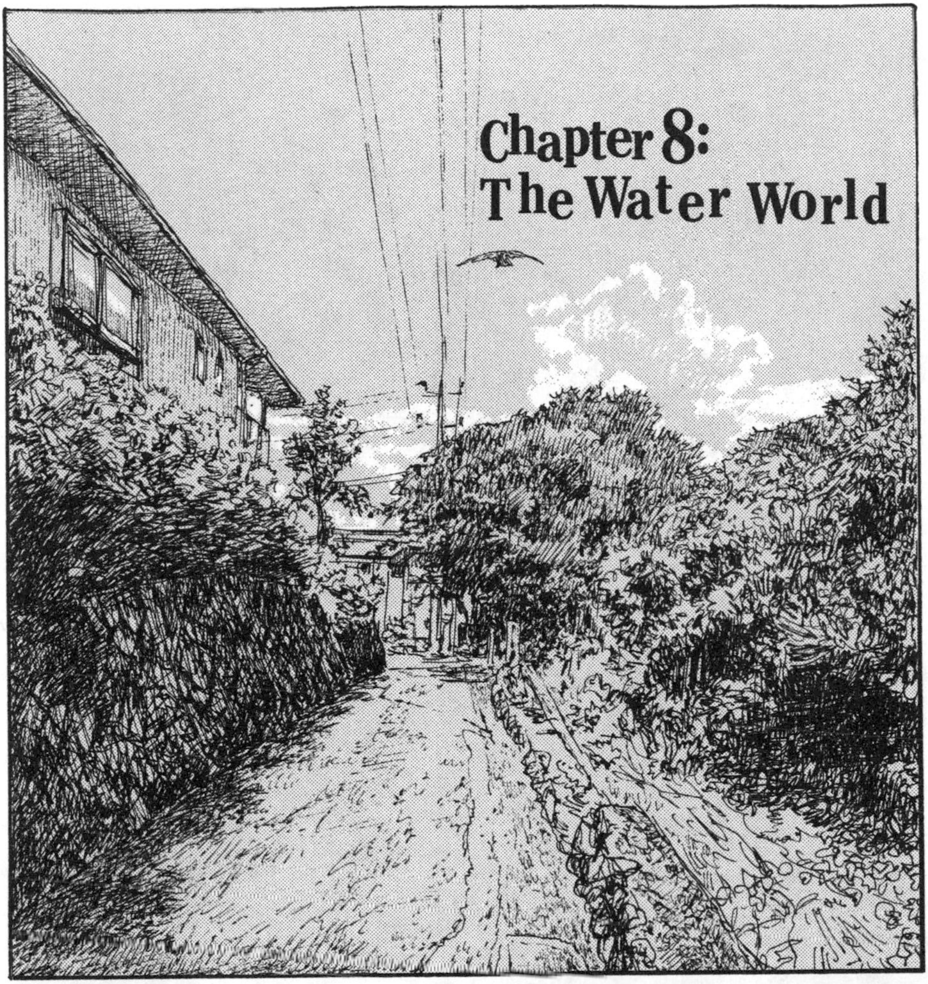
Chapter 8:
The Water World

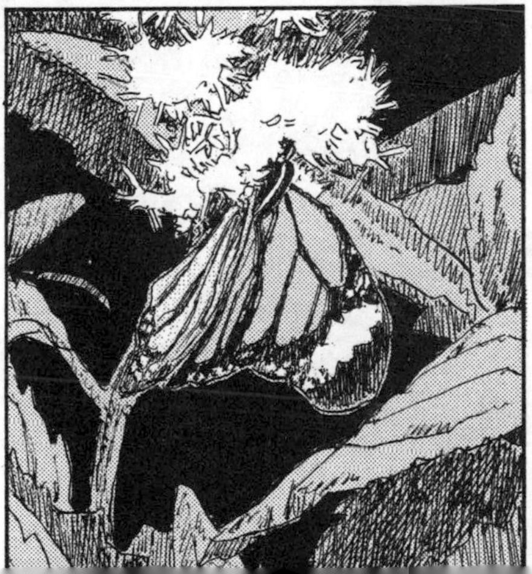

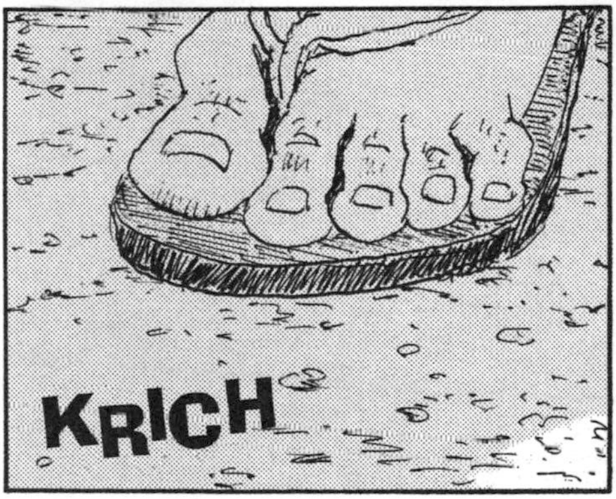
KRICH

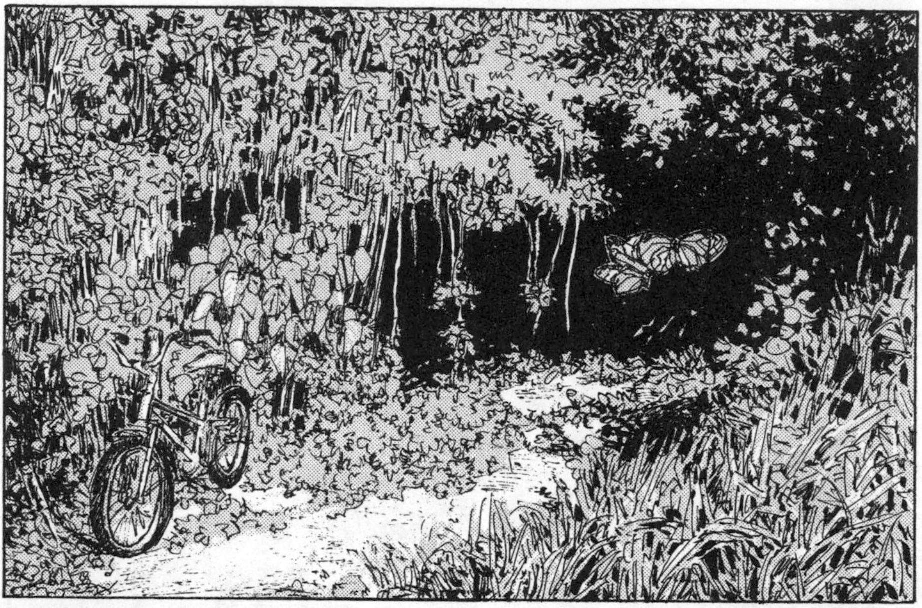
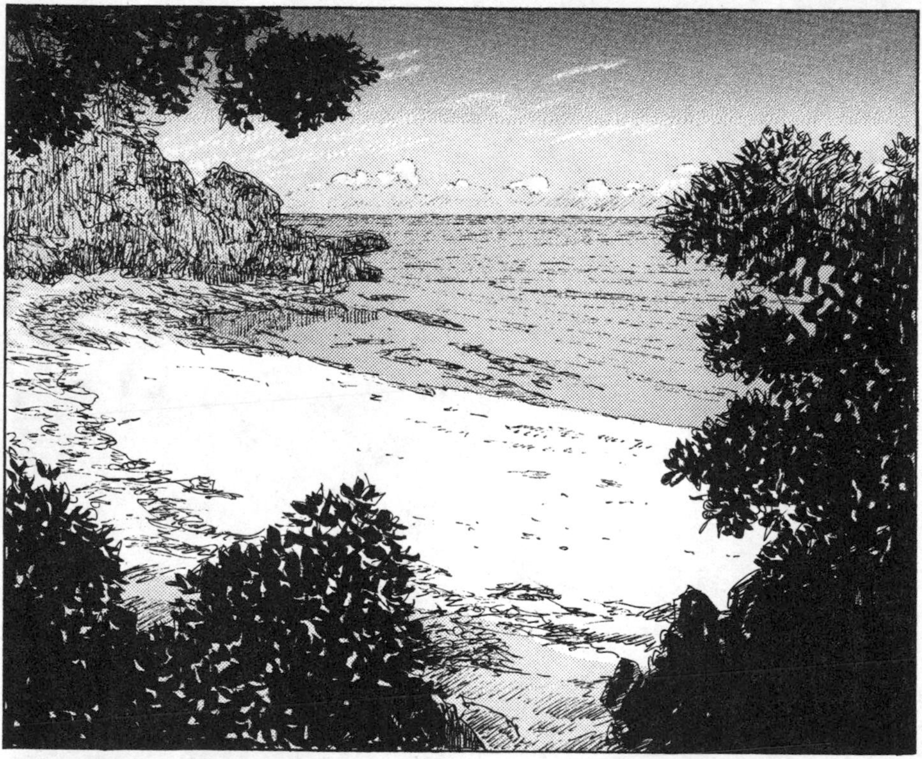

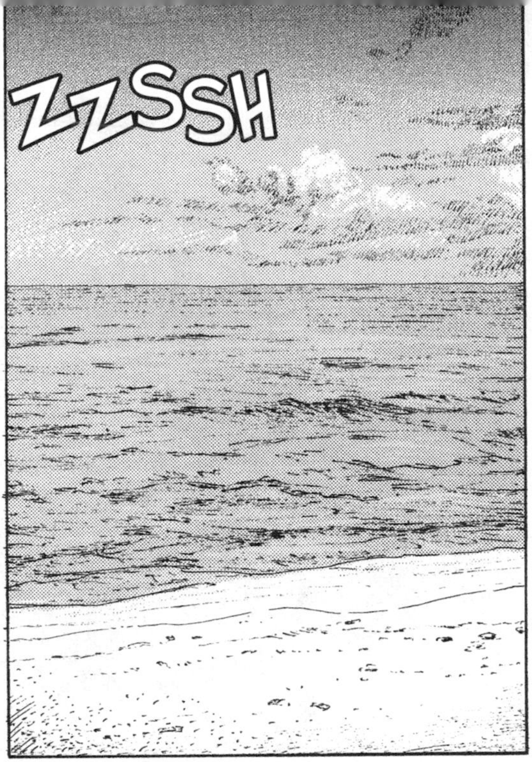
ZZSSH

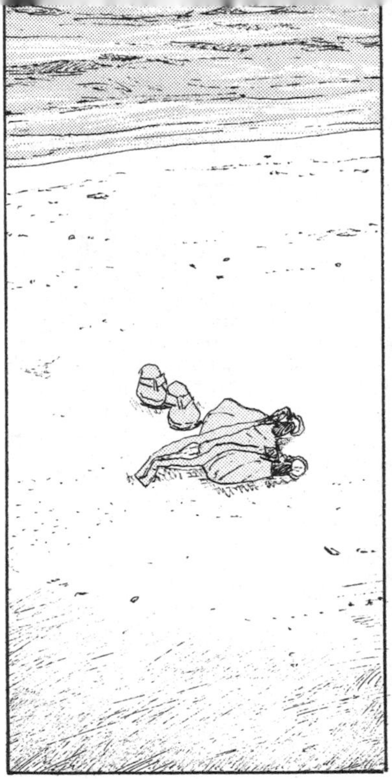

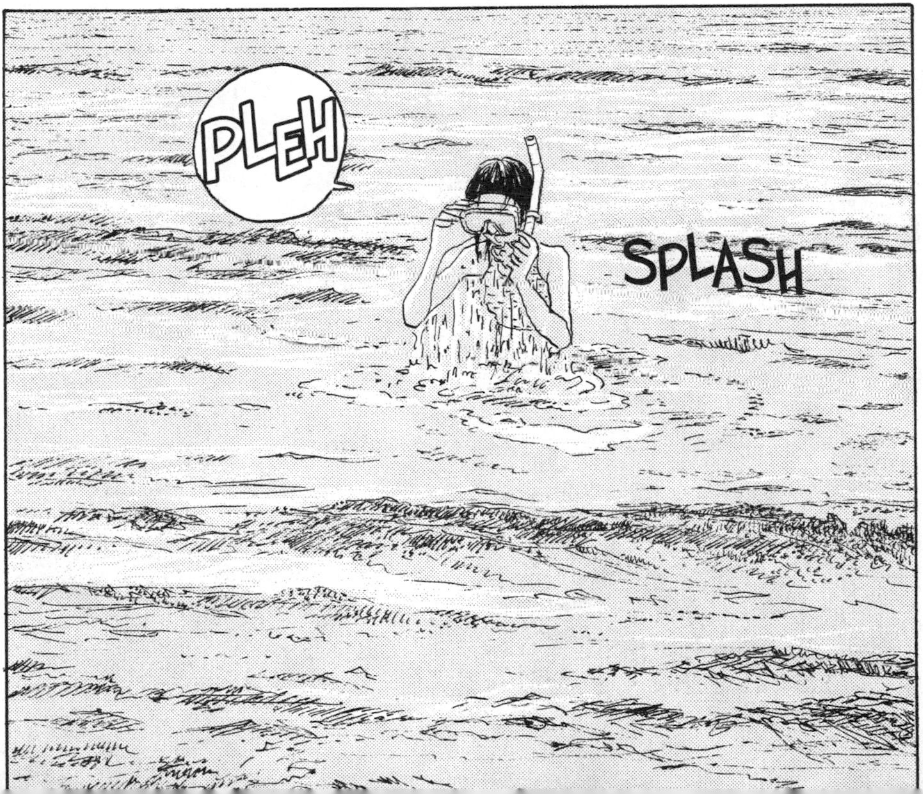
PLEH
SPLASH

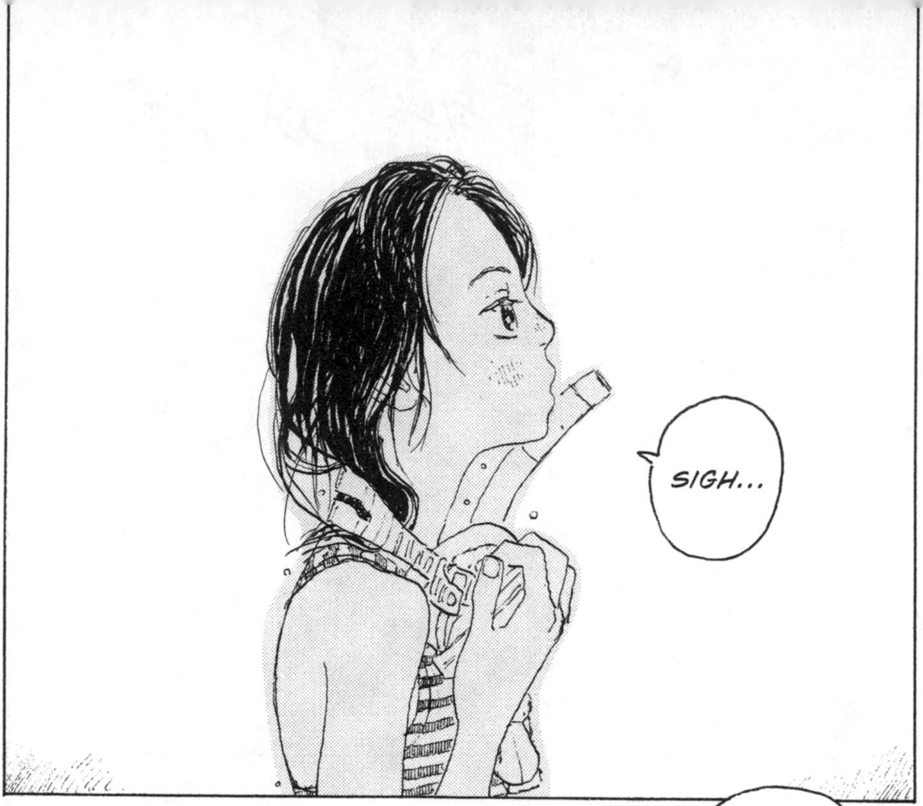
SIGH...

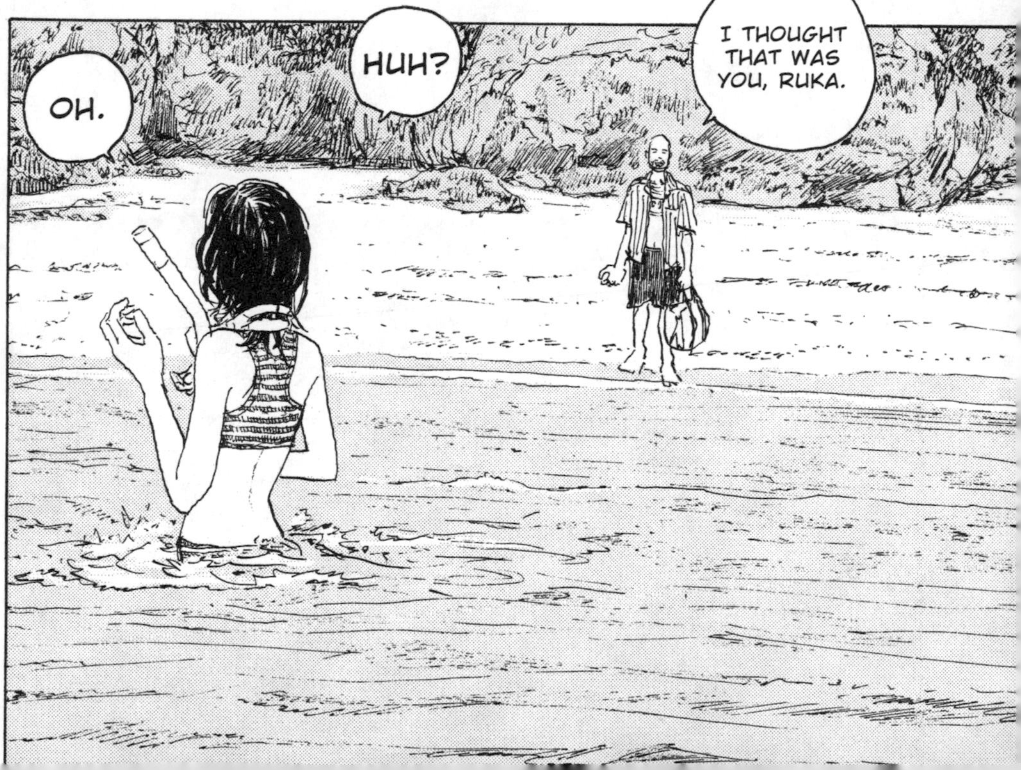
I THOUGHT THAT WAS YOU, RUKA.
HUH?
OH.

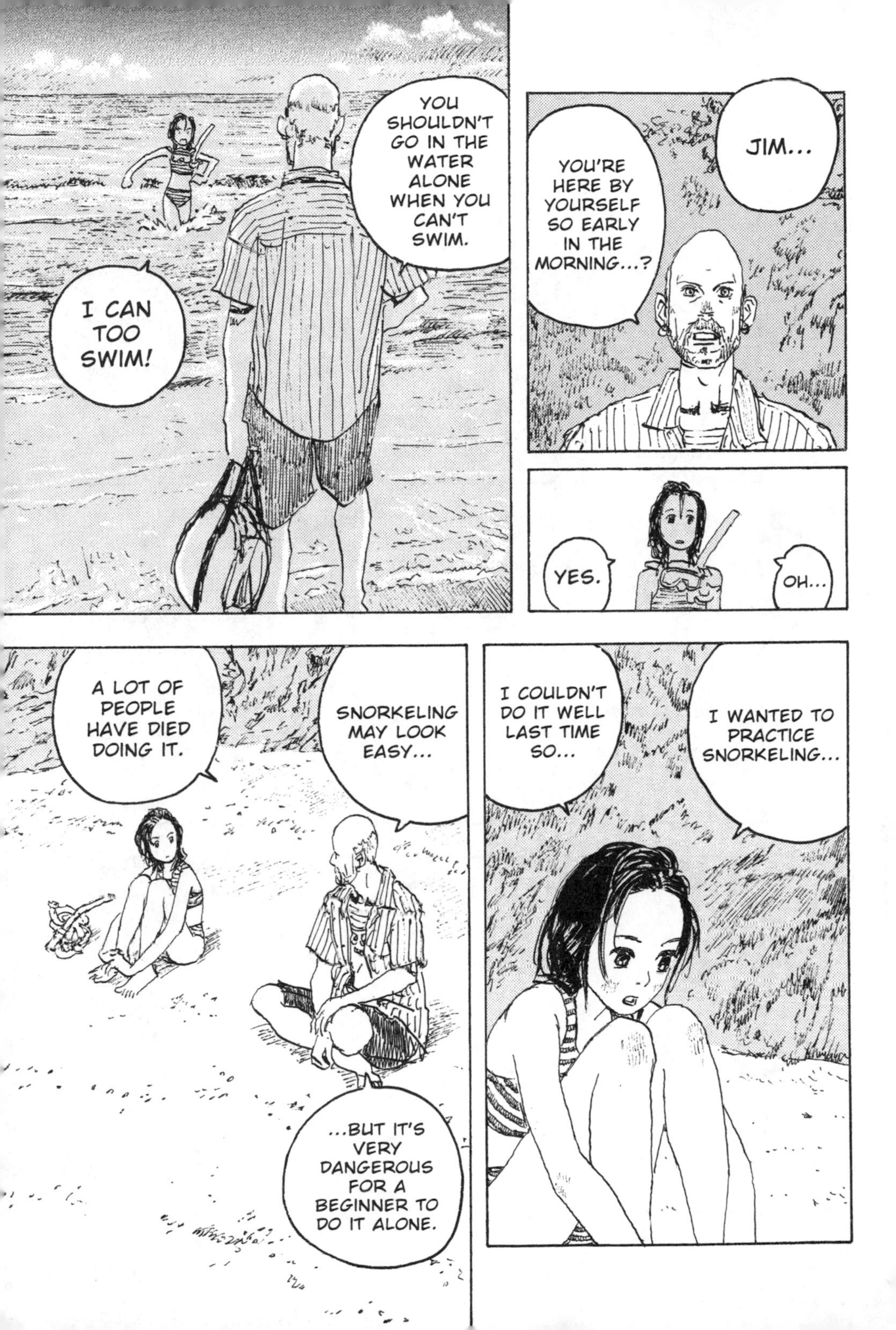
JIM...
YOU'RE HERE BY YOURSELF SO EARLY IN THE MORNING...?
YES.
OH...
YOU SHOULDN'T GO IN THE WATER ALONE WHEN YOU CAN'T SWIM.
I CAN TOO SWIM!
I WANTED TO PRACTICE SNORKELING...
I COULDN'T DO IT WELL LAST TIME SO...
SNORKELING MAY LOOK EASY...
...BUT IT'S VERY DANGEROUS FOR A BEGINNER TO DO IT ALONE.
A LOT OF PEOPLE HAVE DIED DOING IT.

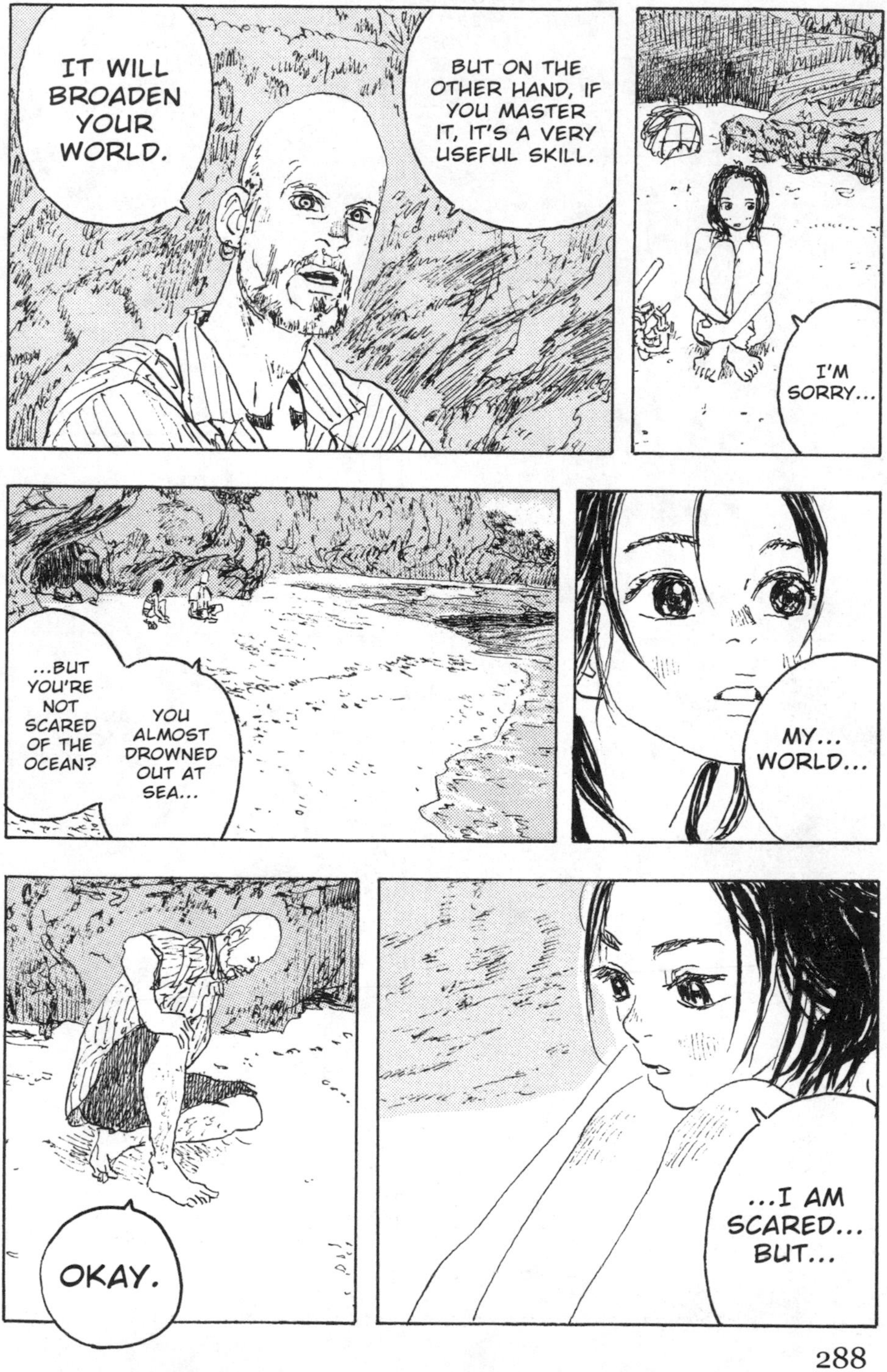
I'M SORRY...
BUT ON THE OTHER HAND, IF YOU MASTER IT, IT'S A VERY USEFUL SKILL.
IT WILL BROADEN YOUR WORLD.
MY... WORLD...
YOU ALMOST DROWNED OUT AT SEA...
...BUT YOU'RE NOT SCARED OF THE OCEAN?
...I AM SCARED... BUT...
OKAY.

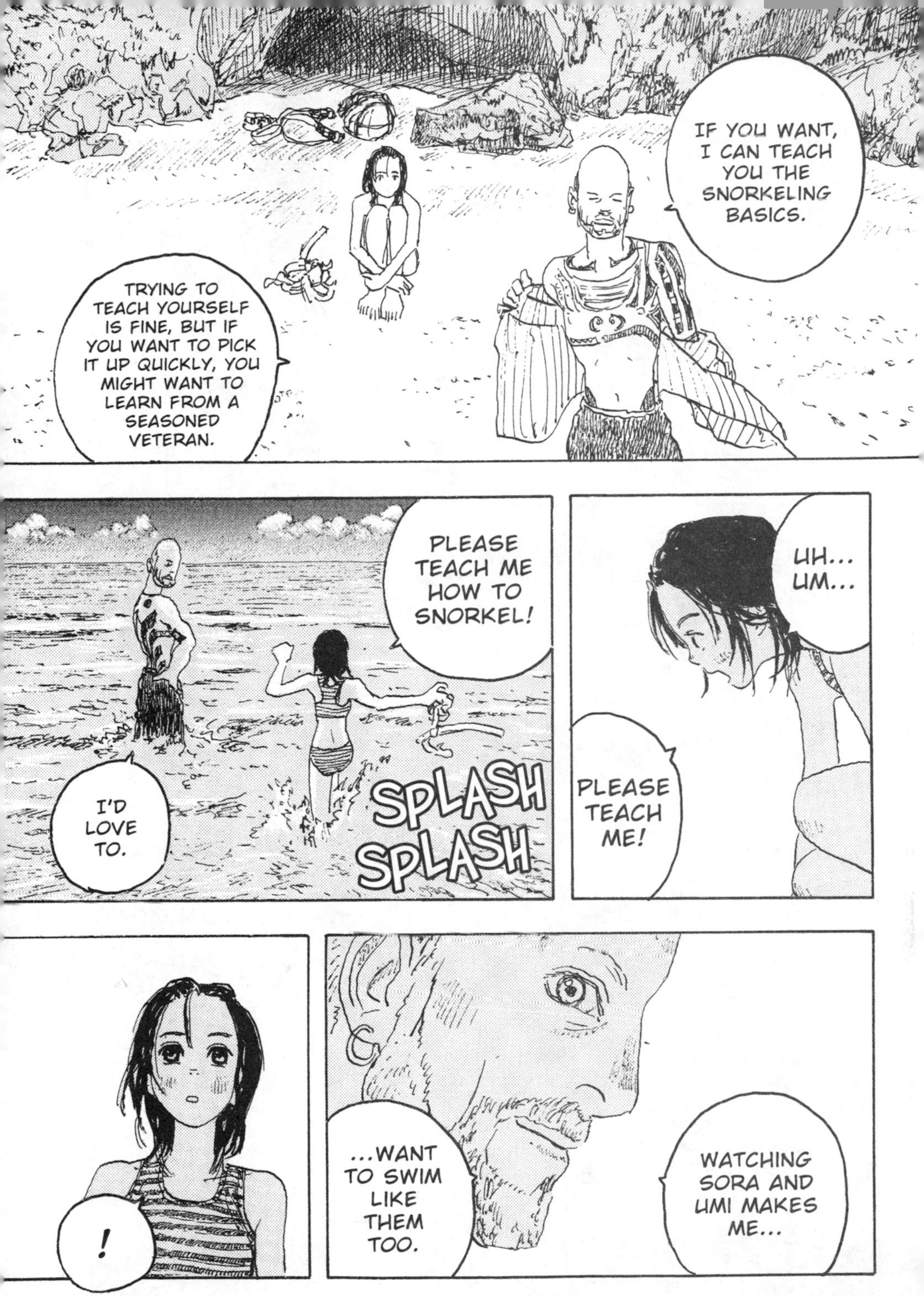
IF YOU WANT, I CAN TEACH YOU THE SNORKELING BASICS.
TRYING TO TEACH YOURSELF IS FINE, BUT IF YOU WANT TO PICK IT UP QUICKLY, YOU MIGHT WANT TO LEARN FROM A SEASONED VETERAN.
UH... UM...
PLEASE TEACH ME!
PLEASE TEACH ME HOW TO SNORKEL!
SPLASH SPLASH
I'D LOVE TO.
WATCHING SORA AND UMI MAKES ME...
...WANT TO SWIM LIKE THEM TOO.
!

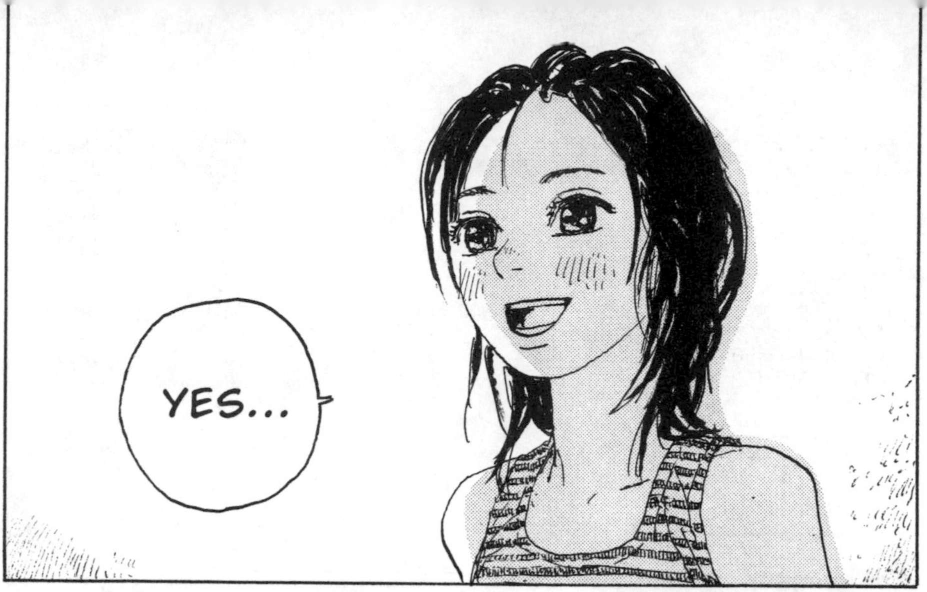
YES...

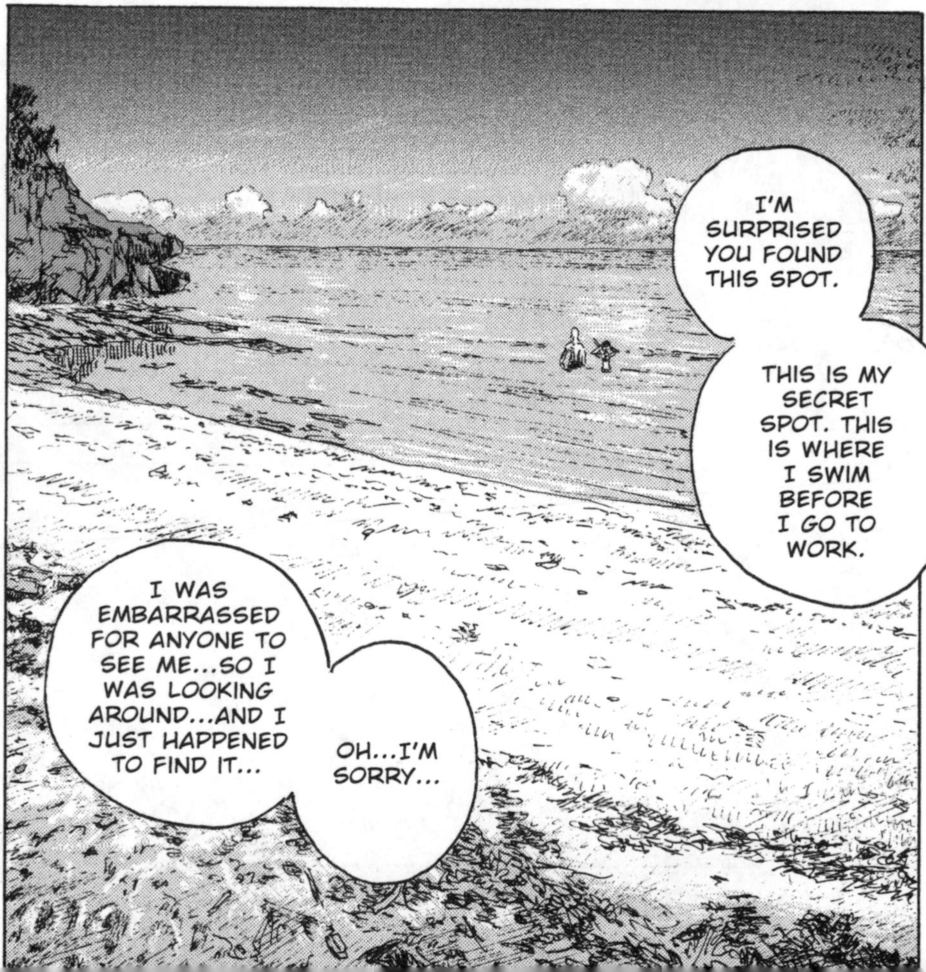
I'M SURPRISED YOU FOUND THIS SPOT.
THIS IS MY SECRET SPOT. THIS IS WHERE I SWIM BEFORE I GO TO WORK.
OH...I'M SORRY...
I WAS EMBARRASSED FOR ANYONE TO SEE ME...SO I WAS LOOKING AROUND...AND I JUST HAPPENED TO FIND IT...

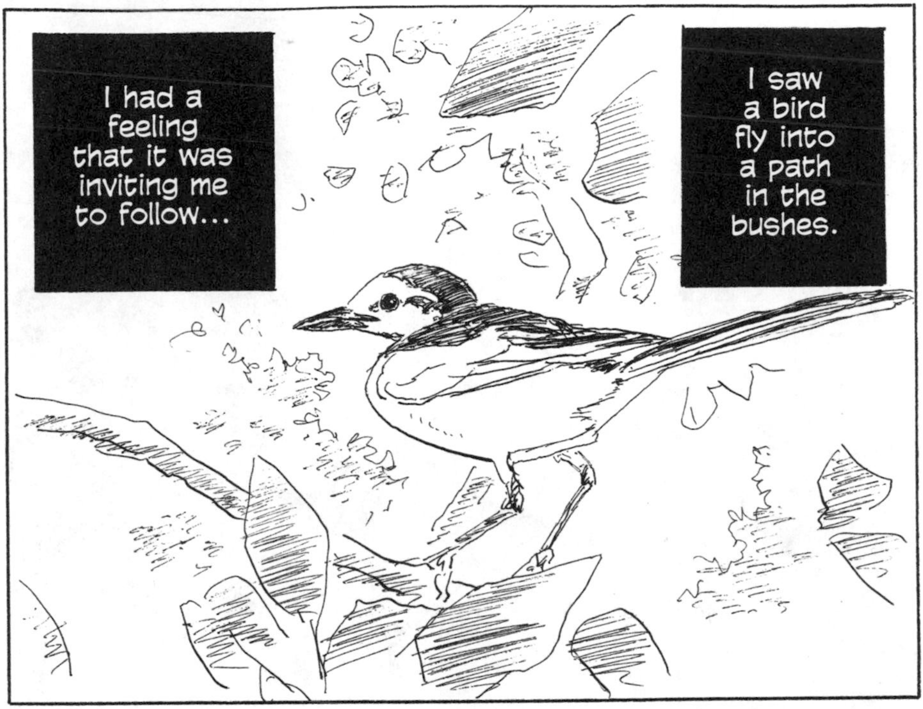
I saw a bird fly into a path in the bushes.
I had a feeling that it was inviting me to follow...

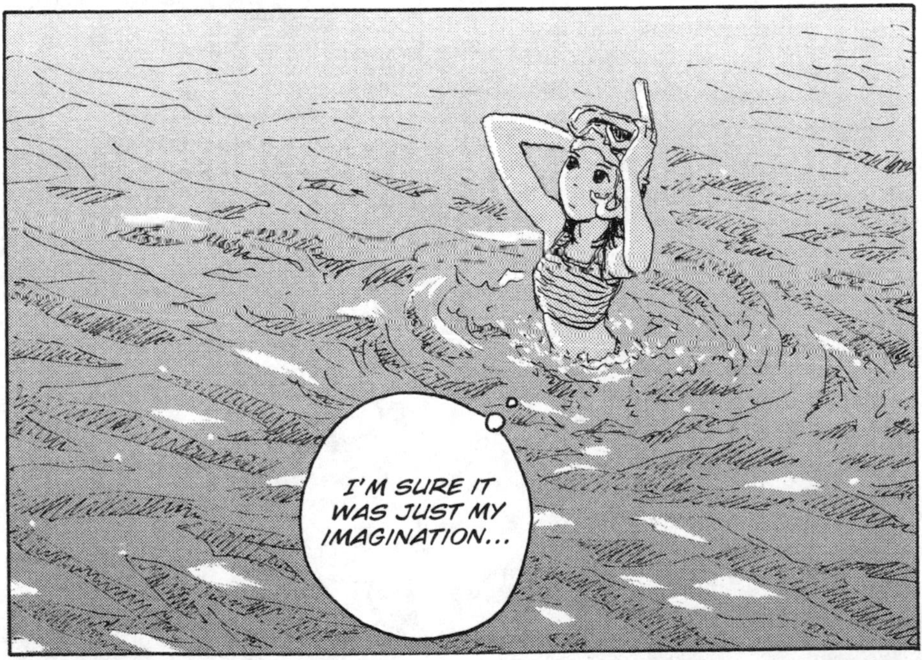
I'M SURE IT WAS JUST MY IMAGINATION...

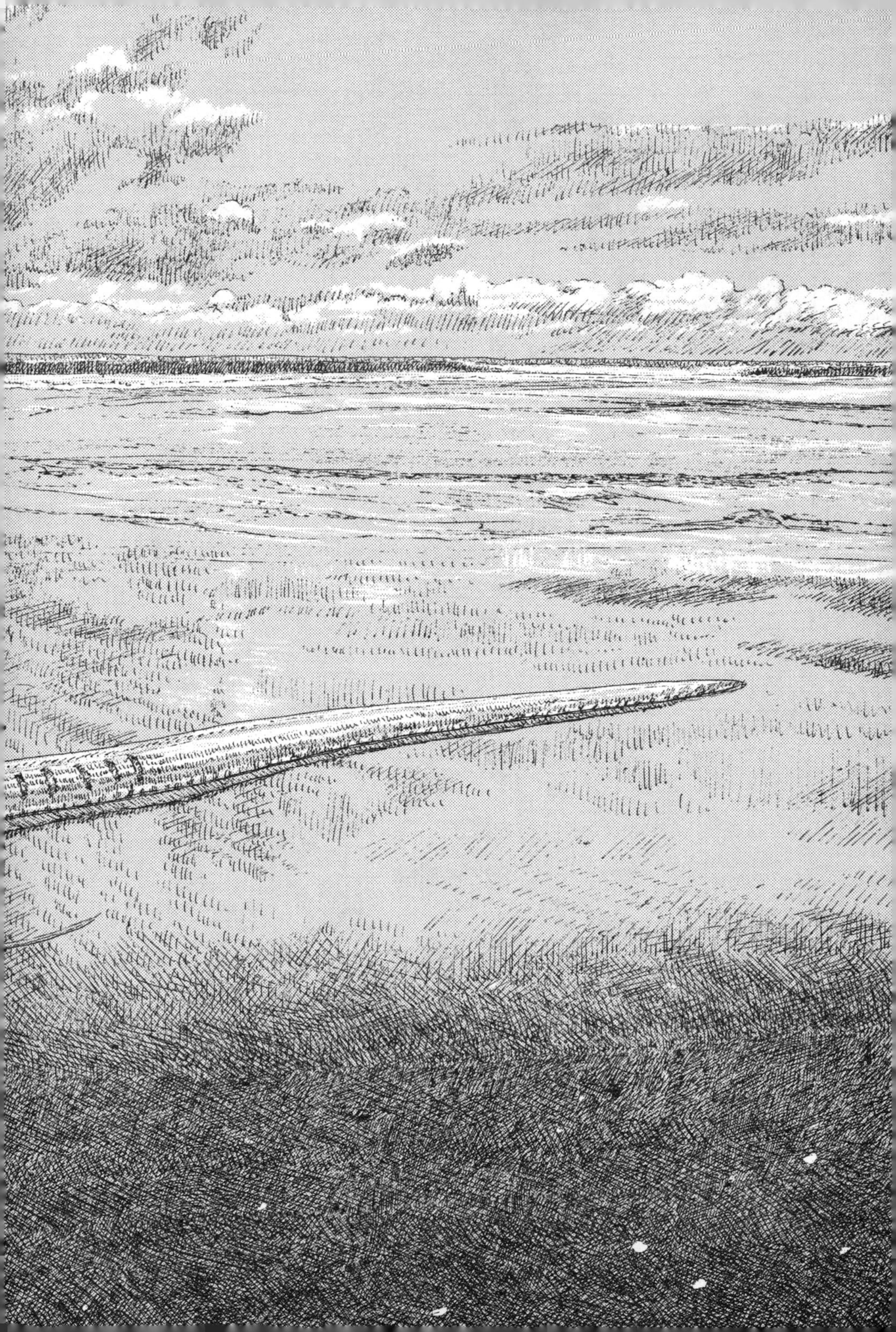

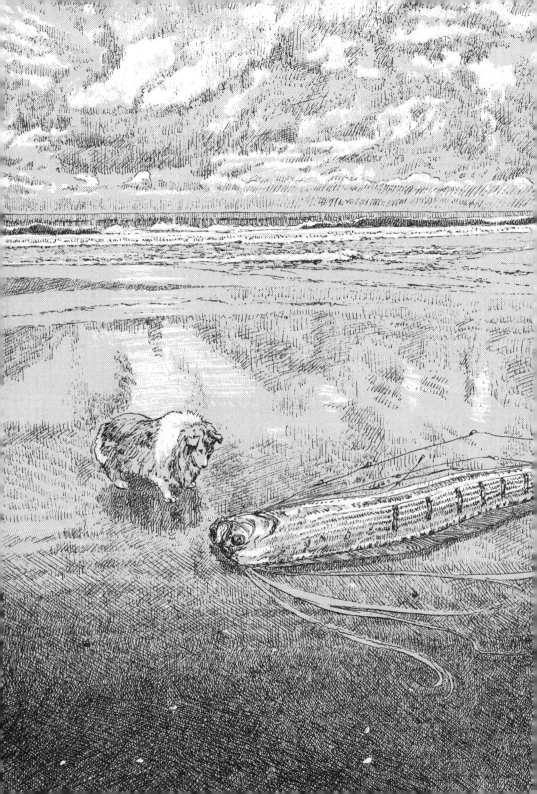

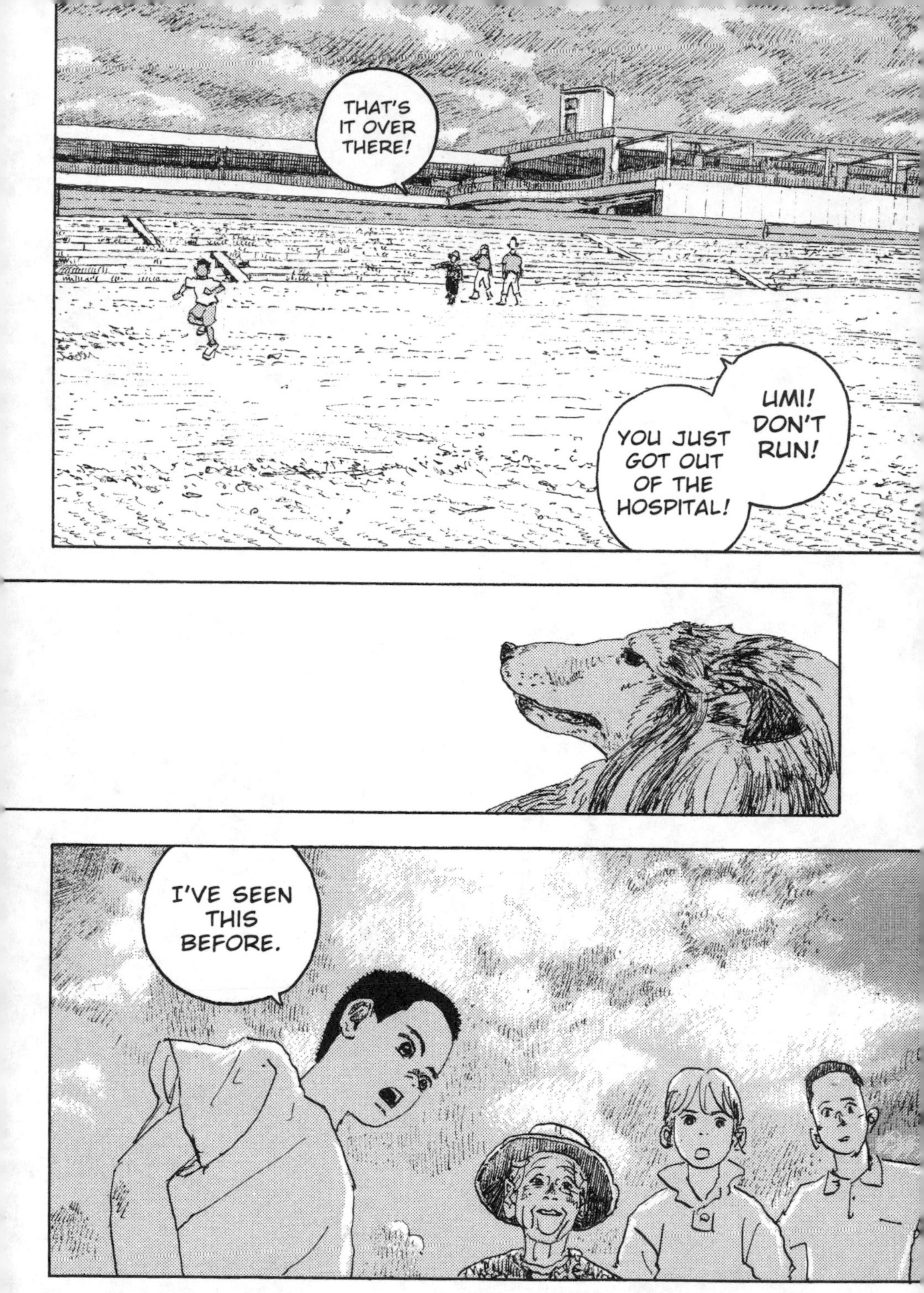
THAT'S IT OVER THERE!
UMI! DON'T RUN!
YOU JUST GOT OUT OF THE HOSPITAL!
I'VE SEEN THIS BEFORE.

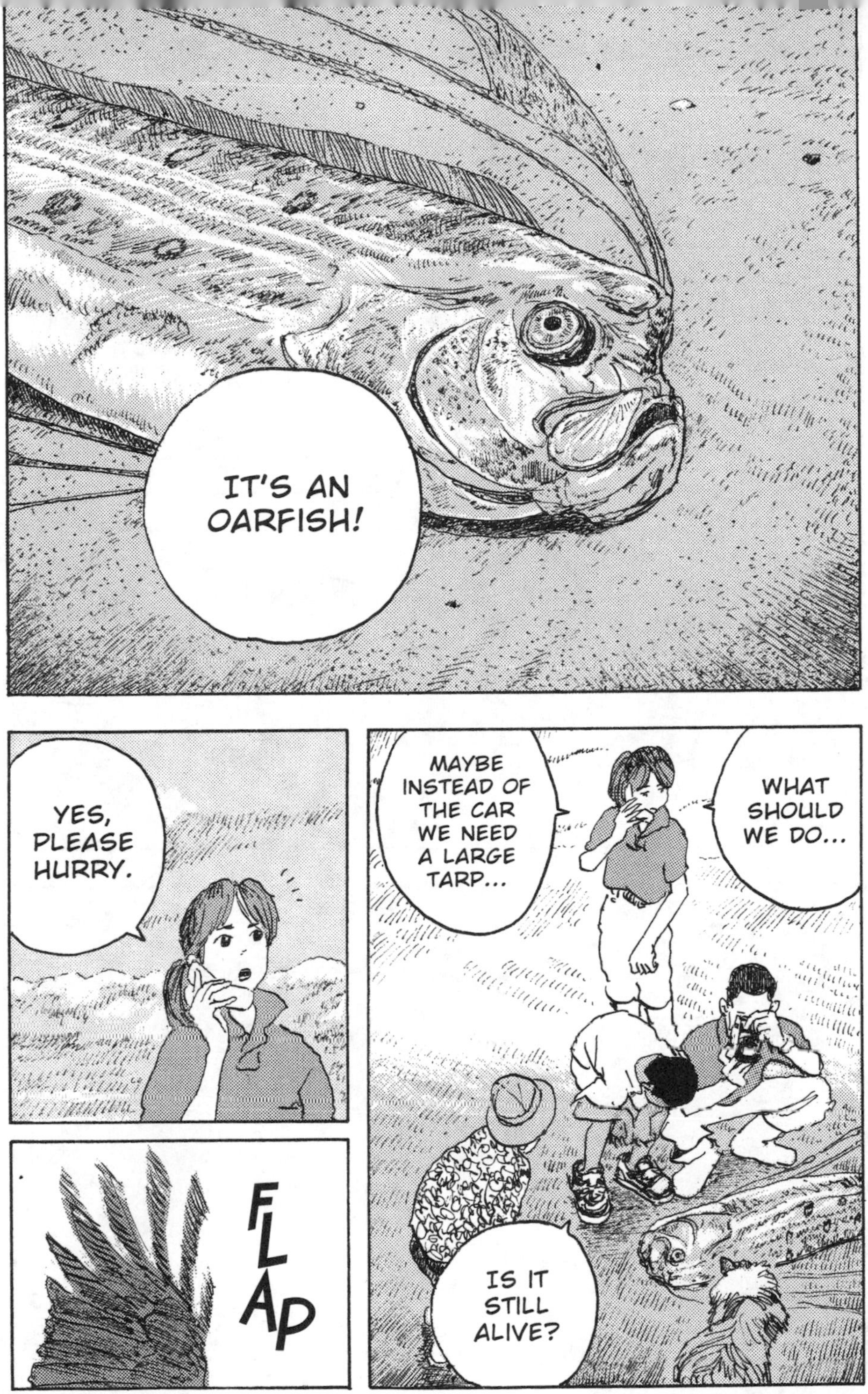
IT'S AN OARFISH!
WHAT SHOULD WE DO...
MAYBE INSTEAD OF THE CAR WE NEED A LARGE TARP...
IS IT STILL ALIVE?
YES, PLEASE HURRY.
FLAP

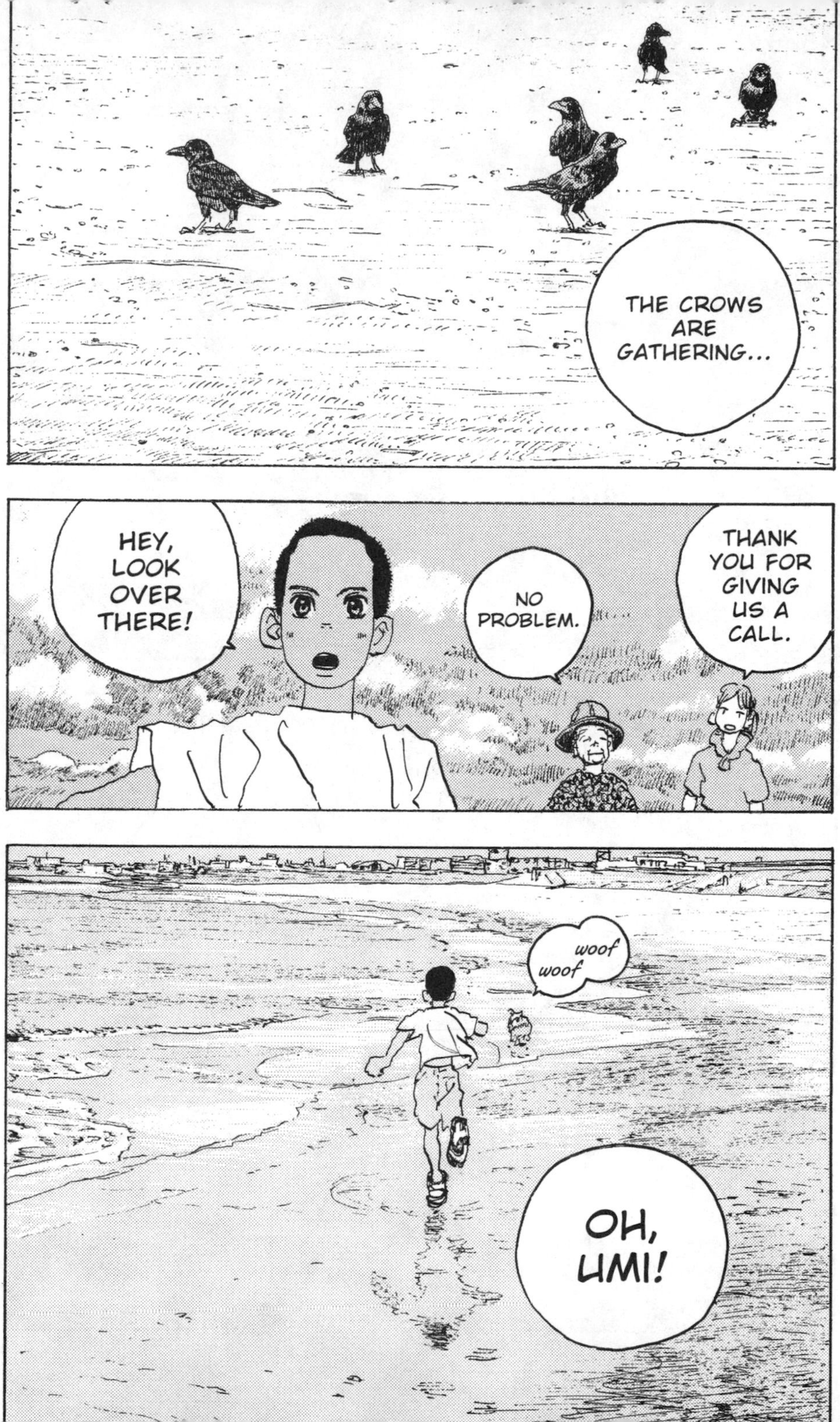
THE CROWS ARE GATHERING...
THANK YOU FOR GIVING US A CALL.
NO PROBLEM.
HEY, LOOK OVER THERE!
woof woof
OH, UMI!

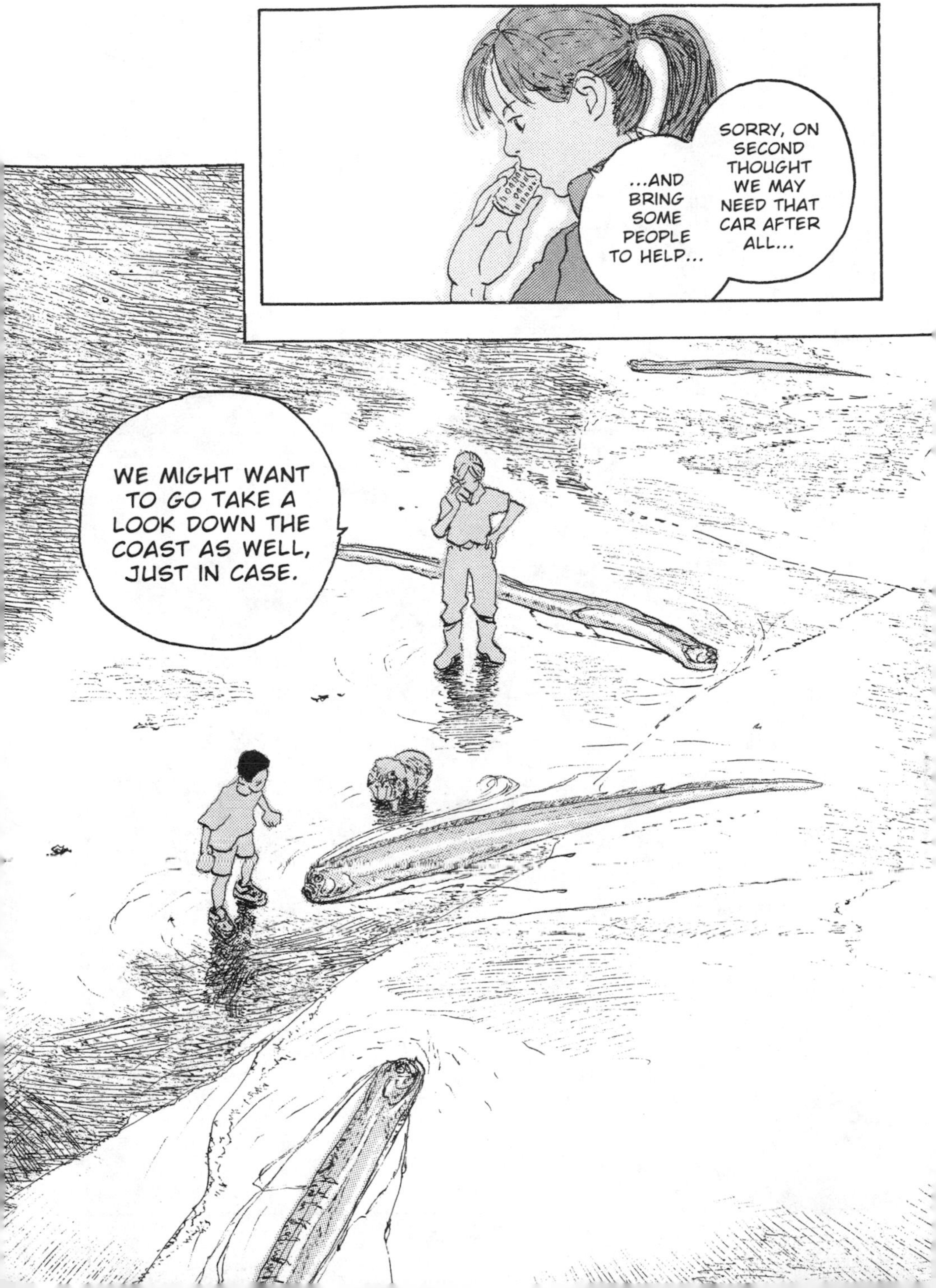
SORRY, ON SECOND THOUGHT WE MAY NEED THAT CAR AFTER ALL...
...AND BRING SOME PEOPLE TO HELP...
WE MIGHT WANT TO GO TAKE A LOOK DOWN THE COAST AS WELL, JUST IN CASE.

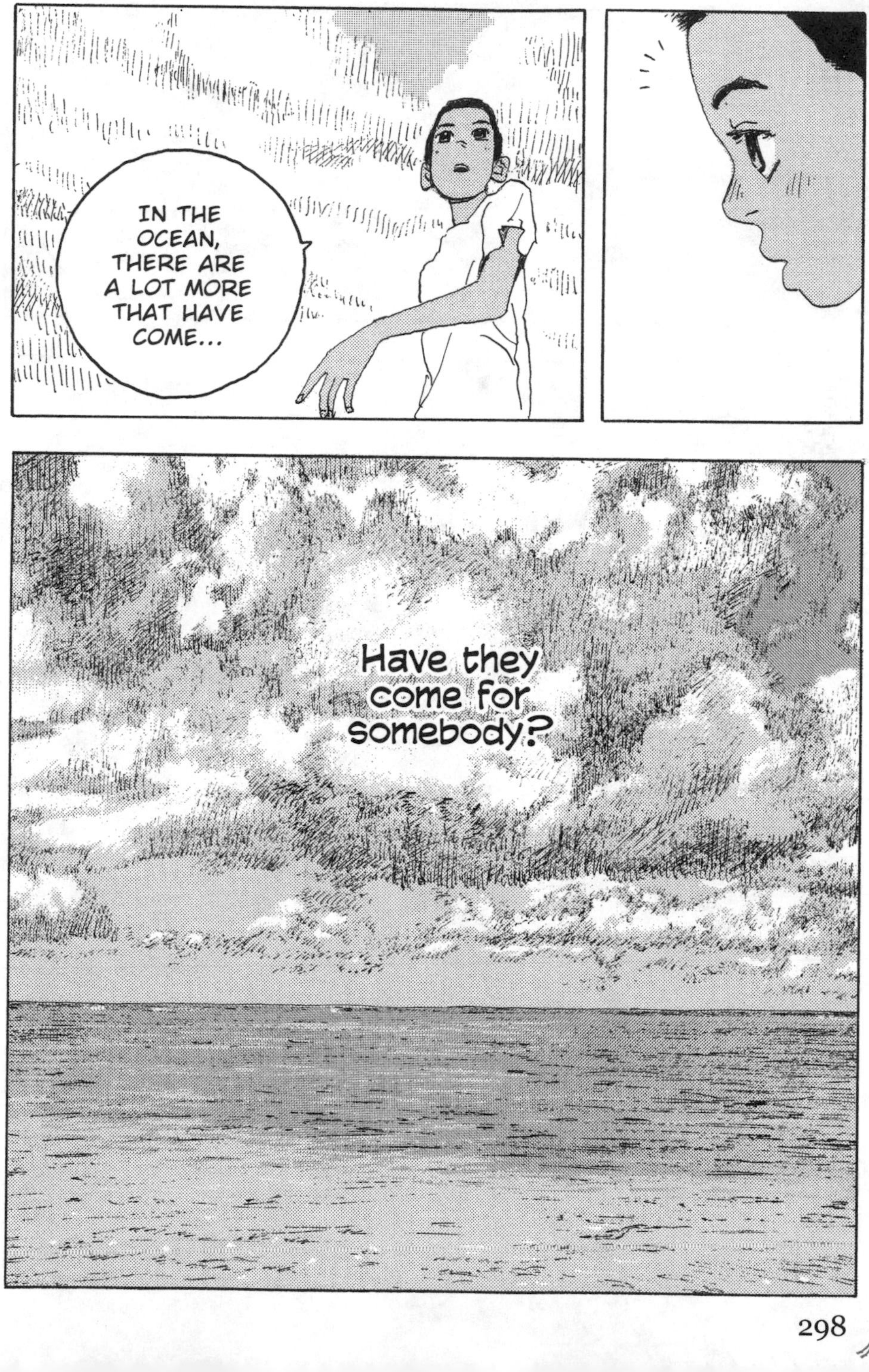
IN THE OCEAN, THERE ARE A LOT MORE THAT HAVE COME...
Have they come for somebody?

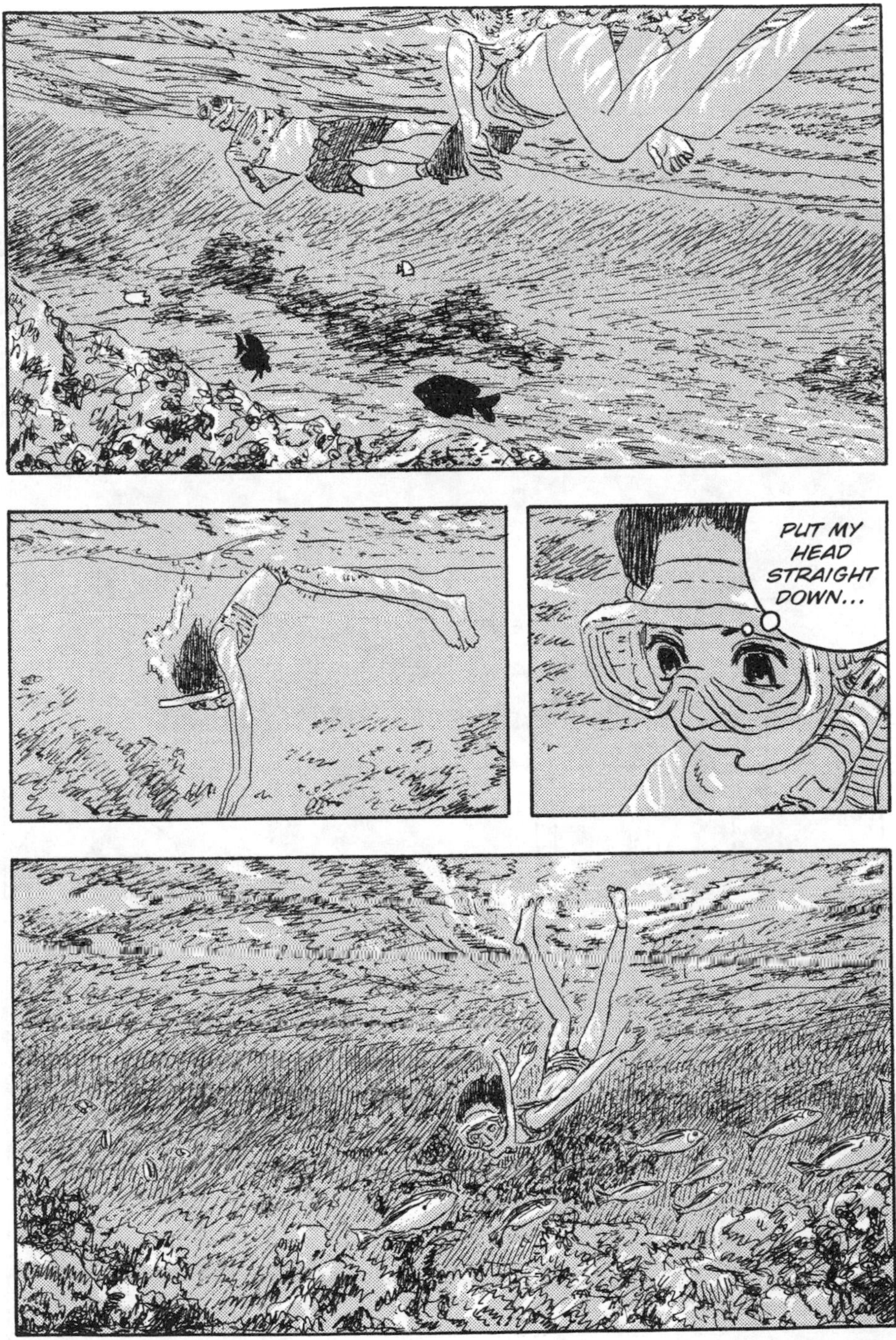
PUT MY HEAD STRAIGHT DOWN...

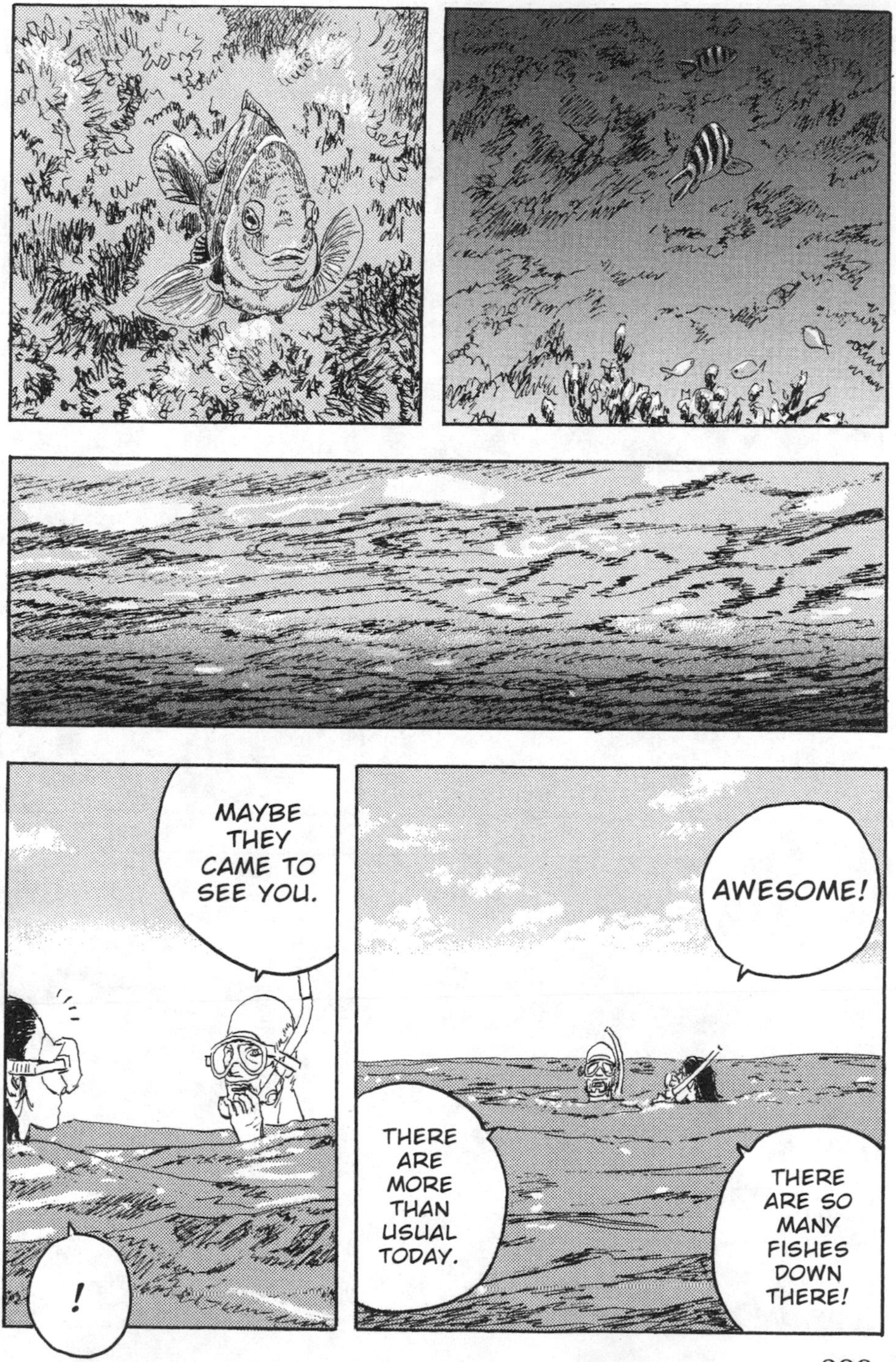
AWESOME!
THERE ARE SO MANY FISHES DOWN THERE!
THERE ARE MORE THAN USUAL TODAY.
MAYBE THEY CAME TO SEE YOU.
!

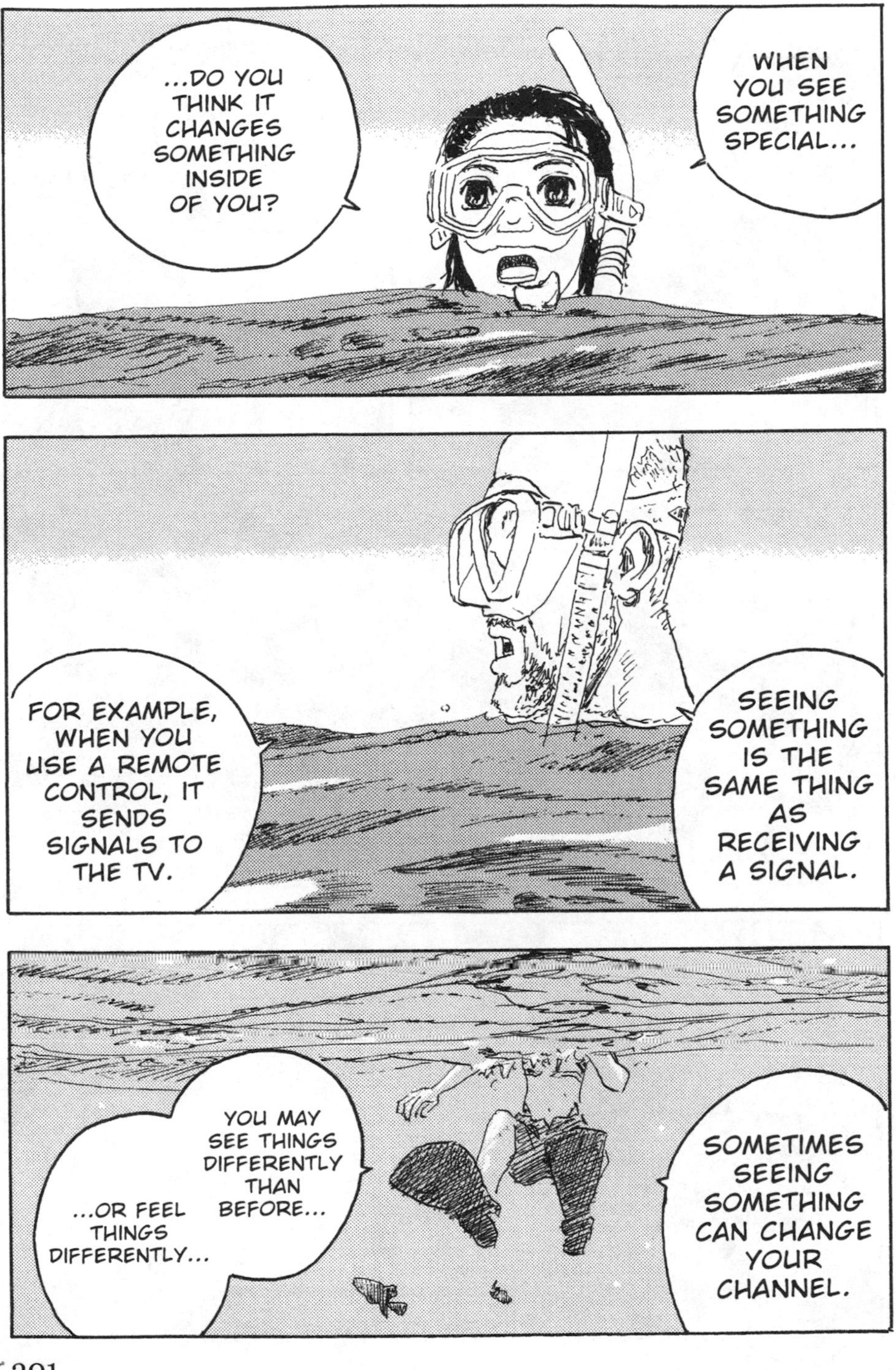
WHEN YOU SEE SOMETHING SPECIAL...
...DO YOU THINK IT CHANGES SOMETHING INSIDE OF YOU?
SEEING SOMETHING IS THE SAME THING AS RECEIVING A SIGNAL.
FOR EXAMPLE, WHEN YOU USE A REMOTE CONTROL, IT SENDS SIGNALS TO THE TV.
SOMETIMES SEEING SOMETHING CAN CHANGE YOUR CHANNEL.
YOU MAY SEE THINGS DIFFERENTLY THAN BEFORE...
...OR FEEL THINGS DIFFERENTLY...

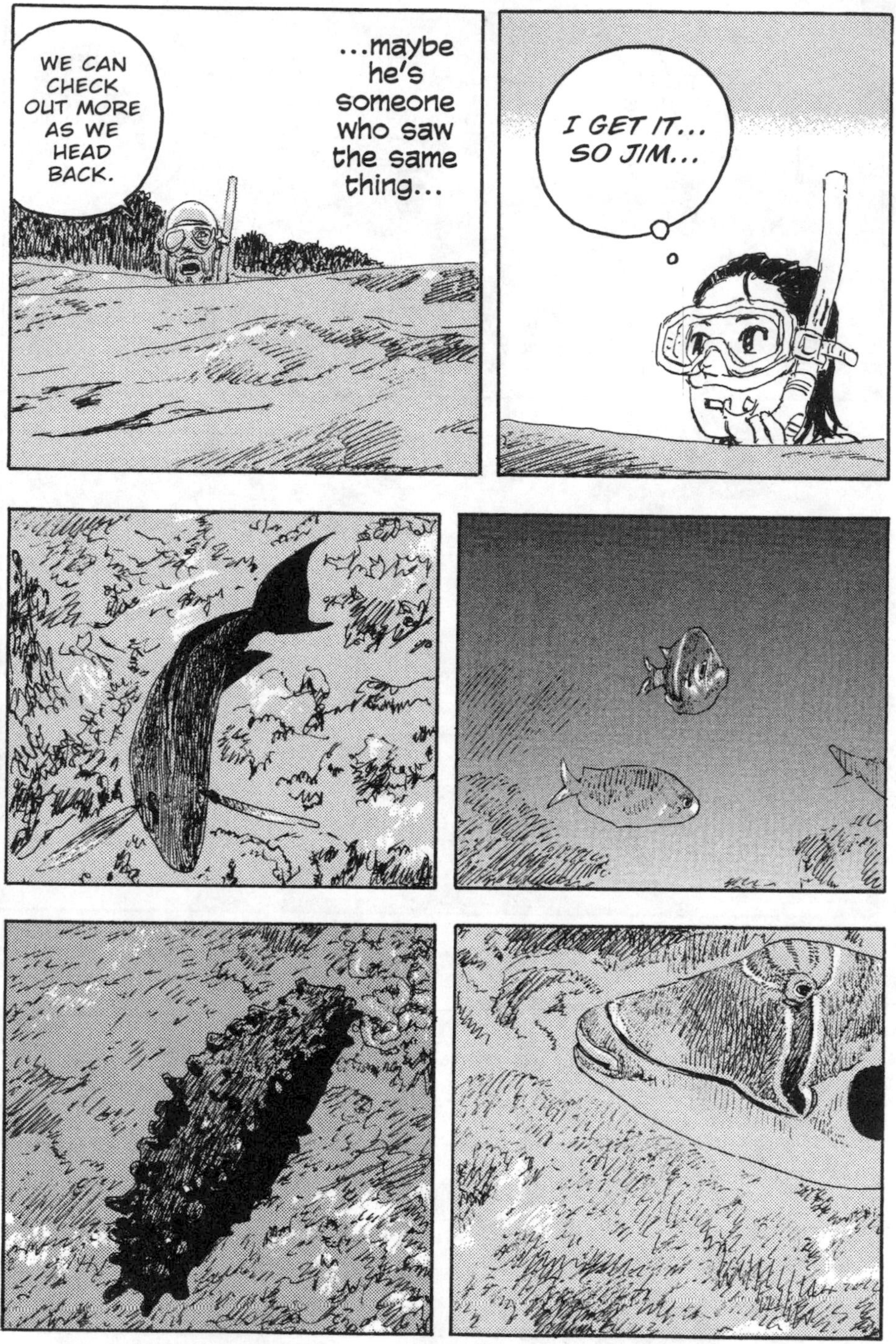
I GET IT... SO JIM...
...maybe he's someone who saw the same thing...
WE CAN CHECK OUT MORE AS WE HEAD BACK.

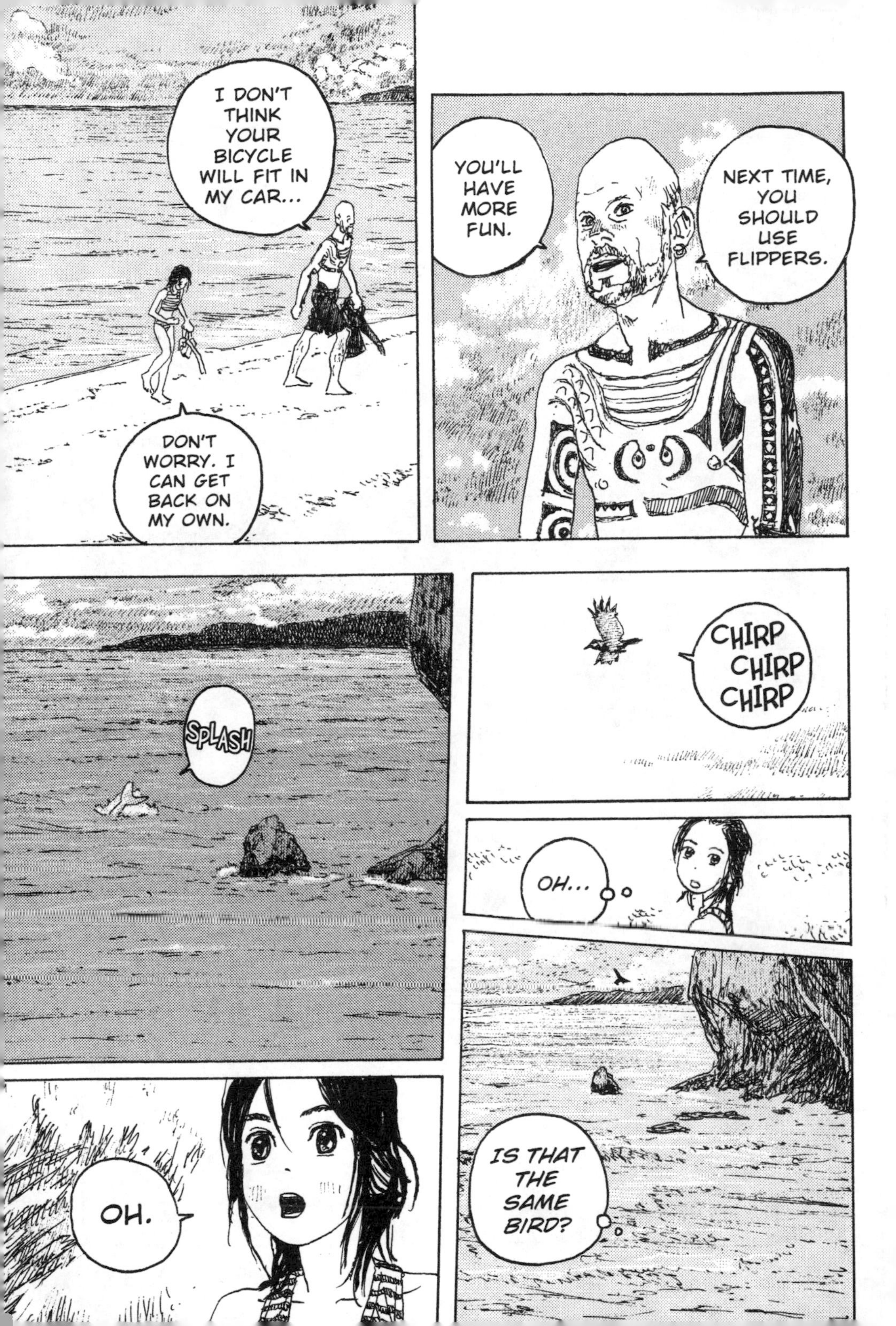
NEXT TIME, YOU SHOULD USE FLIPPERS.
YOU'LL HAVE MORE FUN.
I DON'T THINK YOUR BICYCLE WILL FIT IN MY CAR...
DON'T WORRY. I CAN GET BACK ON MY OWN.
CHIRP CHIRP CHIRP
OH...
IS THAT THE SAME BIRD?
SPLASH
OH.

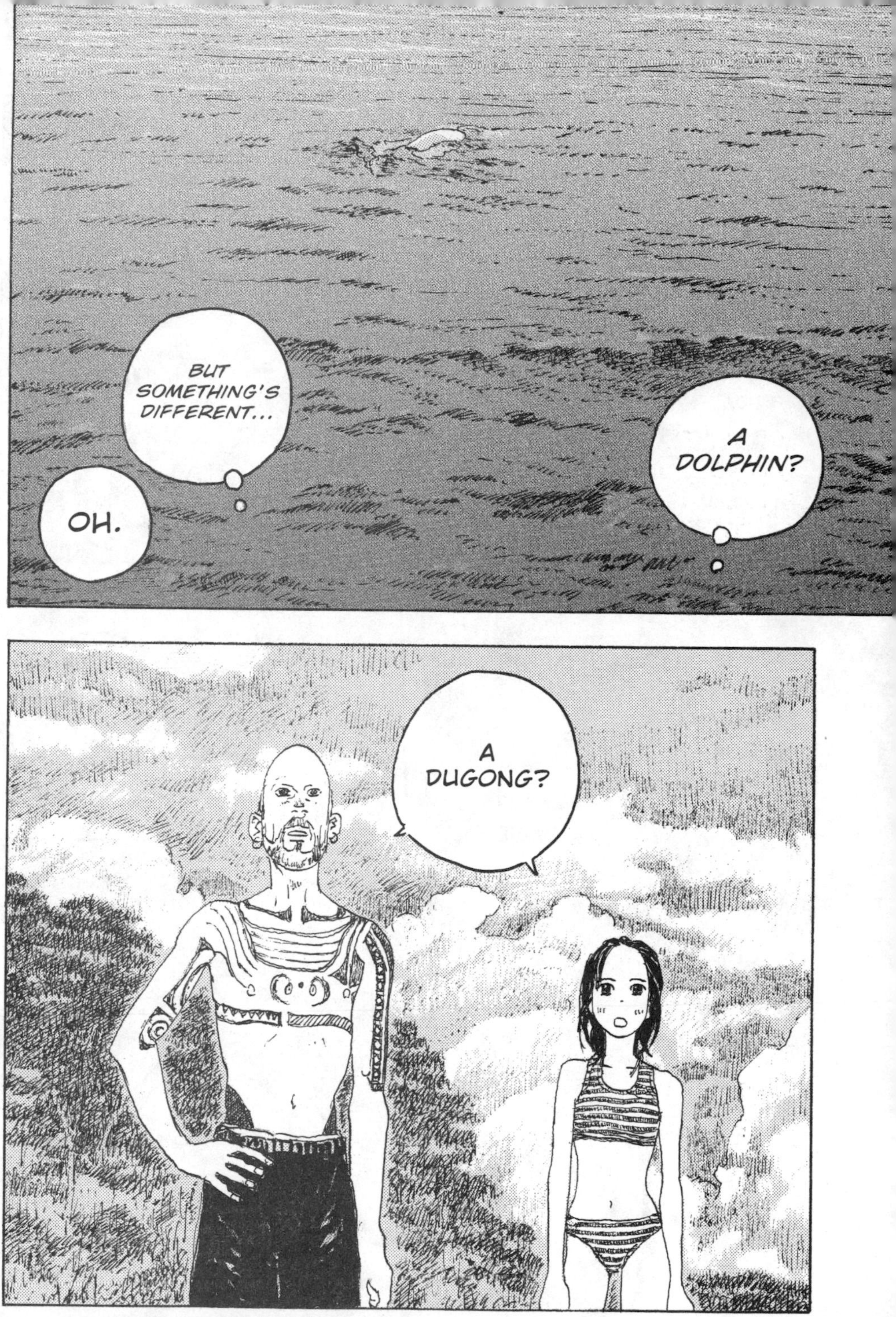
A DOLPHIN?
BUT SOMETHING'S DIFFERENT...
OH.
A DUGONG?

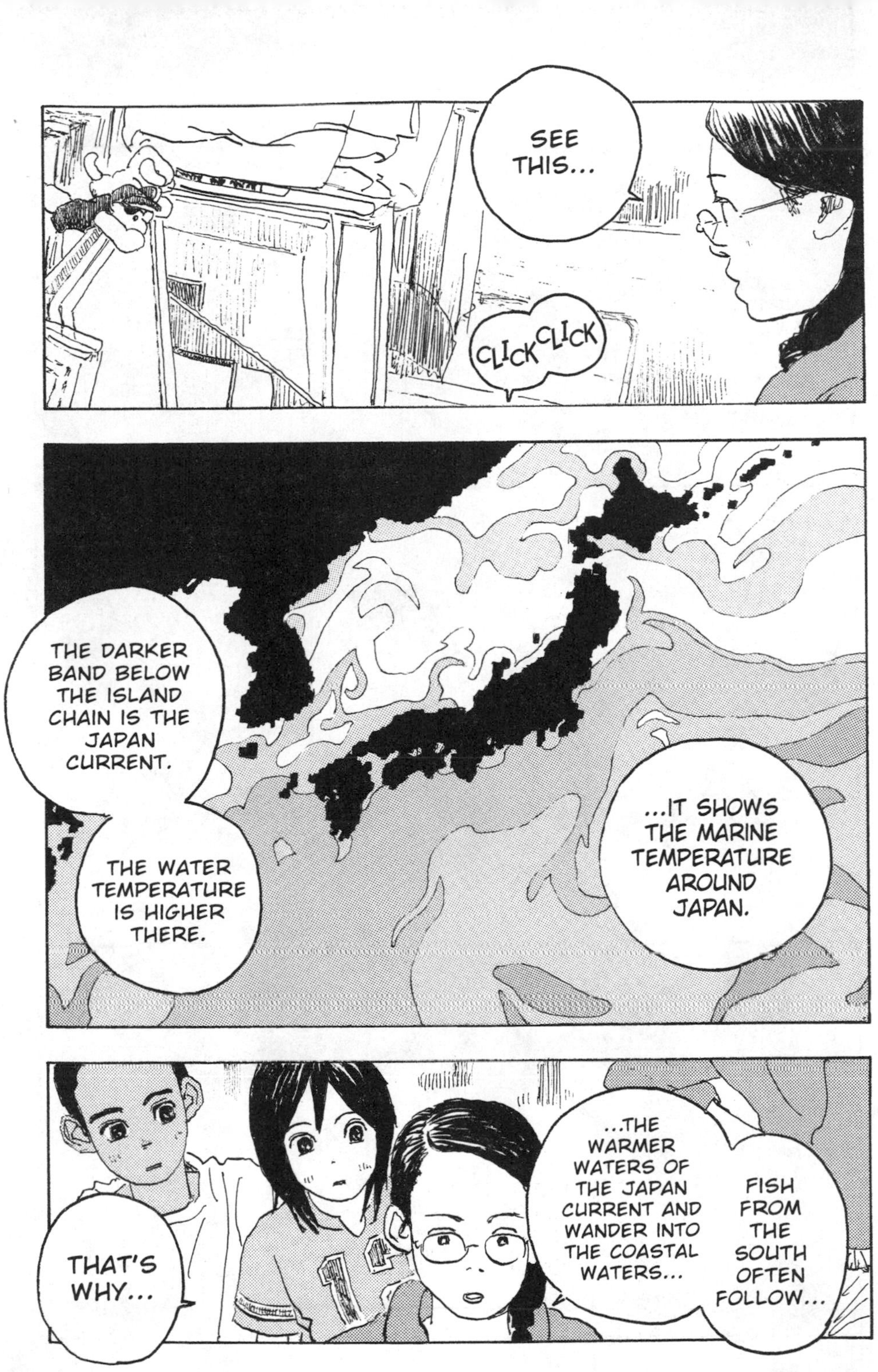
SEE THIS...
CLICK CLICK
...IT SHOWS THE MARINE TEMPERATURE AROUND JAPAN.
THE DARKER BAND BELOW THE ISLAND CHAIN IS THE JAPAN CURRENT.
THE WATER TEMPERATURE IS HIGHER THERE.
FISH FROM THE SOUTH OFTEN FOLLOW...
...THE WARMER WATERS OF THE JAPAN CURRENT AND WANDER INTO THE COASTAL WATERS...
THAT'S WHY...

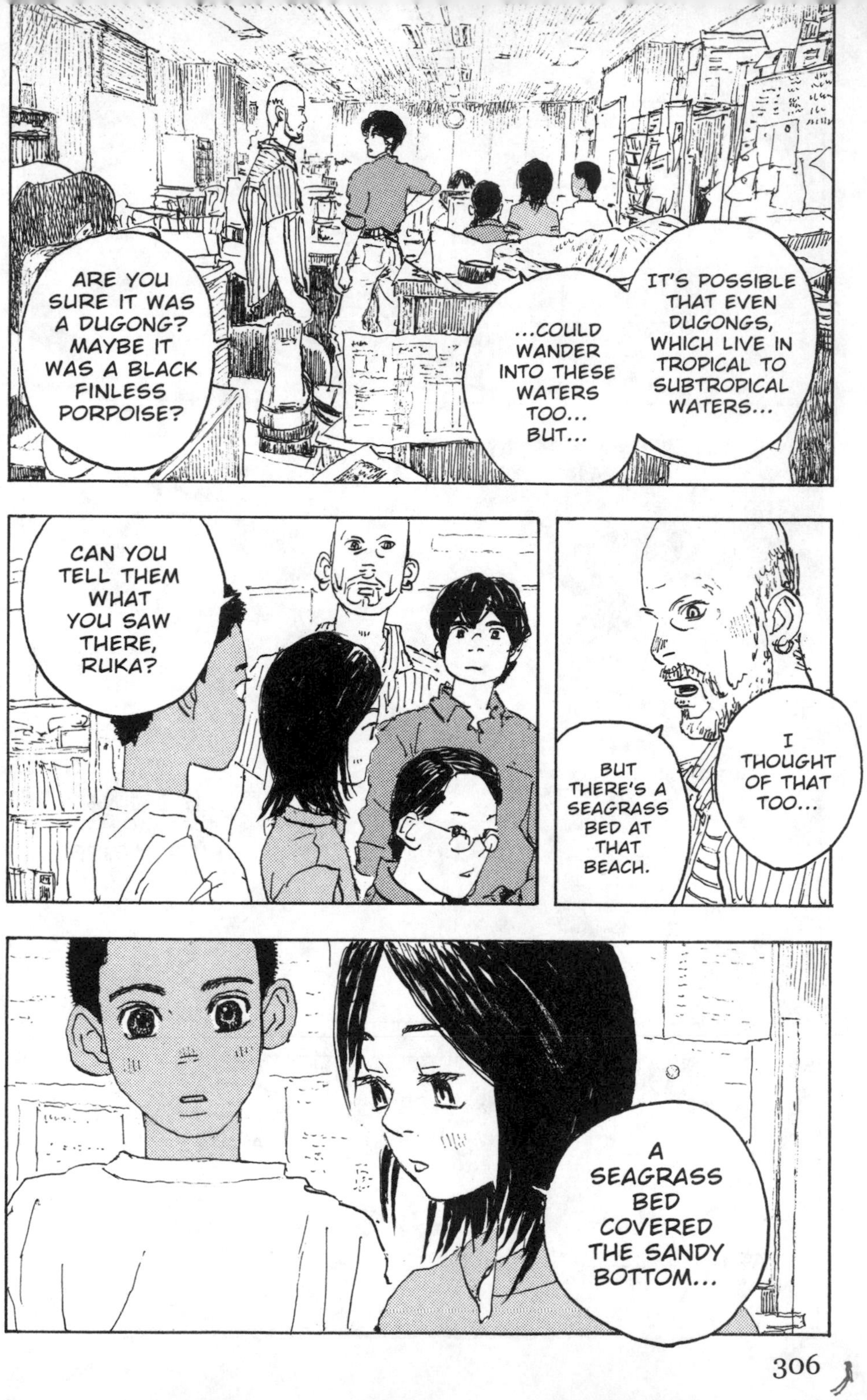
IT'S POSSIBLE THAT EVEN DUGONGS, WHICH LIVE IN TROPICAL TO SUBTROPICAL WATERS...
...COULD WANDER INTO THESE WATERS TOO... BUT...
ARE YOU SURE IT WAS A DUGONG? MAYBE IT WAS A BLACK FINLESS PORPOISE?
I THOUGHT OF THAT TOO...
BUT THERE'S A SEAGRASS BED AT THAT BEACH.
CAN YOU TELL THEM WHAT YOU SAW THERE, RUKA?
A SEAGRASS BED COVERED THE SANDY BOTTOM...

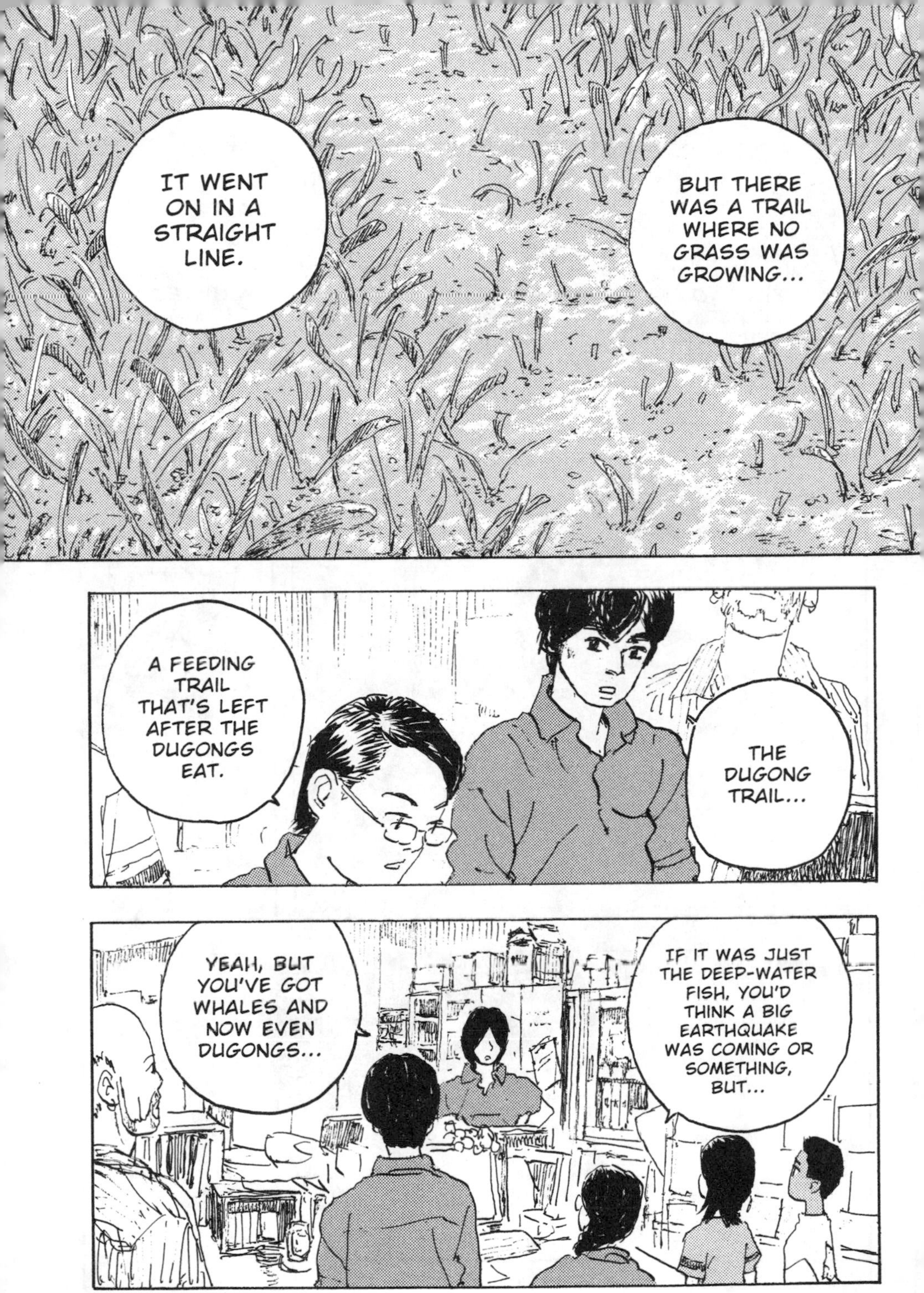
BUT THERE WAS A TRAIL WHERE NO GRASS WAS GROWING...
IT WENT ON IN A STRAIGHT LINE.
THE DUGONG TRAIL...
A FEEDING TRAIL THAT'S LEFT AFTER THE DUGONGS EAT.
IF IT WAS JUST THE DEEP-WATER FISH, YOU'D THINK A BIG EARTHQUAKE WAS COMING OR SOMETHING, BUT...
YEAH, BUT YOU'VE GOT WHALES AND NOW EVEN DUGONGS...

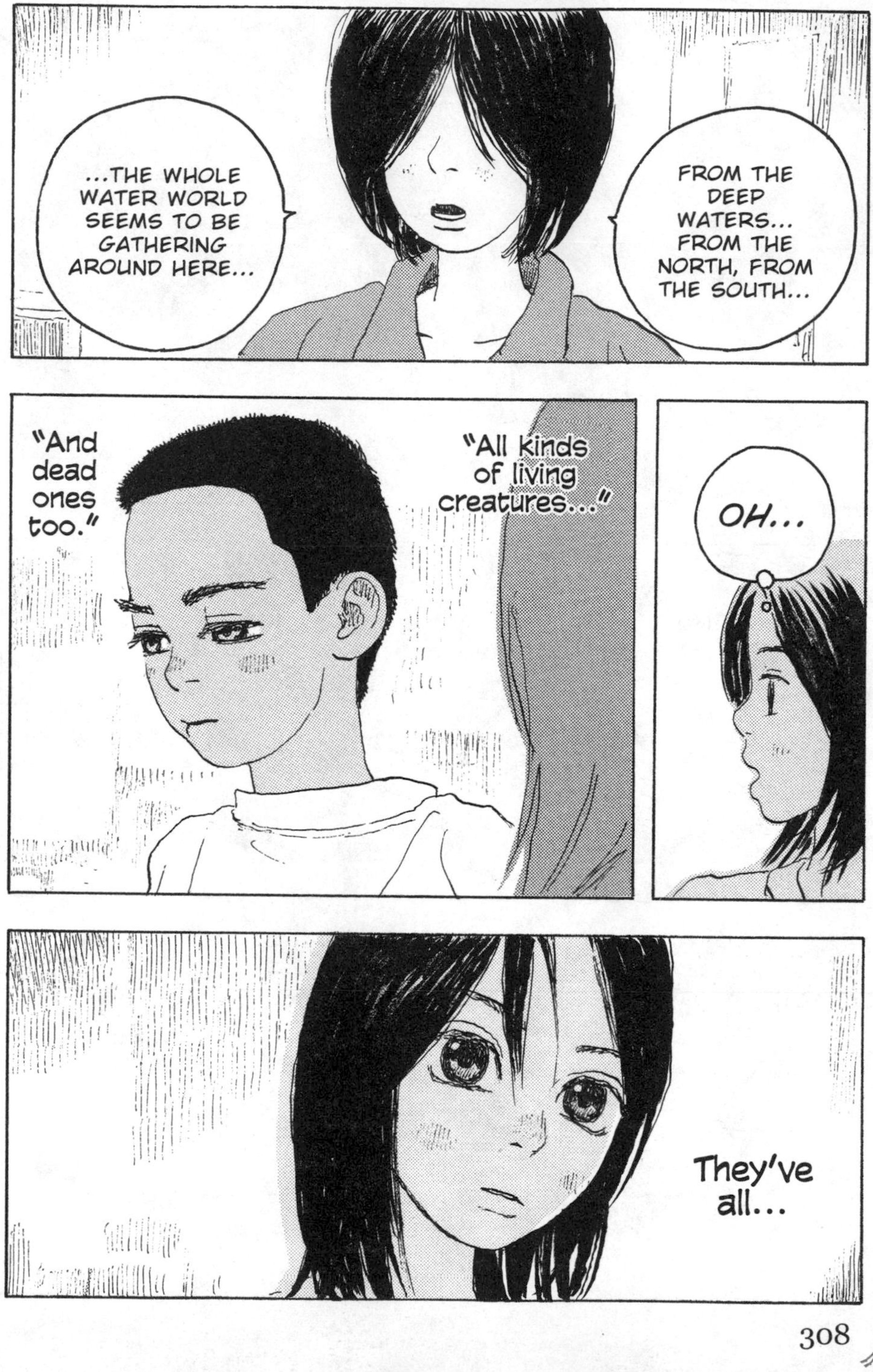
FROM THE DEEP WATERS... FROM THE NORTH, FROM THE SOUTH...
...THE WHOLE WATER WORLD SEEMS TO BE GATHERING AROUND HERE...
OH...
"All kinds of living creatures..."
"And dead ones too."
They've all...

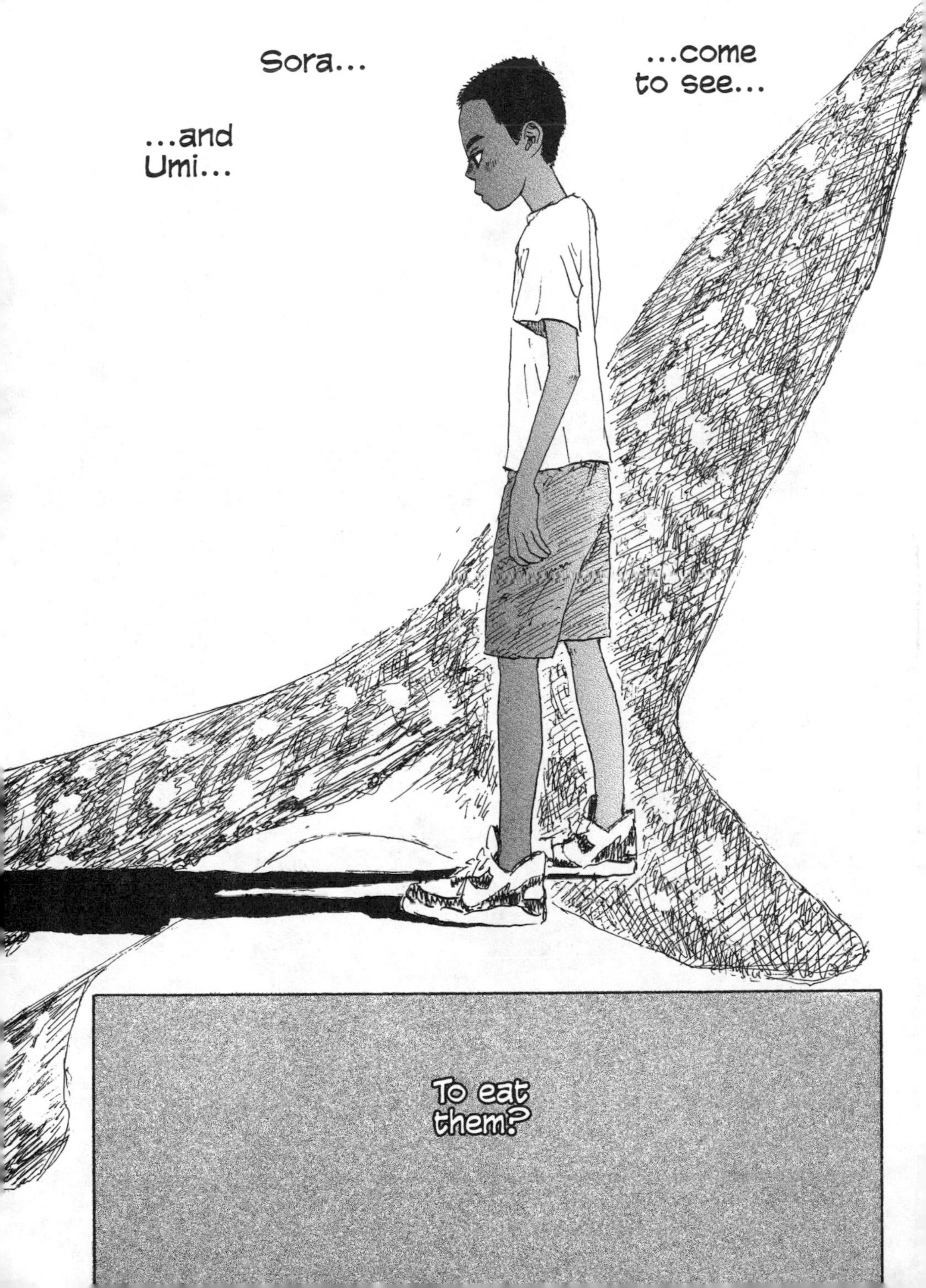
...come to see...
Sora...
...and Umi...
To eat them?

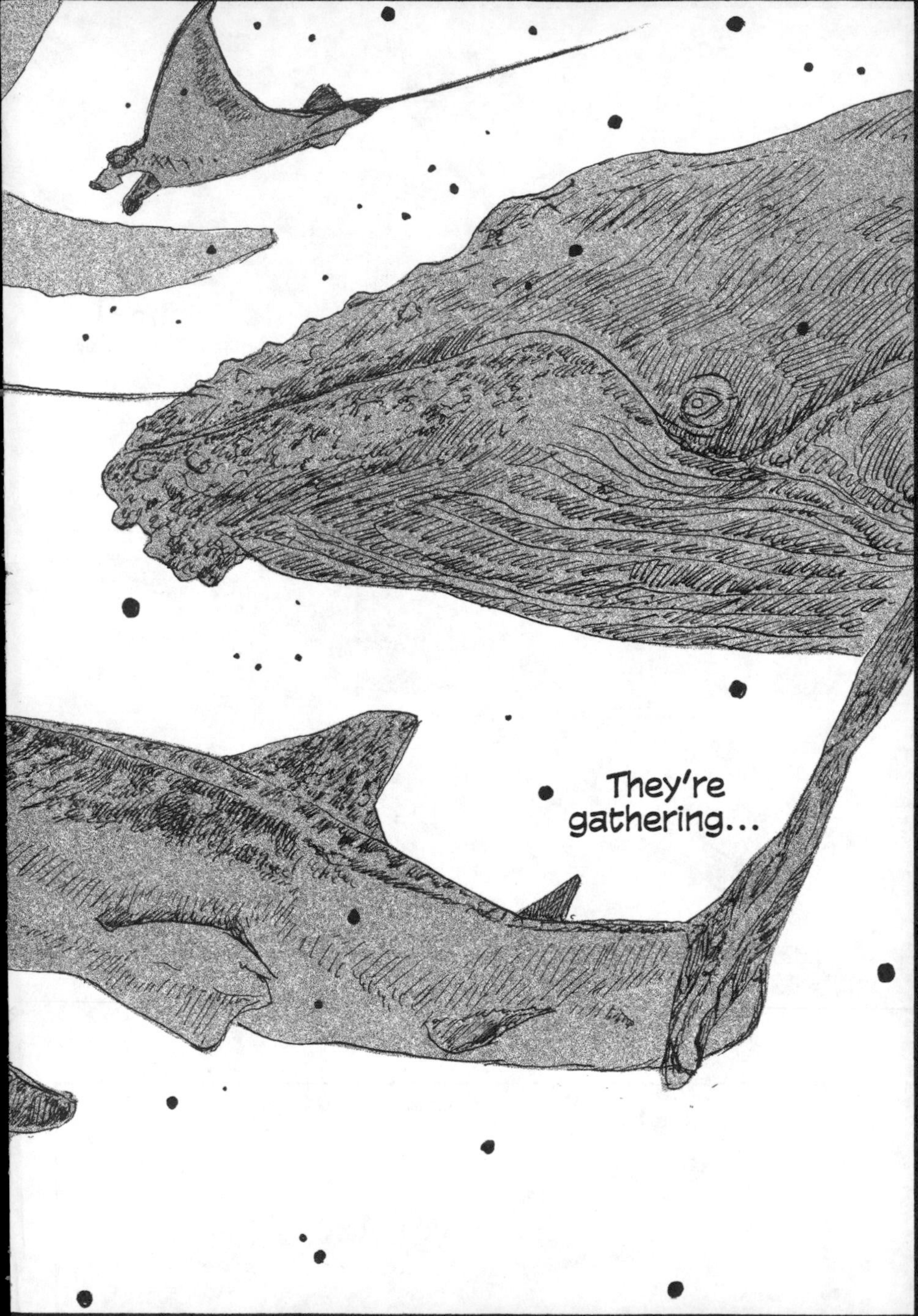
They're gathering...

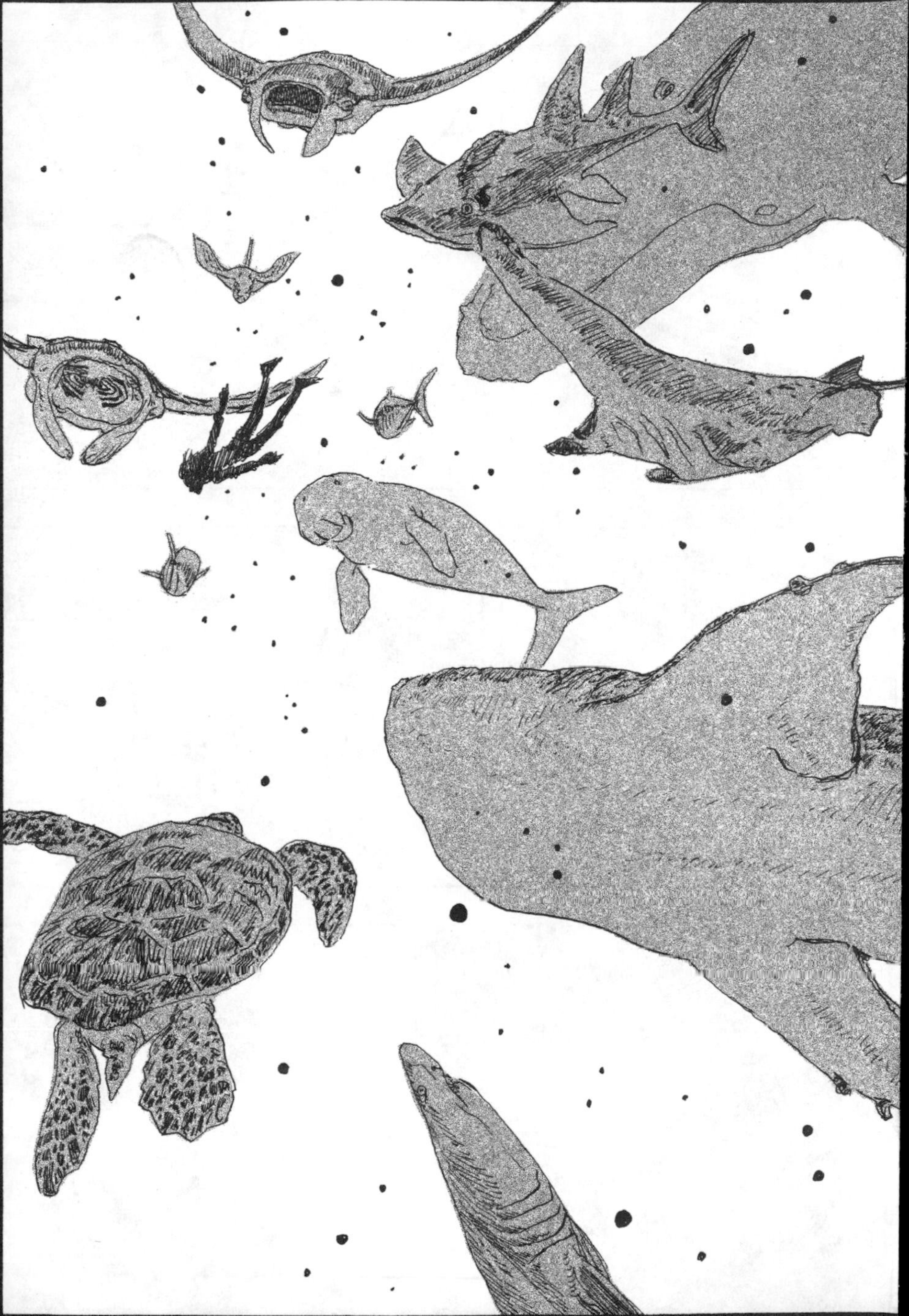

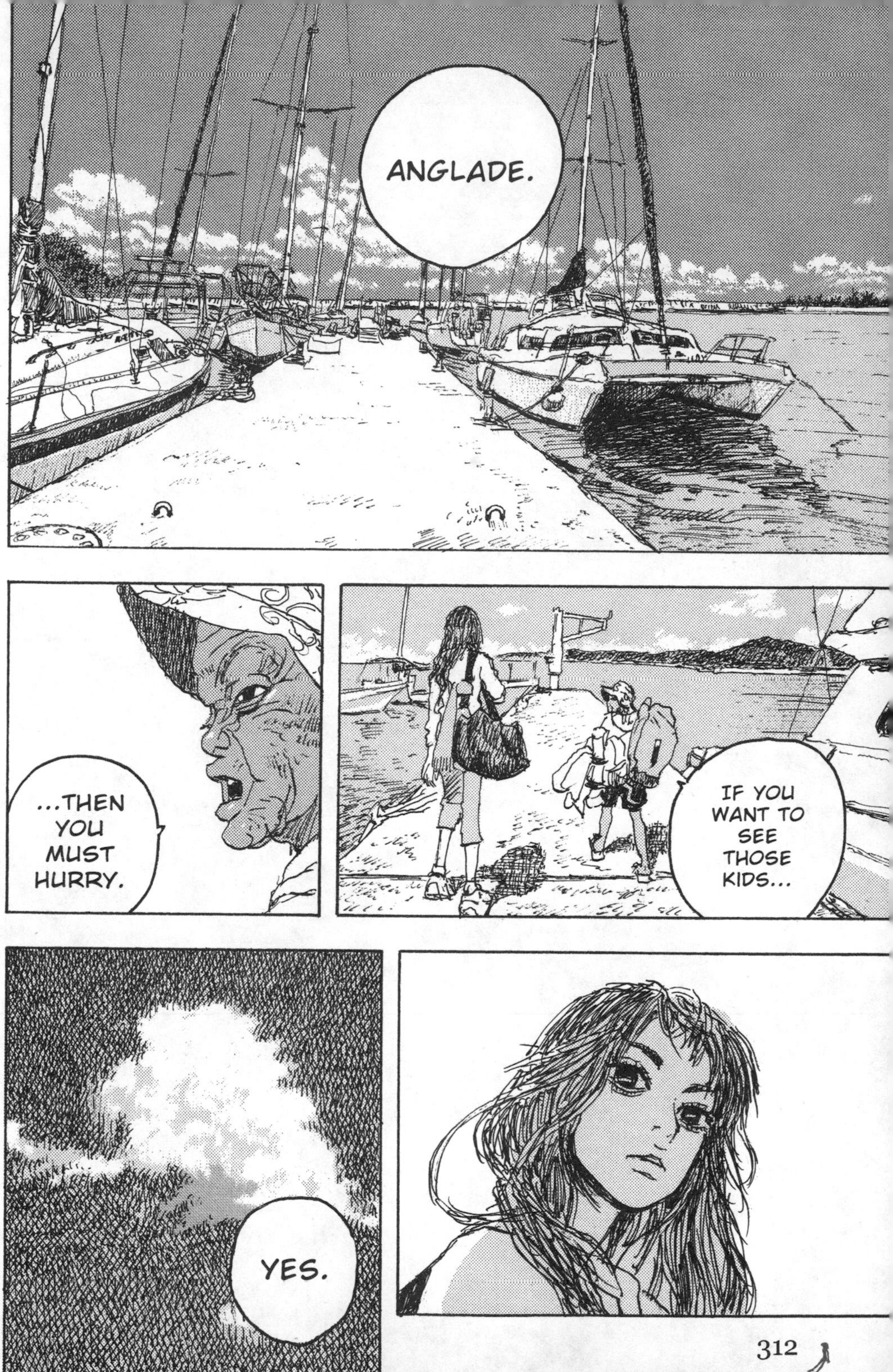
ANGLADE.
IF YOU WANT TO SEE THOSE KIDS...
...THEN YOU MUST HURRY.
YES.

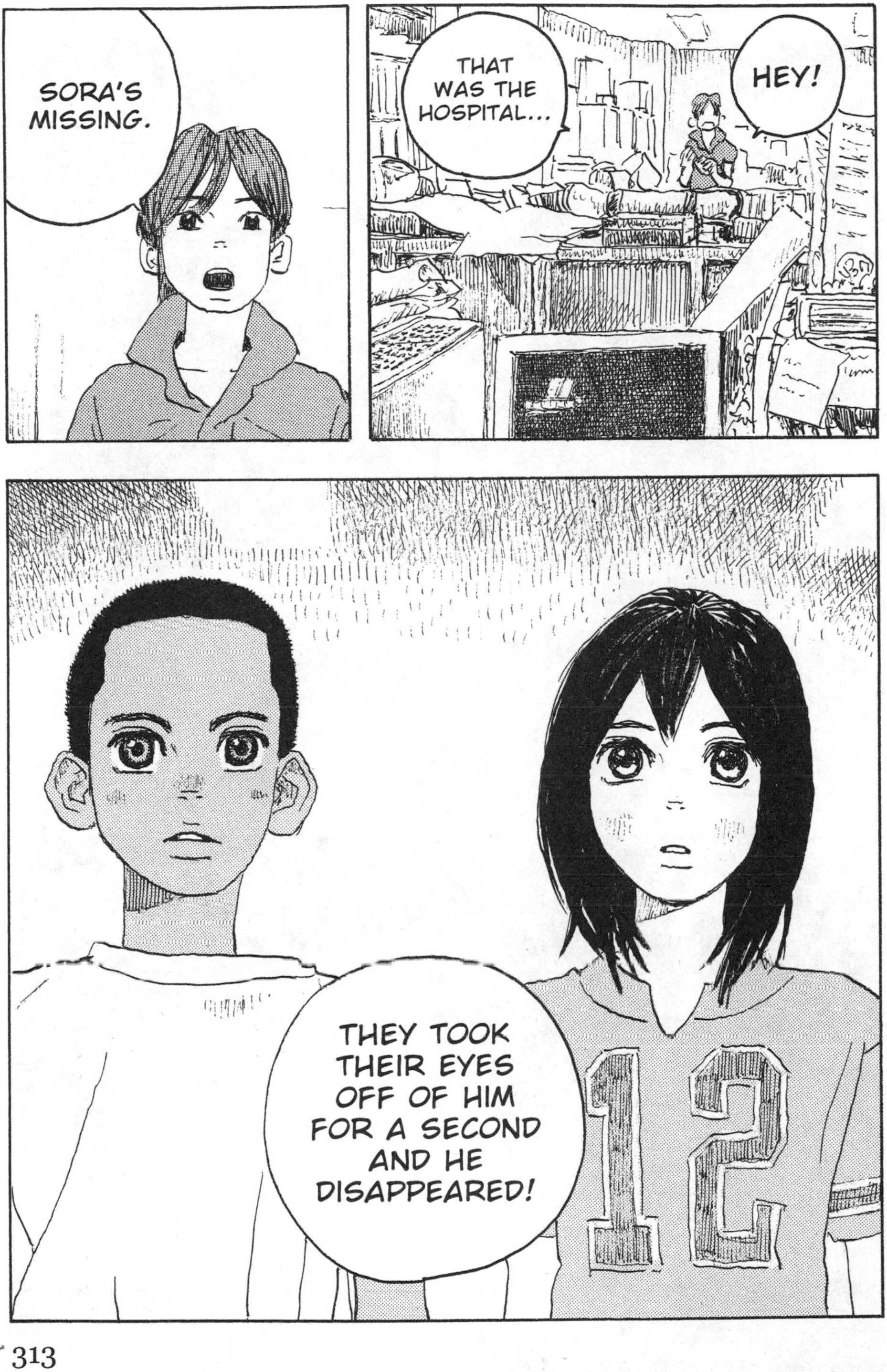
HEY!
THAT WAS THE HOSPITAL...
SORA'S MISSING.
THEY TOOK THEIR EYES OFF OF HIM FOR A SECOND AND HE DISAPPEARED!

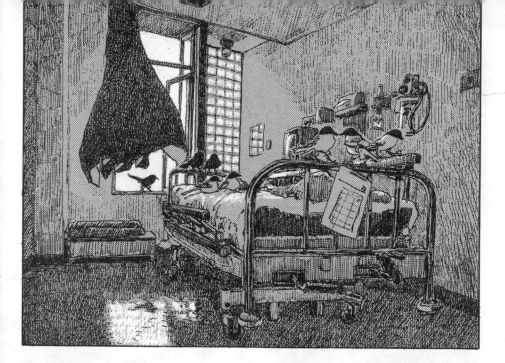

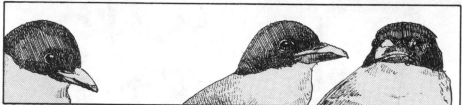

In
retrospect...

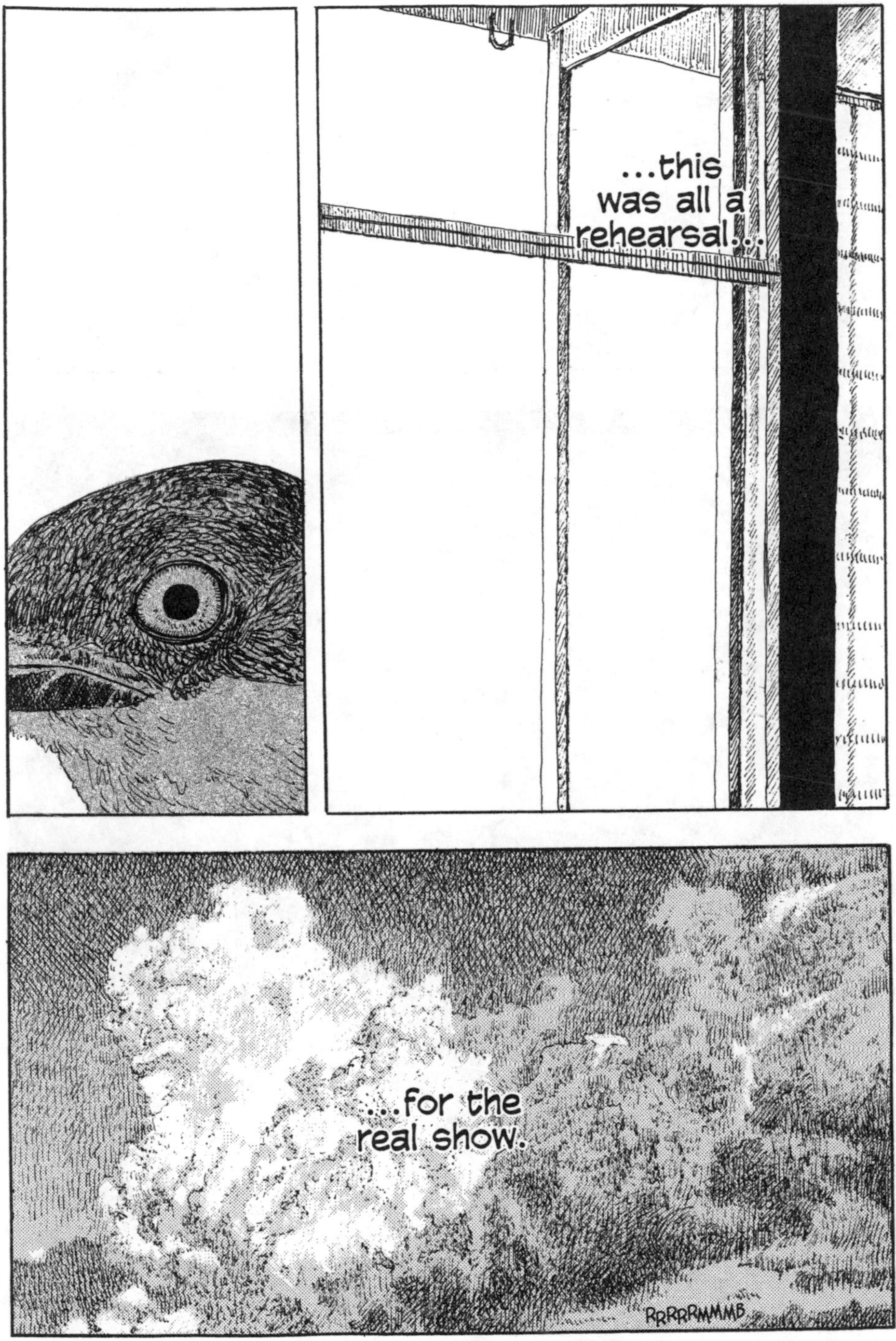
...this was all a rehearsal...
...for the real show.
RRRRRMMMB

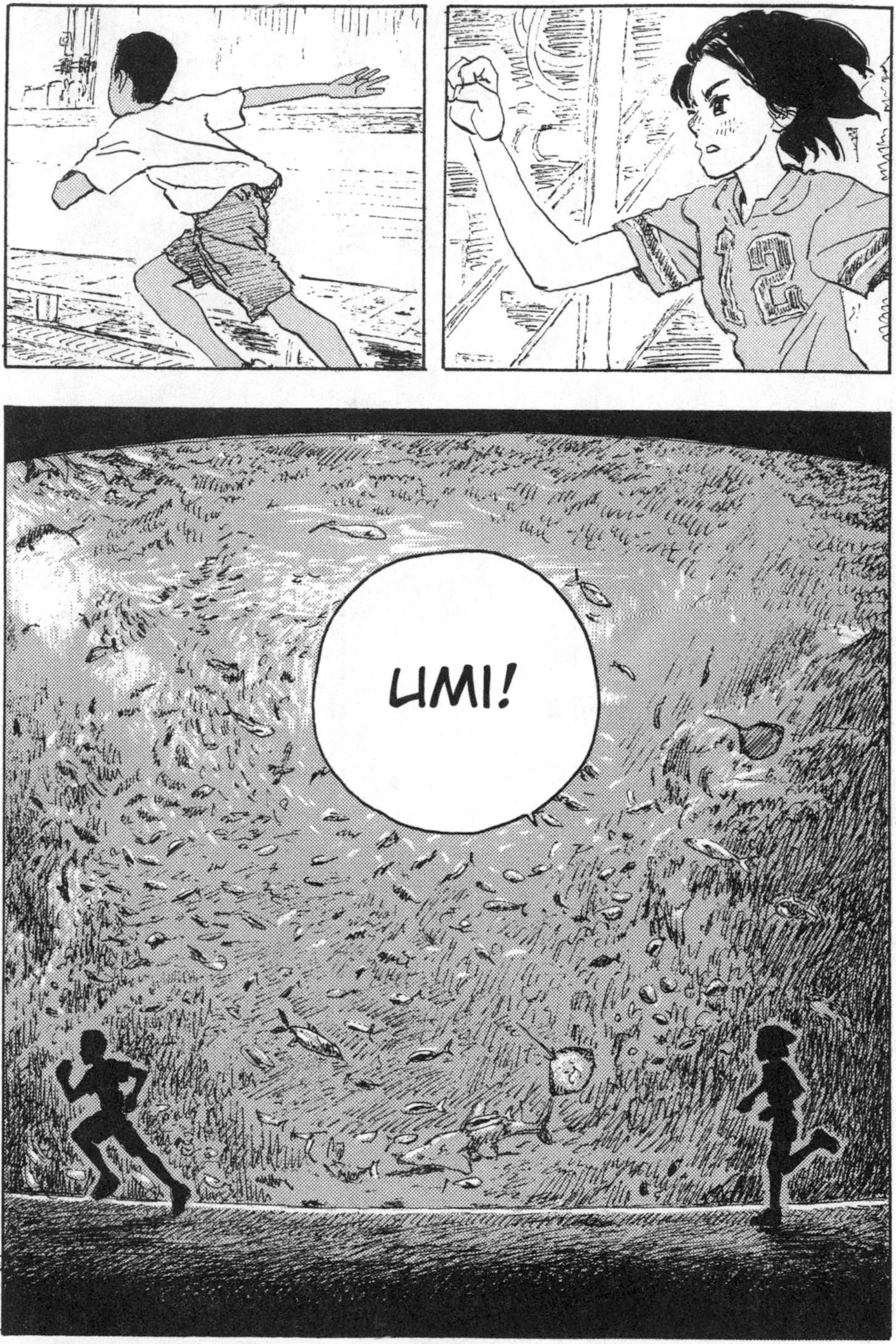
UMI!

Children ~ of the ~ Sea

VOLUME 1
END NOTES

Page 49, panel 2: Shiodome
An area near Tokyo Bay known for its skyscrapers.

Page 70, panel 1: Umi
The kanji is 海 and means "sea" in Japanese.

Page 71, chapter 2: Thunder
The kanji generally used for the word "thunder" is 雷 (kaminari). However, in the chapter title the kanji 神鳴り (kaminari) is used, which means "the sound made by the Gods."

Page 75, panel 1: Recycling
Historically, much more of Japan's trash has been burned than dumped in landfills, due to the country's relative lack of space. In recent years, Japan has begun a serious recycling effort, and municipalities have introduced multiple categories of trash (such as burnable, non-burnable, paper, plastic, etc.) that must be sorted before pickup.

Page 77, panel 5: Thrill-seekers
In Japan they are called *yukaihan* (愉快犯) and commit crimes not for personal gain but to mess with society and get a laugh. The crimes they commit are known by the same name.

Page 83, panel 5: Sora
The kanji is 空 and means "sky" in Japanese.

Page 107, panel 1: Hitodama
This literally means "human soul" and refers to the phenomenon commonly known in English as the will-o'-the-wisp. In Japanese folklore, hitodama (人魂) are said to be disembodied spirits that take the form of fireballs.

Page 123, panel 3: Talisman
The talisman reads *Somin Shôrai shison*. Somin Shôrai is the name of a man in Japanese legend and *shison* means "descendants." Today, the talisman with the kanji of his name (Somin Shôrai shison) is often hung in gateways by a sacred straw rope to ward off evil spirits and misfortune.

Page 125, panel 1: This one says...
The Japanese is *senkyaku banrai* (千客萬来), which means "one after another, many customers come."

Children of the Sea 1

STORY AND ART BY Daisuke Igarashi

TRANSLATION = JN Productions
TOUCH-UP ART & LETTERING = Jose Macasocol
DESIGN = Fawn Lau
EDITOR = Pancha Diaz

EDITOR IN CHIEF, BOOKS = Alvin Lu
EDITOR IN CHIEF, MAGAZINES = Marc Weidenbaum
VP, PUBLISHING LICENSING = Rika Inouye
VP, SALES & PRODUCT MARKETING = Gonzalo Ferreyra
VP, CREATIVE = Linda Espinosa
PUBLISHER = Hyoe Narita

Cooperation and assistance from Enoshima Aquarium

KAIJU NO KODOMO 1 by Daisuke IGARASHI © 2007 Daisuke IGARASHI
All rights reserved. Original Japanese edition published in 2007 by
Shogakukan Inc., Tokyo.
The stories, characters and incidents mentioned in this publication are
entirely fictional.

Printed in the U.S.A.

Published by VIZ Media, LLC
P.O. Box 77010
San Francisco, CA 94107

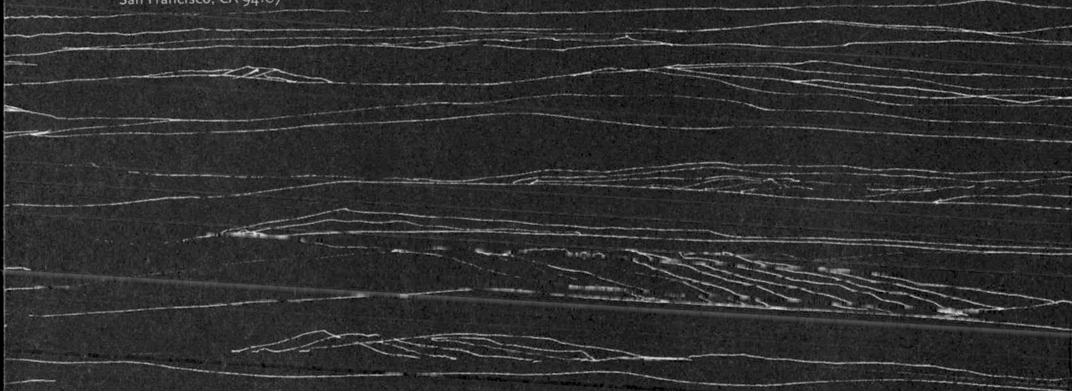

www.viz.com

PARENTAL ADVISORY
CHILDREN OF THE SEA is rated T+ for Older Teen
and is recommended for ages 16 and up. Contains
disturbing imagery.
ratings.viz.com

store.viz.com

VIZ Signature Edition
10 9 8 7 6 5 4 3 2 1
First printing, June 2009

This is the **LAST PAGE** of this book.

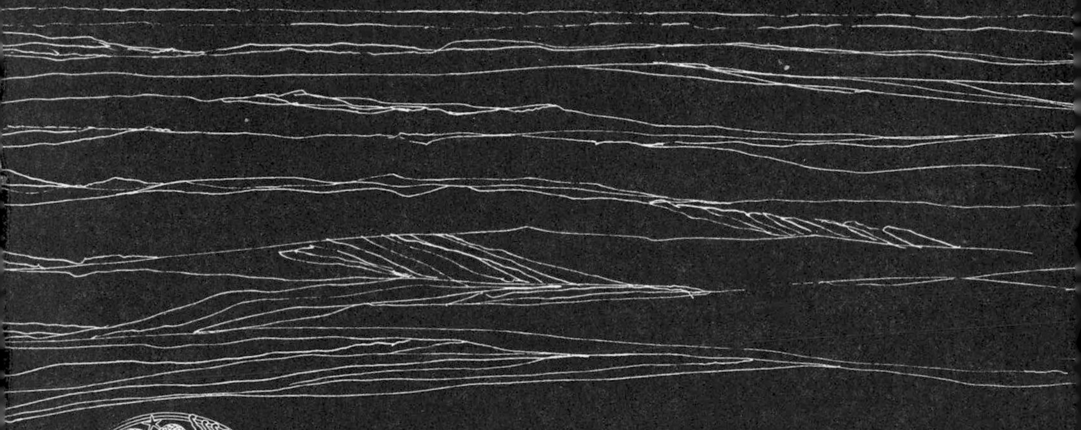

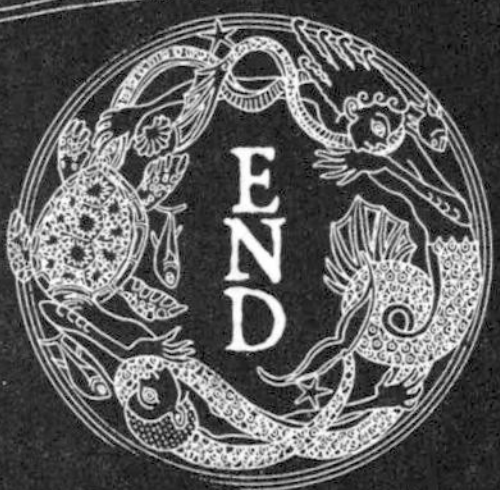
END

CHILDREN OF THE SEA
is printed from RIGHT TO LEFT in the original Japanese format in order to present **DAISUKE IGARASHI'S** stunning artwork the way it was meant to be seen.